Lecture Notes in Artificial Intelligence 9047

Subseries of Lecture Notes in Computer Science

LNAI Series Editors

Randy Goebel
University of Alberta, Edmonton, Canada
Yuzuru Tanaka
Hokkaido University, Sapporo, Japan
Wolfgang Wahlster
DFKI and Saarland University, Saarbrücken, Germany

LNAI Founding Series Editor

Joerg Siekmann
DFKI and Saarland University, Saarbrücken, Germany

T0210558

More information about this series at http://www.springer.com/series/1244

Alexander Gammerman · Vladimir Vovk
Harris Papadopoulos (Eds.)

Statistical Learning and Data Sciences

Third International Symposium, SLDS 2015
Egham, UK, April 20–23, 2015
Proceedings

 Springer

Editors
Alexander Gammerman
University of London
Egham, Surrey
UK

Vladimir Vovk
University of London
Egham, Surrey
UK

Harris Papadopoulos
Frederick University
Nicosia
Cyprus

ISSN 0302-9743   ISSN 1611-3349   (electronic)
Lecture Notes in Artificial Intelligence
ISBN 978-3-319-17090-9   ISBN 978-3-319-17091-6   (eBook)
DOI 10.1007/978-3-319-17091-6

Library of Congress Control Number: 2015935220

LNCS Sublibrary: SL7 – Artificial Intelligence

Springer Cham Heidelberg New York Dordrecht London
ⓒ Springer International Publishing Switzerland 2015

Printed on acid-free paper

Springer International Publishing AG Switzerland is part of Springer Science+Business Media
(www.springer.com)

In memory of Alexey Chervonenkis

Preface

This volume contains the Proceedings of the Third Symposium on Statistical Learning and Data Sciences, which was held at Royal Holloway, University of London, UK, during April 20–23, 2015. The original idea of the Symposium on Statistical Learning and Data Sciences is due to two French academics – Professors Mireille Gettler Summa and Myriam Touati – from Paris Dauphine University. Back in 2009 they thought that a "bridge" was required between various academic groups that were involved in research on Machine Learning, Statistical Inference, Pattern Recognition, Data Mining, Data Analysis, and so on; a sort of multilayer bridge to connect those fields. This is reflected in the symposium logo with the Passerelle Simone-de-Beauvoir bridge. The idea was implemented and the First Symposium on Statistical Learning and Data Sciences was held in Paris in 2009. The event was indeed a great "bridge" between various communities with interesting talks by J.-P. Benzecri, V. Vapnik, A. Chervonenkis, D. Hand, L. Bottou, and many others. Papers based on those talks were later presented in a volume of the *Modulad* journal and separately in a post-symposium book entitled *Statistical Learning and Data Sciences*, published by Chapman & Hall, CRC Press. The second symposium, which was equally successful, was held in Florence, Italy, in 2012.

Over the last 6 years since the first symposium, the progress in the theory and applications of learning and data mining has been very impressive. In particular, the arrival of technologies for collecting huge amounts of data has raised many new questions about how to store it and what type of analytics are able to handle it – what is now known as Big Data. Indeed, the sheer scale of the data is very impressive – for example, the Large Hadron Collider computers have to store 15 petabytes a year (1 petabyte = 10^{15} bytes). Obviously, handling this requires the usage of distributed clusters of computers, streaming, parallel processing, and other technologies. This volume is concerned with various modern techniques, some of which could be very useful for handling Big Data.

The volume is divided into five parts. The first part is devoted to two invited papers by Vladimir Vapnik. The first paper, "Learning with Intelligent Teacher: Similarity Control and Knowledge Transfer," is a further development of his research on learning with privileged information, with a special attention to the knowledge representation problem. The second, "Statistical Inference Problems and their Rigorous Solutions," suggests a novel approach to pattern recognition and regression estimation. Both papers promise to become milestones in the developing field of statistical learning.

The second part consists of 16 papers that were accepted for presentation at the main event, while the other three parts reflect new research in important areas of statistical learning to which the symposium devoted special sessions. Specifically the special sessions included in the symposium's program were:

– Special Session on Conformal Prediction and its Applications (CoPA 2015), organized by Harris Papadopoulos (Frederick University, Cyprus), Alexander Gammerman (Royal Holloway, University of London, UK), and Vladimir Vovk (Royal Holloway, University of London, UK).

- Special Session on New Frontiers in Data Analysis for Nuclear Fusion, organized by Jesus Vega (Asociacion EURATOM/CIEMAT para Fusion, Spain).
- Special Session on Geometric Data Analysis, organized by Fionn Murtagh (Goldsmith College London, UK).

Overall, 36 papers were accepted for presentation at the symposium after being reviewed by at least two independent academic referees. The authors of these papers come from 17 different countries, namely: Brazil, Canada, Chile, China, Cyprus, Finland, France, Germany, Greece, Hungary, India, Italy, Russia, Spain, Sweden, UK, and USA.

A special session at the symposium was devoted to the life and work of Alexey Chervonenkis, who tragically died in September 2014. He was one of the founders of modern Machine Learning, a beloved colleague and friend. All his life he was connected with the Institute of Control Problems in Moscow, over the last 15 years he worked at Royal Holloway, University of London, while over the last 7 years he also worked for the Yandex Internet company in Moscow. This special session included talks in memory of Alexey by Vladimir Vapnik – his long standing colleague and friend – and by Alexey's former students and colleagues.

We are very grateful to the Program and Organizing Committees, the success of the symposium would have been impossible without their hard work. We are indebted to the sponsors: the Royal Statistical Society, the British Computer Society, the British Classification Society, Royal Holloway, University of London, and Paris Dauphine University. Our special thanks to Yandex for their help and support in organizing the symposium and the special session in memory of Alexey Chervonenkis. This volume of the proceedings of the symposium is also dedicated to his memory. Rest in peace, dear friend.

February 2015

Alexander Gammerman
Vladimir Vovk
Harris Papadopoulos

Organization

General Chairs

Alexander Gammerman, UK
Vladimir Vovk, UK

Organizing Committee

Zhiyuan Luo, UK
Mireille Summa, France
Yuri Kalnishkan, UK

Myriam Touati, France
Janet Hales, UK

Program Committee Chairs

Harris Papadopoulos, Cyprus
Xiaohui Liu, UK
Fionn Murtagh, UK

Program Committee Members

Vineeth Balasubramanian, India
Giacomo Boracchi, Italy
Paula Brito, Portugal
Léon Bottou, USA
Lars Carlsson, Sweden
Jane Chang, UK
Frank Coolen, UK
Gert de Cooman, Belgium
Jesus Manuel de la Cruz, Spain
Jose-Carlos Gonzalez-Cristobal, Spain
Anna Fukshansky, Germany
Barbara Hammer, Germany

Shenshyang Ho, Singapore
Carlo Lauro, Italy
Guang Li, China
David Lindsay, UK
Henrik Linusson, Sweden
Hans-J. Lenz, Germany
Ilia Nouretdinov, UK
Matilde Santos, Spain
Victor Solovyev, Saudi Arabia
Jesus Vega, Spain
Rosanna Verde, Italy

Contents

Conformal Prediction and its Applications

New Frontiers in Data Analysis for Nuclear Fusion

Geometric Data Analysis

Invited Papers

Learning with Intelligent Teacher:
Similarity Control and Knowledge Transfer

In memory of Alexey Chervonenkis

Vladimir Vapnik[1,2](✉) and Rauf Izmailov[3]

[1] Columbia University, New York, NY, USA
`vladimir.vapnik@gmail.com`
[2] AI Research Lab, Facebook, New York, NY, USA
[3] Applied Communication Sciences, Basking Ridge, NJ, USA
`rizmailov@appcomsci.com`

Abstract. This paper introduces an advanced setting of machine learning problem in which an Intelligent Teacher is involved. During training stage, Intelligent Teacher provides Student with information that contains, along with classification of each example, additional privileged information (explanation) of this example. The paper describes two mechanisms that can be used for significantly accelerating the speed of Student's training: (1) correction of Student's concepts of similarity between examples, and (2) direct Teacher-Student knowledge transfer.

Keywords: Intelligent teacher · Privileged information · Similarity control · Knowledge transfer · Knowledge representation · Frames · Support vector machines · SVM+ · Classification · Learning theory · Kernel functions · Similarity functions · Regression

1 Introduction

During the last fifty years, a strong machine learning theory has been developed. This theory (see [21], [18], [19], [5]) includes:

- The necessary and sufficient conditions for consistency of learning processes.
- The bounds on the rate of convergence, which, in general, cannot be improved.
- The new inductive principle of Structural Risk Minimization (SRM), which always achieves the smallest risk.
- The effective algorithms (such as Support Vector Machines (SVM)), that realize the consistency property of SRM principle.

This material is based upon work partially supported by AFRL and DARPA under contract FA8750-14-C-0008. Any opinions, findings and / or conclusions in this material are those of the authors and do not necessarily reflect the views of AFRL and DARPA.

© Springer International Publishing Switzerland 2015
A. Gammerman et al. (Eds.): SLDS 2015, LNAI 9047, pp. 3–32, 2015.
DOI: 10.1007/978-3-319-17091-6_1

The general learning theory appeared to be completed: it addressed almost all standard questions of the statistical theory of inference. However, as always, the devil is in the detail: it is a common belief that human students require far fewer training examples than any learning machine. Why?

We are trying to answer this question by noting that a human Student has an Intelligent Teacher[1] and that Teacher-Student interactions are based not only on brute force methods of function estimation. In this paper, we show that Teacher-Student interactions are also based on special mechanisms that can significantly accelerate the learning process. In order for a learning machine to use fewer observations, it has to use these mechanisms as well.

This paper considers the model of learning that includes the so-called Intelligent Teacher, who supplies Student with intelligent (privileged) information during training session. This is in contrast to the classical model, where Teacher supplies Student only with outcome y for event x.

Privileged information exists for almost any learning problem and this information can significantly accelerate the learning process.

2   Learning with Intelligent Teacher: Privileged Information

The existing machine learning paradigm considers a simple scheme: given a set of training examples, find, in a given set of functions, the one that approximates the unknown decision rule in the best possible way. In such a paradigm, Teacher does not play an important role.

In human learning, however, the role of Teacher is important: along with examples, Teacher provides students with explanations, comments, comparisons, metaphors, and so on. In this paper, we include elements of human learning into classical machine learning paradigm. We consider a learning paradigm called *Learning Using Privileged Information (LUPI)*, where, at the training stage, Teacher provides additional information x^* about training example x.

The crucial point in this paradigm is that the privileged information is available only at the training stage (when Teacher interacts with Student) and is not available at the test stage (when Student operates without supervision of Teacher).

In this paper, we consider two mechanisms of Teacher–Student interactions in the framework of the LUPI paradigm:

1. *The mechanism to control Student's concept of similarity between training examples.*

2. *The mechanism to transfer knowledge from the space of privileged information (space of Teacher's explanations) to the space where decision rule is constructed.*

---

[1] Japanese proverb assesses teacher's influence as follows: "better than a thousand days of diligent study is one day with a great teacher."

The first mechanism [20] was introduced in 2006, and here we are mostly reproduce results obtained in [22]. The second mechanism is introduced in this paper for the first time.

2.1 Classical Model of Learning

Formally, the classical paradigm of machine learning is described as follows: given a set of iid pairs (training data)

$$(x_1, y_1), ..., (x_\ell, y_\ell), \quad x_i \in X, \quad y_i \in \{-1, +1\}, \tag{1}$$

generated according to a fixed but unknown probability measure $P(x, y)$, find, in a given set of indicator functions $f(x, \alpha), \alpha \in \Lambda$, the function $y = f(x, \alpha_*)$ that minimizes the probability of incorrect classifications (incorrect values of $y \in \{-1, +1\}$). In this model, each vector $x_i \in X$ is a description of an example generated by Nature according to an unknown generator $P(x)$ of random vectors x_i, and $y_i \in \{-1, +1\}$ is its classification defined according to a conditional probability $P(y|x)$. The goal of Learning Machine is to find the function $y = f(x, \alpha_*)$ that guarantees the smallest probability of incorrect classifications. That is, the goal is to find the function which minimizes the risk functional

$$R(\alpha) = \frac{1}{2} \int |y - f(x, \alpha)| dP(x, y), \tag{2}$$

in the given set of indicator functions $f(x, \alpha)$, $\alpha \in \Lambda$ when the probability measure $P(x, y) = P(y|x)P(x)$ is unknown but training data (1) are given.

2.2 LUPI Model of Learning

The LUPI paradigm describes a more complex model: given a set of iid triplets

$$(x_1, x_1^*, y_1), ..., (x_\ell, x_\ell^*, y_\ell), \quad x_i \in X, \quad x_i^* \in X^*, \quad y_i \in \{-1, +1\}, \tag{3}$$

generated according to a fixed but unknown probability measure $P(x, x^*, y)$, find, in a given set of indicator functions $f(x, \alpha), \alpha \in \Lambda$, the function $y = f(x, \alpha_*)$ that guarantees the smallest probability of incorrect classifications (2).

In the LUPI paradigm, we have exactly the same goal of minimizing (2) as in the classical paradigm, i.e., to find the best classification function in the admissible set. However, during the training stage, we have more information, i.e., we have triplets (x, x^*, y) instead of pairs (x, y) as in the classical paradigm. The additional information $x^* \in X^*$ belongs to space X^* which is, generally speaking, different from X. For any element x_i of training example generated by Nature, Intelligent Teacher generates both its label y_i and the privileged information x_i^* using some unknown conditional probability function $P(x_i^*, y_i|x_i)$.

Since the additional information is available only for the training set and *is not* available for the test set, it is called *privileged information* and the new machine learning paradigm is called *Learning Using Privileged Information.*

Next, we consider three examples of privileged information that could be generated by Intelligent Teacher.

Example 1. Suppose that our goal is to find a rule that predicts the outcome y of a surgery in three weeks after it, based on information x available before the surgery. In order to find the rule in the classical paradigm, we use pairs (x_i, y_i) from past patients.

However, for past patients, there is also additional information x^* about procedures and complications during surgery, development of symptoms in one or two weeks after surgery, and so on. Although this information is not available *before* surgery, it does exist in historical data and thus can be used as privileged information in order to construct a rule that is better than the one obtained without using that information. The issue is how large an improvement can be achieved.

Example 2. Let our goal be to find a rule $y = f(x)$ to classify biopsy images x into two categories y: cancer ($y = +1$) and non-cancer ($y = -1$). Here images are in a pixel space X, and the classification rule has to be in the same space. However, the standard diagnostic procedure also includes a pathologist's report x^* that describes his/her impression about the image in a high-level holistic language X^* (for example, "aggressive proliferation of cells of type A among cells of type B" etc.).

The problem is to use images x along with the pathologist's reports x^* as a privileged information in order to make a better classification rule just in pixel space X: classification by a pathologist is a difficult and time-consuming procedure, so fast decisions during surgery should be made automatically, without consulting a pathologist.

Example 3. Let our goal be to predict the direction of the exchange rate of a currency at the moment t. In this problem, we have observations about the exchange rates before t, and we would like to predict if the rate will go up or down at the moment $t + \Delta$. However, in the historical market data we also have observations about exchange rates *after* moment t. Can this future-in-the-past privileged information be used for construction of a better prediction rule?

To summarize, privileged information is ubiquitous: it usually exists for almost all machine learning problems.

In Section 4, we describe a mechanism that allows one to take advantage of privileged information by controlling Student's concepts of similarity between training examples. However, we first describe statistical properties enabling the use of privileged information.

3   Statistical Analysis of the Rate of Convergence

According to the bounds developed in the VC theory [21], [19], the rate of convergence depends on two factors: how well the classification rule separates the training data

$$(x_1, y_1), ..., (x_\ell, y_\ell), \quad x \in R^n, \ y \in \{-1, +1\} \tag{4}$$

and the VC dimension of the set of functions in which the rule is selected.

The theory has two distinct cases:

1. **Separable case:** there exists a function $f(x, \alpha_\ell)$ in the set of functions $f(x, \alpha), \alpha \in \Lambda$ that separates the training data (4) without errors:

$$y_i f(x_i, \alpha_\ell) > 0 \quad \forall i = 1, ..., \ell.$$

In this case, the function $f(x, \alpha_\ell)$ that minimizes the empirical risk (on training set (4)) with probability $1 - \eta$ has the bound

$$p(yf(x, \alpha_\ell) \leq 0) < O^* \left(\frac{h - \ln \eta}{\ell} \right),$$

where $p(yf(x, \alpha_\ell) \leq 0)$ is the probability of error for the function $f(x, \alpha_\ell)$ and h is VC dimension of the admissible set of functions. Here O^* denotes order of magnitude up to logarithmic factor.

2. **Non-separable case:** there is no function in $f(x, \alpha)$, $\alpha \in \Lambda$ that can separate data (4) without errors. Let $f(x, \alpha_\ell)$ be a function that minimizes the number of errors on (4). Let $\nu(\alpha_\ell)$ be the error rate on training data (4). Then, according to the VC theory, the following bound holds true with probability $1 - \eta$:

$$p(yf(x, \alpha_\ell) \leq 0) < \nu(\alpha_\ell) + O^* \left(\sqrt{\frac{h - \ln \eta}{\ell}} \right).$$

In other words, in the separable case, the rate of convergence has the order of magnitude $1/\ell$; in the non-separable case, the order of magnitude is $1/\sqrt{\ell}$. The difference between these rates[2] is huge: the same order of bounds requires 320 training examples versus 100,000 examples. Why do we have such a large gap?

3.1   Key Observation: SVM with Oracle Teacher

Let us try to understand why convergence rates for SVMs differ so much for separable and non-separable cases. Consider two versions of the SVM method for these cases.

In the separable case, SVM constructs (in space Z which we, for simplicity, consider as an N-dimensional vector space R^N) a maximum margin separating hyperplane. Specifically, in the separable case, SVM minimizes the functional

$$T(w) = (w, w)$$

subject to the constraints

$$(y_i(w, z_i) + b) \geq 1, \quad \forall i = 1, ..., \ell;$$

---

[2] The VC theory also gives more accurate estimate of the rate of convergence; however, the difference remains essentially the same.

while in the non-separable case, SVM minimizes the functional

$$T(w) = (w, w) + C \sum_{i=1}^{\ell} \xi_i$$

subject to the constraints

$$(y_i(w, z_i) + b) \geq 1 - \xi_i, \quad \xi_i \geq 0, \quad \forall i = 1, ..., \ell.$$

That is, in the separable case, SVM uses ℓ observations for estimation of N coordinates of vector w, while in the nonseparable case, SVM uses ℓ observations for estimation of $N + \ell$ parameters: N coordinates of vector w and ℓ values of slacks ξ_i. Thus, in the non-separable case, the number $N + \ell$ of parameters to be estimated is always larger than the number ℓ of observations; it does not matter here that most of slacks will be equal to zero: SVM still has to estimate all ℓ of them. Our guess is that the difference between the corresponding convergence rates is due to the number of parameters SVM has to estimate.

To confirm this guess, consider the SVM with *Oracle Teacher* (Oracle SVM). Suppose that Teacher can supply Student with the values of slacks as privileged information: during training session, Teacher supplies triplets

$$(x_1, \xi_1^0, y_1), ..., (x_\ell, \xi_\ell^0, y_\ell)$$

where ξ_i^0, $i = 1, ..., \ell$ are the slacks for the Bayesian decision rule. Therefore, in order to construct the desired rule using these triplets, the SVM has to maximize the functional

$$T(w) = (w, w)$$

subject to the constraints

$$(y_i(w, z_i) + b) \geq r_i, \quad \forall i = 1, ..., \ell,$$

where we have denoted

$$r_i = 1 - \xi_i^0, \quad \forall i = 1, ..., \ell.$$

One can show that the rate of convergence is equal to $O^*(1/\ell)$ for Oracle SVM. The following (slightly more general) proposition holds true [22].

Proposition 1. *Let $f(x, \alpha_0)$ be a function from the set of indicator functions $f(x, \alpha), \alpha \in \Lambda$ with VC dimension h that minimizes the frequency of errors (on this set) and let*

$$\xi_i^0 = \max\{0, (1 - f(x_i, \alpha_0))\}, \quad \forall i = 1, ..., \ell.$$

Then the error probability $p(\alpha_\ell)$ for the function $f(x, \alpha_\ell)$ that satisfies the constraints

$$y_i f(x, \alpha) \geq 1 - \xi_i^0, \quad \forall i = 1, ..., \ell$$

is bounded, with probability $1 - \eta$, as follows:

$$p(\alpha_\ell) \leq P(1 - \xi_0 < 0) + O^* \left(\frac{h - \ln \eta}{\ell} \right).$$

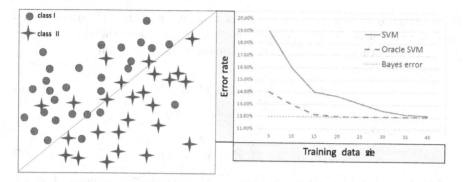

Fig. 1. Comparison of Oracle SVM and standard SVM

That is, for Oracle SVM, the rate of convergence is $1/\ell$ even in the non-separable case. Figure 1 illustrates this: the left half of the figure shows synthetic data for a binary classification problem using the set of linear rules with Bayesian rule having error rate 12% (the diagonal), while the right half of the figure illustrates the rates of convergence for standard SVM and Oracle SVM. While both converge to the Bayesian solution, Oracle SVM does it much faster.

3.2 From Ideal Oracle to Real Intelligent Teacher

Of course, real Intelligent Teacher cannot supply slacks: Teacher does not know them. Instead, Intelligent Teacher, can do something else, namely:

1. define a space X^* of (correcting) slack functions (it can be different from the space X of decision functions);
2. define a set of real-valued slack functions $f^*(x^*, \alpha^*)$, $x^* \in X^*$, $\alpha^* \in \Lambda^*$ with VC dimension h^*, where approximations

$$\xi_i = f^*(x, \alpha^*)$$

of the slack functions[3] are selected;
3. generate privileged information for training examples supplying Student, instead of pairs (4), with triplets

$$(x_1, x_1^*, y_1), ..., (x_\ell, x_\ell^*, y_\ell). \tag{5}$$

---

[3] Note that slacks ξ_i introduced for the SVM method can be considered as a realization of some function $\xi = \xi(x, \beta_0)$ from a large set of functions (with infinite VC dimension). Therefore, generally speaking, the classical SVM approach can be viewed as estimation of two functions: (1) the decision function, and (2) the slack function, where these functions are selected from two different sets, with finite and infinite VC dimension, respectively. Here we consider two sets with finite VC dimensions.

During training session, the algorithm has to simultaneously estimate two functions using triplets (5): the decision function $f(x, \alpha_\ell)$ and the slack function $f^*(x^*, \alpha^*)$. In other words, the method minimizes the functional

$$T(\alpha^*) = \sum_{i=1}^{\ell} \max\{0, f^*(x_i^*, \alpha^*)\} \tag{6}$$

subject to the constraints

$$y_i f(x_i, \alpha) > -f^*(x_i^*, \alpha^*), \quad i = 1, ..., \ell. \tag{7}$$

Let $f(x, \alpha_\ell)$ be a function that solves this optimization problem. For this function, the following proposition holds true [22].

Proposition 2. *The solution $f(x, \alpha_\ell)$ of optimization problem (6), (7) satisfies the bounds*

$$P(yf(x, \alpha_\ell) < 0) \leq P(f^*(x^*, \alpha_\ell^*) \geq 0) + O^* \left(\frac{h + h^* - \ln \eta}{\ell} \right)$$

with probability $1 - \eta$, where h and h^* are the VC dimensions of the set of decision functions $f(x, \alpha)$, $\alpha \in \Lambda$ and the set of correcting functions $f^*(x^*, \alpha^*)$, $\alpha^* \in \Lambda^*$, respectively,

According to Proposition 2, in order to estimate the rate of convergence to the best possible decision rule (in space X) one needs to estimate the rate of convergence of $P\{f^*(x^*, \alpha_\ell^*) \geq 0\}$ to $P\{f^*(x^*, \alpha_0^*) \geq 0\}$ for the best rule $f^*(x^*, \alpha_0^*)$ in space X^*. Note that both the space X^* and the set of functions $f^*(x^*, \alpha^*), \alpha^* \in \Lambda^*$ are suggested by Intelligent Teacher that tries to choose them in a way that facilitates a fast rate of convergence. The guess is that a really Intelligent Teacher can indeed do that.

As shown in the VC theory, in standard situations, the uniform convergence has the order $O(\sqrt{h^*/\ell})$, where h^* is the VC dimension of the admissible set of correcting functions $f^*(x^*, \alpha^*)$, $\alpha* \in \Lambda^*$. However, for special privileged space X^* and corresponding functions $f^*(x^*, \alpha^*), \alpha^* \in \Lambda^*$ (for example, those that satisfy the conditions defined by Tsybakov [15] or the conditions defined by Steinwart and Scovel [17]), the convergence can be faster (as $O([1/\ell]^\delta)$, $\delta > 1/2$).

A well-selected privileged information space X^* and Teacher's explanation $P(x^*, y|x)$ along with sets $f(x, \alpha_\ell), \alpha \in \Lambda$ and $f^*(x^*, \alpha^*), \alpha^* \in \Lambda^*$ engender a convergence that is faster than the standard one. The skill of Intelligent Teacher is being able to select of the proper space X^*, generator $P(x^*, y|x)$, set of functions $f(x, \alpha_\ell), \alpha \in \Lambda$, and set of functions $f^*(x^*, \alpha^*), \alpha^* \in \Lambda^*$: that is what differentiates good teachers from poor ones.

4   SVM+ for Similarity Control in LUPI Paradigm

In this section, we extend SVM to the method called SVM+, which allows one to solve machine learning problems in the LUPI paradigm [22].

Consider again the model of learning with Intelligent Teacher: given triplets

$$(x_1, x_1^*, y_1), ..., (x_\ell, x_\ell^*, y_\ell),$$

find in the given set of functions the one that minimizes the probability of incorrect classifications.[4]

As in standard SVM, we map vectors $x_i \in X$ onto the elements z_i of the Hilbert space Z, and map vectors x_i^* onto elements z_i^* of another Hilbert space Z^* obtaining triples

$$(z_1, z_1^*, y_1), ..., (z_\ell, z_\ell^*, y_\ell).$$

Let the inner product in space Z be (z_i, z_j), and the inner product in space Z^* be (z_i^*, z_j^*).

Consider the set of decision functions in the form

$$f(x) = (w, z) + b,$$

where w is an element in Z, and consider the set of correcting functions in the form

$$f^*(x^*) = (w^*, z^*) + b^*,$$

where w^* is an element in Z^*. In SVM+, the goal is to minimize the functional

$$\mathcal{T}(w, w^*, b, b^*) = \frac{1}{2}[(w, w) + \gamma(w^*, w^*)] + C \sum_{i=1}^{\ell}[(w^*, z_i^*) + b^*]_+$$

subject to the linear constraints

$$y_i((w, z_i) + b) \geq 1 - ((w^*, z^*) + b^*), \quad i = 1, ..., \ell,$$

where $[u]_+ = \max\{0, u\}$.

The structure of this problem mirrors the structure of the primal problem for standard SVM, while containing one additional parameter $\gamma > 0$.

To find the solution of this optimization problem, we use the equivalent setting: we minimize the functional

$$\mathcal{T}(w, w^*, b, b^*) = \frac{1}{2}[(w, w) + \gamma(w^*, w^*)] + C \sum_{i=1}^{\ell}[(w^*, z_i^*) + b^* + \zeta_i] \quad (8)$$

subject to constraints

$$y_i((w, z_i) + b) \geq 1 - ((w^*, z^*) + b^*), \quad i = 1, ..., \ell, \quad (9)$$

and

$$(w^*, z_i^*) + b^* + \zeta_i \geq 0, \quad \forall i = 1, ..., \ell \quad (10)$$

---

[4] In [22], the case of privileged information being available only for a subset of examples is considered: specifically, for examples with non-zero values of slack variables.

and
$$\zeta_i \geq 0, \quad \forall i = 1, ..., \ell. \tag{11}$$

To minimize the functional (8) subject to the constraints (10), (11), we construct the Lagrangian

$$\mathcal{L}(w, b, w^*, b^*, \alpha, \beta) = \tag{12}$$

$$\frac{1}{2}[(w, w) + \gamma(w^*, w^*)] + C\sum_{i=1}^{\ell}[(w^*, z_i^*) + b^* + \zeta_i] - \sum_{i=1}^{\ell}\nu_i\zeta_i -$$

$$\sum_{i=1}^{\ell}\alpha_i\left[y_i[(w, z_i) + b] - 1 + [(w^*, z_i^*) + b^*]\right] - \sum_{i=1}^{\ell}\beta_i[(w^*, z_i^*) + b^* + \zeta_i],$$

where $\alpha_i \geq 0$, $\beta_i \geq 0$, $\nu_i \geq 0$, $i = 1, ..., \ell$ are Lagrange multipliers.

To find the solution of our quadratic optimization problem, we have to find the saddle point of the Lagrangian (the minimum with respect to w, w^*, b, b^* and the maximum with respect to $\alpha_i, \beta_i, \nu_i, i = 1, ..., \ell$).

The necessary conditions for minimum of (12) are

$$\frac{\partial\mathcal{L}(w, b, w^*, b^*, \alpha, \beta)}{\partial w} = 0 \implies w = \sum_{i=1}^{\ell}\alpha_i y_i z_i \tag{13}$$

$$\frac{\partial\mathcal{L}(w, b, w^*, b^*, \alpha, \beta)}{\partial w^*} = 0 \implies w^* = \frac{1}{\gamma}\sum_{i=1}^{\ell}(\alpha_i + \beta_i - C)z_i^* \tag{14}$$

$$\frac{\partial\mathcal{L}(w, b, w^*, b^*, \alpha, \beta)}{\partial b} = 0 \implies \sum_{i=1}^{\ell}\alpha_i y_i = 0 \tag{15}$$

$$\frac{\partial\mathcal{L}(w, b, w^*, b^*, \alpha, \beta)}{\partial b^*} = 0 \implies \sum_{i=1}^{\ell}(\alpha_i - \beta_i) = 0 \tag{16}$$

$$\frac{\partial\mathcal{L}(w, b, w^*, b^*, \alpha, \beta)}{\partial\zeta_i} = 0 \implies \beta_i + \nu_i = C \tag{17}$$

Substituting the expressions (13) in (12) and, taking into account (14), (15), (16), and denoting $\delta_i = C - \beta_i$, we obtain the functional

$$\mathcal{L}(\alpha, \delta) = \sum_{i=1}^{\ell}\alpha_i - \frac{1}{2}\sum_{i,j=1}^{\ell}(z_i, z_j)y_i y_j\alpha_i\alpha_j - \frac{1}{2\gamma}\sum_{i,j=1}^{\ell}(\alpha_i - \delta_i)(\alpha_j - \delta_j)(z_i^*, z_j^*).$$

To find its saddle point, we have to maximize it subject to the constraints

$$\sum_{i=1}^{\ell}y_i\alpha_i = 0 \tag{18}$$

$$\sum_{i=1}^{\ell} \alpha_i = \sum_{i=1}^{\ell} \delta_i \tag{19}$$

$$0 \le \delta_i \le C, \quad i = 1, ..., \ell \tag{20}$$

$$\alpha_i \ge 0, \quad i = 1, ..., \ell \tag{21}$$

Let vectors α^0, δ^0 be the solution of this optimization problem. Then, according to (13) and (14), one can find the approximation to the desired decision function

$$f(x) = (w_0, z_i) + b = \sum_{i=1}^{\ell} \alpha_i^*(z_i, z) + b$$

and to the slack function

$$f^*(x^*) = (w_0^*, z_i^*) + b^* = \sum_{i=1}^{\ell}(\alpha_i^0 - \delta_i^0)(z_i^*, z^*) + b^*$$

The Karush-Kuhn-Tacker conditions for this problem are

$$\begin{cases} \alpha_i^0[y_i[(w_0, z_i) + b] - 1 + [(w_0^*, z_i^*) + b^*]] = 0 \\ (C - \delta_i^0)[(w_0^*, z_i^*) + b^* + \zeta_i] = 0 \\ \nu_i^0 \zeta_i = 0 \end{cases}$$

Using these conditions, one obtains the value of constant b as

$$b = 1 - y_k(w^0, z_k) = 1 - y_k \left[\sum_{i=1}^{\ell} \alpha_i^0(z_i, z_k)\right],$$

where (z_k, z_k^*, y_k) is a triplet for which $\alpha_k^0 \ne 0$ and $\delta_k^0 \ne C$.

As in standard SVM, we use the inner product (z_i, z_j) in space Z in the form of Mercer kernel $K(x_i, x_j)$ and inner product (z_i^*, z_j^*) in space Z^* in the form of Mercer kernel $K^*(x_i^*, x_j^*)$. Using these notations, we can rewrite the SVM+ method as follows: the decision rule in X space has the form

$$f(x) = \sum_{i=1}^{\ell} y_i \alpha_i^0 K(x_i, x) + b,$$

where $K(\cdot, \cdot)$ is the Mercer kernel that defines the inner product for the image space Z of space X (kernel $K^*(\cdot, \cdot)$ for the image space Z^* of space X^*) and α^0 is a solution of the following dual space quadratic optimization problem: maximize the functional

$$\mathcal{L}(\alpha, \delta) = \sum_{i=1}^{\ell} \alpha_i - \frac{1}{2} \sum_{i,j=1}^{\ell} y_i y_j \alpha_i \alpha_j K(x_i, x_j) - \frac{1}{2\gamma} \sum_{i,j=1}^{\ell} (\alpha_i - \delta_i)(\alpha_j - \delta_j) K^*(x_i^*, x_j^*)$$

$$\tag{22}$$

subject to constraints (18) – (21).

Remark. In the special case $\delta_i = \alpha_i$, our optimization problem becomes equivalent to the standard SVM optimization problem, which maximizes the functional

$$\mathcal{L}(\alpha, \delta) = \sum_{i=1}^{\ell} \alpha_i - \frac{1}{2} \sum_{i,j=1}^{\ell} y_i y_j \alpha_i \alpha_j K(x_i, x_j)$$

subject to constraints (18) – (21) where $\delta_i = \alpha_i$.

Therefore, the difference between SVM+ and SVM solutions is defined by the last term in objective function (22). In SVM method, the solution depends only on the values of pairwise similarities between training vectors defined by the Gram matrix K of elements $K(x_i, x_j)$ (which defines similarity between vectors x_i and x_j). The SVM+ solution is defined by objective function (22) that uses two expressions of similarities between observations: one (x_i and x_j) that comes from space X and another one (x_i^* and x_j^*) that comes from space of privileged information X^*. That is, Intelligent Teacher changes the optimal solution by correcting concepts of similarity.

The last term in equation (22) defines the instrument for Intelligent Teacher to control the concept of similarity of Student.

To find value of b, one has to find a sample (x_k, x_k^*, y_k) for which $\alpha_k > 0$, $\delta_k < C$ and compute

$$b = 1 - y_k \left[\sum_{i=1}^{\ell} y_i \alpha_i K(x_i, x_k) \right].$$

Efficient computational implementation of this SVM+ algorithm for classification and its extension for regression can be found in [14] and [22], respectively.

5   Three Examples of Similarity Control Using Privileged Information

In this section, we describe three different types of privileged information (advanced technical model, future events, holistic description), used in similarity control setting [22].

5.1   Advanced Technical Model as Privileged Information

Homology classification of proteins is a hard problem in bioinformatics. Experts usually rely on hierarchical schemes leveraging molecular 3D-structures, which are expensive and time-consuming (if at all possible) to obtain. The alternative information on amino-acid sequences of proteins can be collected relatively easily, but its correlation with 3D-level homology is often poor (see Figure 2). The practical problem is thus to construct a rule for classification of proteins based on their amino-acid sequences as standard information, while using available molecular 3D-structures as privileged information.

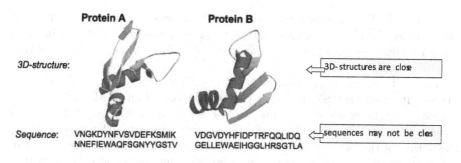

Fig. 2. 3D-structures and amino-acid sequences of proteins

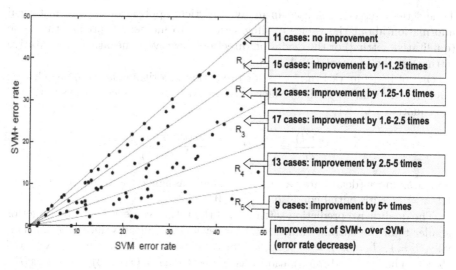

Fig. 3. Comparison of SVM and SVM+ error rates

Since SVM has been successfully used [8], [9] to construct protein classification rules based on amino-acid sequences, the natural next step was to see what performance improvement can be obtained by using 3D-structures as privileged information and applying SVM+ method of similarity control. The experiments used SCOP (Structural Classification of Proteins) database [11], containing amino-acid sequences and their hierarchical organization, and PDB (Protein Data Bank) [2], containing 3D-structures for SCOP sequences. The classification goal was to determine homology based on protein amino-acid sequences from 80 superfamilies (3rd level of hierarchy) with the largest number of sequences. Similarity between amino-acid sequences (standard space) and 3D-structures (privileged space) was computed using the *profile-kernel* [8] and *MAMMOTH* [13], respectively.

Standard SVM classification based on 3D molecular structure had an error rate smaller than 5% for almost any of 80 problems, while SVM classification using protein sequences gave much worse results (in some cases, the error rate was up to 40%).

Figure 3 displays comparison of SVM and SVM+ with 3D privileged information. It shows that SVM+ never performed worse than SVM. In 11 cases it gave exactly the same result, while in 22 cases its error was reduced by more than 2.5 times. Why does the performance vary so much? The answer lies in the nature of the problem. For example, both diamond and graphite consist of the same chemical element, carbon, but they have different molecular structures. Therefore, one can only tell them apart using their 3D structures.

5.2   Future Events as Privileged Information

Time series prediction is used in many statistical applications: given historical information about the values of time series up to moment t, predict the value (qualitative setting) or the deviation direction (positive or negative; quantitative setting) at the moment $t + \Delta$.

One of benchmark time series for prediction algorithms is the quasi-chaotic (and thus difficult to predict) Mackey-Glass time series, which is the solution of the equation [10], [4]

$$\frac{dx(t)}{dt} = -ax(t) + \frac{bx(t-\tau)}{1 + x^{10}(t-\tau)}.$$

Here a, b, and τ (delay) are parameters, usually assigned the values $a = 0.1$, $b = 0.2$, $\tau = 17$ with initial condition $x(\tau) = 0.9$.

The qualitative prediction setting (will the future value $x(t+T)$ be larger or smaller than the current value $x(t)$?) for several lookahead values of T (specifically, $T = 1$, $T = 5$, $T = 8$) was used for comparing the error rates of SVM and SVM+. The standard information was the vector $x_t = (x(t-3), x(t-2), x(t-1), x(t))$ of current observation and three previous ones, whereas the privileged information was the vector $x_t^* = (x(t+T-2), x(t+T-1), x(t+T+1), x(t+T+2))$ of four future events.

The experiments covered various training sizes (from 100 to 500) and several values of T (namely, $T = 1$, $T = 5$, and $T = 8$). In all the experiments, SVM+ consistently outperformed SVM, with margin of improvement being anywhere between 30% and 60%; here the margin was defined as relative improvement of error rate as compared to the (unattainable) performance of the specially constructed Oracle SVM.

5.3   Holistic Description as Privileged Information

This example is an important one, since holistic privileged information is most frequently used by Intelligent Teacher. In this example, we consider the problem of classifying images of digits 5 and 8 in the MNIST database. This database

Complete Images:
(28x28 pixels)

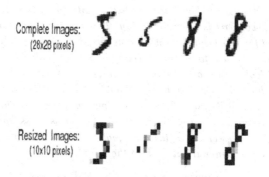

Resized Images:
(10x10 pixels)

Fig. 4. Sample MNIST digits ans their resized images

contains digits as 28*28 pixel images; there are 5,522 and 5,652 images of digits 5 and 8, respectively. Distinguishing between these two digits in 28*28 pixel space is an easy problem. To make it more challenging, the images were resized to 10*10 pixels (examples are shown in Figure 4). A hundred examples of 10*10 images were randomly selected as a training set, another 4,000 images were used as a validation set (for tuning the parameters in SVM and SVM+) and the remaining 1,866 images constituted the test set.

For every training image, its holistic description was created (using natural language). For example, the first image of 5 (see Figure 4) was described as follows:

> *Not absolute two-part creature. Looks more like one impulse. As for two-partness the head is a sharp tool and the bottom is round and flexible. As for tools it is a man with a spear ready to throw it. Or a man is shooting an arrow. He is firing the bazooka. He swung his arm, he drew back his arm and is ready to strike. He is running. He is flying. He is looking ahead. He is swift. He is throwing a spear ahead. He is dangerous. It is slanted to the right. Good snaked-ness. The snake is attacking. It is going to jump and bite. It is free and absolutely open to anything. It shows itself, no kidding. Its bottom only slightly (one point!) is on earth. He is a sportsman and in the process of training. The straight arrow and the smooth flexible body. This creature is contradictory - angular part and slightly roundish part. The lashing whip (the rope with a handle). A toe with a handle. It is an outside creature, not inside. Everything is finite and open. Two open pockets, two available holes, two containers. A piece of rope with a handle. Rather thick. No loops, no saltire. No hill at all. Asymmetrical. No curlings.*

The first image of 8 (Figure 4) was described as follows:

> *Two-part creature. Not very perfect infinite way. It has a deadlock, a blind alley. There is a small right-hand head appendix, a small shoot. The right-hand appendix. Two parts. A bit disproportionate. Almost equal. The upper*

one should be a bit smaller. The starboard list is quite right. It is normal like it should be. The lower part is not very steady. This creature has a big head and too small bottom for this head. It is nice in general but not very self-assured. A rope with two loops which do not meet well. There is a small upper right-hand tail. It does not look very neat. The rope is rather good - not very old, not very thin, not very thick. It is rather like it should be. The sleeping snake which did not hide the end of its tail. The rings are not very round - oblong - rather thin oblong. It is calm. Standing. Criss-cross. The criss-cross upper angle is rather sharp. Two criss-cross angles are equal. If a tool it is a lasso. Closed absolutely. Not quite symmetrical (due to the horn).

These holistic descriptions were mapped into 21-dimensional feature vectors. Examples of these features (with range of possible values) are: `two-part-ness` (0 - 5); `tilting to the right` (0 - 3); `aggressiveness` (0 - 2); `stability` (0 - 3); `uniformity` (0 - 3), and so on. The values of these features (in the order they appear above) for the first 5 and 8 are [2, 1, 2, 0, 1], and [4, 1, 1, 0, 2], respectively. Holistic descriptions and their mappings were created prior to the learning process by an independent expert; all the datasets are publicly available at [12].

The goal was to construct a decision rule for classifying 10*10 pixel images in the 100-dimensional standard pixel space X and to leverage the corresponding 21-dimensional vectors as the privileged space X^*. This idea was realized using the SVM+ algorithm described in Section 4. For every training data size, 12 different random samples selected from the training data were used and the average of test errors was calculated.

To understand how much information is contained in holistic descriptions, 28*28 pixel digits (784-dimensional space) were used instead of the 21-dimensional holistic descriptions in SVM+ (the results shown in Figure 5). In this setting, when using 28*28 pixel description of digits, SVM+ performs worse than SVM+ using holistic descriptions.

6 Transfer of Knowledge Obtained in Privileged Information Space to Decision Space

In this section, we consider one of the most important mechanisms of Teacher-Student interaction: using privileged information to transfer knowledge from Teacher to Student.

Suppose that Intelligent Teacher has some knowledge about the solution of a specific pattern recognition problem and would like to transfer this knowledge to Student. For example, Teacher can reliably recognize cancer in biopsy images (in a pixel space X) and would like to transfer this skill to Student.

Formally, this means that Teacher has some function $y = f_0(x)$ that distinguishes cancer ($f_0(x) = +1$ for cancer and $f_0(x) = -1$ for non-cancer) in the pixel space X. Unfortunately, Teacher does not know this function explicitly (it only exists as a neural net in Teacher's brain), so how can Teacher transfer this construction to Student? Below, we describe a possible mechanism for solving this problem; we call this mechanism *knowledge transfer*.

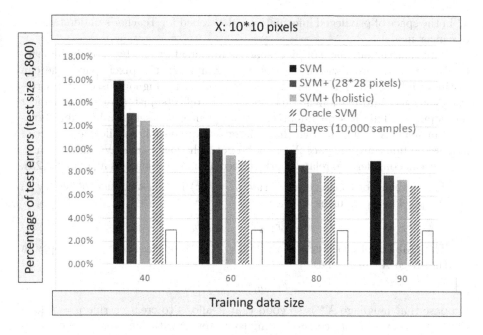

Fig. 5. Error rates for the digit recognition task

Suppose that Teacher believes in some theoretical model on which the knowledge of Teacher is based. For cancer model, he or she believes that it is a result of uncontrolled multiplication of the cancer cells (cells of type B) which replace normal cells (cells of type A). Looking at a biopsy image, Teacher tries to generate privileged information that reflects his or her belief in development of such s process; Teacher can holistically describe the image as:

Aggressive proliferation of cells of type B into cells of type A.

If there are no signs of cancer activity, Teacher may use the description

Absence of any dynamics in the of standard picture.

In uncertain cases, Teacher may write

There exist small clusters of abnormal cells of unclear origin.

In other words, Teacher is developing a special language that is appropriate for description x_i^* of cancer development using the model he believes in. Using this language, Teacher supplies Student with privileged information x_i^* for the image x_i by generating training triplets

$$(x_1, x_1^*, y_1), ..., (x_\ell, x_\ell^*, y_\ell). \tag{23}$$

The first two elements of these triplets are descriptions of an image in two languages: in language X (vectors x_i in pixel space), and in language X^* (vectors

x_i^* in the space of privileged information), developed for Teacher's understanding of cancer model.

Note that the language of pixel space is universal (it can be used for description of many different visual objects; for example, in the pixel space, one can distinguish between male and female faces), while the language used for describing privileged information is very specific: it reflects just a model of cancer development. This has an important consequence: the set of admissible functions in space X has to be rich (has a large VC dimension), while the the set of admissible functions in space X^* may be not rich (has a small VC dimension).

One can consider two related pattern recognition problems using triplets (23):

1. The problem of constructing a rule $y = f(x)$ for classification of biopsy in the pixel space X using data

$$(x_1, y_1), ..., (x_\ell, y_\ell). \tag{24}$$

2. The problem of constructing a rule $y = f^*(x^*)$ for classification of biopsy in the space X^* using data

$$(x_1^*, y_1), ..., (x_\ell^*, y_\ell). \tag{25}$$

Suppose that language X^* is so good that it allows to create a rule $y = f_\ell^*(x^*)$ that classifies vectors x^* corresponding to vectors x with the same level of accuracy as the best rule $y = f_\ell(x)$ for classifying data in the pixel space.[5]

Since the VC dimension of the admissible rules in a special space X^* is much smaller than the VC dimension of the admissible rules in the universal space X and since, the number of examples ℓ is the same in both cases, the bounds on error rate for rule $y = f_\ell^*(x^*)$ in X^* will be better[6] than those for the rule $y = f_\ell(x)$ in X. That is, generally speaking, the classification rule $y = f_\ell^*(x^*)$ will be more accurate than classification rule $y = f_\ell(x)$.

The following problem arises: how one can use the knowledge of the rule $y = f_\ell^*(x^*)$ in space X^* to improve the accuracy of the desired rule $y = f_\ell(x)$ in space X?

6.1   Knowledge Representation

To answer this question, we formalize the concept of representation of the knowledge about the rule $y = f_\ell^*(x^*)$.

Suppose that we are looking for our rule in Reproducing Kernel Hilbert Space (RKHS) associated with kernel $K^*(x_i^*, x^*)$. According to Representer Theorem [7], [16], such rule has the form

$$f_\ell^*(x^*) = \sum_{i=1}^{\ell} \gamma_i K^*(x_i^*, x^*) + b, \tag{26}$$

---

[5] The rule constructed in space X^* cannot be better than the best possible rule in space X, since all information originates in space X.

[6] According to VC theory, the guaranteed bound on accuracy of the chosen rule depends only on two factors: frequency of errors on training set and VC dimension of admissible set of functions.

where γ_i, $i = 1, ..., \ell$ and b are parameters.

Suppose that, using data (25), we found a good rule (26) with coefficients $\gamma_i = \gamma_i^*$, $i = 1, ..., \ell$ and $b = b^*$. This is now our knowledge about our classification problem. Let us formalize the description of this knowledge.

Consider three elements of knowledge representation used in AI [1]:

1. Fundamental elements of knowledge.
2. Frames (fragments) of the knowledge.
3. Structural connections of the frames (fragments) in the knowledge.

We call the *fundamental elements of the knowledge* the smallest number of the vectors $u_1^*...., u_m^*$ from space X^* that can approximate[7] the main part of the rule (26):

$$f_\ell^*(x^*) - b = \sum_{i=1}^{\ell} \gamma_i^* K^*(x_i^*, x^*) \approx \sum_{k=1}^{m} \beta_k^* K^*(u_k^*, x^*). \tag{27}$$

Let us call the functions $K^*(u_k^*, x^*)$, $k = 1, ..., m$ the *frames* (fragments) of knowledge. Our knowledge

$$f_\ell^*(x^*) = \sum_{k=1}^{m} \beta_k^* K^*(u_k^*, x^*) + b$$

is defined as a linear combination of the frames.

6.2   Scheme of Knowledge Transfer Between Spaces

In the described terms, knowledge transfer from X^* into X requires the following:

1. To find the fundamental elements of knowledge $u_1^*, ..., u_m^*$ in space X^*.
2. To find frames (m functions) $K^*(u_1^*, x^*), ..., K^*(u_m^*, x^*)$ in space X^*.
3. To find the functions $\phi_1(x), ..., \phi_m(x)$ in space X such that

$$\phi_k(x_i) \approx K^*(u_k^*, x_i^*) \tag{28}$$

holds true for almost all pairs (x_i, x_i^*) generated by Intelligent Teacher that uses some (unknown) generator $P(x^*, y|x)$.

Note that the capacity of the set of functions from which $\phi_k(x)$ are to be chosen can be smaller than that of the capacity of the set of functions from which the classification function $y = f_\ell(x)$ is chosen (function $\phi_k(x)$ approximates just one fragment of knowledge, not the entire knowledge as function $y = f_\ell^*(x^*)$, which is a linear combination (27) of frames). Also, as we will see in the next section, estimates of all the functions $\phi_1(x), ..., \phi_m(x)$ are done using different pairs as training sets of the same size ℓ. That is, our hope is that transfer of m fragments of knowledge from space X^* into space X can be done with higher accuracy than estimating function $y = f_\ell(x)$ from data (24).

---

[7] In machine learning, they are called the reduced number of support vectors [3].

After finding approximation of frames in space X, the knowledge about the rule obtained in space X^* can be approximated in space X as

$$f_\ell(x) \approx \sum_{k=1}^{m} \delta_k \phi_k(x) + b^*,$$

where coefficients $\delta_k = \beta_k^*$ (taken from (26)) if approximations (28) are accurate. Otherwise, coefficients δ_k can be estimated from the training data, as shown in Section 6.3.

Finding Fundamental Elements of Knowledge. Let our functions ϕ belong to RKHS associated with the kernel $K^*(x_i^*, x^*)$, and let our knowledge be defined by an SVM method in space X^* with support vector coefficients α_i. In order to find the fundamental elements of knowledge, we have to minimize (over vectors $u_1^*, ..., u_m^*$ and values $\beta_1, ..., \beta_m$) the functional

$$R(u_1^*, ..., u_m^*; \beta_1, ..., \beta_m) = \tag{29}$$

$$\left\| \sum_{i=1}^{\ell} y_i \alpha_i K^*(x_i^*, x^*) - \sum_{s=1}^{m} \beta_s K^*(u_s^*, x^*) \right\|_{RKGS}^2 =$$

$$\sum_{i,j=1}^{\ell} y_i y_j \alpha_i \alpha_j K^*(x_i^*, x_j^*) - 2 \sum_{i=1}^{\ell} \sum_{s=1}^{m} y_i \alpha_i \beta_s K^*(x_i^*, u_s^*) + \sum_{s,t=1}^{m} \beta_s \beta_t K^*(u_s^*, u_t^*)$$

The last equality was derived from the following property of the inner product for functions from RKHS [7], [16]:

$$\left(K^*(x_i^*, x^*), K(x_j^*, x^*) \right)_{RKHS} = K^*(x_i^*, x_j^*).$$

Fundamental Elements of Knowledge for Homogenous Quadratic Kernel. For general kernel functions $K^*(\cdot, \cdot)$, minimization of (29) is a difficult computational problem. However, for the special homogenous quadratic kernel

$$K^*(x_i^*, x_j^*) = (x_i^*, x_j^*)^2,$$

this problem has a simple exact solution [3]. For this kernel, we have

$$R = \sum_{i,j=1}^{\ell} y_i y_j \alpha_i \alpha_j (x_i^*, x_j^*)^2 - 2 \sum_{i=1}^{\ell} \sum_{s=1}^{m} y_i \alpha_i \beta_s (x_i^*, u_s^*)^2 + \sum_{s,t=1}^{m} \beta_s \beta_t (u_s^*, u_t^*)^2. \tag{30}$$

Let us look for solution in set of orthonormal vectors $u_i^*, ..., u_m^*$ for which we can rewrite (30) as follows

$$\hat{R} = \sum_{i,j=1}^{\ell} y_i y_j \alpha_i \alpha_j (x_i^*, x_j^*)^2 - 2 \sum_{i=1}^{\ell} \sum_{j=1}^{m} y_i \alpha_i \beta_s (x_i^*, u_s^*)^2 + \sum_{s=1}^{m} \beta_s^2 (u_s^*, u_s^*)^2. \tag{31}$$

Taking derivative of $\hat{R}$ over u_k^*, we obtain that the solutions u_k^*, $k = 1, ..., m$ have to satisfy the equations

$$\frac{d\hat{R}}{du_k} = -2\beta_k \sum_{i=1}^{\ell} y_i \alpha_i x_i^* x_i^{*T} u_k^* + 2\beta_k^2 (u_k^* u_k^{*T}) u_k^* = 0.$$

Introducing notation

$$S = \sum_{i=1}^{\ell} y_i \alpha_i x_i^* x^{*T}, \tag{32}$$

we conclude that the solutions satisfy the equation

$$S u_k^* = \beta_k u_k^*, \quad k = 1, ..., m.$$

That is, the solutions $u_1^*, ..., u_m^*$ are the set of eigenvectors of the matrix S corresponding to non-zero eigenvalues $\beta_1, ..., \beta_m$, which are coefficients of expansion of the classification rule on the frames $(u_k, x^*)^2$, $k = 1, ..., m$.

Using (32), one can rewrite the functional (31) in the form

$$\hat{R} = \mathbf{1}^T S \mathbf{1} - \sum_{k=1}^{m} \beta_k^2, \tag{33}$$

where we have denoted by $\mathbf{1}$ the $(\ell \times 1)$-dimensional matrix of ones.

Therefore, in order to find the fundamental elements of knowledge, one has to solve the eigenvalue problem for $(n \times n)$-dimensional matrix S and then select an appropriate number m of eigenvectors corresponding to m eigenvalues with largest absolute values. One chooses such value of m that makes functional (33) small. The number m does not exceed n (the dimensionality of matrix S).

Finding Images of Frames in Space X. Let us call the conditional average function

$$\phi_k(x) = \int K^*(u_k^*, x^*) p(x^*|x) \, dx^*$$

the image of frame $K^*(u_k^*, x^*)$ in space X. To find m image functions $\phi_k(x)$ of the frames $K(u_k^*, x^*)$, $k = 1, ..., m$ in space X, we solve the following m regression estimation problems: find the regression function $\phi_k(x)$ in X, $k = 1, ..., m$, using data

$$(x_1, K^*(u_k^*, x_1^*)), ..., (x_\ell, K^*(u_k^*, x_\ell^*)), \quad k = 1, ..., m, \tag{34}$$

where pairs (x_i, x_i^*) belong to elements of training triplets (23).

Therefore, using fundamental elements of knowledge $u_1^*, ... u_m^*$ in space X^*, the corresponding frames $K^*(u_1^*, x^*), ..., K^*(u_m^*, x^*)$ in space X^*, and the training data (34), one constructs the transformation of the space X into m-dimensional feature space

$$\phi(x) = (\phi_1(x), ... \phi_m(x)),$$

where k coordinates of vector function $\phi(x)$ are defined as $\phi_k = \phi_k(x)$.

6.3 Algorithms for Knowledge Transfer

1. Suppose that our regression functions can be estimated accurately: for a sufficiently small $\varepsilon > 0$ the inequalities

$$|\phi_k(x_i) - K^*(u_k^*, x_i^*)| < \varepsilon, \quad \forall k = 1, ..., m \quad \text{and} \quad \forall i = 1, ..., \ell$$

hold true for almost all pairs (x_i, x_i^*) generated according to $P(x, x^*, y)$. Then the approximation of our knowledge in space X is

$$f(x) = \sum_{k=1}^{m} \beta_k^* \phi_k(x) + b^*,$$

where β_k^*, $k = 1, ..., m$ are eigenvalues corresponding to eigenvectors $u_1^*, ..., u_m^*$.

2. If, however, ε is not too small, one can use privileged information to employ both mechanisms of intelligent learning: controlling similarity between training examples and knowledge transfer.

In order to describe this method, we denote by vector ϕ_i the m-dimensional vector with coordinates

$$\phi_i = (\phi_1(x_i), ..., \phi_m(x_i))^T.$$

Consider the following problem of intelligent learning: given training triplets

$$(\phi_1, x_1^*, y_1), ..., (\phi_\ell, x_\ell^*, y_\ell),$$

find the decision rule

$$f(\phi(x)) = \sum_{i=1}^{\ell} y_i \hat{\alpha}_i \hat{K}(\phi_i, \phi) + b. \tag{35}$$

Using SVM+ algorithm described in Section 4, we can find the coefficients of expansion $\hat{\alpha}_i$ in (35). They are defined by the maximum (over $\hat{\alpha}$ and δ) of the functional

$$R(\hat{\alpha}, \delta) =$$

$$\sum_{i=1}^{\ell} \hat{\alpha}_i - \frac{1}{2} \sum_{i,j=1}^{\ell} y_i y_j \hat{\alpha}_i \hat{\alpha}_j \hat{K}(\phi_i, \phi_j) - \frac{1}{2\gamma} \sum_{i,j=1}^{\ell} y_i y_j (\hat{\alpha}_i - \delta_i)(\hat{\alpha}_j - \delta_j) K^*(x_i^*, x_j^*)$$

subject to equality constraints

$$\sum_{i=1}^{\ell} \hat{\alpha}_i y_i = 0, \quad \sum_{i=1}^{\ell} \hat{\alpha}_i = \sum_{i=1}^{\ell} \delta_i$$

and inequality constraints

$$\hat{\alpha}_i \geq 0, \quad 0 \leq \delta_i \leq C, \quad i = 1, \ldots, \ell$$

(see Section 4).

Remark. One can use different ideas to represent knowledge obtained in the space X^*. The main factors of these representations are concepts of fundamental elements of the knowledge. They could be, for example, just the support vectors or coordinates x^{t*}, $t = 1, \ldots, d$ of d-dimensional privileged space X^*. However, the fundamental elements defined above have some good properties: for the quadratic kernel, the number m of fundamental elements does not exceed the dimensionality of the space. Also, as was shown in multiple experiments with digit recognition [3], in order to generate the same level of accuracy of the solution, it was sufficient to use m elements, where the value m was at least 20 times smaller than the corresponding number of support vectors.

6.4   Kernels Involved in Intelligent Learning

In this paper, among many possible Mercer kernels (positive semi-definite functions), we consider the following three types:

1. Radial Basis Function (RBF) kernel:

$$K_{RBF_\sigma}(x, y) = \exp\{-\sigma^2(x - y)^2\}.$$

2. INK-spline kernel. Kernel for spline of order one with infinite number of knots. It is defined in the nonnegative domain and has the form

$$K_{INK_1}(x, y) = \prod_{k=1}^{d} \left(1 + x^k y^k + \frac{|x^k - y^k| \max\{x_k, y^k\}}{2} + \frac{(\max\{x^k, y^k\})^3}{3} \right)$$

   where $x^k \geq 0$ and $y^k \geq 0$ are k coordinates of d-dimensional vector x.
3. Homogeneous quadratic kernel

$$K_{Pol_2} = (x, y)^2,$$

   where (x, y) is the inner product of vectors x and y.

The RBF kernel has a free parameter $\sigma > 0$; two other kernels have no free parameters. That was achieved by fixing a parameter in more general sets of functions: the degree of polynomial was chosen to be 2, and the order of INK-splines was chosen to be 1. Note that INK-splines are sensitive to the selection of minimum value a of coordinates x; as illustrated in [6], for reliable performance one should select $a = -3$ and reset all the values smaller than that to a (assuming all the coordinates are normalized to $N(0, 1)$ by subtracting the empirical means and dividing the values by empirical standard deviations).

It is easy to introduce kernels for any degree of polynomials and any order of INK-splines. Experiments show excellent properties of these three types of kernels for solving many machine learning problems. These kernels also can be recommended for methods that use both mechanisms of Teacher-Student interaction.

6.5   Knowledge Transfer for Statistical Inference Problems

The idea of privileged information and knowledge transfer can be also extended to Statistical Inference problems considered in [23], [24].

For simplicity, consider the problem of conditional probability $P(y|x)$ estimation[8] from iid data

$$(x_1, y_1), ..., (x_\ell, y_\ell), \quad x \in X, \ y \in \{0, 1\}, \tag{36}$$

where vector $x \in X$ is generated by a fixed but unknown distribution function $P(x)$ and binary value $y \in \{0, 1\}$ is generated by an unknown conditional probability function $P(y = 1|x)$, $(P(y = 0|x) = 1 - P(y = 1|x))$; this is the function we would like to estimate.

As shown in [23], [24], this requires solving the Fredholm integral equation

$$\int \theta(x - t)P(y = 1|t)dP(t) = P(y = 1, x)$$

if probability functions $P(y = 1, x)$ and $P(x)$ are unknown but iid data (36) generated according to joint distribution $P(y, x)$ are given. Papers [23], [24] describe methods for solving this problem, producing the solution

$$P_\ell(y = 1|x) = P(y = 1|x; (x_1, y_1), ..., (x_\ell, y_\ell)).$$

In this section, we generalize classical Statistical Inference problem of conditional probability estimation to a new model of Statistical Inference with Privileged Information. In this model, along with information defined in the space X, one has the information defined in the space X^*.

Consider privileged space X^* along with space X. Suppose that any vector $x_i \in X$ has its image $x_i^* \in X^*$.

Consider iid triplets

$$(x_1, x_1^*, y_1), ..., (x_\ell, x_\ell^*, y_\ell) \tag{37}$$

that are generated according to a fixed but unknown distribution function $P(x, x^*, y)$. Suppose that, for any triplet (x_i, x_i^*, y_i), there exist conditional probabilities $P(y_i|x_i^*)$ and $P(y_i|x_i)$. Also, suppose that the conditional probability function $P(y|x^*)$ defined in the privileged space X^* is *better* than the conditional probability function $P(y|x)$ defined in space X; here by "better"

---

[8] The same method can be applied to all problems described in [23], [24].

we mean that the *conditional entropy* for $P(y|x^*)$ is smaller than conditional entropy for $P(y|x)$:

$$-\int [\log_2 P(y=1|x^*) + \log_2 P(y=0|x^*)]\, dP(x^*) <$$

$$-\int [\log_2 P(y=1|x) + \log_2 P(y=0|x)]\, dP(x).$$

Our goal is to use triplets (37) for estimating the conditional probability $P(y|x; (x_1, x_1^*, y_1), ..., (x_\ell, x_\ell^*, y_\ell))$ in space X better than it can be done with training pairs (36). That is, our goal is to find such a function

$$P_\ell(y=1|x) = P(y=1|x; (x_1, x_1^*, y_1), ..., (x_\ell, x_\ell^*, y))$$

that the following inequality holds:

$$-\int [\log_2 P(y=1|x; (x_i, x_i^*, y_i)_1^\ell) + \log_2 P(y=0|x; (x_i x_i^*, y_i)_1^\ell)]dP(x) <$$

$$-\int [\log_2 P(y=1|x; (x_i, y_i)_1^\ell) + \log_2 P(y=0|x; (x_i, y_i)_1^\ell,)]dP(x).$$

Consider the following solution for this problem:

1. Using kernel $K(\hat{x}^*, x^*) = (\hat{x}^*, x^*)^2$, the training pairs pairs (x_i^*, y_i) extracted from given training triplets (37) and the methods of solving our integral equation described in [23], [24], find the solution of the problem in space of privileged information X^*:

$$P(y=1|x^*; (x_i^*, y_i)_1^\ell) = \sum_{i=1}^\ell \hat{\alpha}_i(x_i^*, x^*)^2 + b.$$

2. Using matrix $S = \sum_{i=1}^\ell \hat{\alpha}_i x_i^* x_i^{*T}$, find the fundamental elements of knowledge (the eigenvectors $u_1^*, ..., u_m^*$ corresponding to the largest norm of eigenvalues $\beta_1, ..., \beta_m$ of matrix S).
3. Using some universal kernels (say RBF or INK-Spline), find in the space X the approximations $\phi_k(x), k = 1, ..., m$ of the frames $(u_k^*, x^*)^2$, $k = 1, ..., m$.
4. Find the solution of the conditional probability estimation problem $P(y|\phi; (\phi_i, y_i)_1^\ell)$ in the space of pairs (ϕ, y) where $\phi = (\phi_1(x), ..., \phi_m(x))$.

6.6   General Remarks About Knowledge Transfer

What Knowledge Does Teacher Transfer? In previous sections, we linked the knowledge of Intelligent Teacher about the problem of interest in space X to his knowledge about this problem in space X^*. For knowledge transfer, one can consider a more general model. Teacher knows that goal of Student is to construct a good rule in space X with one of the functions from the set $f(x, \alpha)$, $x \in X$, $\alpha \in \Lambda$ with capacity VC_X. Teacher also knows that there exists a rule in space X^* of the same quality which belongs to the set $f^*(x^*, \alpha^*)$, $x^* \in X^*$, $\alpha^* \in \Lambda^*$ that has much smaller capacity VC_{X^*}. This knowledge can be defined by the ratio of the capacities

$$\kappa = \frac{VC_X}{VC_{X^*}}.$$

The larger is κ, the more knowledge Teacher can transfer and fewer examples will Student need to select a good classification rule.

What Are the Roots of Intelligence? In this paper, we defined the roots of intelligence via privileged information produced by Teacher according to Intelligent generator $P(x^*, y|x)$. Existence of triplets[9] (x, x^*, y) in description of the World events reflects *Holism* branch of philosophy, in which any event has multiple descriptions that cannot be reduced to a single point of view. In the opposite *Reductionism* branch of philosophy, descriptions of events can be reduced to a single major point of view (this is reflected in many branches of natural science).

We believe that Intelligent learning reflects Holism philosophy in particular, in multi-level interactions. It appears that intelligent learning is a multi-level representation of events and transfer elements of knowledge between different levels. We also believe that attempts to *significantly* improve the rate of learning in the classical setting using *only* more elaborate mathematical techniques are somewhat akin to Baron Munchausen's feat of pulling himself from a swamp[10]: for a significant improvement in learning process, Student needs *additional* (privileged) information in the same way the real-life Baron would have needed at least a solid foothold for getting out of his predicament.

Holistic Description and Culture. Generally speaking, Student and Teacher can have different sets of functions in Space X^*. In Section 5.3, we presented holistic descriptions of digits 5 and 8 as privileged information for training data reflecting impression of Prof. of Russian Poetry Natalia Pavlovitch. To transform her linguistic representation of privileged information into formal code, Prof. Pavlovitch suggested features for the transformation. One can see that transformation of privileged information from human language into code is very individual. Two different Students can obtain different functions as a result of transfer of the same knowledge given by Teacher. Therefore, in real life, Teacher has to elevate Student on the level of culture where Student can appropriately understand the privileged information.

---

[9] One can generalize the knowledge transfer method for multiple levels of privileged information, say, for two levels using quadruples (x, x^*, x^{**}, y).

[10] Baron Munchausen, the fictional character known for his tall tales, once pulled himself (and his horse) out of a swamp by his hair.

Quadratic Kernel. In the method of knowledge transfer, the special role belongs to the quadratic kernel $(x_1, x_2)^2$. Formally, only two kernels are amenable for simple methods of finding fundamental elements of knowledge (and therefore for knowledge representation): the linear kernel (x_1, x_2) and the quadratic kernel $(x_1, x_2)^2$.

Indeed, if linear kernel is used, one constructs the separating hyperplane in the space of privileged information X^*

$$y = (w^*, x^*) + b^*,$$

where vector of coefficients w^* also belongs to the space X^*, so there is only one fundamental element of knowledge – the vector w^*. In this situation, the problem of constructing the regression function $y = \phi(x)$ from data

$$(x_1, (w^*, x_1^*)), ..., (x_\ell, (w^*, x_\ell^*)) \tag{38}$$

has, generally speaking, the same level of complexity as the standard problem of pattern recognition in space X using data (36). Therefore, one should not expect performance improvement when transferring the knowledge using (38).

With quadratic kernel, one obtains $1 \le m \le d$ fundamental elements of knowledge in d-dimensional space X^*. In this situation, according to the methods described above, one defines the knowledge in space X^* as a linear combination of m frames. That is, one splits the desired function into m (simplified) fragments (a linear combination of which defines the decision rule) and then estimates each of m functions $\phi_k(x)$ separately, using training sets of size ℓ. The idea is that, in order to estimate well a fragment of the knowledge, one can use a set of functions with a smaller capacity than is needed to estimate the entire function $y = f(x)$, $x \in X$. Here privileged information can improve accuracy of estimation of the desired function.

To our knowledge, there exists only one nonlinear kernel (the quadratic kernel) that leads to an exact solution of the problem of finding the fundamental elements of knowledge. For all other nonlinear kernels, the problems of finding the fundamental elements require difficult (heuristic) computational procedures.

Some Philosophical Interpretations. Classical German philosophy had formulated the following general idea (Hegel,1820):

What is reasonable[11] is real and what is real is reasonable.

If we interpret the word "reasonable" as "has a good mathematical justification" and word "real" as "is realized by Nature" we can reformulate this idea as follows:

Models that have a good mathematical justification are realized by the Nature and models that are realized by the Nature have a good mathematical justification.

---

[11] Some translations from German use "rational" instead of "reasonable".

From this point of view, the existence of only one kernel (the quadratic polynomial $(x_i, x_j)^2$) that allows one to find the exact solution of the knowledge
representation problem means that there exists only one good level of structural
complexity for privileged information that can be used by Intelligent Teacher:
not too simple (such as based on linear kernel (x_1, x_2)), but not too complex
(such as based on kernels $(x_1, x_2)^s$, $s > 2$). This claim, however, is not based on
a proof, it is rather based on belief in classical German philosophy.

7   Conclusions

In this paper, we tried to understand mechanisms of human learning that go
beyond brute force methods of function estimation. In order to accomplish this,
we introduced the concept of Intelligent Teacher who generates privileged information during training session. We described two mechanisms that can be used
to accelerate the learning process.

1. The mechanism to control Student's concept of similarity between training
   examples.
2. The mechanism to transfer knowledge from the space of privileged information to the desired decision rule.

*It is quite possible that there exist more mechanisms in Teacher-Student inter-
actions and thus it is important to find them* [12] .

The idea of privileged information can be generalized to any statistical inference problem creating non-symmetric (two spaces) approach in statistics.

Teacher-Student interaction constitutes one of the key factors of intelligent
behavior and it can be viewed as a basic element in understanding intelligence
(in both machines and humans).

Acknowledgments. We thank Professor Cherkassky, Professor Gammerman, and
Professor Vovk for their helpful comments on this paper.

---

[12] In [23], we discuss the idea of replacing the SVM method with the so-called V-matrix
method of conditional probability estimation. As was shown in Section 6.5, privileged
information also can be used for estimation of the conditional probability function.
However, for estimation of this function, Intelligent Teacher can also include in the
privileged information his evaluation of the probability $p(x_i)$ that event x_i belongs
to class $y = 1$ given his guess

$$a_i \le p(x_i) \le b_i,$$

where $0 \le a_i < b_i \le 1$ are some values. For example, in the problem of classification
of a biopsy image x_i, the pathologist can give his assessment of cancer probability (hopefully non-trivial ($a_i > 0, b_i < 1$)). Footnote 10 in [23] shows how such
information can be used for evaluation of conditional probability function.

References

1. Brachman, R., Levesque, H.: Knowledge Representation and Reasoning. Morgan Kaufmann, San Francisco (2004)
2. Berman, H., Westbrook, J., Feng, Z., Gillil, G., Bhat, T., Weissig, H., et al.: The protein data bank. Nucleic Acids Research **28**, 235–242 (2000)
3. Burges, C.: Simplified support vector decision rules. In: 13th International Conference on Machine Learning, pp. 71–77 (1996)
4. Casdagli, M.: Nonlinear prediction of chaotic time series. Physica D **35**, 335–356 (1989)
5. Chervonenkis, A.: Computer Data Analysis (in Russian). Yandex, Moscow (2013)
6. Izmailov, R., Vapnik, V., Vashist, A.: Multidimensional Splines with Infinite Number of Knots as SVM Kernels. In: International Joint Conference on Neural Networks, pp. 1096–1102. IEEE Press, New York (2013)
7. Kimeldorf, G., Wahba, G.: Some Results on Tchebycheffian Spline Functions. Journal of Mathematical Analysis and Applications **33**, 82–95 (1971)
8. Kuang, R., Le, E., Wang, K., Wang, K., Siddiqi, M., Freund, Y., et al.: Profile-Based String Kernels for Remote Homology Detection and Motif Extraction. Journal of Bioinformatics and Computational Biology **3**, 527–550 (2005)
9. Liao, L., Noble, W.: Combining Pairwise Sequence Similarity and Support Vector Machines for Remote Protein Homology Detection. Journal of Computational Biology **10**, 857–868 (2003)
10. Mukherjee, S., Osuna, E., Girosi, F.: Nonlinear Prediction of Chaotic Time Series Using Support Vector Machines. Neural Networks for Signal Processing, 511–520 (1997)
11. Murzin, A., Brenner, S., Hubbard, T., Chothia, C.: SCOP: A Structural Classification of Proteins Database for Investigation of Sequences and Structures. Journal of Molecular Biology **247**, 536–540 (1995)
12. NEC Labs America. http://ml.nec-labs.com/download/data/svm+/mnist. priviledged
13. Ortiz, A., Strauss, C., Olmea, O.: MAMMOTH (Matching Molecular Models Obtained from Theory): An Automated Method for Model Comparison. Protein Science **11**, 2606–2621 (2002)
14. Pechyony, D., Izmailov, R., Vashist, A., Vapnik, V.: SMO-style Algorithms for Learning Using Privileged Information. In: 2010 International Conference on Data Mining, pp. 235–241 (2010)
15. Tsybakov, A.: Optimal Aggregation of Classifiers in Statistical Learning. Annals of Statistcs **31**, 135–166 (2004)
16. Schölkopf, B., Herbrich, R., Smola, A.J.: A Generalized Representer Theorem. In: Helmbold, D.P., Williamson, B. (eds.) COLT 2001 and EuroCOLT 2001. LNCS (LNAI), vol. 2111, p. 416. Springer, Heidelberg (2001)
17. Steinwart, I., Scovel, C. When do support machines learn fast?. In: 16th International Symposium on Mathematical Theory of Networks and Systems (2004)
18. Vapnik, V.: The Nature of Statistical Learning Theory. Springer-Verlag, New York (1995)
19. Vapnik, V.: Statistical Learning Theory. John Wiley & Sons, New York (1998)
20. Vapnik, V.: Estimation of Dependencies Based on Empirical. Data (2nd Edition). Springer, New York (2006)
21. Vapnik, V., Chervonenkis, A.: Theory of Pattern Recognition (in Russian). Nauka, Moscow (1974). German translation: Wapnik W., Tscherwonenkis, A.: Theorie des Zeichenerkennung. Akademie-Verlag, Berlin (1974)

22. Vapnik, V., Vashist, A.: A New Learning Paradigm: Learning Using Privileged Information. Neural Networks **22**, 546–557 (2009)
23. Vapnik, V., Izmailov, R.: Statistical inference problems and their rigorous solutions. In: Gammerman, A., Vovk, V., Papadopoulos, H. (eds.) Statistical Learning and Data Sciences. SLDS 2015, LNCS (LNAI), vol. 9047, pp. 33–71. Springer-Verlag, London (2015)
24. Vapnik, V., Braga, I., Izmailov, R.: A Constructive Setting for the Problem of Density Ratio Estimation. In: SIAM International Conference on Data Mining, pp. 434–442 (2014)

Statistical Inference Problems and Their Rigorous Solutions

In memory of Alexey Chervonenkis

Vladimir Vapnik[1,2]($\boxtimes$) and Rauf Izmailov[3]

[1] Columbia University, New York, NY, USA
vladimir.vapnik@gmail.com
[2] AI Research Lab, Facebook, New York, NY, USA
[3] Applied Communication Sciences, Basking Ridge, NJ, USA
rizmailov@appcomsci.com

Abstract. This paper presents direct settings and rigorous solutions of Statistical Inference problems. It shows that rigorous solutions require solving ill-posed Fredholm integral equations of the first kind in the situation where not only the right-hand side of the equation is an approximation, but the operator in the equation is also defined approximately. Using Stefanuyk-Vapnik theory for solving such operator equations, constructive methods of empirical inference are introduced. These methods are based on a new concept called V-matrix. This matrix captures geometric properties of the observation data that are ignored by classical statistical methods.

Keywords: Conditional probability · Regression · Density ratio · Ill-posed problem · Mutual information · Reproducing kernel hilbert space · Function estimation · Interpolation function · Support vector machines · Data adaptation · Data balancing · Conditional density

1 Basic Concepts of Classical Statistics

In the next several sections, we describe main concepts of Statistics. We first outline these concepts for one-dimensional case and then generalize them for multidimensional case.

1.1 Cumulative Distribution Function

The basic concept of *Theoretical Statistics* and *Probability Theory* is the so-called *Cumulative distribution function* (CDF)

$$F(x) = P(X \leq x).$$

This material is based upon work partially supported by AFRL and DARPA under contract FA8750-14-C-0008. Any opinions, findings and or conclusions in this material are those of the authors and do not necessarily reflect the views of AFRL and DARPA.

© Springer International Publishing Switzerland 2015
A. Gammerman et al. (Eds.): SLDS 2015, LNAI 9047, pp. 33–71, 2015.
DOI: 10.1007/978-3-319-17091-6_2

This function defines the probability of the random variable X not exceeding x. Different CDFs describe different statistical environments, so CDF (defining the probability measure) is the main characteristic of the random events. In this paper, we consider the important case when $F(x)$ is a *continuous* function.

1.2   General Problems of Probability Theory and Statistics

The general problem of Probability theory can be defined as follows:

> *Given a cumulative distribution function $F(x)$, describe outcomes of random experiments for a given theoretical model.*

The general problem of Statistics can be defined as follows:

> *Given iid observations of outcomes of the same random experiments, estimate the statistical model that defines these observations.*

In Section 2, we discuss several main problems of statistics. Next, we consider the basic one: estimation of CDF.

1.3   Empirical Cumulative Distribution Functions

In order to estimate CDF, one introduces the so-called *Empirical Cumulative Distribution function* (ECDF) constructed for iid observations obtained according to $F(x)$:

$$X_1, ..., X_\ell.$$

The ECDF function has the form

$$F_\ell(x) = \frac{1}{\ell} \sum_{i=1}^{\ell} \theta(x - X_i),$$

where $\theta(x - X_i)$ is the step-function

$$\theta(x - X_i) = \begin{cases} 1, \text{ if } x \geq X_i \\ 0, \text{ if } x < X_i \end{cases}$$

Classical statistical theory is based on the fact that ECDF converges to the CDF with increasing number ℓ of observations.

1.4   The Glivenko-Cantelli Theorem and Kolmogorov Type Bounds

In 1933, the following main theorem of statistics, Glivenko-Cantelli theorem, was proven.

Theorem. *Empirical cumulative distribution functions converge uniformly to the true cumulative distribution function:*

$$\lim_{\ell \to \infty} P\{\sup_x |F(x) - F_\ell(x)| \geq \varepsilon\} = 0, \quad \forall \varepsilon > 0.$$

In 1933, Kolmogorov derived asymptotical exact rate of convergence of ECDF to CDF for continuous functions $F(x)$:

$$\lim_{\ell \to \infty} P\{\sqrt{\ell} \sup_x |F(x) - F_\ell(x)| \geq \varepsilon\} = 2 \sum_{k=1}^{\infty} (-1)^{k-1} \exp\{-2\varepsilon^2 k^2\}. \qquad (1)$$

Later, in 1956, Dvoretzky, Kiefer, and Wolfowitz showed the existence of exponential type of bounds for any fixed ℓ:

$$P\{\sup_x |F(x) - F_\ell(x)| \geq \varepsilon\} \leq 2\exp\{-2\varepsilon^2 \ell\} \qquad (2)$$

(Massart [5]). The bound (2) is defined by the first term of the right-hand side of Kolmogorov asymptotic equality (1).

Glivenko-Cantelli theorem and bounds (1), (2) can be considered as a foundation of statistical science since they claim that:

1. It is possible to estimate the true statistical distribution from iid data.
2. The ECDF strongly converges to the true CDF, and this convergence is fast.

1.5 Generalization to Multidimensional Case

Let us generalize the main concepts described above to multidimensional case. We start with CDF.

Joint cumulative distribution function. For the multivariate random variable $x = (x^1, ..., x^d)$, the joint cumulative distribution function $F(x)$, $x \in R^d$ is defined by the function

$$F(x) = P(X^1 \leq x^1, ..., X^d \leq x^d). \qquad (3)$$

As in the one-dimensional case, the main problem of statistics is as follows: estimate CDF, as defined in (3), based on random multivariate iid observations

$$X_1, ..., X_\ell, \quad X_i \in R^d, \quad i = 1, ..., \ell..$$

In order to solve this problem, one uses the same idea of empirical distribution function

$$F_\ell(x) = \frac{1}{\ell} \sum_{i=1}^{\ell} \theta(x - X_i),$$

where $x = (x^1, ..., x^d) \in R^d$, $X_i = (X_i^1, ..., X_i^d) \in R^d$ and

$$\theta(x - X_i) = \prod_{k=1}^{d} \theta(x^k - X_i^k).$$

Note that

$$F(x) = E_u \theta(x - u) = \int \theta(x - u) dF(u),$$

and the generalized (for multidimensional case) Glivenko-Cantelli theorem has
the form

$$\lim_{\ell \to \infty} P \left\{ \sup_x \left| E_u \theta(x - u) - \frac{1}{\ell} \sum_{i=1}^{\ell} \theta(x - X_i) \right| \geq \varepsilon \right\} = 0.$$

This equation describes the uniform convergence of the empirical risks to their
expectation over vectors $u \in R^d$ for the parametric set of multi-dimensional
step functions $\theta(x - u)$ (here $x, u \in R^d$, and u is vector of parameters). Since
VC dimension of this set of functions is equal[1] to d, then, according to the
VC theory [17], [14], [15], the corresponding rate of convergence is bounded as
follows:

$$P \left\{ \sup_x \left| E_u \theta(x - u) - \frac{1}{\ell} \sum_{i=1}^{\ell} \theta(x - X_i) \right| \geq \varepsilon \right\} \leq \exp \left\{ - \left(\varepsilon^2 - \frac{d \ln \ell}{\ell} \right) \ell \right\}. \quad (4)$$

According to this bound, for sufficiently large ℓ, the convergence of ECDF to
the actual CDF does not depend too much on dimensionality of the space. This
fact has important consequences for Applied Statistics.

2   Main Problems of Statistical Inference

The main target of statistical inference theory is estimation (from the data) of
specific models of random events, namely:
1. conditional probability function;
2. conditional density function;
3. regression function;
4. density ratio function.

2.1   Conditional Density, Conditional Probability, Regression, and Density Ratio Functions

Let $F(x)$ be a cumulative distribution function of random variable x. We call
non-negative function $p(x)$ the probability density function if

$$\int_{-\infty}^{x} p(x^*) dx^* = F(x).$$

Similarly, let $F(x, y)$ be the joint probability distribution function of variables x
and y. We call non-negative $p(x, y)$ the joint probability density function of two
variables x and y if

$$\int_{-\infty}^{y} \int_{-\infty}^{x} p(x^*, y^*) dx^* dy^* = F(x, y).$$

---

[1] Since the set of d-dimensional parametric functions $\theta(x - u)$ can shatter, at most, d
vectors.

1. Let $p(x, y)$ and $p(x)$ be probability density functions for pairs (x, y) and vectors x. Suppose that $p(x) > 0$. The function

$$p(y|x) = \frac{p(x, y)}{p(x)}$$

is called the *Conditional Density Function*. It defines, for any fixed $x = x_0$, the probability density function $p(y|x = x_0)$ of random value $y \in R^1$. The estimation of the conditional density function from data

$$(y_1, X_1), ..., (y_\ell, X_\ell) \tag{5}$$

is the most difficult problem in our list of statistical inference problems.

2. Along with estimation of the conditional density function, the important problem is to estimate the so-called *Conditional Probability Function*. Let variable y be discrete, say, $y \in \{0, 1\}$. The function defined by the ratio

$$p(y = 1|x) = \frac{p(x, y = 1)}{p(x)}, \quad p(x) > 0$$

is called *Conditional Probability Function*. For any given vector $x = x_0$, this function defines the probability that value y will take value one (correspondingly $p(y = 0|x = x_0) = 1 - p(y = 1|x = x_0)$). The problem is to estimate the conditional probability function, given data (5) where $y \in \{0, 1\}$.

3. As mentioned above, estimation of the conditional density function is a difficult problem; a much easier problem is the problem of estimating the so-called *Regression Function* (conditional expectation of the variable y):

$$r(x) = \int y p(y|x) dy,$$

which defines expected value $y \in R^1$ for a given vector x.

4. In this paper, we also consider another problem that is important for applications: estimating the ratio of two probability densities [11]. Let $p_{num}(x)$ and $p_{den}(x) > 0$ be two different density functions (subscripts *num* and *den* correspond to numerator and denominator of the density ratio). Our goal is then to estimate the function

$$R(x) = \frac{p_{num}(x)}{p_{den}(x)}$$

given iid data

$$X_1, ..., X_{\ell_{den}}$$

distributed according to $p_{den}(x)$ and iid data

$$X_1', ..., X_{\ell_{num}}'$$

distributed according to $p_{num}(x)$.

In the next sections, we introduce direct settings for these four statistical inference problems.

2.2   Direct Constructive Setting for Conditional Density Estimation

According to its definition, conditional density $p(y|x)$ is defined by the ratio of two densities

$$p(y|x) = \frac{p(x,y)}{p(x)}, \quad p(x) > 0 \tag{6}$$

or, equivalently,

$$p(y|x)p(x) = p(x,y).$$

This expression leads to the following equivalent one:

$$\int \int \theta(y - y')\theta(x - x')p(y|x')dF(x')dy' = F(x,y), \tag{7}$$

where $F(x)$ is the cumulative distribution function of x and $F(x,y)$ is the joint cumulative distribution function of x and y.

Therefore, our setting of the condition density estimation problem is as follows:

Find the solution of the integral equation (7) in the set of nonnegative functions $f(x,y) = p(y|x)$ when the cumulative probability distribution functions $F(x,y)$ and $F(x)$ are unknown but iid data

$$(y_1, X_1), ..., (y_\ell, X_\ell)$$

are given.

In order to solve this problem, we use empirical estimates

$$F_\ell(x,y) = \frac{1}{\ell} \sum_{i=1}^{\ell} \theta(y - y_i)\theta(x - X_i), \tag{8}$$

$$F_\ell(x) = \frac{1}{\ell} \sum_{i=1}^{\ell} \theta(x - X_i) \tag{9}$$

of the unknown cumulative distribution functions $F(x,y)$ and $F(x)$. Therefore, we have to solve an integral equation where not only its right-hand side is defined approximately ($F_\ell(x,y)$ instead of $F(x,y)$), but also the data-based approximation

$$A_\ell f(x,y) = \int \int \theta(y - y')\theta(x - x')f(x',y')dy'dF_\ell(x')$$

is used instead of the exact integral operator

$$Af(x,y) = \int \int \theta(y - y')\theta(x - x')f(x',y')dy'dF(u').$$

Taking into account (9), our goal is thus to find the solution of approximately defined equation

$$\sum_{i=1}^{\ell} \theta(x - X_i) \int_{-\infty}^{y} f(X_i, y')dy' \approx \frac{1}{\ell} \sum_{i=1}^{\ell} \theta(y - y_i)\theta(x - X_i). \tag{10}$$

Taking into account definition (6), we have

$$\int_{-\infty}^{\infty} p(y|x)dy = 1, \quad \forall x \in \mathcal{X}.$$

Therefore, the solution of equation (10) has to satisfy the constraint $f(x, y) \geq 0$ and the constraint

$$\int_{-\infty}^{\infty} f(y', x)dy' = 1, \quad \forall x \in \mathcal{X}.$$

We call this setting *the direct constructive setting* since it is based on direct definition of conditional density function (7) and uses theoretically well-established approximations (8), (9) of unknown functions.

2.3 Direct Constructive Setting for Conditional Probability Estimation

The problem of estimation of the conditional probability function can be considered analogously to the conditional density estimation problem. The conditional probability is defined as

$$p(y = 1|x) = \frac{p(x, y = 1)}{p(x)}, \quad p(x) > 0 \tag{11}$$

or, equivalently,

$$p(y = 1|x)p(x) = p(x, y = 1).$$

We can rewrite it as

$$\int \theta(x - x')p(y = 1|x')dF(x') = F(x, y = 1). \tag{12}$$

Therefore, the problem of estimating the conditional probability is formulated as follows.

In the set of bounded functions $0 \leq p(y = 1|x) \leq 1$, find the solution of equation (12) if cumulative distribution functions $F(x)$ and $F(x, y = 1)$ are unknown but iid data

$$(y_1, X_1), ..., (y_\ell, X_\ell), \quad y \in \{0, 1\}, \quad x \in \mathcal{X}$$

generated according to $F(x, y)$ are given.

As before, instead of unknown cumulative distribution functions we use their empirical approximations

$$F_\ell(x) = \frac{1}{\ell}\sum_{i=1}^{\ell} \theta(x - X_i), \tag{13}$$

$$F_\ell(x, y = 1) = p_\ell F_\ell(x|y = 1) = \frac{1}{\ell}\sum_{i=1}^{\ell} y_i\theta(x - X_i), \tag{14}$$

where p_ℓ ratio of the examples with $y = 1$ to the total number of the observations.

Therefore, one has to solve integral equation (12) with approximately defined right-hand side (13) and approximately defined operator (14):

$$A_{\ell p}(y = 1|x) = \frac{1}{\ell} \sum_{i=1}^{\ell} \theta(x - X_i)p(y = 1|X_i).$$

Since the probability takes values between 0 and 1, our solution has to satisfy the bounds

$$0 \leq f(x) \leq 1, \quad \forall x \in \mathcal{X}.$$

Also, definition (11) implies that

$$\int f(x)dF(x) = p(y = 1),$$

where $p(y = 1)$ is the probability of $y = 1$.

2.4   Direct Constructive Setting for Regression Estimation

By definition, regression is the conditional mathematical expectation

$$r(x) = \int yp(y|x)dy = \int y\frac{p(x,y)}{p(x)}dy.$$

This can be rewritten in the form

$$r(x)p(x) = \int yp(x,y)dy. \tag{15}$$

From (15), one obtains the equivalent equation

$$\int \theta(x - x')r(x')dF(x') = \int \theta(x - x') \int ydF(x',y'). \tag{16}$$

Therefore, the direct constructive setting of regression estimation problem is as follows:

In a given set of functions $r(x)$, find the solution of integral equation (16) if cumulative probability distribution functions $F(x, y)$ and $F(x)$ are unknown but iid data (5) are given.

As before, instead of these functions, we use their empirical estimates. That is, we construct the approximation

$$A_{\ell}r(x) = \frac{1}{\ell} \sum_{i=1}^{\ell} \theta(x - X_i)r(X_i)$$

instead of the actual operator in (16) and the approximation of the right-hand side

$$F_{\ell}(x) = \frac{1}{\ell} \sum_{j=1}^{\ell} y_j\theta(x - X_j)$$

instead of the actual right-hand side in (16), based on the observation data

$$(y_1, X_1), ..., (y_\ell, X_\ell), \quad y \in R, \quad x \in \mathcal{X}. \tag{17}$$

2.5   Direct Constructive Setting of Density Ratio Estimation Problem

Let $F_{num}(x)$ and $F_{den}(x)$ be two different cumulative distribution functions defined on $\mathcal{X} \subset R^d$ and let $p_{num}(x)$ and $p_{den}(x)$ be the corresponding density functions. Suppose that $p_{den}(x) > 0, x \in \mathcal{X}$. Consider the ratio of two densities:

$$R(x) = \frac{p_{num}(x)}{p_{den}(x)}.$$

The problem is to estimate the ratio $R(x)$ when densities are unknown, but iid data

$$X_1, ..., X_{\ell_{den}} \quad \sim F_{den}(x) \tag{18}$$

generated according to $F_{den}(x)$ and iid data

$$X_1', ..., X_{\ell_{num}}' \quad \sim F_{num}(x) \tag{19}$$

generated according to $F_{num}(x)$ are given.

As before, we introduce the constructive setting of this problem: solve the integral equation

$$\int \theta(x - u) R(u) dF_{den}(u) = F_{num}(x)$$

when cumulative distribution functions $F_{den}(x)$ and $F_{num}(x)$ are unknown, but data (18) and (19) are given. As before, we approximate the unknown cumulative distribution functions $F_{num}(x)$ and $F_{den}(x)$ using empirical distribution functions

$$F_{\ell_{num}}(x) = \frac{1}{\ell_{num}} \sum_{j=1}^{\ell_{num}} \theta(x - X_j')$$

for $F_{num}(x)$ and

$$F_{\ell_{den}}(x) = \frac{1}{\ell_{den}} \sum_{j=1}^{\ell_{den}} \theta(x - X_j)$$

for $F_{den}(x)$.

Since $R(x) \geq 0$ and $\lim_{x \to \infty} F_{num}(x) = 1$, our solution must satisfy the constraints

$$R(x) \geq 0, \quad \forall x \in \mathcal{X},$$

$$\int R(x) dF_{den}(x) = 1.$$

Therefore, all main empirical inference problems can be represented via (multidimensional) Fredholm integral equation of the first kind with approximately defined elements. Although approximations converge to the true functions, these problems are computationally difficult due to their ill-posed nature. Thus they require rigorous solutions.[2]

In the next section, we consider methods for solving ill-posed operator equations which we apply in Section 6 to our problems of inference.

3   Solution of Ill-Posed Operator Equations

3.1   Fredholm Integral Equations of the First Kind

In this section, we consider the linear operator equations

$$Af = F, \tag{20}$$

where A maps elements of the metric space $f \in \mathcal{M} \subset E_1$ into elements of the metric space $F \in \mathcal{N} \subset E_2$. Let f be a continuous one-to-one operator and $f(\mathcal{M}) = \mathcal{N}$. The solution of such operator equation exists and is unique:

$$\mathcal{M} = A^{-1}\mathcal{N}.$$

The crucial question is whether this inverse operator is continuous. If it is continous, then close functions in $\mathcal{N}$ correspond to close functions in $\mathcal{M}$. That is, "small" changes in the right-hand side of (20) cause "small" changes of its solution. In this case, we call the operator A^{-1} *stable* [13].

If, however, the inverse operator is discontinuous, then "small" changes in the right-hand side of (20) can cause significant changes of the solution. In this case, we call the operator A^{-1} *unstable*.

Solution of equation (20) is called *well-posed* if this solution

1. *exists;*
2. *is unique;*
3. *is stable.*

Otherwise we call the solution *ill-posed.*

We are interested in the situation when the solution of operator equation *exists*, and *is unique*. In this case, the effectiveness of solution of equation (20) is defined by the *stability* of the operator A^{-1}. If the operator is unstable, then, generally speaking, the numerical solution of equation is impossible.

Here we consider linear integral operator

$$Af(x) = \int_a^b K(x, u)f(u)du$$

defined by the kernel $K(t, u)$, which is continuous almost everywhere on $a \leq t \leq b$, $c \leq x \leq d$. This kernel maps the set of functions $\{f(t)\}$, continuous on $[a, b]$,

---

[2] Various classical statistical methods exist for solving these problems; our goal is to find the most accurate solutions that take into account all available characteristics of the problems.

onto the set of functions $\{F(x)\}$, also continuous on $[c, d]$. The corresponding Fredholm equation of the first kind is

$$\int_a^b K(x, u)f(u)du = F(x),$$

which requires finding the solution $f(u)$ given the right-hand side $F(x)$.

In this paper, we consider integral equation defined by the so-called convolution kernel

$$K(x, u) = K(x - u).$$

Moreover, we consider the specific convolution kernel of the form

$$K(x - u) = \theta(x - u).$$

As stated in Section 2.2, this kernel covers all settings of empirical inference problems.

First, we show that the solution of equation

$$\int_0^1 \theta(x - u)f(u)du = x$$

is indeed ill-posed[3]. It is easy to check that

$$f(x) = 1 \tag{21}$$

is the solution of this equation. Indeed,

$$\int_0^1 \theta(x - u)du = \int_0^x du = x. \tag{22}$$

It is also easy to check that the function

$$f^*(x) = 1 + \cos nx \tag{23}$$

is a solution of the equation

$$\int_0^1 \theta(x - u)f^*(u)du = x + \frac{\sin nx}{n}. \tag{24}$$

That is, when n increases, the right-hand sides of the equations (22) and (24) are getting close to each other, but solutions (21) and (23) are not.

The problem is how one can solve an ill-posed equation when its right-hand side is defined imprecisely.

---

[3] Using the same arguments, one can show that the problem of solving any Fredholm equation of the first kind is ill-posed.

3.2   Methods of Solving Ill-Posed Problems

Inverse Operator Lemma. The following classical inverse operator lemma [13] is the key enabler for solving ill-posed problems.

Lemma. *If A is a continuous one-to-one operator defined on a compact set $\mathcal{M}^* \subset \mathcal{M}$, then the inverse operator A^{-1} is continuous on the set $\mathcal{N}^* = A\mathcal{M}^*$.*

Therefore, the conditions of existence and uniqueness of the solution of an operator equation imply that the problem is well-posed on the compact $\mathcal{M}^*$. The third condition (stability of the solution) is automatically satisfied. This lemma is the basis for all constructive ideas of solving ill-posed problems. We now consider one of them.

Regularization Method. Suppose that we have to solve the operator equation

$$Af = F \tag{25}$$

defined by continuous one-to-one operator A mapping $\mathcal{M}$ into $\mathcal{N}$, and assume the solution of (25) exists. Also suppose that, instead of the right-hand side $F(x)$, we are given its approximation $F_\delta(x)$, where

$$\rho_{E_2}(F(x), F_\delta(x)) \le \delta.$$

Our goal is to find the solution of equation

$$Af = F_\delta$$

when $\delta \to 0$.

Consider a lower semi-continuous functional $W(f)$ (called the *regularizer*) that has the following three properties:

1. the solution of the operator equation (25) belongs to the domain $D(W)$ of the functional $W(f)$;
2. functional $W(f)$ is non-negative values in its domain;
3. all sets

$$\mathcal{M}_c = \{f : W(f) \le c\}$$

   are compact for any $c \ge 0$.

The idea of regularization is to find a solution for (25) as an element minimizing the so-called regularized functional

$$R_\gamma(\hat{f}, F_\delta) = \rho_{E_2}^2(A\hat{f}, F_\delta) + \gamma_\delta W(\hat{f}), \quad \hat{f} \in D(W) \tag{26}$$

with *regularization parameter* $\gamma_\delta > 0$.

The following theorem holds true [13].

Theorem 1. *Let E_1 and E_2 be metric spaces, and suppose for $F \in \mathcal{N}$ there exists a solution $f \in D(W)$ of (26). Suppose that, instead of the exact right-hand side*

F of (26), its approximations[4] $F_\delta \in E_2$ are given such that $\rho_{E_2}(F, F_\delta) \leq \delta$. Consider the sequence of parameter γ such that

$$\gamma(\delta) \longrightarrow 0 \text{ for } \delta \longrightarrow 0,$$

$$\lim_{\delta \longrightarrow 0} \frac{\delta^2}{\gamma(\delta)} \leq r < \infty. \tag{27}$$

Then the sequence of solutions $f_\delta^{\gamma(\delta)}$ minimizing the functionals $R_{\gamma(\delta)}(f, F_\delta)$ on $D(W)$ converges to the exact solution f (in the metric of space E_1) as $\delta \longrightarrow 0$.

In a Hilbert space, the functional $W(f)$ may be chosen as $||f||^2$ for a linear operator A. Although the sets $\mathcal{M}_c$ are (only) weakly compact in this case, regularized solutions converge to the desired one. Such a choice of regularized functional is convenient since its domain $D(W)$ is the whole space E_1. In this case, however, the conditions imposed on the parameter γ are more restrictive than in the case of Theorem 1: namely, γ should converge to zero slower than δ^2.

Thus the following theorem holds true [13].

Theorem 2. *Let E_1 be a Hilbert space and $W(f) = ||f||^2$. Then for $\gamma(\delta)$ satisfying (27) with $r = 0$, the regularized element $f_\delta^{\gamma(\delta)}$ converges to the exact solution f in metric E_1 as $\delta \to 0$.*

4   Stochastic Ill-Posed Problems

In this section, we consider the problem of solving the operator equation

$$Af = F, \tag{28}$$

where not only its right-hand side is defined approximately ($F_\ell(x)$ instead of $F(x)$) but also the operator Af is defined approximately. Such problem are called *stochastic ill-posed problems*.

In the next subsections, we describe the conditions under which it is possible to solve equation (28) where both the right-hand side and the operator are defined approximately.

In the following subsections, we first discuss the general theory for solving stochastic ill-posed problems and then consider specific operators describing particular problems, i.e., empirical inference problems described in the previous sections 2.3, 2.4, and 2.5. For all these problems, the operator has the form

$$A_\ell f = \int \theta(x - u)f(u)dF_\ell(u).$$

We show that rigorous solutions of stochastic ill-posed problem with this operator leverage the so-called V-matrix, which captures some geometric properties of the data; we also describe specific algorithms for solution of our empirical inference problems.

---

[4]   The elements F_δ do not have to belong to the set $\mathcal{N}$.

4.1   Regularization of Stochastic Ill-Posed Problems

Consider the problem of solving the operator equation

$$Af = F$$

under the condition where (random) approximations are given not only for the function on the right-hand side of the equation but for the operator as well (*the stochastic ill-posed problem*).

We assume that, instead of the true operator A, we are given a sequence of random continuous operators A_ℓ, $\ell = 1, 2, ...$ that converges in probability to operator A (the definition of closeness between two operators will be defined later).

First, we discuss general conditions under which the solution of stochastic ill-posed problem is possible and then we consider specific operator equations corresponding to the each empirical inference problem.

As before, we consider the problem of solving the operator equation by the regularization method, i.e., by minimizing the functional

$$R_{\gamma_\ell}^*(f, F_\ell, A_\ell) = \rho_{E_2}^2(A_\ell f, F_\ell) + \gamma_\ell W(f). \tag{29}$$

For this functional, there exists a minimum (perhaps, not unique). We define the closeness of operator A and operator A_ℓ as the distance

$$\|A_\ell - A\| = \sup_{f \in D} \frac{\|A_\ell f - Af\|_{E_2}}{W^{1/2}(f)}.$$

The main result for solving stochastic ill-posed problems via regularization method (29) is provided by the following Theorem [9], [15].

Theorem. *For any $\varepsilon > 0$ and any constants $C_1, C_2 > 0$ there exists a value $\gamma_0 > 0$ such that for any $\gamma_\ell \leq \gamma_0$ the inequality*

$$\begin{aligned} P\{\rho_{E_1}(f_\ell, f) > \varepsilon\} \leq \\ \leq P\{\rho_{E_2}(F_\ell, F) > C_1\sqrt{\gamma_\ell}\} + P\{\|A_\ell - A\| > C_2\sqrt{\gamma_\ell}\} \end{aligned} \tag{30}$$

holds true.

Corollary. As follows from this theorem, if the approximations $F_\ell(x)$ of the right-hand side of the operator equation converge to the true function $F(x)$ in E_2 with the rate of convergence $r(\ell)$, and the approximations A_ℓ converge to the true operator A in the metric in E_1 defined in (30) with the rate of convergence $r_A(\ell)$, then there exists a function

$$r_0(\ell) = \max\{r(\ell), \; r_A(\ell)\}; \quad \lim_{\ell \to \infty} r_0(\ell) = 0,$$

such that the sequence of solutions to the equation converges in probability to the true one if

$$\lim_{\ell \to \infty} \frac{r_0(\ell)}{\sqrt{\gamma_\ell}} = 0, \quad \lim_{\ell \to \infty} \gamma_\ell = 0.$$

4.2   Solution of Empirical Inference Problems

In this section, we consider solutions of the integral equation

$$Af = F$$

where operator A has the form

$$Af = \int \theta(x - u)f(u)dF_1(x),$$

and the right-hand side of the equation is $F_2(x)$. That is, our goal is to solve the integral equation

$$\int \theta(x - u)f(u)dF_1(x) = F_2(x).$$

We consider the case where $F_1(x)$ and $F_2(x)$ are two different cumulative distribution functions. (This integral equation also includes, as a special case, the problem of regression estimation where $F_2(x) = \int y dP(x, y)$ for non-negative y). This equation defines the main empirical inference problem described in Section 2. The problem of density ratio estimation requires solving solving this equation when both functions $F_1(x)$ and $F_2(x)$ are unknown but the iid data

$$X_1^1, ..., X_{\ell_1}^1 \quad \sim F_1 \tag{31}$$

$$X_1^1, ..., X_{\ell_2}^1 \quad \sim F_2 \tag{32}$$

are available. In order to solve this equation, we use empirical approximations instead of actual distribution functions obtaining

$$A_{\ell_1} f = \int \theta(x - u)dF_{\ell_1}(u) \tag{33}$$

$$F_{\ell_k}(x) = \frac{1}{\ell_k} \sum_{i=1}^{\ell_k} \theta(x - X_i^k), \quad k = 1, 2,$$

where $F_{\ell_1}(u)$ is empirical distribution function obtained from data (31) and $F_{\ell_2}(x)$ is the empirical distribution function obtained from data (32).

One can show (see [15], Section 7.7) that, for sufficiently large ℓ, the inequality

$$||A_\ell - A|| = \sup_f \frac{||A_\ell f - Af||_{E_2}}{W^{1/2}(f)} \leq ||F_\ell - F||_{E_2}$$

holds true for the smooth solution $f(x)$ of our equations.

From this inequality, bounds (4), and the Theorem of Section 4.1, it follows that the regularized solutions of our operator equations converge to the actual functions

$$\rho_{E_1}(f_\ell, f) \to_{\ell \to \infty} 0$$

with probability one.

Therefore, to solve our inference problems, we minimize the functional

$$R_\gamma(f, F_\ell, A_{\ell_1}) = \rho_{E_2}^2(A_{\ell_1} f, F_{\ell_2}) + \gamma_\ell W(f). \tag{34}$$

In order to do this well, we have to define three elements of (34):

1. The distance $\rho_{E_2}(F_1, F_2)$ between functions $F_1(x)$ and $F_2(x)$ in E_2.
2. The regularization functional $W(f)$ in space of functions $f \in E_1$.
3. The rule for selecting the regularization constant γ_ℓ.

The next sections describe solution approaches for the first two problems.

5   Solving Statistical Inference Problems with V-matrix

Consider the explicit form of the functional for solving our inference problems. In order to do this, we specify expressions for the squared distance and regularization functional in expression (34).

5.1   The V-matrix

Definition of Distance. Let our distance in E_2 be defined by the L_2 metric

$$\rho_{E_2}^2(F_1(x), F_2(x)) = \int (F_1(x) - F_2(x))^2 \sigma(x) d\mu(x),$$

where $\sigma(x)$ is a *known* positive function defined on $\mathcal{X}$ and $\mu(x)$ is a *known* measure defined on $\mathcal{X}$. To define distance, one can use any non-negative measurable function $\sigma(x)$ and any measure $\mu(x)$. For example, if our equation is defined in the box domain $[0, 1]^d$, we can use uniform measure in this domain and $\sigma(x) = 1$.

Below we define the measure $\mu(x)$ as

$$\mu(x) = \prod_{k=1}^{d} F_\ell(x^k), \tag{35}$$

where each $F_\ell(x^k)$ is the marginal empirical cumulative distribution function of the coordinate x^k estimated from data.

We also consider function $\sigma(x)$ in the form

$$\sigma(x) = \prod_{k=1}^{n} \sigma_k(x^k). \tag{36}$$

In this paper, we consider several weight functions $\sigma(x^k)$:

1. The function

$$\sigma(x^k) = 1.$$

2. For the problem of conditional probability estimation, we consider the function

$$\sigma(x^k) = \frac{1}{F_\ell(x^k|y = 1)(1 - F_\ell(x^k|y = 1)) + \epsilon}, \tag{37}$$

where $\varepsilon > 0$ is a small constant.

3. For the problem of regression estimation, we consider the case where $y \geq 0$ and, instead of $F_\ell(x^k|y=1)$ in (37), use monotonic function

$$F_\ell(x^k) = \frac{1}{\ell \hat{y}_{av}} \sum_{i=1}^{\ell} y_i \theta(x^k - X_i^k),$$

where $\hat{y}_{av}$ is the average value of y in the training data. This function has properties of ECDF.

4. For the problem of density ratio estimation, we consider an estimate of function $F_{num}(x)$ instead of the estimate of function $F(x|y=1)$ in (37).

Remark. In order to justify choice (37) for function $\sigma(x)$, consider the problem of one-dimensional conditional probability estimation. Let $f_0(x)$ be the true conditional probability. Consider the function $\hat{f}_0(x) = p_1 f_0(x)$. Then the solution of integral equation

$$\int \theta(x - u)\hat{f}(u)dF(x) = F(x|y=1)$$

defines the conditional probability $f_0(x) = p_1 f_0(x)$. Consider two functions: the estimate of the right-hand side of equation $F_\ell(x|y=1)$ and the actual right-hand side $F_0(x|y=1)$

$$F_0(x|y=1) = \int_{-\infty}^{x} \hat{f}_0(t)dt.$$

The deviation

$$\Delta = (F_0(x|y=1) - F_\ell(x|y=1))$$

between these two functions has different values of variance for different x. The variance is small (equal to zero) at the end points of an interval and large somewhere inside it. To obtain the *uniform relative deviation* of approximation from the actual function over the whole interval, we adjust the distance in any point of interval proportional to the inverse of variance. Since for any fixed x the variance is

$$\text{Var}(x) = F(x|y=1)(1 - F(x|y=1)), \tag{38}$$

we normalize the squared deviation Δ^2 by (38). Expression (37) realizes this idea.

Definition of Distance for Conditional Probability Estimation Problem. Consider the problem of conditional probability estimation.

For this problem, the squared distance between approximations of the right-hand side and the left-hand side of equation

$$F_\ell(x, y=1) = p_\ell F_\ell(x|y=1) = \frac{1}{\ell} \sum_{i=1}^{\ell} y_i \theta(x - X_i)$$

can be written as follows:

$$\rho^2(A_\ell f, F_\ell) =$$

$$\int \left(\int \theta(x - u)f(u)dF_\ell(u) - \int y_i\theta(x - u)dF_\ell(u) \right)^2 \sigma(x)d\mu(x),$$

where $y_i \in \{0, 1\}$ and $F_\ell(x)$ is the empirical distribution function estimated from training vectors X_i. Therefore, we obtain the expression

$$\rho^2(A_\ell f, F_\ell) = \frac{1}{\ell^2} \sum_{i,j=1}^{\ell} f(X_i)f(X_j) \int \theta(x - X_i)\theta(x - X_j)\sigma(x)d\mu(x) -$$

$$\frac{2}{\ell^2} \sum_{i,j=1}^{\ell} f(X_i)y_j \int \theta(x - X_i)\theta(x - X_j)\sigma(x)d\mu(x) + \qquad (39)$$

$$\frac{1}{\ell^2} \sum_{i,j=1}^{\ell} y_iy_j \int \theta(x - X_i)\theta(x - X_j)\sigma(x)d\mu(x)$$

where the last term does not depend on function $f(x)$.

Since both $\sigma(x)$ and $\mu(x)$ are products of one-dimensional functions, each integral in (39) has the form

$$V_{i,j} = \int \theta(x - X_i)\theta(x - X_j)\sigma(x)\, d\mu(x) =$$

$$\prod_{k=1}^{d} \int \theta(x^k - X_i^k)\theta(x^k - X_j^k)\sigma_k(x^k)d\mu(x^k). \qquad (40)$$

This $(\ell \times \ell)$-dimensional matrix of elements $V_{i,j}$ we call V-matrix of the sample $X_1, ..., X_\ell$, where $X_i = (X_i^1, ... X_i^d)$, $\forall i = 1, ..., \ell$.

Consider three cases:

Case 1: Data belongs to the upper-bounded support $(-\infty, B]^d$ for some B, $\sigma(x) = 1$ on this support, and μ is the uniform measure on it. Then the elements $V_{i,j}$ of V-matrix have the form

$$V_{i,j} = \prod_{k=1}^{d} (B - \max\{X_i^k, X_j^k\}).$$

Case 2: Case where $\sigma(x^k) = 1$ and μ is defined as (35). Then the elements $V_{i,j}$ of V-matrix have the form

$$V_{i,j} = \prod_{k=1}^{d} \nu(X^k > \max\{X_i^k, X_j^k\}).$$

where $\nu(X^k > \max\{X_i^k, X_j^k\})$ is the frequency of X^k from the given data with the values largen than $\max\{X_i^k, X_j^k\}$.

Case 3: where $\sigma(x)$ is defined as (36, 37) and $\mu(x)$ as (35). In this case, the values $V_{i,j}$ also can easily be numerically computed (since both functions are piecewise constant, the integration (40) is reduced to summation of constants).

To rewrite the expression for the distance in a compact form, we introduce the ℓ-dimensional vector Φ

$$\Phi = (f(X_1), ..., f(X_\ell))^T.$$

Then, taking into account (39), we rewrite the first summand of functional (34) as

$$\rho^2(A_\ell f, F_\ell) = \frac{1}{\ell^2} \left(\Phi^T V \Phi - 2\Phi^T V Y + Y^T V Y \right), \tag{41}$$

where Y denotes the ℓ-dimensional vector $(y_1, ..., y_\ell)^T$, $y_i \in \{0, 1\}$.

Distance for Regression Estimation Problem. Repeating the same derivation for regression estimation problem we obtain the same expression for distance

$$\rho^2(A_\ell f, F_\ell) = \frac{1}{\ell^2} \left(\Phi^T V \Phi - 2\Phi^T V Y + Y^T V Y \right),$$

where coordinates of vector Y are values $y \in R$ are given in examples (17) for regression estimation problem.

Distance for Density Ratio Estimation Problem. In the problem of density ratio estimation, we have to solve the integral equation

$$\int \theta(x - u)R(u)dF_{\text{den}}(u) = F_{\text{num}}(x),$$

where cumulative distribution functions $F_{\text{den}}(x)$ and $F_{\text{num}}(x)$ are unknown but iid data

$$X_1, ..., X_{\ell_{\text{den}}} \quad \sim F_{\text{den}}(x)$$

and iid data

$$X'_1, ..., X'_{\ell_{\text{num}}} \quad \sim F_{\text{num}}(x)$$

are available.

Using the empirical estimates

$$F_{\ell_{\text{num}}}(x) = \frac{1}{\ell_{\text{num}}} \sum_{j=1}^{\ell_{\text{num}}} \theta(x - X'_j)$$

and

$$F_{\ell_{\text{den}}}(x) = \frac{1}{\ell_{\text{den}}} \sum_{j=1}^{\ell_{\text{den}}} \theta(x - X_i)$$

instead of unknown cumulative distribution $F_{\text{num}}(x)$ and $F_{\text{den}}(x)$ and repeating the same distance computations as in problems of conditional probability estimation and regression estimation, we obtain

$$\rho^2 = \int \left(\int \theta(x-u)R(u)dF_{\ell_{\text{den}}}(u) - F_{\ell_{\text{num}}}(x) \right)^2 \sigma(x)d\mu(x) =$$

$$\frac{1}{\ell_{\text{den}}^2} \sum_{i,j=1}^{\ell_{\text{den}}} R(X_i)R(X_j) \int \theta(x-X_j)\theta(x-X_j)\sigma(x)d\mu(x) -$$

$$\frac{2}{\ell_{\text{num}}\ell_{\text{den}}} \sum_{i=1}^{\ell_{\text{num}}} \sum_{j=1}^{\ell_{\text{den}}} R(X_i)R(X_j') \int \theta(x-X_i)\theta(x-X_j')\sigma(x)d\mu(x) +$$

$$\frac{1}{\ell_{\text{num}}^2} \sum_{i,j=1}^{\ell_{\text{num}}} \int \theta(x-X_j')\theta(x-X_j')\sigma(x)d\mu(x) = \frac{1}{\ell_{\text{num}}^2} \sum_{i,j=1}^{\ell_{\text{num}}} V_{i,j}^{**} +$$

$$\frac{1}{\ell_{\text{den}}^2} \sum_{i,j=1}^{\ell_{\text{den}}} R(X_i)R(X_j)V_{i,j} - \frac{2}{\ell_{\text{num}}\ell_{\text{den}}} \sum_{i=1}^{\ell_{\text{den}}} \sum_{j=1}^{\ell_{\text{num}}} R(X_i)R(X_j')V_{i,j}^*,$$

where the values $V_{i,j}, V_{i,j}^*, V_{i,j}^{**}$ are calculated as

$$\begin{cases} V_{i,j} = \int \theta(x-X_i)\theta(x-X_j)\sigma(x)d\mu(x), & i,j=1,...,\ell_{\text{den}}, \\ V_{i,j}^* = \int \theta(x-X_i)\theta(x-X_j')\sigma(x)d\mu(x), & i=1,...,\ell_{\text{num}}, \; j=1,...,\ell_{\text{den}}, \\ V_{i,j}^{**} = \int \theta(x-X_i')\theta(x-X_j')\sigma(x)d\mu(x), & i,j=1,...,\ell_{\text{num}}. \end{cases}$$

We denote by V, V^*, and V^{**} (respectively, $\ell_{\text{den}} \times \ell_{\text{den}}$-dimensional, $\ell_{\text{den}} \times \ell_{\text{num}}$-dimensional, and $\ell_{\text{num}} \times \ell_{\text{num}}$-dimensional) the matrices of corresponding elements $V_{i,j}$, $V_{i,j}^*$, and $V_{i,j}^{**}$. We also denote by $1_{\ell_{\text{num}}}$ the ℓ_{num}-dimensional vector of ones, and by R – the ℓ_{den}-dimensional column vector of $R(X_i)$, $i = 1,\ldots,\ell_{\text{den}}$.

Using these notations, we can rewrite the distance as follows:

$$\rho^2 = \frac{1}{\ell_{\text{den}}^2} \left(R^T V R - 2 \left(\frac{\ell_{\text{den}}}{\ell_{\text{num}}} \right) R^T V^* 1_{\ell_{\text{num}}} + \left(\frac{\ell_{\text{den}}}{\ell_{\text{num}}} \right)^2 1_{\ell_{\text{num}}}^T V^{**} 1_{\ell_{\text{num}}} \right).$$

5.2   The Regularization Functionals in RKHS

For each of our inference problems, we now look for its solution in Reproducing Kernel Hilbert Space (RHS).

Reproducing Kernel Hilbert Space. According to Mercer theorem, any positive semi-definite kernel has a representation

$$K(x,z) = \sum_{k=1}^{\infty} \lambda_k \phi_k(x)\phi_k(z), \quad x,z \in \mathcal{X},$$

where $\{\phi_k(x)\}$ is a system of orthonormal functions in L_2 and $\lambda_k \geq 0 \; \forall k$.

Consider the set of functions

$$f(x;a) = \sum_{k=1}^{\infty} a_k \phi_k(x). \tag{42}$$

We say that set of functions (42) belongs to RKHS of kernel $K(x, z)$ if we can define the inner product (f_1, f_2) in this space such that

$$(f_1(x), K(x, y)) = f_1(y). \tag{43}$$

It is easy to check that the inner product

$$(f(x, a), f(x, b)) = \sum_{k=1}^{\infty} \frac{a_k b_k}{\lambda_k},$$

where a_k, $k = 1, \ldots$ and b_k, $k = 1, \ldots$ are the coefficients of expansion of functions $f(x, a)$, and $f(x, b)$, satisfies the reproducing property (43). In particular, the equality

$$(K(x_1, z), K(x_2, z)) = K(x_1, x_2) \tag{44}$$

holds true for the kernel $K(x, x^*)$ that defines RKHS.

The remarkable property of RKHS is the so-called Representer Theorem [3], [4], [8], which states that any function $f(x)$ from RKHS that minimizes functional (34) can be represented as

$$f(x) = \sum_{i=1}^{\ell} c_i K(X_i, x),$$

where c_i, $i = 1, \ldots, \ell$ are parameters and X_i, $i = 1, \ldots, \ell$ are vectors of observations.

Explicit Form of Regularization Functional. In all our Statistical Inference problems, we are looking for solutions in RKHS, where we use the squared norm as the regularization functional:

$$W(f) = (f, f) = ||f||^2. \tag{45}$$

That is, we are looking for solution in the form

$$f(x) = \sum_{i=1}^{\ell} \alpha_i K(X_i, x), \tag{46}$$

where X_i are elements of the observation. Using property (44), we define functional (45) as

$$W(f) = \sum_{i,j=1}^{\ell} \alpha_i \alpha_j K(x_i, x_j).$$

In order to use the matrix form of (34), we introduce the following notations:

1. K is the $(\ell \times \ell)$-dimensional matrix of elements $K(X_i, X_j)$, $i, j = 1, \ldots, \ell$.
2. $\mathcal{K}(x)$ is the ℓ-dimensional vector of functions $K(X_i, x)$, $i = 1, \ldots, \ell$.
3. A is the ℓ-dimensional vector $A = (\alpha_1, \ldots, \alpha_\ell)^T$ of elements α_i, $i = 1, \ldots, \ell$.

In these notations, the regularization functional has the form

$$W(f) = A^T K A, \tag{47}$$

and its solution has the form

$$f(x) = A^T \mathcal{K}(x). \tag{48}$$

6 Solution of Statistical Inference Problems

In this section, we formulate our statistical inference problems as optimization problems.

6.1 Estimation of Conditional Probability Function

Here we present an explicit form of the optimization problem for estimating conditional probability function.

We are looking for the solution in form (48), where we have to find vector A. In order to find it, we have to minimize the objective function

$$T(A) = A^T K V K A - 2A^T K V Y + \gamma A^T K A, \tag{49}$$

where Y is a binary vector (with coordinates $y \in \{0, 1\}$) defined by the observations. The first two terms of the objective function come from distance (41), the last term is the regularization functional (47). (The third term from (49) was omitted in the target functional since it does not depend on the unknown function.) Since the conditional probability has values between 0 and 1, we have to minimize this objective function subject to the constraint

$$0 \le A^T \mathcal{K}(x) \le 1, \quad \forall x \in X. \tag{50}$$

We also know that

$$\int A^T \mathcal{K}(x) dF(x) = p_0, \tag{51}$$

where p_0 is the probability of class $y = 1$.

Minimization of (49) subject to constraints (50), (51) is a difficult optimization problem. To simplify this problem, we minimize the functional subject to the constraints

$$0 \le A^T \mathcal{K}(X_i) \le 1, \ i = 1, ..., \ell, \tag{52}$$

defined only at the vectors X_i of observations. [5]

Also, we can approximate equality (51) using training data

$$\frac{1}{\ell} \sum_{i=1}^{\ell} A^T \mathcal{K}(X_i) = p_\ell, \tag{53}$$

---

[5] One can find the solution in closed form $A = (VK + \gamma I)^{-1} VY$ if constraints (52), (53) are ignored; here I is the identity matrix.

where p_ℓ is frequency of class $y = 1$ estimated from data. Using matrix notation, the constraints (52) and (53) can be rewritten as follows:

$$0_\ell \leq KA \leq 1_\ell, \tag{54}$$

$$\frac{1}{\ell} A^T K 1_\ell = p_\ell. \tag{55}$$

where K is the matrix of elements $K(X_i, X_j)$, $i, j = 1, ..., \ell$ and 0_ℓ, 1_ℓ are ℓ-dimensional vectors of zeros and ones, respectively.

Therefore, we are looking for the solution in form (48), where parameters of vector A minimize functional (49) subject to constraints (54) and (55). This is a quadratic optimization problem with one linear equality constraint and 2ℓ *general* linear inequality constraints.

In Section 6.4, we simplify this optimization problem by reducing it to a quadratic optimization problem with one linear equality constraint and several *box* constraints.

6.2   Estimation of Regression Function

Similarly, we can formulate the problem of regression function estimation, which has the form (46). To find the vector A, we minimize the functional

$$T(A) = A^T KVKA - 2A^T KVY + \gamma A^T KA, \tag{56}$$

where Y is real-valued vector (with coordinates $y_i \in R^1$ of the observations (5)).

Suppose that we have the following knowledge about the regression function:

1. Regression $y = f(x) = A^T K(x)$ takes values inside an interval $[a, b]$:

$$a \leq A^T K(x) \leq b, \quad \forall x \in \mathcal{X}. \tag{57}$$

2. We know the expectation of the values of the regression function:

$$\int A^T K(x) dF(x) = c. \tag{58}$$

Then we can solve the following problem: minimize functional (56) subject to constraints (57), (58).

Usually we do not have knowledge (57), (58), but we can approximate it from the training data. Specifically, we can approximate a by the smallest value of y_i (without loss of generality, we consider $y_i \geq 0$), while b can be approximated by the largest value of y_i from the training set:

$$a_\ell = \min\{y_1, ..., y_\ell\}, \quad b_\ell = \max\{y_1, ..., y_\ell\}.$$

We then consider constraint (57) applied only for the training data:

$$a_\ell \leq A^T K(X_i) \leq b_\ell, \quad i = 1, ..., \ell. \tag{59}$$

Also, we can approximate (58) with the equality constraint

$$\frac{1}{\ell}\sum_{i=1}^{\ell}A^T\mathcal{K}(X_i)=\frac{1}{\ell}\sum_{i=1}^{\ell}y_i. \tag{60}$$

Constraints (59), (60) can be written in matrix notation

$$a_\ell 1_\ell \le KA \le 1_\ell b_\ell, \tag{61}$$

$$\frac{1}{\ell}A^T K 1_\ell = \hat{y}_{av}, \tag{62}$$

where $\hat{y}_{av}$ is the right-hand side of (60). If these approximations[6] are reasonable, the problem of estimating the regression can be stated as minimization of the functional (56) subject to constraints (61), (62). This is a quadratic optimization problem with one linear equality constraint and 2ℓ general linear inequality constraints.

6.3   Estimation of Density Ratio Function

To solve the problem of estimating density ratio function in the form

$$R(x) = A^T\mathcal{K}(x),$$

where A is the ℓ_{den}-dimensional vector of parameters and $\mathcal{K}(x)$ is the ℓ_{den}-dimensional vector of functions $K(X_1, x), ..., K(X_{\ell_{\text{den}}}, x)$, we have to minimize the functional

$$T(A) = A^T KVKA - 2\left(\frac{\ell_{\text{den}}}{\ell_{\text{num}}}\right)A^T KV^* 1_{\ell_{\text{num}}} + \gamma A^T KA, \tag{63}$$

where K is the $\ell_{\text{den}} \times \ell_{\text{den}}$-dimensional matrix of elements $K(X_i, X_j)$ subject to the constraints

$$A^T\mathcal{K}(x) \ge 0, \quad \forall x \in X,$$

$$\int A^T\mathcal{K}(x)dF_{\text{den}}(x) = 1.$$

As above, we replace these constraints with their approximations

$$KA \ge \mathbf{0}_{\ell_{\text{den}}},$$

$$\frac{1}{\ell_{\text{den}}}A^T KV^* 1_{\ell_{\text{num}}} = 1$$

Here K is $(\ell_{\text{den}} \times \ell_{\text{den}})$-dimensional matrix of observations from $F_{\text{den}}(x)$, and V^* is $(\ell_{\text{den}} \times \ell_{\text{num}})$-dimensional matrix defined in Section 5.1.

---

[6] Without constraints, the solution has the closed form (see footnote 7), where $y \in R^1$ are elements of training data for regression.

6.4   Two-Stage Method for Function Estimation: Data Smoothing and Data Interpolation

Solutions of Statistical Inference problems considered in the previous sections require numerical treatment of the general quadratic optimization problem: minimization of quadratic form subject to one linear equality constraint and 2ℓ linear inequality constraints of general type (ℓ linear inequality constraints for density ratio estimation problem).

Numerical solution for such problems can be computationally hard (especially when ℓ is large). In this section, we simplify the problem by splitting it into two parts:

1. Estimating function values at ℓ observation points, i.e., estimating vector $\Phi = (f(X_1), ..., f(X_\ell))^T$.
2. Interpolating the values of function known at the ℓ observation points to other points in the space $\mathcal{X}$.

Estimating Function Values at Observation Points. In order to find the function values at the training data points, we rewrite the regularization functional in objective functions (49), (56), (63) in a different form. In order to do this, we use the equality

$$K = KK^+K,$$

where K^+ is the *pseudoinverse* matrix of matrix[7] K.

In our regularization term of objective functions, we use the equality

$$A^T KA = A^T KK^+ KA.$$

1. Estimation of values of conditional probability. For the problem of estimating the values of conditional probability at ℓ observation points, we rewrite the objective function (49) in the form

$$W(\Phi) = \Phi^T V\Phi - 2\Phi^T VY + \gamma \Phi^T K^+ \Phi, \tag{64}$$

where we have denoted

$$\Phi = KA. \tag{65}$$

In the problem of estimating conditional probability, Y is a binary vector.

In order to find vector Φ, we minimize the functional (64) subject to box constraints

$$0_\ell \leq \Phi \leq 1_\ell,$$

and equality constraint

$$\frac{1}{\ell}\Phi^T 1_\ell = p_\ell.$$

---

[7] Pseudoinverse matrix M^+ of the matrix M (not necessarily symmetric) satisfies the following four conditions: (1) $MM^+M = M$, (2) $M^+MM^+ = M^+$, (3) $(MM^+)^T = MM^+$, and (4) $(M^+M)^T = M^+M$. If matrix M is invertible, then $M^+ = M^{-1}$. Pseudoinverse exists and is unique for any matrix.

2. Estimating values of regression. In order to estimate the vector Φ of values of regression at ℓ observation points, we minimize functional (64) (where Y is a real-valued vector), subject to the box constraints

$$a_\ell 1_\ell \leq \Phi \leq b_\ell 1_\ell,$$

and the equality constraint

$$\frac{1}{\ell} \Phi^T 1_\ell = \hat{y}_{av}.$$

3. Estimating values of density ratio function. In order to estimate the vector Φ of values of density ratio function at ℓ_{den} observation points $X_1, ..., X_{\ell_{\text{den}}}$, we minimize the functional

$$\Phi^T V \Phi - 2 \left(\frac{\ell_{\text{den}}}{\ell_{\text{num}}} \right) \Phi^T V^* 1_{\ell_{\text{num}}} + \gamma \Phi^T K^+ \Phi$$

subject to the box constraints

$$\Phi \geq 0_{\ell_{\text{den}}},$$

and the equality constraint

$$\frac{1}{\ell_{\text{den}}} \Phi^T V^* 1_{\ell_{\text{num}}} = 1.$$

Function Interpolation. In the second stage of our two-stage procedure, we use the estimated function values at the points of training set to define the function in input space. That is, we solve the problem of function interpolation.

In order to do this, consider representation (65) of vector Φ^*:

$$\Phi^* = K A^*. \tag{66}$$

We also consider the RKHS representation of the desired function:

$$f(x) = A^{*T} \mathcal{K}(x). \tag{67}$$

If the inverse matrix K^{-1} exists, then

$$A^* = K^{-1} \Phi^*.$$

If K^{-1} does not exist, there are many different A^* satisfying (66). In this situation, the best interpolation of Φ^* is a (linear) function (67) that belongs to the subset of functions with the smallest bound on VC dimension [15]. According to Theorem 10.6 in [15], such a function either satisfies the equation (66) with the smallest L_2 norm of A^* or it satisfies equation (66) with the smallest L_0 norm of A^*.

Efficient computational implementations for both L_0 and L_2 norms are available in the popular scientific software package Matlab.

Note that the obtained solutions in all our problems satisfy the corresponding constraints only on the training data, but they do not have to satisfy these constraints at any $x \in \mathcal{X}$. Therefore, we truncate the obtained solution functions as

$$f_{tr}(x) = [A^{*T}\mathcal{K}(x)]_a^b,$$

where

$$[u]_a^b = \begin{cases} a, & \text{if } u < a \\ u, & \text{if } a \leq u \leq b \\ b, & \text{if } u > b \end{cases}$$

Additional Considerations. For many problems, it is useful to consider the solutions in the form of a function from a set of RKHS functions with a bias term:

$$f(x) = \sum_{i=1}^{\ell} \alpha_i K(X_i, x) + c = A^T \mathcal{K}(x) + c.$$

To keep computational problems simple, we use fixed bias $c = \hat{y}_{av}$. (One can consider the bias as a variable, but this leads to more complex form of constraints in the optimization problem.)

Using this set of functions, our quadratic optimization formulation for estimating the function values at training data points for the problem of conditional probability and regression estimation is as follows: minimize the functional (over vectors Φ)

$$(\Phi + \hat{y}_{av}1_\ell)^T V(\Phi + \hat{y}_{av}1_\ell) - 2(\Phi + \hat{y}_{av}1_\ell)^T VY + \gamma \Phi^T K^+ \Phi$$

subject to the constraints

$$(a - \hat{y}_{av})1_\ell \leq \Phi \leq (b - \hat{y}_{av})1_\ell,$$

(where $a = 0$, $b = 1$ for conditional probability problem and $a = a_\ell$, $b = b_\ell$ for regression problem) and constraint

$$\Phi^T 1_\ell = 0.$$

For estimating the values of density ratio function at points $(X_1, \ldots, X_{\ell_{den}})$, we choose $c = 1$ and minimize the functional

$$(\Phi + 1_{\ell_{den}})^T V(\Phi + 1_{\ell_{den}}) - 2\left(\frac{\ell_{den}}{\ell_{num}}\right)(\Phi + 1_{\ell_{den}})^T V^* 1_{\ell_{num}} + \gamma \Phi^T K^+ \Phi$$

subject to the constraints

$$-1_{\ell_{den}} \leq \Phi,$$

$$\Phi^T 1_{\ell_{den}} = 0.$$

6.5   Applications of Density Ratio Estimation

Density ratio estimation has many applications, in particular,

- Data adaptation.
- Estimation of mutual information.
- Change point detection.

It is important to note that, in all these problems, it is required to estimate the values $R(X_i)$ of density ratio function at the points $X_1, ..., X_{\ell_{\mathrm{den}}}$ (generated by probability measure $F_{\mathrm{den}}(x)$) rather than function $R(x)$.

Below we consider the first two problems in the pattern recognition setting. These problems are important for practical reasons (especially for unbalanced data): the first problem enables better use of available data, while the second problem can be used as an instrument for feature selection. Application of density ratio to change point detection can be found in [2].

Data Adaptation Problem. Let the iid data

$$(y_1, X_1), ..., (y_\ell, X_\ell) \tag{68}$$

be defined by a fixed unknown density function $p(x)$ and a fixed unknown conditional density function $p(y|x)$ generated according to an unknown joint density function $p(x, y) = p(y|x)p(x)$. Suppose now that one is given data

$$X_1^*, ..., X_{\ell_1}^* \tag{69}$$

defined by another fixed unknown density function $p_*(x)$. This density function, together with conditional density $p(y|x)$ (the same one as for (68)), defines the joint density function $p_*(x, y) = p(y|x)p_*(x)$.

It is required, using data (68) and (69), to find in a set of functions $f(x, \alpha)$, $\alpha \in \Lambda$, the one that minimizes the functional

$$T(\alpha) = \int L(y, f(x, \alpha))p_*(x, y)dydx, \tag{70}$$

where $L(\cdot, \cdot)$ is a known loss function.

This setting is an important generalization of the classical function estimation problem where the functional dependency between variables y and x is the same (the function $p(y|x)$ which is the part of composition of $p(x, y)$ and $p_*(x, y)$), but the environments (defined by densities $p(x)$ and $p_*(x)$) are different.

It is required, by observing examples from one environment (with $p(x)$), to define the rule for another environment (with $p^*(x)$). Let us denote

$$R(x) = \frac{p_*(x)}{p(x)}, \quad p(x) > 0.$$

Then functional (70) can be rewritten as

$$T(\alpha) = \int L(y, f(x, \alpha))R(x)p(x, y)dydx$$

and we have to minimize the functional

$$T_\ell(\alpha) = \sum_{i=1}^{\ell} L(y_i, f(X_i, \alpha)) R(x_i),$$

where X_i, y_i are data points from (68). In this equation, we have multipliers $R(X_i)$ that define the adaptation of data (69) generated by joint density $p(x, y) = p(y|x)p(x)$ to the data generated by the density $p_*(x, y) = p(y|x)p_*(x)$. Knowledge of density ratio values $R(X_i)$ leads to a modification of classical algorithms.

For SVM method in pattern recognition [14], [15], this means that we have to minimize the functional

$$T_\ell(w) = (w, w) + C \sum_{i=1}^{\ell} R(X_i)\xi_i \tag{71}$$

(C is a tuning parameter) subject to the constraints

$$y_i((w, z_i) + b) \geq 1 - \xi_i, \quad \xi \geq 0, \quad y_i \in \{-1, +1\}, \tag{72}$$

where z_i is the image of vector $X_i \in \mathcal{X}$ in a feature space $\mathcal{Z}$.

This leads to the following dual-space SVM solution: maximize the functional

$$T_\ell(\alpha) = \sum_{i=1}^{\ell} \alpha_i - \frac{1}{2} \sum_{i,j=1}^{\ell} \alpha_i \alpha_j y_i y_j K(X_i, X_j), \tag{73}$$

where $(z_i, z_j) = K(X_i, X_j)$ is Mercer kernel that defines the inner product (z_i, z_j) subject to the constraint

$$\sum_{i=1}^{\ell} y_i \alpha_i = 0 \tag{74}$$

and the constraints

$$0 \leq \alpha_i \leq CR(X_i). \tag{75}$$

The adaptation to new data is given by the values $R(x_i)$, $i = 1, ..., \ell$; these values are set to 1 in standard SVM (71).

Unbalanced Classes in Pattern Recognition. An important application of data adaptation method is the case of binary classification problem with unbalanced training data. In this case, the numbers of training examples for both classes differ significantly (often, by orders of magnitude). For instance, for diagnosis of rare diseases, the number of samples from the first class (patients suffering from the disease) is much smaller than the number of samples from the second class (patients without that disease).

Classical pattern recognition algorithms applied to unbalanced data can lead to large false positive or false negative error rates. We would like to construct a method that would allow to control the balance of error rates. Formally, this means that training data are generated according to some probability measure

$$p(x) = p(x|y = 1)p + p(x|y = 0)(1 - p),$$

where $0 \leq p \leq 1$ is a fixed parameter that defines probability of the event of the first class. Learning algorithms are developed to minimize the expectation of error for this generator of random events.

Our goal, however, is to minimize the expected error for another generator

$$p_*(x) = p(x|y = 1)p_* + p(x|y = 0)(1 - p_*),$$

where p_* defines different probability of the first class (in the rare disease example, we minimize expected error if this disease is not so rare); that is, for parameter $p = p_*$.

To solve this problem, we have to estimate the values of density ratio function

$$R(x) = \frac{p_*(x)}{p(x)}$$

from available data. Suppose we are given observations

$$(y_1, X_1), ..., (y_\ell, X_\ell). \tag{76}$$

Let us denote by X_i^1 vectors from (76) corresponding to $y = 1$ and by X_j^0 vectors corresponding to $y = 0$. We rewrite elements of x from (76) generated by $p(x)$ as

$$X_{i_1}^1, ..., X_{i_m}^1, X_{i_{m+1}}^0, ..., X_{i_\ell}^0$$

Consider the new training set that imitates iid observations generated by $p_*(x)$ by having the elements of the first class to have frequency p_*:

$$X_{i_1}^1, ..., X_{i_m}^1, X_{j_1}^1, ...X_{j_s}^1, X_{i_{m+1}}^0, ..., X_{i_\ell}^0, \tag{77}$$

where $X_{j_1}^1, ..., X_{j_s}^1$ are the result of random sampling from $X_{i_1}^1, ..., X_{i_m}^1$ with replacement. Now, in order to estimate values $R(X_i), i = 1, ..., \ell$, we construct function $F_{\ell_{den}}(x)$ from data (76) and function $F_{\ell_{num}}(x)$ from data (77) and use the algorithm for density ratio estimation. For SVM method, in order to balance data, we have to maximize (73) subject to constraints (74) and (75).

Estimation of Mutual Information. Consider k-class pattern recognition problem $y \in \{a_1, ..., a_k\}$.

The *entropy* of nominal random variable y (level of uncertainty for y with no information about corresponding x) is defined by

$$H(y) = -\sum_{t=1}^{k} p(y = a_t) \log_2 p(y = a_t).$$

Similarly, the *conditional entropy* given fixed value x_* (level of uncertainty of y given information x_*) is defined by the value

$$H(y|x_*) = -\sum_{t=1}^{k} p(y = a_t|x_*) \log_2 p(y = a_t|x_*).$$

For any x, the difference (decrease in uncertainty)

$$\Delta H(y|x_*) = H(y) - H(y|x_*)$$

defines the amount of information about y contained in vector x_*. The expectation of this value (with respect to x)

$$I(x, y) = \int \Delta H(y|x)dF(x)$$

is called the *mutual information* between variables y and x. It defines how much information does variable x contain about variable y. The mutual information can be rewritten in the form

$$I(x, y) = \sum_{t=1}^{k} p(y = a_t) \int \left(p(x, y = a_t) \log_2 \frac{p(x, y = a_t)}{p(x)p(y = a_t)} \right) dF(x) \qquad (78)$$

(see [1] for details).

For two densities $(p(x|y = a_t)$ and $p(x))$, the density ratio function is

$$R(x, y = a_t) = \frac{p(x|y = a_t)}{p(x)}.$$

Using this notation, one can rewrite expression (78) as

$$I(x, y) = \sum_{t=1}^{k} p(y = a_t) \int R(y = a_t, x) \log_2 R(y = a_t, x)dF(x), \qquad (79)$$

where $F(x)$ is cumulative distribution function of x.

Our goal is to use data

$$(y_1, X_1), ..., (y_\ell, X_\ell)$$

to estimate $I(x, y)$. Using in (79) the empirical distribution function $F_\ell(x)$ and values $p_\ell(y = a_t)$ estimated from the data, we obtain the approximation $I_\ell(x, y)$ of mutual information (79):

$$I_\ell(x, y) = \frac{1}{\ell} \sum_{t=1}^{m} p(y = a_t) \sum_{i=1}^{\ell} R(X_i, y = a_t) \log_2 R(X_i, y = a_t).$$

Therefore, in order to estimate the mutual information for k-class classification problem, one has to solve the problem of values of density ratio estimation problem k times at the observation points $R(X_i, y = a_t)$, $i = 1, ..., \ell$ and use these values in (79).

In the problem of feature selection, e.g., selection of m features from the set of d features, we have to find the subset of k features that has the largest mutual information.

7   Concluding Remarks

In this paper, we introduced a new unified approach to solution of statistical inference problems based on their direct settings. We used rigorous mathematical techniques to solve them. Surprisingly, all these problems are amenable to relatively simple solutions.

One can see that elements of such solutions already exist in the basic classical statistical methods, for instance, in estimation of linear regression and in SVM pattern recognition problems.

7.1   Comparison with Classical Linear Regression

Estimation of linear regression function is an important part of classical statistics. It is based on iid data

$$(y_1, X_1), ..., (y_\ell, X_\ell),\tag{80}$$

where y is distributed according to an unknown function $p(y|x)$. Distribution over vectors x is a subject of special discussions: it could be either defined by an unknown $p(x)$ or by known fixed vectors. It is required to estimate the linear regression function

$$y = w_0^T x.$$

Linear estimator. To estimate this function, classical statistics uses *ridge regression method* that minimizes the functional

$$R(w) = (Y - \mathbf{X}w)^T (Y - \mathbf{X}w) + \gamma(w, w),\tag{81}$$

where $\mathbf{X}$ is the $(\ell \times n)$-dimensional matrix of observed vectors X, and Y is the $(\ell \times 1)$-dimensional matrix of observations y. This approach also covers the least squares method (for which $\gamma = 0$).

When observed vectors X in (81) are distributed according to an unknown $p(x)$, method (81) is consistent under very general conditions.

The minimum of this functional has the form

$$w_\ell = (\mathbf{X}^T \mathbf{X} + \gamma I)^{-1} \mathbf{X}^T Y.\tag{82}$$

However, estimate (82) is not necessarily the best possible one.

The main theorem of linear regression theory, the *Gauss-Markov* theorem, assumes that input vectors X in (80) are fixed. Below we formulate it in a slightly more general form.

Theorem. *Suppose that the random values* $(y_i - w_0^T X_i)$ *and* $(y_j - w_0^T X_j)$ *are uncorrelated and that the bias of estimate (82) is*

$$\mu = E_y(w_\ell - w_0).$$

Then, among all linear[8] estimates with bias[9] μ, estimate (82) has the smallest expectation of squared deviation:

$$E_y(w_0 - w_\ell)^2 \leq E_y(w_0 - w)^2, \quad \forall w.$$

Generalized linear estimator. Gauss-Markov model can be extended in the following way. Let ℓ-dimensional vector of observations Y be defined by fixed vectors X and additive random noise $\Omega = (\varepsilon_1, ..., \varepsilon_\ell)^T$ so that

$$Y = \mathbf{X}w_0 + \Omega,$$

where the noise vector $\Omega = (\varepsilon_1, ..., \varepsilon_\ell)^T$ is such that

$$E\Omega = 0, \tag{83}$$

$$E\Omega\Omega^T = \Sigma. \tag{84}$$

Here, the noise values at the different points X_i and X_j of matrix $\mathbf{X}$ are correlated and the correlation matrix Σ is *known* (in the classical Gauss-Markov model, it is identity matrix $\Sigma = I$). Then, instead of estimator (82) minimizing functional (81), one minimizes the functional

$$R(w) = (Y - \mathbf{X}w)^T \Sigma^{-1}(Y - \mathbf{X}w) + \gamma(w, w). \tag{85}$$

This functional is obtained as the result of de-correlation of noise in (83), (84). The minimum of (85) has the form

$$\hat{w}_* = (\mathbf{X}^T \Sigma^{-1} \mathbf{X} + \gamma I)^{-1} \mathbf{X}^T \Sigma^{-1} Y. \tag{86}$$

This estimator of parameters w is an improvement of (82) for correlated noise vector.

V-matrix estimator of linear functions. The method of solving regression estimation problem (ignoring constraints) with V matrix leads to the estimate

$$\hat{w}_{**} = (\mathbf{X}^T V \mathbf{X} + \gamma I)^{-1} \mathbf{X}^T V Y.$$

The structure of the V-matrix-based estimate is the same as those of linear regression estimates (82) and (86), except that the V-matrix replaces identity matrix in (82) and inverse covariance matrix in (86).

The significant difference, however, is that both classical models were developed for the known (fixed) vectors X, while V-matrix is defined for random vectors X and is computed using these vectors. It takes into account information that classical methods ignore: the domain of regression function and the geometry of observed data points. The complete solution also takes into accounts the constraints that reflects the belief in estimated prior knowledge about the solution.

---

[8] Note that estimate (82) is linear only if matrix X is fixed.
[9] Note that when $\gamma = 0$ in (81), the estimator (82) with $\gamma = 0$ is unbiased.

7.2   Comparison with SVM Methods for Pattern Recognition

For simplicity, we discuss in this section only pattern recognition problem; we can use the same arguments for the non-linear regression estimation problem.

The pattern recognition problem can be viewed as a special case of the problem of conditional probability estimation. Using an estimate of conditional probability $p(y = 1|x)$, one can easily obtain the classification rule

$$f(x) = \theta(p(y = 1|x) - 1/2).$$

We now compare the solution $\theta(f(x))$ with

$$f(x) = A^T \mathcal{K}(x)$$

obtained for conditional probability problem with the same form of solution that defines SVM.

The coefficients A for LS-SVM have the form [7], [12]

$$A = (K + \gamma I)^{-1} Y.$$

If V-matrix method ignores the prior knowledge about the properties of conditional probability function, the coefficients of expansion have the form

$$A = (KV + \gamma I)^{-1} VY.$$

It is easy, however, to incorporate the existing constraints into solution.

In order to find the standard hinge-loss SVM solution [10], [14], we have to minimize the quadratic form

$$-A^T \mathcal{Y} K \mathcal{Y} A + 2A^T 1_\ell$$

with respect to A subject to the box constraint

$$0_\ell \le A \le C1_\ell$$

and the equality constraint

$$A^T \mathcal{Y} 1_\ell = 0,$$

where C is the (penalty) parameter of the algorithm, and $\mathcal{Y}$ is ($\ell \times \ell$)-dimensional diagonal matrix with $y_i \in \{-1, +1\}$ from training data on its diagonal (see formulas (71), (72), (73), (74), and (75) with $R(x_i) = 1$ in (71) and (75)).

In order to find the conditional probability, we also to have to minimize the quadratic form

$$\Phi^T (V + \gamma K^+) \Phi - 2\Phi VY,$$

with respect to Φ subject to the box constraints[10]

$$0_\ell \le \Phi \le 1_\ell$$

---

[10] Often one has stronger constraints

$$\mathbf{a}_\ell \le \Phi \le \mathbf{b}_\ell,$$

where $0_\ell \le \mathbf{a}_\ell$ and $\mathbf{b}_\ell \le 1_\ell$ are given (by experts) as additional prior information.

and the equality constraint

$$\Phi^T \mathbf{1}_\ell = \ell p_\ell,$$

where γ is the (regularization) parameter of the algorithm (See Section 6.4).

The essential difference between SVM and V-matrix method is that the constraints in SVM method appear due to necessary technicalities (related to Lagrange multiplier method[11]) while in V-matrix method they appear as a result of incorporating existing prior knowledge about the solution: the classical setting of pattern recognition problem does not include such prior knowledge[12].

The discussion above indicates that, on one hand, the computational complexity of estimation of conditional probability is not higher than that of standard SVM classification, while, on the other hand, the V-estimate of conditional probability takes into account not only the information about the geometry of training data (incorporated in V-matrix) but also the existing prior knowledge about solution (incorporated in constraints (54), (55)).

From this point of view, it is interesting to compare accuracy of V-matrix method with that of SVM. This will require extensive experimental research.[13]

---

[11] The Lagrange multiplier method was developed to find the solution in the *dual optimization space* and constraints in SVM method are related to Lagrange multipliers. Computationally, it is much easier to obtain the solution in the dual space given by (73), (74), (75) than in the *primal space* given by (71), (72). As shown by comparisons [6] of SVM solutions in primal and dual settings, (1) solution in primal space is more difficult computationally, (2) the obtained accuracies in both primal and dual spaces are about the same, (3) the primal space solution uses significantly fewer support vectors, and (4) the large number of support vectors in dual space solution is caused by the need to maintain the constraints for Lagrange multipliers.

[12] The only information in SVM about the solution are the constraints $y_i f(x_i, \alpha) \geq 1 - \xi_i$, where $\xi_i \geq 0$ are (unknown) slack variables [18]. However, this information does not contain any prior knowledge about the function f.

[13] In the mid-1990s, the following Imperative was formulated [14], [15]:

"While solving problem of interest, do not solve a more general problem as an intermediate step. Try to get the answer that you need, but not a more general one. It is quite possible that you have enough information to solve a particular problem of interest well, but not enough information to solve a general problem."

Solving conditional probability problem instead of pattern recognition problem might appear to contradict this Imperative. However, while estimating conditional probability, one uses prior knowledge about the solution (in SVM setting, one does not have any prior knowledge), and, while estimating conditional probability with V-matrix methods, one applies rigorous approaches (SVM setting is based on justified heuristic approach of large margin). Since these two approaches leverage different factors and thus cannot be compared theoretically, it is important to compare them empirically.

Acknowledgments. We thank Professor Cherkassky, Professor Gammerman, and Professor Vovk for their helpful comments on this paper.

Appendix: *V*-Matrix for Statistical Inference

In this section, we describe some details of statistical inference algorithms using V-matrix. First, consider algorithms for conditional probability function $P(y|x)$ estimation and regression function $f(x)$ estimation given iid data

$$(y_1, X_1), ..., (y_\ell, X_\ell) \tag{87}$$

generated according to $p(x, y) = p(y|x)p(x)$. In (87), $y \in \{0, 1\}$ for the problem of conditional probability estimation, and $y \in R^1$ for the problems of regression estimation and density ratio estimation. Our V-matrix algorithm consists of the following simple steps.

Algorithms for Conditional Probability and Regression Estimation

Step 1. Find the domain of function. Consider vectors

$$X_1, ..., X_\ell \tag{88}$$

from training data. By a linear transformation in space $\mathcal{X}$, this data can be embedded into the smallest rectangular box with its edges parallel to coordinate axes. Without loss of generality, we also chose the origin of coordinate y such that all $y_i \in [0, \infty]$, $i = 1, ..., \ell$ are non-negative.

Further we assume that data (88) had been preprocessed in this way.

Step 2. Find the functions $\mu(x^k)$. Using preprocessed data (88), construct for any coordinate x^k of the vector x the piecewise constant function

$$\mu_k(x) = \frac{1}{\ell} \sum_{i=1}^{\ell} \theta(x^k - X_i^k).$$

Step 3. Find functions $\sigma(x^k)$. For any coordinate of $k = 1, ..., d$ find the following:

1. The value

$$\hat{y}_{av} = \frac{1}{\ell} \sum_{i=1}^{\ell} y_i$$

(for pattern recognition problem, $\hat{y}_{av} = p_\ell$ is the fraction of training samples from class $y = 1$).

2. The piecewise constant function

$$F_*(x^k) = \frac{1}{\ell \hat{y}_{av}} \sum_{i=1}^{\ell} y_i \theta(x - X_i)$$

(For pattern recognition problem, function $F_*(x^k) = P(x^k|y = 1)$ estimates cumulative distribution function of x^k for samples from class $y = 1$).

3. The piecewise constant function

$$\sigma^k(x) = \left(F_*(x^k)(1 - F_*(x^k)) + \varepsilon\right)^{-1}.$$

Step 4. Find elements of V-matrix. Calculate the values

$$V_{ij}^k = \int \theta(x^k - X_i^k)\theta(x^k - X_j^k)\sigma(x^k)d\mu(x^k) = \int_{\max\{X_i^k, X_j^k\}}^{\infty} \sigma(x^k)d\mu(x^k).$$

Since both $\sigma(x^k)$ and $\mu(x^k)$ are piecewise constant functions, the last integral is a sum of constants.

Step 5. Find V-matrix. Compute elements of V-matrix as

$$V_{ij} = \prod_{k=1}^{d} V_{ij}^k.$$

Remark 1. Since V-matrix in the problems of conditional probability and regression estimation is scale-invariant, one can multiply all elements of this matrix by a fixed constant in order to keep the values of matrix elements within reasonable bounds for subsequent computations.

Remark 2. Any diagonal element V_{tt}^k is not less than elements of the corresponding row V_{tj}^k and column V_{jt}^k. Therefore, in order to compute V-matrix in multidimensional case, it is reasonable to compute the diagonal elements first and, if they are small, just to replace the entries in the corresponding row and column with zeros.

It is possible (especially for large d) that V-matrix can have dominating diagonal elements. In this case, V-matrix can be approximated by a diagonal matrix. This is equivalent to the weighed least squares method where weights are defined by the diagonal values V_{tt}.

Step 6. Find the values of conditional probability or the values of regression at the points of observation. Solve the quadratic optimization problem defined in the corresponding sections (in Section 6.4).

Step 7. Find the conditional probability or regression function. Solve interpolation problem defined in Section 6.4.

Algorithms for Density Ratio Estimation

For the problem of density ratio estimation, the algorithm requires the following modifications:

Step 1a. Find the domain of function. Domain of function is defined using data

$$X_1, ..., X_{\ell_{den}}, X_1', ..., X_{\ell_{num}}', \tag{89}$$

where training vectors X_i and X_j' are distributed according to $F_{den}(x)$ and $F_{num}(x')$, respectively.

Step 2a. Find the functions $\mu(x^k)$. Using (preprocessed) data (89), construct for coordinate x^k, $k = 1, ..., d$ of vector x the piecewise constant function

$$\mu_k(x) = \frac{1}{(\ell_{\text{den}} + \ell_{\text{num}})} \left(\sum_{i=1}^{\ell_{\text{den}}} \theta(x^k - X_i^k) + \sum_{i=1}^{\ell_{\text{num}}} \theta(x^k - X_i'^k) \right).$$

Step 3a. Find functions $\sigma(x^k)$. For any coordinate x^k, $k = 1, ..., d$ find:

– the piecewise constant function

$$F_{**}(x^k) = \frac{1}{\ell_{\text{num}}} \sum_{j=1}^{\ell_{\text{num}}} \theta(x - X_j');$$

– the piecewise constant function

$$\sigma(x^k) = \left(F_{**}(x^k)(1 - F_{**}(x^k)) + \varepsilon \right)^{-1},$$

where $\varepsilon > 0$ is a small value.

Step 4a. Find the V**-matrix and** V^***-matrix.** Estimate the matrices using expressions from corresponding sections.

Step 5a. Find the values of density ratio function at the points of observation. Solve the quadratic optimization problem defined in corresponding sections.

Step 6a. Find the density ratio function. Solve the interpolation problem defined in Section 6.4 (if estimated values of density ratio in ℓ_{den} points are not sufficient for the application, and the function itself has to be estimated).

Choice of Regularization Parameter

The value of regularization parameter γ can be selected using standard cross-validation techniques.

References

1. Cover, T., Thomas, J.: Elements of Information Theory. Wiley, New York (1991)
2. Kawahara Y., Sugiyama, M.: Change-point detection in time-series data by direct density-ratio estimation. In: Proceedings of the 2009 SIAM International Conference on Data Mining, pp. 389–400 (2009)
3. Kimeldorf, G., Wahba, G.: Some Results on Tchebycheffian Spline Functions. Journal of Mathematical Analysis and Applications. **33**, 82–95 (1971)
4. Kimeldorf, G., Wahba, G.: A Correspondence between Bayesian Estimation on Stochastic Processes and Smoothing by Splines. Annals of Mathematical Statistics **41**(2), 495–502 (1970)
5. Massart, P.: The Tight Constant in the Dvoretzky-Kiefer-Wolfowitz Inequality. Annals of Probability **18**(3), 1269–1283 (1990)

6. Osuna, E., Girosi, F.: Reducing the run-time complexity in support vector machines. In: Advances in Kernel Methods, pp. 271–283. MIT Press, Cambridge (1999)
7. Saunders, C., Gammerman, A., Vovk, A.: Ridge regression learning algorithm in dual variables. In: 15th International Conference on Machine Learning, pp. 515–521 (1998)
8. Schölkopf, B., Herbrich, R., Smola, A.J.: A Generalized Representer Theorem. In: Helmbold, D.P., Williamson, B. (eds.) COLT 2001 and EuroCOLT 2001. LNCS (LNAI), vol. 2111, p. 416. Springer, Heidelberg (2001)
9. Stefanyuk, A.: Estimation of the Likelihood Ratio Function in the "Disorder" Problem of Random Processes. Automation and Remote Control 9, 53–59 (1986)
10. Steinwart, I., Scovel, C. When do support machines learn fast? In: 16th International Symposium on Mathematical Theory of Networks and Systems (2004)
11. Sugiyama, M., Suzuki, T., Kanamori, T.: Density Ratio Estimation in Machine Learning. Cambridge University Press (2011)
12. Suykens, J., Vandewalle, J.: Least Squares Support Vector Machine Classifiers. Neural Processing Letters 9(3), 293–300 (1999)
13. Tikhonov, A., Arsenin, V.: Solution of Ill-Posed Problems. Winston & Sons (1977)
14. Vapnik, V.: The Nature of Statistical Learning Theory. Springer, New York (1995)
15. Vapnik, V.: Statistical Learning Theory. John Wiley & Sons, New York (1998)
16. Vapnik, V., Braga, I., Izmailov, R.: A constructive setting for the problem of density ratio estimation. In: SIAM International Conference on Data Mining, pp. 434–442 (2014)
17. Vapnik, V., Chervonenkis, A.: Theory of Pattern Recognition (in Russian). Nauka, Moscow (1974). German translation: Wapnik W., Tscherwonenkis, A.: Theorie des Zeichenerkennung. Akademie-Verlag, Berlin (1974)
18. Vapnik, V., Izmailov, R.: Learning with Intelligent Teacher: Similarity Control and Knowledge Transfer. In: Statistical Learning and Data Sciences. SLDS 2015, LNCS (LNAI), vol. 9047, pp. 3–32. Springer-Verlag, London (2015)
19. Vapnik, V., Stefanyuk, A.: Nonparametric Methods for Estimating Probability Densities. Automation and Remote Control 8, 38–52 (1978)

Statistical Learning and Its Applications

Feature Mapping Through Maximization of the Atomic Interclass Distances

Savvas Karatsiolis[✉] and Christos N. Schizas

Department of Computer Science, University of Cyprus, 1 University Avenue,
2109 Nicosia, Cyprus
karatsioliss@cytanet.com.cy, schizas@ucy.ac.cy

Abstract. We discuss a way of implementing feature mapping for classification problems by expressing the given data through a set of functions comprising of a mixture of convex functions. In this way, a certain pattern's potential of belonging to a certain class is mapped in a way that promotes interclass separation, data visualization and understanding of the problem's mechanics. In terms of enhancing separation, the algorithm can be used in two ways: to construct problem features to feed a classification algorithm or to detect a subset of problem attributes that could be safely ignored. In terms of problem understanding, the algorithm can be used for constructing a low dimensional feature mapping in order to make problem visualization possible. The whole approach is based on the derivation of an optimization objective which is solved with a genetic algorithm. The algorithm was tested under various datasets and it is successful in providing improved evaluation results. Specifically for Wisconsin breast cancer problem, the algorithm has a generalization success rate of 98% while for Pima Indian diabetes it provides a generalization success rate of 82%.

Keywords: Classification · Features · Visualization · Convexity

1 Introduction

During the many decades during which Machine Learning has been evolving, a lot of algorithms have been developed and introduced. While the hypothesis of the generative algorithms like the Bayes classifier may be considered as self-explained and naturally deduced, a discriminative model's hypothesis like the ones calculated by a Neural Network or a Support Vector Machine is difficult to grasp. This phenomenon is really obvious when we deal with a non-linear boundary hypothesis. Real world machine learning problems are very rarely restricted to two or three attributes. On the contrary, the most recently defined Machine Learning problems comprise of tens, hundreds or even thousands of attributes. This phenomenon is stressed by the lately developed belief among the Machine Learning Community that is not the better algorithm that wins at the end of the day but the one supplied with the most data [2]. Fortunately, nowadays collecting data is much easier than it was two decades ago. At the same time, Machine Learning has provided ways to reduce data dimensionality thus allowing partial visualization and data analysis simplification. The problem of using

© Springer International Publishing Switzerland 2015
A. Gammerman et al. (Eds.): SLDS 2015, LNAI 9047, pp. 75–85, 2015.
DOI: 10.1007/978-3-319-17091-6_3

such methods is that they reduce the dimensionality of the input space meaning that the decision of which part of the information could be thrown away is taken in the data space and not the feature space. Another concern with this approach is the fact that significant information may be inevitably disposed, towards the goal of ending up with two or three (transformed) attributes in order to visualize a portion of the data. This high information disposal may prevent the emergence of important data governing relationships. On the other hand, it may be useful to have a feature mapping that can be constrained to two or three dimensions for visualization purposes. Such a mapping naturally encapsulates the data relationships and correlations. By definition, mapping a rather difficult problem into only one, two or three features means that these features must be highly expressive and may comprise of complex functions in order to be able to encapsulate a great amount of the data inter-relations. This approach implies that the derived data representation (feature mapping) is a classification hypothesis for the problem at hand. Effectively, the data is visualized based on a powerful hypothesis that has success rates that are very close to or even better than the success rates of state of the art Machine Learning algorithms.

2   The Feature Mapping Optimization Objective

Let's assume a training data set $D = \{(x^1, y^1), (x^2, y^2), \ldots, (x^M, y^M)\}$ consisting of M labeled patterns such as $x^i \in R^n$ and $y^i \in \{1, 2, 3, \ldots, k\}$ meaning that there are k different labels (classes). The basic task is to construct a hypothesis $h: R^n \rightarrow \{1, 2, \ldots, k\}$ that can predict the label of an unseen data pattern. This hypothesis is based on features that map the characteristics of the different classes of the problem. These features are chosen to be a mixture of convex functions having the problem attributes as variables. The decision of using convex functions has to do with the properties of this special group of functions that are used to accomplish mathematical adequacy. The feature mapping optimization objective is derived assuming two classes for reasons of simplicity so it holds for this discussion that $k = 2$. We will also refer to these classes as the positive and the negative class. To keep the graphs simple the data patterns are restricted to be one dimensional so it further holds that $n = 1$. Finally, we define two random variables X_+ and X_-, one for each problem class. Assuming a feature mapping function f_1 then a certain pattern's feature value is in the form of $\Phi_1^i = f_1(x^i)$. In order to promote inter class separation the expected feature values of the patterns of each class should be separated with a distance d that should be as large as possible.

$$| E[f(X_+)] - E[f(X_-)] | \geq d \tag{1}$$

The optimization objective should be the maximization of separating distance d and is defined as

$$\max_f \{|E[f(X_+)] - E[f(X_-)]|\} \equiv \max_f d \tag{2}$$

Figure 1 demonstrates the rationale behind the defined objective function.

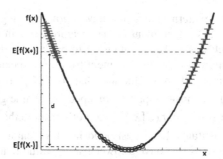

Fig. 1. The feature mapping of a two class problem with the circles representing the negative class patterns and crosses representing the positive class patterns. The feature function $f(x) = x^2$ maps the patterns in a way that the distance d between the expected values of each mapped class is maximized in order to promote class separation. To achieve this goal the feature function must be selected carefully through an optimization process concentrating on getting as large separation as possible.

If the feature functions used in the derived solution are convex or mixtures of convex functions then we can take advantage of Jensen's inequality to establish more strict requirements. More specifically, according to Jensen's inequality for convex functions it holds that

$$f(E[X_+]) \leq E[f(X_+)], f(E[X_-]) \leq E[f(X_-)] \qquad (3)$$

Using this upper bound definition the objective function (2) can be redefined as

$$\max_f \{|f(E[X_+]) - f(E[X_-])|\} \qquad (4)$$

The objective function must be made more stringent and more linked to the desired inter-class separation quality. For this reason we introduce the more sophisticated inter-class distance metric shown in (5) which is called Total Atomic Inter-class Distance (TAID). It will be proved that TAID is a stronger objective function than (4).

$$\frac{1}{M}\sum_{i=1}^{M} \underset{j}{argmin}\{ |f(x_+^i) - f(x_-^j)| \} + \frac{1}{N}\sum_{i=1}^{N} \underset{j}{argmin}\{ |f(x_-^i) - f(x_+^j)| \} \qquad (5)$$

In (5), M is the number of the positive class patterns and N is the number of the negative class patterns in the training set. In practice, this distance metric is the sum of the distances of all feature mapped positive patterns to their nearest negative class mapped pattern atomically plus the total individual distances of the negative patterns after feature mapping to their closest positive class pattern mapping. The proof that the objective function in (4) is a subset of the more enriched Total Atomic Inter-class Distance is fairly simple. Given a dataset of two classes the expected value for the positive class data is $E[X_+]$ and the expected value for the negative class data is $E[X_-]$. Their corresponding feature values are $f(E[X_+])$ and $f(E[X_-])$ respectively as shown in Figure 2. The expected input space values of the two problem classes imply that there are at least four samples placed at minimum distances α, β, γ or δ

away from the expected pattern values and have a lower or higher feature value respectively. This increment or decrement in their feature value in respect to the feature value of the expected classes makes them closer to patterns of the opposite class that are placed on the direction of their displacement from the expected values. For example, a positive pattern mapped on a value less than $f(E[X_-])$ is far more likely to be closer to $f(E[X_-] + \delta)$. A positive pattern mapped on a value greater than $f(E[X_-])$ is far more likely to be closer to $f(E[X_-] - \gamma)$. Let's assume that the pattern having a value of $E[X_+] + \beta$ constitutes the closest opposite class feature value to the B numbered negative class patterns that have a lower feature value than $f(E[X_+])$. Symmetrically $f(E[X_+] - \alpha)$ is the closest positive class feature value to the A negative class patterns that have a higher feature value than $f(E[X_+])$. It should be stated again that there may be a number of negative patterns that have feature values that are closer to $f(E[X_+])$ instead of $f(E[X_+] + \beta)$ or $f(E[X_+] - \alpha)$, but this number is expected to be much smaller than the number of the negative patterns that are indeed closer to the latter two patterns. Furthermore, at the vicinity of the solution the number of negative class patterns having feature values closer to $f(E[X_+] - \alpha)$ should be as small as possible in respect to the number of the negative patterns that are closer to $f(E[X_+] + \beta)$. Accordingly, we assume that $f(E[X_-] + \delta)$ constitutes the closest opposite class feature value to the D positive class patterns that have a lower feature value than $f(E[X_-])$ and $f(E[X_-] - \gamma)$ is the closest negative class feature value for the C positive patterns that have a higher feature value than $f(E[X_-])$. Following the latter definitions we divide the training set into four sub areas and further define their corresponding random variables representing the patterns drawn from these areas. As shown in Figure 2 we have four random variables one for each area of the data distribution, namely $X_{+\gamma}, X_{+\delta}, X_{-\alpha}$ and $X_{-\beta}$.

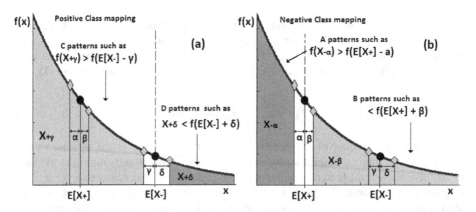

Fig. 2. In order to examine the properties of equation (5) we divide the feature mapping distribution into four areas consisting of A, B, C and D patterns and represented by the random variables $X_{+\gamma}, X_{+\delta}, X_{-\alpha}$ and $X_{-\beta}$. The first subscript of the random variables represents the class and the second the furthest opposite class pattern.

The first subscript of the random variables represents its class and the second subscript the furthest opposite class pattern. Using these definitions the maximum Total Atomic Inter-class Distance equation (5) may be expanded as in (6). It is noted that (6) reflects the maximum TAID because $f(E[X_+] - k), k \in \{\alpha, \beta, \gamma, \delta\}$ are the furthermost opposite class feature mappings values given $E[X_+]$ and $E[X_-]$.

$$\frac{1}{C}\sum_{i=1}^{C}[f(x_{+\gamma}^i) - f(E[X_-] - \gamma)] + \frac{1}{D}\sum_{i=1}^{D}[f(E[X_-] + \delta) - f(x_{+\delta}^i)] +$$

$$\frac{1}{A}\sum_{i=1}^{A}[f(x_{-\alpha}^i) - f(E[X_+] - \alpha)] + \frac{1}{B}\sum_{i=1}^{B}[f(E[X_+] + \beta) - f(x_{-\beta}^i)] =$$

$$E[f(X_{+\gamma})] - f(E[X_-] - \gamma) + f(E[X_-] + \delta) - E[f(X_{+\delta})] + E[f(X_{-\alpha})] -$$
$$f(E[X_+] - \alpha) + f(E[X_+] + \beta) - E[f(X_{-\beta})] \tag{6}$$

$$f(E[X_-] - \gamma) + f(E[X_+] - \alpha) > f(E[X_-] + \delta) + f(E[X_+] + \beta) \rightarrow$$
$$-f(E[X_-] - \gamma) - f(E[X_+] - \alpha) + f(E[X_-] + \delta) + f(E[X_+] + \beta) \equiv \Sigma < 0$$

Replacing the above quantity back to (6) we have

$$TAID = E[f(X_{+\gamma})] - E[f(X_{+\delta})] + E[f(X_{-\alpha})] - E[f(X_{-\beta})] - \Sigma, \Sigma > 0 \tag{7}$$

Equation (7) can be further simplified using the following facts

$$E[f(X_{+\gamma})] = f(E[X_+]) + \delta_1, \delta_1 \geq 0$$
$$E[f(X_{+\delta})] = f(E[X_-]) - \delta_2, \delta_2 > 0$$
$$E[f(X_{-\alpha})] = f(E[X_+]) + \delta_3, \delta_3 > 0$$
$$E[f(X_{-\beta})] = f(E[X_+]) - \delta_4, \delta_4 \geq 0$$

Substituting in (7)

$$TAID = f(E[X_+]) + \delta_1 - f(E[X_-]) + \delta_2 + f(E[X_+]) + \delta_3 - f(E[X_+]) + \delta_4 - \Sigma$$
$$= 2f(E[X_+]) - 2f(E[X_-]) + \Delta - \Sigma \tag{8}$$

Inspecting (8) closer reveals that it essentially includes equation (4) as an embedded sub-goal. Since the TAID metric calculates the sum of the minimum feature distance of the patterns of each class to its nearest opposite class feature value and we are also considering a problem consisting of two classes of data, it is rational to get the multiplier of two for the sub-goal of equation (4). Armed with the basic form of the objective function we are ready to begin formalizing the final expression of the problem. There are still some issues to be solved before there is completeness and ability to implement the method. These concerns are listed below:

• Feature mapping functions should be bounded in order to avoid over fitting and maintain sanity. Fixed upper and lower bounds are implemented which results in rejecting candidate solutions that map any of the data outside this acceptable range. In all experimental runs of the algorithm the bounds are symmetrical in the range -1000 up to 1000.

- Regularization should be added in order to avoid over fitting. Omitting the analysis we just provide the added regularization term r which makes sure that the Σ term never gets zero or extremely low during the search. In practice, the regularization term reflects the number of the boundary range integer values on which at least one positive or one negative pattern is mapped.

$$r = \Sigma_{i=-Bound}^{+Bound} E(i) \quad , \quad E(i) = \begin{cases} 1 & if \quad \exists x^j : \left\lfloor f(x^j) \right\rfloor = i \\ 0 & otherwise \end{cases} \tag{9}$$

- The algorithm should have the ability to construct multiple features in order to deal with problems of high complexity. In this way a number a features can be combined together to provide a decent feature mapping. Having a feature f_1 already constructed using the objective function, a new feature calculation should not ignore its existence and perform its own search in a way that consummates all previous work done so far. This approach provides a whole new perspective to the process of feature mapping the specific problem by adding a different angle of view upon the training patterns. To maintain a different angle of view upon the problem, f_2 should map a specific pattern x^i in a different location on the feature range than f_1 already did. Towards this direction the distance of the two mappings is considered in the objective. In a formal definition, in order to calculate f_2 the objective function of (5) should be modified to reflect the existence of f_1 such as

$$\frac{1}{M}\sum_{i=1}^{M} argmin_{j}\{|f_2(x_+^i) - f_2(x_-^j)|\} + \frac{1}{N}\sum_{i=1}^{N} argmin_{j}\{|f_2(x_-^i) - f_2(x_+^j)|\} \quad +$$

$$\frac{1}{M}\sum_{i=1}^{M} argmin_{j}\{|f_2(x_+^i) - f_1(x^j)|\} + \frac{1}{N}\sum_{i=1}^{N} argmin_{j}\{|f_2(x_-^i) - f_1(x_-^j)|\} \tag{10}$$

Every time a new feature is to be calculated, new sub-goals in the form of function (5) must be included so as to achieve current feature's diversity from the previously constructed features. This increases the complexity of the algorithm exponentially making it very inefficient at a point of losing its practical use. For this reason, the multi- feature objective function (10) is modified in such a way that the requirements of the above discussion are preserved without overwhelming the performance of the solver. The new objective function is using Euclidean distance for the calculation of the current feature function. Every feature mapping at a given point is represented by a vector $\mathring{x}(x^i) = [f_1(x^i)f_2(x^i)...f_k(x^i)]$ whose elements are all previous feature mappings and the one to be calculated $(f_k(x^i))$. Using this approach we have the following objective function. The last term r is the regularization term defined in (9).

$$\frac{1}{M}\sum_{i=1}^{M} argmin_{j}\{\|\mathring{f}(x_+^i) - \mathring{f}(x_-^j)\|_2\} + \frac{1}{N}\sum_{i=1}^{N} argmin_{j}\{\|\mathring{f}(x_-^i) - \mathring{f}(x_+^j)\|_2\} + r$$

- The last modification to the objective function is a term that adds attribute sparseness to the performed feature mapping. The attributes describing the input patterns may be selectively used in an individual feature construction based on their suitability, information content and contribution in respect to all available attributes. This means that   it is preferred, that only a subset of the problem attributes are called forth in calculating a feature. Limiting the number of involved attributes in the feature construction process, favors the usage of the strongest feature elements during each feature   mapping iteration and consequently advances the concentration on a certain angle of view for the problem. This approach is more appropriate when the problem at hand is difficult in the sense that a powerful classification algorithm like a Support Vector Machine or a Neural Network provides somehow lower than desired or expected success rates. There are also situations that a problem has a great number of attributes and it seems rational to construct many features each of which encapsulates a narrow spectrum of the characteristics carried inside the attributes. In such cases the degree of sparseness may be large in order to promote usage of different attributes during the calculation of each problem feature. This approach is similar to sparse auto-encoders currently used by researchers in deep learning algorithms[1]. The feature construction can end when no more unused attributes are used in the lastly constructed feature. At the end of the algorithm execution, it may be observed that some attributes were not used at all, implying that they could be neglected in the training of a classification algorithm. The final objective function intended for maximization is shown below

$$\frac{1}{M}\sum_{i=1}^{M} argmin_{j}\{\|\mathring{f}(x_+^i) - \mathring{f}(x_-^j)\|_2\} + \frac{1}{N}\sum_{i=1}^{N} argmin_{j}\{\|\mathring{f}(x_-^i) - \mathring{f}(x_+^j)\|_2\} +$$

$$r - s\frac{l}{n}, x \in R^n, f_k \in R^l, 0 \le s \le UpperBound \tag{11}$$

The coefficient of sparseness s defines the degree of attributes negligence and the overall sparseness term depends on how many attributes l are actually involved in a specific feature f_k calculation over the total attributes of the problem. The sparseness coefficient can be tuned accordingly depending on the problem at hand.

3   Algorithm Implementation

Having the objective function fully defined in (11), this section deals with how to implement an efficient search method. A gradient based method cannot be used because the objective is not a fixed function with variable parameters and its form cannot be known a priori. The search process should combine and test a great number of convex functions until it reaches a good quality solution. By definition genetic programming algorithms are the best fit for this type of problems. The representation scheme of the genetic programming algorithm consists of a set of convex functions, some primitive operators and some squashing functions. More specifically, the operators used are addition, subtraction, multiplication, division, entropy information, pattern normal value, power function, Gaussian function, logistic function and greater than Boolean functions. The algorithm essentially combines the building blocks of the problem's genome with the goal is to eventually come up with a good feature mapping representation. When a calculation for a pattern falls outside the defined range of the feature mapping the candidate solution is allocated a very small fitness. An initial population goes through the genetic operations of crossover and mutation for several generations until convergence to a state that the best population fitness value does not change any more.

4 Experimental Results

To test the capabilities of the algorithm we first use 2-dimensional artificial datasets because of the natural capability of visualizing the feature mapping surface directly in relation to the input space of the problem. This provides a better understanding of the behavior of the method and reveals its strength and weaknesses. Then we test the algorithm on real world problems, namely the banknotes dataset, the Wisconsin breast cancer dataset and the Pima Indian diabetes dataset[3]. The first artificial dataset generated consists of two inseparable classes of data distributed as in Figure 3. The two features calculated are shown with letters A and B. We observe that features are of satisfactory quality and map the variability of the data classes. One of the greatest advantages of the proposed algorithm is the smoothness of its mapping. Tangled data is given a feature value that implies less confidence than the feature value of patterns placed far away from the opposite class clusters. This smoothness quality is a characteristic of good solutions that generalize well on unseen data. The feature surface of f_2 contributes to the overall problem by emphasizing on distinct feature mapping areas of concern that should get an improvement on their f_1 representation.

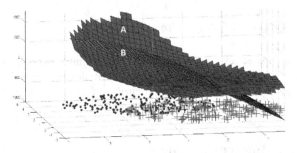

Fig. 3. Two non-separated classes distributed in a two dimensional space are feature mapped with two features A(f_1) and B(f_2) using Total Atomic Inter-class Distance

Constructing only a few enriched features and plotting them in respect to each other provides an insight view to the problem. Besides visualization, the features calculated can be fed directly into a machine learning classification algorithm. Especially when the problem has a great number of attributes, highly sparse feature mapping can make a significant difference in terms of classification results as seen later. The second artificial dataset tested consists of three clusters of inseparable data with the positive class placed between two negative class clusters. Figure 4 shows the data distribution and the feature mapping results. The third dataset consists of multiple separable clusters of data and is shown in Figure 5.

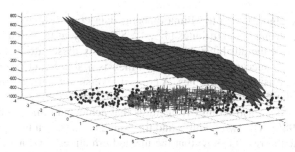

Fig. 4. The mapping results of a two dimensional inseparable problem with three clusters of data, one belonging to the negative class and the other two to the positive class

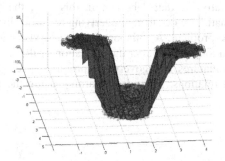

Fig. 5. The mapping results of a two dimensional problem with four separable clusters of data, two belonging to the negative class and the other two to the positive class

Besides the use of artificial datasets, the algorithm was applied to real life problems in order to study its behavior under realistic circumstances. For the separable banknotes dataset the algorithm came up with a single feature function that is doing the job effortless. The histogram of the feature mapping function is shown in Figure 6.

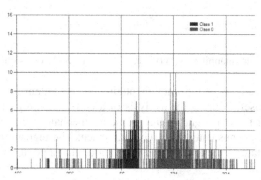

Fig. 6. The feature mapping histogram of the separable banknotes dataset

Applying the algorithm to the Pima diabetes dataset with high sparseness reveals that three really strong data attributes (1st, 4th, 8th) can be used with a classifier while ignoring the rest of the attributes. An SVM using only these attributes can solve the problem with 82% success on the test set which is a significant performance boost over the 75.5% of using all attributes. A comparative survey on various classification approaches for the diabetes dataset can be found in [4]. The Wisconsin breast cancer dataset is solved by constructing two features that achieve an improved classification success rate of 98%. The two features and the boundary is shown in Figure 7.

The experimental results show that the method effectively performs a suitable feature mapping than can be used to advance problem understanding and support the construction of a good classification hypothesis. The next step is to study the possibility of using the algorithm in self-taught feature learning approaches by allowing the absence (partly or totally) of data labeling. In this way, the features will be constructed in respect to naturally occurring underlying relationships and will be enforced by the definition of the problem. A collaborative unsupervised algorithm, for example Expectation-Maximization, could direct the allocation of the labels during the search, thus discovering data features that govern the problem space. After constructing a number of these inter-relations, supervised learning using the given problem labels could follow.

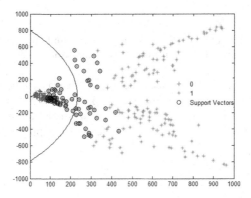

Fig. 7. Feature mapping for WBC dataset with its SVM decision boundary

Studying the outcomes of the implementations, it is evident that the suggested algorithm could be useful during the analysis of a classification problem and can provide the researcher some insight on the problem's mechanics that are otherwise well hidden and deeply encapsulated into the data space. The algorithm also enables the construction of a state of the art hypothesis provided that a good tuning of its parameters is accomplished.

References

1. Raina, R., Battle, A., Lee, H., Packer, B., Ng, A.: Self-taught learning: transfer learning from unlabeled data, pp. 759–766 (2007)
2. Ng, A., Ngiam, J., Foo, C., Mai, Y., Suen, C.: Self-Taught Learning - Ufldl. Ufldlstanfor-dedu (2014). http://ufldl.stanford.edu/wiki/index.php/Self-Taught_Learning (accessed on October 8, 2014)
3. Bache, K., Lichman, M.: UCI Machine Learning Repository. University of California, School of Information and Computer Science, Irvine (2013). http://archive.ics.uci.edu/ml
4. Rahman, R.M.: Comparison of Various Classification Techniques Using Different Data Mining Tools for Diabetes Diagnosis. Journal of Software Engineering and Applications 6(3), 85–97 (2013)

Adaptive Design of Experiments for Sobol Indices Estimation Based on Quadratic Metamodel

Evgeny Burnaev[1,2,3] and Ivan Panin[1,2,3](✉)

[1] Moscow Institute of Physics and Technology, Moscow, Russia
[2] Datadvance llc., Moscow, Russia
evgeny.burnaev@datadvance.net, panin@phystech.edu
[3] Kharkevich Institute for Information Transmission Problems,
Bolshoy Karetny per. 19, Moscow 127994, Russia

Abstract. Sensitivity analysis aims to identify which input parameters of a given mathematical model are the most important. One of the well-known sensitivity metrics is the Sobol sensitivity index. There is a number of approaches to Sobol indices estimation. In general, these approaches can be divided into two groups: Monte Carlo methods and methods based on metamodeling. Monte Carlo methods have well-established mathematical apparatus and statistical properties. However, they require a lot of model runs. Methods based on metamodeling allow to reduce a required number of model runs, but may be difficult for analysis. In this work, we focus on metamodeling approach for Sobol indices estimation, and particularly, on the initial step of this approach — design of experiments. Based on the concept of D-optimality, we propose a method for construction of an adaptive experimental design, effective for calculation of Sobol indices from a quadratic metamodel. Comparison of the proposed design of experiments with other methods is performed.

Keywords: Active learning · Global sensitivity analysis · Sobol indices · Adaptive design of experiments · D-optimality

1 Introduction

Understanding the behaviour of complex mathematical models of complex physical systems is a crucial point for an engineering practice. Discovering knowledge about the most important parameters of the model and learning parameters dependency structure allow to understand better the system behind the model and reveal the way to optimize its performance.

Given some mathematical model, the *sensitivity analysis* tries to find the input parameters which variability has strong effect on the model output and to evaluate this effect quantitatively; to determine how the parts of the model interplay, how the model relates to the real world (see [1]). One of the common metrics to evaluate the sensitivity is a *Sobol sensitivity index*. A lot of Monte Carlo methods were developed for estimation of Sobol indices: direct Monte

© Springer International Publishing Switzerland 2015
A. Gammerman et al. (Eds.): SLDS 2015, LNAI 9047, pp. 86–95, 2015.
DOI: 10.1007/978-3-319-17091-6_4

Carlo simulation, FAST [2], SPF scheme [3] and others. However, these methods require a lot of runs of the analysed model and, therefore, are impractical for a number of industrial applications.

On the other hand, metamodeling methods for Sobol indices estimation allow to reduce the necessary number of model runs. In metamodeling approach, in general, we replace the original model by an approximating *metamodel* (also known as *surrogate model* or *response surface*) which is more computationally efficient and has known internal structure. Approaches based on metamodels consist of the following steps: generation of experimental design and training sample, construction of metamodel and calculation of sensitivity indices using the constructed model. Note that for the last step we can use both prediction based on the constructed model and knowledge about its internal structure, *e.g.* values of its estimated parameters.

This work is devoted to construction of adaptive experimental designs for effective calculation of Sobol indices, *i.e.* calculation using the minimal number of model runs.

There are several approaches related to the experimental design construction for sensitivity analysis problems. Most of them are associated with a uniform (in some sense) space filling design, *e.g.* Latin Hypercube, Sobol sequences and others. These approaches are highly flexible, since specified structure of the analysed model is not required for them. However, these designs, in general, are not optimal in the sense of the fastest convergence of sensitivities to their true values.

Unlike space-filling designs, we try to construct an effective design and, therefore, we make assumptions on the model structure. We assume that the analysed model is quadratic one with a white noise. Although we consider only this simple case, the obtained results can be generalized to a wider class of models, including Polynomial Chaos Expansions and others.

In the above assumptions, we investigate asymptotic behaviour (with respect to the increasing design size) of the proposed estimate for sensitivity index based on quadratic metamodel, prove its asymptotic normality and introduce an optimality criterion for designs. Based on this criterion, we propose a procedure for construction of an effective adaptive experimental design and compare it with other designs.

The paper is organized as follows: in section 2, we review the definition of sensitivity indices and describe their calculation based on quadratic metamodel. In section 3, asymptotic behaviour of index estimate is considered. In section 4, we introduce optimality criterion and propose the procedure for construction of an adaptive experimental design. In section 5, experimental results are given.

2 Calculation of Sensitivity Indices Using Quadratic Metamodel

2.1 Sensitivity Indices

Consider a mathematical model $y = f(\mathbf{x})$, where $\mathbf{x} = (x_1, \ldots, x_d) \in \mathscr{X} \subset \mathbb{R}^d$ is a vector of *(input) features*, $y \in \mathbb{R}^1$ is an *output feature* and $\mathscr{X}$ is a *design space*.

The model is defined as a "black box": its internal structure is unknown, but for the selected *design of experiment* $X = \{\mathbf{x}_i\}_{i=1}^n \in \mathbb{R}^{n \times d}$ we can get a set of model responses and form a *training sample* $L = \{\mathbf{x}_i, y_i = f(\mathbf{x}_i)\}_{i=1}^n$, which allows us to investigate properties of this model.

Let there be given some probability distribution on the design space $\mathscr{X}$ with independent components, and let $\mathbf{x}_\Omega = (x_{i_1}, \ldots, x_{i_p})$ be some subset of input features.

Definition 1. *Sensitivity index of feature set x_Ω is defined as*

$$S_\Omega = \frac{\mathbb{V}(\mathbb{E}(y|x_\Omega))}{\mathbb{V}(y)}, \tag{1}$$

where $\mathbb{E}$ and $\mathbb{V}$ denote a mathematical expectation and a variance.

Remark 1. In this paper, we consider only sensitivity indices of type $S_i \triangleq S_{\{i\}}$, called *first-order* or *main effect sensitivity indices*.

Remark 2. In practice, in order to simulate the variability of input features if no additional information is available, independent uniform distributions are often used with the borders, obtained from physical considerations.

2.2   Metamodeling Approach

Consider calculation of sensitivity indices using the quadratic (meta)model. The model can be represented as

$$y = \alpha_0 + \sum_{i=1}^d \alpha_i x_i + \sum_{i,j=1,\, i \leq j}^d \beta_{ij} x_i x_j, \tag{2}$$

where α_i and β_{ij} are coefficients of the model.

This model can be rewritten as $y = \boldsymbol{\varphi}(\mathbf{x})\boldsymbol{\theta}$, where $\boldsymbol{\theta} = (\alpha_1, \ldots, \alpha_d, \beta_{12}, \ldots, \beta_{(d-1)d}, \beta_{11}, \ldots, \beta_{dd}, \alpha_0) \in \mathbb{R}^q$, $q = d + \frac{d(d-1)}{2} + d + 1$ and

$$\boldsymbol{\varphi}(\mathbf{x}) = (x_1, \ldots, x_d, x_1 x_2, \ldots, x_{d-1} x_d, x_1^2, \ldots, x_d^2, 1). \tag{3}$$

As it was mentioned above, the variability of input features is often modeled via uniform distribution on some interval. Without loss of generality, we assume that $x_i \sim U([-1,1])$, $i = 1, \ldots, d$. Following [4], it is easy to calculate the analytical expressions for sensitivity indices for the quadratic model (2) with uniformly distributed features.

Proposition 1. *Let x_i be i.i.d. and $x_i \sim U([-1,1])$ for $i = 1, \ldots, d$, then the sensitivity indices for the quadratic model (2) have the following form:*

$$S_k = \frac{\frac{1}{3}\alpha_k^2 + \frac{4}{45}\beta_{kk}^2}{\frac{1}{3}\sum_{i=1}^d \alpha_i^2 + \frac{1}{9}\sum_{i,j=1,\, i<j}^d \beta_{ij}^2 + \frac{4}{45}\sum_{i=1}^d \beta_{ii}^2}, \quad k = 1, \ldots, d. \tag{4}$$

Assuming that the original model $f(\mathbf{x})$ is well approximated by some quadratic model, we can obtain an estimate for the sensitivity index S_i of original model using analytical expression for indices (4). Taking into account the results of Proposition 1, we can propose the following procedure for indices estimation:

1. Generate an experimental design $X = \{\mathbf{x}_i\}_{i=1}^n \in \mathbb{R}^{n \times d}$,
2. Simulate the original mathematical model on this design,
3. Form the training sample $L = \{\mathbf{x}_i, y_i = f(\mathbf{x}_i)\}_{i=1}^n$,
4. Construct a quadratic model based on this training sample,
5. Calculate sensitivity indices using estimated coefficients α_i and β_{ij}.

In this paper, we focus on construction of an effective experimental design for this procedure. Note that since $S_k = \psi(\boldsymbol{\alpha}, \boldsymbol{\beta})$ is a nonlinear function of the parameters $\boldsymbol{\alpha}$ and $\boldsymbol{\beta}$, then the existing approaches to the construction of experimental designs, which are effective for estimating α_i and β_{ij} (D-, IV-criterion, see [8]), are not effective for the considered case.

3   Asymptotic Approximation

In this section, we consider asymptotic properties of our indices estimates if the original model is quadratic with Gaussian noise:

$$y = \boldsymbol{\varphi}(\mathbf{x})\boldsymbol{\theta} + \varepsilon, \text{ where } \varepsilon \sim N(0, \sigma^2). \tag{5}$$

Rewrite the formula (4) for sensitivity index using $\boldsymbol{\lambda} = A\boldsymbol{\theta}$:

$$S_k = \frac{\lambda_k^2 + \lambda_{kk}^2}{\sum_{i=1}^d \lambda_i^2 + \sum_{i,j=1,\, i<j}^d \lambda_{ij}^2 + \sum_{i=1}^d \lambda_{ii}^2} \quad k = 1, \ldots, d, \tag{6}$$

where $\boldsymbol{\lambda} = (\lambda_1, \ldots, \lambda_d, \lambda_{12}, \ldots, \lambda_{(d-1)d}, \lambda_{11}, \ldots, \lambda_{dd}) \in \mathbb{R}^{q-1}$, $q = d + \frac{d(d-1)}{2} + d + 1$, normalization matrix $A = [diag(\sqrt{1/3}, \ldots, \sqrt{1/3}, \sqrt{4/45}, \ldots, \sqrt{4/45}, \sqrt{1/9}, \ldots, \sqrt{1/9}), zeros(q-1, 1)] \in \mathbb{R}^{(q-1) \times q}$ consists of a diagonal matrix and a column of zeros; kk denotes the index of the term, corresponding to the squared value of the k-th feature.

Let us assume that the training sample $L = \{\mathbf{x}_i, y_i = f(\mathbf{x}_i)\}_{i=1}^n$ is given, where $X = \{\mathbf{x}_i\}_{i=1}^n \in \mathbb{R}^{n \times d}$ is a design matrix. Let $\hat{\boldsymbol{\theta}}_{\text{OLS}}$ be the Ordinary Least Square estimate of the model parameter $\boldsymbol{\theta}$ based on this training sample, then the estimated index $\hat{S}_k$ has the form:

$$\hat{S}_k = \frac{\hat{\lambda}_k^2 + \hat{\lambda}_{kk}^2}{\sum_{i=1}^d \hat{\lambda}_i^2 + \sum_{i,j=1,\, i<j}^d \hat{\lambda}_{ij}^2 + \sum_{i=1}^d \hat{\lambda}_{ii}^2}, \quad k = 1, \ldots, d, \tag{7}$$

where $\hat{\boldsymbol{\lambda}} = A\hat{\boldsymbol{\theta}}_{\text{OLS}}$.

Using standard results for a linear regression (see [5]), it is not difficult to prove the following proposition.

Proposition 2. *Let $\Psi = \varphi(X) \in \mathbb{R}^{n \times q}$ be an extended design matrix for the training sample in the case of quadratic model, the matrix $\Psi^T \Psi$ is invertible, then*

$$\mathbb{V}(\hat{\lambda}) = \mathbb{V}(A\hat{\theta}) = A \cdot \mathbb{V}(\hat{\theta}) \cdot A^T = \sigma^2 A (\Psi^T \Psi)^{-1} A^T,$$

$$\mathbb{E}\hat{\lambda} = A\theta = \lambda,$$

$$\hat{\delta} = \hat{\lambda} - \lambda \sim \mathcal{N}(0, \sigma^2 A (\Psi^T \Psi)^{-1} A^T).$$

Let $\hat{t}_i \triangleq 2\lambda_i \hat{\delta}_i + \hat{\delta}_i^2$, $\hat{t}_{ij} \triangleq 2\lambda_{ij} \hat{\delta}_{ij} + \hat{\delta}_{ij}^2$, $\hat{t}_{ii} \triangleq 2\lambda_{ii} \hat{\delta}_{ii} + \hat{\delta}_{ii}^2$, $i, j = 1, \ldots, d$, $i \leq j$, and

$$\hat{\mathbf{t}} = (\hat{t}_1, \ldots, \hat{t}_d, \hat{t}_{12}, \ldots, \hat{t}_{(d-1)d}, \hat{t}_{11}, \ldots, \hat{t}_{dd}) \in \mathbb{R}^{q-1}. \tag{8}$$

Let us rewrite formula (7) for estimated sensitivity index in the form

$$\hat{S}_k(\hat{\mathbf{t}}) = \frac{\lambda_k^2 + \lambda_{kk}^2 + \hat{t}_k + \hat{t}_{kk}}{\sum_{i=1}^d (\lambda_i^2 + \hat{t}_i) + \sum_{i,j=1, \, i<j}^d (\lambda_{ij}^2 + \hat{t}_{ij}) + \sum_{i=1}^d (\lambda_{ii}^2 + \hat{t}_{ii})}.$$

The following theorem allows to establish asymptotic properties of this index estimate while new examples are added to the training sample. In this theorem, if some variable has index n, then this variable depends on the training sample of size n.

Theorem 1. *1. Let new points are being added iteratively to experimental design so that*

$$\frac{1}{n} \Psi_n^T \Psi_n \xrightarrow[n \to +\infty]{} \Sigma, \text{ where } \Sigma = \Sigma^T, \det \Sigma > 0. \tag{9}$$

2. Let $\mathbf{t} = (t_1, \ldots, t_d, t_{12}, \ldots, t_{(d-1)d}, t_{11}, \ldots, t_{dd}) \in \mathbb{R}^{q-1}$, $\mathbf{S}(\mathbf{t}) = (S_1(\mathbf{t}), \ldots, S_d(\mathbf{t}))$, where for $k = 1, \ldots, d$

$$S_k(\mathbf{t}) = \frac{\lambda_k^2 + \lambda_{kk}^2 + t_k + t_{kk}}{\sum_{i=1}^d (\lambda_i^2 + t_i) + \sum_{i,j=1, \, i<j}^d (\lambda_{ij}^2 + t_{ij}) + \sum_{i=1}^d (\lambda_{ii}^2 + t_{ii})}.$$

$$G = \left. \left(\frac{\partial \mathbf{S}}{\partial \mathbf{t}} \right) \right|_{\mathbf{t}=0}, \quad \Lambda = diag(\lambda_1, \ldots, \lambda_{q-1}) \tag{10}$$

and holds

$$\det(B\Sigma^{-1}B^T) \neq 0 \tag{11}$$

where $B = G\Lambda A$, **then**

$$\sqrt{n}(\hat{\mathbf{S}}_n - \mathbf{S}) \xrightarrow[n \to +\infty]{\mathfrak{D}} \mathcal{N}(0, 4\sigma^2 B\Sigma^{-1}B^T). \tag{12}$$

Proof. 1. From Proposition 2 we obtain

$$\sqrt{n}\, \hat{\delta}_n \xrightarrow[n \to +\infty]{\mathfrak{D}} \mathcal{N}(0, \sigma^2 A\Sigma^{-1}A^T), \tag{13}$$

$$\sqrt{n}\, \hat{\delta}_n^2 \xrightarrow[n \to +\infty]{\mathfrak{D}} 0. \tag{14}$$

Using Slutsky's theorem ([6]) we obtain from (13) and (14) for $\hat{\mathbf{t}}$:

$$\sqrt{n}\, \hat{\mathbf{t}} \xrightarrow[n \to +\infty]{\mathfrak{D}} \mathcal{N}(0, 4\sigma^2 \Lambda (A\Sigma^{-1}A^T)\Lambda^T). \tag{15}$$

2. Applying δ-method ([7]) on expansion of $\hat{\mathbf{S}}(\hat{\mathbf{t}}) = (\hat{S}_1(\hat{\mathbf{t}}), \ldots, \hat{S}_d(\hat{\mathbf{t}}))$ and asymptotically small parameter $\hat{\mathbf{t}}$, we obtain required expression (12).

The next section provides a method for construction of an experimental design for effective calculation of sensitivity indices.

4 Optimality Criterion and Procedure for Design Construction

Taking into account the results of Theorem 1, the limiting covariance matrix of the indices estimates depends on a) variance σ^2, b) true values of coefficients of quadratic model, defining B, c) experimental design, defining Σ.

In the above assumptions, the asymptotic formula (12) allows to evaluate the quality of the experimental design. Indeed, generally speaking the less covariance matrix norm $\|4\sigma^2 B\Sigma^{-1}B^T\|$ is, the less risk of sensitivity indices estimation is. However, there are two problems on the way of using this formula to construct effective designs. The first one relates to the choice of specific minimized functional for the limiting covariance matrix. The second one refers to the fact that we do not know true values of the coefficients of quadratic model, defining B; therefore, we will not be able to accurately evaluate the quality of the design.

The first problem can be solved in different ways. A number of statistical criteria for design optimality (A-, C-, D-, I-optimality and others, see [8]) are known. In this work, we use D-optimality criterion. D-optimal experimental design minimizes the determinant of the limiting covariance matrix. If the vector of the estimated parameters is normally distributed then D-optimal design allows to minimize the volume of the confidence region for this vector.

The second problem is more complicated: the optimal design for estimation of sensitivity indices depends on the true values of these indices, and it can be constructed only if these true values are known.

There are several approaches to this problem. These approaches are usually associated with either some assumptions about the unknown parameters, or adaptive design construction (see [10]).

Particularly, the minimax-optimal criterion and the averaging-optimal (Bayesian optimal) criterion for design construction use the assumptions about the unknown parameters and allow to achieve design that is optimal in average and independent from the true values of the unknown parameters. However, in this case there is a problem of the choice of an a priori set of possible values (in case of minimax-optimal criterion) or an a priori distribution (in case of the averaged optimal criterion) for the unknown parameters.

On the other hand, in case of adaptive designs, new points are generated sequentially based on current estimate of the unknown parameters, which allows to avoid a priori assumptions on these parameters. However, in this case there is a problem with a confidence of the solution found: if on some step of design construction parameters estimates are very different from their true values, then the design, which is constructed on the basis of these estimates, may lead to new parameters estimates, which are also very different from the real values and so on. In practice, during the construction of adaptive design, assumptions on non-degeneracy of results can be checked at each iteration, and depending on the results one can adjust the current estimates.

In this paper, we propose an adaptive method for construction of design of experiment for calculation of sensitivity indices based on the asymptotic D-optimal criterion (see an algorithm below). As an initial condition, we require an original design to be non-degenerate, *i.e.* such that for an extended design matrix at the initial moment it holds that $\det(\Psi_0^T \Psi_0) \neq 0$. In addition, at each iteration the non-degeneracy of the matrix, defining the minimized criterion, is checked.

In Section 4.1 the details of the optimization procedure are given.

Goal: Construct experimental design for calculation of sensitivity indices

Parameters: initial n_0 and final n numbers of points in the design; set of possible design points Ξ.

Initialization:

- non-degenerate initial design $X_0 = \{\mathbf{x}_i\}_{i=1}^{n_0} \subset \Xi$;
- $\Phi_0 = \sum_{i=1}^{n_0} \varphi(\mathbf{x}_i)\varphi^T(\mathbf{x}_i)$;
- $B_0 = G_0\Lambda_0 A$, where G_0 and Λ_0 (10) are obtained using the initial estimates of the coefficients of a quadratic model;

Iterations: for all i from 1 to $n - n_0$:

- $\mathbf{x}_{n_0+i} = \arg\min_{\mathbf{x}\in\Xi} \det\left[B_{i-1}(\Phi_{i-1} + \varphi(\mathbf{x})\varphi^T(\mathbf{x}))^{-1}B_{i-1}^T\right]$
- Calculate values G_i, Λ_i and $B_i = G_i\Lambda_i A$ using current estimates of the quadratic model coefficients
- $\Phi_i = \Phi_{i-1} + \varphi(\mathbf{x}_{n_0+i})\varphi^T(\mathbf{x}_{n_0+i})$

Output: The design of experiment $X = X_0 \cup X_{add}$, where $X_{add} = \{\mathbf{x}_k\}_{k=n_0+1}^{n}$

4.1　Optimization Details

The idea behind the optimization procedure in the proposed algorithm is analogous to the idea of the Fedorov algorithm for construction of optimal designs [9].

In order to simplify the optimization problem, we need several identities:

- Let A be some non-singular square matrix, $\mathbf{u}$ and $\mathbf{v}$ be vectors such that $1 + \mathbf{v}^T A^{-1}\mathbf{u} \neq 0$, then

$$(A + \mathbf{u}\mathbf{v}^T)^{-1} = A^{-1} - \frac{A^{-1}\mathbf{u}\mathbf{v}^T A^{-1}}{1 + \mathbf{v}^T A^{-1}\mathbf{u}}. \tag{16}$$

– Let A be some non-singular square matrix, $\mathbf{u}$ and $\mathbf{v}$ be vectors of appropriate dimensions, then

$$\det(A + \mathbf{u}\mathbf{v}^T) = \det(A)(1 + \mathbf{v}^T A^{-1}\mathbf{u}). \tag{17}$$

Let $D = B(\Phi + \varphi(\mathbf{x})\varphi^T(\mathbf{x}))^{-1}B^T$, then applying (16) and (17), we obtain

$$\det(D) = \det\left[B\Phi^{-1}B^T - \frac{B\Phi^{-1}\varphi(\mathbf{x})\varphi^T(\mathbf{x})\Phi^{-1}B^T}{1 + \varphi^T(\mathbf{x})\Phi^{-1}\varphi(\mathbf{x})} \right]$$

$$= \det\left[M - \mathbf{u}\mathbf{v}^T \right], \tag{18}$$

where $M = B\Phi^{-1}B^T$, $\mathbf{u} = \frac{B\Phi^{-1}\varphi(\mathbf{x})}{1+\varphi^T(\mathbf{x})\Phi^{-1}\varphi(\mathbf{x})}$, $\mathbf{v} = B\Phi^{-1}\varphi(\mathbf{x})$. Assuming that matrix M is non-degenerate, we obtain

$$\det(D) = \det(M)(1 - \mathbf{v}^T M^{-1}\mathbf{u}) \rightarrow \min$$

The resulting optimization problem is

$$\mathbf{v}^T M^{-1}\mathbf{u} \rightarrow \max \tag{19}$$

or

$$\frac{(\varphi^T(\mathbf{x})\Phi^{-1})B^T(B\Phi^{-1}B^T)^{-1}B(\Phi^{-1}\varphi(\mathbf{x}))}{1 + \varphi^T(\mathbf{x})\Phi^{-1}\varphi(\mathbf{x})} \rightarrow \max_{\mathbf{x}\in\Xi} \tag{20}$$

This problem is easier than the initial one and can be solved with one of the standard methods of optimization.

5 Experimental Results

5.1 Description of Experiments

This section describes the comparison of the proposed approach with some modifications and with other approaches. In the experiments, we assume that the set of possible design points Ξ is a uniform grid in the hypercube $[-1, 1]^d$. At first, we generated some non-degenerate random initial design, and then we used various techniques to add new points iteratively. The sizes of the initial and final designs were $n_0 = 30$ and $n = 60$ points. Normalized empirical quadratic risk was chosen as a metric of quality of the results, normalization coefficient was equal to σ^2/n_i, where n_i is a size of the design on the i-th iteration.

Methods for Testing. iterDoptSI: the proposed method; **iterDopt**: adding a point maximizing the determinant of the information matrix $|\Psi_n^T\Psi_n| \rightarrow \max_{x_n}$ (see [9]). The resulting design is in some sense optimal for estimation of the coefficients of a quadratic model; **rand**: adding a random point from the set of possible design points; **randunif**: adding a random point in the hypercube $[-1, 1]^d$.

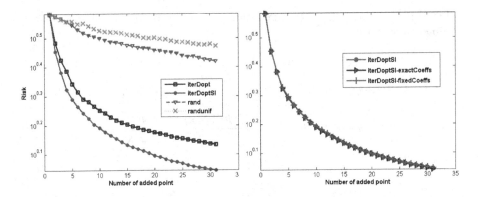

Fig. 1. Quadratic risk in case of different designs. 3-dimensional case

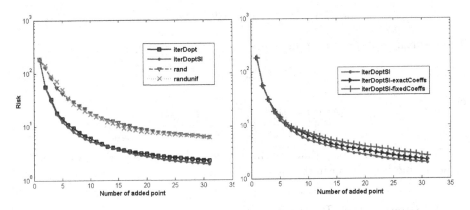

Fig. 2. Quadratic risk in case of different designs. 6-dimensional case

Additional Methods. iterDoptSI-exactCoeffs: variation of the proposed method, in which the estimates of quadratic model coefficients, which are used when adding next points, are replaced with their true values; **iterDoptSI-fixedCoeffs**: variation of the proposed method, in which the estimates of quadratic model coefficients, which are used when adding next points, are fixed to their initial values.

5.2   Description of Results

Figures 1 and 2 demonstrate the performance of different approaches in the case of 3 and 6-dimensional design space. They show the dependence of the normalized quadratic empirical risk on the number of iteration related to adding a new point to the design.

The presented figures illustrate that a) the proposed method **iterDoptSI** allows to get better results than the methods **iterDopt**, **rand** and **randunif**; b) if sensitivity indices are estimated accurately at initial moment, then the performances of the proposed method, **iterDoptSI-exactCoeffs** and **iterDoptSI-fixedCoeffs** are approximately the same, so one can use simplified computational schemes in which the evaluated indices are not updated at each iteration of Algorithm 4; c) method **iterDoptSI** is more efficient at low dimensions.

6   Conclusion

We proposed an asymptotic optimality criterion and method for construction of experimental design which is effective for calculation of sensitivity indices in case of noisy quadratic model. Comparison with other designs shows the superiority of the proposed method over competitors. The proposed approach can be generalized to arbitrary polynomial metamodel and arbitrary continuous distribution of input features. This will be the topic of our future works.

Acknowledgments. The research was conducted in IITP RAS and supported solely by the Russian Science Foundation grant (project 14-50-00150).

References

1. Saltelli, A., Chan, K., Scott, M.: Sensitivity analysis. Probability and statistics series. Wiley, West Sussex (2000)
2. Cukier, R.I., Levine, H.B., Shuler, K.E.: Nonlinear sensitivity analysis of multiparameter model systems. Journal of Computational Physics **26**(1), 142 (1978)
3. Sobol, I.: Global sensitivity indices for nonlinear mathematical models and their Monte Carlo estimates. Mathematics and Computers in Simulation **55**(1–3) (2001)
4. Chen, W., Jin, R.: Analytical variance-based global sensitivity analysis in simulation-based design under uncertainty. Journal of Mechanical Design **127**(5) (2005)
5. Hastie, T., Tibshirani, R., Friedman, J.: Elements of Statistical Learning: Data Mining, Inference and Prediction. Springer, New York (2009)
6. Grimmett, G., Stirzaker, D.: Probability and Random Processes, Oxford (2001)
7. Oehlert, G.W.: A Note on the Delta Method, The American Statistician **46** (1992)
8. Chaloner, K., Verdinelli, I.: Bayesian Experimental Design: A Review. Statistical Science **10**, 273–304 (1995)
9. Miller, A.J., Nguyen, N.-K.: Algorithm AS 295: A Fedorov Exchange Algorithm for D-Optimal Design. Journal of the Royal Statistical Society. Series C (Applied Statistics) **43**(4), 669–677 (1994)
10. Burnaev, E., Panov, M.: Adaptive design of experiments based on gaussian processes. To Appear in Proceedings of the Third International Symposium on Learning and Data Sciences (SLDS 2015), London, England, UK, April 20–22 (2015)

GoldenEye++: A Closer Look into the Black Box

Andreas Henelius[1][✉], Kai Puolamäki[1], Isak Karlsson[2], Jing Zhao[2],
Lars Asker[2], Henrik Boström[2], and Panagiotis Papapetrou[2]

[1] Finnish Institute of Occupational Health, PO Box 40, 00251 Helsinki, Finland
{andreas.henelius,kai.puolamaki}@ttl.fi
[2] Department of Computer and Systems Sciences, Stockholm University, Forum 100,
164 40 Kista, Sweden
{isak-kar,jingzhao,asker,henrik.bostrom,panagiotis}@dsv.su.se

Abstract. Models with high predictive performance are often opaque,
i.e., they do not allow for direct interpretation, and are hence of limited
value when the goal is to understand the reasoning behind predictions.
A recently proposed algorithm, GoldenEye, allows detection of groups
of interacting variables exploited by a model. We employed this technique in conjunction with random forests generated from data obtained
from electronic patient records for the task of detecting adverse drug
events (ADEs). We propose a refined version of the GoldenEye algorithm, called GoldenEye++, utilizing a more sensitive grouping metric.
An empirical investigation comparing the two algorithms on 27 datasets
related to detecting ADEs shows that the new version of the algorithm
in several cases finds groups of medically relevant interacting attributes,
corresponding to prescribed drugs, undetected by the previous version.
This suggests that the GoldenEye++ algorithm can be a useful tool for
finding novel (adverse) drug interactions.

Keywords: Classifiers · Randomization · Adverse drug events

1 Introduction

In some cases, the goal is to find predictive models with the highest possible
performance, e.g., the lowest classification error, for some task of interest. In
other cases, this task is complemented with a desire to understand how the model
makes its predictions, something which may help creating trust in the model
as well as allowing for novel insights. The strongest models, however, are often
opaque, meaning that the logic behind made predictions is very hard to follow in
practice. Examples of such models include support vector machines and random
forests. Recently, the GoldenEye algorithm was proposed [1], which allows for
detecting relations between input variables that are exploited by any type of
classifier, including opaque ones. Although this technique does not provide a
complete picture of the inner workings of the classifier, it allows to gain some
understanding of which variables are exploited and in what context. Moreover,

© Springer International Publishing Switzerland 2015
A. Gammerman et al. (Eds.): SLDS 2015, LNAI 9047, pp. 96–105, 2015.
DOI: 10.1007/978-3-319-17091-6_5

the detection of such interactions may provide useful insights in the particular application domain.

One domain in which one is particularly interested in finding interactions is pharmacovigilance [2]. During clinical trials a typical drug is only tested in isolation or together with a few very common other drugs [3]. This means that when the drug enters the market, very limited empirical evidence has been collected on potential interactions with other drugs. To some extent, potential negative interactions are reported through spontaneous reporting systems, e.g., diuretics and non-steroidal anti-inflammatory drugs [4]. However, it is widely known that such systems suffer from severe under-reporting, e.g., due to the inability of healthcare personnel to accurately identify the involved drugs [5]. Recently, electronic patient records (EPRs) are starting to be used as a complementary source of information, see, e.g., [6]. In addition to containing cases where patients have been prescribed drugs and assigned ADE diagnoses, such EPR data also contain cases with drug prescriptions but without suspected ADEs, in contrast to the spontaneous reporting systems, which only include cases with suspected ADEs. Hence, the EPR data to a larger extent allows for estimating the risk of obtaining a particular ADE, given a set of drugs.

In this study, we will investigate the use of GoldenEye as a tool for finding candidate drug interactions, when applied to EPR data related to 27 different ADE classification tasks. We use random forests [7] to generate the underlying models, which are further analyzed with GoldenEye. The latter employs permutation of input variables to detect any changes in the output predictions. The employed metric for detecting changes is fidelity, i.e., to what extent the class labels change. However, in some cases this metric can be too crude, for example, when the classes are imbalanced. In this work, we also investigate replacing the fidelity metric with a more sensitive one, namely correlation between class membership probabilities for original and randomized data. This allows for detecting changes in the classifier performance even when the output class labels do not change, i.e., when only the class probabilities change.

In the next section, we briefly describe the original technique, GoldenEye, and introduce the revised version, GoldenEye++. We also describe the experimental setup for the empirical investigation. In Section 3, we present the experimental results, and finally, in Section 4, we summarize the main conclusions and point out directions for future work.

2   Method

In this section, we briefly review the GoldenEye algorithm and associated terminology and definitions; for more details, please refer to [1]. We proceed to present an improvement to the GoldenEye algorithm.

2.1   The GoldenEye Algorithm

GoldenEye is an iterative algorithm for finding groups of interacting attributes in a dataset. The finding of groups is formulated as an optimization problem using *fidelity* (the fraction of matching predictions between the original dataset and a randomized dataset) as the goodness measure.

The algorithm works as follows. First, the baseline fidelity fid_b is calculated for a grouping where each attribute is in a group of its own (*all-singleton grouping*). A grouping threshold Δ is defined as $\Delta = \text{fid}_b + \delta$, i.e., the baseline fidelity plus a given constant. Next, the algorithm iteratively removes from the current grouping the attribute which reduces fidelity the least. Attributes are removed from the group one at a time until the fidelity of the current grouping drops below the grouping threshold. At this point, it is determined that a group has been found; the group is stored and the iteration is restarted using the current grouping. Finally, the algorithm outputs the grouping (groups of interacting attributes) for the dataset. A group of attributes means, that the attributes within the group interact, and that this interaction of the variables is exploited by the classifier for predicting the class of an instance.

Figure 1 shows an example of the GoldenEye grouping process for a dataset with four attributes; a, b, c and d, and a grouping threshold $\Delta = 0.8$. Assume that the class y in the dataset is given by the relation $y = (a \oplus b) \vee c$, i.e., attributes a and b interact and must hence occur together in a group when predicting the class, while attribute c is in its own group and attribute d is not needed at all. The path taken by the GoldenEye algorithm is shown by arrows with solid lines. At Level 1, the baseline goodness is calculated. At Level 2, one attribute at a time is detached and the goodness for each grouping is calculated. The grouping $\{\{a, b, c\}, \{d\}\}$ has the highest goodness at this level, and since it also is above Δ, it is used as the starting point for the next iteration on Level 3. On Level 3 it is observed that detaching attribute c lowers the goodness the least, giving the grouping $\{\{a, b\}, \{c\}, \{d\}\}$. Detaching any other attribute at Level 3 would lower the goodness below Δ. Finally, at Level 4, it is observed that detaching the remaining attribute a lowers the goodness below Δ. This terminates the first round of iterations, and the result is the first group: $\{a, b\}$. In the next round of iterations, the starting point is $\{\{c, d\}, \{a\}, \{b\}\}$, i.e., the attributes already in some group are singletons, whereas all currently ungrouped attributes are all initially in the same group. Following the same scheme of detaching one attribute at a time, the singleton group $\{c\}$ is identified after which the grouping process is complete, with the final grouping being $\{\{a, b\}, \{c\}, \{d\}\}$ (boxed on Level 3). Finally, it is investigated whether the singletons c and d are needed for the classification, and it is observed that randomizing d does not affect the goodness, so it can be pruned. The final grouping after pruning is now $\{\{a, b\}, \{c\}\}$, corresponding to the known structure of the data.

Definitions. The dataset X is an $n \times m$ matrix of n observations and m attributes. A subset $S \subseteq [m]$ is called a *group of attributes* and the set of non-overlapping groups of attributes $\mathcal{S} = \{S_1, \ldots, S_k\}$, $S_i \subseteq [m]$ and $S_i \cap S_j = \emptyset \, \forall i \neq j$, is called a *grouping of attributes*. Some attributes $j \in [m]$ may not be part of any group.

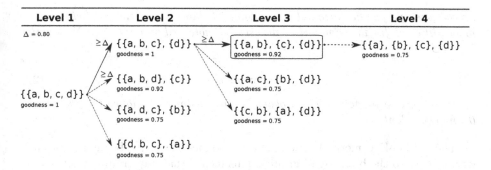

Fig. 1. Illustration of the grouping process using the GoldenEye algorithm

The interpretation is that the attributes in a group are associated and that the relationships between the attributes in a group are needed for the classification task.

Given a dataset X and a grouping $\mathcal{S}$, we define $X_{\mathcal{S}}^*$ as the random permutation of X using $\mathcal{S}$: all attributes in a group are permuted together within-class, and all attributes not occurring in any group are permuted at random. For more details, please refer to Algorithm 1 in [1]. This randomization scheme hence randomizes each group independently, keeping class-dependent associations between attributes in the groups intact.

In the original implementation of the GoldenEye algorithm, *fidelity* g_{fid} is used as the goodness measure in the optimization problem:

$$g_{\text{fid}} = E\left[I\left(y_i = y_i^*\right)\right], \qquad (1)$$

where $I()$ is the indicator function, $y_i = f(X(i, \cdot))$ and $y_i^* = f(X_{\mathcal{S}}^*(i, \cdot))$ are the predicted class labels on the unrandomized data, and on the random permutation $X_{\mathcal{S}}^*$ of the dataset, respectively. See [1] for a more detailed description of the algorithm.

2.2 The GoldenEye++ Algorithm

Fidelity is, in the same way as accuracy, susceptible to class imbalance (see, e.g., [8]), and this might affect the groupings detected by the GoldenEye algorithm. An example of this is if the classifier does not utilize the true relationship between attributes when sufficient performance is reached when the classifier functions as a majority class predictor. For binary classification tasks using classifiers outputting class probabilities, we introduce a new goodness measure g_{cor}, relating class probabilities in the original dataset and in a randomized version of the dataset.

Definition 1. Correlation Goodness *Given a dataset X with binary classes, a classifier f that outputs class probabilities and a grouping of attributes $\mathcal{S}$, Correlation goodness g_{cor} is defined as the correlation between the predicted class* *probabilities p_i for the original unrandomized dataset and the predicted class probabilities p_i^* for the randomized dataset $X_{\mathcal{S}}^*$ obtained by permuting X according to $\mathcal{S}$:*

$$g_{\text{cor}} = \text{cor}\left(p_i, p_i^*\right), \tag{2}$$

where p_i and p_i^* denote the probability that instance i belongs to, e.g., class 0 (or, equivalenty, class 1).

The GoldenEye method relies on the goodness measure being monotonic with respect to the breaking of groups. This means that any grouping deviating from the original will have a goodness equal to or smaller than the original goodness. The goodness g_{cor} is in the interval $[-1, 1]$ and reasonably can be assumed to exhibit the property of monotonicity. The correlation used in the goodness meaure could also be, e.g., rank-order correlation, in which case $g_{\text{cor}} = \text{cor}\left(\text{order}\left(p_i\right), \text{order}\left(p_i^*\right)\right)$.

The goodness measure g_{cor} describes the similarity between the predicted class membership probabilities of the original and the randomized datasets. This correlation-based measure is more sensitive to changes in the predicted classes than accuracy, which allows for a detection of more fine-grained changes in goodness due to the randomizations to be detected.

By GoldenEye++ we refer to the GoldenEye algorithm using correlation goodness, g_{cor}, as the goodness measure instead of fidelity (g_{fid}). The `goldeneye` R-package has been updated to support arbitrary goodness functions, such as correlation goodness used in GoldenEye++ [1].

2.3   Experimental Setup

The behaviour of the GoldenEye++ algorithm was compared to the original GoldenEye algorithm using (i) 13 binary-class datasets from the UCI Machine Learning Repository [10] and (ii) 27 medical datasets.

The twenty-seven datasets were extracted from the Stockholm EPR Corpus[2] [11] for the purpose of illustrating the use of `GoldenEye++` to find known or potential drug-drug interactions. This EPR database contains around 700,000 (anonymized) patients' health records over a two-year period (2009-2010), obtained from Karolinska University Hospital in Stockholm, Sweden. In each of the 27 datasets, the class label was assigned as a specific diagnosis code[3] indicating a certain ADE, and hence the classification task is binary, i.e., whether a patient has been assigned an ADE code or not. In this case, the positive examples are patients who have been assigned the corresponding ADE code, while the negative examples are patients who have

---

[1] Downloadable from https://bitbucket.org/aheneliu/goldeneye/ and easily installed in R using the `devtools` package [9]: `install_bitbucket("aheneliu/goldeneye")`.

[2] This research has been approved by the Regional Ethical Review Board in Stockholm (Etikprövningsnämnden i Stockholm), permission number 2012/834-31/5

[3] The diagnosis in the Stockholm EPR Corpus is encoded by the International Statistical Classification of Diseases and Related Health Problems, 10th Edition (ICD-10)

had been assigned a similar code to the corresponding ADE code. For example, if the class label is G44.4 (drug-induced headache), patients who have had drug-induced headache constitute the positive examples and those who have been assigned a code starting with G44 but other than G44.4 constitute the negative examples.

Features in each dataset are drugs that were prescribed to these patients during the two-year period. The number of features in each dataset ranges from 111 to 987; however, due to heavy computational load and high sparsity of most features, drugs that were taken by less than 10% of patients in each dataset were removed, which results in a reduced number of features ranging from 12 to 84 used in this experiment.

The same learning algorithm was used for both the UCI datasets and for the medical datasets; random forest [7] with 500 trees from the randomForest package [12] for R [13].

3 Results

3.1 UCI Datasets

The experimental results from the grouping of 13 binary-class UCI datasets using GoldenEye and GoldenEye++ are shown in Table 1. In order to compare the similarity of the groupings, we calculated a similarity measure $s(g_1, g_2) = 1 - L_d(g_1, g_2)/N$, where L_d is the Levenshtein distance between g_1 and g_2; string representations of the groupings, and N is the number of attributes in the dataset.

The results show that the groupings from the two algorithms are similar (high s-value), but were not identical for any dataset. Also, the two algorithms appear to find a comparable number of groups for the datasets, but containing a different number of attributes, e.g., diabetes and kr-vs-kp.

It should be noted that a grouping is always a function of both the dataset and the classifier, and in this case also of the optimization criterion, the goodness measure, used to detect the groupings. Based on these results, it appears that the GoldenEye and GoldenEye++ algorithms perform consistently.

3.2 Analyzing Drug Interactions

Among the 27 ADE datasets, GoldenEye found grouped drugs for two datasets, while GoldenEye++ found grouped drugs for nine datasets. The experimental results from the ADE datasets using GoldenEye and GoldenEye++ are shown in Table 2.

As a second step, we continued by manually analysing each group of drugs with respect to their medical relevance. From a causal point of view, we have looked at the groups of drugs and tried to partition the drugs into those that were given to treat the ADE, and those that might possibly have caused the ADE. We have also tried to identify and analyse the medical relevance of any other drug that was present in each group. Note that these datasets contain no temporal information.

Table 1. Groupings of 13 binary-class UCI datasets using GoldenEye and Golden-Eye++. The columns give the following numbers. N: the number of attributes in the dataset, s: similarity between the groupings by GoldenEye and GoldenEye++, *groups*: the number of groups found, *attrs*: the number of attributes contained in the groups, *singl*: the number of singletons and *pruned*: the number of pruned singletons.

dataset	N	s	GoldenEye				GoldenEye++			
			groups	attrs	singl	pruned	groups	attrs	singl	pruned
diabetes	8	0.88	1	5	0	3	1	6	0	2
breast-cancer	9	0.11	1	6	0	3	0	0	8	1
breast-w	9	0.89	0	0	4	5	0	0	5	4
heart-c	13	0.08	1	12	0	1	0	0	9	4
heart-statlog	13	0.77	0	0	5	8	0	0	8	5
credit-a	15	0.80	0	0	4	11	0	0	7	8
vote	16	0.88	0	0	1	15	0	0	3	13
hepatitis	19	0.84	0	0	4	15	0	0	7	12
credit-g	20	0.75	1	7	1	12	1	7	3	10
mushroom	22	0.86	0	0	2	20	0	0	5	17
ionosphere	34	0.88	0	0	13	21	0	0	13	21
kr-vs-kp	36	0.58	2	18	0	18	2	7	6	23
sonar	60	0.83	0	0	16	44	0	0	24	36

Table 2. Groupings of 9 ADE datasets using GoldenEye and GoldenEye++. Table columns as in Table 1.

dataset	N	GoldenEye				GoldenEye++			
		groups	attrs	singl	pruned	groups	attrs	singl	pruned
G44.4	19	0	0	19	0	3	7	12	1
G62.0	57	0	0	57	0	1	8	49	25
I42.7	43	0	0	43	0	1	9	34	25
I95.2	65	0	0	65	0	1	9	56	27
T78.2	12	0	0	12	0	2	8	4	0
T78.3	12	0	0	12	0	2	8	4	0
T78.4	12	1	5	7	6	3	12	0	0
T88.6	49	0	0	49	0	1	9	40	29
T88.7	49	1	9	40	28	1	9	40	12

After discussions with medical experts, we found that for four of the nine datasets, the relationship between the ADE and the grouping found by Golden-Eye++ could be trivially explained as drugs that had been prescribed to treat the particular ADE. Those four datasets contained examples of allergy (T78.4), angioneurotic oedema (T78.3), anaphylactic chock (T78.2), and drug-induced headache (G44.4). Hence the medical relevance could be easily verified, but no causes for any of the ADEs could be identified. For angioneurotic oedema, GoldenEye++ found two groups, each corresponding to groups of drugs that are used to treat varying degrees of angioneurotic oedema depending on severeness; skin rash, respiratory system (breathing), or circulatory system (heart). For allergy, GoldenEye++ found three groups, corresponding to severeness of the allergy; affecting the breathing or the heart.

The remaining five datasets, shown in Table 3, required a more complex analysis of cause and effect for each drug with respect to what would be a likely medical scenario. Here, for each grouping of drugs that was found by GoldenEye++, the drugs were divided into three (possibly overlapping) sets. The first set, shown in column 3 of Table 3, were drugs considered to be characteristic for the patient group. These drugs where used by the medical expert to identify the patient group, shown in column 2 of Table 3. The second set, shown in column 4, contained drugs present in the grouping that are known to cause the specific ADE. In the cases where the medical expert had characterised the patient group as cancer patients undergoing chemotherapy, the ADE was a known adverse effect of the chemotherapy. The third set of drugs, shown in column 5 of Table 3, includes all drugs from the grouping that were characterised as suitable drugs to treat the ADE.

As an example, consider the ADE I42.7 in Table 3, which stands for "Cardiomyopathy due to drug and external agent". GoldenEye++ finds one grouping of drugs which is then further manually subdivided into two groups. The first

Table 3. Medically relevant groupings of attributes found by `GoldenEye++` for 5 of the medical datasets. For each ADE, all the drugs listed in the table were grouped together into one group by `GoldenEye++`. The further division into subgroups (columns 3, 4 and 5) were done manually based on medical relevance. The patient group (column 2) and cause for ADE (column 4) were manually inferred for each ADE based an analysis of all drugs grouped by `GoldenEye++` for that ADE.

ADE	Patient group	Prior Drugs	Drugs causing	Drugs treating
I42.7	Cancer, chemo-therapy	A03FA01, A06AB08, A06AD11, A06AD65, N02AA01	Chemo-theraphy	B01AA03, C07AB07, C07AB02, N05BA04
G62.0	Cancer, chemo-therapy	B01AC06, B03BA01, B05BA03, B05BB01, C10AA01, C10AA01, H02AB01, N02BE01	Chemo-theraphy	*none*
T88.6	Cancer, chemo-therapy, bacterial infection	A06AD65, N02AA01	J01DD01	B01AB01, B05BA03, B05BB01, B05BB02, C01CA24, R03AC02
T88.7	Cancer, chemo-therapy	A02BC01, A03FA01, H02AB01, H02AB06, N02AA01, N02BE01, N05CF01	unspecified	R06AA04, R06AX13
I95.2	Older, Angina Pectoris	B05BA03, B05XA06, C01DA02, C03CA01, C10AA01, N02BE01, N05CF01	01DA02, C03CA01	*none*

subgroup contains Morphine (N02AA01), Metoclopramide (A03FA01), Lactulose (A06AD11), Macrogol (A06AD65), and Sodium picosulfate (A06AB08).
These drugs are all characteristic for the patient group. Cancer patients undergoing chemotherapy experience severe pain and nausea. The pain motivates the
analgesic Morphine while Metoclopramide is used to treat nausea. As a side
effect, Morphine causes constipation, which is treated by the laxatives Macrogol,
Sodium picosulfate, and Lactulose. The second subgroup consists of the remaining drugs, Warfarin (B01AA03), Metoprolol (C07AB02), Bisoprolol (C07AB07),
and Oxazepam (N05BA04), which are all explained by their role as part of the
treatment or diagnosis of the ADE. Warfarin is an anticoagulant (Vitamine K
antagonist), commonly used for heart patients. Bisprolol and Metoprolol are
beta blockers, also commonly prescribed to heart patients. Oxazepam is a Ben-
zodiazepine derivative used to treat anxiety. Heart patients are often prescribed
some drugs to treat the anxiety caused by their illness.

4   Concluding Remarks

In the field of pharmacovigilance, it is important to gain insights into how different drugs interact. However, when investigating the interaction between drugs
using state-of-the art learning algorithms, such as random forest, the black-box
nature of the classifier makes it difficult to understand the basis for predictions.

In this paper, we have extended the GoldenEye algorithm [1] to use instead of
fidelity, a more fine-grained measure based on predicted class probabilities. The
improved algorithm, named GoldenEye++, was compared to the original algorithm using datasets from the UCI machine learning repository. The groupings
detected by the two algorithms were found to be consistent, but not identical.

When applying the GoldenEye++ algorithm on top random forest classifiers
generated from 27 datasets related to adverse drug events, the proposed Gold-
enEye++ algorithm was shown to be able to find medically relevant interactions
between drugs modeled by the random forest classifier.

We conclude that the GoldenEye++ algorithm is a promising technique for
uncovering drug-drug interactions utilized by a classifier.

Acknowledgments. AH and KP were partly supported by the Revolution of Knowledge Work project, funded by Tekes. This work was partly supported by the project
High-Performance Data Mining for Drug Effect Detection at Stockholm University,
funded by Swedish Foundation for Strategic Research under grant IIS11-0053.

References

1. Henelius, A., Puolamäki, K., Boström, H., Asker, L., Papapetrou, P.: A peek into
the black box: exploring classifiers by randomization. Data Mining and Knowledge
Discovery **28**(5–6), 1503–1529 (2014)

2. Härmark, L., Van Grootheest, A.C.: Pharmacovigilance: methods, recent developments and future perspectives. European Journal of Clinical Pharmacology **64**(8), 743–752 (2008)
3. Stricker, B.H.Ch., Psaty, B.M.: Detection, verification, and quantification of adverse drug reactions. BMJ: British Medical Journal **329**(7456), 44 (2004)
4. van Puijenbroek, E.P., Egberts, A.C.G., Heerdink, E.R., Leufkens, H.G.M.: Detecting drug-drug interactions using a database for spontaneous adverse drug reactions: an example with diuretics and non-steroidal anti-inflammatory drugs. European Journal of Clinical Pharmacology **56**(9–10), 733–738 (2000)
5. Milstien, J.B., Faich, G.A., Hsu, J.P., Knapp, D.E., Baum, C., Dreis, M.W.: Factors affecting physician reporting of adverse drug reactions. Drug Information Journal **20**(2), 157–164 (1986)
6. Norén, G.N., Edwards, I.R.: Opportunities and challenges of adverse drug reaction surveillance in electronic patient records. Pharmacovigilance Review **4**(1), 17–20 (2010)
7. Breiman, L.: Random forests. Machine Learning **45**(1), 5–32 (2001)
8. Chawla, N.V.: Data mining for imbalanced datasets: an overview. In: Data mining and Knowledge Discovery Handbook, pp. 853–867. Springer (2005)
9. Wickham, H., Chang, W.: devtools: Tools to make developing R code easier, R package version 1.5 (2014)
10. Bache, K., Lichman, M.: UCI machine learning repository (2014)
11. Dalianis, H., Hassel, M., Henriksson, A., Skeppstedt, M.: Stockholm EPR corpus: a clinical database used to improve health care. In: Swedish Language Technology Conference, pp. 17–18 (2012)
12. Liaw, A., Wiener, M.: Classification and regression by randomforest. R News **2**(3), 18–22 (2002)
13. R Core Team. R: A Language and Environment for Statistical Computing. R Foundation for Statistical Computing, Vienna, Austria (2014)

Gaussian Process Regression for Structured Data Sets

Mikhail Belyaev[1,2,3], Evgeny Burnaev[1,2,3], and Yermek Kapushev[1,2(✉)]

[1] Institute for Information Transmission Problems,
Bolshoy Karetny per. 19, Moscow 127994, Russia
[2] DATADVANCE, llc, Pokrovsky blvd. 3, Moscow 109028, Russia
ermek.kapushev@datadvance.net
[3] PreMoLab, MIPT, Institutsky per. 9, Dolgoprudny 141700, Russia
{mikhail.belyaev,evgeny.burnaev}@datadvance.net

Abstract. Approximation algorithms are widely used in many engineering problems. To obtain a data set for approximation a factorial design of experiments is often used. In such case the size of the data set can be very large. Therefore, one of the most popular algorithms for approximation — Gaussian Process regression — can hardly be applied due to its computational complexity. In this paper a new approach for a Gaussian Process regression in case of a factorial design of experiments is proposed. It allows to efficiently compute exact inference and handle large multidimensional and anisotropic data sets.

Keywords: Gaussian process · Structured data · Regularization

1 Introduction

Gaussian Processes (GP) have become a popular tool for regression which has lots of applications in engineering problems [13]. They combine a simple structure of Bayesian inference and interpretable parameters with an ability to approximate a wide range of functions. However, GP regression is inapplicable for large training sets because its time complexity is $\mathcal{O}(N^3)$ and memory complexity is $\mathcal{O}(N^2)$, where N is a size of the training sample.

Significant amount of research concerns sparse approximation of GP regression reducing time complexity to $\mathcal{O}(M^2N)$ for some $M \ll N$ [1,9,12]. Several papers are dedicated to a Mixture of GPs and a Bayesian Machine Committee [13,14]. However, these are approximations to GP.

Exact GP with reduced time and memory complexity can be achieved by taking into account a structure of a Design of Experiments (DoE). In engineering problems factorial DoEs are often used [10]. In such designs there are several groups of variables — *factors*, in each factor variables take values from a finite set. A size of this set is called a *factor size* and its values are called *levels*. The Cartesian product of factors forms the training set. The size of factorial DoE can be very large as it grows exponentially with dimension of input variables.

© Springer International Publishing Switzerland 2015
A. Gammerman et al. (Eds.): SLDS 2015, LNAI 9047, pp. 106–115, 2015.
DOI: 10.1007/978-3-319-17091-6_6

There are several efficient methods based on splines which consider such structure of the data, e.g. [17]. Several papers describe approaches for GP regression on a lattice which exploit structure of a covariance matrix, e.g. [3]. Such techniques have $\mathcal{O}(N \log N)$ time- and $\mathcal{O}(N)$ memory complexity. A disadvantage of these methods is that they cannot be used in case of *multidimensional factors*.

Another problem which we are likely to encounter is that factor sizes can vary significantly. We will refer to this property of data set as *anisotropy*. Engineers usually use large factors sizes if the corresponding input variables have big impact on function values otherwise the factors sizes are likely to be small, i.e. the factor sizes are often selected using knowledge from a subject domain [15]. Difference between factor sizes can lead to degeneracy of the GP model.

In this paper we propose an algorithm that takes into account factorial nature of the DoE and allows to efficiently calculate exact inference of GP regression. Proposed algorithm is designed for a general case of a factorial DoE when factors are multidimensional. It is also discussed how to introduce regularization to take into account possible anisotropy of the training data set.

1.1 Approximation Problem

Let $f(\mathbf{x})$ be some unknown smooth function. The task is given a data set $\mathcal{D} = \{(\mathbf{x}_i, y_i), \mathbf{x}_i \in \mathbb{R}^d, y_i \in \mathbb{R}\}_{i=1}^N$ of N pairs of inputs $\mathbf{x}_i$ and outputs y_i construct an approximation $\hat{f}(\mathbf{x})$ of the function $f(\mathbf{x})$, assuming that outputs y_i are noisy with additive i.i.d. Gaussian noise:

$$y_i = f(\mathbf{x}_i) + \varepsilon_i, \quad \varepsilon_i \sim \mathcal{N}(0, \sigma_{noise}^2). \tag{1}$$

1.2 Factorial Design of Experiments

In this paper a special case of factorial DoE is considered. Let us refer to sets of points $s_k = \{x_{i_k}^k \in X_k\}_{i_k=1}^{n_k}$, $X_k \subset \mathbb{R}^{d_k}$, $k = \overline{1, K}$ as *factors*. A set of points $\mathbf{S}$ is referred to as a factorial DoE if it is a Cartesian product of factors

$$\mathbf{S} = s_1 \times s_2 \times \cdots \times s_k = \{[x_{i_1}^1, \ldots, x_{i_K}^K], \{i_k = 1, \ldots, n_k\}_{k=1}^K\}. \tag{2}$$

The elements of $\mathbf{S}$ are vectors of the dimension $d = \sum_{i=1}^K d_i$ and the sample size is a product of sizes of all factors $N = \prod_{i=1}^K n_i$. If all the factors are one-dimensional then $\mathbf{S}$ is a full factorial design. But in a more general case factors are multidimensional (see Figure 1). Note that in this paper a factorial design is implemented across continuous real-valued features.

1.3 Gaussian Process Regression

GP regression is a Bayesian approach where a prior distribution over continuous functions is assumed to be a Gaussian Process, i.e.

$$\mathbf{f} \mid \mathbf{X} \sim \mathcal{N}(\boldsymbol{\mu}, \mathbf{K}_f), \tag{3}$$

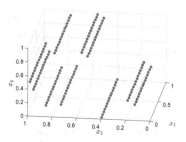

Fig. 1. DoE with 2 factors. x_1 is a 1-dimensional and (x_2, x_3) is a 2-dimensional factor.

where $\mathbf{f} = (f(\mathbf{x}_1), f(\mathbf{x}_2), \dots, f(\mathbf{x}_N))$ is a vector of outputs, $\mathbf{X} = (\mathbf{x}_1^T, \mathbf{x}_2^T, \dots, \mathbf{x}_N^T)^T$ is a matrix of inputs, $\boldsymbol{\mu} = (\mu(\mathbf{x}_1), \mu(\mathbf{x}_2), \dots, \mu(\mathbf{x}_N))$ is a vector of mean function $\mu(\mathbf{x})$, $\mathbf{K}_f = \{k(\mathbf{x}_i, \mathbf{x}_j)\}_{i,j=1}^N$ is a covariance matrix of a priori selected covariance function k.

Without loss of generality the standard assumption of a zero-mean data is made. Also we assume that observations are corrupted with a Gaussian noise $y_i = f(\mathbf{x}_i) + \varepsilon_i$, $\varepsilon_i \sim \mathcal{N}(0, \sigma_{noise}^2)$. For a prediction of $f(\mathbf{x}_*)$ at data point $\mathbf{x}_*$ the posterior mean, conditioned on the observations $\mathbf{y} = (y_1, y_2, \dots, y_N)$, is used

$$\hat{f}(\mathbf{x}_*) = \mathbf{k}(\mathbf{x}_*)^T \mathbf{K}_y^{-1} \mathbf{y}, \tag{4}$$

where $\mathbf{k}(\mathbf{x}_*) = (k(\mathbf{x}_*, \mathbf{x}_1), \dots, k(\mathbf{x}_*, \mathbf{x}_N))^T$, $\mathbf{K}_y = \mathbf{K}_f + \sigma_{noise}^2 \mathbf{I}$ and $\mathbf{I}$ is an identity matrix. Approximation accuracy is evaluated by the posterior variance

$$\mathrm{cov}(\hat{f}(\mathbf{x}_*)) = k(\mathbf{x}_*, \mathbf{x}_*) - \mathbf{k}(\mathbf{x}_*)^T \mathbf{K}_y^{-1} \mathbf{k}(\mathbf{x}_*). \tag{5}$$

Let us denote the vector of hyperparameters by $\boldsymbol{\theta}$. To choose the hyperparameters of our model we consider the log likelihood

$$\log p(\mathbf{y} \,|\, \mathbf{X}, \boldsymbol{\theta}, \sigma_f, \sigma_{noise}) = -\frac{1}{2}\mathbf{y}^T \mathbf{K}_y^{-1} \mathbf{y} - \frac{1}{2}\log |\mathbf{K}_y| - \frac{N}{2}\log 2\pi \tag{6}$$

and optimize it over the hyperparameters [13]. The complexity of learning GP regression is $\mathcal{O}(N^3)$ as it is needed to calculate the inverse of $\mathbf{K}_y$ and the determinant.

2 Proposed Approach

2.1 Tensor and Related Operations

For further discussion we use tensor notation, so let us introduce definition of a tensor and some related operations.

A *tensor* $\mathcal{Y}$ is a K-dimensional matrix of size $n_1 \times n_2 \times \cdots \times n_K$ [8]:

$$\mathcal{Y} = \{y_{i_1, i_2, \dots, i_K}, \{i_k = 1, \dots, n_k\}_{k=1}^K\}. \tag{7}$$

By $\mathcal{Y}^{(j)}$ we denote a matrix consisting of elements of the tensor $\mathcal{Y}$ whose rows are $1 \times n_j$ slices of $\mathcal{Y}$ with fixed indices $i_{j+1}, \ldots, i_K, i_1, \ldots, i_{j-1}$ and altering index $i_j = 1, \ldots, n_j$. For a 2-dimensional tensor it holds $\mathcal{Y}^{(1)} = \mathcal{Y}^T$ and $\mathcal{Y}^{(2)} = \mathcal{Y}$.

Let B be some matrix of size $n_i \times n_i'$. Then the product of the tensor $\mathcal{Y}$ and the matrix B along the direction i is a tensor $\mathcal{Z}$ of size $n_1 \times \cdots \times n_{i-1} \times n_i' \times n_{i+1} \times \cdots \times n_K$ such that $\mathcal{Z}^{(i)} = \mathcal{Y}^{(i)} B$. We will denote this operation by $\mathcal{Y} \otimes_i B$. For a 2-dimensional tensor $\mathcal{Y}$ multiplication along the first and the second directions are left and right multiplications by a matrix: $\mathcal{Y} \otimes_1 B = B^T \mathcal{Y}$, $\mathcal{Y} \otimes_2 B = \mathcal{Y}B$.

Let's consider an operation vec which for every multidimensional matrix $\mathcal{Y}$ returns a vector containing all elements of $\mathcal{Y}$. Then for every tensor $\mathcal{Y}$ of size $n_1 \times n_2 \times \cdots \times n_K$ and $n_i \times p_i$ size matrices B_i, $i = 1, \ldots, K$ it holds that [8]

$$(B_1 \otimes B_2 \cdots \otimes B_K)\text{vec}(\mathcal{Y}) = \text{vec}(\mathcal{Y} \otimes_1 B_1^T \cdots \otimes_K B_K^T), \tag{8}$$

Complexity of calculation of the left hand side of the equation is $\mathcal{O}(N^2)$ assuming that all the matrices B_i are quadratic of size $n_i \times n_i$ and $N = \prod n_i$. The complexity of the right hand side is only $\mathcal{O}(N \sum_i n_i)$.

2.2 Fast Exact Inference

To obtain the benefit of using tensor calculations to perform inference we consider the covariance function which can be represented as a product of covariance functions each depending only on variables from particular factor. The covariance function and the corresponding covariance matrix take the form

$$k(\mathbf{x}_p, \mathbf{x}_q) = \prod_{i=1}^{K} k_i(x_p^i, x_q^i), \quad \mathbf{K}_f = \bigotimes_{i=1}^{K} \mathbf{K}_i,$$

where $x_p^i, x_q^i \in s_i$, $\mathbf{K}_i$ is a covariance matrix defined by the k_i covariance function computed at points from s_i. Such function is still a valid covariance function being the product of separate covariance functions. The most popular squared exponential function can also be represented as a product of squared exponential functions $k_i(x_p^i, x_q^i) = \sigma_{f,i}^2 \exp\left(-\sum_j^{d_i} \left(\theta_i^{(j)}\right)^2 \left(x_p^{(j),i} - x_q^{(j),i}\right)^2\right)$, where $x_p^{(j),i}$ is a j-th component of x_p^i. This covariance function is more general as it allows to take into account features of factors by choosing different k_i for different factors. Note that factors can be multidimensional.

Let $\mathbf{K}_i = \mathbf{U}_i \mathbf{D}_i \mathbf{U}_i^T$ be a Singular Value Decomposition (SVD), where $\mathbf{U}_i$ is an orthogonal matrix of eigenvectors of matrix $\mathbf{K}_i$ and $\mathbf{D}_i$ is a diagonal matrix of eigenvalues. Using properties of the Kronecker product we obtain

$$\mathbf{K}_y^{-1} = \left(\bigotimes_{i=1}^{K} \mathbf{U}_i\right) \left(\left[\bigotimes_{i=1}^{K} \mathbf{D}_i\right] + \sigma_{noise}^2 \mathbf{I}\right)^{-1} \left(\bigotimes_{i=1}^{K} \mathbf{U}_i^T\right). \tag{9}$$

Equations (4), (5), (6) do not require explicit inversion of $\mathbf{K}_y$. In each equation it is multiplied by a vector. Calculation of (9) requires $\mathcal{O}(N^2)$ operations, but to compute $\mathbf{K}_y^{-1}\mathbf{y}$ much more efficient expression can be derived. Let $\mathcal{Y}$ be a tensor such that $\mathrm{vec}(\mathcal{Y}) = \mathbf{y}$. Applying identities (8) and (9) $\mathbf{K}_y^{-1}\mathbf{y}$ can be written as

$$\mathbf{K}_y^{-1}\mathbf{y} = \mathrm{vec}\left[\left((\mathcal{Y} \otimes_1 \mathbf{U}_1 \cdots \otimes_K \mathbf{U}_K) * \mathcal{D}^{-1}\right) \otimes_1 \mathbf{U}_1^T \cdots \otimes_K \mathbf{U}_K^T\right], \qquad (10)$$

where $\mathcal{D}$ is a tensor constructed by transforming the diagonal of $\mathbf{D} = \left[\bigotimes_k \mathbf{D}_k\right] + \sigma_{noise}^2\mathbf{I}$ into a tensor. The elements of the tensor $\mathcal{D}$ are eigenvalues of $\mathbf{K}_y$, so

$$|\mathbf{K}_y| = \prod_{i_1,\ldots,i_K} \mathcal{D}_{i_1,\ldots,i_K}. \qquad (11)$$

Taking into account the complexity of computing the right hand side of (8) and SVD the following proposition is obtained.

Proposition 1. *The computational complexity of the log likelihood (6), where $\mathbf{K}_y^{-1}\mathbf{y}$ and $|\mathbf{K}_y|$ are calculated using (10) and (11), is $\mathcal{O}\left(\sum_{i=1}^{K} n_i^3 + N\sum_{i=1}^{K} n_i\right)$.*

Supposing that $n_i \ll N$ (the number of factors is large and their sizes are close). we obtain that $\mathcal{O}(N\sum_i n_i) = \mathcal{O}(N^{1+\frac{1}{K}})$. This is much less than $\mathcal{O}(N^3)$.

For a gradient based method which is used for optimization of the log likelihood over parameters $\boldsymbol{\theta}$ the derivatives are required. They take the form

$$\frac{\partial}{\partial\theta}\left(\log p(\mathbf{y}|\mathbf{X}, \sigma_f, \sigma_{noise})\right) = -\frac{1}{2}\mathrm{Tr}(\mathbf{K}_y^{-1}\mathbf{K}') + \frac{1}{2}\mathbf{y}^T\mathbf{K}_y^{-1}\mathbf{K}'\mathbf{K}_y^{-1}\mathbf{y}, \qquad (12)$$

where θ is one of the parameters of covariance function (component of θ_i, σ_{noise} or $\sigma_{f,i}, i = 1,\ldots,d$) and $\mathbf{K}' = \frac{\partial\mathbf{K}}{\partial\theta}$. $\mathbf{K}'$ is also the Kronecker product $\mathbf{K}' = \mathbf{K}_1 \otimes \cdots \otimes \mathbf{K}_{i-1} \otimes \frac{\partial\mathbf{K}_i}{\partial\theta} \otimes \mathbf{K}_{i+1} \otimes \cdots \otimes \mathbf{K}_K$, where θ is a parameter of the i-th covariance function. Denoting by $\mathcal{A}$ a tensor such that $\mathrm{vec}(\mathcal{A}) = \mathbf{K}_y^{-1}\mathbf{y}$ the second term in (12) is efficiently computed using the same technique as in (10):

$$\frac{1}{2}\mathbf{y}^T\mathbf{K}_y^{-1}\mathbf{K}'\mathbf{K}_y^{-1}\mathbf{y} = \left\langle \mathcal{A}, \mathcal{A} \otimes_1 \mathbf{K}_1^T \otimes_2 \cdots \otimes_{i-1} \mathbf{K}_{i-1}^T \otimes_i \right.$$
$$\left. \frac{\partial\mathbf{K}_i^T}{\partial\theta} \otimes_{i+1} \mathbf{K}_{i+1}^T \otimes_{i+2} \cdots \otimes_K \mathbf{K}_K^T \right\rangle. \qquad (13)$$

Using properties of the trace and the Kronecker product we can obtain

$$\mathrm{Tr}(\mathbf{K}_y^{-1}\mathbf{K}') = \left\langle \mathrm{vec}\left(\mathcal{D}^{-1}\right), \bigotimes_{i=1}^{K} \mathrm{diag}\left(\mathbf{U}_i\mathbf{K}_i'\mathbf{U}_i\right) \right\rangle, \qquad (14)$$

where $\mathrm{diag}(A)$ is a vector of diagonal elements of a matrix A.

For the derivatives the following statement holds.

Proposition 2. *The computational complexity of calculating derivatives of the log likelihood is $\mathcal{O}\left(\sum_{i=1}^{K} n_i^3 + N\sum_{i=1}^{K} n_i\right)$.*

2.3   Anisotropy

In an engineering practice sizes of factors often differ significantly. It is a common case for the GP regression to become degenerate in this case (see Figures 3, 4). Suppose that the given DoE consists of two one-dimensional factors with sizes n_1, n_2 and $n_1 \ll n_2$. Then the length-scale for the first factor is expected to be much greater than the length-scale for the second factor (or $\theta_1 \ll \theta_2$). However, in practice the opposite is often observed. The reason is that the optimization algorithm stacks in a local maximum as the log likelihood is non-convex function with lots of local maxima.

Let us denote length-scales as $l_k^{(i)} = \left(\theta_k^{(i)}\right)^{-1}$, where $\theta_k^{(i)}$ is a k-th component of a vector of parameters of i-th covariance function. To incorporate knowledge about factor sizes in GP we introduce a regularization by imposing beta-prior on $\boldsymbol{\theta}$ with parameters α and β and rescaled to some interval $\left[a_k^{(i)}, b_k^{(i)}\right]$:

$$\frac{\theta_k^{(i)} - a_k^{(i)}}{b_k^{(i)} - a_k^{(i)}} \sim \mathcal{B}e(\alpha, \beta), \ \{i = 1, \ldots, d_k\}_{k=1}^{K}, \tag{15}$$

Let $B(\alpha, \beta)$ be a beta function. Then the log likelihood has the form

$$\log p(\mathbf{y} \,|\, \mathbf{X}, \boldsymbol{\theta}, \sigma_f, \sigma_{noise}) = -\frac{1}{2} \mathbf{y}^T \mathbf{K}_y^{-1} \mathbf{y} - \frac{1}{2} \log |\mathbf{K}_y| - \frac{N}{2} \log 2\pi - d \log(B(\alpha, \beta)) +$$
$$\sum_{k,i} \left((\alpha - 1) \log \left(\frac{\theta_k^{(i)} - a_k^{(i)}}{b_k^{(i)} - a_k^{(i)}} \right) + (\beta - 1) \log \left(1 - \left(\frac{\theta_k^{(i)} - a_k^{(i)}}{b_k^{(i)} - a_k^{(i)}} \right) \right) \right), \tag{16}$$

It is not known a priori large or small should be the length-scales, so prior should impose nearly the same penalties on the intermediate values of $\boldsymbol{\theta}$. Setting $\alpha = \beta = 2$ leads to the desired shape of the prior (Figure 2).

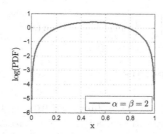

Fig. 2. Logarithm of Beta distribution probability density function, $\alpha = \beta = 2$

Numerous references use a gamma-prior, e.g. [11]. Preliminary experiments showed that GP models with such prior often degenerate. Prior distribution with compact support restricts $\theta_k^{(i)}$ to belong to interval $[a_k^{(i)}, b_k^{(i)}]$ therefore prohibiting too small and too large length-scales and excluding every possibility to degenerate (if intervals $[a_k^{(i)}, b_k^{(i)}]$ are chosen properly).

It seems reasonable that the length-scale is not needed to be much less than the distance between points. That is why we choose the lower bound to be $c_k *$ $\min\limits_{x,y \in s_k, x^{(i)} \neq y^{(i)}} \|x^{(i)} - y^{(i)}\|$ and the upper bound to be $C_k * \max\limits_{x,y \in s_k} \|x^{(i)} - y^{(i)}\|$. The value c_k should be close to 1. If c_k is too small we are taking risks to overfit the data by allowing small length-scales. If c_k is too large we are going to underfit the data by allowing only large length-scales. Constants C_k must be much greater than c_k to permit large length-scales and preserve flexibility. Constants $c_k = 0.5$ and $C_k = 100$ worked rather good in our test cases.

Figure 5 illustrates GP regression with introduced regularization. The parameters were chosen such that the approximation is non-degenerate.

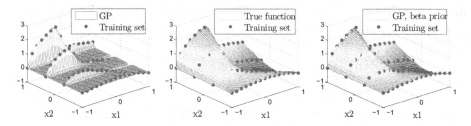

Fig. 3. Degeneracy of the GP model   **Fig. 4.** True function   **Fig. 5.** The GP model with proposed prior distribution

2.4   Initialization

It is also important to choose reasonable initial values of parameters in order to converge to a good solution during parameters optimization. The kernel-widths for different factors should be proportional to the factor sizes. So it seems reasonable to use average distance between points in a factor as an initial value

$$\theta_k^{(i)} = \left[\frac{1}{n_k} \left(\max_{x \in s_k}(x^{(i)}) - \min_{x \in s_k}(x^{(i)}) \right) \right]^{-1}. \tag{17}$$

3   Experimental Results

The algorithms were tested on a set of functions from [5,18]. Sample sizes N varied from 100 to about 200000, input dimensions — from 2 to 6. For each function several factorial anisotropic DoE were generated. Compared algorithms are proposed approach without (tensorGP) and with regularization (tensorGP-reg), Fully Independent Training Conditional GP (FITC) [16], Sparse Spectrum GP (SSGP) [9] and Multivariate Adaptive Regression Splines (MARS) [7]. For FITC and SSGP the number of inducing points (or spectral points for SSGP) M varied from 500 to 70 as complexity of algorithms is $\mathcal{O}(M^2 N)$.

To assess quality of approximation a mean squared error was used

$$\text{MSE} = \frac{1}{N_{test}} \sum_{i=1}^{N_{test}} (\hat{f}(\mathbf{x}_i) - f(\mathbf{x}_i))^2, \tag{18}$$

where $N_{test} = 50000$ is a size of a test set. The test sets were generated randomly.

To compare performance of algorithms on a number of problems it is convenient to use Dolan-Moré curves [4]. The idea of Dolan-Moré curves is as follows. Let $t_{p,a}$ be a quality measure of an a-th algorithm on a p-th problem and $r_{p,a}$ be a performance ratio, $r_{p,a} = \frac{t_{p,a}}{\min_s(t_{p,s})}$. Then Dolan-Moré curve is a graph of $\rho_a(\tau)$

$$\rho_a(\tau) = \frac{1}{n_p}\text{size}\{p : r_{p,a} \leq \tau\},$$

which can be thought of as a probability for the a-th algorithm to have performance ratio within factor $\tau \in \mathbb{R}_+$. The higher the curve $\rho_a(\tau)$ is located the better works the a-th algorithm. $\rho_a(1)$ is a ratio of problems on which the a-th algorithm performed the best.

As tensorGP is an exact GP it performs better than the approximations of GP, i.e. FITC and SSGP. The tensorGP-reg algorithm has better quality due to regularization (see Figure 6). Figure 7 presents Dolan-Moré curves for training time. Time perfor-

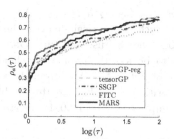
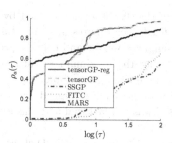

Fig. 6. Dolan-Moré curves for approxima- **Fig. 7.** Dolan-Moré curves for run-times
tion quality comparison   comparison

mance of proposed approach is comparable to that of MARS algorithm and outperforms FITC and SSGP techniques. For $N = 1000$ training time of tensorGP-reg is about 1 sec, for $N = 400000$ — 480 sec Training time of standard GP model for $N = 1000$ is about 120 sec, for $N = 400000$ it cannot be fitted due to memory limitation.[1]

3.1   Rotating Disc Problem

Let us consider a real world problem of a rotating disc shape design. Such kind of problems often arises during aircraft engine design and in turbomachinery [2]. In this problem a disc of an impeller rotating around the shaft is considered. The geometrical

---

[1] Experiments were conducted on a PC with Intel i7 2.8 GHz processor and 4 GB RAM.

114   M. Belyaev et al.

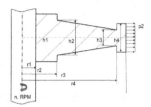

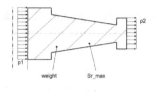

Fig. 8. Rotating disc parametrization   **Fig. 9.** Rotating disc objectives

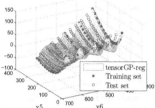

Fig. 10. 2D slice along x_5 and x_6 variables of FITC. MSE = 86.703.   **Fig. 11.** 2D slice along x_5 and x_6 variables of tensorGP-reg. MSE = 0.398.

shape of the disc is parameterized by 6 variables $\mathbf{x} = (h_1, h_2, h_3, h_4, r_2, r_3)$ (r_1 and r_4 are fixed), see Figures 8, 9. The task is to find such geometrical shape of the disc that minimizes weight and contact pressure p_1 between the disc and the shaft while constraining the maximum radial stress Sr_{max} to be less than some threshold. It is a common practice to build approximations of objective functions to analyze and optimize them [6]. We applied the proposed algorithm and FITC to this problem. The DoE was full factorial and anisotropic, the sample size was 14400, factor sizes — $[1, 8, 8, 3, 15, 5]$.

Figures 10 and 11 depict 2D slices of contact pressure approximations along x_5, x_6 variables (other variables are fixed). As you can see tensorGP-reg provides much more accurate approximation than FITC.

4   Conclusion

Gaussian Processes are often used for building approximations for small data sets. However, the structure of the given data set contains important information which allows to efficiently compute exact inference even for large data sets.

Introduced regularization combined with reasonable initialization has proven to be an efficient way to struggle degeneracy in case of anisotropic data. Algorithm proposed in this paper takes into account the special factorial structure of the data set and is able to handle huge samples preserving power and flexibility of GP regression. Our approach has been successfully applied to toy and real problems.

Acknowledgments. The research was conducted in the IITP RAS and solely supported by the Russian Science Foundation grant (project 14-50-00150).

References

1. Abdel-Gawad, A.H., Minka, T.P., et al.: Sparse-posterior gaussian processes for general likelihoods. arXiv preprint arXiv:1203.3507 (2012)
2. Armand, S.C.: Structural Optimization Methodology for Rotating Disks of Aircraft Engines. NASA technical memorandum, National Aeronautics and Space Administration, Office of Management, Scientific and Technical Information Program (1995)
3. Chan, G., Wood, A.T.: Algorithm as 312: An algorithm for simulating stationary gaussian random fields. Journal of the Royal Statistical Society: Series C (Applied Statistics) **46**(1), 171–181 (1997)
4. Dolan, E.D., Moré, J.J.: Benchmarking optimization software with performance profiles. Mathematical Programming **91**(2), 201–213 (2002)
5. Evoluationary computation pages – the function testbed: Laappeenranta University of Technology. http://www.it.lut.fi/ip/evo/functions/functions.html
6. Forrester, A.I.J., Sobester, A., Keane, A.J.: Engineering Design via Surrogate Modelling - A Practical Guide. J. Wiley (2008)
7. Friedman, J.H.: Multivariate adaptive regression splines. The Annals of Statistics, 1–67 (1991)
8. Kolda, T.G., Bader, B.W.: Tensor decompositions and applications. SIAM Review **51**(3), 455–500 (2009)
9. Lázaro-Gredilla, M., Quiñonero-Candela, J., Rasmussen, C.E., Figueiras-Vidal, A.R.: Sparse spectrum gaussian process regression. The Journal of Machine Learning Research **11**, 1865–1881 (2010)
10. Montgomery, D.C.: Design and Analysis of Experiments. John Wiley & Sons (2006)
11. Neal, R.M.: Monte carlo implementation of gaussian process models for bayesian regression and classification. arXiv preprint physics/9701026 (1997)
12. Quiñonero-Candela, J., Rasmussen, C.E.: A unifying view of sparse approximate gaussian process regression. The Journal of Machine Learning Research **6**, 1939–1959 (2005)
13. Rasmussen, C.E., Williams, C.: Gaussian Processes for Machine Learning. MIT Press (2006)
14. Rasmussen, C.E., Ghahramani, Z.: Infinite mixtures of gaussian process experts. In: Advances in Neural Information Processing Systems 14, pp. 881–888. MIT Press (2001)
15. Rendall, T., Allen, C.: Multi-dimensional aircraft surface pressure interpolation using radial basis functions. Proc. IMechE Part G: Aerospace Engineering **222**, 483–495 (2008)
16. Snelson, E., Ghahramani, Z.: Sparse gaussian processes using pseudo-inputs. In: Advances in Neural Information Processing Systems 18, pp. 1257–1264 (2005)
17. Stone, C.J., Hansen, M., Kooperberg, C., Truong, Y.K.: Polynomial splines and their tensor products in extended linear modeling. Ann. Statist. **25**, 1371–1470 (1997)
18. Swiss International Institute of Technology. http://www.tik.ee.ethz.ch/sop/download/supplementary/testproblems/

Adaptive Design of Experiments
Based on Gaussian Processes

Evgeny Burnaev[1,2,3] and Maxim Panov[1,2,3]($\boxtimes$)

[1] Institute for Information Transmission Problems,
Bolshoy Karetny per. 19, Moscow 127994, Russia
[2] DATADVANCE, LLC, Pokrovsky blvd. 3, Moscow 109028, Russia
[3] PreMoLab, MIPT, Institutsky per. 9, Dolgoprudny 141700, Russia
evgeny.burnaev@datadvance.net, panov.maxim@gmail.com

Abstract. We consider a problem of adaptive design of experiments for Gaussian process regression. We introduce a Bayesian framework, which provides theoretical justification for some well-know heuristic criteria from the literature and also gives an opportunity to derive some new criteria. We also perform testing of methods in question on a big set of multidimensional functions.

Keywords: Active learning · Computer experiments · Sequential design · Gaussian processes

1 Introduction

Construction of an approximation for an unknown dependency is one of the main steps of surrogate modelling (modelling based on the data) [1,2]. One of the most popular approaches is based on the Gaussian process model [3,4]. It is used in a variety of applied projects including conceptual design, structural optimization, multicriteria optimization, design in aerospace and automobile industries.

In many engineering applications the number of evaluations of a target function $f(\mathbf{x})$ is sufficiently limited due to a long execution time of one evaluation and/or its high cost. That's why the problem of creating methods for construction of a training set D_N of limited size N in a way to get the best possible quality of approximation is of the great importance. The design of experiments (DoE), which optimizes some statistical criterion, is called optimal design of experiments. For parametric models the problem of design of experiments, which optimizes the quality of approximation, is very close to the problem of optimal experimental design for estimation of the model's parameters. The theory of optimal DoE for parametric models is well-developed, see [5,6] and many others. However, in the situation, when approximation model is non-parametric (for example, Gaussian process regression model), we come to the different statement of the DoE problem [7,8], in which the DoE is constructed in a way to obtain the best possible prediction of the target function value. In this paper we will consider the adaptive variant of such a problem which recently gained much

© Springer International Publishing Switzerland 2015
A. Gammerman et al. (Eds.): SLDS 2015, LNAI 9047, pp. 116–125, 2015.
DOI: 10.1007/978-3-319-17091-6_7

attention [1,9]. The adaptive DoE process constructs training set iteratively and on each iteration design points are selected based on the properties of the approximation constructed on the previous iteration.

In this paper we focus on the adaptive design of experiments for Gaussian process (or kriging) regression models. This kind of models along with a prediction of the unknown function $f(\mathbf{x})$ allows to estimate a variance of the prediction $\sigma^2(\mathbf{x})$. Such a point-wise error estimate gives an opportunity to construct different strategies for reducing uncertainty of the approximation and therefore improving its quality. This area of research originates from the field of design and analysis of computer experiments [10–12]. The adaptive sampling strategies for improving the quality of approximation are closely related to the surrogate-based optimization [13], sequential designs for estimating the probability of a failure [14] and adaptive designs for estimating the sensitivity indices [15].

This paper makes a contribution in two main directions. First of all, we provide a Bayesian framework which allows to define optimal adaptive sampling strategies. Then we show, that many of the commonly used adaptive sampling criteria are approximations of optimal one-step look-ahead strategies. Also some new adaptive sampling strategies are obtained as optimal one-step look-ahead solutions. Second, we make an extensive testing of the most of currently used adaptive sampling approaches for the Gaussian process regression and compare them numerically.

2   Gaussian Process Regression

Let $y = f(\mathbf{x})$ be some unknown function with input vector $\mathbf{x} \in \mathbb{X} \subset \mathbb{R}^n$ and output $y \in \mathbb{R}$, $D_N = (X_N, \mathbf{y}_N) = \{(\mathbf{x}_i, y_i = f(\mathbf{x}_i)), i = 1, \ldots, N\}$ be a training set. Let's assume that $f(\mathbf{x})$ is a realization of a Gaussian process. Gaussian process, being a one of the possible ways to define a distribution on the functional space, is completely defined by its mean $m(\mathbf{x}) = \mathbb{E}[f(\mathbf{x})]$ and covariance function $k(\mathbf{x}, \tilde{\mathbf{x}}) = \mathbb{E}[(f(\mathbf{x}) - m(\mathbf{x}))(f(\tilde{\mathbf{x}}) - m(\tilde{\mathbf{x}}))]$. In applications the weighted exponential covariance function $k(\mathbf{x}, \tilde{\mathbf{x}}) = \sigma^2 \exp(-\sum_{i=1}^{n} \theta_i^2 (x^i - \tilde{x}^i)^2)$ is widely used.

Let us assume without loss of generality that $m(\mathbf{x}) \equiv 0$. If the covariance function $k(\mathbf{x}, \tilde{\mathbf{x}})$ is known, then the posterior process is also Gaussian:

$$\mathbb{P}_N(f) = \mathbb{P}(f|D_N) \sim GP\big(\hat{f}_N(\mathbf{x}), \hat{K}_N(\mathbf{x}, \tilde{\mathbf{x}})\big), \tag{1}$$

where the posterior mean of the Gaussian process $f(\mathbf{x})$ at some set of test points X^* can be written as follows [16]:

$$\hat{f}_N(X^*) = \hat{f}(X^*|D_N) = K_* K^{-1} \mathbf{y}_N, \tag{2}$$

where $K_* = \big[k(\mathbf{x}_i^*, \mathbf{x}_j), i = 1, \ldots, N_*; j = 1, \ldots, N\big]$, $K = \big[k(\mathbf{x}_i, \mathbf{x}_j), i, j = 1, \ldots, N\big]$.

The posterior covariance matrix at test points is given by

$$\hat{K}_N(X^*) = \hat{K}(X^*|X_N) = K_{**} - K_* K^{-1} K_*^T, \tag{3}$$

where $K_{**} = \big[k(\mathbf{x}_i^*, \mathbf{x}_j^*), i, j = 1, \dots, N_*\big]$. Then the posterior variance $\hat{\sigma}_N^2(X^*) = \hat{\sigma}^2(X^*|X_N) = \mathrm{diag}(\hat{K}_N(X^*))$.

The posterior mean at test points can be used for prediction of function values (approximation) and the posterior variance provides corresponding point-wise errors estimates. Let us note that here we described only basic idea of the Gaussian process regression. For more details about the model and parameters estimation algorithms please see [16–18]. Formulas (2) and (3) allow for simple iterative updates when new points are added to the training set.

Proposition 1. *Let for a Gaussian process $f(\mathbf{x})$ a mean and a covariance functions are equal to $\hat{f}_0(\mathbf{x}) \equiv 0$ and $\hat{K}_0(\mathbf{x}, \tilde{\mathbf{x}}) = k(\mathbf{x}, \tilde{\mathbf{x}})$ correspondingly. Then the following update equations can be used to calculate the mean and the covariance function of the posterior process for $i = 1, \dots, N$:*

$$\hat{f}_i(\mathbf{x}) = \hat{f}_{i-1}(\mathbf{x}) + \frac{\hat{K}_{i-1}(\mathbf{x}, \mathbf{x}_i)}{\hat{K}_{i-1}(\mathbf{x}_i, \mathbf{x}_i)} \big(y_i - \hat{f}_{i-1}(\mathbf{x})\big),$$

$$\hat{K}_i(\mathbf{x}, \tilde{\mathbf{x}}) = \hat{K}_{i-1}(\mathbf{x}, \tilde{\mathbf{x}}) - \frac{\hat{K}_{i-1}(\mathbf{x}, \mathbf{x}_i)\hat{K}_{i-1}(\mathbf{x}_i, \tilde{\mathbf{x}})}{\hat{K}_{i-1}(\mathbf{x}_i, \mathbf{x}_i)}.$$

Moreover, due to the fact, that a Gaussian random measure is completely defined by the mean and the covariance functions, the corresponding iterative update is available for the posterior Gaussian measure (1).

Corollary 1. *There exists a functional ϕ such that $\mathbb{P}_l = \phi(\mathbf{x}_l, y_l, \mathbb{P}_{l-1}), l = 1, \dots, N$.*

3   Adaptive Design of Experiments

The area of adaptive design of experiments has been paid much attention in recent decades and numerous criteria have been proposed. To the best of our knowledge, all the criteria are obtained from the common sense arguments, such as uniform filling of the design space, reduction of the error predicted by Gaussian process model, etc. However, it seems reasonable to develop criteria which are optimal in terms of some statistical functional. We are going to introduce Bayesian framework which allows to formally state the adaptive design of experiments problem and start with some definitions.

Definition 1. *Let $\rho = \rho(f, \hat{f})$ be some measurable functional. We will call it error function (see particular examples below).*

Definition 2. *Let $q_\rho(D_l) = \mathbb{E}\big[\rho(f, \hat{f}_l)\big|D_l\big]$, where expectation is taken as conditional given fixed sample D_l. Let's call $q_\rho(D_l)$ a mean posterior risk.*

Definition 3. *The optimal experimental plan X_N is a solution of the following optimization problem:*

$$J^* = \min_{X_N \in \mathbb{X}^N} \mathbb{E}_{\mathbf{y}_N}\left[\sum_{i=1}^{N} Q_\rho(\mathbf{x}_i, y_i, D_{i-1})\right], \tag{4}$$

where $Q_\rho(\mathbf{x}_i, y_i, D_{i-1}) = q_\rho(D_{i-1} \cup (\mathbf{x}_i, y_i)) - q_\rho(D_{i-1})$.

Let us note, that (4) is equivalent to minimizing the error at the final iteration:

$$J^* = \min_{X_N \in \mathbb{X}^N} \mathbb{E}_{\mathbf{y}_N} \left[q_\rho(D_N) \right] - q_\rho(D_0),$$

where we set $q_\rho(D_0) = \mathbb{E}\rho(f, \hat{f}_0)$, $\hat{f}_0 = 0$.

Due to Corollary 1 the problem (4) is a stochastic dynamic programming problem and we can write the Bellman equations for it:

$$J_r(D_{r-1}) = \min_{\mathbf{x}_r \in \mathbb{X}} \mathbb{E}_{y_r} \left[Q_\rho(\mathbf{x}_r, y_r, D_{r-1}) + J_{r+1}(D_{r-1} \cup (\mathbf{x}_r, y_r)) \right], r = 1, \ldots, N,$$

where $J_r(D_{r-1})$ is a value function at r-th step and $J_{N+1} \equiv 0$. Unfortunately, this stochastic dynamic programming problem is infinite dimensional and can not be solved explicitly. That is why in the next section we consider various one-step look-ahead solutions.

4 One-Step Look-Ahead Solutions

Value function for the last step of the stochastic dynamic programming problem (4) is given by the following formula:

$$J_N(D_{N-1}) = \min_{\mathbf{x}_N \in \mathbb{X}} \mathbb{E}_{y_N} \left[Q_\rho(\mathbf{x}_N, y_N, D_{N-1}) \right].$$

Thus, the criterion for choosing an optimal one-step look-ahead point has the form:

$$\mathbf{x}_N = \arg \min_{\mathbf{x} \in \mathbb{X}} \mathcal{I}_\rho(\mathbf{x}), \tag{5}$$

where $\mathcal{I}_\rho(\mathbf{x}) = \mathbb{E}_{y_N} \left[Q_\rho(\mathbf{x}, y_N, D_{N-1}) \right]$.

Depending on the choice of the error function $\rho(f, \hat{f})$ different types of criteria will follow. We consider the following types of the error function:

1. L_2-norm of difference between f and $\hat{f}_N$: $\rho_2(f, \hat{f}_N) = \frac{1}{|\mathbb{X}|} \int_{\mathbb{X}} (f(\mathbf{u}) - \hat{f}_N(\mathbf{u}))^2 d\mathbf{u}$.
2. L_1-norm of difference between f and $\hat{f}_N$: $\rho_1(f, \hat{f}_N) = \frac{1}{|\mathbb{X}|} \int_{\mathbb{X}} |f(\mathbf{u}) - \hat{f}_N(\mathbf{u})| d\mathbf{u}$.
3. L_∞-norm of difference between f and $\hat{f}_N$: $\rho_\infty(f, \hat{f}_N) = \max_{\mathbf{u} \in \mathbb{X}} |f(\mathbf{u}) - \hat{f}_N(\mathbf{u})|$.

4.1 L_2 Error Function

Proposition 2. *If the error function is $\rho(f, \hat{f}_N) = \rho_2(f, \hat{f}_N)$, then the optimal one-step look-ahead criterion has the form*

$$\mathcal{I}_{\rho_2}(\mathbf{x}) = \int_{\mathbb{X}} (\hat{\sigma}^2(\mathbf{u}|X_{N-1} \cup \mathbf{x}) - \hat{\sigma}^2(\mathbf{u}|X_{N-1})) d\mathbf{u}.$$

We will denote this criterion as IntegratedMseGain. Due to the fact that $\hat{\sigma}^2(\mathbf{u}|X_{N-1})$ is independent of $\mathbf{x}_N$ this criterion coincides with the well known criterion IMSE [10]:

$$\mathcal{I}_{IMSE}(\mathbf{x}) = \frac{1}{|\mathbb{X}|} \int_{\mathbb{X}} \hat{\sigma}^2(\mathbf{u}|X_{N-1} \cup \mathbf{x}) d\mathbf{u}.$$

Proposition 3. *Change of the posterior variance at point* $\mathbf{v}$ *after point* $\mathbf{x}$ *is added to the sample, can be written as:*

$$\hat{\sigma}^2(\mathbf{v}|X_{N-1} \cup \mathbf{x}) - \hat{\sigma}^2(\mathbf{v}|X_{N-1}) = -\frac{\hat{K}_{N-1}^2(\mathbf{x}, \mathbf{v})}{\hat{\sigma}^2(\mathbf{x}|X_{N-1})}.$$

Corollary 2. *The criterion* $\mathcal{I}_{\rho_2}(\mathbf{x})$ *can be rewritten as:*

$$\mathcal{I}_{\rho_2}(\mathbf{x}) = -\frac{1}{|\mathbb{X}|} \int_{\mathbb{X}} \frac{\hat{K}_{N-1}^2(\mathbf{x}, \mathbf{v})}{\hat{\sigma}^2(\mathbf{x}|X_{N-1})} d\mathbf{v}.$$

This corollary allows to compute $\mathcal{I}_{\rho_2}$ more effectively and increase its computational stability compared to IMSE, as no direct inversion of the covariance matrix for a full training set $(X_{N-1} \cup \mathbf{x})$ is needed.

In some important particular cases the criterion can be computed analytically. For example, for a widely used in applications weighted exponential covariance function we can state the following preposition.

Proposition 4. *Let* $k(\mathbf{x}, \tilde{\mathbf{x}}) = \sigma^2 \exp(-\sum_{i=1}^n \theta_i^2 (x^i - \tilde{x}^i)^2)$, *and* $\mathbb{X} = \prod_{i=1}^n [a_i, b_i]$. *Define* $\mathbf{k}(\mathbf{x}) = \{k(\mathbf{x}, \mathbf{x}_i)\}_{i=1}^{N-1}$. *Then*

$$\mathcal{I}_{\rho_2}(\mathbf{x}) = \frac{\operatorname{trace}(\mathbf{k}(\mathbf{x})\mathbf{k}^T(\mathbf{x})C) - 2\mathbf{k}^T(\mathbf{x})\mathbf{c}(\mathbf{x}) + c_{NN}(\mathbf{x})}{|\mathbb{X}|\hat{\sigma}^2(\mathbf{x}|X_{N-1})},$$

where $\mathbf{c}(\mathbf{x}) = [c_{iN}]_{i=1}^{N-1}, C = [c_{ij}]_{i,j=1}^{N-1}$, $\operatorname{erf}(x) = \frac{2}{\sqrt{\pi}} \int_0^x e^{-t^2} dt$,

$$c_{ij} = \sigma^4 \prod_{k=1}^n \frac{\sqrt{\pi} \exp(-\frac{1}{2}\theta_k^2 (x_i^k - x_j^k)^2)}{\sqrt{8}\theta_k(b_k - a_k)} \left[\operatorname{erf}\left(\sqrt{2}\theta_k \left(a_k - \frac{x_i^k + x_j^k}{2}\right)\right) - \right.$$

$$\left. - \operatorname{erf}\left(\sqrt{2}\theta_k \left(b_k - \frac{x_i^k + x_j^k}{2}\right)\right) \right],$$

where for the ease of notations we denoted $\mathbf{x} = \mathbf{x}_N$.

4.2 L_1 Error Function

Proposition 5. *If the error function is* $\rho(f, \hat{f}_N) = \rho_1(f, \hat{f}_N)$, *then the optimal one-step look-ahead criterion has the form*

$$\mathcal{I}_{\rho_1}(\mathbf{x}) = \int_{\mathbb{X}} \sqrt{\frac{2}{\pi}} (\hat{\sigma}(\mathbf{u}|X_{N-1} \cup \mathbf{x}) - \hat{\sigma}(\mathbf{u}|X_{N-1})) d\mathbf{u}.$$

To the best of our knowledge this criterion has no analogues in the literature, but its computation is complicated due to the structure of the formula inside the integral.

4.3 L_∞ Error Function

Proposition 6. *If the error function is* $\rho(f, \hat{f}_N) = \rho_\infty(f, \hat{f}_N)$*, then the optimal one-step look-ahead criterion has the form*

$$\mathcal{I}_{\rho_\infty}(\mathbf{x}) = \mathbb{E}\left[\max_{\mathbf{u}\in\mathbb{X}}\left|f(\mathbf{u})-\hat{f}(\mathbf{u}|D_{N-1}\cup(\mathbf{x},y_N))\right| - \max_{\mathbf{u}\in\mathbb{X}}\left|f(\mathbf{u})-\hat{f}(\mathbf{u}|D_{N-1})\right|\,\middle|\,D_{N-1}\right].$$

Let us note that this criterion can't be computed analytically. In order to compute it one can use approximation techniques for the distribution of the maximum of the posterior Gaussian random process. In many common situations the maximum is proportional to the maximal value of the posterior variance [19], which justifies usage of the popular criterion Maximum Variance (MaxVar) [10]

$$\mathcal{I}_{MV}(\mathbf{x}) = \hat{\sigma}^2(\mathbf{x}|X_{N-1}).$$

5 Towards More Robust Adaptive DoE Criterion

It is of the great importance that the optimization problem (5) is always multimodal and its complexity highly depends on the complexity of the criterion in question. Some popular criteria as IMSE, have very complicated surface with multiple narrow local optima, which makes their optimization a hard task. In this work we consider a simple multiplicative combination of criteria IntegratedMseGain and Maximum Variance (IntegratedMseGainMaxVar):

$$\mathcal{I}_{IGMV}(\mathbf{x}) = \frac{\hat{\sigma}^2(\mathbf{u}|X_{N-1})}{|\mathbb{X}|}\int_{\mathbb{X}}(\hat{\sigma}^2(\mathbf{u}|X_{N-1}\cup\mathbf{x}) - \hat{\sigma}^2(\mathbf{u}|X_{N-1}))\mathrm{d}\mathbf{u} =$$

$$= \frac{1}{|\mathbb{X}|}\int_{\mathbb{X}}[k(\mathbf{x},\mathbf{u}) - k(\mathbf{x},X)^T K^{-1}k(\mathbf{u},X)]^2\,\mathrm{d}u = \frac{1}{|\mathbb{X}|}\int_{\mathbb{X}}\hat{K}_{N-1}^2(\mathbf{x},\mathbf{u})\mathrm{d}u.$$

This criterion takes into account global behaviour of the function as IntegratedMseGain does, but is more numerically stable then IntegratedMseGain and MaxVar (see behaviours of these criteria for 2D example in Figure 1).

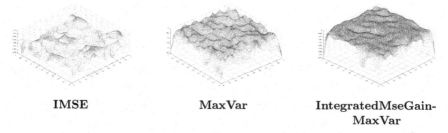

IMSE   MaxVar   IntegratedMseGain-
                                              MaxVar

Fig. 1. Surfaces of IMSE, MaxVar and IntegratedMseGainMaxVar criteria

6   Experiments

6.1   Model Experiments

For the experiments we used a big set of artificial functions which are commonly
used for testing optimization algorithms [20–22]. The idea behind such a choice
is that approximation models are very often used as substitutes for real target
functions during surrogate-based optimization process [13].

We performed testing on 10 different functions with 3 and 4 dimensional
inputs. For every function we generated 10 independent initial DoEs with the
size (10 * dimensionality) points. Adaptive DoE was performed starting from
each initial DoE and for each criterion, described in Section 4, except criteria
$\mathcal{I}_{\rho_1}$ and $\mathcal{I}_{\rho_\infty}$ as they are hard to compute even numerically. As a benchmark
we used the method of random sampling and the non-adaptive method which

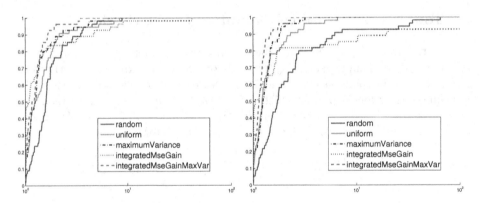

Fig. 2. Dolan-More curves for test functions, 30 added points

Fig. 3. Dolan-More curves for test functions, 50 added points

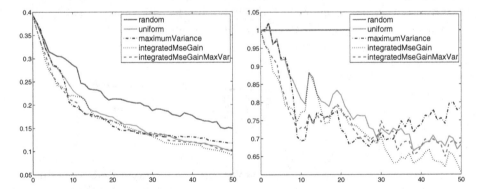

Fig. 4. Error curves for Michalewicz function

Fig. 5. Error curves for Michalewicz function (normed by the error curve of the random sampling)

Table 1. Input parameters for compression spring design problem

Input parameter	d	D	n	h_f
Lower bound	0.25 mm	1 cm	70	2.5 cm
Upper bound	5 mm	2 cm	100	100 cm

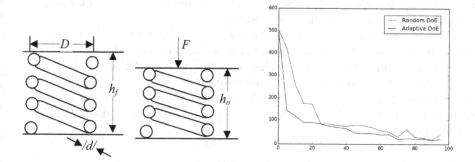

Fig. 6. Compression spring and its para-   **Fig. 7.** RMS on the test set depending on
meters   the number of points added to DoE

generates new points maximizing minimum inter-point distance, i.e. provides a maximum to the following criterion: $\mathcal{I}_{uniform}(\mathbf{x}) = \min_{\mathbf{v} \in X_{N-1}} d(\mathbf{x}, \mathbf{v})$, where $d(\mathbf{x}, \mathbf{v})$ is a Euclidean distance between points $\mathbf{x}$ and $\mathbf{v}$.

On every iteration we add to the DoE one point optimizing the criterion in question and re-estimate parameters of Gaussian process regression using maximum likelihood approach. Results are compared by means of the root mean squared error on big test set of 10000 points. For convenience results are presented in the form of Dolan-More curves [23]. The higher curve is on the plot, the better is the quality obtained by the corresponding algorithm. Results are presented for 30 adaptively added points (see Figure 2) and for 50 adaptively added points (see Figure 3).

Let us note that IntegratedMseGain criterion provides good results in the most cases (the value of the Dolan-More curve at zero). However for many test functions this criterion also shows bad performance due to numerical instability (the corresponding Dolan-More curve reaches the maximal level with significant delay compared to the curves for other criteria). IntegratedMseGainMaxVar criterion is more robust and provides better results.

Also let's consider an example how the error of approximation changes from iteration to iteration of adaptive DoE process. We consider Michalewicz function in the domain $[0, 1]^2$. On Figures 4 and 5 we plot the dependence of the approximation error on a number of iteration of the adaptive DoE process (the results are averaged over 5 initial train samples). It can be easily seen, that adaptive methods are much better then the random sampling with the error of the best method 1.7 times smaller then the error, obtained in case the random sampling is used.

6.2 Spring Design

We consider a physical model of a compression spring [24]. We wish to construct a DoE which provides an accurate approximation of a force of the spring at its pre-load height, $h_0 = 2.5$ cm. The input design parameters are wire diameter d, coil diameter D, number of coils in the spring n and spring free height h_f, see Figure 6. We provide parameters bounds in Table 1. The force of a spring is computed by means of the physical model [24].

We generated two designs: a random design with 200 points and an adaptive design of the same size, generated using IntegratedMseGainMaxVar criterion (starting from an initial random design with 100 points). We computed a root mean squared error on a big test sample for each iteration of a DoE generation algorithm, see Figure 7. We conclude, that the adaptive design for this test case ensures decreasing trend for the approximation error and better quality than the random design.

7 Conclusions

In this work we propose an approach to adaptive design of experiments for a Gaussian process regression which allows to formulate it as stochastic dynamic programming problem. Optimal one-step look-ahead solutions of this problem allow to justify many criteria of adaptive design of experiments, well known from the literature. Also in this work we introduce new criterion IntegratedMseGainMaxVar, which in simple form combines well-known criteria, but achieves better numerical stability. Experimental results show the benefits of adaptive designs compared to the random sampling. The proposed criterion provides better results then the other criteria. As a direction of future research we plan to construct solutions of dynamic programming problem with horizon of few steps and obtain new, more accurate criteria of adaptive design of experiments.

Acknowledgments. The research was conducted in IITP RAS and supported solely by the Russian Science Foundation grant (project 14-50-00150).

References

1. Forrester A., Sobester A., Keane A.: Engineering Design via Surrogate Modelling. A Practical Guide, pp. 238. Wiley (2008)
2. Bernstein A.V., Burnaev E.V., Kuleshov A.P.: Intellectual data analysis in meta-modelling. In: Proceedings of 17th Russian Seminar "Neuroinformatics and its Applications to Data Analysis", pp. 23–28, Krasnoyarsk (2009)
3. Giunta, A., Watson, L.T.: A comparison of approximation modeling technique: polynomial versus interpolating models. In: 7th AIAA/USAF/NASA/ISSMO Symposium on Multidisciplinary Analysis and Optimization, pp. 392–404. AIAA, Reston (1998)
4. Batill, S.M., Renaud, J.E., Gu, X.: Modeling and simulation uncertainty in multidisciplinary design optimization. In: AIAA Paper, pp. 2000–4803, September 2000

5. Fedorov, V.V.: Theory of Optimal Experiments. Academic Press (1972)
6. Pukelsheim, F.: Optimal Design of Experiments. Wiley, New York (1993)
7. Fedorov, V.V.: Design of spatial experiments: model fitting and prediction. In: Handbook of Statistics, pp. 515–553. Elsevier, Amsterdam (1996)
8. Zimmerman, D.L.: Optimal network design for spatial prediction, covariance parameter estimation, and empirical prediction. Environmetrics **17**(6), 635–652 (2006)
9. Chen, R.J.W., Sudjianto, A.: On sequential sampling for global metamodeling in engineering design. In: Proceedings of DETC 2002, Montreal, Canada, September 29-October 2 (2002)
10. Sacks, J., Welch, W.J., Mitchell, T.J., Wynn, H.P.: Design and Analysis of Computer Experiments. Statistical Science **4**(4), 409–423 (1989). doi:10.1214/ss/1177012413
11. Currin, C., Mitchell, T., Morris, M., Ylvisaker, D.: A Bayesian approach to the design and analysis of computer experiments. Journal of the American Statistical Association **86**(416), 953–963 (1991)
12. Welch, W.J., Buck, R.J., Sacks, J., Wynn, H.P., Mitchell, T.J., Morris, M.D.: Screening, predicting and computer experiments. Technometrics **34**, 15–25 (1992)
13. Jones, D.R., Schonlau, M., William, J.: Efficient global optimization of expensive black-box functions. J. Glob. Optim. **13**(4), 455–492 (1998)
14. Bect, J., Ginsbourger, D., Li, L., Picheny, V., Vazquez, E.: Sequential design of computer experiments for the estimation of a probability of failure. Statistics and Computing **22**(3), 773–793 (2012)
15. Burnaev, E., Panin, I.: Adaptive design of experiments for sobol indices estimation based on quadratic metamodel. In: Proceedings of the Third International Symposium on Learning and Data Sciences (SLDS 2015), London, England, UK, April 20–22 (to appear, 2015)
16. Rasmussen, C.E., Williams, C.K.I.: Gaussian Processes for Machine Learning. The MIT Press (2006)
17. Burnaev, E., Zaytsev, A., Panov, M., Prikhodko, P., Yanovich, Yu.: Modeling of nonstationary covariance function of Gaussian process on base of expansion in dictionary of nonlinear functions. In ITaS-2011, Gelendzhik, October 2-7 (2011)
18. Belyaev, M., Burnaev, E., Kapushev, Y.: Gaussian process regression for large structured data sets. In: Proceedings of the Third International Symposium on Learning and Data Sciences (SLDS 2015), London, England, UK, April 20–22 (to appear, 2015)
19. Adler, R.J., Taylor, J.E.: Random Fields and Geometry. Springer, 2007
20. Saltelli, A., Sobol, I.M.: About the use of rank transformation in sensitivity analysis of model output. Reliab. Eng. Syst. Safety **50**(3), 225–239 (1995)
21. Ishigami, T., Homma, T.: An importance qualification technique in uncertainty analysis for computer models. In: Proceedings of the Isuma 1990, First International Symposium on Uncertainty Modelling and Analysis. University of Maryland (1990)
22. Rönkkönen, J., Lampinen, J.: An extended mutation concept for the local selection based differential evolution algorithm. In: Proceedings of Genetic and Evolutionary Computation Conference, GECCO 2007, London, England, UK, July 7–11 (2007)
23. Dolan, E.D., More, J.J.: Benchmarking optimization software with performance profiles. In: Mathematical Programmming, Ser. A 91, pp. 201–213 (2002)
24. Fox, R.L.: Optimization methods for engineering design. Addison-Wesley, Massachusetts (1971)

Forests of Randomized Shapelet Trees

Isak Karlsson[⊠], Panagotis Papapetrou, and Henrik Boström

Department of Computer and Systems Sciences, Stockholm University, Forum 100,
164 40 Kista, Sweden
{isak-kar,panagiotis,henrik.bostrom}@dsv.su.se

Abstract. Shapelets have recently been proposed for data series classification, due to their ability to capture phase independent and local
information. Decision trees based on shapelets have been shown to provide not only interpretable models, but also, in many cases, state-of-
the-art predictive performance. Shapelet discovery is, however, computationally costly, and although several techniques for speeding up this
task have been proposed, the computational cost is still in many cases
prohibitive. In this work, an ensemble-based method, referred to as Random Shapelet Forest (RSF), is proposed, which builds on the success of
the random forest algorithm, and which is shown to have a lower computational complexity than the original shapelet tree learning algorithm.
An extensive empirical investigation shows that the algorithm provides
competitive predictive performance and that a proposed way of calculating importance scores can be used to successfully identify influential
regions.

Keywords: Data series classification · Shapelets · Decision trees ·
Ensemble

1 Introduction

In many applications, measurements of some quantity are made over time or
over some other logical ordering. For example, data series have been analyzed
to classify human heart rates [15], to recognize image shapes [10], and to find
anomalies in periodic light curves [20]. Although the measurements are ordered,
the resulting data series are often treated as ordinary feature vectors, allowing for
classification using standard machine learning algorithms, such as support vector
machines [7], random forests [5], and nearest neighbor classifiers (k-NN) [2].
Experimental evidence, however, suggests that treating time series data as one
dimensional series and applying nearest neighbor classifiers with elastic distance
measures, such as dynamic time warping (DTW) [3] or its constrained version
(cDTW) [21], results in state-of-the-art predictive performance [23]. It has also
been observed that the performance of elastic measures converges to that of
using the euclidean distance when the size of the training sets increase [23].

As alternatives to the k-NN classifier, several competitive approaches based
on *shapelets* have been suggested, such as shapelet-based decision trees [24], logical combinations of shapelets [17], and data pre-processing approaches using

© Springer International Publishing Switzerland 2015
A. Gammerman et al. (Eds.): SLDS 2015, LNAI 9047, pp. 126–136, 2015.
DOI: 10.1007/978-3-319-17091-6_8

shapelet transformations [1,13]. A shapelet is a phase-independent subsequence of a longer data series used as a local primitive for classification. In this setting, the idea is to find the closest matching position within each data series to a particular shapelet, and use this similarity as a discriminatory feature for classification. In the original shapelet classifier [24], the shapelet extraction is embedded in a decision tree classifier. However, since the search for the most informative shapelet is a very time consuming task, a significant amount of research has focused on improving the speed of which shapelets can be explored and utilized. For example, by *early abandoning* and *entropy pruning* [24], by using approximation methods [19], by random traversal orderings [12] and online normalization with re-ordered early abandoning [18]. While these approaches make the search for shapelet candidates more efficient and, hence, shapelet classification usable in a wider range of applications, decision trees are not the most accurate classifier. For standard machine learning tasks, it has been observed that single decision trees are frequently outperformed by more elaborate classifiers such as random forests [5], neural networks [22], and SVMs [7]. Thus, although shapelet based classifiers can perform well on many tasks and are able to provide insights that may help practitioners understand why and how a classification is made [24], their classification accuracy and training performance are often prohibitive [19].

If the goal is to maximize classification accuracy when using decision trees, one straightforward and effective approach is to combine a set of single trees into an ensemble, e.g., using bagging [4]. One of the main reasons for trees being suitable as ensemble members is due to their variability, i.e., slight changes in the training sample can result in completely different trees. The idea is that by combining a set of models, all performing better than random and making errors to some extent independently, the probability of the ensemble making an error will decrease with the number of ensemble members (trees). One way of achieving this, popularized by, e.g,, the random forest, is hence to introduce randomness in the tree generation process [4,5]. The purpose of this study is to describe and investigate a novel data series classifier building on the idea of random forests to improve classification accuracy of shapelet trees. The main contributions include a description the Random Shapelet Forest (RSF) algorithm, an extensive empirical investigation of the classification performance and the description of an importance score for identifying influential data series regions.

The remainder of this paper is organized as follows. In the next section, we briefly discuss related work on data series classification. In Section 3, we present the novel algorithm for generating forests of randomized shapelet trees and discuss some implementation choices. In Section 4, we present the experimental setup and the empirical investigation. Finally in Section 5, we summarize the main findings and point out directions for future work.

2 Background

A data series is an (often temporally) ordered series of data points, sampled using some specified method, e.g., for time series, sampling is typically made using fixed and regular time intervals. Let us denote a dataset of n such data series as $\mathcal{D} = \{d_1, \ldots, d_n\}$ and assume, similar to many other studies on data series analysis, that each data series $d_i \in \mathcal{D}$, $\langle d_{i1}, \ldots, d_{im} \rangle$ is of length m. Then given a vector of class labels $y_1, \ldots, y_n \in Y$, the goal of data series classification (DSC) is to find a function $f : \mathcal{D} \to Y$ that as accurately as possible[1] approximates the true function h used to generate the data.

As briefly described in the introduction, a shapelet is any subsequence extracted from a data series d_i. More formally, $s^i_{j,k}$ is a continuous sequence from d_i of length k starting at position j. Every subsequence in every data series in the database is a possible candidate. If the set of all possible candidates of length k from d_i is denoted as s^i_k, then all possible candidates of that length are denoted as $s_k = \{s^1_k \cup s^2_k \cup \ldots \cup s^n_k\}$, and finally the set of all possible candidates is $S = \{s_1 \cup s_2 \cup \ldots \cup s_m\}$. Since shapelets must be invariant to scale and offset to detect localized shape similarities, they are individually z-normalized. Hence, shapelets are usually extracted in a brute-force manner by searching and normalizing all possible candidates between some pre-defined lengths l (lower) and u (upper). Let $f(p, q)$ be a function (e.g., the Euclicean distance) used to calculate the distance between two data series p, q of equal length m. The distance between a data series d_j and a shapelet candidate s'_k, can be found by calculating the distance to all subsequences of length k in d_i and taking the minimum, i.e., $f_{sub}(d_j, s'_k) = min_{s \in s^j_k} f(d_j, s)$. The minimum distance of a candidate s' and all data series in D can be used to generate a vector of n distances $D_{s'}$, which in turn can be used to assess the classification quality of shapelets in terms of, e.g., entropy or gini [6,24].

3   Forests of Randomized Shapelet Trees

Random forest is an ensemble classifier consisting of a set of classification (or regression) trees [5]. The main idea of learning ensembles is to generate sufficiently accurate members which, in the optimal case, make errors independently from each other. By combining the predictions of these members, the resulting generalization error can be expected to be smaller than that of the individual models. In the random forest algorithm, randomization in the generation of ensemble members are usually injected by employing bagging [4], i.e., randomly selecting with replacement n examples to include during training; and by sample a small subset of features to evaluate at each node of the trees [14].

In this study, a related idea is utilized when generating forests of shapelet trees where randomization is injected both in the selection of data series to include during training and in the selection of shapelet candidates used during the construction of each tree, aggregating them to a forest of randomized shapelet trees. Algorithm 1 presents the main procedure for generating such a forest. The algorithm expects a database consisting of n data series, $\mathcal{D} = \{d_1, \ldots, d_n\}$, where each data series d_i is a vector of consecutive measurements $\langle d_{i1}, \ldots, d_{im} \rangle$ and

---

[1] Usually assessed by the classification error on an independent validation set.

each $d_{ij} \in \mathcal{R}$. Furthermore, the algorithm expects a vector of output variables $y_1, \ldots, y_n \in Y$ from the domain $\mathcal{Y}$ and a parameter indicating the number of random shapelet trees to generate, t.

Given the database of data series, Algorithm 1 draws a random sample of indices from $\mathcal{D}$. Although, the function Sample can be implemented in a number of ways, the traditional bootstrap approach [4] described earlier are chosen here. Hence, Sample returns a vector of n indices drawn with replacement from the range $[0, n]$. Using this sample, the algorithm continues by generating the kth tree (sequentially or in parallel) using the procedure RandomShapeletTree and the data series included in the sample $\mathcal{D}_{d_k}$.

Algorithm 1. SHAPELETFOREST($\mathcal{D}$: database, Y: target, t: trees, l, u, r)

Input : $\mathcal{D} = \{d_1, \ldots, d_n\}$ and class labels $y_1, \ldots, y_n \in Y$.
Output: An ensemble of random shapelet trees $T_1, \ldots, T_t$

   for $k \leftarrow 0$ **to** t **do**
1      $d_k \leftarrow$ Sample($\mathcal{D}$);
2      $T_k \leftarrow$ RandomShapeletTree($\mathcal{D}_{d_k}$, $\mathcal{Y}_{d_k}$, l, u, r);
      $\mathcal{T} \leftarrow \mathcal{T} \cup \{t'\}$;
   return $T_1, \ldots, T_t$

The RandomShapeletTree function first samples r shapelet candidates from the set of all possible candidates S. Instead of sampling candidates from a pre-calculated database, SampleShapelet is implemented to randomly and uniformly select a single data series $d_i \in \mathcal{D}$ and extract a shapelet $s^i_{j,k}$ from d_i by uniformly picking a length k in the range $k = rand([l, u])$ and a start position in the range $j = rand([0, m - k])$, where l and u denotes minimum and maximum shapelet size. This results in a subset $\bar{S} \in S$ of all possible candidates. The BestSplit function determines which shapelet, $\bar{s} \in \bar{S}$, and distance threshold, τ, should be selected as the test condition. The chosen test condition is subsequently used to separate the data series into two groups, those with a distance $f_{sub}(d, \bar{s}) \leq \tau$ and those with a distance $f_{sub}(d, \bar{s}) > \tau$. To efficiently obtain the threshold τ for a particular shapelet, the distances from the shapelet to all data series in the database need to be calculated, after which one can sort the examples according to their distance and select the best threshold from the midpoints between two adjacent sorted values, analogous to how numeric features are discretized during tree growth [11]. The utility of a split is then be determined by an impurity measure such as gini-index or entropy, the latter being selected here. The entropy is calculated as $\sum_{y \in \mathcal{Y}} p(y) \log_2 p(y)$, where $p(y)$ denote the fraction of examples having a particular class label. Using the entropy, the utility of a split is calculated as the information gain, ΔI, which is the difference between the sum of entropy at the child nodes, weighted by the fraction of examples at a particular node, and the entropy at the parent node. To resolve conflicts in information gain, i.e. two or more thresholds with the same gain, the threshold that maximizes the separation gap is chosen [19].

The `Distribute` function partitions the examples according to the chosen split point, i.e., *left* contains the examples with a distance less than or equal to τ and vice versa for *right*. If no examples are partitioned to the *left* or to the *right*, a leaf node is created predicting the most probable class. Otherwise the partitions are subsequently used to recursively build sub-trees. The recursion continues until there are no more informative shapelets or the node is pure, i.e., containing examples from one class only. Even though the original shapelet tree algorithm [24] has a run-time complexity of $O(m^3 n^2 \log m^3 n)$, the computational cost is reduced to $O(Trn^2 \log rn)$ for the shapelet forest algorithm; and, since T and r are constants, the amortized computational cost is reduced to $O(n^2 \log n)$.

Algorithm 2. RANDOMSHAPELETTREE($\mathcal{D}$: dataset, Y: target, l, u, r)

Input : $\mathcal{D} = \{d_1, \ldots, d_n\}$ and class label $y_1, \ldots, y_n \in Y$.
Output: A randomized shapelet tree, T.

  $\bar{S} \leftarrow \emptyset$;
  for $s \leftarrow 0$ **to** r **do**
1 | $s' \leftarrow$ SampleShapelet$(\mathcal{D}, l, u)$;
2 | $\bar{S} \leftarrow \bar{S} \cup \{s'\}$;
  end
3 $\tau, \bar{s} \leftarrow$ BestSplit$(\mathcal{D}, Y, \bar{S})$;
4 $left, right \leftarrow$ Distribute$(\mathcal{D}, Y, \bar{s}\ \tau)$;
  if $\mathcal{D}_{left} = \emptyset$ *or* $\mathcal{D}_{right} = \emptyset$ **then**
   | $T \leftarrow$ MakeLeaf(Y);
  else
   | $T_{left} \leftarrow$ RandomShapeletTree$(\mathcal{D}_{left}, Y_{left}, l, u, S)$;
   | $T_{right} \leftarrow$ RandomShapeletTree$(\mathcal{D}_{right}, Y_{right}, l, u, S)$;
   | $T \leftarrow \{(\tau, \bar{s}, T_{left}), (\tau, \bar{s}, T_{right})\}$;
  end
  return T

Similar to traditional classification trees, one of the most important contributions introduced in the original shapelet classification algorithm is the ability to identify important features by manually inspecting the generated trees [24]. In the context of decision trees, Breiman et. al., (1984) [6] showed that this process could be automated by defining the measure of importance for a given variable. In a single decision tree, the use of surrogate splits is necessary to account for masking effects of correlated variables. However, due to randomization, masking effects present in single decision trees are decreased for random forests. Hence, in Breiman (2001) [5] the importance of a variable X_j is calculated by adding up, for each tree $T_1, \ldots, T_m$, the weighted impurity decrease $\frac{N_t}{N} \Delta I(c_t, t)$ for all nodes where X_j is used, giving the importance of X_j as $\frac{1}{M} \sum_{m=1}^{M} \sum_{t \in T_m} 1(j_t = j) \frac{N_t}{N} \Delta I(c_t, t)$, where $\frac{N_t}{N}$ is the fraction of examples reaching node t, and $1(j_t = j)$ is 1 if X_j is used for splitting node t and 0 otherwise. This measure is often denoted as *Mean Decrease Impurity* (MDI).

The random shapelet tree-algorithm requires two hyper-parameters to be tuned, the minimum and maximum length of sampled candidate shapelets. Hence, one important aspect when optimizing these parameters is to understand how important different lengths are for predicting Y. One approach, suggested by Hills et al. (2014) [13], estimates an appropriate shapelet length by randomly and repeatedly sampling a small subset of data series and, from these, extracting the best shapelets of all possible lengths. The best candidates from each data series are then merged and sorted by length. The minimum and maximum lengths are then given by the longest shapelet of the first quartile and shortest shapelet of the fourth quartile, respectively. For the RSF, another approach is to calculate the mean decrease in impurity of the shapelet lengths used in the forests. Hence, the standard MDI can be re-defined to, instead of considering a particular variable X_j, consider whether or not a particular length k is included in a split c_t.

Since forests of randomized shapelet trees consist of multiple trees, it is difficult to interpret and identify shapelets important for classifying a particular data series. For the interval-based time series forest, a measure of importance based on intervals has been suggested [9]. The entropy for different interval-based features are added up over all nodes in the forest, giving an importance score for each position in the data series. In this work, a similar approach is taken, where each position is given an importance score based on the MDI. The importance of position p for predicting Y is calculated by summing the weighted impurity decrease $\frac{N_t}{N} \frac{\Delta I(c_t^s,t)}{k}$ for all positions included in shapelet s of length k, i.e. $\frac{1}{M} \sum_{m=1}^{M} \sum_{t \in T_m} 1(j_t = j) \frac{N_t}{N} \frac{\Delta I(s_t,t)}{k}$.

4 Experiments

4.1 Experimental Setup

The datasets in the UCR Time Series Repository [16] represent a wide range of different classification tasks varying from image outline classification, e.g., OSU Leaf, to motion classification, e.g., Gun Point, and sensor reading classification, e.g., Fatal ECG of different sizes (from 16 to 1800 examples) and lengths (from 24 to 1882 measurements) [16]. Frequently, only a subset of the (current) 45 datasets in this repository is used when estimating the performance of shapelet-based classifiers due to the computational burden [12,13,19,24]. In contrast, we will here use all the 45 datasets, thanks to the limited computational cost of the shapelet forest algorithm.

To evaluate the performance of machine learning models on unseen data, an independent test set should be employed. If plenty of data are available, one simple approach is to split the data into two halves, and use one for training the model and the other one for evaluating its performance. However, when data is scarce, cross-validation is a viable approach for estimating the performance. Since already created training and validation sets are provided in the UCR Time Series Repository [16] together with baseline error estimates, we here opt for

the former. The baseline error estimates are calculated for 1-nearest neighbors
with Euclidean distance (1-NN), dynamic time warping with optimized warping
windows (1-NN DTW-best) and dynamic time warping with an unconstrained
warping window (1-NN DTW-no) [16]. In this study, the miss-classification rate
(i.e. the fraction of miss-classifications) is used as performance metric, since
this is the most commonly employed metric when comparing the classification
performance on data series classification [12,13,19,24]. However, we note that
other measures, such as the area under ROC curve, can be more suitable in some
cases, e.g., when the class distribution differ between training and testing.

As described in Section 3, the forest of randomized shapelet trees requires a
number of hyper-parameters to be set: the minimum shapelet length l, the maximum shapelet length u, the number of shapelets to sample r, and the number
of trees in the forest T. Usually, the optimal parameter settings are found by
repeated k-fold cross-validation, selecting the parameters with the lowest validation error. However, here we opt for a more ad-hoc approach, selecting 100
shapelets ($r = 100$) randomly in the range 2 ($l = 2$) to m ($u = m$). Furthermore,
to investigate the effect of forest size, an increasing number of trees is generated.
The considered forest sizes are 10, 25, 50, 100, 250 and 500; where forests of the
largest size are to be compared with the baseline approaches. Since the forest
generating algorithm is stochastic, changes in the random shapelet candidates
can affect predictive performance. However, the number of grown trees is rather
large and this risk is therefore neglected here. Finally, to detect if there are any
significant deviations in predictive performance between the forest of randomized shapelet trees and the baseline approaches, as measured by the error rate,
a Friedman test followed by a Nemenyi post-hoc test is performed [8].

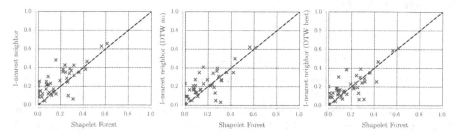

Fig. 1. Error rates for the random shapelet forest (RSF) with 500 trees compared to
the baseline approaches. For every point above the diagonal, RSF has a lower error.
Each point represents one dataset from the UCR Time Series Repository [16].

4.2   Empirical Results

The error rates for the Random Shapelet Forest with 500 trees and the baseline
approaches are shown in Fig. 1 and Fig. 2. In Fig. 2, where the error rates for
different forest sizes together with the baselines are provided, it can be seen that
the average error rate for the RSF slowly converges after 100 trees have been

added. Moreover, in Fig. 1, the error rates for all datasets are represented as points, where the x-axis represents the RSF and the y-axis the error rate for the baseline approaches. Hence, the diagonal line represents equal error rates and for every point above this line, the RSF classifier has a lower error estimate than the corresponding baseline classifier. Although Fig. 1 shows the absolute error rates for each algorithm and dataset, statistical tests for determining whether differences in predictive performance are significant are computed using the performance ranks of the algorithms [8].

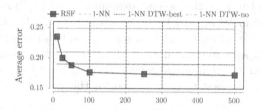

Fig. 2. Error rate for each forest size, averaged over every dataset, compared to the average error rate of the baseline approaches

As seen in Fig. 1, RSF performs better than the baseline approaches on a majority of the datasets. A Friedman test confirms that the observed differences in error ranks deviate significantly ($p < 0.01$) from what can be expected under the null hypothesis. To detect if there are any significant pair-wise deviations between the RSF and the baseline approaches, a post-hoc Nemenyi test is performed, which reveals that there is a significant ($p < 0.01$) difference in error rank between the RSF and the 1-NN, and between RSF and the unconstrained 1-NN DTW ($p < 0.01$). However, no significant differences can be detected for the constrained 1-NN DTW. The latter can perhaps be explained by the fact that no parameter optimizations where conducted for the RSF. Interestingly, RSF beats the baselines with a large margin for the image outline classification tasks, e.g., for Swedish Leaf and OSU Leaf, RSF have an error rate of 0.09 and 0.157 compared to 0.157 and 0.384 for the best baseline respectively.

To explore the proposed importance measure, two datasets where the RSF algorithm performs especially good are explored in greater detail. The chosen

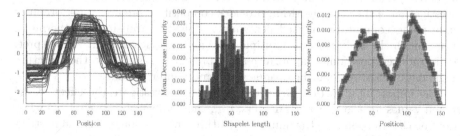

Fig. 3. Length and Position importance for the Gun Point dataset

datasets are `Gun Point` and `ECG five Days`, where the former concerns the prediction of human motion and the latter the prediction of human heart beats [16]. The data series and their corresponding importance scores are shown in Fig. 3 and Fig. 4 respectively. As seen in Fig. 3 (center), the most informative lengths for the `Gun Point` dataset seem to be somewhere between 30–70 data points, which by ocular inspection of Fig. 3 (left) seems rather intuitive. Similarly to the shapelet identified by Ye and Keogh (2009), the most important region seems to be around positions 40 and 120 [24]. The error rate for this dataset is 0.0, which, to the best of our knowledge, is better than the best reported result in the literature. In the second example, the `ECG Five Days` dataset, extracted from PhysioNet.org [16,19], is shown in Fig. 4 (left). According to the positional importance score, the elevation at around time-point 80 carries the most significant shapes for classifying the ECG series, which is also confirmed in [19]. Finally, the random shapelet forest is able to achieve 100% accuracy, which again is better than the best result reported for this dataset [19].

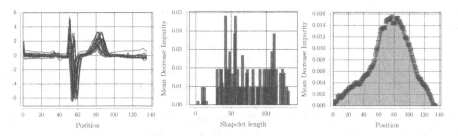

Fig. 4. The time-series in the *ECG five days* dataset with the respective length and positional importance scores

5   Concluding Remarks

In this study, a novel randomization-based ensemble algorithm, RSF, for classifying data series based on shapelets was introduced and empirically evaluated against state-of-the-art methods based on constrained and unconstrained dynamic time warping. The results show that there is a significant difference in predictive performance as measured by error rate. The main conclusion from the investigation is that the algorithm provides competitive predictive performance while being computationally efficient and simple to parallelize. Furthermore, even though the RSF contains multiple trees and is hence difficult to interpret, the introduced positional importance score provides insights into the structure of the data series, making the opaque forest more interpretable.

One important direction for future work is to investigate the effect of the chosen values for the hyper-parameters, e.g., the number of inspected shapelets could be chosen similar to the number of features in a random forest. Of particular interest would be to study their effect on the average predictive performance of the trees in the ensemble and their diversity, by decomposing the mean square error of the forest. Another, related, direction for future work is to investigate how the shapelet sampling algorithm affects the predictive performance. For example, since shapelets are local primitives, one might benefit from weighting the sampling procedure towards shorter subsequences. Finally, another possible direction for future work is to incorporate other, randomized, data series primitives to support additional ways of defining similarity.

Acknowledgments. This work was partly supported by the project High-Performance Data Mining for Drug Effect Detection at Stockholm University, funded by Swedish Foundation for Strategic Research under grant IIS11-0053.

References

1. Bagnall, A., Davis, L.M., Hills, J., Lines, J.: Transformation basedensembles for time series classification. In: SDM, vol.12, pp. 307–318. SIAM (2012)
2. Batista, G.E., Wang, X., Keogh, E.J.: A complexity-invariant distance measure for time series. In: SDM, vol. 11, pp. 699–710. SIAM (2011)
3. Berndt, D.J., Clifford, J.: Using dynamic time warping to find patterns in time series. In: KDD workshop, vol. 10, pp. 359–370. Seattle, WA (1994)
4. Breiman, L.: Bagging predictors. Machine Learning **24**(2), 123–140 (1996)
5. Breiman, L.: Random forests. Machine Learning **45**(1), 5–32 (2001)
6. Breiman, L., Friedman, J., Stone, C.J., Olshen, R.A.: Classification and regression trees. CRC Press (1984)
7. Cortes, C., Vapnik, V.: Support-vector networks. Machine Learning **20**(3)
8. Demšar, J.: Statistical comparisons of classifiers over multiple data sets. The Journal of Machine Learning Research **7**, 1–30 (2006)
9. Deng, H., Runger, G., Tuv, E., Vladimir, M.: A time series forest for classification and feature extraction. Information Sciences **239**, 142–153 (2013)
10. Ding, H., Trajcevski, G., Scheuermann, P., Wang, X., Keogh, E.: Querying and mining of time series data: experimental comparison of representations and distance measures. Proc. of the VLDB Endowment **1**(2), 1542–1552 (2008)
11. Fayyad, U.M., Irani, K.B.: On the handling of continuous-valued attributes in decision tree generation. Machine Learning **8**(1), 87–102 (1992)
12. Gordon, D., Hendler, D., Rokach, L.: Fast randomized model generation for shapelet-based time series classification. arXiv preprint arXiv:1209.5038 (2012)
13. Hills, J., Lines, J., Baranauskas, E., Mapp, J., Bagnall, A.: Classification of time series by shapelet transformation. Data Mining and Know. Discovery **28**(4) (2014)
14. Ho, T.K.: The random subspace method for constructing decision forests. IEEE Trans. on Pat. Analysis and Machine Intelligence **20**(8), 832–844 (1998)
15. Kampouraki, A., Manis, G., Nikou, C.: Heartbeat time series classification with support vector machines. Inf. Tech. in Biomedicine **13**(4) (2009)
16. Keogh, E., Zhu, Q., Hu, B., Hao, Y., Xi, X., Wei, L., Ratanamahatana, C.A.: The ucr time series classification/clustering homepage, www.cs.ucr.edu/eamonn/time_series_data/
17. Mueen, A., Keogh, E., Young, N.: Logical-shapelets: an expressive primitive for time series classification. In: Proc. 17th ACM SIGKDD. ACM (2011)

18. Rakthanmanon, T., Campana, B., Mueen, A., Batista, G., Westover, B., Zhu, Q., Zakaria, J., Keogh, E.: Searching and mining trillions of time series subsequences under dynamic time warping. In: Proc. of the 18th ACM SIGKDD. ACM (2012)
19. Rakthanmanon, T., Keogh, E.: Fast shapelets: a scalable algorithm for discovering time series shapelets. In: Proc. 13th SDM. SIAM (2013)
20. Rebbapragada, U., Protopapas, P., Brodley, C.E., Alcock, C.: Finding anomalous periodic time series. Machine Learning **74**(3), 281–313 (2009)
21. Sakoe, H., Chiba, S.. In: Transactions on ASSP, vol. 26, pp. 43–49
22. Schmidhuber, J.: Deep learning in neural networks: An overview. arXiv preprint arXiv:1404.7828 (2014)
23. Wang, X., Mueen, A., Ding, H., Trajcevski, G., Scheuermann, P., Keogh, E.: Experimental comparison of representation methods and distance measures for time series data. Data Mining and Knowl. Discovery **26**(2) (2013)
24. Ye, L., Keogh, E.: Time series shapelets: a new primitive for data mining. In: Proc. of the 15th ACM SIGKDD. ACM (2009)

Aggregation of Adaptive Forecasting Algorithms Under Asymmetric Loss Function

Alexey Romanenko$^{(\boxtimes)}$

Moscow Institute of Physics and Technology, 9 Institutskiy per., Dolgoprudny, Moscow Region 141700, Russian Federation
alexromsput@gmail.com

Abstract. The paper deals with applying the strong aggregating algorithm to games with asymmetric loss function. A particular example of such games is the problem of time series forecasting where specific losses from under-forecasting and over-forecasting may vary considerably. We use the aggregating algorithm for building compositions of adaptive forecasting algorithms. The paper specifies sufficient conditions under which a composition based on the aggregating algorithm performs as well as the best of experts. As a result, we find a theoretical bound for the loss process of a given composition under asymmetric loss function. Finally we compare the composition based on the aggregating algorithm to other well-known compositions in experiments with real data.

Keywords: Aggregating algorithm · Time series forecasting · Asymmetric loss function

1 Introduction

In this paper we consider the following situation. Suppose we are given an *outcome space* Ω and a *prediction space* Γ. There is a loss function $\lambda \colon \Omega \times \Gamma \to [0, +\infty]$. The triple $\langle \Omega, \Gamma, \lambda \rangle$ is called *game* [1]. Suppose we are also given a set of *experts* $\mathfrak{A}$ and a *learner*. The learner and the experts try to predict a sequence $x_1, \ldots, x_T \in \Omega^T$ according to the following protocol:

at each step $t = 0, 1, \ldots, T$

1. each expert $A \in \mathfrak{A}$ makes a forecast $\hat{x}_{t+1}^A \in \Gamma$ of the next element $x_{t+1} \in \Omega$;
2. the learner makes its own prediction $\hat{x}_{t+1} \in \Gamma$ based on the forecasts of the experts;
3. the actual value $x_{t+1} \in \Omega$ is observed;
4. the experts incur the loss $\lambda\left(x_{t+1}, \hat{x}_{t+1}^A\right)$ and the learner incurs the loss $\lambda\left(x_{t+1}, \hat{x}_{t+1}\right)$.

The *loss process* of expert A is the sum of its losses at each step: $\text{Loss}_T^A = \sum_{t=1}^T \lambda(x_t, \hat{x}_t^A)$. The loss process of the learner is $\text{Loss}_T = \sum_{t=1}^T \lambda(x_t, \hat{x}_t)$. The goal is to suggest a method for the learner to be able to predict as close as

A. Gammerman et al. (Eds.): SLDS 2015, LNAI 9047, pp. 137–146, 2015.
DOI: 10.1007/978-3-319-17091-6_9

Data: $(x_1, \ldots, x_T)$ — a sequence from Ω^T;
$A^1, \ldots, A^M$ — experts;
$\beta \in (0, 1)$ — parameter of learning rate;
$\rho_0 \in \mathbb{R}^M$ — initial expert weights distribution;
$S \colon \mathbb{R}^\Omega \to \Gamma$ — substitution function;
Result: γ_{t+1} — forecast of the next element of the sequence at each step
$\quad t = 1, \ldots T.$

for $t = 1$ **to** T **do**
$\quad$ **for** $j = 1$ **to** M **do**
$\quad\quad \hat{x}_{t+1}^j = A^j(x_1, \ldots, x_t);$
$\quad\quad g_t(x) = \log_\beta \left(\sum_{j=1}^M p_t^j \cdot \beta^{\lambda(x, \hat{x}_{t+1}^j)} \right);$
$\quad\quad p_{t+1}^j = p_t^j \cdot \beta^{\lambda(x_{t+1}, \hat{x}_{t+1}^j)};$
$\quad\quad p_{t+1}^j = \frac{p_{t+1}^j}{\sum_{k=1}^M p_{t+1}^k};$
$\quad\quad \gamma_{t+1} = S(g_t(x)).$
$\quad$ **end**
end

1: Aggregating Algorithm

possible to the best expert in terms of loss process. A more general statement of
the problem is formulated in [2].

As a strategy for the learner V. Vovk suggested the (strong) aggregating
algorithm 1 in [3,4].

Function $g_t(x)$ is called generalized action [4]. Substitution function S defines
a forecast value $\hat{x}_{t+1}$, based on generalized action $g_t(x)$ by the following condition:

$$\forall x \in \Omega \;\; \lambda(x, \hat{x}_{t+1}) \le c(\beta) \cdot g_t(x). \tag{1}$$

V. Vovk proved in [3] that in many games where the aggregating algorithm
is used as a learner on a finite set of experts $\mathfrak{A} = \{A^1, \ldots, A^M\}$ the following
upper bound holds:

$$\mathrm{Loss}_T \le c(\beta) \cdot \mathrm{Loss}_T^A + a(\beta) \cdot \ln(M), \;\; \forall A \in \mathfrak{A}. \tag{2}$$

It was shown that in such games $c(\beta) \ge 1$, and $a(\beta) = c(\beta)/\ln(1/\beta)$ and
that upper bound (2) cannot be improved. A game in which for some $\beta \in (0, 1)$
$c(\beta) = 1$ is called β-*mixable* game. A game is called mixable if it is β-mixable
for some $\beta \in (0, 1)$.

1.1   Time Series Forecasting

A particular case of the situation above is the time series forecasting problem.
This problem has the following characteristics.

First, the outcome space and the prediction space are equal and are subsets
of the real axis $\Omega = \Gamma = [Y_1, Y_2] \subset \mathbb{R}$. Let us call a sequence of elements
$X_T = x_1, \ldots, x_T \in \Omega$ ordered by time a time series.

Next, the loss function is asymmetric and often can be described as a function of difference $x - \hat{x}$

$$\lambda(x, \hat{x}) = \begin{cases} k_1 \cdot (\hat{x} - x)^p & , x < \hat{x}, \\ k_2 \cdot (x - \hat{x})^p & , x \geq \hat{x}, \end{cases} \tag{3}$$

where $k_1 > 0$, $k_2 > 0$, $p > 1$. Parameters k_1 and k_2 describe the difference between specific losses from under-forecasting and over-forecasting. The power p designates dependence of the losses on the difference $x - \hat{x}$. Henceforward we will call the game with $\Omega = \Gamma = [Y_1, Y_2]$ and loss function (3) an asymmetric game. We do not consider the situation where $p = 1$ because such game is not mixable [1,5].

Finally, the experts in the time series forecasting problem are usually simple adaptive algorithms like exponential smoothing model, Holter-Winters model, or Theil-Wage model [6]. In this paper we explore the aggregating algorithm for building compositions under finite set $\mathfrak{A} = \{A^1, \ldots, A^M\}$ of simple adaptive algorithms, hereinafter *base algorithms*[1], in the asymmetric loss game.

We proceed as follows. In the first part, some theoretical results about mixability of an asymmetric game are presented. We also discuss conditions for parameters of the aggregating algorithm under which inequality (2) will be satisfied. In the second part, we provide some practical results about compositions based on the aggregating algorithm. We conclude with a description of experiments that compare the aggregating algorithm to other well–known approaches to building compositions of time series forecasting algorithms.

2 Mixability of Asymmetric Games and Parameters of the Aggregating Algorithm

This section derives theoretical conditions on the parameters of the aggregating algorithm for an asymmetric game to be mixable.

2.1 Mixability of the Asymmetric Game

Lemma 1 from [5] gives a general expression of the necessary and sufficient conditions on the learning rate β for an asymmetric game due to [8]:

$$\beta \geq \exp\left(\frac{(p-1)(Y_2 - Y_1)}{p \cdot \max\limits_{\gamma \in [Y_1, Y_2]} \left(k_2(Y_2 - \gamma)^p(\gamma - Y_1) + k_1(\gamma - Y_1)^p(Y_2 - \gamma)\right)} \right).$$

Since Y_1, Y_2 and p are given, the bound for β follows from the solution of the maximization task:

$$\max\limits_{\gamma \in [Y_1, Y_2]} \left(k_2(Y_2 - \gamma)^p(\gamma - Y_1) + k_1(\gamma - Y_1)^p(Y_2 - \gamma)\right). \tag{4}$$

For some p it can be easy to find.

---

[1] In this paper we define experts as base algorithms. However, there are other ways to select experts for the aggregating algorithm in the time series forecasting problem [7].

Theorem 1. *For $p = 2$ the asymmetric game is mixable if and only if*

$$\beta \geq \exp\left(-\frac{1}{2 \cdot K \cdot (Y_2 - Y_1)^2}\right), \tag{5}$$

where $K = \frac{2k_1 - k_2 - k^*}{3(k_1 - k_2)} \cdot \frac{k_1 - 2k_2 + k^*}{3(k_1 - k_2)} \cdot \frac{k_1 + k_2 + k^*}{3}, \ k^* = \sqrt{(k_1 - k_2)^2 + k_1 \cdot k_2}.$

Mixability conditions of a symmetric game can be easily derived from Theorem 1. A symmetric loss function is obtained from (3) under conditions $k_1 \to k$, $k_2 \to k$. In this case $K \to \frac{k}{4}$ and the condition of mixability (5) converts to $\beta \geq \exp\left(-2/\left(k \cdot (Y_2 - Y_1)^2\right)\right)$. This result complies with Lemma 2 from [3] when $k = 1$, $Y_1 = -1$, $Y_2 = 1$.

However, solving problem (4) at each step t of aggregating algorithm 1 involves time consuming calculations. The following estimation is more appropriate in practical cases (sufficient condition).

Theorem 2. *An asymmetric game is β-mixable if β lies significantly close to 1:*

$$\beta \geq \exp\left(-\frac{2(p-1)}{\left(\max\{k_1, k_2\}\left(\frac{2p}{p+1}\right)^{p+1} + p \cdot \min\{k_1, k_2\}\right) \cdot \hat{Y}^p}\right), \tag{6}$$

where $\hat{Y} = \frac{Y_2 - Y_1}{2}.$

Proof. The proof lies in solving maximization task (4). Let us estimate the maximum of the function

$$F(\gamma) = \left(k_2 \cdot (Y_2 - \gamma)^p(\gamma - Y_1) + k_1 \cdot (\gamma - Y_1)^p(Y_2 - \gamma)\right)$$

First of all we notice that $F(Y_2) = F(Y_1) = 0$, therefore

$$\max_{\gamma \in [Y_1, Y_2]} F(\gamma) = \max_{\gamma \in (Y_1, Y_2)} F(\gamma) =$$

$$= \max_{\gamma \in (Y_1, Y_2)} \left(k_2(Y_2 - \gamma)^p(\gamma - Y_1) + k_1(\gamma - Y_1)^p(Y_2 - \gamma)\right) =$$

$$= \max_{y \in (-\hat{Y}, \hat{Y})} \left(k_2(\hat{Y} - y)^p(y + \hat{Y}) + k_1(y + \hat{Y})^p(\hat{Y} - y)\right) =$$

$$= \max_{y \in [-\hat{Y}, \hat{Y}]} \left(k_2 f_2(y) + k_1 f_1(y)\right),$$

where $\hat{Y} = \frac{Y_2 - Y_1}{2}$, $f_1(y) = (\hat{Y} - y)(y + \hat{Y})^p$, $f_2(y) = (\hat{Y} - y)^p(y + \hat{Y})$.
It is easy to see that $f_1(y) = f_2(-y)$ and

$$\arg\max_{y \in (-\hat{Y}, \hat{Y})} f_1(y) = -\arg\max_{y \in (-\hat{Y}, \hat{Y})} f_2(y) = \frac{(1-p)\hat{Y}}{p+1},$$

so

$$\max_{y \in (-\hat{Y}, \hat{Y})} f_1(y) = \max_{y \in (-\hat{Y}, \hat{Y})} f_2(y) = \frac{1}{p}\left(\frac{2p}{p+1}\right)^{p+1} \cdot \hat{Y}^{p+1}.$$

A more detailed analysis of the first derivative of $f_1(y)$ shows that $f_1(y)$ monotonically decreases from $\frac{(1-p)\cdot\hat{Y}}{p+1}$ to $\hat{Y}$, and $f_2(y)$ monotonically increases from $-\hat{Y}$ to $\frac{(p-1)\cdot\hat{Y}}{p+1}$. Consequently

$$\frac{1}{p}\left(\frac{2p}{p+1}\right)^{p+1}\cdot\hat{Y}^{p+1} > f_1(0) = f_2(0) = \hat{Y}^{p+1}.$$

Summarizing all points above we obtain:

$$\max_{\gamma\in[Y_1,Y_2]} F(\gamma) = \max_{y\in[-\hat{Y},\hat{Y}]}\left(\max\{k_1,k_2\}\cdot f_2(y) + \min\{k_1,k_2\}\cdot f_2(-y)\right) <$$

$$< \max\{k_1,k_2\}\cdot \max_{y\in[-\hat{Y},\hat{Y}]}\left(f_2(y)\right) + \min\{k_1,k_2\}\cdot f_2(0) \le$$

$$\le \left(\frac{\max\{k_1,k_2\}}{p}\left(\frac{2p}{p+1}\right)^{p+1} + \min\{k_1,k_2\}\right)\cdot\hat{Y}^{p+1}.$$

2.2 Parameters ρ_0 and $S(x)$

If the conditions of Theorem 2 are met, there exists an initial distribution of expert weights ρ_0 and a substitution function $S(x)$ such that inequality (2) holds for $c(\beta) = 1$. The choice of parameters ρ_0, and $S(x)$ of the aggregating algorithm should be based on the following lemma:

Lemma 1. *Let the conditions of Theorem 2 be fulfilled. Inequality (2) will hold with $c(\beta) = 1$ if the following sufficient conditions are met:*

1. *the initial distribution $\rho_0 = \{\rho_0^1,\ldots,\rho_0^M\}$ of base algorithms $\mathfrak{A} = \{A^1,\ldots,A^M\}$ is such that $\min\limits_{j=1,\ldots,M} \rho_0^j > 0$.*
2. *substitution function $S(g)$ takes such values that*

$$\lambda(Y_1,S(g))\in[0,g(Y_1)]; \quad \lambda(Y_2,S(g))\in[0,g(Y_2)]. \tag{7}$$

This lemma is a simple modification of Lemma 3 from [1] for the case of a finite set of experts $\mathfrak{A}$.

The second condition has a clear geometric interpretation. If we display a curve $\left(\lambda(Y_1,\hat{x}),\lambda(Y_2,\hat{x})\right)$, where $\hat{x}\in[Y_1,Y_2]$, on a Cartesian plane the substitution function should take only such values out of $[Y_1,Y_2]$ that correspond to the points of the curve within the rectangle $[0,g(Y_1)]\times[0,g(Y_2)]$. The illustration of this interpretation is provided in Figure 1 (see the experimental section).

$$S_1(g) = \frac{Y_2\sqrt[p]{k_2 g(Y_1)} + Y_1\sqrt[p]{k_1 g(Y_2)}}{\sqrt[p]{k_2 g(Y_1)} + \sqrt[p]{k_1 g(Y_2)}}. \tag{8}$$

2.3   Loss Process Bound

Having applied a uniform initial distribution of expert weights $\rho_0^j = 1/M$ for $j = 1, \ldots, M$ and substitution function (8), we obtain composition AA_1. Theorem 2, Lemma 1 and inequality (2) result in the upper bound of the loss process of this composition.

Corollary 1. *Under conditions of Theorem 2, for every set of experts $\mathfrak{A} = \{A^1, \ldots, A^M\}$ in an asymmetric game the loss process of AA_1 is estimated as*

$$\mathrm{Loss}_T^{AA_1} \leq \min_{i=1,\ldots,M} \mathrm{Loss}_T^{A^i} +$$

$$+ \frac{(Y_2 - Y_1)^p}{(p-1)} \left(\max\{k_1, k_2\} \left(\frac{p}{p+1} \right)^{p+1} + \frac{p}{2^{p+1}} \min\{k_1, k_2\} \right) \cdot \ln(M). \tag{9}$$

Therefore, the loss process of composition AA_1 amplifies at a speed not greater than that of the loss process of the best base algorithm. Since the loss process is defined as the loss accumulated by the point of time T, the marginal addition of the second item to the sum of inequality (9) declines over time. Time-complexity of composition AA_1 has a linear dependency on the number of base algorithms M and the length of the time series T: $O(M \cdot T)$.

3   Experiments

The experiments were conducted on sales data of a retailer Lama (Tomsk, Russian Federation). Each time series describes daily sales of SKU (Stock Keeping Unit) in one shop of the retail chain from 2005/01/01 to 2010/01/01. Some time series contain clear trend and seasonality, but it is not the case for the whole data set. Since a lot of time series are not stationary, ARMA and ARIMA models cannot be applied. Many time series have NaN (not–a–number) values, the number of which varies from 50 to 1500 per time series. There are 1913 different time series in total, however, only subsets are used for test purposes and each experiment is conducted on a different subset.

Sales forecasting in retail chains requires an asymmetric loss function. The asymmetry is justified by substantially different losses under over- and under-forecast. Over-forecast occurs when the forecasted value is larger than the actual value of the time series and leads to overstock, larger logistic costs, a greater portion of expired goods, and stock depreciation. Under-forecast, in turn, leads to a market share loss and a decrease in stock rotation. The difference between over- and under-forecasted values depends greatly on the kind of goods under consideration. In the present experiments we used an asymmetric loss function with various values for k_1 and k_2 in loss function (3). We describe only the experiments run on $p = 2$ for the sake of briefness and clarity. However, we also carried out the experiments for other values for p and obtained similar results.

3.1 Base Algorithms

We use the following models as base algorithms: exponential smoothing (ES) with smoothing parameter α, adaptive exponential smoothing model (AES) with parameter of adaptation γ according to Trigg-Leach approach, linear Brown model (BL) with discount parameter β, and seasonal model of Theil-Wage (TW) with parameter of mean α_1, parameter of trend α_2 and parameter of seasonality α_3 [6]. Approaches to generalize ES, BL and TW for the time series forecasting problem under asymmetric loss function are described in [9]. Let us note that time-complexity of all these models is linear along the length of time series.

3.2 Compositions Based on the Aggregating Algorithm

Compositions of base algorithms are built using the aggregating algorithm with the following parameters. The parameter of learning rate β is tuned on 250 representative time series, the optimal value of β is in range [0.90, 0.99]. The initial expert weights distribution is uniform. Substitution function (8) is used in composition AA_1 and the following function is used in composition AA_2.

$$S_2\left(g\right) = \frac{k_2 Y_1 - k_1 Y_2}{k_1 - k_2} - \frac{\sqrt{k_2 k_1 (Y_1 - Y_2)^2 + g(Y_1) - g(Y_2)}}{k_1 - k_2}. \tag{10}$$

Figure 1 shows that forecast values γ_1^* and γ_2^* correspond to substitution functions (8) and (10) respectively and comply with Lemma 1.

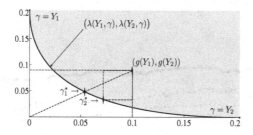

Fig. 1. Forecasts for S_1 and S_2

3.3 Comparison with Base Algorithms

In this experiment we investigate how well forecast composition AA_1 performs compared to base algorithms. The asymmetric loss function (3) has parameters $p = 2$ and $k_1 = 1$, $k_2 = 2$. Seven algorithms are used as experts: A^1, A^2 are ES with different parameters of smoothing, A^3 is BL, A^4–A^7 are TW with different parameters of level, trend and seasonality.

Figure 2 contains graphs of time-averaged loss processes $MSE = \frac{1}{T} \cdot \text{Loss}_T$ of composition AA_1 and base algorithms for a sample time series. We see that between steps 400 and 500 a change of the best base algorithm occurs. It is interesting that AA_1 captures that change and starts to outperform even the best expert. Figure 3 shows time-averaged and time series-averaged loss processes on 1000 time series where composition AA_1 performs as well as the best base algorithm and at the end outperforms the best expert.

We also find that for sufficiently large time spaces (over 100 points) theoretical bound (9) exceeds the actual loss process of the composition AA_1 by no more than 30% (Figure 4).

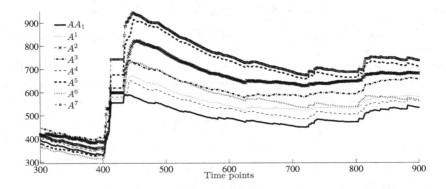

Fig. 2. MSE of composition AA_1 and base algorithms on one time series

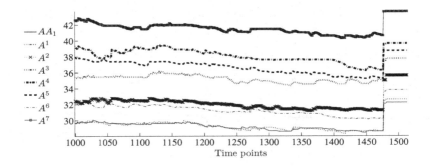

Fig. 3. MSE of composition AA_1 and base algorithms on 1000 time series

Table 1 shows MSE of AA_1, its theoretical bound (TB) and MSE of the best expert (BE) at different values k_1 and k_2 on 1000 time series.

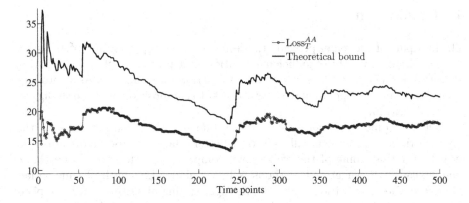

Fig. 4. *MSE* of composition AA_1 and its theoretical bound on 1000 time series

Table 1. MSE of AA_1 and the best expert

k_1/k_2	1	2	5	10	15	20
AA_1	**21.69**	**32.24**	**57.33**	**80.96**	**110.7**	**139.9**
BE	22.05	32.63	58.24	81.79	111.5	140.6
TB	25.16	38.2	71.80	99.44	141.1	179.7

3.4   Comparison with Other Compositions

The quality of the suggested compositions is now compared with the compositions built with standard methods. In our previous work [7] we compared AA_1 and AA_2 with such compositions as AFTER [10], InverseWeights [11] and some other models under symmetric loss function ($k_1 = k_2 = 1$). There we showed that AA_1 and AA_2 outperformed other compositions by 3%–5%.

Here we present the comparison of compositions AA_1, AA_2 with the quantile regression (QR) [12] under asymmetric loss function with different values of parameters k_1, k_2 and $p = 2$ (Table 2). As we can see both AA_1 and AA_2 show better results than QR. This can be explained by the fact that QR optimizes an absolute instead of square loss function.

Table 2. The loss process of compositions at different values k_1 and k_2

k_1/k_2	AA_1	AA_2	QR
2	**2344**	2375	2804
10	**2694**	2863	4978
100	**7700**	8605	12223

4 Conclusion

The first part of the paper presents the results concerning mixability of an asymmetric loss game. We obtain sufficient condition on β–parameter of the aggregating algorithm for a game with asymmetric loss function to be mixable. As a corollary result we obtain an upper bound of loss process of a composition based on the aggregating algorithm.

When it comes to experimental results, the suggested compositions for the asymmetric loss game generally perform better than the base algorithms and even better than some of the well-known compositions. Moreover, algorithmic complexity of the suggested methods is linear along the length of time series. Therefore, the compositions based on the aggregating algorithm can be applied in practice for time series forecasting in the case of asymmetric loss functions.

Acknowledgments. I am grateful to Yury Kalnishkan and my advisor Konstantin Vorontsov for providing information and recommendations.

References

1. Vovk, V.: Competitive on-line statistics. International Statistical Review **69** (2001)
2. Vovk, V., Zhdanov, F.: Prediction with expert advice for the Brier game. Journal of Machine Learning Research **10**, 2445–2471 (2009)
3. Vovk, V.: A Game of Prediction with Expert Advice. Journal of Computer and System Sciences **56**, 153–173 (1998)
4. Vovk, V., Watkins, C.: Universal portfolio selection. In: Proceedings of the Eleventh Annual Conference on Computational Learning Theory, COLT, pp. 12–23 (1998)
5. Kalnishkan, Y., Vyugin, M.V.: Mixability and the existence of weak complexities. In: Kivinen, J., Sloan, R.H. (eds.) COLT 2002. LNCS (LNAI), vol. 2375, pp. 105–120. Springer, Heidelberg (2002)
6. Lukashin, Y.P.: Adaptive methods of short-term time series forecasting. Financy i statistica **415**, Moscow (2003) (in Russian)
7. Romanenko, A.A.: Aggregation of adaptive forecast algorithms. Reports of the 15th Russian Conference on Mathematical Methods of Image Recognition, pp. 170–173, Moscow (2011) (in Russian)
8. Haussler, D., Kivinen, J., Warmuth, M.K.: Sequential prediction of individual sequences under general loss functions. IEEE Trans. on Information Theory **5**, 1906–1925 (1998)
9. Cipra, T.: Asymmetric recursive methods for time series. Applications of Mathematics **39**(3), 203–214 (1994)
10. Yang, Y.: Combining forecasting procedures: some theoretical results. Econometric Theory **20**, 176–222 (2004)
11. Timmermann, A.G.: Forecast Combinations. CEPR Discussion Papers (2006). http://ideas.repec.org/p/cpr/ceprdp/5361.html
12. Postnikova, E.: Quantile Regression. NSU **34** (2000) (in Russian)

Visualization and Analysis of Multiple Time Series by Beanplot PCA

Carlo Drago[1]([⊠]), Carlo Natale Lauro[2], and Germana Scepi[2]

[1] University of Rome "Niccolo Cusano", Via Don Carlo Gnocchi 3,
20016 Roma, Italy
carlo.drago@unicusano.it
[2] University of Naples "Federico II", Via Cinthia 26, 80126 Naples, Italy

Abstract. Beanplot time series have been introduced by the authors as an aggregated data representation, in terms of peculiar symbolic data, for dealing with large temporal datasets. In the presence of multiple beanplot time series it can be very interesting for interpretative aims to find useful syntheses. Here we propose an extension, based on PCA, of the previous approach to multiple beanplot time series. We show the usefulness of our proposal in the context of the analysis of different financial markets.

Keywords: Beanplots · Symbolic data analysis

1 The Statistical Problem

In the presence of large temporal datasets, the authors [4,6] have already shown the relevance of introducing beanplot data for visualizing and interpreting usefully the data structure. In particular, the visualization and the analysis of these representations can be very interesting in the identification of intra-period patterns (intra-day by example) and their inter-period changes.

In this work, we propose an extension, based on PCA, of this approach to multiple beanplot series. Our aim is to find and to show patterns in the data to construct composite indicators on multiple time series, and to easily identify change points. This paper is organized as follows: in section 2 some remarks on the beanplot time series data approach are reported, showing this representation for the Dow Jones time series index. Section 3 presents a parameterization of the beanplots useful for the research of a synthesis in the presence of multiple time series. In section 4, the PCA based approach to multiple time series is presented. Section 5 reports an application on real financial time series data. Some remarks on possible perspectives conclude the paper.

2 Beanplot Time Series

Traditional time series do not faithfully describe phenomena showing a high degree of variability or where the variable is observed at a given frequency but,

© Springer International Publishing Switzerland 2015
A. Gammerman et al. (Eds.): SLDS 2015, LNAI 9047, pp. 147–155, 2015.
DOI: 10.1007/978-3-319-17091-6_10

the interest is in the lower frequency analysis. In these situations, temporal aggregations based on observed distributions have been introduced [2,4].

Beanplots [8] are representations obtained by a combination of a 1-dimensional scatterplot and a density trace. In this sense a density trace at time t with $t = 1 \ldots T$ can be defined as:

$$B_t^K = \frac{1}{nh} \sum_{i=1}^{n} K\left(\frac{x - x_i}{h}\right) \tag{1}$$

where K is a kernel function, h is a smoothing parameter defined as a bandwidth and n is the number of x_i intra-period observations.

Various kernels (K) can be generally chosen (Gaussian, uniform, Epanechnikov, triweight, exponential, cosine between others) in order to represent adequately the observed density function. In fig.1 [1] we show an example of a beanplot shape obtained by using a combination of several Gaussian kernels.

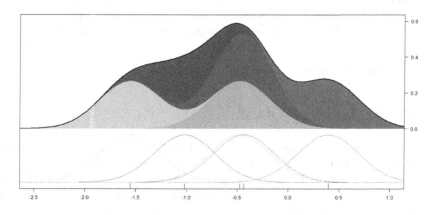

Fig. 1. Beanplot based on Gaussian kernel function

For the bandwidth choice, we can consider: low, high bandwiths, or the Sheather-Jones approach [11]. With low bandwidths we tend to show many bumps and to maximize the number of bumps by beanplot, while with high bandwidths more regular shape of the density traces are obtained. However the risk with a high bandwidth is to lose interesting information. Finally, by using the Sheather Jones method, the bandwidth changes beanplot by beanplot, so the bandwidth becomes an indicator of variability.

A beanplot time series can be defined as an ordered sequence of beanplot data over the time.

In fig.2 [5] we show, as an example, a beanplot time series related to the Dow Jones Index from 1996 to 2010. The chosen temporal aggregation interval in this example is only instrumental to show the potential of this tool in the visualization of particular financial aspects.

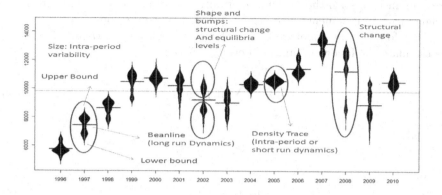

Fig. 2. Beanplot Time Series: Dow Jones Index 1996-2010

We highlight that the beanplot time series easily show: structural changes (for example in 2008) expressed by changes in the mean, the intra-period variability expressed by the size of the different beanplots, and the equilibria levels of the series expressed by the different bumps of the beanplot shape.

In general we can detect some typical taxonomies in the beanplots: unimodality (data tend to gather over one mode in a regular way as in fig.2 the beanplot observed for 2005), multimodality (data tend to gather over two modes as in fig.2 for the year 2002) and break (data tend to gather in two modes but there is at least one break between the observations).

Therefore the visualization of a beanplot time series can be useful for descriptive aims; in fact the beanplots capture interesting aspects relating to the structural changes of the original series.

The different temporal aggregations can have relevant impacts on the shapes of the beanplots. By choosing higher aggregation we tend to lose some relevant features of the time series like cycles. As well it is possible to lose relevant information related to the intra-period structural changes. Otherwise with lower aggregation we can obtain too many beanplots which can be redundant and not significant. Therefore a problem of this approach consists in the identification of a significant aggregation interval. Here we choose the interval only by using an empirical criteria based on the the aim of the analysis.

3   Model-Based Beanplots: Parameterization

The nonparametric approach based on beanplot representations is very useful for the visualization of univariate large temporal datasets. In the presence of multivariate large time series, and for clustering or forecasting aims, it could be appropriate to search a density function of which the beanplot can be considered the graphical representation. By considering the nature of beanplots and how the shape of a beanplot is computed, we choose to estimate it with a finite mixture density. The J individual distributions, called mixture components $f_j(x)$ that are combined to form the mixture distribution $(j = 1...J)$, are characterized by weights (p_j) and moments, like means and variance and so on.

Therefore in a beanplot time series for each beanplot, at time t $(t = 1..T)$, we calculate the following mixture density function:

$$B_t^* = \sum_{j=1}^{J} p_j f(x|\theta_j) \tag{2}$$

where:

$$0 \le p_j \le 1 \tag{3}$$

and

$$p_1 + p_2 + \cdots + p_J = 1. \tag{4}$$

In the case of mixture of normal distributions (equation 2) is completely defined by weights, means (μ_J) and variances (σ_j^2). In our approach we limit ourselves to consider only mixture based on Gaussians distributions. The parameters of these distributions have an interesting interpretation in the financial context:

- Each μ_j represents the intra-period mean, for example price values of a stock gathered over time. Changes in the μ_j can occur in the presence of structural changes and relevant events.
- Each σ_j represents the intra-period variability, as in financial terms, volatility. Changes in σ_j can occur in presence of financial news (higher or lower intra-period volatility).
- Each p_j represent the weight of each component. Changes in p_j can be seen as intra-period structural changes.

Various approaches have been proposed in literature in order to select the number of components in a mixture (see for example [7, 10]).

In the financial context, the different components seem to show different financial behaviours. Therefore, considering the applicative aim of our approach, we decide to choose the number of components on the basis of empirical simulations. Here we perform some simulations with the aim of showing that large temporal series, observed on a finer scale, are well approximated by mixtures of two Gaussian components. We perform 900 simulations of time series with 3500 observations. We decide to take in to account, in the experimental design, three different levels of volatility, structural changes and seasonality, typical characteristics of financial data. For each simulation, we represent the aggregated beanplot based on the all 3500 observations and in fig.3, we show the different types of obtained beanplots. In particular, we obtain nine types of different beanplots representing the different levels of simulated financial characteristics (different levels of volatility in the first row, different levels of structural changes in the second row, different levels of seasonality in the third row). We calculate a mixture distribution for each simulated time series ([9]). We consider a mixture distribution based on two Gaussian components. We measure the goodness of fit of each mixture distribution on the basis of the index presented in Du ([7]). The results show that in about 90% of the cases of the data in the first row, the null hypothesis of the adequacy of the models cannot be refused; in about 80% in second row, the null hypothesis cannot be refused, in about 70% of the cases in the third row the null hypothesis cannot be refused.

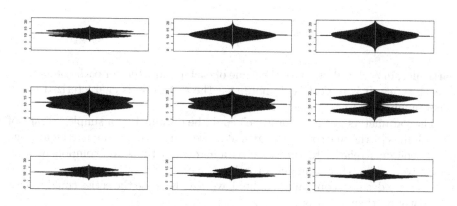

Fig. 3. Beanplot Data: Simulation

We highlight that, in general, in applicative contexts, the choice of number of components seems to be a compromise between comparability, simplicity and usability.

4   Multiple Beanplot Time Series

Multiple Beanplot time series can be defined as the simultaneous observation of more than one Beanplot time series. We can observe, for example, the beanplot time series related to more than one financial time series.

We start to consider n beanplots time series for $t = 1..T$. At each time t, we parametrize each of the n beanplot by the approach proposed in section 3 and derive a vector of parameters for each beanplot. If we consider only three parameters and J components, for each beanplot, we have a vector with $J \times 3$ columns and 1 row.

Therefore we can observe the time series of the vector of parameters for each of the n series.

We now search for each time, t a synthesis of these vectors for the n series, in order to obtain a unique vector of parameters. Our aim is to find an "average beanplot" called a "prototype beanplot". The time series of this prototype can be considered for analyzing the global dynamics of the series.

Aiming to obtain a syntesis of the n series, we define for each time t, the following matrix:

The data matrix $Y_t(n, 3J)$ is organized as follows: in the rows, we have the different n series while in the columns, we have the $3 \times J$ different parameters. In

$$Y_t = \begin{array}{c} \\ 1 \\ 2 \\ 3 \\ \\ n \end{array} \begin{array}{|cccccccccccc|} \hline p_1\ p_2\ \cdots\ p_J\ m_1\ m_2\ \ldots\ m_J\ s_1\ s_2\ \ldots\ s_J \\ \vdots \quad \cdots \qquad\qquad \cdots \qquad\qquad\quad \vdots \\ \vdots \quad \cdots \qquad\qquad \cdots \qquad\qquad\quad \vdots \\ \\ \vdots\ \vdots\ \vdots \qquad\qquad \vdots \qquad\qquad\quad \vdots \\ \\ \vdots\ \vdots \qquad\qquad\quad \cdots \qquad\qquad\quad \vdots \\ \hline \end{array}$$

particular, in each cell, we have the value of each parameter, for each component, in each series. It is important to note that the matrix Y_t is characterized by an equal number of J components for each series.

The parameters of the "prototype" could be obtained by a simple average of the columns of the matrix Y. In particular, we can calculate the partial average of the columns related to the same parameter and the same component and, successively, for each parameter a total average.

Here, we decide to obtain a weighted average, because the series could weight differently on their synthesis.

For assigning these weights to the different n series we perform an PCA on the transposed matrix of Y_t, called H_t.

Therefore we obtain $k \leq n$ eigenvectors associated to the k eigenvalues of the matrix $H_t' H_t$.

We weight the original variables of the matrix H_t with the elements of the eigenvectors and finally we obtain k vectors of synthesis. In these syntheses we have the parameters of k "prototypes".

In order to define the most significant "prototypes", it is possible to consider the percentage of variance explained:

$$\lambda_i / \sum_{i=1}^{n} \lambda_i \tag{5}$$

If we consider, for each time t the vector of the parameters associated to the highest eigenvalue, we can derive t different mixture models based on J Gaussian components. For to represent the different t models with t different "prototype" beanplots, we simulate data described by the parameters of these models.

5   Application on Real Data

The aim of this application is to visualize multiple financial time series by means of beanplots and to obtain the prototype time series. We examine the closing prices of 7 different markets representative of the Euro-American and Asia zone (France, Mexico, Argentina, Germany, Switzerland, Singapore and Taiwan). The data are extracted from Yahoo Finance. The observations are related to the period 1-1-2001 to 31-12-2008. Data are collected daily, the single beanplot is

Table 1. PCA Explained Variance (EV) by the first PC (column 2), normalized eigenvectors (columns 3-9), PCA beanplot parameters (columns 10-15)

t	EV	FCHI	MXX	MERV	GDAXI	SSMI	STI	TWII	P1	P2	M1	M2	S1	S2
1	99.92	0.16	0.20	0.01	0.19	0.23	0.06	0.16	0.59	0.41	5149	6014	457	279
2	99.92	0.14	0.24	0.01	0.15	0.21	0.06	0.19	0.25	0.75	4731	5215	242	622
3	99.78	0.13	0.26	0.03	0.12	0.20	0.06	0.20	0.46	0.54	4258	5107	207	351
4	99.77	0.11	0.31	0.03	0.12	0.17	0.06	0.19	0.72	0.28	6233	6493	551	115
5	99.91	0.11	0.36	0.04	0.12	0.16	0.06	0.16	0.50	0.50	7788	8917	311	664
6	99.90	0.10	0.40	0.03	0.12	0.16	0.05	0.13	0.55	0.45	11225	12682	421	1063
7	99.97	0.09	0.45	0.03	0.11	0.14	0.05	0.13	0.42	0.58	16382	17835	754	659
8	99.62	0.08	0.48	0.04	0.11	0.12	0.04	0.13	0.25	0.75	16078	16388	1075	2606

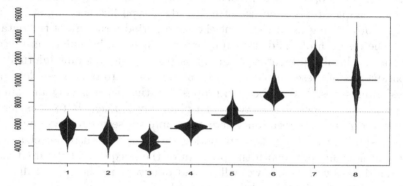

Fig. 4. PCA Beanplot Prototype Time Series. (beanplot 1 corresponds to 2001)

built yearly. In order to define a "prototype" of the overall market, we apply the approach proposed in section 4.

We highlight that in this application, we fix $J = 2$ Gaussian components of the mixture models by taking in to account the results of the empirical simulations proposed in section 3. Furthermore, as in column 2. of table 1. is shown, we choose for each time t only the parameters associated to the first eigenvalue (which explains in each time t about 99% of the variance).

In particular, in column 3-9 of table 1., we can observe the different weights calculated for the different markets in each time. We note that the Mexican market (MXX) seems to weight more than other markets over the time. France (FCHI), Germany (GDAXI), Switzerland (SSMI) seem to be similar in their behavior. The prototype parameters are shown in columns 9-15. The results of the different eigenvectors impacted on the final prototype obtained. In this sense the Mexico and Argentina series influenced the impact of each component on the final prototype. It is possible to interpret the prototype parameters in terms of structural growth and volatility: the parameters M_1 and M_2, show the growth of the markets over the period 2004-2008. In the years 2005-2009, it is possible to see an increase in the variability (parameters S_1 and S_2).

Finally in 2007 there is a relevant change-point (as shown by the parameters p_1 and p_2). In 2008 there is the financial crisis and the economic cycle tends to change and markets fall. In fig.4 we show the beanplot prototypes time series. The beanplots structure for the years 2005 and 2006 shows similarities, which can be interpreted as economic stability in these years. The beanplot structure for 2008 is very different from the others, as we expected. The change in the structure for 2007-2008 is well visualized in the beanplot prototype time series. The stability structure for the first three beanplots corresponds to a stability of the market in the associated years.

6   Conclusions

In this work we propose an approach for dealing with multiple time series by means of beanplot tools. The use of a new data type like a beanplot has the advantage of allowing us to represent the intra-period structure of the data at time t. The research of the density function of which the beanplot can be considered a graphical representation allows us to keep the relevant information. The parameters of these functions can be used in order to build beanplot "prototypes" time series. The application proposed in this paper is only an example for showing the proposed approach. The main development is to consider an application on daily aggregation where our approach seems to show more significant results in capturing the intra period variability. In future developments we will consider more in depth the problem of the adequacy of the used models to the data. Furthermore we will extend our work to the case of different components and distributions than those used.

Acknowledgments. The authors thanks the two anonymous referees for their helpful comments and suggestions.

References

1. A.A.V.V. R Graph Gallery. http://gallery.r-enthusiasts.com/ (2013)
2. Arroyo, J., Maté, C.: Forecasting histogram time series with k-nearest neighbours methods. International Journal of Forecasting **25**(1), 192–207 (2009)
3. Billard, L., Diday, E.: From the Statistics of Data to the Statistics of Knowledge. Journal of the American Statistical Association **98**, 470–487 (2003)
4. Drago, C., Scepi, G.: Visualizing and exploring high frequency financial data: beanplot time series. In: New Perspectives in Statistical Modeling and Data Analysis: Proceedings of the 7th Conference of the Classification and Data Analysis Group of the Italian Statistical Society, Catania, 2009, vol. 7, p. 283. Springer (9–11 September 2011)
5. Drago, C., Scepi, G.: Time Series Clustering from High Dimensional Data. Working Paper also presented at CHDD 2012 International Workshop on Clustering High Dimensional Data, Napoli, May 2012
6. Drago, C., Lauro, C., Scepi, G.: Beanplot Data Analysis in a Temporal Framework Workshop in Symbolic Data Analysis. Working Paper also presented at eight Meeting of the Classification and Data Analysis Group of the Italian Statistical Society, Pavia, September 2011

7. Du, J.: Combined algorithms for constrained estimation of finite mixture distributions with grouped data and conditional data (Doctoral dissertation, McMaster University) (2002)
8. Kampstra, P.: Beanplot: A Boxplot Alternative for Visual Comparison of Distributions. Journal Of Statistical Software **28**(November), 1–9 (2008)
9. Macdonald, P. and with contributions from Du, J. mixdist: Finite Mixture Distribution Models. R package (2012)
10. Sheng, H.Y., Walker, J.J., Ogren, D.E.: A stepwise method for determining the number of component distributions in a mixture. Mathematical Geology **18**(2), 153–160 (1986)
11. Sheather, S.J., Jones, C.: A reliable data-based bandwidth selection method for kernel density estimation. Journal of the Royal Statistical Society Series B Methodological **53**(3), 683–690 (1991)
12. Verde, R., Irpino, A.: Dynamic clustering of histogram data: using the right metric. In: Brito, P., Bertrand, P., Cucumel, G., De Carvalho, F.: Selected contributions in data analysis and classification, pp. 123–134. Springer, Berlin (2007)

Recursive SVM Based on TEDA

Dmitry Kangin[1(✉)] and Plamen Angelov[1,2]

[1] Data Science Group, School of Computing and Communications,
Lancaster University, Lancaster, UK
[2] Chair of Excellence, University Carlos III, Madrid, Spain
{d.kangin,p.angelov}@lancaster.ac.uk

Abstract. The new method for incremental learning of SVM model incorporating recently proposed TEDA approach is proposed. The method updates the widely renowned incremental SVM approach, as well as introduces new TEDA and RDE kernels which are learnable and capable of adaptation to data. The slack variables are also adaptive and depend on each point's 'importance' combining the outliers detection with SVM slack variables to deal with misclassifications. Some suggestions on the evolving systems based on SVM are also provided. The examples of image recognition are provided to give a 'proof of concept' for the method.

Keywords: SVM · TEDA · Incremental learning · Evolving system

1 Introduction

Nowadays, there are plenty of models for object classification. Some of them are aimed on off-line classification, which takes all the samples at once, other are aimed for the incremental classification, which work sample-by-sample. Those which do not require to hold all the sample set, are referred as 'online'. Finally, 'evolving' models are designed to change the structure of the system taking into account recent changes and forget those patterns which occurred long ago.

The problem stated in the article is raised by different approaches: SVM models, novel TEDA data analysis concept, and evolving systems.

SVM was first proposed as Generalised Portrait Algorithm by Vapnik and Lerner in 1963 [1], with some works together with Chervonenkis [2], but was not widely used until the beginning of the 1990-s, when new contributions by Vapnik and other authors were proposed [3], [4]. Now, the SVM family contains a huge number of different algorithms, capable of most widely known machine learning problems (clustering[5], outlier detection[6], structured learning[7]).

TEDA approach has recently emerged and gives promising results on data outlier detection[8], classification [9] and other machine learning problems [10]. It is based on data and provides attractive concept of learning the parameters by data, not by some pre-defined constraints.

Evolving systems describe the ability of structural adaptation "from scratch" to consider the changes in the data stream[11], [12]. The distinctive feature of such a system is that it takes into consideration more recent patterns in data, forgetting those

© Springer International Publishing Switzerland 2015
A. Gammerman et al. (Eds.): SLDS 2015, LNAI 9047, pp. 156–168, 2015.
DOI: 10.1007/978-3-319-17091-6_11

that happened many time ago and hence may be not relevant, by changing the structure of the classifier and forgetting the patterns which are not relevant. One of the popular applications of such systems is classification [13], [14], [15]. Such methods are based on fuzzy systems, as well as neural networks [16].

The outline of the article is as follows:

— first, the SVM systems are reviewed;
— second, the TEDA background and TEDA SVM statement is given;
— third, the novel TEDA kernel is proposed;
— fourth, incremental update procedure is formulated;
— fifth, the new samples incremental update procedure is proposed;
— sixth, the experimental results are discussed.

The article is finalised by conclusion, describing the research results.

2   SVM Model Formulation

Here the accurate statement of the supervised learning problem is performed. Let us have some object set, which we designate as Ω, and a finite space of object classes, referred as Y. Then, let us have a subset, $\Omega_L \subset \Omega$, named training set, for each the following function is defined: $F_L : \Omega_L \rightarrow Y$. The problem is to build a function $F : \Omega \rightarrow Y$, approximating the function F_L on the set Ω_L. The assumption is that F will be a good mapping for further objects, Ω_V where the index V denotes validation. $\Omega_V \cap \Omega_L = \emptyset$; $\Omega_V, \Omega_L \subset \Omega$. The method we propose has its roots in the SVM problem statement [4, 17]. Here we introduce the basic formulation of SVM problem with slack variables and notation we further use. Consider a two class classification problem, where

$$\Omega_L = \{x_1, x_2, \dots, x_k\}, Y = \{-1, 1\}, F(x_n) = t_n, n \in [1 \dots k]. \tag{1}$$

Here k is the number of the data samples.
Here we state the problem for overlapping classes (C-SVM) [17]

$$\frac{1}{2}\|w\|^2 + C\sum_{n=1}^{k} \Xi_n \rightarrow \min_{w,b,\Xi_n}, \tag{2}$$

w.r.t. following constraints:

$$t_n y(x_n) \geq 1 - \Xi_n, \Xi_n \geq 0, n = 1 \dots k. \tag{3}$$

Here Ξ_n are so-called 'slack variables', C is the so-called 'box constraint' parameter [17]. This problem statement allows some misclassification of the training set for hardly-divisible data, and $y(x) = w^T x + b$, where w, b are the parameters of the hyperplane. This formulation is widely used [4, 17,18]. If we write down Lagrangian, differentiate it and find an extremum [17], we get the dual problem

$$\bar{L}(\alpha) = -\frac{1}{2}\sum_{n=1}^{k}\sum_{m=1}^{k}\alpha_n\alpha_m t_n t_m [\phi(\pmb{x}_n)]^T\phi(\pmb{x}_m) + \sum_{n=1}^{k}\alpha_n \to \min_{\alpha,b}, \tag{4}$$

$$0 \le \alpha_n \le C, \sum_{n=1}^{k}\alpha_n t_n = 0.$$

Then, we can consider another problem (v-SVM) [18]:

$$\frac{1}{2}\|\pmb{w}\|^2 - v\gamma + \frac{1}{k}\sum_{n=1}^{k}\Xi_n \to \min_{w,b,\gamma,\Xi_n} \tag{5}$$

w.r.t. the following constraints:

$$t_n y(\pmb{x}_n) \ge \gamma - \Xi_n, \Xi_n \ge 0, \qquad n = 1, \dots, k, \tag{6}$$

The parameter v gives a lower bound for the fraction of support vectors, as well as an upper bound for the fraction of margin errors in case of $\gamma > 0$. This formulation can be proven to be equivalent to C-SVM with $\hat{C} = \frac{1}{k\gamma}$, if $\gamma > 0$ [18].

Then we can denote a kernel function $K(\pmb{x}_n, \pmb{x}_m) = [\phi(\pmb{x}_n)]^T\phi(\pmb{x}_m)$, where $\phi(\cdot)$ is some mapping function, taken from the (possibly infinite) mapping functions space. It can be recognised as a replacement to the ordinary scalar product, introducing non-linearity into the model. The widely known kernels are: linear, Mahalanobis [19], cosine [20], Gaussian [21], histogram intersection [22] or survival [23] kernels). One can also restore it based on the data using metric learning techniques. Hence, the feature transformation (for finite or infinite space) can be replaced by changing the distance metric, given by the kernel.

3   TEDA Approach Summary

TEDA framework provides a novel systematic method of a "per point" online data analysis [8], [9].

Consider that we have object space $\Omega \subseteq \mathbb{R}^p$ containing data samples, where p is the data dimensionality. This space is equipped with some distance (i.e. Euclidean, L_1, cosine or any others). Further we refer this distance as $d(\pmb{x}, \pmb{y})$. We can pick data samples sequence from this object space:

$$\{\pmb{x}_1, \pmb{x}_2 \dots \pmb{x}_k \dots\}, \pmb{x}_k \in \Omega, k \in \mathbb{N}, \tag{7}$$

where k is a sequence number of the object which can be represented as the instant of time, when the data sample has arrived. For this reason, index k will be referred to as time instant further for simplicity. We can construct sum distance to some particular point $\pmb{x} \in \Omega$, for each element up to the k-th one [8], [10]:

$$\pi^k(\pmb{x}) = \sum_{i=1}^{k} d(\pmb{x}, \pmb{x}_i), k \ge 1. \tag{8}$$

Based on this definition, we define the eccentricity at the time instant k:

$$\xi^k(\pmb{x}) = \frac{2\pi^k(\pmb{x})}{\sum_{i=1}^{k}\pi^k(\pmb{x}_i)} = 2\frac{\sum_{i=1}^{k}d(\pmb{x},\pmb{x}_j)}{\sum_{i=1}^{k}\sum_{j=1}^{k}d(\pmb{x}_i,\pmb{x}_j)}, k \ge 2, \sum_{i=1}^{k}\pi^k(\pmb{x}) > 0. \tag{9}$$

The complement of eccentricity, typicality is defined as:

$$\tau^k(x) = 1 - \xi^k(x). \tag{10}$$

The eccentricity and typicality are both bounded [8], [10]:

$$0 \le \xi^k(x) \le 1, \sum_{i=1}^{k} \xi^k(x_i) = 2, k \ge 2, \sum_{i=1}^{k} \pi^k(x_i) > 0. \tag{11}$$

$$0 \le \tau^k(x) \le 1, \sum_{i=1}^{k} \tau^k(x_i) = k - 2, k \ge 2, \sum_{i=1}^{k} \pi^k(x_i) > 0. \tag{12}$$

Normalised eccentricity and typicality can also be defined as [8], [10]:

$$\zeta^k(x) = \frac{\xi^k(x)}{2}, \sum_{i=1}^{k} \zeta^k(x_i) = 1, k \ge 2, \sum_{i=1}^{k} \pi^k(x_i) > 0. \tag{13}$$

$$t^k(x) = \frac{\tau^k(x)}{k-2}, \sum_{i=1}^{k} \tau^k(x_i) = 1, k > 2, \sum_{i=1}^{k} \pi^k(x_i) > 0. \tag{14}$$

The method's capability of online problems resolution follows from existence of the formulae of the incremental update [8], [9]. There exist convenient formulae for incremental calculation for Euclidean and Mahalanobis distance [19], but here we do not discuss it. Generally, for any distance, we can use the formula $\pi^{k+1}(x) = \pi^k(x) + d(x, x_{k+1})$ and calculate all other quantities based on it.

4   The TEDA SVM Statement

In the classical formulation of SVM given above we aim to give an upper bound of the fraction of margin errors. But here we are targeting aiming to make it dependent on the 'importance' of each of the support vectors, i.e. make more *'typical'* support vectors penalised more for being out of boundaries, rather than *'anomalous'*. In other words, we care less for anomalous data samples and more for typical ones to be covered well by the classifier; we do not try to cover all data sample equally, but proportionally to their typicality.

Here, the "local" typicality in regards to each of the classes is proposed as a weight for each of the support vectors. For each class c_m we define typicality [8]

$$\tau_c^k(x) = 1 - 2 \frac{\sum_{x_j \in X_c} d(x, x_j)}{\sum_{x_i \in X_c} \sum_{x_j \in X_c} d(x_i, x_j)}, c \in \{c_m, c_{\bar{m}}\}, c_m \in C, c_{\bar{m}} = C \backslash c_m. \tag{15}$$

Here X_c denotes the objects with labels from the set c, which we build here by the scheme 'one versus the rest'. For each of the classes we build the following model:

$$\frac{1}{2} \|w\|^2 + \sum_{n=1}^{k} C \tau_{c_m}^k(x_n)[y_n > 0]\Xi_n + \sum_{n=1}^{k} C \tau_{c_{\bar{m}}}^k(x_n)[y_n < 0]\Xi_n \to \min_{w, \Xi, b} \tag{16}$$

w.r.t. following constraints:

$$t_n y(x_n) \ge 1 - \Xi_n, \Xi_n \ge 0, n = 1 \dots k. \tag{17}$$

We can see that this model preserves the upper boundary property γ for the margin errors [1817], where $\gamma = \frac{1}{k\bar{C}}$, $C > 0$, as the upper boundary is known: $C\tau^k_{c_{\{m,\overline{m}\}}}(x) \leq C$. But what we gain additionally is possibility to control the 'importance' of each data samples. The algorithm takes into account our desire to 'sacrifice' the correct recognition only for the most 'anomalous' data. The more typical is data in the model, the higher will be the box constraint for it because of higher typicality. Opposite case, when the object is more anomalous, is penalised less due to lower typicality in order to avoid fitting the model to anomalous cases.

5   TEDA Kernel

Further to TEDA formulation, we propose also novel formulation of a kernel within the TEDA framework. We define the following TEDA-like kernel:

$$\ddot{\zeta}^k(x,y) = \langle x,y \rangle (\zeta^k(x)\zeta^k(y))^\gamma,$$

$$\ddot{\zeta}^k(x,y) = \langle x,y \rangle \left(\frac{\sum_{i=1}^k d(x_i,x) \sum_{i=1}^k d(x_i,y)}{\left(\sum_{i=1}^k \sum_{j=1}^k d(x_i,x_j)\right)^2} \right)^\gamma, \sum_{i=1}^k \sum_{j=1}^k d(x_i,x_j) > 0. \tag{18}$$

Here $\zeta^k(x)$ is a normalised data eccentricity, $\gamma > 0$ is some parbameter, showing the data eccentricity involvement. It helps us to take into account not only scalar product itself, but also the importance of each of the points. The interpretation of the kernel is to increase the kernel values for the 'anomalous' points, and at the same time decrease the kernel values between 'typical' points, bringing it closer in the data space.

To be the kernel, $\ddot{\zeta}^k$ should meet the following requirements:

1. $\ddot{\zeta}^k(x,y) = \ddot{\zeta}^k(y,x)$.
2. $\ddot{\zeta}^k$ is positive semi-definite, i.e. $\forall y_1, y_2, \ldots y_m \in \Omega, \forall x_1, x_2, \ldots x_k \in \Omega$, where Ω is a Hilbert space, the matrix $M \in \mathbb{R}^{m \times m}$, $M_{ij} = \ddot{\zeta}^k(y_i, y_j)$ is non-negative definite, that is for any $\alpha \in \mathbb{R}^m$ $\alpha^T M \alpha \geq 0$.
   Proof sketch:

1. $\ddot{\zeta}^k(x,y) = \langle x,y \rangle \left(\frac{\sum_{i=1}^k d(x_i,x) \sum_{i=1}^k d(x_i,y)}{\left(\sum_{i=1}^k \sum_{j=1}^k d(x_i,x_j)\right)^2} \right)^\gamma = \langle y,x \rangle \left(\frac{\sum_{i=1}^k d(x_i,y) \sum_{i=1}^k d(x_i,x)}{\left(\sum_{i=1}^k \sum_{j=1}^k d(x_i,x_j)\right)^2} \right)^\gamma =$
$$= \ddot{\zeta}(y,x).$$

2. For Euclidean distance, it can be proven to be equivalent to:

$$\ddot{\zeta}^k(x,y) \propto \langle x,y \rangle \left(\left(\|x - \mu^k\|^2 + \sigma^{k^2} \right) \left(\|y - \mu^k\|^2 + \sigma^{k^2} \right) \right)^\gamma, \tag{19}$$

where μ^k is the mean over $x_1, x_2, \ldots x_k$, σ^k is a variance over $x_1, x_2, \ldots x_k$ which depend on the data set and are the values derived from data. It can be proven to be a particular case of the polynomial kernel multiplied on the linear kernel.

The scalar product can be replaced here by any kernel $K(x,y)$, to get this expression:

$$\zeta^k(x,y) \propto K(x,y)\left(\left(\|x-\mu^k\|^2 + \sigma^{k^2}\right)\left(\|y-\mu^k\|^2 + \sigma^{k^2}\right)\right)^T, \tag{20}$$

We can also make the similar statement via RDE [12]:

$$D(x,y) = 1/(1 + \|x-y\|^2 + \Sigma_k - \|\mu_k^2\|). \tag{21}$$

It is equivalent to Cauchy kernel [12] (up to the multiplier), and Cauchy kernel itself can be proven to be a proper kernel, hence it is also a kernel:

$$D(x,y) \propto \frac{1}{1+\|x-y\|^2/\alpha}, \alpha > 0. \tag{22}$$

6   TEDA SVM Incremental Update

Here the standard problem of the incremental update is stated.

Let us have a training data sequence $\{x_1, \dots, x_k \dots\}$, $x_k \in \Omega$ which arrives one-by one, where k is an order number of the data element. For each x_k there is a label $y_k \in Y$. Up to the k-th element we have the problem (16).

Then, the $(k+1)$-th element arrives, and the problem is re-formulated as

$$\frac{1}{2}\|w\|^2 + \sum_{i=1}^{k+1} C\tau_{cm}^i(x_i)[y_i > 0]\Xi_n + \sum_{i=1}^{k+1} C\tau_{c\overline{m}}^i(x_i)[y_i < 0]\Xi_i \to \min_{w,\Xi,b} \tag{23}$$

w.r.t. following constraints:

$$t_i y(x_i) \geq 1 - \Xi_i, \Xi_i \geq 0, i = 1 \dots k+1. \tag{24}$$

Also, we should take into account that

$$y(x) = w^T \phi(x) + b, \tag{25}$$

as it was mentioned before, and $\phi(x)$ is a feature mapping. Hence, we should also update the feature mapping $\phi(x)$. Generally, it is not feasible as the mapping can be set on functional spaces including infinite-dimensional ones. It can be shown, that dual problem transition allows us to express $y(x)$ in terms of the kernel $K(x_i, x_j) = \phi^T(x_i)\phi(x_j)$ (this notation denotes scalar product, although the mapping can be given in infinite-dimensional space). Hence we need to update the kernel matrix $K \in \mathbb{R}^{N \times N}$ only, where $K_{ij} = K(x_i, x_j)$.

Then we can see, that the incremental update consists of several stages:

— kernel update (section 6.2);
— solution update for the updated kernel (section 6.2);
— solution update for the updated box constraints (section 6.3);
— solution update incorporating the new data (section 6.1).

Then we can write down the dual problem as

$$L(\alpha) = \frac{1}{2}\sum_{i=1}^{k}\sum_{j=1}^{k}\alpha_i\alpha_j t_i t_j [\phi(x_i)]^T \phi(x_j) - \sum_{i=1}^{k}\alpha_i + b\sum_{n=1}^{k} t_i\alpha_i =$$

$$= \frac{1}{2}\sum_{i=1}^{k}\sum_{j=1}^{k}\alpha_i\alpha_j t_i t_j K\left(x_i, x_j\right) - \sum_{i=1}^{k}\alpha_i + b\sum_{i=1}^{k} t_i\alpha_i \rightarrow \min_{\alpha, b}, \qquad (26)$$

$$0 \le \alpha_i \le C_i, \forall i \in [1, k], \sum_{i=1}^{k}\alpha_i t_i = 0.$$

Differentiating the dual problem, we obtain Karush-Kuhn-Tucker conditions (KKT):

$$g_j(x_j) = \frac{\partial L(\alpha)}{\partial \alpha_j} = \sum_{i=1}^{k}\alpha_i t_i t_j K\left(x_i, x_j\right) - 1 + t_j b = t_j y(x_j) - 1,$$

$$\frac{\partial \check{L}(\alpha)}{\partial b} = \sum_{i=1}^{k} t_i\alpha_i = 0, g_j(x_j)\begin{cases} > 0, & \alpha_j = 0, \\ = 0, & 0 < \alpha_j < C_j. \\ < 0, & \alpha_j = C_j. \end{cases} \qquad (27)$$

Let us denote all the training set as Ω_L. This set is divided onto three disjoined sets: margin vectors S, for which $g_j(x_j) = 0$, error support vectors E, for which $g_j(x_j) < 0$, and the rest of the vectors vectors R, for which $g_j(x_j) > 0$, which are not included into the existing solution.

6.1   Adding new Samples

The incremental learning method for SVM was first described in [24].

Apart of this previously proposed method, here we do not choose one global box constraint C for every element of the SVM problem, but use its own box constraint for every object. More, we do not even make it constant, but update it from data.

When transferring from the problem (26) for k elements to the problem for $k + 1$ elements, we should ensure, that the data is in equilibrium, i.e. the conditions of the problem are satisfied.

Let us denote for notation simplicity $M = k + 1$.

We denote as $Q_{ij} = t_i t_j K(x_i, x_j)$.

Then, we begin to change the new vector's coefficient α_M until the configuration within the system changes:

$$\Delta g_j(x_j) = Q_{jM}\Delta\alpha_M + \sum_{n\in S} Q_{jn}\Delta\alpha_M + t_j\Delta b, \forall j \in \Omega_L \cup \{M\},$$

$$0 = t_M\Delta\alpha_M + \sum_{n\in S} t_n\Delta\alpha_n. \qquad (28)$$

Then, we can define

$$\Theta = \begin{bmatrix} 0 & t_{s_1} & \cdots & t_{s_{l(S)}} \\ t_{s_1} & Q_{s_1 s_1} & \cdots & Q_{s_1 s_{l(s)}} \\ \vdots & \vdots & \ddots & \vdots \\ t_{s_{l(S)}} & Q_{s_{l(s)} s_1} & \cdots & Q_{s_{l(s)} s_{l(s)}} \end{bmatrix} \qquad (29)$$

and write the KT conditions changing equations   in the vector form as

$$\Theta[\Delta b \quad \Delta\alpha_{s_1} \quad \cdots \quad \Delta\alpha_{s_{l(S)}}]^T = -[y_M \quad Q_{s_1M} \quad \cdots \quad Q_{s_{l(S)}M}]^T \Delta\alpha_M \quad (30)$$

for the support vector set.
Then we can continue with

$$\Delta b = \beta\Delta\alpha_M, \quad (31)$$

$$\Delta\alpha_j = \beta_j\Delta\alpha_M, \forall j \in D. \quad (32)$$

$$[\beta \quad \beta_{s_1} \quad \cdots \quad \beta_{s_{l(s)}}]^T = -\Theta^{-1}[y_M \quad Q_{s_1M} \quad \cdots \quad Q_{s_{l(s)}M}]^T \quad (33)$$

for all support vectors, and $\beta_n = 0 \; \forall n \in T\backslash S$.
Then

$$\Delta g_j(x_j) = \Gamma_j\Delta\alpha_M, \forall j \in T \cup \{M\}; \Gamma_j = Q_{jM} + \sum_{n\in S} Q_{jn}\beta_n + t_j\beta, \forall j \notin S. \quad (34)$$

After that, we find the maximal increment until the following event occur:

- $g_M \leq 0$, with M joining S when $g_M = 0$;
- $\alpha_M \leq 0$, with M joining E when $\alpha_M = 0$;
- $0 \leq \alpha_j \leq C_j, j \in S$ with $\alpha_j = 0$ when j-th vector transfers from S to R, and $\alpha_j = C_j$ when transferring from S to E;
- $g_j \leq 0, \forall j \in E$, with $g_j = 0$ when j-th vector transfers from E to S;
- $g_j \geq 0, \forall j \in R$, with $g_j = 0$ when j-th vector transfers from R to S.

After this procedure, the new support vectors should be added to the matrix Θ^{-1}. It can be proven that

$$\Theta^{-1} \leftarrow \begin{bmatrix} \Theta^{-1} & 0 \\ & \vdots \\ 0 & \cdots & 0 \end{bmatrix} +$$
$$+ \frac{1}{\Gamma_M}[\beta \quad \beta_{s_1} \quad \cdots \quad \beta_{s_{l(s)}} \quad 1]^T[\beta \quad \beta_{s_1} \quad \cdots \quad \beta_{s_{l(s)}} \quad 1]. \quad (35)$$

This formula allows us to add a vector into S.

The procedure is repeated until no transition between subsets R, E, and S occurs. Also, it should be noticed, that the procedure is proven to be reversible [24]. The process of deletion data during the learning process is referred as decremental learning [24].

6.2 Updating the Kernel

Here we address the learnable kernel update problem in SVM:

$$L_k(\alpha) = \frac{1}{2}\sum_{i=1}^{k}\sum_{j=1}^{k}\alpha_i\alpha_jt_it_jK(x_i,x_j) - \sum_{i=1}^{k}\alpha_i + b\sum_{i=1}^{k}t_i\alpha_i \to \min_{\alpha,b}. \quad (36)$$

The problem is replaced by one with the new kernel $\widehat{K}$

$$L_{k+1}(\alpha) = \frac{1}{2}\sum_{i=1}^{k}\sum_{j=1}^{k}\alpha_i\alpha_j t_i t_j \check{K}\left(\boldsymbol{x}_i, \boldsymbol{x}_j\right) - \sum_{i=1}^{k}\alpha_i + b\sum_{i=1}^{k}t_i\alpha_i \to \min_{\alpha,b} \tag{37}$$

Again, the problems are constrained as in (26).

Therefore, the problem differs in kernel we use. As before, we denote

$$Q_{ij} = t_i t_j K(\boldsymbol{x}_i, \boldsymbol{x}_j), \hat{Q}_{ij} = t_i t_j \check{K}(\boldsymbol{x}_i, \boldsymbol{x}_j). \tag{38}$$

Let us denote also

$$\hat{Q}_{ij} - Q_{ij} = \Delta Q_{ij}. \tag{39}$$

Then we consider

$$\Delta g_j(x_j) = \sum_{n \in S}(Q_{jn} + \beta\Delta Q_{jn})\Delta\alpha_n + \beta\sum_{n \in S}\Delta Q_{jn}\alpha_n + t_j\Delta b, \sum_{n \in S}t_n\Delta\alpha_n = 0. \tag{40}$$

Here $0 \le \beta \le 1$. The problem is to express the corrections of $\Delta\alpha_n$ as a function of some coefficient $\beta \in [0,1]$.

Here we denote Θ as in (29) and

$$\tilde{\Theta} = \begin{bmatrix} 0 & 0 & \cdots & 0 \\ 0 & \Delta Q_{s_1 s_1} & \cdots & \Delta Q_{s_1 s_{l_S}} \\ \vdots & \vdots & \ddots & \vdots \\ 0 & \Delta Q_{s_{l_S} s_1} & \cdots & \Delta Q_{s_{l_S} s_{l_S}} \end{bmatrix}. \tag{41}$$

Then

$$(\Theta + \beta\tilde{\Theta})\begin{bmatrix} \Delta b & \Delta\alpha_{s_1} & \cdots & \Delta\alpha_{s_{l_S}} \end{bmatrix}^T = \beta\tilde{\Theta}\begin{bmatrix} b & \alpha_{s_1} & \cdots & \alpha_{s_{l_S}} \end{bmatrix}^T. \tag{42}$$

In this case

$$\begin{bmatrix} \Delta b & \Delta\alpha_{s_1} & \cdots & \Delta\alpha_{s_{l_S}} \end{bmatrix}^T = \beta(\Theta + \beta\tilde{\Theta})^{-1}\tilde{\Theta}\begin{bmatrix} b & \alpha_{s_1} & \cdots & \alpha_{s_{l_S}} \end{bmatrix}^T =$$

$$= \begin{bmatrix} b & \alpha_{s_1} & \cdots & \alpha_{s_{l_S}} \end{bmatrix}^T - (\Theta + \beta\tilde{\Theta})^{-1}\Theta\begin{bmatrix} b & \alpha_{s_1} & \cdots & \alpha_{s_{l_S}} \end{bmatrix}^T. \tag{43}$$

The maximal increment condition is the same as for the new data update, but additionally we should mind $\beta \in [0,1]$. The update of the matrix is performed the same way like Θ.

6.3   Updating Box Constraints

In this case, we use the same update equations, as the standard update for the new data, but here we check if the KKT constraints are violated on the first stage due to the change of the box constraints.

We remember, that for each of the objects we have (27) with the old constraints. For the stage $k + 1$ we should have

$$g_j(x_j) \begin{cases} > 0, & \alpha_j = 0, \\ = 0, & 0 < \alpha_j < C_j^{k+1}, \\ < 0, & \alpha_j = C_j^{k+1}. \end{cases} \tag{44}$$

but for some of the vectors $D \subset \Omega_L$ the conditions can be broken: $\alpha_j > C_j^{k+1}$. Also, because generally $C_j^{k+1} \neq C_j^k$, some transitions between sets E and R may occur. Hence, we need to correct the solution w.r.t. all the vectors violating the conditions.

The procedure is proposed in a following way. For each vector x_m, violating the KKT conditions, we perform the procedure exactly the same way as for the new vector, considering that it is a newly-added vector to k-vector SVM problem with training set $D \backslash x_m$ and new C_i. For the sets E and S, the vector should be preliminarily deleted by decremental learning procedure should be as [24].

7 Suggestions on the Method Implementation

Additionally, even despite the given method is not *'evolving'* but *'online'*, as it does not discard the previous data samples, the decremental learning procedure can be proposed, as the incremental procedure for SVM is reversible. The following simplest method can be considered:

- for each sample x, update its within-class typicality $\tau_c^k(x)$;
- inspect all the samples which appeared in the train sequence up to the newest element x_k: $\{x_1, ..., x_n ... x_k\}$, $x_n \in \Omega$. If their typicality is lower than some given threshold T, we can state, that the sample should be rejected.
- For the sample set elements to be rejected, perform decremental learning, analogous to that described in [24].

Using this modification, we can employ all the benefits of evolving systems, such as possibility to adopt to the changes on the data neglecting those patterns that appeared long ago, but base it on the SVM framework, rather than fuzzy systems or neural networks. Usage of the SVM framework, instead of fuzzy rule-based evolving systems, gives us an opportunity of using strict optimisation problem statements, which gives benefits of better generalisation of the method.

8 Demonstrations for the Experimental Data

For the proof of concept, an example of human activities images classification was provided (**Fig. 1**, data set [25]). The feature transformation method was exactly borrowed from the previous research described in [13] and is composed from Haar and gist [26] features.

Fig. 1. Human activities data samples

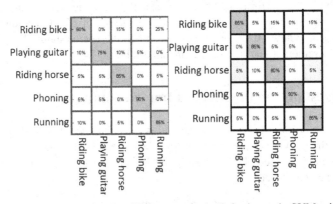

Fig. 2. Results of the recognition for different methods (left picture is SVM with histogram intersection kernel, accuracy rate is 79%, right picture is SVM with TEDA kernel, combined with histogram intersection kernel, and TEDA box constraints, accuracy rate is 81%).

For the experiments, the following methods were compared:

— SVM with Gaussian kernel with $\sigma = 34.4725$, $C = 30$.
— SVM with TEDA kernel, combined with Gaussian kernel, with $\sigma = 34.4725$, $\gamma = 2$, $C = 30$, and TEDA weights.

Here the Gaussian kernel is

$$K_G (x, y) = \exp(-(x - y)^T (x - y)/(2\sigma^2)). \tag{45}$$

In contrast to Gaussian distribution probability density, the multiplier is neglected, just because the solution will be the same for any constant.

By TEDA kernel combined with Gaussian kernel we denote

$$K_{\text{TEDA}} (x, y) = K_G (x, y) \times \left(\left(\|x - \mu^k\|^2 + \sigma^{k^2} \right) \left(\|y - \mu^k\|^2 + \sigma^{k^2} \right) \right)^\gamma. \tag{46}$$

No other modifications are introduced into the model except the TEDA kernel and TEDA weights. Therefore, we suppose that the improvement in the kernel and box variables leads to the increase of the quality of the recognition.

The training data set contains 200 items, 40 images for each of the classes. The testing data set consists of 100 items, 20 images per class. Although the method was initially designed for handwritten symbol images, it can be also applied to describe any other images as well.

The results are given as it is depicted in **Fig. 2**. On the left part of the image, the results for Gaussian kernel are proposed. At the right part of the image, SVM was augmented with TEDA 'box constraints' and uses TEDA kernel, combined with Gaussian kernel. One can see, that the results were (slightly) improved. However, the method has more perspectives, as it makes the model more flexible giving different values to the 'box constraints' and enabling kernel learning 'from scratch'.

9   Conclusion

In this paper, the new modification of the SVM with slack variables for classification was proposed which changes slack variables independently for each of the data samples taking into account the 'typicality' of each data sample and forcing more 'anomalous' data to be misclassified sooner than typical ones. For this purpose, the novel 'box constraints' update model was developed based on the recently proposed TEDA framework, and the novel learnable kernels based on TEDA and RDE were proposed. The incremental SVM was modified to take into account changes of the box variables during the training process, as well as learnable kernels. Though the model, proposed here, is not evolving yet, the ideas were described how to make the model 'evolving'. In the experimental section, a few examples were given to approve the ideas of SVM with new learnable box constraints.

Acknowledgements. Plamen Angelov would like to acknowledge the support of Chair of Excellence award which he was given by Santander Bank, Spain for the period March-September 2015 which is being hosted by Carlos III University, Madrid, Spain.

References

1. Vapnik, V., Lerner, A.: Pattern recognition using generalised portrait method. Automation and Remote Control **24**, 774–780 (1963)
2. Vapnik, V.N., Ya, A., Chervonenkis.: Teorija raspoznavanija obrazov: Statisticheskie problemy obuchenija. (Russian) = Theory of pattern recognition: Statistical problems of learning. Nauka, Moscow (1974)
3. Boser, B.E., Guyon, I.M., Vapnik, V.N.: A training algorithm for optimal margin classifiers. In: COLT 1992: Proceedings of the Fifth Annual Workshop on Computational Learning Theory, pp. 144–152. ACM Press, New York (1992)
4. Vapnik, V.N.: The Nature of Statistical Learning Theory. Springer-Verlag New York, Inc. (1995)
5. Yang, J., Estivill-Castro, V., Chalup, S.K.: Support vector clustering through proximity graph modelling. In: Proceedings of the 9th International Conference on Neural Information Processing, ICONIP 2002, vol. 2. IEEE (2002)
6. Chen, Y., Zhou, X., Huang, T.S.: One-class SVM for learning in image retrieval. In: Proceedings of the International Conference on Image Processing, vol. 1. IEEE (2001)
7. Tsochantaridis, I., et al.: Support vector machine learning for interdependent and structured output spaces. In: Proceedings of the Twenty-First International Conference on Machine Learning. ACM (2004)

8. Angelov, P.: Outside the Box: An Alternative Data Analytics Framework. Journal of Automation, Mobile Robotics and Intelligent Systems **8**(2), 53–59 (2014)
9. Kangin, D., Angelov, P.: New Autonomously Evolving Classifier TEDAClass. IEEE Transactions on Cybernetics (2014, submitted)
10. Angelov, P.: Anomaly detection based on eccentricity analysis. In: 2014 IEEE Symposium Series on Computational Intelligence, 9-12 December, Orlando, Florida (2014, to appear, accepted to publication)
11. Angelov, P., Filev, D., Kasabov, N. (eds.) Evolving Intelligent Systems: Methodology and Applications. IEEE Press Series on Computational Intelligence, p. 444. John Willey and Sons (April 2010) ISBN: 978-0-470-28719-4
12. Angelov, P.: Autonomous Learning Systems: From Data Streams to Knowledge in Real time. John Willey and Sons (December 2012) ISBN: 978-1-1199-5152-0
13. Angelov, P., Kangin, D., Zhou, X., Kolev, D.: Symbol recognition with a new autonomously evolving classifier autoclass. In 2014 IEEE Conference on Evolving and Adaptive Intelligent Systems, pp. 1–6. IEEE (2014); DOI BibTeX
14. Angelov, P., Yager, R.: A new type of simplified fuzzy rule-based systems. International Journal of General Systems **41**(2), 163–185 (2012)
15. Angelov, P., Zhou, X., Klawonn, F.: Evolving fuzzy rule-based classifiers. In: First 2007 IEEE International Conference on Computational Intelligence Applications for Signal and Image Processing, April 1-5, Honolulu, Hawaii, USA, pp. 220–225 (2007)
16. Kasabov, N., Liang, L., Krishnamurthi, R., Feigin, V., Othman, M., Hou, Z., Parmar, P.: Evolving Spiking Neural Networks for Personalised Modelling of Spatio-Temporal Data and Early Prediction of Events: A Case Study on Stroke. Neurocomputing **134**, 269–279 (2014)
17. Bishop, C.M.: Pattern recognition and machine learning, pp. 325–358. Springer, New York (2006)
18. Schölkopf, B., Smola, A., Williamson, R.C., Bartlett, P.L.: New support vector algorithms. Neural Computation **12**, 1207–1245 (2000)
19. Mahalanobis, P.C.: On the generalised distance in statistics. Proceedings of the National Institute of Sciences of India **2**(1), 49–55 (1936)
20. Li, B., Han, L.: Distance weighted cosine similarity measure for text classification. In: Yin, H., Tang, K., Gao, Y., Klawonn, F., Lee, M., Weise, T., Li, B., Yao, X. (eds.) IDEAL 2013. LNCS, vol. 8206, pp. 611–618. Springer, Heidelberg (2013)
21. Keerthi, S.S., Lin, C.-J.: Asymptotic behaviors of support vector machines with Gaussian kernel. Neural Computation **15**(7), 1667–1689 (2003)
22. Maji, S., Berg, A.C., Malik, J.: Classification using intersection kernel support vector machines is efficient. In: IEEE Conference on Computer Vision and Pattern Recognition, CVPR 2008. IEEE (2008)
23. Chen, B., Zheng, N., Principe, J.C.: Survival kernel with application to kernel adaptive filtering. In: The 2013 International Joint Conference on IEEE Neural Networks (IJCNN) (2013)
24. Cauwenberghs, G., Poggio, T.: Incremental and Decremental Support Vector Machine Learning. NIPS, pp. 409–415 (2000)
25. Li, L.-J., Fei-Fei, L.: What, where and who? Classifying events by scene and object recognition. In: IEEE 11th International Conference on Computer Vision, ICCV 2007, pp. 1–8 (2007)
26. Oliva, A., Torralba, A.: Modeling the shape of the scene: a holistic representation of the spatial envelope. International Journal of Computer Vision **42**(3), 145–175 (2001). Gist Descriptor (Matlab code). http://people.csail.mit.edu/torralba/code/spatialenvelope/b

RDE with Forgetting: An Approximate Solution for Large Values of k with an Application to Fault Detection Problems

Clauber Gomes Bezerra[1]([✉]), Bruno Sielly Jales Costa[2], Luiz Affonso Guedes[3], and Plamen Parvanov Angelov[4,5]

[1] Federal Institute of Rio Grande do Norte - IFRN, Campus EaD, Natal, Brazil
clauber.bezerra@ifrn.edu.br
[2] Federal Institute of Rio Grande do Norte - IFRN,
Campus Zona Norte, Natal, Brazil
bruno.costa@ifrn.edu.br
[3] Department of Computer Engineering and Automation - DCA,
Federal University of Rio Grande do Norte - UFRN, Natal, Brazil
affonso@dca.ufrn.br
[4] Data Science Group, School of Computing and Communications,
Lancaster University, Lancaster LA1 4WA, UK
[5] Chair of Excellence, Carlos III University, Madrid, Spain
p.angelov@lancaster.ac.uk

Abstract. Recursive density estimation is a very powerful metric, based on a kernel function, used to detect outliers in a n-dimensional data set. Since it is calculated in a recursive manner, it becomes a very interesting solution for on-line and real-time applications. However, in its original formulation, the equation defined for density calculation is considerably conservative, which may not be suitable for applications that require fast response to dynamic changes in the process. For on-line applications, the value of k, which represents the index of the data sample, may increase indefinitely and, once that the mean update equation directly depends on the number of samples read so far, the influence of a new data sample may be nearly insignificant if the value of k is high. This characteristic creates, in practice, a stationary scenario that may not be adequate for fault detect applications, for example. In order to overcome this problem, we propose in this paper a new approach to RDE, holding its recursive characteristics. This new approach, called RDE with forgetting, introduces the concept of moving mean and forgetting factor, detailed in the next sections. The proposal is tested and validated on a very well known real data fault detection benchmark, however can be generalized to other problems.

Keywords: Outlier detection · Novelty detection · Fault detection · Recursive density estimation

© Springer International Publishing Switzerland 2015
A. Gammerman et al. (Eds.): SLDS 2015, LNAI 9047, pp. 169–178, 2015.
DOI: 10.1007/978-3-319-17091-6_12

1 Introduction

A general dataset may contain elements with particular features that are considerably different from the other elements. This type of element is called outlier. Outlier detection is a statistical problem that is applicable in several research areas, such as military surveillance of enemy activities, intrusion detection in cyber security, fraud detection for credit cards, insurance or health care and fault detection in safety critical systems [1].

Considering a discrete signal from an industrial plant, an outlier may represent a process abnormality. Sometimes, such abnormality indicates an occurring fault, which can cause severe problems to the process, such as unexpected stoppages, production losses, reduction of equipment lifetime and accidents with environmental or human life consequences [2]. Therefore, fault detection in industrial processes is a problem that has been widely researched in recent years [22,23].

For this type of application, it is imperative that the data be monitored in real time. Thus, one needs to use a fast processing data analysis technique in order to follow complex signal dynamics. The algorithm, then, must work with low computational effort and memory usage.

The idea of the RDE calculation was introduced by Angelov & Buswell [3], first named in Angelov et al. [6] and its latest version is a part of a patent application [4]. The general idea was broadly used in many different applications, such as object tracking [6] and novelty detection [7] in video streams, flight data analysis [8] and, more recently, on industrial fault detection [19–21].

The main concept is based on the Cauchy kernel, that has similar properties as Gaussian function, however does not need to follow any pre-defined distributions and can be recursively updated. This particular feature means that only a very small amount of data are required to be stored in the memory, which is essential for real-time applications and limited computational resources. Therefore, RDE allows an infinite (theoretical) amount of data to be processed exactly in real-time, very fast.

However, in its original formulation RDE has conservative characteristics, which may not be the most suitable for some kinds of applications, such as industrial processes analysis. In this type of application, data is analyzed for long time periods, resulting in a large amount of data. Thus, the RDE can not provide a fast response to changes in process dynamics. To solve this problem, we present a new RDE formulation, called RDE with forgetting.

The remainder of this paper is organized as follows: Section 2 describes the RDE algorithm. In section 3, RDE with forgetting formulation is present as a new alternative to traditional RDE. In section 4, DAMADICS benchmark, which is used as case of study for this proposal, is presented. Section 5 presents the results obtained using RDE with forgetting in comparison to traditional RDE. Finally, section 6 presents some brief conclusions on RDE with forgetting.

2 Recursive Density Estimation

By definition, "let all measurable physical variables from the vector, $x \in R^n$ are divided into clusters. Then, for any input vector $x \in R^n$, its Λ-th cluster density value is calculated for Euclidean type distance as" [5]:

$$d_\Lambda = \frac{1}{1 + \frac{1}{N_\Lambda} + \sum_{i=1}^{N_\Lambda} \|x_k - x_i\|^2} \tag{1}$$

where d_Λ denotes the local density of cluster Λ; N_Λ denotes the number of data samples associated with the cluster Λ. For general purposes, x_k represents the feature vector with values for the instant k.

Distance is, then, calculated between the input vector x_k and other vectors that belong to the same cluster as x (measured at previous time instances). Equation 1 can be used to calculate the local density of clusters in off-line mode. However, in real-time applications, the calculation must be on-line. This equation 1, then, can be derived as an exact (not approximated or learned) quantity as [5]:

$$D(x_k) = \frac{1}{1 + \|x_k - \mu_k\|^2 + X_k - \|\mu\|^2} \tag{2}$$

where both the mean, μ_k, and the scalar product, X_k, can be updated recursively as follows:

$$\mu_k = \frac{k-1}{k}\mu_{k-1} + \frac{1}{k}x_k, \qquad \mu_1 = x_1 \tag{3}$$

$$X_k = \frac{k-1}{k}X_{k-1} + \frac{1}{k}\|x_k\|^2, \qquad X_1 = \|x_1\|^2 \tag{4}$$

For real-time applications, the input data is collected continuously, in on-line mode, from the source, which, depending on the application, may be an industrial plant, a video camera, a microphone and so on. Some of the new data reinforce and confirm the information contained in the previous data and other data, however, bring new information, which could indicate a change in operating conditions, a novelty, a fault or simply a more significant change in the dynamic of the process [6]. The value of the information that they bring is closely related to the information from the data collected so far. The informative potential of the new data depends on the spatial proximity to the already existing data cluster, that represents the value of "normality".

In order to detect outliers within a data stream, one first need to select a set of features that, when assuming an "invariant" value, it represents the normal behavior of the system. The term "invariant" means, thus, a data sample that is not considerably oscillatory but, obviously, may vary within the operating regime boundaries for a real industrial system. The input vector x_k is an n-dimensional vector, composed of the values of the n selected features.

The feature extraction (or feature selection) task can be classified as either quantitative, such as principal component analysis (PCA) [9], partial least squares (PLS) [10], linear discriminant analysis (LDA) [11], or qualitative, for example expert systems [12] or trend modeling methods [13]. For more information on the use of feature extraction methods, the reader is referred to Anzanello [14], Levine [15] and Liu et al [16].

3   Recursive Density Estimation with Forgetting

Although very powerful, the RDE algorithm is susceptible to a few problems, specially when dealing with real applications. In that case, the amount of data samples can grow considerably over time. The problem occurs when the value of k, which represents the index of the current sample, grows indefinitely.

Analyzing the equations 3 and 4 of the algorithm (mean and scalar product calculations), one can understand that the terms $(k-1)/k$ and $1/k$ are used as weight coefficients: while the first referred term is the weight of the past values, the second one is the weight of the current data sample in all equations.

Since k varies from 1 to an indefinite value, it is possible to see that, when the value of k is high, the term $1/k$ becomes nearly irrelevant, thus, a considerably eccentric recently read data sample will have no interference at all on the mean calculation, for example. This characteristic may cause important distortions on the calculated terms.

As an example, let us consider a general process with a sampling period of 1s. As one can see in table 1, after less than two minutes, the term $(k-1)/k$ already possesses a weight of 99% in the equation. Furthermore, as k grows, the referred term tends to 100% given the limited computer numerical representation.

Table 1. Evolution of k and weights on RDE equations over time

Timestamp	k	$\frac{k-1}{k}$	$\frac{1}{k}$
00:00:01	1	0	1
00:00:10	10	0.9	0.1
00:00:50	50	0.98	0.02
00:01:40	100	0.99	0.01
00:16:40	1000	0.999	0.001
02:46:40	10000	0.9999	0.0001
$\vdots$	$\vdots$	$\vdots$	$\vdots$
24:00:00	86400	$\simeq 1$	$\simeq 0$

We, then, propose in this paper a slight change in the RDE algorithm, named RDE with forgetting. This update consists of using a forgetting factor α in the equations 3 and 4, replacing the weights $(k-1)/k$ and $1/k$. Thus, the equations can be rewritten as:

$$\mu_k = \alpha\mu_{k-1} + (1-\alpha)x_k, \qquad \mu_1 = x_1 \tag{5}$$

$$X_k = \alpha X_{k-1} + (1-\alpha)\|x_k\|^2, \qquad X_1 = \|x_1\|^2 \tag{6}$$

where α is the forgetting factor, with $0 \le \alpha \le 1$.

The use of a forgetting factor enables static weights over time, since the first value of k until its maximum value. Using the same previous example, the values of weights during a day for $\alpha = 0.9$ are shown in table 2.

Table 2. Evolution of k and weights on RDE with forgetting equations over time

Timestamp	k	α	$1-\alpha$
00:00:01	1	0.9	0.1
00:00:10	10	0.9	0.1
00:00:50	50	0.9	0.1
00:01:40	100	0.9	0.1
00:16:40	1000	0.9	0.1
02:46:40	10000	0.9	0.1
$\vdots$	$\vdots$	$\vdots$	$\vdots$
24:00:00	86400	0.9	0.1

4 Case of Study

The study and validation of the proposed approach was performed on the fault detection benchmark DAMADICS. It is one of the most used benchmarks for fault detection and diagnosis applications and is advantageous in the sense of enabling to perform the experiments using real industrial data and serving as a fair basis of comparison to other techniques.

DAMADICS is the acronym for Development and Applications of Methods for Actuator Diagnosis in Industrial Control Systems, first introduced in Bartys et al. [17]. It is an openly available benchmark system, based on the industrial operation of the sugar factory Cukrownia Lublin SA, Poland. The benchmark considers many details of the physical and electro-mechanical properties of a real industrial actuator valve, figure 1 operating under challenging process conditions.

With DAMADICS, it is possible to simulate nineteen abnormal events, along with the normal operation, from three actuators. A faulty state is composed by the type of the fault followed by the failure mode, which can be abrupt or incipient. Moreover, the benchmark also provides a set of off-line data files, each one containing the data from 24-hour use of the plant, including artificial insertion of faults in specific hours.

5 Experiment and Results

In this section we present the results obtained from the application of RDE with forgetting to a set of off-line data files from DAMADICS benchmark. The set of data provides, among others, the following measured variables: CV (process control variable), PV (output process variable) and X (rod displacement of the servo motor).

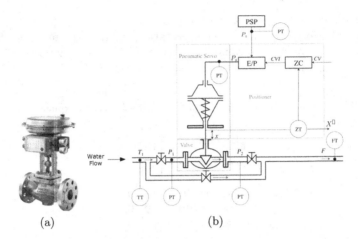

(a)   (b)

Fig. 1. Actuator model of DAMADICS benchmark [18]: (a) external view e (b) internal schema

Each of these variables has a total of 86400 samples, which corresponds to a sampling period of 1s. In the following results we use the signals CV, PV and X resulting in the input vector $x = \{CV, PV, X\}$. In this case, according to the proposal of the RDE, each input x either belongs or not to the "normal" cluster. The charts of Figure 2 show the behavior of these three variables during the first 12 hours of a given day, which is considered the fault-free period.

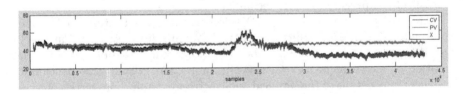

Fig. 2. Signals CV, PV e X during the first 12 hours of a given day

Using the same data, the density and mean density were calculated using the RDE algorithm for the same period of time, again, considering only the fault-free case. The mean of density is calculated by:

$$\overline{D}_k = \frac{k-1}{k}\overline{D}_{k-1} + \frac{1}{k}D_k, \qquad \overline{D}_1 = D_1 \qquad (7)$$

The results obtained are shown in Figure 3.

By analyzing the chart of Figure 3(a) one can observe that the mean density signal is not able to follow the density when there is a considerably density drop. This is due to the fact that the value of k is high enough to prevent that the current data sample have a considerable influence on the density mean calculation, as shown in equation 7. For a specific group of applications, that

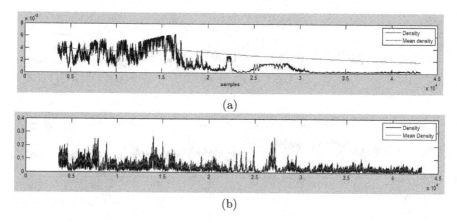

(a)

(b)

Fig. 3. density and mean density of x for the first 12 hours of a given day using (a) RDE and (b) RDE with forgetting

behavior may not be adequate, specially when dealing with real-time problems, where the response to oscillations should be immediate.

The same experiment was performed using RDE with forgetting algorithm with a forgetting factor $\alpha = 0.99$. The mean density, in this case, is calculated by:

$$\overline{D}_k = (1 - \alpha)\overline{D}_{k-1} + \alpha D_k, \qquad \overline{D}_1 = D_1 \qquad (8)$$

The results are shown in Figure 3(b). Note that, the signal of mean is able to quickly cope with density oscillations.

We observe, then, that RDE with forgetting is suitable for applications where one needs to detect abrupt changes in the behavior of a system. As case of study, thus, in this work we are using a fault detection of an industrial process application as basis of comparison to RDE traditional approach.

By analyzing the last 12 hours of the day, we are able to identify 3 different faults. The algorithms RDE and RDE with forgetting were used to calculate the density of data from that period. A forgetting factor $\alpha = 0.99$ was used in RDE with forgetting. The results for both approaches are shown in Figure 4.

By analyzing the charts on Figure 4 one can observe that the results obtained are very similar and both approaches present considerable density changes during the faults. These alterations occur both in amplitude and in frequency, which demonstrates that RDE with forgetting can be used successfully in fault detection applications. In relation to the processing time, the two algorithms also obtained very similar results. It is important to highlight that a complementary signal processing technique must be associated with RDE or RDE with forgetting in order to determine the beginning and end of the faults, as those presented in Costa et al. [19–21], for example.

After repeating the experiments with a diferent fault provided by the benchmark and using the variables X and CV as input, the obtained results are shown in Figure 6. Notice that, the input signals, after the second vertical dashed bar, do not return to the previous "zone of normality" (prior to the first vertical

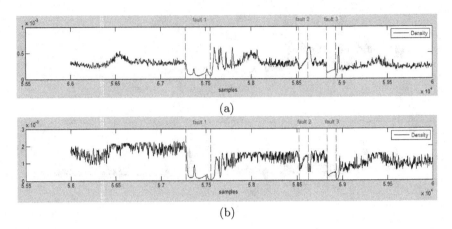

Fig. 4. density calculated for the last 12 hours of a given day using (a) RDE e (b) RDE with forgetting

dashed bar), which results in lack of detection of the end of the fault by RDE. RDE with forgetting, on the other hand, is sensitive to the status change and, after a while, is able to rise the calculated density, resulting in a more proper detection of the end of the referred fault.

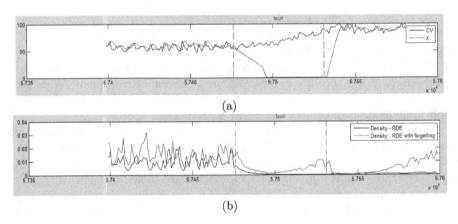

Fig. 5. (a) input data and (b) density calculated using RDE and RDE with forgetting

6   Conclusion

In this work we proposed a new algorithm, called RDE with forgetting, to be used as an alternative to the traditional and well known RDE technique in specific applications that require fast response to dynamic process changes. The proposal was developed aiming to improve the weight coefficient calculations used in traditional RDE, maintaining one of its most important features - recursivity -, which enables practical on-line and real-time applications.

The proposed algorithm uses a parameter α, which represents the desired forgetting factor. This parameter value may be estimated according to the desired weight for the current data item. In presented results, we use a fixed value for , but a complementary study is required to estimate the best choice of values for this parameter in each application. In future work, a study can be done in such a way that this parameter can be updated adaptively, according to the read data. The greater the value of , the closer RDE with forgetting is to traditional RDE in concern to the slow response to system changes.

It is important to highlight that the traditional RDE is a powerful tool to on-line data analysis, however, may not be suitable for very specific applications, where systems require fast response to changes even when there is a substantial amount of historical data read so far.

The new technique was successfully applied to a real set of fault data from a very well known fault detection benchmark, however it is generic and can be used to other outlier and novelty detection applications.

References

1. Singh, K., Upadhyaya, S.: Outlier Detection: Applications And Techniques. International Journal of Computer Science Issues (2012)
2. Venkatasubramanian, V.: Abnormal events management in complex process plants: Challenges and opportunities in intelligent supervisory control, em Foundations of Computer-Aided Process Operations, pp. 117–132 (2003)
3. Angelov, P., Buswell, R.: Evolving rule-based models: A tool for intelligent adaptation. In: Joint 9th IFSA World Congress and 20th NAFIPS International Conference, vol. 2, pp. 1062–1067 (2001)
4. Angelov, P.: Anomalous system state identification, patent GB1208542.9, priority date: May 15, 2012 (2012)
5. Angelov, P.: Autonomous Learning Systems: From Data to Knowledge in Real Time. John Willey and Sons (2012)
6. Angelov, P., Ramezani, R., Zhou, X.: Autonomous novelty detection and object tracking in video streams using evolving clustering and takagi-sugeno type neuro-fuzzy system. In: IEEE International Joint Conference on Neural Networks, IJCNN 2008. IEEE World Congress on Computational Intelligence, pp. 1456–1463 (2008)
7. Ramezani, R., Angelov, P., Zhou, X.: A fast approach to novelty detection in video streams using recursive density estimation. In: 4th International IEEE Conference on Intelligent Systems, IS 2008, vol. 2, pp 142–147 (2008)
8. Kolev, D., Angelov, P., Markarian, G., Suvorov, M., Lysanov, S.: ARFA: Automated real time flight data analysis using evolving clustering, classifiers and recursive density estimation. In: Proceedings of the IEEE Symposium Series on Computational Intelligence, SSCI 2013, Singapore, pp. 91–97 (2013)
9. Malhi, A., Gao, R.: PCA-based feature selection scheme for machine defect classification. IEEE Transactions on Instrumentation and Measurement **53**(6), 1517–1525 (2004)
10. Kembhavi, A., Harwood, D., Davis, L.: Vehicle detection using partial least squares. IEEE Transactions on Pattern Analysis and Machine Intelligence **33**(6), 1250–1265 (2011)

11. Song, F., Mei, D., Li, H.: Feature selection based on linear discriminant analysis. In: 2010 International Conference on Intelligent System Design and Engineering Application (ISDEA), vol. 1, pp. 746–749 (2010)
12. Pande, S.S., Prabhu, B.S.: An expert system for automatic extraction of machining features and tooling selection for automats. Computer-Aided Engineering Journal 7(4), 99–103 (1990)
13. Dash, S., Rengaswamy, R., Venkatasubramanian, V.: Fuzzy-logic based trend classification for fault diagnosis of chemical processes. Computers & Chemical Engineering 27(3), 347–362
14. Anzanello, M.J.: Feature Extraction and Feature Selection: A Survey of Methods in Industrial Applications. John Wiley & Sons, Inc. (2010)
15. Levine, M.: Feature extraction: A survey. Proceedings of the IEEE 57(8), 1391–1407 (1969)
16. Liu, H., Chen, G., Jiang, S., Song, G: A survey of feature extraction approaches in analog circuit fault diagnosis. In: Pacific-Asia Workshop on Computational Intelligence and Industrial Application, PACIIA 2008, vol. 2, pp. 676–680 (2008)
17. Bartys, M., Patton, R., Syfert, M., de las Heras, S., Quevedo, J.: Introduction to the DAMADICS actuator FDI benchmark study. Control Engineering Practice 14(6), 577–596 (2006) ISSN 0967–0661
18. DAMADICS Information Web site. http://diag.mchtr.pw.edu.pl/damadics/
19. Costa, B.S.J., Angelov, P.P., Guedes, L.A.: Real-time fault detection using recursive density estimation. Journal of Control, Automation and Electrical Systems 25(4), 428–437 (2014)
20. Costa, B.S.J., Angelov, P.P., Guedes, L.A.: Fully unsupervised fault detection and identification based on recursive density estimation and self-evolving cloud-based classifier. Neurocomputing 150, 289–303 (2014)
21. Costa, B.S.J., Angelov, P.P., Guedes, L.A.: A new unsupervised approach to fault detection and identification. In: 2014 International Joint Conference on Neural Networks (IJCNN), pp. 1557–1564, July 6–11 (2014)
22. Chen, W., Khan, A.Q., Abid, M., Ding, S.X.: Integrated design of observer based fault detection for a class of uncertain nonlinear systems. Applied Mathematics and Computer Science 21(3), 423–430 (2011)
23. Lemos, A., Caminhas, W., Gomide, F.: Adaptive fault detection and diagnosis using an evolving fuzzy classifier. Inf. Sci. 220, 64–85 (2013)

Sit-to-Stand Movement Recognition Using Kinect

Erik Acorn[1]([⊠]), Nikos Dipsis[1], Tamar Pincus[2], and Kostas Stathis[1]

[1] Department of Computer Science, Royal Holloway University of London,
Egham, Surrey TW20 0EX, UK
Erik.Acorn.2013@live.rhul.ac.uk
[2] Department of Psychology, Royal Holloway University of London, Egham,
Surrey TW20 0EX, UK

Abstract. This paper examines the application of machine-learning techniques to human movement data in order to recognise and compare movements made by different people. Data from an experimental set-up using a sit-to-stand movement are first collected using the Microsoft Kinect input sensor, then normalized and subsequently compared using the assigned labels for correct and incorrect movements. We show that attributes can be extracted from the time series produced by the Kinect sensor using a dynamic time-warping technique. The extracted attributes are then fed to a random forest algorithm, to recognise anomalous behaviour in time series of joint measurements over the whole movement. For comparison, the k-Nearest Neighbours algorithm is also used on the same attributes with good results. Both methods' results are compared using Multi-Dimensional Scaling for clustering visualisation.

Keywords: Machine-learning · Movement recognition · Kinect · Sit-to-stand

1 Introduction

The use of computers to collect, analyse and interpret human movement is becoming increasingly popular. In particular, we are witnessing the development of natural interfaces that allow users to interact with computers while performing ordinary movements. Key to such interfaces is the detection, categorisation and analysis of body movements made by people with different body shapes and physical characteristics.

Because of their intuitive and ordinary application, natural user interfaces can only be expected to increase in prevalence, especially with the introduction of cheaper hardware providing input sensing and supporting enhanced processing techniques. A case in support of this position is the introduction of motion sensing devices such as the Microsoft Kinect [1], which are conveniently used by a wide audience in their home environment.

Although there may be a multitude of uses for which it is necessary to process motion capture data for further analysis, we are motivated by applications such as that proposed by Bragaglia et al [2], who discuss an architecture based on Kinect to recognise home exercises by people, including fall recognition for elderly patients. We are particularly interested in applications that would support people who are suffering

© Springer International Publishing Switzerland 2015
A. Gammerman et al. (Eds.): SLDS 2015, LNAI 9047, pp. 179–192, 2015.
DOI: 10.1007/978-3-319-17091-6_13

from back pain. Low back pain has recently been estimated as the number one ranking cause of daily disability worldwide [3] and there is a great incentive for patients to be able to carry out rehabilitation in their homes.

However, there are expected complications with the use of input devices such as Kinect, in particular those arising from noisy data and variability between examples of a similar action. In a real world example, noise can be due to background movements and inaccurate interpretation of body parts by the capturing software. Variability can be due to differing distances from the capturing device, different body shapes, determination of the start of a motion and duration of the motion.

To address these issues we aim to create an experiment for collecting human movement data with emphasis on compromised movement due to back pain. Our objective is to apply machine-learning to analyse the data and to create enough human movement data from different subjects to be able to effectively apply an algorithm for comparison and to identify anomalies. To make the discussion concrete, we study the movement of standing up from a seated position with a view to categorising the same motion performed by various participants.

One benefit of bringing this kind of movement analysis into the home is that it will allow people with medical problems to be monitored and treated remotely, saving hospital care time and resources. It also has the potential of allowing physiotherapy exercises from home with expert feedback. Such feedback would either be asynchronous feedback from a physiotherapist examining the data after collection or directly from the machine-learning algorithm whereby the anomaly can be identified by means of a trained computer model.

The work provides a framework whereby movement data based on sit-to-stand movements are extracted from a dataset based on joint behaviour. The main contribution underlying subsequent data analysis is the production of the warp distance matrix as a new application of Dynamic Time Warping to human motion data. The matrix produced eliminates the time dimension in the data. This new approach is shown to produce good results when used as input for all of the machine- learning techniques applied. We also show how a bagging implementation of k-Nearest Neighbours (kNN) can average the results over a large number of out-of-bag validations, at the same time producing a kNN distance matrix allowing the use of Multi-Dimensional Scaling for cluster visualisation.

The paper is structured as follows. Section 2 discusses the background work, other work in related fields, the history of movement recognition, different purposes for its use and methods of analysis employed. Section 3 describes the framework of our approach including a description of the set-up, general approach to the boundaries of the work, data structures set up for use in evaluation code, visualization tools and explanations of data analysis algorithms used. Section 4 is the main evaluation, presenting the intermediate processes applied to the data, results of the various techniques used including graphical representations to demonstrate outcomes of the analytical procedures, explanations of results and values of error rates attained. Finally section 5 provides discussion and conclusions of the attained results including a summary of the achievements of the project as well as an outline of further work.

2　Movement Recognition: Analysis and Models

Motion capture and movement recognition using computational techniques starting with Marker Based Systems (MBS) was described in early work of Cappozzo et al [4]. MBS set-ups such as Vicon use sophisticated stereophotogrammetrics and actors with carefully placed markers on key body joints or anatomical landmarks. This is necessarily carried out in a specialised environment with expensive equipment and requires time consuming preparation. The system cost alone is US$96-120k according to Han et al [5]. Recent developments have seen low cost Markerless Motion Capture (MMC) devices becoming available including Sony Playstation Eye, Prime Sense Sensor, Intel's Creative Camera and Microsoft Kinect. With these depth cameras and Natural User Interface libraries such as Kinect SDK, OpenNI/NITE, Evoluce SDK and others (Shingade & Ghotkar [6]), motion recognition can be carried out in a non-specialised environment.

Fig. 1. Kinect sensor

The Microsoft Kinect sensor is an RGB-D camera costing about US$200. It records colour video and uses an Infra-red emitter, projecting a structured IR light onto the scene in order to calculate depth measurements. The sensor was launched in 2010 with a description of use by Shotton et al [7]. Microsoft's Natural User Interface for Kinect web page [1] contains documents describing skeletal tracking using Kinect. The cost effectiveness of setting up MMC systems has led to increased use in many areas such as motion capture for games and films (Sinthanayothin et al [8]), NUI using hand gestures (Elgendi et al [9]), and chronic pain rehabilitation using 'serious games' (Schonauer et al [10]). A few studies have compared the two methods (MBS and MMC) for relative accuracy. Studies by Bonnechere et al [11] on static body segment recognition concluded that Kinect is very reliable if measurements are calibrated. Linear regression used to equate measurements from the Vicon MBS with Kinect data. The MBS data is taken as a gold standard. The same group performed another study [12] to compare motion analysis, considering body angles as well as body segment lengths during a deep squat action. This time the conclusion was that the angles at large joints i.e. shoulder, hip and knee were reliable after regression analysis in comparison with MBS. Limb end segments and angles were found not to be reliable; in particular hands feet, forearm and elbow.

Machine-learning techniques were researched for this problem because the data is multi-dimensional. Recognising patterns over the whole data context including over time is extremely complicated and adding to that variation in body shapes and other factors augments the complexity. Machine-learning techniques can be used to reduce the dimensionality and the variability of the data. Data sample alignment is necessary in order to compare like portions of the movement data. Okada & Hasegawa [13] described Data Time Warping (DTW) for this purpose, minimizing Euclidean distance between datasets by warping in the time domain.

Dynamic Time Warping allows two time series that are similar but locally out of phase to align in a non-linear manner. According to Ratanamahatana & Keogh [14], DTW is the best solution known for time series problems in a variety of domains. Their work gives a good insight into bounding constraints and distance metrics when configuring DTW. Han et al [5] use the result of the DTW calculation as a measure of similarity between data-sets. Action recognition is performed on Kinect data in order to compare results with a Vicon (MBS) set-up. The results of this calculation would be applicable to a k-Nearest Neighbours (kNN) algorithm for example.

Herzog et al [15] describe a variation of DTW tailored to account for their Parametrised Hidden Markov Model (PHMM) which considers the hidden state. PHMM is discussed in the following subsection describing Models. Chandola et al [16] suggest two ways to tackle anomaly detection in time series. One is to reduce the contextual anomaly detection problem to a point anomaly detection problem. This may be done using rigid or elastic alignment of time series for example DTW. The second is to model the structure in the data and use the model to detect anomalies. Modelling the structure effectively means reducing dimensions and Han et al [5] use Kernel Principal Component Analysis for this purpose.

Brandao et al [17] presented a comparative analysis of three algorithms applied to human pose recognition using RGB-D images from a Kinect sensor with Kinect SDK. The static pose is represented by coordinates in a bounding box with sides of between 8 and 64 units in different trials. The algorithms used for comparison were C4.5 Gain Ratio Decision Tree, Naive Bayes Classifier, and k-Nearest Neighbour Classifier and were implemented in the data mining tool Weka. The conclusion was that the best classifier was found to be kNN although the Decision Tree Classifier was almost as good; the larger the number of cells used to describe the body part positions, the better the prediction although 8x8 was almost as good as 64x64; and the pose predictions were greater than 90% even when using participants with different body shapes for the data capture.

Herzog et al [15] detail the implementation of Parametric HMM models for recognition of movement using Gaussian output distributions and considering transition probabilities between states which follow each other in the action; the other transition probabilities being zero. The probabilities are calculated using Baum/Welch expectation maximization (EM) for a given training set. As mentioned in the previous section, they used a modified DTW for data alignment to account for the hidden state, first setting up a global HMM model using the whole training set and secondly training local HMMs aligning with reference to the global HMM. This uses the idea that HMMs are temporally invariant.

Random forests are successfully used for human pose recognition by many authors (Shotton et al [18], Rogez et al [19]). Classification of a depth image from a static pose is predicted with random forests grown using a large training dataset.

3   Experimental Set-Up and Framework

Data collection experiments were performed in a controlled environment in order to minimize noise and external factors. Window blinds were closed to maintain constant lighting. A plastic based swivel chair without castors was placed at a fixed distance from the sensor which was mounted on a computer desk 1m above floor level and 2.5m from the chair. The motion capture was performed with each participant three times facing the Kinect sensor and three times at 45° to the line of the sensor. It was decided that imaging with the subject facing at 90° side-on to the sensor was unreliable because Kinect software tries to interpret body parts which are occluded with this aspect.

Thirty-one random volunteers participated in the collection of the experimental data, 21 men and 10 women of heights between 1.52m to 1.94m. The volunteers were shown a short video describing how to stand up from a seated position. They were then each asked to stand in front of the Kinect sensor, sit down and stand up while a motion capture was performed. During this process, each participant was filmed separately using a video camera in order for later reviewing by a physiotherapist. In this way each participant produced six data samples. Thus 93 example data sets were produced for each of the two aspects. On assessment these examples were confirmed as being a smooth action with balanced weight positioning and without twisting and thus were labelled as normal.

In addition to the normal participants, three additional participants performed purposefully faulty actions of four different categories according to the guidelines, producing 12 extra data sets facing the sensor and 12 angled 45° to the sensor. The faulty actions were: (i) starting with feet too far forward; (ii) standing with head too far back; (iii) twisting one shoulder while standing and (iv) starting with trunk too far back (>45° at hip joint).

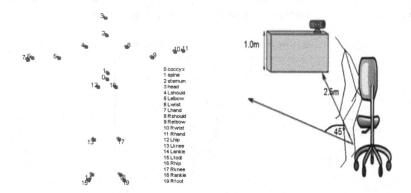

Fig. 2. (a) Kinect anatomical landmarks   (b) Experiment facing 45° to line of Kinect

The data produced by the Kinect sensor is given as 20 body points with x, y and z coordinates relative to an origin, at a frequency of 30Hz. Thus every second 20 x 3 x 30 data points are produced. A data reader was used to store the raw data representing human body movement. This collecting software written in C++ buffers the data stream to RAM in real time and periodically a separate thread writes the data to disk. The figure shows the 20 body points measured by the Kinect API software.

3.1   Data Visualization

We have developed a *Reanimator Tool* to visualize a full joint data set over the duration of a given example. Any data example can be replayed as a 3-d animation (see Fig. 3). Reviewing the animated data is helpful in determining the start of the action and any anomalies or corruptions in the captured data up to the start of the action.

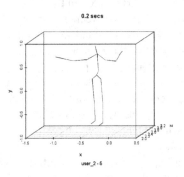

Fig. 3. A data frame taken from the Reanimator Tool

Any joint can be plotted against its warped plot and the reference plot using a function written for this visualisation. The reverse warp from the reference plot to the example is also plotted for comparison. This demonstrates the effect of dynamic time warping with respect to a reference data example on a given example, for a given joint in axis x, y or z. The figure below shows an example of warp plots.

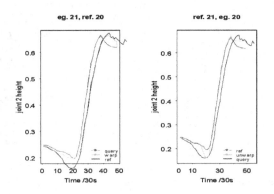

Fig. 4. Warp plot function output

Any joint can be plotted in a given axis consecutively for each participant. This gives an idea of the form of the joint's movement over time for various examples and can be applied to the excised data from the start or to the whole data sample. Any abnormal examples can be spotted. Fig. 5 shows a joint plot of 4 successive participants.

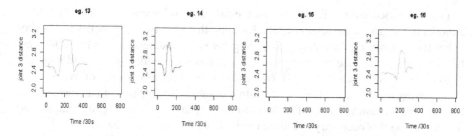

Fig. 5. Head joint plots with time for different participants

3.2   Analysis

It is necessary to determine the start and end points of the action by applying recognisable conditions in the data. Similarly it will be useful to determine a finite number of intermediate key points during conditional recognisable actions in the data to enable alignment. Using DTW allows continuous realignment of data over time measurement intervals as well as providing a way of calculating an averaged distance metric with respect to a reference dataset. This distance is useful as a metric in any classification technique. The principal of DTW will be discussed here and its application to the data is discussed in the Evaluation section.

To compare two similar vectors of time series data of lengths m and n, dynamic time warping algorithm creates an mxn matrix of distances between all elements of each vector. The lowest cost contiguous path from the starting point to the end point is the chosen path whereby indices of the two vectors are mapped effectively dilating and compressing the time line to produce the best fit. Various configurations can be chosen for the distance metric and matrix path.

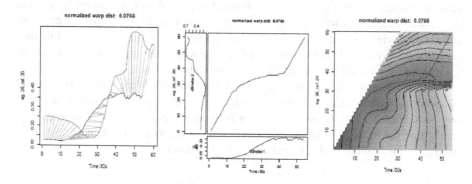

Fig. 6. Three views of a warp between sternum plots of an example and a reference example

Plotting the warp is a good way of determining the configurations producing the most appropriate warp. The 3 plots in **Fig. 6** show different representations of the warp of example 26 against example 20. The chosen step configuration is asymmetric which is why the density plot is missing the upper left corner.

Having carried out pre-processing on the raw data, further work is necessary to fit a model to categorise movement types. Broadly, there are two approaches for categorising the motion; the first being clustering based on likeness or otherwise to other labelled data and the second being to create models representing proper and improper movements. Both methods would involve the analysis of a sequence of events, each event having a context i.e. time series with a number of independent parameters such as body segment angles. The difficulty is to identify anomalies in a set of contexts and for this reason it is necessary to reduce or eliminate the time dimension.

The less complicated approach is to use transduction to categorise by association though it may not supply intuitive reasons for improper movements, which limits the usefulness of a diagnosis. Clustering algorithms use similarity or difference measurements between data points to classify points into groups. There are many different possibilities for the way of measuring similarity. Euclidean distance is a commonly used metric. kNN is the transductive method chosen based on the background reading and its implementation is described in section 4.6.

Using induction to create a model is more complicated but may give more information about the reasons for an improper movement. A method used in some studies is Hidden Markov Model for which transition matrices could be determined for proper and improper movements transitioning between the key intermediate stages of the action. However this requires the identification of those key 'hidden states'. Janssen et al [20] discuss four phases of the sit-to-stand motion identified by Shenkman et al [21] but note the major influence in characteristics of a sit-to-stand action in a range of studies where chair heights and types varied.

Decision trees have the advantage of giving an intuitive explanation of the reason for a prediction model, the most important attribute being at the top of the tree. However, decision tree models may vary widely with different data sets so random forests are appropriate particularly with small data sets. Random forests are formed by applying decision trees on bootstrapped examples chosen from the data pool. Averaging the results leads to lower variance and this method known as bagging maximises the use of the available data for producing a model and validating it. Random forests can be configured in various ways, using randomly chosen subsets of attributes up to the full complement and can be averaged over any number of sample selections without causing over-fitting.

The data sets available in this project are limited and any prediction method should be tested using data examples and comparing real outcomes with predictions. This may be achieved using cross-validation or bagging methods. The advantage of bagging is that the model can be averaged over a large number of random samples thus making the most of labelled data and also reducing variance.

4   Evaluation

4.1   Extracting Action Data

The Data collected includes in most cases standing in front of the sensor while waiting for Kinect to recognize the body joints, then assuming the seated position before carrying out the action of standing up. There may then be trailing actions which, along with any data recorded before the action, should be trimmed from the data. Functions were written in order to programmatically retrieve the required data. Doing this programmatically means that some rules need to be decided which may be fairly complicated in order to be applied correctly to all data sets. However, it is useful to be able to prepare the data automatically so that it is somewhat uniform. The two data measurement techniques used, namely with subject face-on to sensor and 45° angled, are considered completely separately because the 3-d data measurements produced are unrelated. The idea is to produce two sets of results for comparison.

In order to remove any preliminary movement from the data sets, the variation of values of the distance of the head from the sensor is used. In normal circumstances, the seated position places the head at its furthest distance from the sensor during the sensor-facing experiments and furthest to the right of the sensor during the angled experiments. Before searching for the start point, a minimum point is verified in the majority of cases where the participant started from a standing position. In the 3 cases where the participant started seated, this minimum value is ignored.

Similarly to the determination of starting, the end point is determined programmatically but using the height of the sternum which is expected to increase following the start of the action and reach a steady value at the end of the action. When height values stay within a small distance of each other for more than 10 readings (1/3 of a second) this is taken as the end of the movement. Typical plots of the sternum height are shown below before and after data excision.

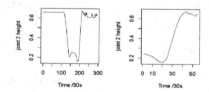

Fig. 7. A sternum plot before and after start and finish indexing

4.2   Warp Distance Matrix

Using one of the data sets as a reference, time warping was obtained based on the height of the sternum joint during the action. The reference example used was example 20 which corresponds to User2-2 and User2-5 in the face-on and 45° aspects and is compatible with all other examples for the purpose of warping. The sternum is chosen as the reference joint for the warp because it is central and most representative of the time sequence of the whole body movement.

Having calculated the warp indices for each example data set, the sternum-based warp is used to map the time series data from the remaining joints with their corresponding joint from the reference example. By this method, difference measurements are calculated between the mapped measurements and summed over the full period. The normalized distance for each joint and axis is calculated by averaging with respect to time elapsed. Thus a 3-dimensional matrix of distances is created with a single value for each joint in each of 3 axes. These values are used as attributes in building decision trees and the other predictive algorithms.

4.3   Classification

For the purpose of this study, all actions performed by normal participants were initially labelled as not faulty. The examples 1-12 corresponding to the 3 participants who performed faulty standing actions are labelled as FALSE, and examples 13-105 are labelled as TRUE. Although some of the normal participants were assessed with minor faults, the training algorithms will use the more exaggerated faults in the creation of models with the hope of assessing the other examples.

4.4   Decision Trees

The decision trees built with all of the data from each of the two data sets give only one classification error for the face-on data tree and none for the other tree. These trees show the important attributes used to match the trees to the data and distinguish actions labelled faulty. The values however are only relevant to the data set produced against the reference example and have no meaning as absolute values. The closer the value to 0, the more alike that attribute is to that of the reference example after normalization. The figure below shows the trees built from the two sets of data with attribute values at decision points described by axis and joint location. These trees model the full data sets but are not validated and it can be assumed that that the data is over-fitted.

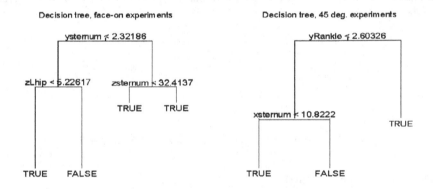

Fig. 8. Decision tree plots showing dimension and joint of decision splits

Rather than using k-fold cross-validation and averaging error estimation, the random forest algorithm is a better method for prediction and evaluation using decision trees. Random forest results follow this sub-section.

4.5   Random Forests

Random forests were grown with the parameters: maximum number of nodes, number of attributes for decision trees, and number of trees to grow. Best results were obtained with trees of size 3. All attributes from the frames were used which includes 10 joints in x and y axes for face-on data and all 3 axes for 45° data.

The confusion matrices show out-of-bag prediction error rates of 6.7% and 4.8% respectively for the two data sets, almost all of the errors coming from the FALSE classifications. In this case, error rates for false positive classification (classifying a FALSE result as TRUE) were 58% and 33% respectively. These results may vary using different seeds as the process is stochastic. In fact the 45° data set consistently showed better classification of faulty actions. Given the high rate of correct classification of non-faulty actions, greater than 50% correct classification of faulty actions results in the low overall out-of-bag prediction error rates stated (see tables below).

Table 1. Face-on random forest results 45° random forest results

	FALSE	TRUE	error		FALSE	TRUE	error
FALSE	5	7	0.58333	FALSE	8	4	0.33333
TRUE	0	92	0	TRUE	1	91	0.01087

Using proximity matrices produced by the random forest algorithm which is a square matrix of distances between every pair of examples, a multi-dimensional scaling plot can be produced which graphically demonstrates distances of examples where most are clustered closely. This shows a trend in the faulty examples because the random forest was able to distinguish them successfully; but also some examples of the non-faulty trials which lie outside of the main cluster. The 45° data shows good clustering of a group of faulty trials some distance from the main cluster of non-faulty examples.

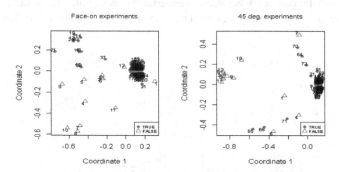

Fig. 9. Labelled Multi-Dimensional Scaling plots of Random Forest distances

In the face-on plot in Fig. 9 the 11 examples in the top left are outside of the normal cluster, identified in the plot by their data example numbers. In the 45° plot the 3 examples in the bottom centre are outside of the normal cluster. These represent examples labelled as normal which show some abnormalities according to the algorithm.

4.6   K-Nearest Neighbours with Bagging

The k-Nearest Neighbours algorithm was used on the scaled attribute data with a bagged sample over 500 sample selections and the out-of-bag predictions averaged to produce a confusion matrix. The implementation stores predicted results for out-of-bag samples on each bag selection. After 500 selections each example is awarded a classification based on which classification was predicted more often for that example. The following error rates are produced with k=2 giving 1.9% and 0 out-of-bag prediction error rates respectively.

Table 2. Face-on kNN results, k=2 45° kNN results, k=2

	FALSE	TRUE	error		FALSE	TRUE	error
FALSE	11	1	0.083333	FALSE	12	0	0
TRUE	1	91	0.010870	TRUE	0	92	0

The actions of a single user may be expected to be close to one another so using a higher value of k may give a more realistic error rate. Using k=5 implies a majority of 3 neighbours in the training set determine the result of the test set. Table 3 shows the results with k=5, giving 4.8% and 0.96% error rates.

Table 3. Face-on kNN results, k=5 45° kNN results, k=5

	FALSE	TRUE	error		FALSE	TRUE	error
FALSE	7	5	0.41667	FALSE	11	1	0.083333
TRUE	0	92	0	TRUE	0	92	0

kNN uses a distance matrix between every example set of attributes and every other to calculate the nearest neighbours. This can be plotted using multi-dimensional scaling

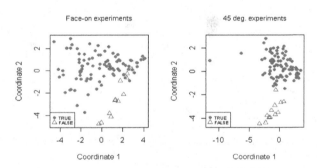

Fig. 10. Labelled Multi-Dimensional Scaling plot of kNN distances

Dynamic time warp distances are used as the attributes and each example has a TRUE or FALSE label. The plot shown in Fig. 10 shows why the results for kNN bagging prediction error are so low, particularly for the 45° experiments. The clusters for faulty and non-faulty actions are well defined.

5   Discussion and Conclusions

We have presented an experiment for collecting human movement data using the Kinect depth sensor motion camera with emphasis on variation in movement due to back pain. Various machine-learning techniques were used to analyse the data and effectively applied to identify anomalies. A general method of comparing data sets acquired from experiments was devised. Results show that attribute sets created using a technique based on dynamic time warping can be successfully used in machine-learning algorithms to identify anomalous actions. Results using random forests and using k-Nearest Neighbours with bagging showed good clustering and good out-of-bag validation results with overall error rates below 7%. Best results were obtained on the 45° experiments which when analysed using kNN with k=5 give an overall error rate of <1% and false positive rate of only 8% meaning 92% of the anomalous actions were identified. Classification predictions could be made using the models created against new examples of the same action. Multi-dimensional scaling techniques were used to visualize distance matrices produced by the two methods.

Further work could use machine-learning methods to detect the action within a full data set. This is an important part of the overall process. It is important to build a larger database of experimental data including clinical participants with back pain. In such a case the heuristic approach we used to identify the offset of the action within a data set becomes less feasible. While matching a part of the overall action using machine-learning, the same process based on dynamic time warping could be used to identify anomalies. In this case, the dynamic time warp would have to be free to match the start rather than anchored to the start of the data. Using a non-anchored configuration with dynamic time warping was not found to be satisfactory so a new approach to the DTW algorithm could be considered. Other models such as Hidden Markov Models could also be considered for this approach.

References

1. Natural User Interface for Kinect Microsoft. http://msdn.microsoft.com/en-us/library/hh855352.aspx
2. Bragaglia, S., Di Monte, S., Mello, P.: A Distributed system using MS kinect and event calculus for adaptive physiotherapist rehabilitation. In: Eighth International Conference on Complex, Intelligent and Software Intensive Systems 2014 (2014)
3. Balagué, F., et al.: Non-specific low back pain. The Lancet **379**(9814), 482–491 (2012)
4. Cappozzo, A., Catani, F., Leardini, A., Croce, U.: Position and orientation in space of bones during movement: anatomical frame definition and determination. Clinical Biomechanics (1995)
5. Han, S., Achar, M., Lee, S., Pena-Mora, F.: Empirical assessment of RGB-D sensor on motion capture and action recognition for construction worker monitoring. Visualization in Engineering, June 2014
6. Shingade, A., Ghotkar, A.: Animation of 3D Human Model Using Markerless Motion Capture Applied to Sports. International Journal of Computer Graphics & Animation, January 2014

7. Shotton, J., Fitzgibbon, A., Cook, M., Sharp, T., Finocchio, M., Moore, R., Kipman, A., Blake, A.: Real-time human pose recognition in parts from single depth images. In: Proceedings of the IEEE Conference on Computer Vision and Pattern Recognition, CVPR 2011 (2011)
8. Sinthanayothin, C., Wongwaen, N., Bholsithi, W.: Skeleton Tracking using Kinect Sensor & Displaying in 3D Virtual Scene. International Journal of Advancements in Computing Technology (IJACT), June 2013
9. Elgendi, M., Picon, F., Magnenat-Thalmann, N.: Real-Time Speed Detection of Hand Gesture using Kinect. Institute for Media Innovation paper
10. Schonauer, C., Pintaric, T., Kaufmann, H.: Chronic pain rehabilitation with a serious game using multimodal input. In: Proceedings of International Conference on Virtual Rehabilitation (June 2011)
11. Bonnechere, B., Jansen, B., Silva, P., Bouzahouene, H., Sholukha, V., Cornelius, J., Rooze, M., Van Sint Jan, S.: Determination of the precision and accuracy of morphological measurements using the Kinect sensor: comparison with standard stereophotogrammetry. Ergonomics, April 2014
12. Bonnechere, B., Jansen, B., Silva, P., Bouzahouene, H., Omelina, L., Cornelius, J., Rooze, M., Van Sint Jan, S.: Can the Kinect sensors be used for Motion Analysis?. Transaction on Electrical and Electronic Circuits and Systems, January 2013
13. Okada, S., Hasegawa, O.: Motion recognition based on dynamic time warping method with self-organizing incremental neural network. In: Proceeding of 19th International Conference on Pattern Recognition, ICPR 2008 (2008)
14. Ratanamahatana, C., Keogh, E.: Everything you know about Dynamic Time Warping is Wrong. University of California paper
15. Herzog, D., Kruger, V., Grest, D.: Parametric Hidden Markov Models for Recognition and Synthesis of Movements. Aalborg University Copenhagen paper
16. Chandola, V., Banerjee, A., Kumar, V.: Anomaly Detection: a Survey. ACM Computing Surveys, September 2009
17. Brandao, A., Fernandes, L., Clua, E.: A comparative analysis of classification algorithms applied to M5AIE-extracted human poses. In: Proceedings of SBGames (October 2013)
18. Shotton, J., Girshick, R., Firzgibbon, A., Sharp, T., Cook, M., Finocchio, M., Moore, R., Kohli, P., Criminisi, A., Kipman, A., Blake, A.: Efficient human pose estimation from single depth images. In: Advances in Computer Vision and Pattern Recognition (2013)
19. Rogez, G., Rihan, J., Ramalingam, S., Orrite, C., Tor, P.H.: Randomized trees for human pose detection. In: IEEE Computer Society Conference 2008 Computer Vision and Pattern Recognition (2008)
20. Janssen, W., Bussmann, H., Stam, H.: Determinants of the Sit-To-Stand Movement: A review. Physical Therapy Journal (2002)
21. Shenkman, M., Berger, R., Riley, P., et al.: Whole-body movements during rising to standing from sitting. Physical Therapy Journal (1990)

Additive Regularization of Topic Models for Topic Selection and Sparse Factorization

Konstantin Vorontsov[1](✉), Anna Potapenko[2], and Alexander Plavin[3]

[1] Moscow Institute of Physics and Technology,
Dorodnicyn Computing Centre of RAS,
National Research University Higher School of Economics, Moscow, Russia
voron@forecsys.ru
[2] National Research University Higher School of Economics, Moscow, Russia
anya_potapenko@mail.ru
[3] Moscow Institute of Physics and Technology, Moscow, Russia
alexander@plav.in

Abstract. Probabilistic topic modeling of text collections is a powerful tool for statistical text analysis. Determining the optimal number of topics remains a challenging problem in topic modeling. We propose a simple entropy regularization for topic selection in terms of *Additive Regularization of Topic Models* (ARTM), a multicriteria approach for combining regularizers. The entropy regularization gradually eliminates insignificant and linearly dependent topics. This process converges to the correct value on semi-real data. On real text collections it can be combined with sparsing, smoothing and decorrelation regularizers to produce a sequence of models with different numbers of well interpretable topics.

Keywords: Probabilistic topic modeling · Regularization · Probabilistic latent sematic analysis · Topic selection · EM-algorithm

1 Introduction

Topic modeling is a rapidly developing branch of statistical text analysis [1]. Topic model reveals a hidden thematic structure of the text collection and finds a highly compressed representation of each document by a set of its topics. From the statistical point of view, a probabilistic topic model defines each topic by a multinomial distribution over words, and then describes each document with a multinomial distribution over topics. Such models appear to be highly useful for many applications including information retrieval, classification, categorization, summarization and segmentation of texts. More ideas and applications are outlined in the survey [2].

Determining an appropriate number of topics for a given collection is an important problem in probabilistic topic modeling. Choosing too few topics results in too general topics, while choosing too many ones leads to insignificant and highly similar topics. *Hierarchical Dirichlet Process*, HDP [3,4] is the

© Springer International Publishing Switzerland 2015
A. Gammerman et al. (Eds.): SLDS 2015, LNAI 9047, pp. 193–202, 2015.
DOI: 10.1007/978-3-319-17091-6_14

most popular Bayesian approach for number of topics optimization. Nevertheless, HDP sometimes gives very unstable number of topics and requires a complicated inference if combined with other models.

To address the above problems we use a non-Bayesian semi-probabilistic approach — *Additive Regularization of Topic Models*, ARTM [5,6]. Learning a topic model from a document collection is an ill-posed problem of approximate stochastic matrix factorization, which has an infinite set of solutions. In order to choose a better solution, we maximize the log-likelihood with a weighted sum of regularization penalty terms. These regularizers formalize additional requirements for a topic model. Unlike Bayesian approach, ARTM avoids excessive probabilistic assumptions and simplifies the inference of multi-objective topic models.

The aim of the paper is to develop topic selection technique for ARTM based on entropy regularization and to study its combinations with other useful regularizers such as sparsing, smoothing and decorrelation.

The rest of the paper is organized as follows. In section 2 we introduce a general ARTM framework, the regularized EM-algorithm, and a set of regularizers including the entropy regularizer for topic selection. In section 3 we use semi-real dataset with known number of topics to show that the entropy regularizer converges to the correct number of topics, gives a more stable result than HDP, and gradually removes linearly dependent topics. In section 4 the experiments on real dataset give an insight that optimization of the number of topics is in its turn an ill-posed problem and has many solutions. We propose additional criteria to choose the best of them. In section 5 we discuss advantages and limitations of ARTM with topic selection regularization.

2   Additive Regularization of Topic Models

Let D denote a set (collection) of texts and W denote a set (vocabulary) of all terms that appear in these texts. A term can be a single word or a keyphrase. Each document $d \in D$ is a sequence of n_d terms $(w_1, \ldots, w_{n_d})$ from W. Denote n_{dw} the number of times the term w appears in the document d.

Assume that each term occurrence in each document refers to some latent topic from a finite set of topics T. Then text collection is considered as a sample of triples (w_i, d_i, t_i), $i = 1, \ldots, n$ drawn independently from a discrete distribution $p(w, d, t)$ over a finite space $W \times D \times T$. Terms w and documents d are observable variables, while topics t are latent variables. Following the "bag of words" model, we represent each document as a subset of terms $d \subset W$.

A probabilistic topic model describes how terms of a document are generated from a mixture of given distributions $\phi_{wt} = p(w \mid t)$ and $\theta_{td} = p(t \mid d)$:

$$p(w \mid d) = \sum_{t \in T} p(w \mid t) p(t \mid d) = \sum_{t \in T} \phi_{wt} \theta_{td}. \tag{1}$$

Learning a topic model is an inverse problem to find distributions ϕ_{wt} and θ_{td} given a collection D. This problem is equivalent to finding an approximate representation of frequency matrix $F = \left(\frac{n_{dw}}{n_d}\right)_{W \times D}$ with a product $F \approx \Phi\Theta$ of two unknown matrices — the matrix $\Phi = (\phi_{wt})_{W \times T}$ of *term probabilities for the topics* and the matrix $\Theta = (\theta_{td})_{T \times D}$ of *topic probabilities for the documents*. Matrices F, Φ and Θ are *stochastic*, that is, their columns are non-negative, normalized, and represent discrete distributions. Usually $|T| \ll |D|$ and $|T| \ll |W|$.

In *Probabilistic Latent Semantic Analysis*, PLSA [7] a topic model (1) is learned by log-likelihood maximization with linear constrains:

$$L(\Phi, \Theta) = \sum_{d \in D} \sum_{w \in d} n_{dw} \ln \sum_{t \in T} \phi_{wt} \theta_{td} \to \max_{\Phi, \Theta}; \tag{2}$$

$$\sum_{w \in W} \phi_{wt} = 1, \quad \phi_{wt} \ge 0; \qquad \sum_{t \in T} \theta_{td} = 1, \quad \theta_{td} \ge 0. \tag{3}$$

The product $\Phi\Theta$ is defined up to a linear transformation $\Phi\Theta = (\Phi S)(S^{-1}\Theta)$, where matrices $\Phi' = \Phi S$ and $\Theta' = S^{-1}\Theta$ are also stochastic. Therefore, in a general case the maximization problem (2) has an infinite set of solutions.

In *Additive Regularization of Topic Models*, ARTM [5] a topic model (1) is learned by maximization of a linear combination of the log-likelihood (2) and r regularization penalty terms $R_i(\Phi, \Theta)$, $i = 1, \ldots, r$ with nonnegative *regularization coefficients* τ_i:

$$R(\Phi, \Theta) = \sum_{i=1}^{r} \tau_i R_i(\Phi, \Theta), \qquad L(\Phi, \Theta) + R(\Phi, \Theta) \to \max_{\Phi, \Theta}. \tag{4}$$

The Karush–Kuhn–Tucker conditions for (4), (3) give (under some technical restrictions) the necessary conditions for the local maximum in a form of the system of equations [6]:

$$p_{tdw} = \frac{\phi_{wt} \theta_{td}}{\sum_{s \in T} \phi_{ws} \theta_{sd}}; \tag{5}$$

$$\phi_{wt} \propto \left(n_{wt} + \phi_{wt} \frac{\partial R}{\partial \phi_{wt}} \right)_+; \qquad n_{wt} = \sum_{d \in D} n_{dw} p_{tdw}; \tag{6}$$

$$\theta_{td} \propto \left(n_{td} + \theta_{td} \frac{\partial R}{\partial \theta_{td}} \right)_+; \qquad n_{td} = \sum_{w \in d} n_{dw} p_{tdw}; \tag{7}$$

where $(z)_+ = \max\{z, 0\}$. Auxiliary variables p_{tdw} are interpreted as conditional probabilities of topics for each word in each document, $p_{tdw} = p(t \mid d, w)$.

The system of equations (5)–(7) can be solved by various numerical methods. Particularly, the simple-iteration method is equivalent to the EM algorithm, which is typically used in practice. The pseudocode of Algorithm 2.1 shows its rational implementation, in which E-step (5) is incorporated into M-step (6)–(7), thus avoiding storage of 3D-array p_{tdw}.

The strength of ARTM is that each additive regularization term results in a simple additive modification of the M-step. Many models previously developed within Bayesian framework can be easier reinterpreted, inferred and combined using ARTM framework [6], [8].

Algorithm 2.1. The regularized EM-algorithm for ARTM

Input: document collection D, number of topics $|T|$;
Output: Φ, Θ;
1 initialize vectors ϕ_t, θ_d randomly;
2 **repeat**
3      $n_{wt} := 0$, $n_{td} := 0$ for all $d \in D$, $w \in W$, $t \in T$;
4   **for all** $d \in D$, $w \in d$
5          $p(w \mid d) := \sum_{t \in T} \phi_{wt}\theta_{td}$;
6   increase n_{wt} and n_{td} by $n_{dw}\phi_{wt}\theta_{td}/p(w \mid d)$ for all $t \in T$;
7      $\phi_{wt} \propto \left(n_{wt} + \phi_{wt}\frac{\partial R}{\partial \phi_{wt}}\right)_+$ for all $w \in W$, $t \in T$;
8      $\theta_{td} \propto \left(n_{td} + \theta_{td}\frac{\partial R}{\partial \theta_{td}}\right)_+$ for all $t \in T$, $d \in D$;
9 **until** Φ and Θ *converge*;

To find a reasonable number of topics we propose to start from a wittingly large number and gradually eliminate insignificant or excessive topics from the model. To do this we perform the entropy-based sparsing of distribution $p(t) = \sum_d p(d)\theta_{td}$ over topics by maximizing KL-divergence between $p(t)$ and the uniform distribution over topics [8]:

$$R(\Theta) = \frac{n}{|T|} \sum_{t \in T} \ln \sum_{d \in D} p(d)\theta_{td} \;\rightarrow\; \max.$$

Substitution of this regularizer into the M-step equation (7) gives

$$\theta_{td} \propto \left(n_{td} - \tau \frac{n}{|T|} \frac{n_d}{n_t}\theta_{td}\right)_+.$$

Replacing θ_{td} in the right-hand side by its unbiased estimate $\frac{n_{td}}{n_d}$ gives an interpretation of the regularized M-step as a row sparser for the matrix Θ:

$$\theta_{td} \propto n_{td}\left(1 - \tau \frac{n}{|T|n_t}\right)_+.$$

If n_t counter in the denominator is small, then all elements of a row will be set to zero, and the corresponding topic t will be eliminated from the model. Values τ are normally in $[0, 1]$ due to the normalizing factor $\frac{n}{|T|}$.

Our aim is to understand how the entropy-based topic sparsing works and to study its behavior in combinations with other regularizers. We use a set of three regularizers — sparsing, smoothing and decorrelation proposed in [6] to divide topics into two types, $T = S \sqcup B$: domain-specific topics S and background topics B.

Domain-specific topics $t \in S$ contain terms of domain areas. They are supposed to be sparse and weakly correlated, because a document is usually related to a small number of topics, and a topic usually consists of a small number of domain-specific terms. Sparsing regularization is based on KL-divergence maximization between distributions ϕ_{wt}, θ_{td} and corresponding uniform distributions.

Decorrelation is based on covariance minimization between all topic pairs and helps to exclude common lexis from domain-specific topics [9].

Background topics $t \in B$ contain common lexis words. They are smoothed and appear in many documents. Smoothing regularization minimizes KL-divergence between distributions ϕ_{wt}, θ_{td} and corresponding uniform distributions. Smoothing regularization is equivalent to a maximum a posteriori estimation for LDA, *Latent Dirichlet Allocation* topic model [10].

The combination of all mentioned regularizers leads to the M-step formulas:

$$\phi_{wt} \propto \left(n_{wt} - \beta_0 \underbrace{\beta_w[t \in S]}_{\substack{\text{sparsing} \\ \text{specific} \\ \text{topic}}} + \beta_1 \underbrace{\beta_w[t \in B]}_{\substack{\text{smoothing} \\ \text{background} \\ \text{topic}}} - \underbrace{\gamma[t \in S]\, \phi_{wt} \sum_{s \in S \setminus t} \phi_{ws}}_{\text{topic decorrelation}} \right)_+ ; \quad (8)$$

$$\theta_{td} \propto \left(n_{td} - \alpha_0 \underbrace{\alpha_t[t \in S]}_{\substack{\text{sparsing} \\ \text{specific} \\ \text{topic}}} + \alpha_1 \underbrace{\alpha_t[t \in B]}_{\substack{\text{smoothing} \\ \text{background} \\ \text{topic}}} - \underbrace{\tau[t \in S]\frac{n}{|T|}\frac{n_d}{n_t}\theta_{td}}_{\substack{\text{topic} \\ \text{selection}}} \right)_+ ; \quad (9)$$

where regularization coefficients α_0, α_1, β_0, β_1, γ, τ are selected experimentally, distributions α_t and β_w are uniform.

3 Number of Topics Determination

In our experiments we use NIPS dataset, which contains $|D| = 1740$ English articles from the Neural Information Processing Systems conference for 12 years. We use the version, preprocessed by A. McCallum in BOW toolkit [11], where changing to low-case, punctuation elimination, and stop-words removal were performed. The length of the collection in words is $n \approx 2.3 \cdot 10^6$ and the vocabulary size is $|W| \approx 1.3 \cdot 10^4$.

In order to assess how well our approach determines the number of topics, we generate semi-real (synthetic but realistic) datasets with the known number of topics. First, we run 500 EM iterations for PLSA model with T_0 topics on NIPS dataset and generate synthetic dataset $\Pi_0 = (n^0_{dw})$ from Φ, Θ matrices of the solution: $n^0_{dw} = n_d \sum_{t \in T} \phi_{wt}\theta_{td}$. Second, we construct a parametric family of semi-real datasets $\Pi_\alpha = (n^\alpha_{dw})$ as a mixture $n^\alpha_{dw} = \alpha n_{dw} + (1-\alpha)n^0_{dw}$, where $\Pi_1 = (n_{dw})$ is the term counters matrix of the real NIPS dataset.

From synthetic to real dataset. Fig. 1 shows the dependence of revealed number of topics on the regularization coefficient τ for two families of semi-real datasets, obtained with $T_0 = 50$ and $T_0 = 25$ topics. For synthetic datasets ARTM reliably finds the true number of topics for all τ in a wide range. Note, that this range does not depend much on the number of topics T_0, chosen for datasets generation. Therefore, we conclude that an approximate value of regularization coefficient $\tau = 0.25$ from the middle of the range is recommended for determining number of topics via our approach.

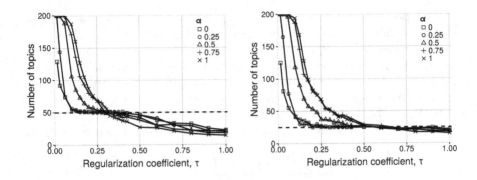

Fig. 1. ARTM for semi-real datasets with $T_0 = 50$ (left) and $T_0 = 25$ (right)

However as the data changes from synthetic Π_0 to real Π_1, the horizontal part of the curve diminishes, and for NIPS dataset there is no evidence for the "best" number of topics. This corresponds to the intuition that real text collections do not expose the "true number of topics", but can be reasonably described by models with different number of topics.

Comparison of ARTM and HDP models. In our experiments we use the implementation[1] of HDP by C. Wang and D. Blei. Fig. 2(b) demonstrates that the revealed number of topics depends on the parameter of the model not only for ARTM approach (Fig. 1, $\alpha = 1$ case), but for HDP as well. Varying the concentration coefficient γ of Dirichlet process, we can get any number of topics.

Fig. 2(a) presents a bunch of curves, obtained for several random starts of HDP with default $\gamma = 0.5$. Here we observe the instability of the method in two ways. Firstly, there are incessant fluctuations of number of topics from iteration to iteration. Secondly, the results for several random starts of the algorithm significantly differ. Comparing Fig. 2(a) and Fig. 2(c) we conclude that our approach is much more stable in both ways. The numbers of topics, determined by two approaches with recommended values of parameters, are similar.

Elimination of linearly dependent topics. One more important question is which topics are selected for exclusion from the model. To work it out, we extend the synthetic dataset Π_0 to model linear dependencies between the topics. 50 topics obtained by PLSA are enriched by 20 convex combinations of some of them; and new vector columns are added to Φ matrix. The corresponding rows in Θ matrix are filled with random values drawn from a bag of elements of original Θ, in order to make values in the new rows similarly distributed. These matrices are then used as synthetic dataset for regularized EM-algorithm with topic selection to check whether original or combined topics remain. Fig. 2(d) demonstrates that the topic selection regularizer eliminates excessive linear combinations, while more sparse and diverse topics of the original model remain.

---

[1] http://www.cs.princeton.edu/~chongw/resource.html.

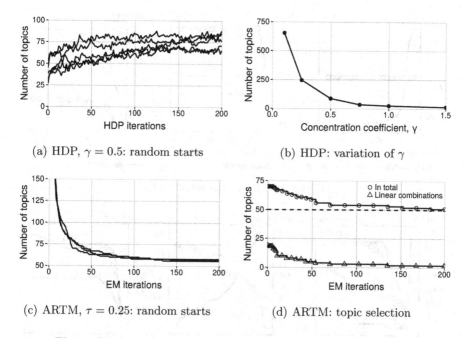

(a) HDP, $\gamma = 0.5$: random starts

(b) HDP: variation of γ

(c) ARTM, $\tau = 0.25$: random starts

(d) ARTM: topic selection

Fig. 2. ARTM and HDP models for determining number of topics

4   Topic Selection in a Sparse Decorrelated Model

The aim of the experiments in this section is to show that the proposed topic selection regularizer works well in combination with other regularizers. The topic model quality is evaluated by multiple criteria.

The *hold-out perplexity* $\mathscr{P} = \exp\left(-\frac{1}{n}L(\Phi, \Theta)\right)$ is the exponential average of the likelihood on a test set of documents; the lower, the better.

The *sparsity* is measured by the ratio of zero elements in matrices Φ and Θ over domain-specific topics S.

The *background ratio* $\mathscr{B} = \frac{1}{n}\sum_{d \in D}\sum_{w \in d}\sum_{t \in B} n_{dw}p(t \mid d, w)$ is a ratio of background terms over the collection. It takes values from 0 to 1. If $\mathscr{B} \to 0$ then the model doesn't distinguishes common lexis from domain-specific terms. If $\mathscr{B} \to 1$ then the model is degenerated, possibly due to excessive sparsing.

The *lexical kernel* W_t of a topic t is a set of terms that distinguish the topic t from the others: $W_t = \{w : p(t \mid w) > \delta\}$. In our experiments $\delta = 0.25$. We use the notion of lexical kernel to define two characteristics of topic interpetability.

The *purity* $\sum_{w \in W_t} p(w \mid t)$ shows the cumulative ratio of kernel in the topic.

The *contrast* $\frac{1}{|W_t|}\sum_{w \in W_t} p(t \mid w)$ shows the diversity of the topic.

The *coherence of a topic* $\mathscr{C}_t^k = \frac{2}{k(k-1)}\sum_{i=1}^{k-1}\sum_{j=i}^{k} \mathrm{PMI}(w_i, w_j)$ is defined as the average pointwise mutual information over word pairs, where w_i is the i-th word in the list of k most probable words in the topic. Coherence is commonly

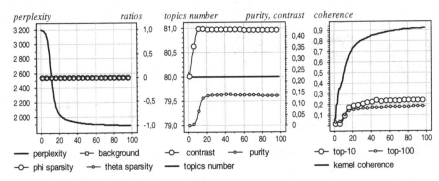

Fig. 3. Baseline: LDA topic model

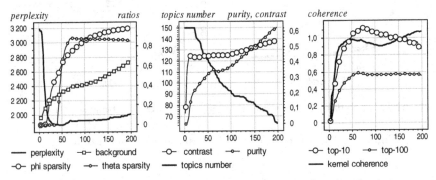

Fig. 4. Combination of sparsing, decorrelation, and topic selection

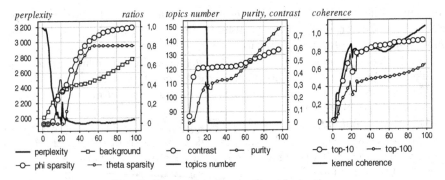

Fig. 5. Sequential phases of regularization

used as the interpretability measure of the topic model [12]. We estimate the coherence for top-10, top-100, and besides, for lexical kernels.

Finally, we define the corresponding measures of purity, contrast, and coherence for the topic model by averaging over domain-specific topics $t \in S$.

Further we represent each quality measure of the topic model as a function of the iteration step and use several charts for better visibility. Fig. 3 provides such charts for a standard LDA model, while Fig. 5 and Fig. 4 present regularized models with domain-specific and background topics. We use constant parameters for smoothing background topics $|S| = 10$, $\alpha_t = 0.8$, $\beta_w = 0.1$.

The model depicted in Fig. 4 is an example of simultaneous sparsing, decorrelating and topic selection. Decorrelation coefficient grows linearly during the first 60 iterations up to the highest value $\gamma = 200000$ that does not deteriorate the model. Topic selection with $\tau = 0.3$ is turned on later, after the 15-th iteration. Topic selection and decorrelation are used at alternating iterations because their effects may conflict; in charts we depict the quality measures after decorrelating iterations. To get rid of insignificant words in topics and to prepare insignificant topics for further elimination, sparsing is turned on staring from the 40-th iteration. Its coefficients α_t, β_w gradually increase to zeroize 2% of Θ elements and 9% of Φ elements each iteration. As a result, we get a sequence of models with decreasing number of sparse interpretable domain-specific topics: their purity, contrast and coherence are noticeably better then those of LDA topics.

Another regularization strategy is presented in Fig. 5. In contrast with the previous one, it has several sequential phases for work of different regularizers. Firstly, decorrelation makes topics as different as possible. Secondly, topic selection eliminates excessive topics and remains 80 topics of 150. Note, that in spite of small $\tau = 0.1$, many topics are excluded at once due to the side effect of the first phase. The remained topics are significant, and none of them manage to be excluded later on. The final phase performs both sparsing and decorrelating of the remained topics to successfully improve their interpretability.

It is curious that the number of topics 80, determined by this strategy, corresponds to the results of the previous strategy quite well. In Fig. 4 we observe two regions of perplexity deterioration. The first one concerns Θ sparsing; after that the perplexity remains stable for a long period till the 150-th iteration, when the number of topics becomes less than 80. This moment indicates that all the remained topics are needed and should not be further eliminated.

5   Conclusions

Learning a topic model from text collection is an ill-posed problem of stochastic matrix factorization. Determining the number of topics is an ill-posed problem too. In this work we develop a regularization approach to topic selection in terms of non-Bayesian ARTM framework. Starting with excessively high number of topics we gradually make them more and more sparse and decorrelated, and eliminate unnecessary topics by means of entropy regularization. This approach gives more stable results than HDP and during one learning process generates a sequence of models with quality measures trade-off. The main limitation, which should be removed in future work, is that regularization coefficients are not optimized automatically, and we have to choose the regularization strategy manually.

Acknowledgments. The work was supported by the Russian Foundation for Basic Research grants 14-07-00847, 14-07-00908, 14-07-31176, Skolkovo Institute of Science and Technology (project 081-R), and by the program of the Department of Mathematical Sciences of RAS "Algebraic and combinatoric methods of mathematical cybernetics and information systems of new generation".

References

1. Blei, D.M.: Probabilistic topic models. Communications of the ACM **55**(4), 77–84 (2012)
2. Daud, A., Li, J., Zhou, L., Muhammad, F.: Knowledge discovery through directed probabilistic topic models: a survey. Frontiers of Computer Science in China **4**(2), 280–301 (2010)
3. Teh, Y.W., Jordan, M.I., Beal, M.J., Blei, D.M.: Hierarchical Dirichlet processes. Journal of the American Statistical Association **101**(476), 1566–1581 (2006)
4. Blei, D.M., Griffiths, T.L., Jordan, M.I.: The nested chinese restaurant process and bayesian nonparametric inference of topic hierarchies. J. ACM **57**(2), 7:1–7:30 (2010)
5. Vorontsov, K.V.: Additive regularization for topic models of text collections. Doklady Mathematics **89**(3), 301–304 (2014)
6. Vorontsov, K.V., Potapenko, A.A.: Additive regularization of topic models. Machine Learning, Special Issue on Data Analysis and Intelligent Optimization (2014). doi:10.1007/s10994-014-5476-6
7. Hofmann, T.: Probabilistic latent semantic indexing. In: Proceedings of the 22nd Annual International ACM SIGIR Conference on Research and Development In Information Retrieval, pp. 50–57. ACM, New York (1999)
8. Vorontsov, K.V., Potapenko, A.A.: Tutorial on probabilistic topic modeling: additive regularization for stochastic matrix factorization. In: Ignatov, D.I., et al (eds.) AIST 2014. CCIS, vol. 436, pp. 29–46. Springer, Heidelberg (2014)
9. Tan, Y., Ou, Z.: Topic-weak-correlated latent dirichlet allocation. In: 7th International Symposium Chinese Spoken Language Processing (ISCSLP), pp. 224–228 (2010)
10. Blei, D.M., Ng, A.Y., Jordan, M.I.: Latent Dirichlet allocation. Journal of Machine Learning Research **3**, 993–1022 (2003)
11. McCallum, A.K.: Bow: A toolkit for statistical language modeling, text retrieval, classification and clustering (1996). http://www.cs.cmu.edu/~mccallum/bow
12. Newman, D., Noh, Y., Talley, E., Karimi, S., Baldwin, T.: Evaluating topic models for digital libraries. In: Proceedings of the 10th Annual Joint Conference on Digital libraries, JCDL 2010, pp. 215–224. ACM, New York (2010)

Social Web-Based Anxiety Index's Predictive Information on S&P 500 Revisited

Rapheal Olaniyan[1], Daniel Stamate[1]([⊠]), and Doina Logofatu[2]

[1] Data Science and Soft Computing Lab, Department of Computing, Goldsmiths
College, University of London, London, UK
d.stamate@gold.ac.uk
[2] Department of Computer Science, Frankfurt University of Applied Sciences,
Frankfurt, Germany

Abstract. There has been an increasing interest recently in examining the possible relationships between emotions expressed online and stock markets. Most of the previous studies claiming that emotions have predictive influence on the stock market do so by developing various machine learning predictive models, but do not validate their claims rigorously by analysing the statistical significance of their findings. In turn, the few works that attempt to statistically validate such claims suffer from important limitations of their statistical approaches. In particular, stock market data exhibit erratic volatility, and this time-varying volatility makes any possible relationship between these variables non-linear, which tends to statistically invalidate linear based approaches. Our work tackles this kind of limitations, and extends linear frameworks by proposing a new, non-linear statistical approach that accounts for non-linearity and heteroscedasticity.

1 Introduction

According to the investment theory, stock market is operating under the Efficient Market Hypothesis (EMH), in which stock prices are assumed to incorporate and reflect all known information. Sprenger et al. [15] strongly disagree with EMH by saying that the market is inefficient and therefore abnormal returns can be earned. In search for abnormal earning, researchers now 'listen' to news and mine online aggregated social data all in the course for these attractive profits.

Schumaker and Chen [14] are among the early researchers to investigate whether emotions can predict the stock market. Machine learning algorithms such as SVM, Naive Bayes, etc, are utilised to develop predictive models used to claim that financial news have a statistically significant impact on the stock market. Bollen et al. [4] present an interesting machine learning based approach to examine if emotions influence stock prices. Their results support the claim that emotions do influence the stock market.

The linear Granger causality analysis is employed by Gilbert and Karahalios [8] as a method to illustrate that web blog contained sentiment has predictive

© Springer International Publishing Switzerland 2015
A. Gammerman et al. (Eds.): SLDS 2015, LNAI 9047, pp. 203–213, 2015.
DOI: 10.1007/978-3-319-17091-6_15

information on the stock market, but this method proved to have clear limitations as explained later in this paper. A linear model and the Granger causality test are used also by Mao et al. [12] to examine the influence of social blogs on the stock market. The authors do raise some concerns about the possible non-linear nature in the relationship, but such concerns are not further explored. The non-linear Granger causality test, which relies on a Self-Organising Fuzzy Neural Network model, is unpopular in this area of work as it is thought not to be strong enough to capture volatile stock market movements, as revealed by Jahidul et al. [10]. Mittal and Goel [13] use machine learning algorithms to investigate if stock blogs, as a proxy for news, can predict this complex financial movement. Their findings make the same claim that stock blogs can be used to predict stock prices, and they use some level of accuracy of the predictive models to support their results.

Stock market is highly volatile. Therefore, capturing its movement and identifying relationships between stock prices and possible predictive variables require the use of appropriate approaches. These approaches should normally meet two requirements. The first requirement is to generate models for prediction, and the second requirement is to rigorously prove the models' predictive value.

As illustrated earlier in this section, there is a growing research work trying to establish that online expressed emotions have predictive information on the stock market. Most of these works fulfill the first requirement by devising and proposing various predictive models, but very few works attempt to fulfill also the second requirement by rigorously / statistically proving the predictive value of these models. Gilbert and Karahalios [8] are among the very few that do consider both requirements, by proposing a statistical approach, which is based on the Granger causality analysis and Monte Carlo simulations. We recognise the large interest and potential generated by [8] in inspiring further research that demonstrates the link between the online expressed emotions and the stock market. Our work builds upon the approach presented in [8], and does so by critically analysing it, by clearly identifying its drawbacks and limitations, by tackling these limitations and by extending the approach and the results presented in the paper. As such, we establish our findings on data which has been obtained from the [8] 's authors website.

The remainder of this paper is organized as follows. Section 2 briefly revisits the empirical analysis of Gilbert and Karahalios [8]. In particular it presents the data, and the Anxiety Index's building process. In addition, we discuss the essential limitations of the approach of [8], and provide and discuss the results of our alternative Monte Carlo simulations. Section 3 presents our new statistical based approach which captures efficiently the stock market volatility, and the predictive information relationship direction between stock prices and emotion. Section 4 entails our findings and conclusion.

2   Discussion on the Web Blog Based Anxiety Index

Four stationary daily time series variables were explored in Gilbert and Karahalios [8]: the Anxiety Index (AI), the stock return, and two control variables which are the trading volume and the stock volatility. All the variables were generated from the stock market data S&P 500, except for the Anxiety Index AI.

[8] introduced the Anxiety Index using 20 million posts and blogs from Live-Journal, that had been gathered within three periods of 2008: January 25th to June 13th; August 1st to September 30th, and November 3rd to December 18th. Two sets of linguistic classifiers trained with a LiveJournal mood corpus from 2004 were employed to build the Anxiety Index metric. First, a corpus of 624,905 mood-annotated LiveJournal posts from Balog et al. [3] was used. 12,923 posts that users tagged as 'anxious', 'worried', 'nervous' or 'fearful' were extracted. Then two classifiers were trained to distinguish between 'anxious' and 'non anxious' posts. The first classifier $C1$, which was a boosted decision tree, as introduced by Yoav and Robert [16], used the most informative 100 word stems as features. The second classifier $C2$ consisting of a bagged Complement Naive Bayes model [11], used 46,438 words obtained from the 2004 corpus mentioned above. $C1_t$ and $C2_t$ were defined as the standard proportions of posts classified as 'anxious' by $C1$ and $C2$, respectively, during the closing trading day t. $C1_t$ and $C2_t$ were integrated in the series C defined by $C_t = max(C1_t, C2_t)$. The Anxiety Index was finally defined as the series $A_t = log(C_{t+1}) - log(C_t)$. 174 values were generated for this series from the available data.

The S&P 500 index was used as a proxy for the stock market, and was employed to generate three variables participating in the development of predictive models, namely the stock market acceleration metric denoted as M, the return volatility denoted as V, and the volume of stock trading denoted as Q. The stock return at time t was defined as $R_t = log(SP_{t+1}) - log(SP_t)$, where SP is the closing stock price. The stock market acceleration metric was obtained from the stock return as $M_t = R_{t+1} - R_t$. The stock return volatility was expressed as $V_t = R_{t+1} * R_{t+1} - R_t * R_t$, and finally Q_t was expressed as the first difference of the lagged trading volume.

2.1   Findings and Limitations

The two OLS models employed by Gilbert and Karahalios in [8] are:

$$M1: M_t = \alpha + \Sigma_{i=1}^{3}\beta_i M_{t-i} + \Sigma_{i=1}^{3}\gamma_i V_{t-i} + \Sigma_{i=1}^{3}\delta_i Q_{t-i} + \epsilon_t \qquad (1)$$

$$M2: M_t = \alpha + \Sigma_{i=1}^{3}\beta_i M_{t-i} + \Sigma_{i=1}^{3}\gamma_i V_{t-i} + \Sigma_{i=1}^{3}\delta_i Q_{t-i} +$$
$$\Sigma_{i=1}^{3}\eta_i A_{t-i} + \epsilon_t \qquad (2)$$

The models $M1$ and $M2$ were used to measure the influence of the Anxiety Index on stock prices. The difference in the models is that $M1$ does not include the Anxiety Index variable, it only uses the lagged market variables mentioned above in this section. $M2$ adds the lagged Anxiety Index to the $M1$'s variables. If $M2$ performs better than $M1$, one could conclude that the Anxiety Index has predictive information on the stock market. The first two columns of Table 1 show that $M2$, with the Anxiety Index included in the analysis, would outperform $M1$, judging from the Granger causality F statistics $F_{3,158} = 3.006$, and the corresponding p-value $p_{Granger} = 0.0322$.

Table 1. Granger Causality results and Monte Carlo Simulation. $MCp_{Gausskern}$, MCp_{inv} and MCp_{boot} are the p-values of the simulations using a Gaussian kernel assumption, the inverse transform sampling, and bootstrap sampling respectively.

$F_{3,158}$	$p_{Granger}$	$MCp_{Gausskern}$	MCp_{inv}	MCp_{boot}
3.006	0.0322	0.045	0.045	0.045

The main disadvantage of the approach of Gilbert and Karahalios [8] was that the Granger causality analysis's linear models M1 and M2 were actually not valid from a statistical point of view. In particular these models suffered of major shortcomings as for instance residuals were non-normally distributed, and they presented a heterogeneity of the variance. As such, although the p-value $p_{Granger} < 0.05$ suggests that the Anxiety Index adds significantly some predictive information on the stock market, such a conclusion is not supported by a valid statistical reasoning.

Due to the mentioned pitfalls, [8] proposed also a Monte Carlo simulation with a Gaussian kernel distribution assumption for the Anxiety Index, in an attempt to retrieve the same conclusion as in the non-statistically supported Granger causality analysis. The authors generated 1 million sets of samples for the Anxiety Index. These new series were used in (2) by iterating 1 million times to generate the same number of F statistic values, and then to classify these values based on if any F statistic is at least 3.01. The total number of F statistic's values that were at least 3.01 was then divided by the number of iteration to obtain the Monte Carlo experimental p-value, $MCp_{Gausskern} = 0.045$, shown in Table 1.

Although $MCp_{Gausskern} < 0.05$ seemed to confirm the conclusion of the Granger causality analysis, the Monte Carlo simulation suffered at its turn of the issue of retrieving a significantly different experimental p-value with respect to $p_{Granger}$. This issue seemed to be the consequence of another issue, consisting of the fact that the empirical distribution of the F-statistic computed in the Monte Carlo experiments significantly deviated from the expected F-distribution, as confirmed by the Kolmogorov-Smirnov test, i.e. $D = 0.0337$, $p < 0.001$ [8].

This realization constitutes a nontrivial reason to question the Monte Carlo estimates, and a natural question which arises is: would the assumption of the Gaussian kernel distribution for the Anxiety Index have possibly introduced a bias in the simulation? To answer the question, we apply other non-parametric Monte Carlo simulation methods based on the inverse transform sampling method using the continuous version of the empirical distribution function corresponding to the original Anxiety Index's sample, and bootstrap sampling. We follow the same procedure as that used in [8]. Our Monte Carlo p-values are presented in the columns four and five of Table 1, where MCp_{inv} and MCp_{boot} denote p-values issued from the use of the inverse transform sampling and the bootstrap sampling methods. Both simulations led to a similar value of 0.045. Moreover, in both cases the empirical distribution of the F-statistic computed in the Monte Carlo experiments is different from the expected F-distribution. These shortcomings confirm once again that proving the relationship between the Anxiety Index and stock prices is problematic if linear models are involved.

To this end we propose a new statistical approach to solve the limitations in [8] and to also reveal the relationship direction between the variables of interest.

3 Anxiety Index's Predictive Information on the Stock Market, Revisited

We follow the guidelines from Diks and Panchenko [6] (see [7] for detailed explanation and software) to examine the line of Granger causality between the variables involved in our analysis. The idea of the non-parametric statistical technique for detecting nonlinear causal relationships between the residuals of linear models was proposed by Baek and Brock [2]. It was later modified by Hiemstra and Jones [9] and this has become one of the most popular techniques for detecting nonlinear causal relationships in variables.

Consider two series X_t and Y_t as follows: let the Lx and Ly be the lag length of the lag series X_t^{Lx} and Y_t^{Ly} of X_t and Y_t respectively, and let us denote the k-length lead vector of Y_t by Y_t^k. In other words,

$$Y_t^k \equiv (Y_t, Y_{t+1}, ..., Y_{t+k-1}), k = 1, 2, ..., t = 1, 2, ..,$$

$$Y_t^{Ly} \equiv (Y_{t-Ly}, Y_{t-Ly+1}, ..., Y_{t-1}), Ly = 1, 2, ..., t = Ly + 1, Ly + 2, ..., \quad (3)$$

$$X_t^{Lx} \equiv (X_{t-Lx}, X_{t-Lx+1}, ..., Y_{t-1}), Ly = 1, 2, ..., t = Lx + 1, Lx + 2, ...,$$

Given arbitrary values for $k, Lx, Ly \geq 1$ and $\varepsilon > 0$, then X_t does not strictly nonlinearly Granger cause Y_t if:

$$Pr(\| Y_t^k - Y_s^k \| < \varepsilon \mid \| Y_t^{Ly} - Y_s^{Ly} \| < \varepsilon, \| X_t^{Lx} - X_s^{Lx} \| < \varepsilon)$$
$$= Pr(\| Y_t^k - Y_s^k \| < \varepsilon \mid \| Y_t^{Ly} - Y_s^{Ly} \| < \varepsilon) \quad (4)$$

where $Pr(A \mid B)$ denotes the probability of A given B, $\| \cdot \|$ is the maximum norm, i.e. for a vector $V \equiv (v_1, v_2, ..., v_m)$, $\| V \| = max\{v_1, ..., v_m\}$, $s, t = max(Lx, Ly) + 1, ..., N - k + 1$, N is the length of the time series and ε is N-dependent and typically has values between 0.5 and 1.5 after normalising the time series to unit variance. The left hand side in (4) is the conditional probability which implies that two arbitrary k-length lead vectors of Y_t are within a distance ε, given that two associating Lx- length lag vector of X_t and two associating Ly-length lag vector of Y_t are within a distance of ε. The right hand side in (4) is the probability that two arbitrary k-length lead vectors of Y_t are within a distance of ε, given that the two corresponding Ly-length lag vector of Y are within the distance of ε.

Eq.(4) can be rewritten using conditional probabilities in terms of the ratios of joint probabilities as follows:

$$\frac{CI(k+Ly, Lx, \varepsilon)}{CI(Ly, Lx, \varepsilon)} = \frac{CI(k+Ly, \varepsilon)}{CI(Ly, \varepsilon)} \tag{5}$$

The joint probabilities are defined as:

$$
\begin{aligned}
CI(k+Ly, Lx, \varepsilon) &\equiv Pr(\| Y_t^{k+Ly} - Y_s^{k+Ly} \| < \varepsilon, \| X_t^{Lx} - X_s^{Lx} \| < \varepsilon), \\
CI(Ly, Lx, \varepsilon) &\equiv Pr(\| Y_t^{Ly} - Y_s^{Ly} \| < \varepsilon, \| X_t^{Lx} - X_s^{Lx} \| < \varepsilon), \\
CI(k+Ly, \varepsilon) &\equiv Pr(\| Y_t^{k+Ly} - Y_s^{k+Ly} \| < \varepsilon), \\
CI(Ly, \varepsilon) &\equiv Pr(\| Y_t^{Ly} - Y_s^{Ly} \| < \varepsilon)
\end{aligned} \tag{6}
$$

The Correlation-Integral estimators of the joint probabilities expressed in Eq. (6) measure the distance of realizations of a random variable at two different times. They are proportions defined as the number of observations within the distance ε to the total number of observations. Let us denote the time series of realizations of X and Y as x_t and y_t for $t = 1, 2, ..., N$ and let y_t^k, y_t^{Ly} and x_t^{Lx} denote the k-length lead, and Lx-length lag vectors of x_t and the Ly-length lag vectors of y_t as defined in (3). In addition, let $I(Z_1, Z_2, \varepsilon)$ denote a kernel that equals 1 when two conformable vectors Z_1 and Z_2 are within the maximum-norm distance ε of each other and 0 otherwise. The Correlation-Integral estimators of the joint probabilities in equation (6) can be expressed as:

$$
\begin{aligned}
CI(k+Ly, Lx, \varepsilon, n) &\equiv \frac{2}{n(n-1)} \sum\sum_{t<s} I(y_t^{k+Ly}, y_s^{k+Ly}, \varepsilon) \cdot I(x_t^{Lx}, x_s^{Lx}, \varepsilon), \\
CI(Ly, Lx, \varepsilon, n) &\equiv \frac{2}{n(n-1)} \sum\sum_{t<s} I(y_t^{Ly}, y_s^{Ly}, \varepsilon) \cdot I(x_t^{Lx}, x_s^{Lx}, \varepsilon), \\
CI(k+Ly, \varepsilon, n) &\equiv \frac{2}{n(n-1)} \sum\sum_{t<s} I(y_t^{k+Ly}, y_s^{k+Ly}, \varepsilon), \\
CI(Ly, \varepsilon, n) &\equiv \frac{2}{n(n-1)} \sum\sum_{t<s} I(y_t^{Ly}, y_s^{Ly}, \varepsilon),
\end{aligned} \tag{7}
$$

where $t, s = max(Lx, Ly) + 1, ..., N - k + 1$, $n = N + 1 - k - max(Lx, Ly)$.

Given that two series, X and Y, are strictly stationary and meet the required mixing conditions mentioned in Denker and Keller [5], under the null hypothesis that X does not strictly Granger cause Y, the test statistics T is asymptotically normally distributed and it follows that:

$$T = \sqrt{n}\left(\frac{CI(k+Ly, Lx, \varepsilon, n)}{CI(Ly, Lx, \varepsilon, n)} - \frac{CI(k+Ly, \varepsilon, n)}{CI(Ly, \varepsilon, n)}\right) \sim N\left(0, \sigma^2(k, Ly, Lx, \varepsilon)\right) \tag{8}$$

where $n = N + 1 - k - max(Lx, Ly)$ and $\sigma^2(\cdot)$, the asymptotic variance of the modified Baek and Brock test statistics, and an estimator for it are defined in the Appendix in Hiemstra and Jones [9].

To test our variables for a possibly non-linear relation, we start by introducing the general framework of our models. Consider a regression modeling with a constant conditional variance, $VAR(Y_t \mid X_{1,t}, ..., X_{m,t}) = \sigma_\epsilon^2$. Then regressing Y_t on $X_{1,t}, ..., X_{m,t}$ can be generally denoted as:

$$Y_t = f(X_{1,t}, ..., X_{m,t}) + \epsilon_t, \tag{9}$$

where ϵ_t is independent of $X_{1,t}, ..., X_{m,t}$ with expectation zero and constant conditional variance σ_ϵ^2. $f(\cdot)$ is the conditional expectation of $Y_t \mid X_{1,t}, ..., X_{m,t}$. Eq.(9) can be extended to include conditional heteroscedasticity as follows:

$$Y_t = f(X_{1,t}, ..., X_{m,t}) + \sigma(X_{1,t}, ..., X_{m,t})\epsilon_t \tag{10}$$

where $\sigma^2(X_{1,t}, ..., X_{m,t})$ is the conditional variance of $Y_t \mid X_{1,t}, ..., X_{m,t}$ and ϵ_t has the mean 0 and the conditional variance 1. Since $\sigma(X_{1,t}, ..., X_{m,t})$ is a standard deviation, it is captured using a non-linear non-negative function in order to maintain its non-negative structure. This leads us to GARCH models. Comparing Eq.(9) and Eq.(10), the first part of the right hand side of Eq.(9) is the same with that of Eq.(10). This is a linear model. The second part of the right hand side of Eq.(9) are residuals of the linear process. They represent the second part of the right hand side of Eq.(10). Eq.(9) can finally be presented in the VAR framework as:

$$M_t = c + \Sigma_{i=1}^3 h_i M_{t-i} + \Sigma_{i=1}^3 \gamma_i V_{t-i} + \Sigma_{i=1}^3 \delta_i Q_{t-i} + \\ \Sigma_{i=1}^3 \eta_i A_{t-i} + a_t \tag{11}$$

$$A_t = c + \Sigma_{i=1}^3 h_i M_{t-i} + \Sigma_{i=1}^3 \gamma_i V_{t-i} + \Sigma_{i=1}^3 \delta_i Q_{t-i} + \\ \Sigma_{i=1}^3 \eta_i A_{t-i} + a_t \tag{12}$$

Following the second part of the right hand side of Eq.(10), the residuals a_t from Eq.(11) and Eq.(12) are presented in GARCH(1,1) as:

$$a_t = \sigma_t \epsilon_t \tag{13}$$

where $\sigma_t = \sqrt{w + \alpha_1 a_{t-1}^2 + \beta_1 \sigma_{t-1}^2}$, in which w, α_1 and β_1 are constants. We finally derive the GARCH(1,1)-filtered residuals, standardized residuals, as

$$\epsilon_t = \frac{a_t}{\sigma_t} \tag{14}$$

We obtain the residuals from the VAR model in Eq. (11) and (12). The test statistic in Eq. (8) is then applied to these residuals to detect the causal relation between the Anxiety Index and stock prices. Diks and Panchenko [6] provide some important improvement to the Non-linear Granger Causality test. [6] demonstrates that the value to be arbitrarily assigned to the distance ε is highly conditional on the length n of the time series. The larger the value n, the smaller the assigned value for ε and, the better and more accurate the results.

Most of the related works choose $k = Lx = Ly = 1$. The length of the series we are analysing is less than 200, so choosing $\varepsilon = 1.5$ conforms with Table 2. Given $\varepsilon = 1.5$, $k = Lx = Ly = 1$, the results from the test are presented in Table 3.

Table 2. Assigning values to ε, as of Diks and Panchenko [6]

n	100	200	500	1000	2000	5000	10,000	20,000	60,000
ε	1.5	1.5	1.5	1.2	1	0.76	0.62	0.51	0.37

Our first result in this framework seems to support the idea that the Anxiety Index has predictive information on the stock market, as this is based on the p-value of 0.017 shown in the first row of Table 3. Some re-considerations are necessary though.

Hiemstra and Jones [9] state that the non-linear structure of series is related to ARCH errors. Anderson [1] proves that the volatility of time series contains predictive information flow. But Diks and Panchenko [6] warn that the presence of conditional heteroscedasticity in series could produce spurious results. To avoid any possible bias in our results, the residuals are applied to Eq.(13) to filter out any conditional heteroscedasticity in the residuals of the VAR models. We also rely on the GARCH(1,1)-filtered residuals to re-establish our findings.

We are able to identify, using the GARCH(1,1) results, that a_t from Eq.(11) is a GARCH process with ϵ_t being a Gaussian white noise (having the p-values $\alpha = 0.003$, $\beta < 0.001$ and Shapiro-Wilk $= 0.383$) and that a_t from Eq.(12) does not contain significant heteroscedasticity except that ϵ_t is an i.i.d. white noise with a heavy-tailed distribution (having the p-values $\alpha = 0.136$, $\beta = 0.454$ and Shapiro-Wilk $= 0.018$). We obtain GARCH(1,1)-filtered residuals and the test statistic in Eq.(8) is re-applied to three sets of residuals: OLS residuals from Eq.(11) and Eq.(12); GARCH(1,1)-filtered residuals of stock returns and OLS residuals from Eq.(12); and GARCH(1,1)-filtered residuals from both stock returns and Anxiety Index. The results we present in rows 2 and 3 of Table 3 show p-values > 0.05 and thus confirm that our earlier result presented in row 1 of Table 3 is biased by the presence of heteroscedasticity in the residuals. We are thus able to show that the Anxiety Index does not possess any significant predictive information on the stock market.

In view of our results above, we therefore claim that the conclusion from Gilbert and Karahalios [8] according to which the Anxiety Index has predictive information on the stock market is not valid, which is supported also by the fact that the statistical conditions to validate their results are not met.

Table 3. Non-linear Granger non-causality test

$AI => SP$		$SP => AI$	
Lx=Ly=1	p	**Lx=Ly=1**	p
Before filtering	0.017	Before filtering	0.182
$GARCH(1,1)_{SP}$	0.349	$GARCH(1,1)_{SP}$	0.922
$GARCH(1,1)_{SP,AI}$	0.718	$GARCH(1,1)_{SP,AI}$	0.685

4   Conclusion

This paper proposes a new approach to statistically demonstrating the predictive information relationship direction between stock prices and emotions expressed online. In particular it proves that the Anxiety Index introduced by Gilbert and Karahalios [8] does not possess predictive information with respect to S&P 500. Our work does so by addressing the statistical limitations present in, and by extending the approach of [8].

The main drawback of the approach in [8] to proving the existence of the predictive information of the Anxiety Index with respect to the stock market was that this approach used a Granger causality analysis based on producing and assessing predictive linear models, which were actually not valid from a statistical point of view. In particular these models suffered of major shortcomings as for instance residuals were non-normally distributed, and they presented a heterogeneity of the variance. In an attempt to partially correct the above shortcomings, the Monte Carlo simulation performed by assuming a Gaussian kernel based density for the Anxiety Index, was also biased as the empirical distribution of the employed F statistic significantly deviated from the expected F-distribution [8].

We note that Monte Carlo simulations using the Gaussian kernel density approach have their own bandwidth selection problem, which may bias the simulations - see Zambom and Dias [17]. We therefore re-designed the Monte Carlo simulation presented in [8] by using bootstrap samples of the Anxiety Index first, and the inverse transform sampling based on the continuous version of the empirical distribution function corresponding to the original Anxiety Index sample. The results showed no improvement. This re-confirms the non-linear nature in the relationship between the stock market and emotion, and the erratic volatility in the variables. Linear models appear to be too 'basic' to capture these complexities.

We have therefore extended the approach of [8] by proposing a more capable framework based on the non-linear models introduced in [6]. Our first result, based on a p-value of 0.017 obtained in the non-linear Granger non-causality test, capturing the predictive information of the Anxiety Index with respect to S&P 500, is biased by the presence of heteroscedasticity. We filtered out the heteroscedasticity in the residuals using Eq. (13) and our GARCH(1,1)-filtered residuals were used with the test statistic in Eq. (7). Our results, based on p-values > 0.05, express the true non-causality relationship of Anxiety Index with respect to S&P 500.

Although our work has established that the Anxiety Index does not have predictive information with respect to the stock market, by proposing a new approach which is statistically sound and more conclusive, there are still some concerns on how the Anxiety Index was built, based on incomplete data, non-specific LiveJournal posts, corpus challenges, non-representative data sample, among others. Further refining the process of defining the Anxiety Index by addressing the above mentioned concerns, may help to fine-tune our empirical results and provide us with a more reliable predictive model.

References

1. Anderson, T.G.: Return volatility and trading volume: an information flow interpretation of stochastic volatility. Journal of Finance **51**, 169–204 (1996)
2. Baek, E., Brock, W.: A general test for nonlinear Granger causality: bivariate model. Working paper. Iowa State University (1992)
3. Balog, K., Gilad, M., de Maarten, R.: Why are they excited? Identifying and explaining spikes in blog mood levels. In: Proceedings of 11th Conference of the European Chapter of the Association for Computational Linguistics (EACL) (2006)
4. Bollen, J., Mao, H., Zeng, X.: Twitter mood predicts the stock market. Journal of Computational Science **2**(1), 1–8 (2011)
5. Denker, M., Keller, G.: On U-statistics and von-Mises statistics for weakly dependent processes. Z. Wahrscheinlichkeitsthorie und Verwandte Gebiete **64**, 505–522 (1983)
6. Diks, C., Panchenko, V.: A new statistic and practical guidelines for nonparametric Granger causality testing. Journal of Economic Dynamics and Control **30**(9–10), 1647–1669 (2006)
7. http://www1.fee.uva.nl/cendef/whoiswho/showHP/default.asp?selected=40&pid=6
8. Gilbert, E., Karahalios, K.: Widespread worry and the stock market. In: Proceedings of the 4th International Conference on Weblogs and Social Media, pp. 58–65 (2010)
9. Hiemstra, C., Jones, J.D.: Testing for linear and nonlinear Granger causality in the stock price-volume relation. Journal of Finance **49**, 1639–1664 (1994)
10. Jahidul, A., Mohammad, A.H., Rajib, H.: Analyzing public emotion and predicting stock market using social media. American Journal of Engineering Research **2**(9), 265–275 (2013)
11. Jason, D.M.R., Lawrence, S., Jaime, T., David, R.K.: Tackling the poor assumptions of naive bayes text classifiers. In: Proceedings of the Twentieth International Conference on Machine Learning, pp. 616–623 (2003)
12. Mao, H., Counts, A., Bollen, J.: Predicting financial markets: comparing survey, news, twitter and search engine data. arXiv preprint. arXiv:1112.1051 (2011)
13. Mittal, A., Goel, A.: Stock prediction using twitter sentiment analysis. Project report, Stanford (2012)
14. Schumaker, R.P., Chen, H.: Textual analysis of stock market prediction using breaking financial news: The AZFin text system. ACM Transactions on Information Systems **27**(2), 12:1–12:19 (2009)

15. Sprenger, T.O., Tumasjan, A., Sandner, P.G., Welpe, I.M.: Tweets and trades: the information content of stock microblogs. European Financial Management **20**(5), 926–957 (2014)
16. Yoav, F., Robert, E.S.: A decision-theoretic generalization of on-line learning and an application to boosting. Journal of Computer and System Science **49**, 119–139 (1997)
17. Zambom, A.Z., Dias, R.: A review of kernel density estimation with application to Econometrics. arXiv:1212.2812v1 (2012)

Exploring the Link Between Gene Expression and Protein Binding by Integrating mRNA Microarray and ChIP-Seq Data

Mohsina Mahmuda Ferdous[1]([✉]), Veronica Vinciotti[3],
Xiaohui Liu[1,2], and Paul Wilson[4]

[1] Department of Computer Science, Brunel University London,
Uxbridge UB8 3PH, UK
mohsina.ferdous@brunel.ac.uk
[2] Faculty of Engineering, King Abdulaziz Unviersity, Jeddah 21589, Saudi Arabia
[3] Department of Mathematics, Brunel University London, Uxbridge UB8 3PH, UK
[4] GlaxoSmithKline Medicine Research Centre, Stevenage SG1 2NY, UK

Abstract. ChIP-sequencing experiments are routinely used to study genome-wide chromatin marks. Due to the high-cost and complexity associated with this technology, it is of great interest to investigate whether the low-cost option of microarray experiments can be used in combination with ChIP-seq experiments. Most integrative analyses do not consider important features of ChIP-seq data, such as spatial dependencies and ChIP-efficiencies. In this paper, we address these issues by applying a Markov random field model to ChIP-seq data on the protein Brd4, for which both ChIP-seq and microarray data are available on the same biological conditions. We investigate the correlation between the enrichment probabilities around transcription start sites, estimated by the Markov model, and microarray gene expression values. Our preliminary results suggest that binding of the protein is associated with lower gene expression, but differential binding across different conditions does not show an association with differential expression of the associated genes.

Keywords: Protein binding · Gene regulation · Markov random field

1 Introduction

The development and maintenance of any organism is regulated by a set of chemical reactions that switch specific loci of the genome off and on at strategic times and locations. Epigenetics is the study of these reactions that control gene expression levels and the factors that influence them. Although the relationship between epigenetics and phenotypes is not always straightforward, studying tissues of affected and unaffected subjects and maintaining the study prospective may help identify the differences between causal associations and non-causal associations [1]. DNA microarray and ChIP-seq technologies play a crucial role

© Springer International Publishing Switzerland 2015
A. Gammerman et al. (Eds.): SLDS 2015, LNAI 9047, pp. 214–222, 2015.
DOI: 10.1007/978-3-319-17091-6_16

in understanding this relationship, by investigating structural and functional characteristics of genomes. DNA microarray technology, which enables measurement of the expression level of a large number of genes simultaneously, has been used in functional genomic studies, system biology, epigenetic research and so on. ChIP-seq, which is a comparatively new technology, has been used to describe the locations of histone post-translational modifications and DNA methylation genome-wide in many studies and to study alterations of chromatin structure which influence gene expression levels.

Next generation sequencing has undoubtedly several advantages over microarray experiments and it is often the choice for many studies. However, microarray experiments still have a place in bioinformatics, due to the cost-effectiveness and relative simplicity of this technique [2]. Hurd et al. [3] have predicted that in the near future, these two technologies may also complement each other and form a symbolic relationship. Integration of results from these two technologies might open new doors for epigenetic research.

Several attempts have been made to combine protein binding and mRNA expression data over the years. Markowetz et al. [4] have explored how histone acetylation around Transcription Start Sites (TSSs) correlates with gene expression data. In their study, ChIP-ChIP is used for measuring acetylation levels. Qin et al. and Guan et al. [5,6] have proposed a web-based server to analyse interactions between transcription factors and their effect on gene expression, by using information on bound and non-bound regions. Other attempts have also been made to infer relationships between gene expression and histone modification where absolute tag counts around a feature, such as promoter, is considered. Hoang et al. [7] have shown how, incorporating the spatial distribution of enrichment in the analysis, can improve the result. In general, it is absolutely vital to measure the level of acetylation and probability of enrichment accurately in order to find possible relationships between ChIP-seq and gene expression data. There are several characteristics of ChIP-seq data that are needed to be considered while modelling such data before we attempt to combine it with gene expression data.

In a typical ChIP-seq experiment, an antibody is used in the immunoprecipitation step to isolate specific DNA fragments that are in direct physical contact with a protein of interest. Figure 1 [14] gives an overview of how ChIP-seq technology works. Those fragments are called reads/tags. The reads are then mapped back to the reference genome and the resulting mapped reads are further analyzed to find out peaks or enriched regions where the protein in question is actually bound. It is common to divide the genome into fixed sized windows/bins and then summarize the counts per bin. Finally, a statistical model is used to detect the windows with a significant number of counts, that is the regions that are bound by the protein in question. While generating the data, some random DNA sequences are also collected with the bound sequences. These are usually scattered across the genome and form a background noise. Due to the particular antibody used and to the difficult protocol that each experiment needs to follow, it is common to observe varying background to signal ratios for different

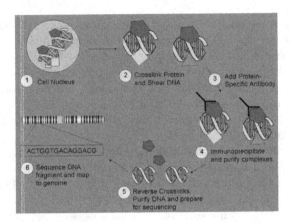

Fig. 1. Schematic representation of ChIP-seq technology. 1: Cell nucleus 2: A protein of interest is cross-linked with DNA sites it binds to in an in vivo environment. 3: The DNA is sheared by sonication or other mechanism. 4: Antibody is added 5: Crosslinked DNAs are filtered out with antibody by the immunoprecipitation technique 6: These DNA fragments are sequenced, forming reads, and are mapped back to the genome.

experiments. This poses an issue when multiple ChIP-seq experiments need to be modelled together and when comparative analyses with other data sources need to be carried out. Bao *et al.* [8] have proposed a mixture model where multiple experiments can be modelled together while taking into account the efficiency of individual experiments. However, there are other issues related to ChIP-seq data. Due to an often ad-hoc division of the genome in fixed-size windows, it is possible for an enrichment profile to cross neighbouring regions. This induces spatial dependencies in the count data, which is often observed for ChIP-seq data. All these issues are addressed in the approach proposed by Bao et al. [9]. In this proposed approach, a Markov random Field (MRF) model has been implemented that accounts for the spatial dependencies in ChIP-seq data as well as the different ChIP-seq efficiencies of individual experiments. In this paper, we have applied this model to the analysis of ChIP-seq data for the Brd4 protein.

Investigating enrichment around a feature in the genome such as promoter, TSS etc is very common while studying relationships between binding of a protein/TF and gene regulation. TSS is where transcription of the genes into RNA begins, therefore it is often considered in comparative analyses of binding and expression data. After analysing the ChIP-seq data using the MRF model, we have used the estimated probability of enrichment around the transcription start (TS) and performed comparative analysis on the associated gene expression data generated in the same biological condition.

In Section 2, we describe the data that has been used for this paper. We also give a brief overview of the MRF model for ChIP-seq data and how the parameters are estimated, as well as the differential expression analysis of the microarray data. In Section 3, we show our current results in comparing ChIP-seq and microarray data. Finally, we draw some conclusions in Section 4.

2   Data and Methods

2.1   Description of the Data

In this study, we have used the ChIP-seq data for the Brd4 protein provided by Nicodeme *et al.* [11]. Illumina beadarray technology was also used to collect gene expression data on the same experimental conditions as ChIP-Seq. The data was collected from samples that are treated with a synthetic compound (I-BET) that, by 'mimicking' acetylated histones, disrupts chromatin complexes responsible for the expression of key inflammatory genes in activated macrophages (Drug data) and also from sample simulated with lipopolysaccharide (LPS) (control data). The ChIP-seq data was collected at three time points: 0, 1 and 4 hours (0H, 1H, 4H) and microarray data at four time points (0H, 1H, 2H and 4H). For the ChIP-seq data, one replicate is available for each condition, whereas three replicates per condition are available in the microarray study.

2.2   Analysis of ChIP-seq Data

The ChIP-seq reads are aligned against the mouse genome (version mm9) using bowtie [10] and only uniquely mapped reads were retained for further analysis. The reference genome was obtained from UCSC Genome Browser. The percentage of reads that are aligned ranges from 60.86% to 78.03%. In this experiment, for simplicity, we have considered only Chromosome 1. So, we have selected only those reads that are found in Chromosome 1 of the mouse genome. We have divided the length of Chromosome 1 into 200bp windows and generated count data per windows. These count data are then supplied as the input for MRF model, described in the next section.

2.3   A Brief Description of MRF Model

We have followed the methodology proposed by Bao *et al.* [9] for the analysis of ChIP-seq data. Given the data, the model associates to each window a probability of being enriched or not. Additional information such as enrichment information of neighbouring regions is also considered while calculating this probability. A brief overview of the model is given below.

Let M be the total number of bins and Y_{mcr} the counts in the mth bin, $m = 1, 2, \ldots, M$, under condition c and replicate r. In our case, the condition c stands for a particular protein and/or a particular time point, and $r = 1, \ldots, R_c$ is the number of replicates under condition c. The counts Y_{mcr} are either drawn from a background population (non-enriched region) or a from a signal population (enriched region). Let X_{mc} be the unobserved random variable specifying if the mth bin is enriched ($X_{mc} = 1$) or non-enriched ($X_{mc} = 0$) under condition c. A mixture model for Y_{mcr} is defined as follows [8]:

$$Y_{mcr} \sim p_c f(y|\theta_{cr}^S) + (1 - p_c)f(y|\theta_{cr}^B),$$

where $p_c = P(X_{mc} = 1)$ is the mixture portion of the signal component and $f(y, \theta_{cr}^S)$ and $f(y, \theta_{cr}^B)$ are the signal and background densities for condition c and replicate r, respectively. An attractive feature of this model is the fact that the probability p_c of a region being enriched does not depend on ChIP efficiencies. However the parameters, signal and background distributions θ_{cr}^S and θ_{cr}^B depend on ChIP efficiencies of replicates r. This allows to combine multiple ChIP-seq experiments, while accounting for the individual ChIP efficiencies.

As the signal and background densities can take any form, the signal can be modelled using Poisson or Negative Binomial and their zero-inflated extensions to account for the excess number of zeros typical of this type of data. So for the mixture components $f(y, \theta_{cr}^S)$ and $f(y, \theta_{cr}^B)$, we consider:

$$Y_{mc}|X_{mc} = 0 \sim ZIP(\pi_c, \lambda_{0c}) \quad \text{or} \quad ZINB(\pi_c, \mu_{0c}, \phi_{0c}),$$
$$Y_{mc}|X_{mc} = 1 \sim Poisson(\lambda_{1c}) \quad \text{or} \quad NB(\mu_{1c}, \phi_{1c})$$

In our study, we have used zero inflated negative Binomial for modelling the background and Negative binomial for modelling the signal for all our ChIP-seq datasets.

In order to account for spatial dependencies, the latent variable X_{mc}, which represents the binding profile, is further assumed to satisfy one-dimensional first order Markov properties. Given the adjacent bins states, $X_{m-1}, c = i$, and $c = j$, with $i, j \in \{0, 1\}$

$$Y_{mcr}|X_{m-1,c} = i, X_{m+1,c} = j \sim p_{c,ij} f(y, \theta_{cr}^S) + (1 - p_{c,ij}) f(y, \theta_{cr}^B)$$

Thus, the enrichment of a region depends on the state of the two adjacent regions. All the parameters in this model are estimated using a Bayesian approach, which is implemented in the R package enRich. The method returns the posterior probability of enrichment for each region of the genome.

Finally to decide whether a region is enriched or not, a threshold is set on these probabilities. Different criteria can be used to set this cut-off. In our study, we set a cut-off corresponding to a chosen FDR. If D is the set of declared enriched regions corresponding to a particular cut-off on the posterior probabilities, then the estimated false discovery rate for this cut-off is given by

$$\widehat{FDR} = \frac{\sum_{m \in D} \hat{P}(X_{mc} = 0|\mathbf{Y})}{|D|}.$$

In our study, we used this approach for all 200bp regions in Chromosome 1. We then further refine the output to only consider the regions that contain TSs.

2.4   Analysis of Microarray Data

Microarray data have been preprocessed using the R package beadarray [12]. Then the processed data has been normalised and analysed for differential expression using the package limma [13]. This returns an adjusted p-value for differential expression between drug and control using an empirical Bayes method. We use these p-values to select the differentially expressed genes.

2.5 TSS Selection

We have downloaded TSS information of the mouse genome (chromosome 1) using NCBI mm9 assembly. Each txStart (Transcription start) and txEnd (Transcription end) coordinates are then linked with the associated genes. Many genes have several TSSs, and also some txStarts are at the same co-ordinate and others may reside within 200 bp regions to each other. Firstly, we remove the duplicate TSSs from the list. As we select enrichment probability within regions of 200bp, for each gene we select only one TSS within this window. From UCSC we downloaded 55419 TSSs and retained 38156 after this selection. As we consider only transcription start point for this experiment, we then retrieve the estimated probability of enrichment from the ChIP-seq analysis per TS.

3 Results and Discussion

3.1 ChIP-seq Analysis

We have analysed the ChIP-seq data with both the latent mixture model [8] and the MRF model [9]. For each condition, Table 1 shows the number of regions bound by Bdr4 at 5% FDR. The efficiency for each experiment estimated by the model is also given in the fourth column.

Table 1. Comparison of mixture model and MRF model in terms of number of regions bound by Brd4 at 5% FDR

Conditions	MRF model	Mixture model	IP efficiency
0H control	3394	1475	0.8201
0H drug	3185	930	0.8501
1H control	3161	614	0.8937
1H drug	3265	926	0.8937
4H control	3354	1345	0.8347
4H drug	2810	281	0.7809

At 5% FDR, the MRF model produces more enriched regions for each condition than the mixture model. By inspection of the regions detected by MRF but not by the mixture model, we have found out that MRF can assign a high probability to a region that has relatively low tag counts but has neighbouring regions with a large number of counts, as it incorporates spatial dependency in the model. On the other hand, the mixture model will assign a very low enrichment probability to those regions, thus discarding potentially useful information.

3.2   Expression Data versus Enrichment Probability

Nicodeme *et al.* [11] suggests that the impact of the drug I-BET on LPS-inducible gene expression is highly selective and it has no effect on the expression of housekeeping genes. Our key interest has been to investigate whether differential binding or differential enrichment of the protein Brd4 around TSS between drug and control data is associated with differential expression of the corresponding genes.

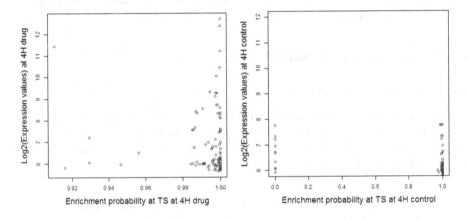

Fig. 2. Investing correlation between differential binding with differential expression result. (Left) At time point 4H and for the drug condition, TS regions with very high probabilities of enrichment are plotted versus the corresponding gene expression (log2) values. (Right) The low expressed genes found in the left plot are investigated in control data to check the effect of differential binding on regulation of genes.

At time point 4H, we select the TSs that have high probabilities of enrichment in the drug condition (at 5% FDR) and isolate 115 regions. The left plot in Figure 2 shows the gene expression values (in the log scale) versus the probabilities of enrichment for these regions. The plot shows a cluster of 84 genes in the bottom right corner that have very low expression values (below the median overall expression of 6.22). This was observed also at different time points. To find out whether binding of Brd4 in those regions play any role in the down-regulation of genes, we consider the binding and expression of these genes on the control data. The Right plot in Figure 2 shows that there is a small number of non-bound regions. However, these genes do not have a significantly higher expression value than in the drug samples. Thus, in this study, we found that differential bindings did not play a direct role in down-regulation of genes between drug and control experiments.

To investigate whether differential acetylation levels is associated with differential expression, we have selected differentially expressed genes at 4H between drug and control with a 1% cutoff on the adjusted p-values. We have subtracted expression values (log2) of control data from drug data (i.e. taking log ratios) and have done the same with enrichment probabilities. In Figure 3, Left plot shows the differential expression versus differential probability. Overall, few changes are found in the probabilities of enrichment between different conditions, suggesting that the genes are bound or not bound in both conditions and that the probabilities are either close to 0 or close to 1. Therefore, the plot does not show any association between differential probabilities of enrichment and differential expression. However, we are considering using different measures of acetylation levels than posterior probabilities. Similar results were obtained when comparing two time points (1H and 4H, respectively), as shown in the right plot of Figure 3. Here there are some regions with different probabilities of enrichment, but with no associated down or up regulation.

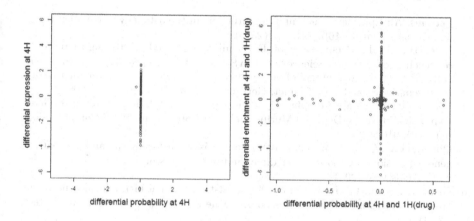

Fig. 3. Investing correlation between differential probability with differential expression result. (Left) Plot for differential probability versus differential expression(log2) between drug and control data at 4H. (Right) Plot for differential probability versus differential expression(log2) between 4H and 1H for drug data.

4   Conclusion

In this study, we have investigated a possible association between gene expression and protein binding data, from mRNA microarray and ChIP-seq data respectively. We have emphasized the need to account for important features of ChIP-seq data in the detection of the enriched regions and have therefore opted for the use of a Markov random field model for the analysis of ChIP-seq data. Our results show that protein binding is associated with lower expression values, but that differential binding between different conditions, e.g. drug and control or different time points, is not associated with up or down regulation of the corresponding genes.

A number of steps will be considered in the future to consolidate the research in this study. Firstly, we will extend the analysis from Chromosome 1 to the whole genome, to check whether the results generalise to this case, as well as to different proteins (the data in [11] is for five proteins). Secondly, we will consider different ways of measuring acetylation levels, while still considering the issue of different ChIP efficiencies of individual experiments. Finally, we will consider other chromatin markers, such as promoters, to explore a possible association between these and gene regulation, as well as possible combinatorial patterns between chromatin markers and gene regulation.

Acknowledgments. This work is supported by EPSRC and GlaxoSmithKline [Industrial CASE Award (EP/J501864/1)].

References

1. Petronis, A.: Epigenetics as a unifying principle in the aetiology of complex traits and diseases. Nature **465**, 721–727 (2010)
2. Xiao, H., et al.: Perspectives of DNA microarray and next-generation DNA sequencing technologies. Science in China Series C: Life Sciences **52**(1), 7–16 (2009)
3. Hurd, P.J., et al.: Advantages of next-generation sequencing versus the microarray in epigenetic research. Brief Funct. Genomics Proteomics **8**, 174–183 (2009)
4. Markowetz, F., et al.: Mapping Dynamic Histone Acetylation Patterns to Gene Expression in Nanog-Depleted Murine Embryonic Stem Cells. PLoS Comput. Biol. **6**(12), e1001034 (2010)
5. Qin, J., et al.: ChIP-Array: combinatory analysis of ChIP-seq/chip and microarray gene expression data to discover direct/indirect targets of a transcription factor. Nucl. Acids Res. (2011)
6. Guan, D., et al.: PTHGRN: unraveling post-translational hierarchical gene regulatory networks using PPI, ChIP-seq and gene expression data. Nucl. Acids Res. (2014)
7. Hoang, S.A., et al.: Quantification of histone modification ChIP-seq enrichment for data mining and machine learning applications. BMC Research Notes **4**, 288 (2011)
8. Bao, Y., et al.: Accounting for immunoprecipitation efficiencies in the statistical analysis of ChIP-seq data. BMC Bioinformatics **14**, 169 (2013)
9. Bao, Y., et al.: Joint modeling of ChIP-seq data via a Markov random field model. Biostat. **15**(2), 296–310 (2014)
10. Langmead, B., et al.: Ultrafast and memory-efficient alignment of short DNA sequences to the human genome. Genome Biol. **10**, R25 (2009)
11. Nicodeme E., et al.: Suppression of inflammation by a synthetic histone mimic. Nature 23, 468 (7327), 1119–1123 (2010)
12. Dunning, M.J., et al.: beadarray: R classes and methods for Illumina bead-based data. Bioinformatics **23**(16), 2183–2184 (2007)
13. Smyth, G.K.: Limma: linear models for microarray data. In: Gentleman, R., Carey, V., Dudoit, S., Irizarry, R., Huber, W. (eds.): Bioinformatics and Computational Biology Solutions Using R and Bioconductor, pp. 397–420. Springer, New York (2005)
14. wikipedia entry. http://www.wikipedia.org

Evolving Smart URL Filter
in a Zone-Based Policy Firewall for Detecting
Algorithmically Generated Malicious Domains

Konstantinos Demertzis[✉] and Lazaros Iliadis

Democritus University of Thrace, 193 Pandazidou st., 68200 Orestiada, Greece
{kdemertz,liliadis}@fmenr.duth.gr

Abstract. Domain Generation Algorithm (DGA) has evolved as one of the most dangerous and "undetectable" digital security deception methods. The complexity of this approach (combined with the intricate function of the fast-flux "botnet" networks) is the cause of an extremely risky threat which is hard to trace. In most of the cases it should be faced as zero-day vulnerability. This kind of combined attacks is responsible for malware distribution and for the infection of Information Systems. Moreover it is related to illegal actions, like money mule recruitment sites, phishing websites, illicit online pharmacies, extreme or illegal adult content sites, malicious browser exploit sites and web traps for distributing virus. Traditional digital security mechanisms face such vulnerabilities in a conventional manner, they create often false alarms and they fail to forecast them. This paper proposes an innovative fast and accurate evolving Smart URL Filter (eSURLF) in a Zone-based Policy Firewall (ZFW) which uses evolving Spiking Neural Networks (eSNN) for detecting algorithmically generated malicious domains names.

Keywords: Domain generation algorithm · Fast-Flux · Evolving spiking neural network · Botnet · Feed forward neural network · Particle swarm optimization

1 Introduction

The most common malware types, aim for the recovery of communication with the Command & Control (C2RS) remote servers and its retention on a regular basis. This is done in order for the botmasters to gather or distribute information and upgrades towards the undermined devices (bots). This communication is usually achieved with the use of hardcoded address or with pool addresses which are controlled by the malware developer or by the botmaster. Modern programming techniques offer malware developers, the chance to use thousands alternating IP addresses of different subnet in order to communicate with the C2RS. However it is easy for the network engineers to trace these IPs, to put them in blacklists.

It is a fact that most recent malware generations use new extremely complicated and smarter ways to communicate with the C2RS under the framework of botnets. More specifically, the communication is achieved by the use of custom distributed

© Springer International Publishing Switzerland 2015
A. Gammerman et al. (Eds.): SLDS 2015, LNAI 9047, pp. 223–233, 2015.
DOI: 10.1007/978-3-319-17091-6_17

dynamic DNS services which are executed in high port numbers. This is done in order to avoid to be traced by security programs located in the gateway of networks. In this way fast-flux botnets are created, whose target is the mapping of a fully qualified domain name to hundreds of IP addresses. These IPs are interchanged too fast, with a combination of random IP addresses and a very small Time-To-Live (TTL) for each partial DNS Resource Record. In this way a domain name can change its corresponding IP address very often (e.g. every 3 minutes). Another usual approach is the blind proxy redirection (BPR) technique. The BPR continuously redirects the applications received by frontend systems to backend servers, in order to spoil the traces and the data that designate an attack. In this way the complexity of the botnets increases [1].

DGA or *"Domain Fluxing"* is the most recent and smarter technique used by the creators of sophisticated malware. This method increases the complexity of the networks exponentially. Its algorithm creates a big number of domain names with specific specification characteristics that can be traced only by their creator. Some of these domains are the actual contact points with the C2RS of the botnets and they are used on a temporal basis and for minimum time intervals. This makes them much more difficult to be spotted. For example the following algorithm 1 creates domains according to a DGA perspective, where each domain is determined based on a date.

Algorithm 1. Generates a domain by the current date [2]

1. defgenerate_domain(year, month, day):
2.   """Generates a domain by the current date"""
3.   domain = ""
4. for i in range(32):
5.   year = ((year ^ 8 * year) >> 11) ^ ((year & 0xFFFFFFF0) << 17)
6.   month = ((month ^ 4 * month) >> 25) ^ 9 * (month & 0xFFFFFFF8)
7.   day = ((day ^ (day << 13)) >> 19) ^ ((day & 0xFFFFFFFE) << 12)
8.   domain += chr(((year ^ month ^ day) % 25) + 97)
9.   domain += '.com'
10. return domain

E.g., on June 18th, 2014, this method would generate the following domain names:

k.com	kafph.com	kafphogvi.com	kafphogvifahu.com
ka.com	kafpho.com	kafphogvif.com	kafphogvifahut.com
kaf.com	kafphog.com	kafphogvifa.com	kafphogvifahutb.com
kafp.com	kafphogv.com	**kafphogvifah.com**	kafphogvifahutbl.com

Every time that the botmaster wishes to contact the bots in a predefined strike-time, it creates the proper DNS records for one of the newly created names in the C2RS. In the above example, the strike time is the 18th of June 2014. At this point DNS records are activated only for the domain name **kafphogvifah.com**. Some minutes before the strike-time the C2RS are activated in order to establish communication. Right afterwards, the botmaster deletes the registrations of the DNS service and deactivates the

C2RS. The thousands domains created by the DGA algorithm daily, the huge complexity of the fast-flux botnets and the distributed function of the C2RS for some minutes per day, make designation of these servers a very tedious task [3].

This research paper proposes the development of an innovative system, capable of protecting from fast-flux botnets that use domain names created with the DGA methodology. Existing methods focus in DNS traffic analysis [4] [5] [6]. This paper proposes an Evolving Smart URL Filter in a Zone-based Policy Firewall for detecting Algorithmically Generated Malicious Domains Names. It is a biologically inspired Artificial Intelligence (AI) security technique as it uses evolving Spiking Neural Networks. The eSNN are the third generation neural networks, emulating the function of the human brain in the most efficient way. This research effort is an enhancement of previous [7] [8] [9] [10]. The efficiency of the proposed eSURLF approach has been compared to other evolving and bio-inspired learning methods, namely: Feed Forward Neural Networks using Particle Swarm Optimization (FNNPSO) technique and Gene Expression Programming (GEP).

1.1   Literature Review

Gu et al. (2007) [11] proposed a method to detect the infection and coordination dialog of botnets by matching a state-based infection sequence model. Based on URL extraction from spam mail Ma, et al. [12], studied a number of machine learning methods for classification web site. Characteristics, such as IP addresses, whois records and lexical features of phishing URLs have been analyzed by McGrath and Gupta [13]. Xie et al [14] in focus on detecting spamming botnets by developing regular expression based signatures from a dataset of spam URLs. Etienne, et al. [15] proposed a technique for the detection and mitigating botnet infection on a network. They use multiple features from DNS queries such as A and NS Records, IP ranges, TTL and alphanumeric characters from domains. In their experiment, they applied Naive Bayesian. Nhauo et al. [16] proposed a method for Classification of Malicious Domains using Support Vector Machine and Bi-gram algorithm using only domain names and their results showed that features extracted by bi-gram were performing a lot better than single alphanumeric character. Antonakakis et. al. [17] uses a combination of clustering and classification algorithms to detecting the DGA-Based Malware. Zhao et al. [18] select a set of attributes from the network flows and then applies a Bayes network and a decision tree algorithm to classify malicious traffic. Also, a number of approaches have been studied in [19] [20] [21] [22] which use the spam emails as the primary information source, for detecting fast-flux domains.

2   URL Filtering

URL filtering is a technique which controls network traffic, by allowing or forbidding access to specific websites based on the information contained in the requested URL. Filters can be applied in various ways such as software, proxy servers, DNS services and firewalls. The ZFW method is an advanced technique used in modern firewalls. It functions in a flexible way employing control zones. Each zone controls traffic based on the IP and the redirection of the requests from one zone to the other, according to the rules that have been defined for each security level by the system administrator [23]. ZFW offers URL filtering in the following manner:

- *Local URL List* which can include URLs or IP addresses that have been traced as risky (black list records) and URLs in which the user wishes to have access (white list records). Before the use of a URL it is checked if it is included in one of the black or white lists and access is forwarded or stopped. The difficulty in regular updating this lists and the non-spotting of zero-day threats are the main disadvantages.

- *URL Filter Servers* containing information related to the malware content, which are updated regularly. Before using a URL an HTTP request is sent to the URL filter server in order to be checked and to allow or restrict access. If the URL filter server is not responding the next one is searched. A serious drawback is the potential that filter servers do not respond whereas there is no mechanism for tracing zero-day threats.

- *Local URL lists with URL filter servers*. It is a hybrid model of the above two cases that combines advantages and disadvantages.

3   Datasets

Two datasets namely the *dga_timestamp* and the *dga_dictionary* were constructed and used for testing. As legit domains 100,000 domain names were used. They were chosen randomly from the database with the 1 million most popular domain names of Alexa [24]. For the malicious domains the updated list of the Black Hole DNS database was used [25]. This list includes 16,374 records from domains that have been traced and characterized as dangerous. More over in the *dga_time stamp* dataset 15,000 domain name records were added labeled as malicious. They were created based on the time stamp DGA algorithm, with length from 4 to 56 characters of the form *18cbth51n205gdgsar1io1t5.com*. In the *dga_dictionary* dataset 15,000 domain name records were added labeled as malicious, which were created with the use of words of phrases coming from an English dictionary. Their length varied from 4 to 56 characters of the form *hotsex4rock69burningchoir.com*. In both of the cases the characteristics used as independent parameters were: *length* (the length of the strings of the domains) *entropy* (the entropy of each domain as degree of uncertainty, with the higher values met in the DGA domains), *alexa_grams* (the degree of coherence between the domain and the list of domains originating from Alexa. This is done with the technique of the probability linguistic model for the forecasting of the next n-gram element), *word_grams* (the degree of coherence between the domain and a list of 479,623 words or widely used characters. It is estimated with the same method as in the previous one), *differences* (the difference between the values of alexa_grams and word_grams). The depended variable was the *class* of the domain (*legit* or *malicious*) [26]. Duplicate records and records with incompatible characters were removed. Also the outliers and the extreme values spotted were removed based on the Inter Quartile

Range (IQR) technique [27]. After this preprocessing operation the *dga _time stamp* dataset was left with 116,756 records from which the 90,338 are class *legit* and the rest 26,418 are class *dga*, whereas the *dga_dictionary* dataset includes 116,071 records from which the 90,445 are class *legit* and the rest 25,626 class *malicious*.

4   Methods and Materials

4.1   Evolving Spiking Neural Network

The eSNNs based on the "Thorpe" neural model [28] are modular connectionist-based systems that evolve their structure and functionality in a continuous, self-organized, on-line, adaptive, interactive way from incoming information [29]. In order to classify real-valued data sets, each data sample, is mapped into a sequence of spikes using the Rank Order Population Encoding (ROPE) technique [30] [31]. In this encoding method neurons are organized into neuronal maps which share the same synaptic weights. Whenever the synaptic weight is modified, the same modification is applied to the entire population of neurons within the map. Inhibition is also present between each neuronal map. If a neuron spikes, it inhibits all the neurons in the other maps with neighboring positions. This prevents all the neurons from learning the same pattern. When propagating new information, neuronal activity is initially reset to zero. Then, as the propagation goes on, each time one of their inputs fire, neurons are progressively desensitized. This is making neuronal responses dependent upon the relative order of firing of the neuron's afferents [32] [33]. Also in this model the neural plasticity is used to monitor the learning algorithm by using one-pass learning method. The aim of this learning scheme is to create a repository of trained output neurons during the presentation of training samples [34].

4.2   Feed Forward Neural Networks and Heuristic Optimization Methods

A common form of ANN are the feed forward ones (FNN) with three layers (Input, Hidden and Output). A typical training process includes the following steps [35]:

- The weighted sums of the inputs are calculated based on function (1):

$$s_j = \sum_{i=1}^{n}(W_{ij}X_i) - \theta_j \quad j=1,2,...,h \tag{1}$$

where n,h,m are the number of input, hidden and output nodes respectively and W_{ij} is the connection weight from the ith node of the input layer to the jth node of the hidden layer. Also θ_j is the bias (threshold).

- The output for each hidden node is estimated with the following equation (2):

$$S_j = sigmoid_{(s_j)} = \frac{1}{(1+exp(-s_j))} j=1,2,...,h \tag{2}$$

- The final output is estimated based on the equations (3) and (4) below:

$$O_k = \sum_{j=1}^{h}\left(W_{jk}S_j\right) - \theta'_k \quad k=1,2,...,m \tag{3}$$

$$O_k = sigmoid_{(o_k)} = \frac{1}{(1+exp(-o_k))} k=1,2,...,m \tag{4}$$

Various heuristic optimization methods have been used to train FNNs such as Genetic Algorithms (GAs) and Particle Swarm Optimization (PSO) algorithms. Generally, there are three heuristic approaches used to train or optimize FNNs. First, heuristic algorithms are used to find a combination of weights and biases which provide the minimum error for a FNN. Second, heuristic algorithms are employed to find the optimal architecture for the network related to a specific case. The last approach is to use an evolutionary algorithm to tune the parameters of a gradient-based learning algorithm, such as the learning rate and momentum [36]. In this research effort PSO has been employed to provide the optimal FNN model.

4.2.1 Particle Swarm Optimization

PSO is an evolutionary computation technique which is proposed by Kennedy and Eberhart. It was inspired by social behavior of bird flocking or fish schooling. PSO shares many similarities with evolutionary computation techniques such as GA. The system is initialized with a population of random solutions and searches for optima by updating generations. However, unlike GA, PSO has no evolution operators such as crossover and mutation. In PSO, the potential solutions, called particles, fly through the problem space by following the current optimum particles. Each particle keeps track of its coordinates in the problem space which are associated with the best solution (fitness) it has achieved so far. (The fitness value is also stored.) This value is called "*pbest*". Another "best" value that is tracked by the particle swarm optimizer is the best value obtained so far by any particle in its neighbors. This location is called "*lbest*". When a particle takes all the population as its topological neighbors, the best value is a global best and is called "*gbest*". According to the PSO at each time step there is a change in the velocity (acceleration) of each particle toward its *pbest* and *lbest* locations (local version of PSO). Acceleration is weighted by a random term, with separate random numbers being generated for acceleration toward *pbest* and *lbest* locations. PSO was mathematically modeled as follows [36]:

$$v_i^{t+1} = wv_i^t + c_1 \times rand \times (pbest_i - x_i^t) + c_2 \times rand \times \left(gbest\text{-}x_i^t\right) \tag{5}$$

$$x_i^{t+i} = x_i^t + v_i^{t+i} \tag{6}$$

Where v_i^t is the velocity of particle i at iteration t, w is a weighting function, c_j is an acceleration coefficient, *rand* is a random number between 0 and 1, x_i^t is the current position of particle i at iteration t, $pbest_i$ is the pbest of agent i at iteration t, and *gbest* is the best solution so far. Where wv_i^t, provides exploration ability for PSO, the

$$c_1 \times rand \times (pbest_i - x_i^t) + c_2 \times rand \times \left(gbest\text{-}x_i^t\right) \tag{7}$$

represent private thinking and collaboration of particles. The PSO starts by randomly placing the particles in a problem space. During each iteration, the velocities of particles are calculated using equation (5). After defining the velocities, the positions of particles can be calculated as shown in equation (6). The process of changing particles' positions continues until an end criterion is met.

4.3   Gene Expression Programming

The GEP is an evolutionary algorithm that uses populations of individuals and chooses the optimal ones based on a fitness function. Then it imports new individuals or potential solutions in the population, by using one or more genetic operators. The substantial difference between the GEP and the GA and Genetic Programming (GP) is in the nature of the individuals. Specifically, GA uses a sequence of symbols of stable length whereas GP uses nonlinear entities (parse trees) of various length and shape. GEP employs both above forms of individuals. Initially they are encoded like linear strings of stable length (genotype of chromosome) and then they are expressed as expression trees (EXTR) with different shape and size (phenotype). The correlation between the chromosomes and the EXTR in GEP declares an exclusive translation system from the language of the chromosomes to the one of the EXTR. The set of the genetic operators applied to GEP and import new individuals they always create syntactically correct EXTR [37].

5   Description of the Proposed Method

The proposed herein methodology uses an eSNN classification approach in order to detect and verify the DGA domain names. The topology of the developed eSNN is strictly feed-forward, organized in several layers and weight modification occurs on the connections between the neurons of the existing layers. The encoding is performed by ROPE technique with 20 Gaussian Receptive Fields (GRF) per variable. The data are normalized to the interval [-1, 1] and so the coverage of the Gaussians is determined by using i_min and i_max. Each input variable is encoded independently by a group of one-dimensional GRF. The GRF of neuron i is given by its center μ_i by equation (8) and width σ by equation (9)

$$\mu_i = I^n_{min} + \frac{2i-3}{2}\frac{I^n_{max} - I^n_{min}}{M-2} \qquad (8)$$

$$\sigma = \frac{1}{\beta}\frac{I^n_{max} - I^n_{min}}{M-2} \qquad (9)$$

where $1 \leq \beta \leq 2$ and the parameter β directly controls the width of each Gaussian receptive field. When a neuron reaches its threshold, it spikes and inhibits neurons at equivalent positions in the other maps so that only one neuron will respond at any location. Every spike triggers a time based Hebbian-like learning rule that adjusts the synaptic weights. For each training sample i with class label l which represent a *legit* domains, a new output neuron is created and fully connected to the previous layer of neurons, resulting in a real-valued weight vector $w^{(i)}$ with $w_j^{(i)} \in R$ denoting the connection between the pre-synaptic neuron j and the created neuron i. In the next step, the input spikes are propagated through the network and the value of weight $w_j^{(i)}$ is computed according to the order of spike transmission through a synapse

$$j: w_j^{(i)} = (m_l)^{order(j)} \tag{10}$$

where j is the pre-synaptic neuron of i. Function $order(j)$ represents the rank of the spike emitted by neuron j. The firing threshold $\theta^{(i)}$ of the created neuron i is defined as the fraction $c_l \in R$, $0 < c_l < 1$, of the maximal possible potential

$$u_{max}^{(i)}: \theta^{(i)} \leftarrow c_l u_{max}^{(i)} \tag{11}$$

$$u_{max}^{(i)} \leftarrow \sum_j w_j^{(i)} (m_l)^{order(j)} \tag{12}$$

The weight vector of the trained neuron is compared to the weights corresponding to neurons already stored in the repository. Two neurons are considered too "similar" if the minimal *Euclidean* distance between their weight vectors is smaller than a specified similarity threshold s_l. Both the firing thresholds and the weight vectors were merged according to equations (13) and (14):

$$w_j^{(k)} \leftarrow \frac{w_j^{(i)} + N w_j^{(k)}}{1 + N} \tag{13}$$

$$\theta^{(k)} \leftarrow \frac{\theta^{(i)} + N \theta^{(k)}}{1 + N} \tag{14}$$

Integer N denotes the number of samples previously used to update neuron k. The merging is implemented as the average of the connection weights, and of the two firing thresholds. After merging, the trained neuron i is discarded and the next sample processed. If no other neuron in the repository is similar to the trained neuron i, the neuron i is added to the repository as a new output.

6   Results

The performance of the employed algorithms for the case of the *dga_dictionary* dataset has been quite high as the obtained correlation shows. On the other hand, in the *dga_timestamp* dataset there was quite a lot of noise, due to the unstructured text of domain names that cannot be easily understood by machines. Regarding the overall efficiency of the methods, the results show that the eSNN has much better generalization performance and more accurate classification output. The accuracy comparison of the evolving algorithms with 10-fold cross validation is shown in table 1 and the confusion matrices in tables 2, 3 and 4

Table 1. Accuracy (ACC) Comparison between FFNN PSO, GEP and eSNN

	dga_dictionary dataset	dga _timestamp dataset
Classifier	**ACC**	**ACC**
FNNPSO	95.5%	91.9%
GEP	92.1%	90.6%
eSNN	**95.8%**	**92.4%**

Table 2. Confusion matrix for FNNPSO

CONFUSION MATRIX FOR FFNNPSO					
	dga_dictionary dataset			dga _timestamp dataset	
	Legit	DGA	Accuracy	Legit	DGA	Accuracy
Legit	**86556**	3889	95,7%	**84105**	6233	93,1%
DGA	1204	**24422**	95,3%	2457	**23961**	90,7%
	Overall Accuracy		**95.5%**	**Overall Accuracy**		**91.9%**

Table 3. Confusion matrix for GEP

CONFUSION MATRIX FOR GEP					
	dga_dictionary dataset			dga _timestamp dataset	
	Legit	DGA	Accuracy	Legit	DGA	Accuracy
Legit	**83933**	6512	92,8%	**81666**	8672	90,4%
DGA	2204	**23422**	91,4%	2430	**23988**	90,8%
	Overall Accuracy		**92.1%**	**Overall Accuracy**		**90.6%**

Table 4. Confusion matrix for eSNN

CONFUSION MATRIX FOR eSNN					
	dga_dictionary dataset			dga _timestamp dataset	
	Legit	DGA	Accuracy			
Legit	**87732**	2713	97%	**84647**	5691	93,7%
DGA	1384	**24242**	94,6%	2351	**24067**	91,1%
	Overall Accuracy		**95.8%**	**Overall Accuracy**		**92.4%**

7   Discussion – Conclusions

An innovative biologically inspired artificial intelligence computer security technique
has been introduced in this paper. An evolving Smart URL Filter in a Zone-based
Policy Firewall proposed for detecting Algorithmically Generated Malicious Domains
Names. It performs classification by using eSNN for the detection of DGA with high
accuracy and generalization. The classification performance and the accuracy of the
eSNN model were experimentally explored based on different datasets and compared
with other evolving algorithms and reported very promising results. In this way it
adds a higher degree of integrity to the rest of the security infrastructure of a ZFW.

As a future direction, aiming to improve the efficiency of the proposed method, it would be essential to try feature minimization using Principal Component Analysis or other existing approaches. Also additional computational intelligence methods could be explored and compared on the same security task. Finally the eSURLF could be improved towards a better online learning with self-modified parameter values.

References

1. www.damballa.com
2. www.crowdstrike.com
3. DGAs and Cyber-Criminals: A Case Study, Research Note. www.damballa.com
4. Yadav, S., Reddy, A.K.K., Reddy, A.L.N., Ranjan, S.: Detecting Algorithmically Generated Domain-Flux Attacks With DNS Traffic Analysis. ACM **20**(5) (2012)
5. Perdisci, R., Corona, I., Giacinto, G.: Early Detection of Malicious Flux Networks via Large-Scale Passive DNS Traffic Analysis. By the IEEE Computer Society (2012)
6. Bilge, L., Kirda, E., Kruegel, C., Balduzzi, M.: EXPOSURE: Finding Malicious Domains Using Passive DNS Analysis. TISSEC **16**(4), Article No. 14 A (2014)
7. Demertzis, K., Iliadis, L.: A hybrid network anomaly and intrusion detection approach based on evolving spiking neural network classification. In: Sideridis, A.B. (ed.) E-Democracy 2013. CCIS, vol. 441, pp. 11–23. Springer, Heidelberg (2014)
8. Demertzis, K., Iliadis, L.: Evolving computational intelligence system for malware detection. In: Iliadis, L., Papazoglou, M., Pohl, K. (eds.) CAiSE Workshops 2014. LNBIP, vol. 178, pp. 322–334. Springer, Heidelberg (2014)
9. Demertzis, K., Iliadis, L.: Bio-Inspired hybrid artificial intelligence framework for cyber security. In: Proceedings of the 2nd Conference on CryptAAF, Athens, Greece (2014)
10. Demertzis, K., Iliadis, L.: Bio-Inspired Hybrid Intelligent Method for Detecting Android Malware. In: Proceedings of the 9th KICSS Conference, Limassol, Cyprus (2014)
11. Gu, G., Porras, P., Yegneswaran, V., Fong, M., Lee W.: Bothunter: detecting malware infection through ids-driven dialog correlation. In: 16th USENIX, pp. 1--16 (2007)
12. Ma, J.: Beyond blacklist: learning to detect malicious website from suspicious URLs. In: SIGKDD Conference, Paris, France (2009)
13. McGrath, D.K., Gupta, M.: Behind phishing: an examination of phisher modi operandi. In: USENIX on Large-scale Exploits and Emergent Threats (LEET) (2008)
14. Xie, Y., Yu, F., Achan, K., Panigrahy, R., Hulten, G., Osipkov, I.: Spamming botnets: signatures and characteristics. ACM SIGCOMM Comp. Comm. Review (2008)
15. Stalmans, E.: A framework for DNS based detection and mitigation of malware infections on a network. In: Information Security South Africa Conference (2011)
16. Nhauo, D., Sung-Ryul, K.: Classification of malicious domain names using support vector machine and bi-gram method. J. of Security and its Applications **7**(1) (2013)
17. Antonakakis, M., Perdisci, R., Nadji, Y., Vasiloglou, N., Abu, S., Lee, W., Dagon, D.: From Throw-Away Traffic to Bots: Detecting the Rise of DGA-Based Malware (2012)
18. Zhao, D., Traore, I., Sayed, B., Lu, W., Saad, S., Ghorbani, A.: Botnet detection based on traffic behavior analysis and flow intervals. J. Computer Security **39**, 2–16 (2013)
19. Holz, T., Gorecki, C., Rieck, K., Freiling, F.: Measuring and detecting fast-flux service networks. In: Network & Distributed System Security Symposium, NDSS 2008 (2008)
20. Passerini, E., Paleari, R., Martignoni, L., Bruschi, D.: Fluxor: detecting and monitoring fast-flux service networks. In: DIMVA 2008 (2008)

21. Nazario, J., Holz, T.: As the net churns fast-flux botnet observations. In: MALWARE (2008)
22. Konte, M., Feamster, N., Jung, J.: Dynamics of online scam hosting infrastructure. In: Passive and Active Measurement Conference, PAM 2009 (2009)
23. Cisco Router and Security Device Manager 2.4 User's Guide. www.cisco.com
24. http://www.alexa.com/
25. http://www.malwaredomains.com/
26. https://www.clicksecurity.com/
27. Upton, G., Cook, I.: Understanding Statistics. Oxford University Press, p. 55 (1996)
28. Thorpe, S.J., Delorme, A., Rullen, R.: Spike-based strategies for rapid processing (2001)
29. Schliebs, S., Kasabov, N.: Evolving spiking neural network—a survey. Springer (2013)
30. Delorme, A., Perrinet, L., Thorpe, S.J.: Networks of Integrate-and-Fire Neurons using Rank Order Coding. Pub. in Neurocomputing **38-40**(1-4), 539–545 (2000)
31. Thorpe, S.J., Gautrais, J.: Rank order coding. In: CNS 1997: 6th Conf. on Computational Neuroscience: Trends in Research, pp. 113–118. Plenum Pr. (1998)
32. Kasabov, N.: Evolving connectionist systems: Methods and Applications in Bioinformatics, Brain study and intelligent machines. Springer (2002)
33. Wysoski, S.G., Benuskova, L., Kasabov, N.: Adaptive learning procedure for a network of spiking neurons and visual pattern recognition. In: Blanc-Talon, J., Philips, W., Popescu, D., Scheunders, P. (eds.) ACIVS 2006. LNCS, vol. 4179, pp. 1133–1142. Springer, Heidelberg (2006)
34. Schliebs, S., Defoin-Platel, M., Kasabov, N.: Integrated feature and parameter optimization for an evolving spiking neural network. In: Köppen, M., Kasabov, N., Coghill, G. (eds.) ICONIP 2008, Part I. LNCS, vol. 5506, pp. 1229–1236. Springer, Heidelberg (2009)
35. Iliadis, L.: Intelligent Information Systems and applications in risk estimation. A. Stamoulis publication, Thessaloniki (2008) ISBN: 978-960-6741-33-3
36. Mirjalili, S., Hashim, S., Sardroudi, H.: Training feedforward neural networks using hybrid particle swarm optimization and gravitational search algorithm. Elsevier (2012)
37. Ferreira, C.: Gene Expression Programming: Mathematical Modeling by an Artificial Intelligence, 2nd edn., Springer (2006)

Lattice-Theoretic Approach to Version Spaces in Qualitative Decision Making

Miguel Couceiro[1](✉) and Tamás Waldhauser[2]

[1] LORIA (CNRS - Inria Nancy Grand Est - Université de Lorraine),
Equipe Orpailleur – Bâtiment B, Campus Scientifique, B.P. 239,
54506 Vandœuvre-íes-Nancy Cedex, France
miguel.couceiro@inria.fr
[2] Bolyai Institute, University of Szeged, Aradi vértanúk tere 1,
Szeged H-6720, Hungary
twaldha@math.u-szeged.hu

Abstract. We present a lattice-theoretic approach to version spaces in multicriteria preference learning and discuss some complexity aspects. In particular, we show that the description of version spaces in the preference model based on the Sugeno integral is an NP-hard problem, even for simple instances.

1 Motivation

We consider an instance of supervised learning, where given a set $\mathbf{X}$ of objects (or alternatives), a set L of labels (or evaluations) and a finite set $S \subseteq \mathbf{X} \times L$ of labeled objects, the goal is to predict labels of new objects.

In the current paper, our motivation is found in the field of preference modeling and learning (prediction). We take the decomposable model to represent preferences over a set $\mathbf{X} = X_1 \times \cdots \times X_n$ of alternatives (e.g., houses to buy) described by n attributes X_i (e.g., price, size, location, color). In this setting, preference relations $\preceq$ are represented by mappings $U \colon \mathbf{X} \to L$ valued in a scale L, and called "overall utility functions", using the following rule:

$$\mathbf{x} \preceq \mathbf{y} \quad \text{if and only if} \quad U(\mathbf{x}) \leq U(\mathbf{y}).$$

In other words, an alternative $\mathbf{x}$ is less preferable than an alternative $\mathbf{y}$ if the score of $\mathbf{x}$ is less than that of $\mathbf{y}$. This representation of preference relations is usually refined by taking into account "local preferences " $\preceq_i$ on each X_i, modeled by mappings $\varphi_i \colon X_i \to L$ called "local utility functions", which are then merged through an aggregation function $p \colon L^n \to L$ into an overall utility function U:

$$U(\mathbf{x}) = p\left(\phi(\mathbf{x})\right) = p\left(\varphi_1(x_1), \ldots, \varphi_n(x_n)\right). \tag{1}$$

T. Waldhauser—This research is supported by the Hungarian National Foundation for Scientific Research under grant no. K104251 and by the János Bolyai Research Scholarship.

A. Gammerman et al. (Eds.): SLDS 2015, LNAI 9047, pp. 234–238, 2015.
DOI: 10.1007/978-3-319-17091-6_18

Loosely speaking, p merges the local preferences in order to obtain a global preference on the set of alternatives. In the qualitative setting, the aggregation function of choice is the *Sugeno integral* that can be regarded [10] as an *idempotent lattice polynomial function*, and the resulting global utility function (1) is then called a *pseudo-polynomial function*. This observation brings the concept of Sugeno integral to domains more general than scales (linearly ordered sets) such as distributive lattices and Boolean algebras. Apart from the theoretic interest, such generalization is both natural and useful as it allows incomparability amongst alternatives, a situation that is most common in real-life applications.

In this setting, we consider the learning scenario where given a training set consisting of pairs of alternatives together with their evaluations, we would like to determine all models (1) that are consistent with it. Formally we consider the following *supervised learning task*:

- **Given:**
  - a distributive lattice L (evaluation space)
  - a training set T of pairs $(\mathbf{x}, l_{\mathbf{x}}) \in \mathbf{X} \times L$
- **Find:** all pseudo-polynomials $U \colon \mathbf{X} \to L$ s.t. $U(\mathbf{x}) = l_{\mathbf{x}}$ for all $(\mathbf{x}, l_{\mathbf{x}}) \in T$.

In other words, we would like to describe the *version space* (see, e.g., [1,11]) in this qualitative setting, which asks for all lattice polynomial functions $p \colon L^n \to L$ and all local utility functions $\varphi_i \colon X_i \to L$, $i \in [n] := \{1, \ldots, n\}$, such that for every $(\mathbf{x}, l_{\mathbf{x}}) \in T$, $\mathbf{x} = (x_1, \ldots, x_n)$, we have $p\left(\phi(\mathbf{x})\right) = l_{\mathbf{x}}$.

Remark 1. This task of describing the version space was formalized mathematically in [3,5] as an interpolation problem. In this sense, we assume that the function f_T determined by T (i.e., $f_T(\mathbf{x}) = l_{\mathbf{x}}$ for each $(\mathbf{x}, l_{\mathbf{x}}) \in T$) is well-defined.

Remark 2. We would like to stress the fact that, despite motivated by a problem rooted in preference learning (see [7] for general background and a thorough treatment of the topic), our setting differs from the standard setting in machine learning. This is mainly due to the fact that we aim to describing utility-based preference models that are consistent with existing data (version spaces) rather than aiming to learning utility-based models by optimization (minimizing loss measures and coefficients) such as in, e.g., the probabilistic approach of [2] or the approach based on the Choquet integral of [12], and that naturally accounts for errors and inconsistencies in the learning data. Another difference is that, in the latter, data is supposed to be given in the form of feature vectors (thus assuming that local utilities over attributes are known a priori), an assumption that removes the additional difficulty that we face, namely, that of describing local utility functions that enable models based on the Sugeno integral that are consistent with existing data. It is also worth noting that we do not assume any structure on attributes and that we allow incomparabilities in evaluation spaces, which thus subsume preferences that are not necessarily rankings.

The complete description of the version space in the multicriteria setting still eludes us, but using some lattice-theoretic techniques developed in [3] (recalled in Section 2), we present in Section 3 explicit descriptions of version spaces when the local utility functions $\varphi_i \colon X_i \to L$ are known a priori.

2   When the Local Utility Functions are Identity Maps

Recall that a *polynomial function* over a distributive lattice L is a mapping $p \colon L^n \to L$ that can expressed as a combination of the lattice operations $\wedge$ and $\vee$, projections and constants. In the case when L is bounded, i.e., with a least and a greatest element denoted by 0 and 1, resp., Goodstein [8] showed that polynomial functions $p \colon L^n \to L$ coincide exactly with those lattice functions that are representable in *disjunctive normal form* (DNF for short) by

$$p(\mathbf{x}) = \bigvee_{I \subseteq [n]} \left(c_I \wedge \bigwedge_{i \in I} x_i \right), \quad \text{where } \mathbf{x} = (x_1, \ldots, x_n) \in L^n. \tag{2}$$

In fact he provided a canonical DNF where each c_I is of the form $p(\mathbf{1}_I)$, where $\mathbf{1}_I$ denotes the "indicator function" of $I \subseteq [n]$.

Recall that the Birkhoff-Priestley representation theorem [6] states that we can embed L into a Boolean algebra B. For the sake of canonicity, we assume that L generates B, so that B is uniquely determined up to isomorphism. We also denote the boundary elements of B by 0 and 1. The complement of an element $a \in B$ is denoted by a'.

In [3], we showed that the version space when the local utility functions are identity maps (i.e., $X_i = L$ and the models are lattice polynomial functions) can be thought of as an interval lower and upper bounded by polynomials p^- and p^+, resp., defined as follows. Let T be a training set as above and consider the corresponding function $f_T \colon D \to L$ (D comprises the first components of couples in T). Define the following two elements in B for each $I \subseteq [n]$:

$$c_I^- := \bigvee_{\mathbf{a} \in D} \left(f_T(\mathbf{a}) \wedge \bigwedge_{i \notin I} a_i' \right) \quad \text{and} \quad c_I^+ := \bigwedge_{\mathbf{a} \in D} \left(f_T(\mathbf{a}) \vee \bigvee_{i \in I} a_i' \right).$$

and let p^- and p^+ be the polynomial functions over B given by:

$$p^-(\mathbf{x}) := \bigvee_{I \subseteq [n]} \left(c_I^- \wedge \bigwedge_{i \in I} x_i \right) \quad \text{and} \quad p^+(\mathbf{x}) := \bigvee_{I \subseteq [n]} \left(c_I^+ \wedge \bigwedge_{i \in I} x_i \right).$$

Theorem 1 ([3]). *Let $p \colon B^n \to B$ be a polynomial function over B given by (2) and let D be the set of the first components of couples in a training set T. Then $p|_D = f_T$ if and only if $c_I^- \leq c_I \leq c_I^+$ (or, equivalently, $p^- \leq p \leq p^+$).*

Remark 3. From Theorem 1 it follows that a necessary and sufficient condition for the existence of a polynomial function $p \colon B^n \to B$ such that $p|_D = f_T$ is $c_I^- \leq c_I^+$, for every $I \subseteq [n]$. Moreover, if for every $I \subseteq [n]$, there is $c_I \in L$ such that $c_I^- \leq c_I \leq c_I^+$, then and only then the version space over L is not empty.

3   When the Local Utility Functions are Known A Priori

We now assume that the local utility functions $\varphi_i \colon X_i \to L$ are known a priori. So given a training set $T \subseteq \mathbf{X} \times L$, our goal to find all polynomial functions p over L such that the pseuo-polynomial function U given by (1) is consistent with T, i.e., $U|_D = f_T$. Let us consider an arbitrary polynomial function p over B in its disjunctive normal form (2). The corresponding pseudo-polynomial function $U = p(\varphi_1, \ldots, \varphi_n)$ verifies $U|_D = f_T$ if and only if $p|_{D'} = f_{T'}$ where D' is the set of first components of couples in $T' = \{(\phi(\mathbf{x}), f_T(\mathbf{x})) \colon (\mathbf{x}, f_T(\mathbf{x})) \in T\}$. Using the construction of Section 2 for T', we define coefficients $c^-_{I,\phi}$ and $c^+_{I,\phi}$ for every $I \subseteq [n]$ as follows:

$$c^-_{I,\phi} := \bigvee_{\mathbf{a} \in D} \left(f_T(\mathbf{a}) \wedge \bigwedge_{i \notin I} \varphi_i(a_i)' \right) \quad \text{and} \quad c^+_{I,\phi} := \bigwedge_{\mathbf{a} \in D} \left(f_T(\mathbf{a}) \vee \bigvee_{i \in I} \varphi_i(a_i)' \right).$$

Denoting the corresponding polynomial functions by p^-_ϕ and p^+_ϕ, Theorem 1 yields the following explicit description of version spaces.

Theorem 2. Let $T \subseteq \mathbf{X} \times L$ and D as before. For any $\varphi_i \colon X_i \to L \, (i \in [n])$ and any polynomial function $p \colon B^n \to B$ given by (2), we have that $U = p(\phi)$ verifies $U|_D = f_T$ if and only if $c^-_{I,\phi} \leq c_I \leq c^+_{I,\phi}$ for all $I \subseteq [n]$ (or, equivalently, $p^-_\phi \leq p \leq p^+_\phi$).

Remark 4. Note that if there exist couples $(\mathbf{a}, f_T(\mathbf{a})), (\mathbf{b}, f_T(\mathbf{b})) \in T$ such that $f_T(\mathbf{a}) \neq f_T(\mathbf{b})$ but $\phi(\mathbf{a}) = \phi(\mathbf{b})$, then the corresponding version space in the current multicriteria setting is void. We invite the reader to verify that this situation cannot occur if the condition of Theorem 2 is satisfied.

4   Concluding Remarks and Further Directions

Theorem 2 describes the version space for given local utility functions $\varphi_i \colon X_i \to L$. It still remains an open problem to determine all such local utility functions for which an interpolating polynomial function exists. Looking for interpolating polynomials over B, this amounts to solving the system of inequalities $c^-_{I,\phi} \leq c^+_{I,\phi}$ for the unknown values $\varphi_i(a_i)$. As the following example illustrates, this is a computationally hard problem, even in the simpler case of *quasi-polynomial functions*, where it is assumed that $X_1 = \cdots = X_n = X$ and $\varphi_1 = \cdots = \varphi_n = \varphi$.

Example 1. We define an instance of our interpolation problem for any finite simple graph $G = (V, E)$. Let $L = \{0, 1\}$ be the two-element chain, let $X = V \dot{\cup} \{s, t\}$, let $D = \{(u, v) \colon uv \in E\} \cup \{(t, s), (s, s), (t, t), (s, t)\}$, and let $f_T(t, s) = 1, f_T(s, s) = 0, f_T(t, t) = f_T(s, t) = 1$ and $f_T(u, v) = 1$ for all $uv \in E$. Since there are only 4 polynomials over L (namely 0, 1, $x_1 \wedge x_2$ and $x_1 \vee x_2$), it is easy to verify that $p(\varphi(x_1), \varphi(x_2))$ interpolates f_T if and only if $p = x_1 \vee x_2$, $\varphi(s) = 0, \varphi(t) = 1$ and $\{v \in V \colon \varphi(v) = 1\}$ is a covering set of the graph G. Hence, already in this simple case, it is an NP-hard problem to describe the whole version space, as it involves finding all covering sets (in part., all minimal covering sets) in a graph.

Despite the above example, the corresponding decision problem (is there an interpolating pseudo-polynomial?) might be tractable. Also, in some special cases, such as when all the sets X_i as well as L are finite chains and one considers only order-preserving local utility functions $\varphi_i : X_i \to L$ (which is the case in many applications), it might be feasible to construct the full version space. These problems constitute topics of further research of the authors.

References

1. Cornuéjols, A., Miclet, L.: Apprentissage artificiel - Concepts et algorithmes. Eyrolles (2010)
2. Cao-Van, K., De Baets, B., Lievens, S.: A probabilistic framework for the design of instance-based supervised ranking algorithms in an ordinal setting. Annals Operations Research **163**, 115–142 (2008)
3. Couceiro, M., Dubois, D., Prade, H., Rico, A., Waldhauser, T.: General interpolation by polynomial functions of distributive lattices. In: Greco, S., Bouchon-Meunier, B., Coletti, G., Fedrizzi, M., Matarazzo, B., Yager, R.R. (eds.) IPMU 2012. CCIS, vol. 299, pp. 347–355. Springer, Heidelberg (2012)
4. Couceiro, M., Waldhauser, T.: Axiomatizations and factorizations of Sugeno utility functions. Internat. J. Uncertain. Fuzziness Knowledge-Based Systems **19**(4), 635–658 (2011)
5. Couceiro, M., Waldhauser, T.: Interpolation by polynomial functions of distributive lattices: a generalization of a theorem of R. L. Goodstein. Algebra Universalis **69**(3), 287–299 (2013)
6. Davey, B.A., Priestley, H.A.: Introduction to Lattices and Order. Cambridge University Press, New York (2002)
7. Fürnkranz, J., Hüllermeier, E. (eds.): Preference learning. Springer, Berlin (2011)
8. Goodstein, R. L.: The Solution of Equations in a Lattice. Proc. Roy. Soc. Edinburgh Section A 67, 231–242 (1965/1967)
9. Grätzer, G.: General Lattice Theory. Birkhäuser Verlag, Berlin (2003)
10. Marichal, J.-L.: Weighted lattice polynomials. Discrete Mathematics **309**(4), 814–820 (2009)
11. Mitchell, T.: Machine Learning. McGraw Hill (1997)
12. Tehrani, A.F., Cheng, W., Hüllermeier, E.: Preference Learning Using the Choquet Integral: The Case of Multipartite Ranking. IEEE Transactions on Fuzzy Systems **20**(6), 1102–1113 (2012)

Conformal Prediction
and its Applications

A Comparison of Three Implementations of Multi-Label Conformal Prediction

Huazhen Wang[1,2]([✉]), Xin Liu[1], Ilia Nouretdinov[2], and Zhiyuan Luo[2]

[1] College of Computer Science and Technology, Huaqiao University,
Quanzhou, China
{wanghuazhen,xliu}@hqu.edu.cn
[2] Computer Learning Research Centre, Royal Holloway,
University of London, Egham, UK
{ilia,zhiyuan}@cs.rhul.ac.uk

Abstract. The property of calibration of Multi-Label Learning (MLL) has not been well studied. Because of the excellent calibration property of Conformal Predictors (CP), it is valuable to achieve calibrated MLL prediction via CP. Three practical implementations of Multi-Label Conformal Predictors (MLCP) can be established. Among them are Instance Reproduction MLCP (IR-MLCP), Binary Relevance MLCP (BR-MLCP) and Power Set MLCP (PS-MLCP). The experimental results on benchmark datasets show that all three MLCP methods possess calibration property. Comparatively speaking, BR-MLCP performs better in terms of prediction efficiency and computational cost than the other two.

Keywords: Multi-Label Learning · Threshold calibration · Conformal predictor · Nonconformity measure · K nearest neighbors

1 Introduction

Multi-Label Learning (MLL) is a different machine learning classification problem with traditional machine learning, where each instance is always assigned to multiple labels simultaneously and the predictor predicts a set of labels (*labelset*). An MLL classifier tries to construct a confidence function to measure the confidence of each label being a true label. Given a predefined threshold, a set of labels with confidence scores higher than the threshold can be collected to establish the predicted *labelset*[9]. A representative work is ML-KNN (K-Nearest Neighbors) algorithm, which computes the posterior probability of each label as the confidence measurement, and selects those labels whose posterior probability is larger than 0.5 to construct the region prediction[10]. However, it is always difficult to figure out the prior distribution of a dataset properly in machine learning literature. Consequently, the posterior probability always cannot provide valid confidence for MLL prediction. Few studies have involved the calibration property of prediction *labelset* which guarantees its error rate hedged by the corresponding threshold. In a previous study, we applied Conformal Predictors (CP) to produce calibrated MLL prediction[8]. Recently, Papadopoulos

© Springer International Publishing Switzerland 2015
A. Gammerman et al. (Eds.): SLDS 2015, LNAI 9047, pp. 241–250, 2015.
DOI: 10.1007/978-3-319-17091-6_19

also proposed another method of using CP to provide MLL predictions [5]. CP is a confidence machine that predicts a well-calibrated prediction for traditional single-label test instance [7]. CP has been applied to many real-world problems in different machine learning settings, including classification, regression, and clustering[1]. Because of the excellent calibration property of CP, it is valuable to extend CP to MLL setting to achieve calibrated prediction. The implementation of calibrated MLL via CP constructs a general framework, i.e., Multi-Label Conformal Predictors (MLCP). This study is to consider three practical implementations of MLCP, i.e., Instance Reproduction MLCP(IR-MLCP), Binary Relevance MLCP(BR-MLCP) and Power Set MLCP(PS-MLCP). The calibration properties of the three different implementations of MLCP are then investigated, as well as the prediction efficiencies and computational complexities are analyzed.

2   Related Work

2.1   Multi-Label Learning

The learning setting of MLL can be described as follows: the learning data is given as (x, Y) , where x is the instance and $Y \subseteq \mathcal{Y} = \{1, 2, ..., Q\}$ is the *labelset* while $\mathcal{Y}$ is the whole set of labels containing Q labels. An MLL classifier tries to learn a real valued function $f(x, y), y \in \mathcal{Y}$ which measures the confidence of y being the proper label of x. Thus, given a specified threshold $t(x)$, the MLL classifier outputs the predicted *labelset*: $h(x) = \{y | f(x, y) > t(x), y \in \mathcal{Y}\}$, where $h(x)$ obviously is a region prediction.

   A large variety of algorithms have been proposed to construct the confidence measure $f(x, y)$. Generally, existing MLL algorithms can be divided into two groups using the categorization scheme of transformation method[6]. One is Pattern Transformation (PT), which splits the multi-label examples straightforward into single-label examples and then applies single-label machine learning algorithms to tackle the multi-pattern recognition problem. Among the PT methods, only three approaches are really valuable, including decomposing a multi-label example into several single-label examples or into several independent binary classification problems, or wrapping independently each *labelset* as a new single-label class. And the other is Algorithmic Adaption(AA) method, which adapts traditional single-label algorithms for the multi-label example and constructs corresponding MLL classifier. Nevertheless, most AA approaches in essence are in conjunction with the PT methods [3]. Therefore, we adopt three PT methods as the underlying algorithm for CP, and then construct three implementations of MLCP respectively.

2.2   Conformal Predictor

Given a training example sequence $Z^{(n)} = (z_1, z_2, ..., z_n)$ and a testing instance x_{n+1}, CP applies transductive inference to incorporate the test instance to learn the predicted label. Specifically, CP iterates through each possible label $y \in \{1, 2, ..., C\}$, where C is the number of labels, to establish a respective testing example $z_{n+1}^y = (x_{n+1}, y)$. Then the test example is incorporated with the training data $Z^{(n)}$ to construct the corresponding testing data sequence, i.e., $z_1, z_2, ..., z_n, z_{n+1}^y$. After that, CP executes the algorithmic randomness test to evaluate the fitness of testing data sequence being i.i.d.. In order to fit the multi-dimensional data, a compromise is reached on that uses a particular non-conformity function Λ to map the testing data sequence into a sequence of real score, i.e,

$$\alpha_i = \Lambda(\{z_1, \ldots, z_{i-1}, z_{i+1}, \ldots, z_n, z_{n+1}^y\}, z_i) \qquad (1)$$

As a necessity, each score α_i reflects the nonconformity of the example z_i with the rest examples. Next, a smoothed p-value is computed as follows,

$$p_{n+1}^y = \frac{\left|\{i = 1, 2, ..., n+1 : \alpha_i > \alpha_{n+1}^y\}\right| + \lambda \cdot \left|\{i = 1, 2, ..., n+1 : \alpha_i = \alpha_{n+1}^y\}\right|}{n+1}$$

$$(2)$$

where λ is a random value in $[0, 1]$.

In the end, given a predefined significance level ε, CP outputs the prediction set as follows:

$$\tau_{n+1}^\varepsilon = \{y : p_{n+1}^y > \varepsilon, y = 1, 2, ..., C\} \qquad (3)$$

The virtue of CP is that the error rate has been theoretically proved to be bounded by the significance level ε, i.e.,

$$P\{y_{n+1} \notin \tau_{n+1}^\varepsilon\} \leq \varepsilon \qquad (4)$$

where y_{n+1} is the true label of the test instance x_{n+1}. The formality of Equation (4) is well known as the calibration property of CP.

3   The Implementations of Multi-Label Conformal Predictor

Consider the learning setting of MLCP : given a training example sequence $Z^{(n)} = ((x_1, Y_1), (x_2, Y_2), ..., (x_n, Y_n))$, the task is output a *labelset* for the testing instance x_{n+1}. With three PT methods being the underlying algorithms of CP, three implementations of MLCP, i.e., Instance Reproduction MLCP (IR-MLCP), Binary Relevance MLCP (BR-MLCP) and Power Set MLCP (PS-MLCP) can be constructed respectively.

IR-MLCP and PS-MLCP have been introduced in recent two papers[5,8], and BR-MLCP is the new one firstly proposed in this paper. All three algorithms are described in detail as follows.

3.1   Instance Reproduction MLCP

The implementation of IR-MLCP has been proposed in our previous study[8]. The pseudo-code of IR-MLCP is demonstrated in Algorithm 1.

Algorithm 1. Instance Reproduction MLCP

Data: training set $\mathbf{Z}^{(n)}$, testing instance x_{n+1}
Result: predicted *labelset* $\hat{Y}_{n+1}$
initialization;

1. $\mathbf{Z}^{(n)} \to \mathbf{Z}^{(n')}$ where $n' \geq n$ representing the size of enlarged single-label dataset.
   for $i = 1$ **to** n **do**
   - given $Y_i = \{h_1, h_2, ..., h_{l_i}\}$, where $\{h_1, h_2, ..., h_{l_i}\} \subseteq \{1, 2, ..., Q\}$ and l_i is the size of the *labelset* Y_i. The instance x_i is replicated $(l_i - 1)$ times to propagate l_i identical instances.
   - each pair of $(x_i, h_j), j = 1, 2, ..., l_i$ is added to the new single-label dataset
   end

2. the test instance x_{n+1} is committed to the new dataset $\mathbf{Z}^{(n')}$ for prediction.
3. applying basic procedure of conformal prediction, i.e., Equation (1) and (2), to output a region prediction as follows,

$$\tau_{n+1}^{\varepsilon} = \{q : p_{n+1}^q > \varepsilon, q = 1, 2, ..., Q\} \tag{5}$$

4. using τ_{n+1}^{ε} as the prediction *labelset* $\hat{Y}_{n+1}$

It is worth noting that MLL classifier, as well as IR-MLCP, is essentially a region predictor. Consequently, many evaluation metrics rather than accuracy rate have been studied. The performance of IR-MLCP has been studied using some MLL-specified evaluation criteria, i.e., Hamming loss,one-error,etc.[8]. Furthermore, in order to explore the calibration property of IR-MLCP, a definition of error is needed. In this scenario, an error occurs if the label in true *labelset* Y_{n+1} is not present in the prediction τ_{n+1}^{ε} ,

$$\text{err}_{n+1}^{h_j} = \begin{cases} 1 & h_j \notin \tau_{n+1}^{\varepsilon}, h_j \in Y_{n+1} \\ 0 & otherwise \end{cases} \tag{6}$$

Therefore, IR-MLCP is *valid* if it satisfies the calibration property

$$P\{\text{err}_{n+1} \leq \varepsilon\} \leq \varepsilon \tag{7}$$

where $\text{err}_{n+1} = \frac{1}{|Y_{n+1}|} \sum_{h_j \in Y_{n+1}} \text{err}_{n+1}^{h_j}$.

3.2   Binary Relevance MLCP

The implementation of BR-MLCP is a new method first proposed in this paper. The underlying PT method is using one-against-all method to convert Q single-label datasets into the binary classification problem. The pseudo-code of BR-MLCP is given in Algorithm 2.

It's worth noting that a label is chosen to be a predicted result with its p-value greater than ε/Q instead of ε. It is derived from the integrating effect of multiple p-values which possess the valid property,i.e., $P\{p \leq \varepsilon\} \leq \varepsilon$ [4]. Actually, BR-MLCP also outputs a *labelset*. An error occurs if the true *labelset* Y_{n+1} is not a subset of the prediction set τ_{n+1}^{ε} . Therefore, BR-MLCP is *valid* if it satisfies the theorem as follows:

Algorithm 2. Binary Relevance MLCP

Data: training set $\mathbf{Z}^{(n)}$, testing instance x_{n+1}
Result: predicted *labelset* $\hat{Y}_{n+1}$
initialization;

1. $\mathbf{Z}^{(n)} \rightarrow \{\mathbf{Z}^{(n)q} = (z_1^q, z_2^q, ..., z_n^q), q = 1, 2, ..., Q\}$
   for $q = 1$ **to** Q **do**
   - construct a binary dataset $\mathbf{Z}^{(n)q}$ with the example like $z_i^q = (x_i, b_i)$, where $b_i \in \{q, -q\}$ with $b_i = q$ if $q \in Y_i$ and $-q$ otherwise.
   - the test instance x_{n+1} is committed to the new dataset $\mathbf{Z}^{(n)q}$ for prediction.
   - applying basic procedure of conformal prediction, i.e., Equation (1) and (2), to output the confidence measure, i.e., p-value p_{n+1}^q

   end
2. Collecting all Q p-values, i.e., $p_{n+1}^q, q = 1, 2, ..., Q$ to output a region prediction, as follows,

$$\tau_{n+1}^\varepsilon = \{q : p_{n+1}^q > \varepsilon/Q, q = 1, 2, ..., Q\} \tag{8}$$

3. using τ_{n+1}^ε as the prediction *labelset* $\hat{Y}_{n+1}$

Theorem 1. *BR-MLCP satisfies the following validity property:*

$$P\{Y_{n+1} \not\subset \tau_{n+1}^\varepsilon\} \leq \varepsilon \tag{9}$$

Proof. The event $Y_{n+1} \not\subset \tau_{n+1}^\varepsilon$ may happen if there exists at least one $q \in \{1, 2, ..., Q\}$, such that $q \in Y_{n+1}$ but $q \notin \tau_{n+1}^\varepsilon$. In terms of a binary problem, this means: $z_{n+1}^q = q$ but $p_{n+1}^q \leq \varepsilon/Q$. By validity of two-class CP, the probability of this is at most ε/Q for each q. So the overall probability is at most ε.

$$P\{Y_{n+1} \not\subset \tau_{n+1}^\varepsilon\} \leq \varepsilon \tag{10}$$

3.3 Power Set MLCP

PS-MLCP has been proposed by Papadopoulos [5]. The pseudo-code of PS-MLCP is demonstrated in Algorithm 3.

Obviously, the deficiency of PS-MLCP is the sophisticated output, which contains a set of *labelsets*. Generally, the output of PS-MLCP is not the final result. It usually should be further submitted to practitioner for clarification. An error occurs if the true *labelset* Y_{n+1} is not in the predicted *labelsets*. Obviously, due to the consistence with ordinary conformal prediction, PS-MLCP should be valid.

4 Experimental Results

Two of the most commonly used benchmark datasets in MLL, i.e., *scene* and *yeast*, were used in the experiments. Both datasets can be downloaded from the benchmark sources of MLL (http://mulan.sourceforge.net/datasets.html).

Algorithm 3. Power Set MLCP

Data: training set $\mathbf{Z}^{(n)}$, testing instance x_{n+1}
Result: predicted *labelsets*
initialization;

1. $Z^{(n)} \rightarrow Z'^{(n)}$
   for $i = 1$ **to** n **do**
   - (x_i, Y_i) is transform to be (x_i, γ_i) where the new class γ_i is in the label power-set space, i.e., $\gamma_i \in \{1, 2, ..., 2^Q\}$
   end
2. the test instance x_{n+1} is committed to the new single-label dataset $\mathbf{Z}'^{(n)} = ((x_1, \gamma_1), (x_2, \gamma_2), ..., (x_n, \gamma_n))$ for prediction.
3. applying basic procedure of conformal prediction, i.e., Equations (1) and (2), to output a predicted *labelsets* as follows,

$$\tau_{n+1}^{\varepsilon} = \{\gamma : p_{n+1}^{\gamma} > \varepsilon, \gamma = 1, 2, ..., 2^Q\} \tag{11}$$

4. using τ_{n+1}^{ε} to be a set of *labelsets* as the prediction result for x_{n+1}

The first data set, *scene*, is an image dataset that assigns each image with one or more labels, coming from the whole set of six labels, i.e., beach, sunset, field, fall-foliage, mountain, and urban. The index of Label Cardinality (LC) which computes the average number of labels per example is quite low 1.08 in *scene*. Furthermore, many *labelsets* (e.g. mountains+sunset +field) are extremely rare. So the number of Actual *Labelsets*(AL) is far less than that of Bound of *Labelsets*(BL). In addition, the index of *Labelsets* Diversity (LD) which is used to describe the proportion of distinct *Labelsets* appeared in *scene*, is 23%. The second data set, *yeast*, is a biomedical data set that represents each gene with several gene functions (labels) coming from a complete set of 14 labels. The characteristics of *yeast* as well as *scene* are summarized in Table 1.

Table 1. Characteristics of datasets

	#examples	#attributes	#labels	BL	AL	LD	LC
scene	2407	294	6	64	15	23%	1.08
yeast	2417	103	14	2417	198	8%	4.25

According to Algorithms 1-3, the common phase in three different implementations of MLCP is the basic procedure of conformal prediction, which requires a design of nonconformity measure to compute the sequence of nonconformity scores in Equation (1). For the sake of consistency and comparability, we chose the same nonconformity measure in each algorithm. Specially, we used the widely known KNN-based nonconformity measure, i.e., $\alpha_i = \frac{\sum_{j=1}^{K} D_{ij}^{y_i}}{\sum_{j=1}^{K} D_{ij}^{-y_i}}, i = 1, 2, ...,$ where α_i is the nonconformity score of the example in terms of (x_i, y_i). Notably, the set of classes containing y_i and $-y_i$ is diversity, i.e., Q classes for IR-MLCP, 2 classes for BR-MLCP and 2^Q classes for PS-MLCP. And $D_{ij}^{y_i}$ and $D_{ij}^{-y_i}$ is the *jth* shortest distance between instance x_i and the instances labelled same and differently from x_i respectively. And K is the number of nearest neighbours. In our experiments, the parameter K was set to be $K = 3$, and Euclidean distance was used to obtain the distance between two instances. All the three algorithms were executed in online mode.

4.1   Comparisons of Calibration Property

In this subsection, we present the empirical exploration of the calibration property of three MLCP implementations. The distributions of error rate against significance level are depicted in Fig. 1 for IR-MLCP, in Fig. 2 for BR-MLCP and in Fig. 3 for PS-MLCP respectively.

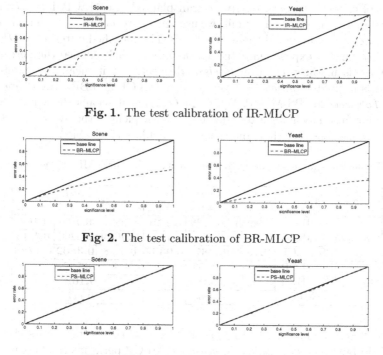

Fig. 1. The test calibration of IR-MLCP

Fig. 2. The test calibration of BR-MLCP

Fig. 3. The test calibration of PS-MLCP

It can be seen in Fig. 1, the baseline serves as ideal property, i.e., exact calibration, where the error rate is exactly equal to the predefined significance level. Obviously, the distributions of IR-MLCP in both cases of *scence* and *yeast* are all lower than their corresponding base calibration lines, i.e., the error rates are always smaller than the corresponding significance levels, which shows that IR-MLCP performs conservative calibration. Fig. 2 shows that the distributions of BR-MLCP is also under the baselines, which illustrates the property of conservative calibration. While for PS-MLCP in Fig. 3, the calibration lines are closely attached to the baseline, which demonstrates excellent calibration property.

In conclusion, all the three implementations of MLCP, i.e, IR-MLCP, BR-MLCP and PS-MLCP, are valid. It manifests that calibrated MLL prediction via conformal predictors is feasible. In return, it reveals that conformal prediction preserves effective ways of adapting its framework to MLL. Therefore, the implementations of IR-MLCP, BR-MLCP and PS-MLCP can provide calibrated prediction to make the error rate bounded by the predefined significance level.

4.2   Comparisons of Prediction Efficiency

Except for the test calibration property, the prediction efficiency is another main consideration of MLCP methods. According to CP, there are two kinds of efficiency criteria: ε-dependent efficiency criteria and ε-free efficiency criteria[2]. The two sets of criteria can accordingly be transplanted into MLCP, but need some modifications. Due to the page limit, we used two criteria chosen from each of the sets of criteria and modified them for MLCP. The modified criteria are OE_{MLL} and OF_{MLL} in our experiments. In case of OE_{MLL}, it is defined the percentage of false labels in the prediction *labelset*. Respectively, it mean the number of false labels in prediction *labelset* over Q for IR-MLCP and BR-MLCP, and over Actual *Labelsets* for PS-MLCP. While for OF_{MLL}, it means the average of all p-values for false labels for a test instance. Consequently, the averaged OF_{MLL} and OE_{MLL} across the whole dataset were calculated in Table 2.

Table 2. Comparison of prediction efficiency for three MLCP methods

Criteria	Method	scene			yeast		
		$\varepsilon = 0.05$	$\varepsilon = 0.1$	$\varepsilon = 0.2$	$\varepsilon = 0.05$	$\varepsilon = 0.1$	$\varepsilon = 0.2$
OE_{MLL}	IR-MLCP	0.8933	0.6236	0.2621	0.9801	0.9596	0.9183
	BR-MLCP	0.2436	0.1806	0.1196	**0.5689**	0.5266	0.4615
	PS-MLCP	**0.1559**	**0.0873**	**0.0392**	0.6508	**0.3502**	**0.1743**
OF_{MLL}	IR-MLCP	0.1653			0.737		
	BR-MLCP	**0.0215**			**0.1027**		
	PS-MLCP	0.0363			0.1174		

Note that the smaller of OE_{MLL} or OF_{MLL} , the better is. As shown in Table 2, in both cases of *scene* and *yeast*, PS-MLCP performs the best in terms of OE_{MLL}, with the gap between PS-MLCP and the others is enlarged when ε is large. While BR-MLCP illustrates its better efficiency in terms of OF_{MLL}. Theoretically, high prediction efficiency of MLCP methods stems from two aspects, i.e., the effectiveness of multi-label transformation and the effectiveness of conformal prediction. Obviously, PS-MLCP owes to its ability of attracting complete potential correlations among labels. While PS-MLCP may dramatically worsen when it handles with a large amount of classes in conformal prediction. While the factor of effective conformal prediction contributes to the superiority of BR-MLCP. Because conformal prediction tends to be successful in the binary classification tasks. Furthermore, the KNN-based nonconformity measure also promotes the superiority of BR-MLCP, because it always deals well with class-imbalance when K is small. When it comes IR-MLCP, the relatively poor efficiency might be due to the ignorance of label correlations and the large amount of multiple classes in conformal prediction.

4.3   Comparisons of Computational Complexity

From the comparative respective, computational complexity is an important issue. The computational cost of MLCP method depends on the computational complexity of multi-label data transformation method and the basic procedure of conformal prediction. Especially, by using the same KNN-based nonconformity measure in different MLCP methods, the computational complexity of conformal prediction is similar. That is, suppose the number of train data is n, the number of features is p and the number of labels is Q, the computational cost of KNN-based conformal prediction is $\mathcal{O}(Q \cdot n \cdot p)$. However, the actual value of $\mathcal{O}(Q \cdot n \cdot p)$ is determined by the computational complexity of different multi-label data transformation methods.

For IR-MLCP, the computational cost is $\mathcal{O}(Q \cdot n' \cdot p)$. The expansion of train dataset $Z^{(n)} \rightarrow Z^{(n')}$ makes up a great portion of computational cost when the label cardinality is large. For BR-MLCP, the basic conformal prediction must be executed Q times. So there is a multiplier Q for the time complexity. However, each basic conformal prediction consists of binary labels. Consequently, the computational cost is $\mathcal{O}(Q \cdot 2 \cdot n \cdot p)$. For PS-MLCP, the *labelset* transformation from Y_i to $\gamma_i \in \{1, 2, ..., 2^Q\}$ contributes to the computation burden. In extreme cases, the computational cost of PS-MLCP is $\mathcal{O}(2^Q \cdot n \cdot p)$, while the computational burden can reduce when labelsets diversity is small.

Table 3. Averaged execution time (Second) of three MLCP methods

dataset	IR-MLCP	BR-MLCP	PS-MLCP
scene	**145.61**	339.97	275.39
yeast	4802.69	**529.61**	3426.05

Besides the theoretical complexity analysis, we recorded the averaged time of 10 runs of three MLCP methos in Table 3. From Table 3 we can see IR-MLCP runs fastest in *scene* dataset and BR-MLCP runs almost ten times more quickly than the other two MLCP methods in *yeast* dataset. While BR-MLCP is the slowest for *scene* dataset, IR-MLCP is the slowest in *yeast* dataset. Obviously, the label cardinality factor determines the performance of IR-MLCP in the experiments. Consider BR-MLCP in the case of *yeast* with 14 labels, it obtains excellent performance when the number of labels is large. While for PS-MLCP, it does not have an advantage in terms of computation efficiency.

5 Conclusion

This paper presents the first summary of three implementations of multi-label conformal predictors, i.e., IR-MLCP, BR-MLCP and PS-MLCP, which illustrated and compared in detail the respective pros and cons of each method. The experimental results showed that all the three methods have calibration property that guarantees theoretical reliability in prediction. Comparatively, in case of prediction efficiency, BR-MLCP always benefits from effective conformal prediction, while PS-MLCP can take advantage of attracting complete potential correlations among labels. While in terms of computational cost, both IR-MLCP and BR-MLCP have advantages. Further work should establish additional implementation of MLCP for multi-label learning task. Furthermore, the adaption of traditional single-label nonconformity measures to fit the multi-label example would also be crucial for the success of multi-label conformal prediction. In addition, the reduction of computational burden of PS-MLCP could be investigated when the union of the outputted *labelsets* is informative.

Acknowledgments. The authors thank Professor Alex Gammerman and Professor Vladimir Vovk for them pointing out the directions for this research. This work is supported by EPSRC grant EP/K033344/1 (Mining the Network Behaviour of Bots); by the National Natural Science Foundation of China (No.61128003) grant; the Natural Science Foundation of Fujian Province in China under Grant (No.2012J01274).

References

1. Balasubramanian, V., Ho, S.S., Vovk, V.: Conformal Prediction for Reliable Machine Learning: Theory. Adaptations and Applications. Morgan Kaufmann, Massachusetts (2014)
2. Fedorova, V.: Conformal prediction and testing under on-line compression models. PhD Thesis, Royal Holloway University of London (2014)
3. Madjarov, G., Kocev, D., Gjorgjevikj, D., Dzeroski, S.: An extensive experimental comparison of methods for multi-label learning. Pattern Recognition **45**(9), 3084–3104 (2012)
4. Nouretdinov, I., Melluish, T., Vovk, V.: Ridge regression confidence machine. In: ICML, pp. 385–392. Citeseer (2001)
5. Papadopoulos, H.: A Cross-Conformal Predictor for Multi-label Classification. In: Iliadis, L., Maglogiannis, I., Papadopoulos, H., Sioutas, S., Makris, C. (eds.) AIAI 2014 Workshops. IFIP AICT, vol. 437, pp. 241–250. Springer, Heidelberg (2014)
6. Tsoumakas, G., Katakis, I.: Multi-label classification: An overview. International Journal of Data Warehousing and Mining (IJDWM) **3**(3), 1–13 (2007)
7. Vovk, V., Gammerman, A., Shafer, G.: Algorithmic Learning in a Random World. Springer, New York (2005)
8. Wang, H., Liu, X., Lv, B., Yang, F., Hong, Y.: Reliable multi-label learning via conformal predictor and random forest for syndrome differentiation of chronic fatigue in traditional chinese medicine. PLoS ONE **9**(6), e99565 (2014)
9. Zhang, M.L., Zhou, Z.H.: A review on multi-label learning algorithms. IEEE Transactions on Knowledge and Data Engineering **26**(8), 1819–1837 (2014)
10. Zhang, M., Zhou, Z.: Ml-knn: A lazy learning approach to multi-label learning. Pattern Recognition **40**(7), 2038–2048 (2007)

Modifications to p-Values of Conformal Predictors

Lars Carlsson[1]([✉]), Ernst Ahlberg[1], Henrik Boström[2], Ulf Johansson[3], and Henrik Linusson[3]

[1] Drug Safety and Metabolism, AstraZeneca Innovative Medicines and Early Development, Mölndal, Sweden
{lars.a.carlsson,ernst.ahlberg}@astrazeneca.com
[2] Department of Systems and Computer Sciences, Stockholm University, Stockholm, Sweden
henrik.bostrom@dsv.su.se
[3] School of Business and IT, University of Borås, Borås, Sweden
{ulf.johansson,henrik.linusson}@hb.se

Abstract. The original definition of a p-value in a conformal predictor can sometimes lead to too conservative prediction regions when the number of training or calibration examples is small. The situation can be improved by using a modification to define an approximate p-value. Two modified p-values are presented that converges to the original p-value as the number of training or calibration examples goes to infinity.

Numerical experiments empirically support the use of a p-value we call the interpolated p-value for conformal prediction. The interpolated p-value seems to be producing prediction sets that have an error rate which corresponds well to the prescribed significance level.

1 Introduction

Conformal predictors [6] provide an excellent way of generating hedged predictions. Given a prescribed significance level, ϵ, they make errors when predicting new examples at a rate corresponding to ϵ. The conformal predictor is said to be a valid predictor. This property is attained by predicting sets of possible labels rather than individual labels which is often the case for standard machine-learning methods. However, all conformal predictors are conservatively valid which means that the error rate usually is smaller than the required significance level. Conservative validity leads to less or non-optimal efficiency for a predictor and the ideal situation would be for any conformal predictor to be exactly valid, not only because the relation to efficiency but also because we do not want the predictions to deviate from our expectation with respect to the

---

This work was supported by the Swedish Foundation for Strategic Research through the project High-Performance Data Mining for Drug Effect Detection (IIS11-0053) and the Knowledge Foundation through the project Big Data Analytics by Online Ensemble Learning (20120192).

A. Gammerman et al. (Eds.): SLDS 2015, LNAI 9047, pp. 251–259, 2015.
DOI: 10.1007/978-3-319-17091-6_20

error rate. Reduced efficiency has been observed when using inductive conformal predictors on typical regression datasets from the drug-discovery domain [4]. The observation was that for predictions at low significance levels, prediction ranges sometimes exceeded the observed label range, which could be perceived by users of such predictors as the conformal prediction theory is not very useful. In ongoing work where we use trees for inductive conformal predictions and condition on examples in end leaves of the trees, we observe a similar pattern [5]. In both these examples the problem seems to originate from a limited number of calibration examples leading to an insufficient resolution in p-values.

Given that the exchangeability assumption is fulfilled, the main vehicle for achieving improved efficiency is through improved definitions of the nonconformity scores. This is an area of active research and there are many different ways to construct nonconformity scores through for example using different machine-learning algorithms as part of the definition of nonconformity scores. This is a trial and error process. Another possibility would be to see if there are alternative ways of using the nonconformity scores when computing p-values. We are not aware of any previous approaches and this is why we will attempt to put forward suggestions for alternative definitions of p-values.

The organization of this paper is the following. In the next section we propose another definition of a p-value and also a more generally described p-value. We show that they converge to the p-value suggested in [6] as the number of training examples goes to infinity. Then, in section 3, we empirically study validity and efficiency of all three types of p-values. We conclude the paper in the last section discussing the results.

2   Modifications of the P-value

We are considering a set of examples $\{z_1, \ldots, z_n\}$. A general definition of a smoothed conformal predictor is given in [6], however in this section we will study a non-smoothed p-value or its modifications without loss of generality. The definition of a non-smoothed p-value can be expressed as

$$p = \frac{|\{i = 1, \ldots, n : \alpha_i \geq \alpha_n\}|}{n}, \tag{1}$$

and we will refer to this as the *original p-value*. In this case α_n is the nonconformity score of a new example z_n. This example can be predicted using a set predictor

$$\Gamma^\epsilon(z_1, \ldots, z_{n-1}) : \{z | p > \epsilon\}, \tag{2}$$

and the nonconformity scores are defined by

$$(\alpha_1, \ldots, \alpha_n) := A(z_1, \ldots, z_n), \tag{3}$$

where A is a nonconformity function producing nonconformity scores for z_i under the exchangeability model. In (1) the nonconformity score α_n, corresponding to the new example z_n, is assumed to belong to the same probability distribution as the nonconformity scores of the previously observed examples and is included in the distribution when its relative position (based on size) is determined. Since all different α_i that we have observed are random discrete variables, we can define a probability density function

$$f(t) = \sum_{i=1}^{n} \frac{1}{n}\delta(t - \alpha_i), \tag{4}$$

where δ is the Dirac delta function. Furthermore, assume $\alpha_i \in [\alpha_{min}, \alpha_{max}]$ and $\alpha_{min}, \alpha_{max} \in \mathbf{R}$. Then

$$F(\alpha_n) := Pr(t \geq \alpha_n) = \int_{\alpha_n}^{\alpha_{max}} \sum_{i=1}^{n} \frac{1}{n}\delta(t - \alpha_i)dt$$

$$= \frac{1}{n}\sum_{i=1}^{n} \big(\theta(\alpha_{max} - \alpha_i) - \theta(\alpha_n - \alpha_i)\big), \tag{5}$$

where θ is the Heaviside step function. If we assume that all α_i are different and that $\alpha_{min} < \alpha_n < \alpha_{max}$ then (5) becomes

$$F(\alpha_n) = \frac{1}{n}\sum_{i=1}^{n} \big(1 - \theta(\alpha_n - \alpha_i)\big). \tag{6}$$

With $\theta(0) := 0$ we get $F(\alpha_n) \equiv p$ and since all α_i are exchangeable the probability that the set predictor Γ^ϵ will make an error is ϵ as $n \to \infty$.

Let us consider an alternative view where we exclude α_n from the distribution of random discrete variables. After all, given the set of previous observations $\{z_1, \ldots, z_{n-1}\}$ we want to assess how nonconforming z_n is. All examples are still equally probable and we do not change the assumption of exchangeability. The probability density function with z_n excluded is

$$\tilde{f}(t) = \sum_{i=1}^{n-1} \frac{1}{n-1}\delta(t - \alpha_i), \tag{7}$$

corresponding to (5) a *modified p-value* can be defined as

$$\tilde{p} := \tilde{F}(\alpha_n) = \frac{1}{n-1}\sum_{i=1}^{n-1} \big(1 - \theta(\alpha_n - \alpha_i)\big). \tag{8}$$

To see what effect our alternative view has we form the difference between the original and modified p-value

$$p - \tilde{p} = \left(\frac{1}{n} - \frac{1}{n-1}\right)\sum_{i=1}^{n-1} \big(1 - \theta(\alpha_n - \alpha_i)\big) + \frac{1}{n}$$

$$= \frac{1 - \tilde{F}(\alpha_n)}{n}$$

$$= \frac{1 - \tilde{p}}{n}. \tag{9}$$

Rearranging this last expression leads to $\tilde{p} = (np - 1)/(n - 1)$ and as $n \to \infty$ the modified p-value converges to the original p-value. Thus, we have shown the following proposition.

Proposition 1. *A conformal predictor based on the p-value in (8) is asymptotically conservatively valid.*

An alternative way of representing the modified p-value is

$$\tilde{p} = \frac{|\{i = 1, \ldots, n-1 : \alpha_i \geq \alpha_n\}|}{n-1}, \tag{10}$$

and smoothing can be applied similarly to how it is applied to the original p-value, since smoothing is a way to ensure that p-values ultimately are distributed uniformly even though there are two or more nonconformity scores that are identical. It is interesting to observe that, given that the nonconformity scores are sorted and renumbered in increasing order, for one particular i then $\alpha_{i-1} < \alpha_n < \alpha_i$ where $i = 2, \ldots, n - 1$. For any α_n within these bounds the p-value will be constant. In the following in addition to sorted nonconformity scores, also assume that $0 \leq t \leq 1$ and $t \in \mathbf{R}$. Furthermore, let there exist a monotonically increasing function $g(t)$ with known values $g(t_0 := 0) = \alpha_{min}$, $g(t_{n-1} := 1) = \alpha_{max}$, $g(t_n) = \alpha_n$ and $g(t_i) = \alpha_i$ for $i = 1, \ldots, n - 2$. The corresponding probability density function is

$$f_g(t) = \sum_{i=1}^{n-1} g(t)\big(\theta(t - t_{i-1}) - \theta(t - t_i)\big), \tag{11}$$

with a p-value defined as

$$p_g := F_g(t_n) = Pr(t \geq t_n) = \frac{\int_{t_n}^1 f_g(t)dt}{\int_0^1 f_g(t)dt}. \tag{12}$$

NB we do not have to explicitly compute this expression as long as $\tilde{p} \leq p_g$ and this is obviously true for any α_n and i such that $\alpha_{i-1} < \alpha_n < \alpha_i$ where $i = 1, \ldots, n - 1$. Hence, we only need to estimate t_n to get p_g. To conclude this section, we have now shown the following proposition.

Proposition 2. *A conformal predictor based on the p-value in (12) is asymptotically conservatively valid.*

3   Empirical Results of Modified P-values

In this section we will empirically study the validity and efficiency of conformal predictors based on the three different p-values described in the previous section. We are particularly interested in the case of small calibration sets. But first we will define a p-value corresponding to (12). Given that the nonconformity scores of the already learnt examples are sorted in increasing order with respect to their index, that is $\alpha_i < \alpha_{i+1}$, find a $k = 0, \ldots, n-2$ such that $\alpha_k < \alpha_n < \alpha_{k+1}$. Then an alternative expression to (12) based on determining t_n by linear interpolation using $g(t_k)$, $g(t_{k+1})$ and $g(t_n)$ is,

$$p_g = \frac{|\{i = 1, \ldots, n-1 : \alpha_i \geq \alpha_n\}| - 1}{n - 1} + \frac{1 - \dfrac{\alpha_n - \alpha_k}{\alpha_{k+1} - \alpha_k}}{n - 1}. \tag{13}$$

The second term comes from the linear interpolation and we remark that other approximations can be used to more accurately describe $g(t_n)$ as long as they are monotonically increasing. Even for this p-value, smoothing can be applied in exactly the same way as it is applied for the original p-value. We will in the remainder of this paper refer to the p-value in (1) as the *original p-value*, to (10) as the *modified p-value* and finally to (13) as the *interpolated p-value*.

For the numerical experiments, we have used both binary classification responses and regression responses. We used the random forest implementation of the scikit-learn package [1] with default parameters and always 100 trees. The nonconformity scores for classification was defined as

$$\alpha = 1 - \hat{P}(y \mid h(x)), \tag{14}$$

and for regression it was

$$\alpha = \frac{|h(x) - y|}{\sigma(x)}, \tag{15}$$

where $h(x)$ is a prediction of an object x and y the object's label. $\hat{P}$ is what scikit-learn denotes probability. In the case of regression, we trained a second model on log-residual errors and the corresponding prediction of an object is $\sigma(x)$. The prediction sets for classification were calculated using (2) and in the regression case the following expression was used to compute the prediction range for a given significance level ϵ

$$\hat{Y}^\epsilon = h(x) \pm \alpha_\epsilon \sigma(x), \tag{16}$$

and the midpoint of the range, $y = h(x)$. The datasets used in the empirical study are listed in Table 1. All datasets were taken from UCI [3] except `anacalt`, which was taken from KEEL [2]. The response variables of the regression datasets were linearly scaled to have values in the range $[0, 1]$ and the objects were not scaled. The procedure we followed to generate the empirical results is outlined in Algorithm 1.

Table 1. Datasets

(a) Classification

Dataset	Features
balance-scale	4
diabetes	8
mushroom	121
spambase	57
tic-tac-toe	27

(b) Regression

Dataset	Features
abalone	8
anacalt	7
boston	13
comp	12
stock	9

for $iter \in \{1, 20\}$ **do**
    for $dataset \in datasets$ **do**
        for $calibrationSize \in \{29, 49, 99\}$ **do**
            trainX, testY = dataset.drawrandom(200)
            testX, testY = dataset.drawrandom(100)
            calX, calY = dataset.drawrandom(calibrationSize)
            model = train(trainX, trainY)
            nonconformityScores = calibrate(model, calX, calY)
            predict(testX, model, nonconformityScores, original)
            predict(testX, model, nonconformityScores, modified)
            predict(testX, model, nonconformityScores, interpolated)
        end
    end
end

Algorithm 1. This represents how the numerical experiments were conducted. The function `dataset.drawrandom(n)` randomly draws, without replacement, a subset of size n from dataset.

The results for classification and regression were calculated averaging the results for each individual dataset and they are presented in Figures 1 and 2, respectively and are shown for significance levels from 0 to 0.2. The main observation is that for both types of labels, in terms of error rate as well as for efficiency, the interpolated p-value seems to be upper bounded by the original p-value and lower bounded by the modified p-value. Also, the interpolated p-value changes smoothly as opposed to the other two that have a saw-toothed shape. The order of the p-values in terms of increasing efficiency is original, to interpolated and then to modified. In terms of increasing error rate the order is reversed.

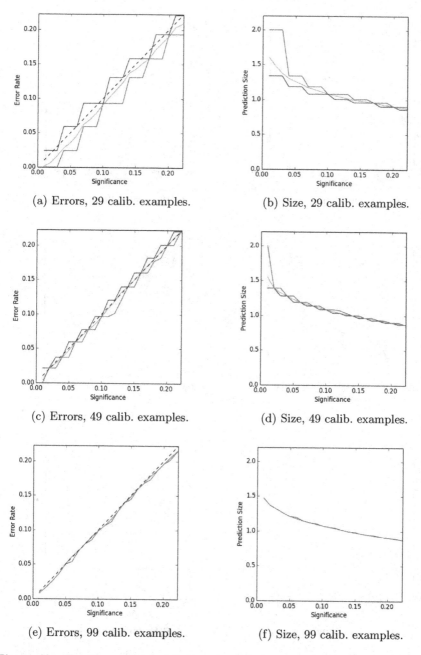

(a) Errors, 29 calib. examples.

(b) Size, 29 calib. examples.

(c) Errors, 49 calib. examples.

(d) Size, 49 calib. examples.

(e) Errors, 99 calib. examples.

(f) Size, 99 calib. examples.

Fig. 1. Classification error rates (left) and prediction sizes (right, average number of classes per prediction) for original p-values (red), modified p-values (blue), interpolated p-values (cyan)

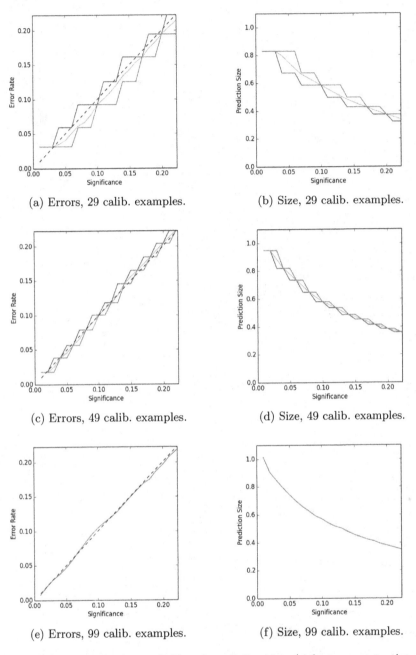

(a) Errors, 29 calib. examples.

(b) Size, 29 calib. examples.

(c) Errors, 49 calib. examples.

(d) Size, 49 calib. examples.

(e) Errors, 99 calib. examples.

(f) Size, 99 calib. examples.

Fig. 2. Regression error rates (left) and prediction sizes (right, average portion of the label space covered per prediction) for original p-values (red), modified p-values (blue), interpolated p-values (cyan)

4 Discussion

We have introduced a new type of p-value which is based on interpolated nonconformity scores. The interpolated p-value is shown to be asymptotically conservatively valid and empirically more close to being exactly valid than the original p-value proposed in [6]. We remark that these differences are only observed when the learnt distribution of calibrations examples are relatively small *i.e.* under 100 examples. For larger samples there does not seem to be a difference and our theoretical analysis show that all p-values covered in this paper converge to the same value for one particular set of examples as the example size goes to infinity. The computational complexity of the interpolated p-value is of the same order as the original p-value. In future work, we will try to compare the original p-value to the interpolated p-value when applied to different datasets and also with different nonconformity functions.

References

1. scikit-learn 0.15 (2014). http://scikitlearn.org/
2. Alcalá, J., Fernández, A., Luengo, J., Derrac, J., García, S., Sánchez, L., Herrera, F.: Keel data-mining software tool: Data set repository, integration of algorithms and experimental analysis framework. Journal of Multiple-Valued Logic and Soft Computing **17**, 255–287 (2010)
3. Bache, K., Lichman, M.: UCI machine learning repository (2013). http://archive.ics.uci.edu/ml
4. Eklund, M., Norinder, U., Boyer, S., Carlsson, L.: Application of conformal prediction in QSAR. In: Iliadis, L., Maglogiannis, I., Papadopoulos, H., Karatzas, K., Sioutas, S. (eds.) AIAI 2012 Workshops. IFIP AICT, vol. 382, pp. 166–175. Springer, Heidelberg (2012)
5. Johansson, U., Ahlberg, E., Boström, H., Carlsson, L., Linusson, H., Sönströd, C.: Handling small calibration sets in mondrian inductive conformal regressors (2014). Submitted to SLDS 2015
6. Vovk, V., Shafer, G., Gammerman, A.: Algorithmic learning in a random world. Springer, New York (2005)

Cross-Conformal Prediction
with Ridge Regression

Harris Papadopoulos[✉]

Computer Science and Engineering Department, Frederick University,
7 Y. Frederickou St., Palouriotisa, 1036 Nicosia, Cyprus
h.papadopoulos@frederick.ac.cy

Abstract. Cross-Conformal Prediction (CCP) is a recently proposed
approach for overcoming the computational inefficiency problem of Conformal Prediction (CP) without sacrificing as much informational efficiency as Inductive Conformal Prediction (ICP). In effect CCP is a
hybrid approach combining the ideas of cross-validation and ICP. In
the case of classification the predictions of CCP have been shown to be
empirically valid and more informationally efficient than those of the
ICP. This paper introduces CCP in the regression setting and examines
its empirical validity and informational efficiency compared to that of
the original CP and ICP when combined with Ridge Regression.

Keywords: Conformal prediction · Cross-validation · Inductive conformal prediction · Prediction regions · Tolerance regions

1 Introduction

Conformal Prediction (CP) is a machine learning framework for extending conventional machine learning algorithms and producing methods, called Conformal
Predictors (CPs), that produce prediction sets satisfying a given level of confidence. These sets are guaranteed to include the correct labels with a probability
equal to or higher than the required confidence level. To date many CPs have
been developed and have been shown to produce valid and useful in practice set
predictions; see e.g. [2,4,5,8,9,11]. The main drawback of the methods developed
following the original version of the CP framework is that they are much more
computationally inefficient than the conventional algorithms they are based on.
A modification of the framework, called Inductive Conformal Prediction (ICP),
overcomes this problem by using different parts of the training set for the two
stages of the CP process. This however, has the undesirable side-effect of losing
some of the informational efficiency of the original version of the framework. That
is the resulting prediction sets are larger than those produced by the original
framework.

In an effort to get the best of both worlds a new modification of the framework was proposed in [12], called Cross-Conformal Prediction (CCP), which
combines the idea of ICP with that of cross-validation. In [12] CCP was studied

© Springer International Publishing Switzerland 2015
A. Gammerman et al. (Eds.): SLDS 2015, LNAI 9047, pp. 260–270, 2015.
DOI: 10.1007/978-3-319-17091-6_21

in the Classification setting and was shown to produce empirically valid confidence measures with higher informational efficiency than those of the ICP. This, combined with its comparable to ICP computational efficiency makes CCP the best option when the computational time required by the original CP is too much.

This paper introduces CCP in the case of regression and examines its empirical validity and informational efficiency. The particular method examined in this work is based on the well known Ridge Regression algorithm, which is the first algorithm to which regression CP has been applied and one of the only two algorithms for which the original version of CP was developed (the second algorithm is Nearest Neighbours Regression). However the approach described here can be followed with any regression algorithm. This is actually an additional advantage of CCP and ICP over the original CP as the latter can only be combined with particular algorithms in the case of regression. Furthermore unlike the original CP, CCP can be used with all normalized nonconformity measures (see [7,8]), which were shown to improve the informational efficiency of ICP.

The rest of this paper starts with a description of the CP framework and its inductive version in Section 2. Then Section 3 details the CCP approach and explains the way it can be followed in the case of Regression. Section 4 gives the definition of a normalized nonconformity measure, first proposed in [7] for the Ridge Regression ICP, which was used in the experiments performed. This is followed by the experimental examination of CCP and its comparison with the original CP and ICP in Section 5. Finally Section 6 gives the concluding remarks and future directions of this work.

2   Conformal and Inductive Conformal Prediction

We are given a training set of l observations $\{z_1, \ldots, z_l\}$, where each $z_i \in \mathbf{Z}$ is a pair (x_i, y_i) consisting of an object $x_i \in \mathbf{X}$ and an associated label $y_i \in \mathbf{Y}$ (dependent variable). We are also given a new object x_{l+1} and our aim is to produce a prediction set, or region that will contain the correct label y_{l+1} with a predefined confidence with the only assumption that all $z_i \in \mathbf{Z}$ are exchangeable.

CP assumes every possible label $\tilde{y} \in \mathbf{Y}$ of x_{l+1} in turn and calculates the *nonconformity scores*

$$\alpha_i^{\tilde{y}} = A(\{z_1, \ldots, z_{i-1}, z_{i+1}, \ldots, z_l, z_{l+1}^{\tilde{y}}\}, z_i), \quad i = 1, \ldots, l, \tag{1a}$$

$$\alpha_{l+1}^{\tilde{y}} = A(\{z_1, \ldots, z_l\}, z_{l+1}^{\tilde{y}}), \tag{1b}$$

where $z_{l+1}^{\tilde{y}} = (x_{l+1}, \tilde{y})$ and $A(S_i, z_j)$ is a numerical score indicating how strange it is for the example z_j to belong to the examples in the set $S_i \subset \mathbf{Z}$. In effect the function A, called the *nonconformity measure* of the CP, uses a conventional machine learning algorithm, called the *underlying algorithm* of the CP, to assess the nonconformity of z_j to the set S_i. The resulting nonconformity scores can then be used to calculate the *p-value* of $\tilde{y}$ as

$$p(z_1, \ldots, z_l, z_{l+1}^{\tilde{y}}) = \frac{|\{i = 1, \ldots, l : \alpha_i^{\tilde{y}} \geq \alpha_{l+1}^{z_{l+1}^{\tilde{y}}}\}| + 1}{l + 1}, \tag{2}$$

also denoted as $p(\tilde{y})$. The p-value function (2) guarantees that $\forall \delta \in [0, 1]$ and for all probability distributions P on $\mathbf{Z}$,

$$P^{\tilde{y}}\{((x_1, y_1), \ldots, (x_l, y_l), (x_{l+1}, y_{l+1})) : p(y_{l+1}) \leq \delta\} \leq \delta, \tag{3}$$

where y_{l+1} is the true label of x_{l+1}; a proof can be found in [13]. After calculating the p-value of all possible labels $\tilde{y} \in \mathbf{Y}$, the CP outputs the prediction set, or prediction region (PR) in the case of regression,

$$\{\tilde{y} : p(\tilde{y}) > \delta\}, \tag{4}$$

which has at most δ chance of being wrong, i.e. of not containing y_{l+1}.

Of course in the case of regression it would be impossible to explicitly consider every possible label $\tilde{y} \in \mathbb{R}$. A procedure that makes it possible to compute the PR (4) with Ridge Regression for the standard regression nonconformity measure

$$\alpha_i = |y_i - \hat{y}_i| \tag{5}$$

was proposed in [5]. The same idea was followed in [13] and [8] for the k-nearest neighbours regression algorithm. Still however this approach has two important drawbacks

1. it is very computationally inefficient compared to the algorithm the CP is based on, and
2. it cannot be followed with all regression algorithms.

Inductive Conformal Prediction (ICP) overcomes these problems by dividing the training set into two smaller sets, the *proper training set* with m examples and the *calibration set* with $q = l - m$ examples. The proper training set is then used for training the underlying algorithm of the ICP and only the examples in the calibration set are used for calculating the p-value of each possible classification for every test example. More specifically, ICP calculates the p-value of each possible classification $\tilde{y}$ of x_{l+1} as

$$p(\tilde{y}) = \frac{|\{i = m + 1, \ldots, m + q : \alpha_i \geq \alpha_{l+1}^{\tilde{y}}\}| + 1}{q + 1}, \tag{6}$$

where

$$\alpha_i = A(\{z_1, \ldots, z_m\}, z_{m+i}), \quad i = 1, \ldots, q, \tag{7a}$$

$$\alpha_{l+1}^{\tilde{y}} = A(\{z_1, \ldots, z_m\}, z_{l+1}^{\tilde{y}}), \tag{7b}$$

and $z_{l+1}^{\tilde{y}} = (x_{l+1}, \tilde{y})$.

As with the original CP approach in the case of regression it is impossible to explicitly consider every possible label $\tilde{y} \in \mathbb{R}$ and calculate its p-value. However, in this case both the nonconformity scores of the calibration set examples $\alpha_{m+1}, \ldots, \alpha_{m+q}$ and the underlying algorithm prediction $\hat{y}_{l+1}$ are not affected by the value of $\tilde{y}$, only the nonconformity score α_{l+1} is affected. Therefore $p(\tilde{y})$

changes only at the points where $\alpha_{l+1}^{\tilde{y}} = \alpha_i$ for some $i = m+1, \ldots, m+q$. As a result, for a confidence level $1 - \delta$ we only need to find the biggest α_i such that when $\alpha_{l+1}^{\tilde{y}} = \alpha_i$ then $p(\tilde{y}) > \delta$, which will give us the maximum and minimum $\tilde{y}$ that have a p-value bigger than δ and consequently the beginning and end of the corresponding PR. More specifically, we sort the nonconformity scores of the calibration examples in descending order obtaining the sequence

$$\alpha_{(m+1)}, \ldots, \alpha_{(m+q)}, \tag{8}$$

and output the PR

$$(\hat{y}_{l+1} - \alpha_{(m+s)}, \hat{y}_{l+1} + \alpha_{(m+s)}), \tag{9}$$

where

$$s = \lfloor \delta(q + 1) \rfloor. \tag{10}$$

3   Cross-Conformal Prediction for Regression

As ICP does not include the test example in the training set of its underlying algorithm, the latter needs to be trained only once and in the case of regression the approach can be combined with any underlying algorithm. However the fact that it only uses part of the training set for training its underlying algorithm and for calculating its p-values results in lower informational efficiency, i.e. looser PRs. Cross-Conformal Prediction, which was recently proposed in [12], tries to overcome this problem by combining ICP with cross-validation. Specifically, CCP partitions the training set in K subsets (folds) $S_1, \ldots, S_K$ and calculates the nonconformity scores of the examples in each subset S_k and of $(x_{l+1}, \tilde{y})$ for each possible label $\tilde{y}$ as

$$\alpha_i = A(\cup_{m \neq k} S_m, z_i), \quad z_i \in S_k, \quad m = 1, \ldots, K, \tag{11a}$$

$$\alpha_{l+1}^{\tilde{y},k} = A(\cup_{m \neq k} S_m, z_{l+1}^{\tilde{y}}), \quad m = 1, \ldots, K, \tag{11b}$$

where $z_{l+1}^{\tilde{y}} = (x_{l+1}, \tilde{y})$. Note that for $z_{l+1}^{\tilde{y}}$ K nonconformity scores $\alpha_{l+1}^{\tilde{y},k}$, $k = 1, \ldots, K$ are calculated, one with each of the K folds. Now the p-value for each possible label $\tilde{y}$ is computed as

$$p(\tilde{y}) = \frac{\sum_{k=1}^{K} |\{z_i \in S_k : \alpha_i \geq \alpha_{l+1}^{\tilde{y},k}\}| + 1}{l + 1}. \tag{12}$$

Again in the case of regression the possible labels $\tilde{y} \in \mathbb{R}$ are infinite. Still though, like in the case of the ICP, only the nonconformity score of z_{l+1} is affected by changes to the value of $\tilde{y}$. As a result $p(\tilde{y})$ can change only at the values of $\tilde{y}$ for which $\alpha_{l+1}^{\tilde{y}} = \alpha_i$ for some $i = 1, \ldots, l$. Note that in this case however we have K different predictions $\hat{y}_{l+1}^1, \ldots, \hat{y}_{l+1}^K$, where $\hat{y}_{l+1}^k$ was produced by training the underlying algorithm on $\cup_{m \neq k} S_m$, $m = 1, \ldots, K$. Specifically nonconformity measure (5) in this case for an example $z_i \in S_k$ is actually

$$\alpha_i = |y_i - \hat{y}_i^k|; \tag{13}$$

for $\alpha_{l+1}^{\tilde{y},k}$ replace y_i with $\tilde{y}$. As a result, each $\tilde{y}$ is associated with K nonconformity scores $\alpha_{l+1}^{\tilde{y},1}, \ldots, \alpha_{l+1}^{\tilde{y},K}$ and each $\alpha_{l+1}^{\tilde{y},k}$ is compared with the nonconformity scores of the examples in S_k. So in order to find the values for which $p(\tilde{y}) > \delta$ we map each nonconformity score α_i to the $\tilde{y}$ values for which $\alpha_{l+1}^{\tilde{y}} = \alpha_i$ generating the lists

$$\nu_i = \hat{y}_{l+1}^k - \alpha_i, \quad z_i \in S_k, \quad i = 1, \ldots, l, \tag{14a}$$

$$\xi_i = \hat{y}_{l+1}^k + \alpha_i, \quad z_i \in S_k, \quad i = 1, \ldots, l. \tag{14b}$$

Now $p(\tilde{y})$ changes only at the points where $\tilde{y} = \nu_i$ or $\tilde{y} = \xi_i$ for some $i = 1, \ldots, l$. So if $\tilde{y}_1, \ldots, \tilde{y}_{2l}$ are the values $\nu_1, \ldots, \nu_l, \xi_1, \ldots, \xi_l$ sorted in ascending order and if $\tilde{y}_0 = -\infty$ and $\tilde{y}_{2l+1} = \infty$, then $p(\tilde{y})$ remains constant in each interval $(\tilde{y}_0, \tilde{y}_1), (\tilde{y}_1, \tilde{y}_2), \ldots, (\tilde{y}_{2l}, \tilde{y}_{2l+1})$.

The p-value in each interval $(\tilde{y}_i, \tilde{y}_{i+1})$ can be calculated as

$$p_i = \frac{|\{i = 1, \ldots, l : \nu_i \le \tilde{y}_i\}| - |\{i = 1, \ldots, l : \xi_i \le \tilde{y}_i\}| + 1}{l+1}. \tag{15}$$

Consequently for any confidence level $1 - \delta$ the resulting PR is:

$$\bigcup_{i:p_i>\delta} [\tilde{y}_i, \tilde{y}_{i+1}]. \tag{16}$$

Note that these PRs may have 'holes' in them. This however should happen very rarely, if ever, for the low values of δ we are interested in.

Although CCP needs to train its underlying algorithm K times as opposed to just one for ICP, it is still much more computationally efficient than the original CP. It also can be combined with any underlying algorithm in the case of regression. In comparison with ICP it generates its PRs based on a much richer set of nonconformity scores, resulting from all training examples rather than just the calibration examples. Furthermore, in most cases (depending on K) the underlying algorithm of the CCP is trained on a larger training set compared to the proper training set of the ICP.

4   Normalized Nonconformity Measures

In addition to the typical nonconformity measure (5) some additional nonconformity measures for regression have been proposed in [6–8] for Ridge Regression, Nearest Neighbours Regression and Neural Networks Regression. These measures normalize (5) by the expected accuracy of the underlying algorithm being used. The intuition behind this is that if two examples have the same nonconformity score as defined by (5) and the prediction $\hat{y}$ of the underlying algorithm for one of them was expected to be more accurate than the other, then the former is actually less conforming than the latter. This leads to PRs that are larger for the examples which are more difficult to predict and smaller for the examples which are easier to predict.

Almost all such nonconformity measures however, cannot be used in conjunction with TCP, with the exception of only two out of the six such measures proposed in [8]. This is an additional advantage of CCP over TCP, since the former, like ICP, can be combined with any nonconformity measure.

As this work focuses on Ridge Regression (RR) as underlying algorithm, this section will describe the nonconformity measure proposed in [7] for this algorithm. This measure is defined as

$$\alpha_i = \frac{|y_i - \hat{y}_i|}{\exp(\mu_i)}, \tag{17}$$

where μ_i is the RR prediction of the value $\ln(|y_i - \hat{y}_i|)$. Specifically, after training the RR algorithm on the training set we calculate the residuals $\ln(|y_j - \hat{y}_j|)$ for all training examples and train a linear RR on the pairs $(x_j, \ln(|y_j - \hat{y}_j|))$. The use of the logarithmic instead of the direct scale ensures that the estimate is always positive.

The resulting PRs in the case of CCP can be generated by calculating ν_i and ξ_i as

$$\nu_i = \hat{y}_{l+1}^k - \alpha_i \exp(\mu_i), \quad z_i \in S_k, \quad i = 1, \ldots, l, \tag{18a}$$

$$\xi_i = \hat{y}_{l+1}^k + \alpha_i \exp(\mu_i), \quad z_i \in S_k, \quad i = 1, \ldots, l, \tag{18b}$$

and following the steps described in Section 3.

5   Experiments and Results

Experiments were performed on four benchmark data sets of different sizes from the UCI [1] and DELVE [10] repositories: Boston Housing, Concrete Compressive Strength, Abalone and Pumadyn (the 8nm variant). Table 1 lists the number of examples and attributes comprising each data set together with the width of the range of its labels. The aim was to examine the validity and informational efficiency of Cross-Conformal Prediction with Ridge Regression as underlying algorithm using nonconformity measures (5) and (17). The informational efficiency was assessed in comparison to those of the corresponding original (Transductive) and Inductive Ridge Regression Conformal Predictors [5,7] under exactly the same setting.

Evaluation was performed on the results obtained from 10 random runs of a cross-validation process. Based on their sizes the two smaller data sets (Boston Housing and Concrete Compressive Strength) were split into 10 folds, whereas the Abalone data set was split into 5 folds and the Pumadyn data set was split into 2 folds; this cross-validation process was for generating the training and test sets the algorithms were evaluated on, not to be confused with the internal cross-validation of CCP. The input attributes of each data set were normalized setting their mean value to 0 and their standard deviation to 1. An RBF kernel was used in the Ridge Regression underlying algorithm, while the kernel parameter (σ) and ridge factor (a) were optimized on each data set

Table 1. Main characteristics and experimental setup for each data set

	Housing	Concrete	Abalone	Pumadyn
Examples	506	1030	4177	8192
Attributes	13	8	8	8
Label range	45	80.27	28	21.17
Folds (evaluation)	10	10	5	2
Calibration size	99	299	1099	1299

Table 2. PR tightness and empirical validity on the Boston Housing data set

Method/ Measure		Mean Width			Median Width			Errors (%)		
		90%	95%	99%	90%	95%	99%	90%	95%	99%
ICP	(5)	9.199	12.435	28.469	9.194	12.170	25.743	10.32	5.24	0.97
	(17)	9.099	12.178	26.804	9.037	11.790	24.556	9.82	5.38	1.15
CCP $K = 5$	(5)	9.511	12.573	25.713	9.351	12.420	25.241	8.10	3.52	0.75
	(17)	9.385	12.220	24.936	9.143	11.913	24.457	7.92	3.70	0.61
CCP $K = 10$	(5)	9.044	12.000	24.496	8.991	11.915	24.242	9.19	4.15	0.83
	(17)	8.965	11.583	23.508	8.801	11.336	22.971	9.05	4.23	0.79
CCP $K = 20$	(5)	8.834	11.673	24.194	8.821	11.647	23.909	9.62	4.47	0.85
	(17)	8.742	11.239	22.982	8.592	11.039	22.586	9.64	4.45	0.79
TCP	(5)	10.524	13.448	24.810	7.829	10.036	18.536	9.72	4.80	0.79

by minimizing the radius/margin bound for the first three data sets and (due to its size) the validation error on half the training set for the Pumadyn data set using the gradient descent approach proposed in [3] and the corresponding code provided online[1]. In the case of ICP the calibration set size in was set to $q = 100n - 1$, where n was chosen so that q was the closest value less than one third of the training set; i.e. $n = \lfloor \frac{l}{300} \rfloor$, where l is the training set size. Along with the characteristics of each data set Table 1 gives the number of folds it was split into and calibration set size q used with ICP.

In order to assess the informational efficiency of the Ridge Regression Cross-Conformal Predictor (RR-CCP) Tables 2–5 report the mean and median widths of the PRs produced by RR-CCP with K set to 5, 10 and 20 for the 90%, 95% and 99% confidence levels, along with those produced by the original Transductive version of CP (TCP) and those produced by ICP for each data set. In the case of CCP and ICP the widths obtained with both nonconformity measures (5) and (17) are reported. However with TCP only nonconformity measure (5) can be used. The same Tables report the percentage of errors made by each method

---

[1] The code is located at http://olivier.chapelle.cc/ams/

Table 3. PR tightness and empirical validity on the Concrete data set

Method/ Measure		Mean Width 90%	95%	99%	Median Width 90%	95%	99%	Errors (%) 90%	95%	99%
ICP	(5)	18.720	24.879	46.303	18.650	24.784	45.503	9.94	5.03	0.94
	(17)	18.079	23.853	47.210	17.921	23.570	43.691	9.81	4.87	0.92
CCP $K = 5$	(5)	18.516	24.251	41.612	18.082	23.776	41.154	7.06	2.97	0.45
	(17)	17.910	22.990	40.094	17.305	22.236	39.089	7.07	2.55	0.50
CCP $K = 10$	(5)	17.324	22.643	38.411	17.061	22.319	38.134	8.46	3.68	0.54
	(17)	16.675	21.231	36.954	16.255	20.579	36.078	8.39	3.53	0.61
CCP $K = 20$	(5)	16.780	21.878	37.289	16.706	21.700	36.795	9.10	4.14	0.65
	(17)	16.142	20.408	35.610	15.753	19.866	34.752	9.33	4.33	0.76
TCP	(5)	19.513	24.593	38.254	14.176	17.881	27.632	9.82	5.15	0.97

Table 4. PR tightness and empirical validity on the Abalone data set

Method/ Measure		Mean Width 90%	95%	99%	Median Width 90%	95%	99%	Errors (%) 90%	95%	99%
ICP	(5)	6.700	9.090	14.883	6.682	9.064	14.848	10.06	4.99	1.02
	(17)	6.385	8.380	13.469	6.379	8.370	13.405	10.10	5.01	1.01
CCP $K = 5$	(5)	6.750	9.038	14.961	6.721	9.017	14.983	9.43	4.73	0.93
	(17)	6.425	8.307	13.437	6.404	8.275	13.388	9.48	4.63	0.93
CCP $K = 10$	(5)	6.698	8.994	14.901	6.684	8.980	14.919	9.67	4.85	0.96
	(17)	6.368	8.210	13.276	6.330	8.160	13.193	9.71	4.73	0.96
CCP $K = 20$	(5)	6.673	8.971	14.875	6.660	8.971	14.883	9.80	4.92	0.98
	(17)	6.343	8.152	13.172	6.298	8.088	13.082	9.82	4.87	0.97

Table 5. PR tightness and empirical validity on the Pumadyn data set

Method/ Measure		Mean Width 90%	95%	99%	Median Width 90%	95%	99%	Errors (%) 90%	95%	99%
ICP	(5)	4.153	5.139	7.355	4.159	5.128	7.337	10.17	5.10	1.02
	(17)	4.148	5.099	7.210	4.137	5.076	7.186	10.16	5.14	1.00
CCP $K = 5$	(5)	4.182	5.167	7.312	4.162	5.148	7.319	8.57	4.11	0.76
	(17)	4.174	5.146	7.196	4.145	5.118	7.163	8.59	3.96	0.69
CCP $K = 10$	(5)	4.070	5.033	7.138	4.064	5.026	7.121	9.26	4.55	0.90
	(17)	4.053	5.012	7.017	4.032	4.990	6.990	9.32	4.43	0.83
CCP $K = 20$	(5)	4.020	4.974	7.049	4.007	4.964	7.025	9.56	4.76	0.98
	(17)	4.006	4.944	6.926	3.986	4.925	6.901	9.66	4.68	0.91

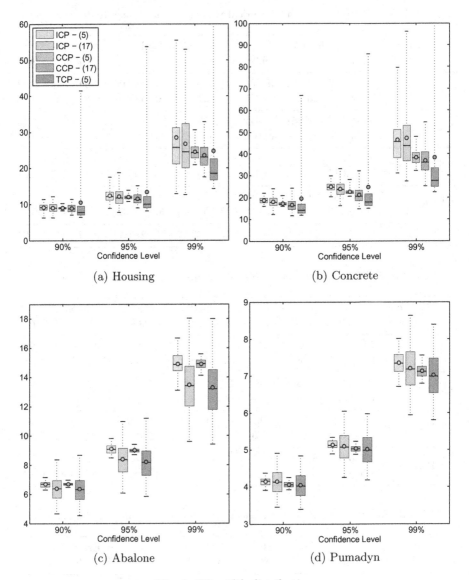

(a) Housing

(b) Concrete

(c) Abalone

(d) Pumadyn

Fig. 1. PR width distribution

for every confidence level to evaluate the empirical validity of the corresponding PRs.

Figure 1 complements the information reported in Tables 2-5 by displaying boxplots for each data set showing the median, upper and lower quartiles and 2nd and 98th percentiles of the PR widths produced by each method for the three confidence levels. The mean widths are also marked with a circle. For CCP the widths obtained with $K = 10$ were used here. In the case of the TCP with the

99% confidence level the 98th percentile of the obtained widths extends much higher than the maximum value displayed in the plots.

In terms of empirical validity the error percentages displayed in Tables 2–5 demonstrate that the error rates of the PRs produced by CCP are always lower than the required significance level. The change of K, at least up to $K = 20$, does not seem to affect validity. In many cases the PRs of CCP seem more conservative than those of the two other methods, since the error percentages of the latter are nearer to the corresponding significance levels. This suggests that there might be room for further improvement.

By comparing the mean and median widths of the PRs produced by CCP with the three different values of K, it seems that increasing K improves informational efficiency. However it is not clear if much larger values of K will still have the same effect. Also the extent of improvement is not always significant. In comparing the widths of the PRs produced by CCP with those of the ICP with the same nonconformity measure, one can see that in all cases, with the exception of the abalone data set with nonconformity measure (5), CCP with K set to 10 and 20 gives overall tighter PRs. In the case of the TCP it seems that while most of its PRs are tighter than those of the CCP and ICP, some are extremely loose and result in a mean width that is higher than that of the CCP.

6   Conclusion

This work introduced Cross-Conformal Prediction in the case of regression and examined its empirical validity and informational efficiency when combined with Ridge Regression as underlying algorithm. CCP does not suffer from the computational inefficiency problem of the original CP approach while it makes a more effective use of the available training data than ICP. Additionally, on the contrary to the original CP it can be combined with any conventional regression algorithm and any regression nonconformity measure.

The experimental results presented show that the PRs produced by CCP are empirically valid while being tighter than those of the ICP. Although the PRs of the original CP approach are tighter for the majority of cases, for some examples they become extremely loose, thing that does not happen with CCP.

A first future direction of this work is to examine the empirical validity and performance of CCP when using one-sided nonconformity measures and combining the resulting upper and lower prediction rays to obtain the overall PR. This makes the computation of the PRs simpler and it is interesting to see if the resulting PRs are also tighter. Moreover it would be interesting to study how the performance of CCP is affected in comparison to that of the TCP and ICP as the size of the data set in question increases. Finally the application of CCP to real world problems where the provision of valid PRs is desirable is an important future aim.

References

1. Bache, K., Lichman, M.: UCI machine learning repository (2013). http://archive.ics.uci.edu/ml
2. Bhattacharyya, S.: Confidence in predictions from random tree ensembles. In: Proceedings of the 11th IEEE International Conference on Data Mining (ICDM 2011), pp. 71–80. Springer (2011)
3. Chapelle, O., Vapnik, V., Bousquet, O., Mukherjee, S.: Choosing multiple parameters for support vector machines. Machine Learning **46** (2002)
4. Lambrou, A., Papadopoulos, H., Gammerman, A.: Reliable confidence measures for medical diagnosis with evolutionary algorithms. IEEE Transactions on Information Technology in Biomedicine **15**(1), 93–99 (2011)
5. Nouretdinov, I., Melluish, T., Vovk, V.: Ridge regression confidence machine. In: Proceedings of the 18th International Conference on Machine Learning (ICML 2001), pp. 385–392. Morgan Kaufmann, San Francisco (2001)
6. Papadopoulos, H., Haralambous, H.: Reliable prediction intervals with regression neural networks. Neural Networks **24**(8), 842–851 (2011). http://dx.doi.org/10.1016/j.neunet.2011.05.008
7. Papadopoulos, H., Proedrou, K., Vovk, V., Gammerman, A.: Inductive confidence machines for regression. In: Elomaa, T., Mannila, H., Toivonen, H. (eds.) ECML 2002. LNCS (LNAI), vol. 2430, pp. 345–356. Springer, Heidelberg (2002)
8. Papadopoulos, H., Vovk, V., Gammerman, A.: Regression conformal prediction with nearest neighbours. Journal of Artificial Intelligence Research **40**, 815–840 (2011). http://dx.doi.org/10.1613/jair.3198
9. Proedrou, K., Nouretdinov, I., Vovk, V., Gammerman, A.: Transductive confidence machines for pattern recognition. In: Elomaa, T., Mannila, H., Toivonen, H. (eds.) ECML 2002. LNCS (LNAI), vol. 2430, pp. 381–390. Springer, Heidelberg (2002)
10. Rasmussen, C.E., Neal, R.M., Hinton, G.E., Van Camp, D., Revow, M., Ghahramani, Z., Kustra, R., Tibshirani, R.: DELVE: Data for evaluating learning in valid experiments (1996). http://www.cs.toronto.edu/delve/
11. Saunders, C., Gammerman, A., Vovk, V.: Transduction with confidence and credibility. In: Proceedings of the 16th International Joint Conference on Artificial Intelligence, vol. 2, pp. 722–726. Morgan Kaufmann, Los Altos (1999)
12. Vovk, V.: Cross-conformal predictors. Annals of Mathematics and Artificial Intelligence (2013). http://dx.doi.org/10.1007/s10472-013-9368-4
13. Vovk, V., Gammerman, A., Shafer, G.: Algorithmic Learning in a Random World. Springer, New York (2005)

Handling Small Calibration Sets
in Mondrian Inductive Conformal Regressors

Ulf Johansson[1]([✉]), Ernst Ahlberg[2], Henrik Boström[3],
Lars Carlsson[2], Henrik Linusson[1], and Cecilia Sönströd[1]

[1] Department of Information Technology, University of Borås, Borås, Sweden
{ulf.johansson,henrik.linusson,cecilia.sonstrod}@hb.se
[2] Drug Safety and Metabolism, AstraZeneca Innovative Medicines and Early
Development, Mölndal, Sweden
{ernst.ahlberg,lars.a.carlsson}@astrazeneca.com
[3] Department of Systems and Computer Sciences, Stockholm University,
Stockholm, Sweden
henrik.bostrom@dsv.su.se

Abstract. In inductive conformal prediction, calibration sets must contain an adequate number of instances to support the chosen confidence level. This problem is particularly prevalent when using Mondrian inductive conformal prediction, where the input space is partitioned into independently valid prediction regions. In this study, Mondrian conformal regressors, in the form of regression trees, are used to investigate two problematic aspects of small calibration sets. If there are too few calibration instances to support the significance level, we suggest using either extrapolation or altering the model. In situations where the desired significance level is between two calibration instances, the standard procedure is to choose the more nonconforming one, thus guaranteeing validity, but producing conservative conformal predictors. The suggested solution is to use interpolation between calibration instances. All proposed techniques are empirically evaluated and compared to the standard approach on 30 benchmark data sets. The results show that while extrapolation often results in invalid models, interpolation works extremely well and provides increased efficiency with preserved empirical validity.

1 Introduction

A conformal predictor outputs prediction sets instead of point predictions. For regression, which is the focus of this study, the prediction sets become prediction intervals. A conformal predictor is always valid [11], i.e., the error rate, on novel data, is bounded by a preset significance level. Conformal predictors rely on *nonconformity functions* that measure the strangeness (the nonconformity) of an instance. When used for predictive modeling, conformal prediction

This work was supported by the Swedish Foundation for Strategic Research through the project High-Performance Data Mining for Drug Effect Detection (IIS11-0053) and the Knowledge Foundation through the project Big Data Analytics by Online Ensemble Learning (20120192).

A. Gammerman et al. (Eds.): SLDS 2015, LNAI 9047, pp. 271–280, 2015.
DOI: 10.1007/978-3-319-17091-6_22

often utilizes nonconformity functions based on an underlying machine learning model. In regression, the most commonly used nonconformity function is simply the absolute error made by the model on a specific instance.

Inductive conformal prediction (ICP) [6,11] can be applied on top of any predictive model, but requires a set of instances, called the calibration set, that was not used for the training of the model. The nonconformity function is applied to all instances in the calibration set, thus producing a set of nonconformity scores. In regression, the boundaries of the prediction intervals can be obtained immediately from this set of nonconformity scores. More specifically, we would first order the nonconformity scores and then simply pick the one corresponding to the desired significance level [6,8,11]. As an example, if we have exactly 4 nonconformity scores, and the significance level is $\epsilon = 0.2$, we would pick the highest nonconformity score, expecting that, in the long run, exactly 20% of test instances would be at most as nonconforming. When using absolute error as the nonconformity function, the resulting prediction interval thus becomes the point prediction from the model $\pm$ the nonconformity score, and we can expect this to be valid in the long run.

There are, however, a couple of subtleties involved when using ICP. First of all, the calibration set must be large enough to support the chosen significance level. If the calibration set contains too few instances, it is simply not granular enough, thus making it impossible to pick an instance corresponding to the desired significance level. As an example, $\epsilon = 0.2$ requires 4 instances, while $\epsilon = 0.05$ requires 19 instances. In general, the minimum number of required calibration instances is $\epsilon^{-1} - 1$. Another potential problem is that even if there are enough calibration instances to support the significance level, there might be no specific instance corresponding exactly to the significance level, i.e., one instance is too pessimistic and the next too optimistic. In the general formula, this is handled by always picking the more nonconforming instance, thus preserving the validity guarantee. The resulting interval will, however, be unnecessarily large. For instance, if we for $\epsilon = 0.2$ have 7 calibration instances, we would still pick the most nonconforming instance to create the prediction interval, but this interval is overly conservative; as a matter of fact, the expected error rate is as low as $1/7 \approx 0.143$. In general, we need exactly $k\epsilon^{-1} - 1$ calibration instances, where k is an arbitrary integer, for an inductive conformal regressor to remain exactly valid.

Both problems described above apply mainly to small data sets when using standard ICP. However, another situation where calibration sets may become small, even if the data set is large to begin with, is when *Mondrian* ICP (MICP) [11] is used. An MICP is, simply put, an ICP where the problem space is somehow divided into subspaces. If individual sets of instances, each belonging to a specific subspace, are used for calibration, the resulting MICP will be valid for each and every subspace.

The overall purpose of this paper is to suggest and evaluate techniques for handling the problems associated with small calibration sets. In the experimentation, regression trees are used as the underlying model for MICP. With this setup, every leaf, which corresponds to a rule expressed as the path from the root to that leaf, will be valid, but the price paid is that different calibration sets must be used for each leaf.

2   Background

2.1   Conformal Prediction

An inductive conformal regressor [6] utilizes an arbitrary real-valued measure of strangeness, called a nonconformity function, together with a statistical test to construct statistically valid prediction intervals, meaning that, given a significance level ϵ, the resulting prediction interval contains the true target value with probability $1-\epsilon$. In predictive modeling, nonconformity functions are often based on the prediction error of a traditional machine learning model — if the model makes a large prediction error on a certain instance, this instance is deemed stranger than one for which the model makes a smaller prediction error. A standard nonconformity function for regression problems [7,8] is

$$A(\boldsymbol{x}_i, y_i, h) = |y_i - h(\boldsymbol{x}_i)|, \tag{1}$$

where h is the *underlying model* of the conformal regressor, i.e., a regression model trained on the regression problem at hand.

An inductive conformal regressor is trained using the following procedure:

1. Divide the training data Z into two disjoint subsets:
   - a proper training set Z^t and
   - a calibration set Z^c.
2. Train the underlying model h on Z^t.
3. Use the nonconformity function to measure the nonconformity of the instances in Z^c, obtaining a list of calibration scores $\alpha_1, ..., \alpha_q$, where $q = |Z^c|$, sorted in descending order.

For a new test instance $\boldsymbol{x}_{k+1}$, a prediction region is constructed as

$$\hat{Y}^\epsilon_{k+1} = h(\boldsymbol{x}_{k+1}) \pm \alpha_p, \tag{2}$$

where $p = \lfloor \epsilon(q+1) \rfloor$.

While each prediction made by an inductive conformal regressor contains the true output with probability $1 - \epsilon$, it is still possible that errors are distributed unevenly within the problem space. For example, if the underlying model is a regression tree, it is possible that some leaf nodes in the tree make more errors than expected, while other leaf nodes make fewer errors than expected [5]. Mondrian conformal predictors [12] resolve this by dividing the problem space into several disjoint subcategories $\kappa_1, ..., \kappa_m$ and providing a confidence $1 - \epsilon$ for each κ_j separately. As an example, for classification, each κ_j can be mapped to a possible class label, thus ensuring that errors are not unevenly distributed over the classes. Similarly, the problem space can be divided w.r.t. to the feature space, and then all the corresponding conformal predictors, i.e., one for each feature sub-space, will be valid. To construct a Mondrian conformal regressor, α_p is selected, not from the full set of calibration scores, but from a subset $\{\alpha_i : \alpha_i \in \alpha_1, ..., \alpha_q \wedge \kappa(\boldsymbol{x}_i) = \kappa(\boldsymbol{x}_{k+1})\}$. The rest of the procedure is unchanged.

2.2   Regression Trees as MICPs

The popularity of decision tree learning is due to its fairly high accuracy cou-
pled with an ability to produce interpretable models. Furthermore, generating
a decision tree is relatively fast and requires a minimum of parameter tuning.
The two most famous decision tree algorithms are C4.5/C5.0 [9] and CART
[4]. Building a decision tree consists of recursively splitting the data set on the
independent variables. At the root node, all possible ways of splitting the entire
data set are evaluated using some *purity gain* measure. The purity gain is the
difference in impurity between the original data set and the resulting subsets, if
that split is chosen. The split resulting in the highest purity gain is selected, and
the procedure is then repeated recursively for each subset in this split, until a
terminal condition is met. The final nodes are called leaf nodes, and represent the
predictions produced by the model. The impurity measure used varies between
different decision tree algorithms; C4.5 uses *entropy* while CART optimizes the
Gini index. In regression trees, which is the focus of this study, a typical leaf node
simply contains a value, which is the mean or median of the training instances
falling in that leaf.

Fig. 1 below shows an induced regression tree for the Laser data set. Training
parameters were set to produce a very compact tree, but despite this, the tree is
fairly accurate with a test set *rmse* of 0.11 and a correlation coefficient[1] of 0.78.

```
x1<46.5
|     x1<26.5
|     |     x2<106.5:
|     |     |     y=0.100
|     |     x2>=106.5
|     |     |     y=0.062
|     x1>=26.5
|     |     y=0.158
x1>=46.5
|     x3<57.5:
|     |     y=0.475
|     x3>=57.5
|     |     y=0.256
```

Fig. 1. Sample regression tree for Laser data set

If we apply MICP to a regression tree, not only the entire model, but also all
leaves, each corresponding to a rule with conditions obtained by following a path
from the root node to that leaf, will be valid. In Fig. 2 below, an MICP based
on the regression tree from Fig. 1 above is shown. In this MICP, two different

---

[1] The Pearson correlation between the true output values of the test set and the
predictions made by the regression model.

prediction intervals are presented for each leaf, obtained from two different confidence levels; 80% and 95%, respectively. Note that the use of two levels here is for the purpose of illustration only; in practice, just one level would be used. It can be seen that for the 95% confidence level, most intervals are quite wide. Still, it must be noted that the MICP operates as expected, since interval sizes vary between leaves. For standard ICP, all intervals would have the same size.

```
x1<46.5
|     x1<26.5
|     |     x2<106.5:
|     |     |    y=[0.036,0.164]  (80%)     y=[0,0.279]  (95%)
|     |     x2>=106.5
|     |     |    y=[0.029,0.096]  (80%)     y=[0.019,0.106]  (95%)
|     x1>=26.5
|     |    y=[0.066,0.250]  (80%)     y=[0,0.338]  (95%)
x1>=46.5
|     x3<57.5:
|     |    y=[0.198,0.751]  (80%)     y=[0.031,0.918]  (95%)
|     x3>=57.5
|     |    y=[0.133,0.377]  (80%)     y=[0.076,0.434]  (95%)
```

Fig. 2. Sample MICP for Laser data set

3   Method

In this section, we first consider alternative ways of handling the problem of small calibration sets, which, as pointed out in the introduction, may result in overly conservative predictions. Then, the setup for the empirical investigation of the alternative approaches is described.

3.1   Suggested Solutions to Small Calibration Sets

In this paper, we investigate three different techniques aimed at handling the problem with few calibration instances and evaluate these techniques on MICPs built on top of regression trees.

The first technique works by ensuring that there are enough calibration instances to support the significance level, without the need for extrapolation. More specifically, a regression tree is first generated in standard fashion using training data. After this, the resulting tree is pruned until each leaf contains enough calibration instances to support the chosen significance level. It must be noted that although this strategy uses the calibration instances when producing the final tree, their targets are not revealed, and hence this procedure does not violate the demand that calibration instances must constitute a fresh data set. The second technique proposed uses standard interpolation to find a nonconformity score exactly matching the desired significance level. The third investigated technique employs extrapolation in case the number of calibration instances is lower than the required $1/\epsilon - 1$ [2].

3.2 Experimental Setup

All experimentation was performed in MatLab with regression trees built using the MatLab version of CART, called *rtree*. All parameter values were left at their defaults. Pruning was implemented separately, and operates iteratively by first calculating the number of calibration instances falling in each leaf; if this is smaller than the required number necessary to support the chosen significance level, that leaf node, and all its siblings, are pruned. This is repeated until no leaf node contains too few instances. For both interpolation and extrapolation, the built-in option in MatLab called *interp1*, setting the mode to 'spline', i.e., a cubic spline interpolation, is used.

The first experiment compares the standard procedure, i.e., rounding down and picking a slightly pessimistic calibration instance, to the proposed method of using interpolation. In this experiment, the two techniques operate on identical pruned trees, so the only difference is whether interpolation is used or not. In the second experiment, we investigate the option of extrapolating, again using the cubic spline method in MatLab. This method requires at the very least 4 instances, but different values are tried by setting them as goals for the pruning procedure. Naturally, there is a trade-off here, since larger trees are expected to be more accurate. The question is thus if valid, but more efficient MICPs, can be obtained by using extrapolation and fewer calibration instances than required by the significance level. In the experiments, 30 publicly available medium-sized data sets were used, ranging from approximately 1000 to 9500 instances. All data sets are from the UCI [2], Delve [10] or KEEL [1] repositories. For the actual experimentation, standard 10-fold cross-validation was used. For each fold, the training data was divided $2:1$ into a true training set and a calibration set.

The three variants of MICP used in the experimentation are:

MICP-std — standard MICP
MICP-ip — MICP using interpolation
MICP-ip-ep — MICP using interpolation and extrapolation

4 Results

Table 1 below shows the results from Experiment 1. Looking first at the tree sizes, we see that the pruning, as expected, produced more compact trees when the significance level is lowered. Specifically, when $\epsilon = 0.01$ some trees are exceptionally small; for some data sets even a single node. Comparing error rates, it is obvious that the standard approach is indeed quite conservative, while the approach using interpolation achieves empirical error rates very close to the chosen significance level.

---

[2] We investigate interpolation of nonconformity scores further in the paper *Modifications to p-values of Conformal Predictors*, also presented at COPA 2015.

Table 1. Error rates of MICPs with and without interpolation

	$\epsilon = 0.2$			$\epsilon = 0.1$			$\epsilon = 0.05$			$\epsilon = 0.01$		
	treeSize	std	ip	treeSize	std	ip	treeSize	std	ip	treeSize	std	ip
abalone	131	.180	.195	74	.092	.101	46	.042	.050	11	.008	.010
airfoil	103	.164	.194	36	.092	.102	19	.043	.055	4	.008	.011
anacalt	32	.182	.217	10	.101	.110	3	.053	.058	1	.004	.012
bank8fh	221	.188	.201	124	.090	.099	83	.042	.049	19	.008	.010
bank8fm	409	.175	.204	202	.086	.100	109	.041	.049	22	.009	.012
bank8nh	173	.188	.198	90	.099	.107	60	.048	.053	11	.010	.010
bank8nm	331	.179	.199	165	.085	.095	92	.040	.046	21	.008	.010
comp	275	.184	.201	141	.087	.099	81	.043	.050	4	.010	.010
concrete	55	.168	.196	27	.080	.096	14	.036	.041	1	.004	.007
cooling	56	.147	.178	25	.087	.111	13	.025	.036	3	.005	.010
deltaA	146	.191	.201	66	.093	.098	35	.042	.045	10	.009	.010
deltaE	227	.185	.196	121	.089	.097	69	.044	.049	22	.007	.009
friedm	62	.166	.189	35	.093	.113	19	.038	.048	3	.006	.009
heating	55	.188	.214	21	.107	.117	11	.048	.053	3	.012	.012
kin8fh	461	.174	.207	231	.083	.103	130	.041	.052	27	.007	.011
kin8fm	551	.162	.191	265	.078	.098	134	.037	.047	28	.007	.011
kin8nh	337	.180	.201	180	.086	.100	98	.039	.046	23	.006	.008
kin8nm	405	.181	.204	194	.090	.103	96	.045	.053	23	.008	.010
laser	39	.196	.209	20	.092	.103	14	.042	.047	2	.004	.009
mg	70	.188	.211	32	.084	.096	18	.040	.044	3	.006	.009
mortage	67	.174	.199	33	.071	.084	16	.038	.046	1	.008	.008
puma8fh	236	.182	.196	122	.087	.098	81	.041	.050	27	.009	.010
puma8fm	383	.172	.197	220	.080	.096	126	.037	.049	29	.008	.011
puma8nh	278	.178	.198	153	.090	.101	101	.043	.053	21	.010	.012
puma8nm	465	.170	.197	249	.079	.099	129	.041	.048	23	.007	.009
stock	45	.174	.191	19	.097	.106	10	.041	.051	1	.006	.014
treasury	57	.172	.195	33	.073	.087	18	.041	.052	1	.013	.014
wineRed	42	.175	.194	26	.082	.105	15	.032	.039	2	.006	.007
wineWhite	67	.190	.197	33	.097	.105	24	.045	.050	7	.007	.009
wizmir	97	.173	.201	50	.092	.110	24	.035	.049	4	.010	.012
Mean	196	.178	.199	100	.088	.101	56	.041	.049	12	.008	.010
#Invalid	0	0		0	0		0	0		0	0	
#Conserv.	22	0		17	0		18	0		4	0	

In order to analyze the results further, standard binomial tests are employed to compare the obtained results against the significance levels. More specifically, we tested, at the significance level $\alpha = 0.05$, whether the results are consistent with the chosen ϵ-values. For this analysis, we performed one series of tests with the null hypothesis that the technique does not produce conservative MICPs, and another series of tests with the null hypothesis that the technique results in valid MICPs. Since a large number of statistical tests are performed, the correction procedure recommended by Benjamini and Yekutieli [3] is employed.

The last two rows in Table 1 show the number of data sets where the specific technique produced conservative or invalid MICPs, respectively. As expected, the standard approach often resulted in conservative MICPs. Actually, the MICPs are significantly conservative on a majority of all data sets, for all significance levels but $\epsilon = 0.01$. Notably, there are no statistically significant invalid MICPs. Turning to Experiment 2, Table 2 below shows aggregated results over all 30 data sets.

Table 2. MICPs without interpolation and extrapolation (MICP-std), with just interpolation (MICP-ip) and with both interpolation and extrapolation (MICP-ip-ep)

	Req. inst.	treeSize	rmse	r	intSize	err. rate	#Cons.	#Invalid
				$\epsilon = 0.2$				
MICP-std	4	196	.085	.832	.218	.178	22	0
MICP-ip	4	196	.085	.832	.204	.199	0	0
				$\epsilon = 0.1$				
MICP-std	9	100	.090	.822	.297	.088	17	0
MICP-ip	9	100	.090	.822	.280	.101	0	0
MICP-ip-ep	4	196	.085	.832	.273	.110	0	9
MICP-ip-ep	7	122	.088	.826	.277	.103	0	1
				$\epsilon = 0.05$				
MICP-std	19	56	.097	.798	.406	.041	18	0
MICP-ip	19	56	.097	.798	.382	.049	0	0
MICP-ip-ep	4	196	.085	.832	.341	.085	0	30
MICP-ip-ep	10	92	.091	.820	.358	.053	0	2
MICP-ip-ep	15	67	.094	.810	.369	.050	0	0
				$\epsilon = 0.01$				
MICP-std	99	12	.140	.579	.827	.008	4	0
MICP-ip	99	12	.140	.579	.798	.010	0	0
MICP-ip-ep	4	196	.085	.832	.459	.104	0	30
MICP-ip-ep	30	39	.104	.789	.621	.017	0	20
MICP-ip-ep	50	25	.116	.731	.672	.011	0	2
MICP-ip-ep	75	17	.126	.672	.718	.011	1	0

Starting with the underlying regression tree models, the first column shows the number of instances required in each leaf node before the pruning stopped. The second column shows the resulting tree sizes, and the next two columns present predictive performance, as *rmse* and correlation coefficient. As expected, the general pattern is that larger trees are also more accurate. Examination of interval sizes and error rates reveals that while the techniques using extrapolation are more efficient (produce smaller prediction intervals), there is a clear risk that using extrapolation results in invalid MICPs. Inspecting the last column, which shows the number of data sets where the technique produced MICPs with empirical error rates significantly higher than the desired significance level, it is seen that extrapolation requires a fairly high number of calibration instances. For smaller calibration sets, extrapolation often results in invalid MICPs. Having said that, the corresponding prediction intervals are always smaller, mostly due to the fact that the underlying model is larger and thus more accurate. On many data sets, the difference is substantial, especially when $\epsilon = 0.01$. Looking at the different significance levels one by one, we first note that when $\epsilon = 0.2$, there is no point in using extrapolation (at least not the method employed here) since four points (instances) are still required. For $\epsilon = 0.1$, requiring four points is not enough. Even requiring seven points fairly often results in invalid MICPs. With this in mind, our recommendation is to require at least nine points, making extrapolation unnecessary. When $\epsilon = 0.05$, using 15 instances and extrapolation, instead of the nominally required 19 instances, seems to produce valid and more efficient MICPs. Finally, for $\epsilon = 0.01$, using fewer than the required instances and extrapolation appears to be the best choice. Specifically, requiring either 50 or 75 calibration instances will lead to larger and more accurate trees, while the resulting MICPs are generally still empirically valid.

5   Concluding Remarks

When having a small set of calibration instances, something which is common for Mondrian conformal predictors in particular, there is a risk of being too conservative, if the chosen instance in the calibration set for determining the size of the output prediction region does not perfectly correspond to the percentile that is prescribed by the chosen significance level. Moreover, for very small calibration sets, or low significance values, there may not even be a sufficient number of instances to guarantee validity. To address the first problem, an approach which employs interpolation among the calibration instances was proposed. Furthermore, using extrapolation was identified as an option when the second problem occurs. Results from an extensive empirical investigation were presented, comparing the interpolation approach to the standard, possibly conservative approach, and also in a separate experiment, investigating the effect of using extrapolation. The empirical results clearly show the benefit of employing the interpolation approach; for the 30 investigated data sets, the standard approach generated intervals that were statistically significant conservative in 22 cases, while this was not the case for any of the data sets when using interpolation. This was achieved without sacrificing validity and hence the study presents strong evidence in favor of employing interpolation when having small data sets. The second experiment shows that although substantial improvements in efficiency, i.e., smaller output interval sizes, can be obtained by performing extrapolation, this comes at the cost of frequently violating validity. Extrapolation should hence be used with care.

One direction for future work is to investigate what guarantees can be provided for interpolation to be not only efficient and valid in practice, but also in theory. Other directions involve considering alternative approaches to reducing conservatism, e.g., sampling approaches, and studying other Mondrian conformal predictors, in which the problem of handling small calibration sets occurs frequently.

References

1. Alcalá-Fdez, J., Fernández, A., Luengo, J., Derrac, J., García, S.: Keel data-mining software tool: Data set repository, integration of algorithms and experimental analysis framework. Multiple-Valued Logic and Soft Computing **17**(2–3), 255–287 (2011)
2. Bache, K., Lichman, M.: UCI machine learning repository (2013). http://archive.ics.uci.edu/ml
3. Benjamini, Y., Yekutieli, D.: The control of the false discovery rate in multiple testing under dependency. Annals of Statistics **29**, 1165–1188 (2001)
4. Breiman, L., Friedman, J., Stone, C.J., Olshen, R.A.: Classification and Regression Trees. Chapman & Hall/CRC (1984)
5. Johansson, U., Sönströd, C., Boström, H., Linusson, H.: Regression trees for streaming data with local performance guarantees. In: IEEE International Conference on Big Data. IEEE (2014) (in press)
6. Papadopoulos, H.: Inductive conformal prediction: Theory and application to neural networks. Tools in Artificial Intelligence **18**, 315–330 (2008)
7. Papadopoulos, H., Haralambous, H.: Neural networks regression inductive conformal predictor and its application to total electron content prediction. In: Diamantaras, K., Duch, W., Iliadis, L.S. (eds.) ICANN 2010, Part I. LNCS, vol. 6352, pp. 32–41. Springer, Heidelberg (2010)
8. Papadopoulos, H., Haralambous, H.: Reliable prediction intervals with regression neural networks. Neural Networks **24**(8), 842–851 (2011)
9. Quinlan, J.R.: C4.5: Programs for machine learning. Morgan Kaufmann Publishers Inc. (1993)
10. Rasmussen, C.E., Neal, R.M., Hinton, G., van Camp, D., Revow, M., Ghahramani, Z., Kustra, R., Tibshirani, R.: Delve data for evaluating learning in valid experiments (1996). www.cs.toronto.edu/delve
11. Vovk, V., Gammerman, A., Shafer, G.: Algorithmic Learning in a Random World. Springer-Verlag New York, Inc. (2005)
12. Vovk, V., Gammerman, A., Shafer, G.: Algorithmic learning in a random world. Springer (2005)

Conformal Anomaly Detection of Trajectories with a Multi-class Hierarchy

James Smith[1], Ilia Nouretdinov[1]([✉]), Rachel Craddock[2], Charles Offer[2], and Alexander Gammerman[1]

[1] Computer Learning Research Center,
Royal Holloway University of London, Egham, UK
{James.Smith.2009,ilia,alex}@cs.rhul.ac.uk
[2] Thales UK, London, UK
{Rachel.Craddock,Charles.Offer}@uk.thalesgroup.com

Abstract. The paper investigates the problem of anomaly detection in the maritime trajectory surveillance domain. Conformal predictors in this paper are used as a basis for anomaly detection. A multi-class hierarchy framework is presented for different class representations. Experiments are conducted with data taken from shipping vessel trajectories using data obtained through AIS (Automatic Identification System) broadcasts and the results are discussed.

1 Introduction

Detecting anomalous behaviour in the maritime domain is an important task since it involves the safety and security of ships. Automated methods for such detection are highly beneficial as they can lower operator workload, freeing up the operator's time to address tasks which cannot be automated. There has been a large amount of research conducted in the Anomaly Detection domain [1]. In this paper we use the terms 'anomalies','abnormalities' or 'outliers' to describe some patterns in the data that do not conform to typical behaviour. We use the term 'normal' to describe patterns that do conform to typical behaviour.

We focus on the anomaly detection of trajectories. A trajectory is a journey between two different points, for example between two harbours.

Some examples of 'anomalous' trajectories include: travelling to unusual locations, taking unfamiliar routes and sudden changes of speed or direction.

Conformal Anomaly Detection [9] is an application of Conformal Predictors [4] for Anomaly Detection. The key advantage of conformal predictors is their provably valid confidence measures that are provided alongside their predictions. The only assumption they make is that the data is independently and identically distributed (i.i.d.);

In our problem we have some previous trajectories $z_1, z_2, ..., z_n$, and we assume all 'normal' trajectories come from the same probability distribution P. Conformal predictors make no further assumptions about the distribution.

Conformal Anomaly Detection is based on Hawkin's definition of an outlier [2]: "An outlier is an observation which deviates so much from the other

A. Gammerman et al. (Eds.): SLDS 2015, LNAI 9047, pp. 281–290, 2015.
DOI: 10.1007/978-3-319-17091-6_23

observations as to arouse suspicions that it was generated by a different mechanism". Therefore conformal prediction relies on using a 'normal' class and we calculate the likelihood of a new object (trajectory) originating from the same distribution.

One of the main advantages of Conformal Anomaly Detection over most anomaly detection techniques is that they allow the calibration of the false-positive rate. It can be essential in real-world applications to control the number of false positives.

Several previous papers have studied anomaly detection with conformal predictors [6–10]. Typically they use all the previous data in a single class of 'normal', throughout this paper we will call this the the global class. Most previous papers [6,8–10] predict the likelihood of a new trajectory having originated from the global class. One of the previous papers [7] solely uses classes based on the vessel type (Passenger/Cargo/Tanker), but no comparison to the global class is presented.

In this paper we propose putting all the trajectories into a three-level artificial hierarchy of classes as seen in Fig 1. The **global class** contains all the previous data of the 'normal' class at the top layer, this is split as we progress down the hierarchy. At the next layer, the data is split into **type classes**, one for each vessel type. The final layer of the data is separated into **local classes**, one for each vessel.

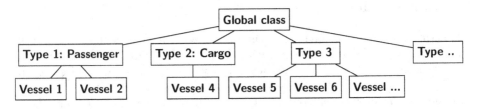

Fig. 1. Visualisation of the multi-class hierarchy

Our approach of having multiple 'normal' classes adds more complexity to the problem, and in this paper we investigate if in practice any benefits can be gained by using the different classes.

2   Method

The Conformal Anomaly Detection technique calculates the likelihood that a new object z_n was produced by the same distribution as the previous objects $z_1, z_2, ..., z_{n-1}$. The outputted p-value p_n is that likelihood. The standard Conformal Anomaly Detection algorithm [6] is as follows:

When producing predictions it is useful to use a level of significance ϵ. According to the validity property [4], if all the data objects $z_1, \ldots, z_n$ are really generated by the same distribution, then the probability that $p_n \leq \epsilon$ is at most ϵ.

Conformal Anomaly Detection

Input   : Non-Conformity Measure A, significance level ϵ, training objects
$z_1, z_2, ..., z_{n-1}$ and new object z_n
Output: P-value p_n, boolean variable Anomaly

$D = \{z_1, ..., z_n\}$
for $i \leftarrow 1$ to n do
$\quad | \quad \alpha_i \leftarrow A(D \setminus z_i, z_i)$
end
$\tau \leftarrow U(0, 1)$
$p_n \leftarrow \frac{|\{i: a_i > a_n\}| + \tau |\{i: a_i = a_n\}|}{n}$
if $p_n < \epsilon$ then
$\quad | \quad Anomaly \leftarrow$ **true**
else
$\quad | \quad Anomaly \leftarrow$ **false**
end

In the context of anomaly detection this means that if z_n is not an anomaly, it will be classified as anomaly with probability at most ϵ. This allows the false positive rate to be calibrated with the significance parameter ϵ [9], it should be noted that this is only guaranteed for the online case when the true type of a predicted vessel becomes known soon after the prediction.

The Non-Conformity Measure (NCM) A is a type of information distance between an object and a bag of objects. In the experiments in this paper we focus on the k-nearest neighbour Hausdorff distance non-conformity measure [6] to compare a trajectory against a bag of trajectories. In particular we use the one nearest neighbour non-conformity measure, using the symmetrical Hausdorff distance metric as the one nearest neighbour algorithm has shown good performance compared to others in [10].

Multi-class Hierarchy

In previous applications of applying conformal anomaly detection to trajectories, typically one global class of 'normal' is used to encompass all previous data. However with vessel trajectories there exists an information hierarchy as introduced earlier in Fig 1.

In trajectory data some vessels such as passenger vessels will make the same repeated journeys, for these vessels it is normal to make repeated trips along a route and 'abnormal' if they deviate from these routes. This leads to the idea of treating every vessel as its own local class. The immediate benefit is that it is likely that a vessel only conducts a subset of journeys from the global class and that a more focused set of previous examples could be used to save computational resources.

The vessel type classes may be beneficial as they contain more data than local classes, but will not contain all the trajectories. In our data the observed vessels come from 16 types of vessel including passenger, cargo, pleasure, tankers, dredgers, pilot vessels and many others.

By comparison the global class is the simplest to implement. It allows predictions to be made for trajectories belonging to vessels that have no prior data in the training set. The global class is also better suited if there is no information available on the type of the vessel. One weakness of the global class is that is unable to distinguish between vessels of different types and will not be able to detect if a passenger vessel starts conducting journeys similar to that of a military vessel. There are also vessels that due to their nature may not follow any previous trajectories, such as search and rescue vessels conducting searches. These 'deviations' are considered as typical behaviour for such vessels and in this case the global class may perform worse.

The main advantage of producing multiple p-values like this is to attempt to better understand trajectories that are classified as 'anomalous'. The trajectory may be anomalous in the global context, but 'normal' for its local context and vice versa. We could determine under which class the trajectories are 'anomalous' or 'normal' and use this to gain insight.

To use this in practice we shall generate a p-value to indicate the likelihood of the trajectory belonging to each of its three associated classes these being: p_{global}, p_{type} and p_{local}. In the p_{global} case all prior trajectories are used regardless of which vessel they come from. p_{type} is calculated from using previous trajectories from the same type of vessel. p_{local} is calculated from using previous trajectories from the same vessel. In practice this requires extra processing and in this paper we restrict the task to the case when all vessels' types and IDs are known.

In Figure 2 $filter$ is a function for filtering the previous trajectories for either vessels of the same $type$ or trajectories from the same $local$ vessel. In the case of $type$ it will only return objects that match the type of the new object, in the case of $self$ it will only return trajectories that belong to the same vessel.

Note in the multi-class algorithm Figure 2 the decision rule $min(p_{global}, p_{type}, p_{self}) < \epsilon$ is used, and we predict that the object is 'anomalous' if any of its p-values indicate that it is anomalous, we shall later investigate this rule in our experiments. Aggregating the p-values in this manner does affect the property of a well-calibrated false positive rate. Instead of the decision rule being bounded by ϵ, it is bounded by $min(3\epsilon, 1)$; this is because each p-value may contribute ϵ false-positives and the maximum false-positive rate is 1.

3   Experiments and Data

In our data for all trajectories we know both the vessel type and ship IDs. Automated Identification System (AIS) is a system for tracking vessels, vessels that use AIS are fitted with a transceiver that broadcasts the position of the vessel (acquired from an on-board GPS unit), and the vessel ID alongside a timestamp and other information every few seconds. Not all vessels are mandated to use AIS but all passenger and tanker vessels and vessels weighing 300 gross tons or more are required to do so under the International Maritime Organisation's

---

Conformal Anomaly Detection: Multi-Class Hierarchy

Input   : Non-Conformity Measure A, significance level ϵ, training objects
$z_1, z_2, ..., z_{n-1}$ and new object z_n
Output: P-values: p_{global}, p_{type} and p_{self}, Boolean variable *Anomaly*

$D = \{z_1, ..., z_n\}$
for $i \leftarrow 1$ to n do
  | $\alpha_{global,i} \leftarrow A(D \setminus z_i, z_i)$
end
$\tau \leftarrow U(0,1)$
$p_{global} \leftarrow \frac{|\{i:a_{global,i} > a_{global,n}\}| + \tau |\{i:a_{global,i} = a_{global,n}\}|}{n}$
$D = filter(D, type, z_n);$
$N \leftarrow = |D|$
for $j \leftarrow 1$ to N do
  | $\alpha_{type,j} \leftarrow A(D \setminus z_j, z_j)$
end
$p_{type} \leftarrow \frac{|\{j:a_{type,j} > a_{type,N}\}| + \tau |\{j:a_{type,j} = a_{type,N}\}|}{N}$
$D = filter(D, self, z_n);$
$N \leftarrow = |D|$
for $m \leftarrow 1$ to N do
  | $\alpha_{self,k} \leftarrow A(D \setminus z_m, z_m)$
end
$p_{self} \leftarrow \frac{|\{m:a_{self,m} > a_{self,N}\}| + \tau |\{m:a_{self,m} = a_{self,N}\}|}{N}$

if $min(p_{global}, p_{type}, p_{self}) < \epsilon$ then
  | *Anomaly* $\leftarrow$ **true**
else
  | *Anomaly* $\leftarrow$ **false**

Fig. 2. Conformal Anomaly Detection: Multi-Class Hierarchy algorithm

regulations [3]. We use AIS data collected from Portsmouth on the south coast of England during 2012.

In this paper we represent trajectories as a sequence of discrete $4D$ points $(x, y, x_{velocity}, y_{velocity})$ in a similar method to [7]. The original broadcasts are linearly interpolated such that they are spaced at 200m intervals to reduce the problem of over and under-saturation of data as a single receiver may not be able to capture all broadcasts due to a variety of factors such as range, weather and obstacles.

The algorithm for splitting the broadcasts into trajectories is similar to [6]. If a vessel leaves the observation area for a period of 10 minutes or more, or if the vessel is stationary for a period of 5 minutes or more we consider this as the end of a trajectory. Therefore a *trajectory* is a sequence of $4D$ points which are moving and can have any length. The $4D$ points are normalised such that $x, y \in [0,1]$ and $x_{velocity}, y_{velocity} \in [-1,1]$.

In our experiments we consider trajectories generated over a several week time period. All the experiments are conducted using a batch offline mode in which the data is split into training and test sets. The testing and training sets being chosen from a randomly shuffled set of trajectories. Most of the experiments are comparing p-values, in these cases the decision rule is that a trajectory is classed as 'anomalous' if $p_{value} < \epsilon$ otherwise it is classed as 'normal'. Recall that we use 16 different types of vessel in our experiments as introduced in the method section.

We also do not investigate the possibility of 'anomalies' existing in the training set. This would lead to a different distribution being represented in the training set.

Anomaly Generation: Random Walks

One of the big challenges is that there is a lack of real-world labelled anomalous datasets for AIS trajectories - at the time of writing the authors are unaware of any publicly available AIS dataset with labelled anomalies. Therefore it is necessary for empirical purposes to create artificial anomalies.

One previously suggested approach [6] is to select a pre-existing trajectory, pick a random point on the trajectory and simulate a random walk for a specified distance. It can be argued that randomness may not truly represent real world anomalies however it does give an indication of ability to distinguish trajectories generated from a different distribution. In this paper random walks are generated to a distance of 600m. Once generated the random walk trajectories will report the same vessel ID as the vessel ID from the pre-existing trajectory.

Wrong Type Behaviour Anomalies

In our study of using type and local classes it is useful to demonstrate the property that using a global class does not distinguish if a trajectory is 'normal' for in the context of a particular vessel. Wrong type anomalies are designed to represent this problem. To generate wrong type anomalies we choose a trajectory and assign it a new random vessel ID matching another in our database. The anomalous trajectory will then be compared against the same type as the one, the new vessel ID came from. This emulates a vessel behaving in a manner possibly unexpected for itself.

3.1   Experiment 1: Comparing p_{global}, p_{local} and p_{type} Directly

In this experiment we seek to directly compare p_{global}, p_{local} and p_{type} when they are all given the same data. In this experiment we filter the available trajectories to only those of vessels with at least 600 trajectories leaving us with 16 vessels. We then use 200 trajectories from each vessel in the training set and 200 in the testing set. We add 100 artificial random-walk anomalies to the testing set. This leads to a testing set of 3300 trajectories and a training set of 3200 trajectories. For each trajectory we then compute each of the 3 p-values using its given type and vessel ID.

3.2 Experiment 2: Maintaining Computational Cost

In this experiment we examine what happens in the case in which we have limited computational resources and can only compare a new trajectory against a fixed number of previous trajectories. This is tested by comparing the performance of the p_{local}, p_{type} and p_{global} p-values using the same number of previous trajectories when calculating all p-values. We will only use the 11 vessels with the most trajectories in our dataset that such that there are at least 1000 trajectories available from each vessel. We first split the trajectories such that there are 500 trajectories from each vessel in both the training and testing set for calculating p_{local}, the same testing set throughout this experiment. The training set used for calculating each p_{type} is created by selecting 500 trajectories randomly from the training sets used for calculating p_{local} of matching vessel type.

In the case of the global class the training set is generated by adding 50 trajectories for each vessel, leading to a training set of 550 trajectories when calculating p_{global}, this is slightly higher than the size of the training sets of p_{type} and p_{local} but not that separating trajectories by type and vessel ID requires more processing.

Finally we generate 100 random walk anomalies using any the trajectory in the training and test sets as a starting point from the random walks and these random walk 'anomalous' trajectories are then added to the testing set.

3.3 Experiment 3: Wrong Behaviour Type Anomalies

In this experiment we aim to test how robust the different p-values are to a vessel acting in a manner that is peculiar for itself or its type, yet similar to other vessels.

To do this we create a training set from the 13 most active vessels in our dataset using 110 trajectories from each vessel. The testing set consists of a further 110 trajectories from each vessel alongside a total of 100 random walk anomalies and a total of 100 wrong type behaviour anomalies. We then generate p-values for all trajectories in the testing set.

3.4 Experiment 4: Hybrid Rule

This experiment investigates what happens if we merge all the three p-values together with a decision rule such that a trajectory is predicted as an anomaly if: $min(p_{global}, p_{type}, p_{self}) < \epsilon$. This experiment uses the same training and testing sets from experiment 1.

4 Results

Below are the tables of the results gathered from the experiments mentioned in the previous section. The tables show the number of true positives (tp) (i.e.

Table 1. Results of experiment 1: Direct comparison

ϵ	p_{global} tp	p_{global} fp	p_{type} tp	p_{type} fp	p_{local} tp	p_{local} fp
0.01	71%	0.8 %	**85 %**	0.8 %	73 %	0.8%
0.02	86%	1.6 %	**91 %**	1.9 %	88 %	1.5%
0.03	93%	3.0 %	93 %	2.7 %	**94 %**	2.2%
0.05	**94%**	4.3 %	**94 %**	4.2 %	**94 %**	3.9%
0.10	96%	8.5 %	**97 %**	9.6 %	**97 %**	9.5%

Table 2. Results of experiment 2: Comparison with the same computational cost

ϵ	p_{global} tp	p_{global} fp	p_{type} tp	p_{type} fp	p_{local} tp	p_{local} fp
0.01	49 %	0.5 %	71 %	0.9 %	**76 %**	0.7%
0.02	54 %	0.8 %	80 %	2.5 %	**86 %**	1.8%
0.03	60 %	1 %	89 %	3.7 %	**90 %**	2.9%
0.05	84 %	4.1 %	91 %	4.9 %	**96 %**	5.0%
0.10	89 %	8.9 %	94 %	10%	**97 %**	10.4%

Table 3. Results of experiment 3: Wrong type behaviour anomalies

ϵ	p_{type} tp	p_{type} fp	p_{local} tp	p_{local} fp
0.01	**54 %**	1.3 %	52.5 %	0.9%
0.02	**76 %**	2.4 %	68.5 %	1.5%
0.03	**78 %**	3.5 %	77.5 %	2.4%
0.05	**81 %**	5.9 %	80 %	4.5%
0.10	85 %	10.1 %	**89 %**	10.8%

Table 4. Results of experiment 4: Hybrid rule

ϵ	hybrid tp	hybrid fp	$\frac{\epsilon}{3}$	hybrid tp	hybrid fp
0.01	93%	1.8 %	$\frac{0.01}{3}$	75 %	0.4 %
0.02	96%	3.6 %	$\frac{0.02}{3}$	87 %	1.3 %
0.03	99%	5.5 %	$\frac{0.03}{3}$	93 %	1.8 %
0.05	99%	8.4 %	$\frac{0.05}{3}$	95 %	2.8 %
0.10	99%	15.8%	$\frac{0.10}{3}$	99 %	5.8 %

anomalies captured) and the number of false positives (fp) - (i.e. 'normal' trajectories mis-classified as anomalies). A bold font has been used to denote the p-value that captures the most true anomalies for a given significance level ϵ.

In table 1 we see that when using all the information together p_{type} generally better captures the anomalies than the other p-values. For significances 0.03, 0.05 and 0.10 the performance offered by all them is rather similar (within 1% difference). p_{local} also outperforms p_{global} at the lower significances 0.01,0.02. This reveals that it is clear that with large amounts of training data p_{type} and p_{local} are capable of out performing p_{global}, and if a vessel's ID is unavailable knowing its type is enough in most cases. p_{type} performs better than p_{local} for the lower significances of 0.01 and 0.02 where arguably performance is most important. However p_{local} consistently has a lower number of false positives than all other the p-values indicating the best performance for significances 0.03, 0.05 and 0.10.

Table 2 shows the performance of the p-values for experiment 2, the case where we consider equal computational resources. It is clear that p_{local} outperforms p_{type}, and p_{type} outperforms p_{global} at identifying a superior number of anomalies for all ϵ, this indicates that having a more focused history of prior examples improves classification performance.

Experiment 3 shows that the type class performs well at detecting 'anomalies' of vessels demonstrating behaviour from other types .

Experiments 1-3 in most cases show that the significance parameter ϵ does provide a well-calibrated false-positive rate in most cases, even though there is no guarantee of this in the offline mode that is used.

Experiment 4 shows that the hybrid rule performs far better at detecting the random walk anomalies than any of the single p-values in experiment 1. It is important to note that ϵ doesn't calibrate the number of false-positives close to ϵ as the other p-values do on their own. The hybrid rule adds false positives from the 3 p-values possibly tripling the number of false-positives relative to ϵ but it is clear there is an overlap of the false-positives from each p-value. In addition, we carried out experiments using $\frac{\epsilon}{3}$ to take into account that the false positive rate of the hybrid rule is expected to be below $min(3\epsilon, 1)$. This allows fair comparison to the false positives rates seen in experiment 1. Comparing table 1 and the right side of table 4, we see that the hybrid method shows the best true positive results for $\epsilon = 0.03$ and $\epsilon = 0.05$ when preserving the same false-positive rate bound.

5   Conclusion

Past approaches using conformal prediction for anomaly detection typically focus on using a global class, or split the classes with little overlap. In this paper we have proposed a new multi-class hierarchy framework for the anomaly detection of trajectories. We have also presented a study of this approach showing that there are several benefits from using alternative classes to the global class. We generate three p-values p_{global}, p_{type} and p_{local} for new trajectories. We have discussed the pros and cons of each of the p-values.

We demonstrated that in practice using these extra p-values can lead to the detection of more anomalies for less false-positives.

We have also shown it is possible to combine all the p-values by taking a hybrid approach using the minimum p-value of p_{global}, p_{type} and p_{local}. Experiment 3 showed that it is possible to detect more anomalies when using this approach than when using individual p-values. This highlights that each p-value is able to detect different anomalies better than the others.

Local classes perform better at detecting anomalies when provided with the same amount of previous trajectories as both the global and type classes. This indicates that local classes are a better option when computational cost is considered.

The multi-class hierarchy framework could potentially be reused for other anomaly detection problems that involve a class hierarchy.

In future work it would be interesting to investigate further the multi-class hierarchy of trajectory data as there are still many unanswered questions. A particularly interesting problem is attempting to predict the type or vessel ID of a new trajectory and to answer whether a trajectory with unknown type/ID of vessel is an 'anomaly' or not. Also it may be interesting to attempt to find similar vessels.

Acknowledgments. James Smith is grateful for a PhD studentship jointly funded by Thales UK and Royal Holloway, University of London. This work is supported by EPSRC grant EP/K033344/1 ("Mining the Network Behaviour of Bots"); and by grant 'Development of New Venn Prediction Methods for Osteoporosis Risk Assessment' from the Cyprus Research Promotion Foundation. We are also grateful to Vladimir Vovk and Christopher Watkins for useful discussions. AIS Data was provided by Thales UK.

References

1. Chandola, V., Banerjee, A., Kumar, V.: Anomaly Detection A Survey. ACM Computing Surveys (CSUR) (2009). http://dl.acm.org/
2. Hawkins, D.: Identification of outliers, vol. 11. Chapman and Hall, London (1980)
3. International Maritime Organisation.: Regulation 19 - Carriage requirements for shipborne navigational systems and equipment. International Convention for the Safety of Life at Sea (SOLAS) Treaty. Chapter V (last amendment: May 2011)
4. Vovk, V., Gammerman, A., Shafer, G.: Algorithmic learning in a random world. Springer (2005)
5. Gammerman, A., Vovk, V.: Hedging predictions in machine learning. The Computer Journal **50**(2), 151–163 (2007)
6. Laxhammar, R., Falkman, G.: Sequential conformal anomaly detection in trajectories based on hausdorff distance. In: 2011 Proceedings of the 14th International Conference on Information Fusion (FUSION) (2011)
7. Laxhammar, R., Falkman, G.: Conformal prediction for distribution-independent anomaly detection in streaming vessel data. In: Proceedings of the First International Workshop on Novel Data Stream Pattern Mining Techniques, pp. 47–55. ACM (2010)
8. Laxhammar, R., Falkman, G.: Online detection of anomalous sub-trajectories: A sliding window approach based on conformal anomaly detection and local outlier factor. In: Iliadis, L., Maglogiannis, I., Papadopoulos, H., Karatzas, K., Sioutas, S. (eds.) AIAI 2012 Workshops. IFIP AICT, vol. 382, pp. 192–202. Springer, Heidelberg (2012)
9. Laxhammar, R.: Conformal anomaly detection: Detecting abnormal trajectories in surveillance applications. PhD Thesis, University of Skovde (2014)
10. Smith, J., Nouretdinov, I., Craddock, R., Offer, C., Gammerman, A.: Anomaly detection of trajectories with kernel density estimation by conformal prediction. In: Iliadis, L., Maglogiannis, I., Papadopoulos, H., Sioutas, S., Makris, C. (eds.) AIAI 2014 Workshops. IFIP AICT, vol. 437, pp. 271–280. Springer, Heidelberg (2014)

Model Selection Using Efficiency of Conformal Predictors

Ritvik Jaiswal and Vineeth N. Balasubramanian[(✉)]

Department of Computer Science and Engineering,
Indian Institute of Technology, Hyderabad 502205, India
{cs11b031,vineethnb}@iith.ac.in

Abstract. The Conformal Prediction framework guarantees error calibration in the online setting, but its practical usefulness in real-world problems is affected by its efficiency, i.e. the size of the prediction region. Narrow prediction regions that maintain validity would be the most useful conformal predictors. In this work, we use the efficiency of conformal predictors as a measure to perform model selection in classifiers. We pose this objective as an optimization problem on the model parameters, and test this approach with the k-Nearest Neighbour classifier. Our results on the USPS and other standard datasets show promise in this approach.

Keywords: Conformal prediction · Efficiency · Model selection · Optimisation

1 Introduction

The Conformal Predictions (CP) framework was developed by Vovk, Shafer and Gammerman [1]. It is a framework used in classification and regression which outputs labels with a guaranteed upper bound on errors in the online setting. This makes the framework extremely useful in applications where decisions made by machines are of critical importance. The framework has grown in its awareness and use over the last few years, and has now been adapted to various machine learning settings such as active learning, anomaly detection and feature selection [2]. It has also been applied to various domains including biometrics, drug discovery, clinical diagnostics and network analysis in recent years.

The CP framework has two important properties that define its utility: *validity* and *efficiency*, as defined in [1]. The *validity* of the framework refers to its error calibration property, i.e, keeping the frequency of errors under a pre-specified threshold ε, at the confidence level $1-\varepsilon$. The *efficiency* of the framework corresponds to the size of the prediction (or output) sets: smaller the size of the prediction set, higher the efficiency. While the validity of the CP framework is proven to hold for any classification or regression method (assuming data is exchangeable and a suitable conformity measure can be defined on the method) [3], the efficiency of the framework can vary to a large extent based on the choice of classifiers and classifier parameters [4]. The practical applicability of

© Springer International Publishing Switzerland 2015
A. Gammerman et al. (Eds.): SLDS 2015, LNAI 9047, pp. 291–300, 2015.
DOI: 10.1007/978-3-319-17091-6_24

the CP framework can be limited by the efficiency of the framework; satisfying the validity property alone may cause all class labels to occur in predictions thus rendering the framework incapable of decision support.

The study of efficiency of the framework has garnered interest in recent years (described in Section 2). Importantly, efficiency can be viewed as a means of selecting model parameters in classifiers, i.e. the model parameter that provides the most narrow conformal prediction regions, while maintaining validity, would be the best choice for the classifier for a given application. We build upon this idea in this work. In particular, we explore the use of the *S-criterion* of efficiency (average sum of p-values across classes), as defined by Vovk et al. in [5], of the CP framework for model selection in different classifiers. This model selection is posed as an optimisation problem, i.e. the objective is to optimise the value of the *S-criterion* metric of efficiency, when written in terms of the model parameters. Such an approach gives us the value of the parameters which maximise the performance of the classifier. We validate this approach to model selection using the k-Nearest Neighbour (k-NN) classifier [6].

The remainder of the paper is organised as follows. Section 2 reviews earlier works that have studied efficiency or model selection using conformal predictors. Section 3 describes the proposed methodology of this paper including the criterion of efficiency used, the formulation of the objective function and the solution (model parameter) obtained by solving the ranking problem derived from the objective function. Section 4 details the experiments and results of applying this method to different datasets. Section 5 summarises the work and also mentions possible future additions and improvements to this work.

2   Related Work

Earlier works that have studied efficiency in the CP framework or model selection using conformal predictors can broadly be categorised into three kinds: works that have attempted to improve the efficiency of the framework using appropriate choice of model parameters; another which studies a closely related idea on model selection using conformal predictors, specifically developed for Support Vector Machines (SVM); and lastly, a recent work that has performed a detailed investigation of efficiency measures for conformal predictors. We describe each of these below.

Balasubramanian et al. [4] proposed a Multiple Kernel Learning approach to learn an appropriate kernel function to compute distances in the kernel k-NN classifier. They showed that the choice of the kernel function/parameter in kernel k-NNs can greatly influence efficiency, and hence proposed a maximum margin methodology to learn the kernel to obtain efficient conformal predictors. Pekala and Llorens [7] proposed another methodology based on local distance metric learning to increase the efficiency of k-NN based conformal predictors. In their approach, they defined a Leave-One-Out estimate of the expected number of predictions containing multiple class labels (which is a measure of efficiency of CPs), which they minimised by formulating a distance metric learning problem.

Yang et al. [8] studied a very similar idea to learn distance metrics that increase the efficiency of conformal predictors using three different metric learning methods: Large Margin Nearest Neighbours, Discriminative Component Analysis, and Local Fisher Discriminant Analysis. While each of these methods can be considered complementary to the proposed work, none of these efforts viewed their methods as one of model selection, which we seek to address in this work.

Hardoon et al. [9] [2] proposed a methodology for model selection using nonconformity scores - in particular, for SVMs, and had an objective similar to the proposed work. However, in their approach, K models, each with different model parameters, are trained on a given dataset, and the error bound ϵ is decided at run-time for each test point by choosing the error bound (called $\epsilon_{critical}$) of the model (among all the K trained models) that results in a singleton prediction set. In contrast, here we seek to develop a model selection approach that selects the unique value of a given model parameter that provides maximal classifier performance on a test set (in terms of accuracy) using an optimisation strategy.

Vovk et al. recently investigated different metrics for measuring the efficiency of conformal predictors in [5], which we build on in this work. Among the different criteria of efficiency are the *S-criterion*, which measures the average sum of the p-values of the data points, the *N-criterion*, which uses the average size of the prediction sets, the *U-criterion*, which measures the average unconfidence, i.e. the average of the second largest p-values of the data points, the *F-criterion*, which measures the average fuzziness, or the sum of all p-values apart from the largest one, of the data points, the *M-criterion*, which measures the percentage of test points for which the prediction set contains multiple labels, and the *E-criterion*, which measures the average amount by which the size of the prediction set exceeds 1. [5] also introduced the concept of observed criteria of efficiency, namely, OU, OF, OM and OE. These criteria are simply the *observed* counterparts of the aforementioned *prior* criteria of efficiency. A detailed explanation of each of the different criteria of efficiency can be found in [5]. We develop our model selection methodology using the *S-criterion* for efficiency, which we describe in Section 3.

3   Proposed Methodology

In this paper, we propose a new methodology for model selection in classifiers by optimising the *S-criterion* measure of efficiency of conformal predictors [5]. We validate our methodology on the k-NN classifier by formulating an optimisation problem, and choosing that value for k which minimises the *S-criterion* measure. We view the optimisation formulation as a ranking problem, and select the k that minimises the objective function score. We found, in our experiments, that this value of k also provides very high performance of the classifier in terms of accuracy of class label predictions. Our methodology is described below.

Let $\{(x_1, y_1), (x_2, y_2), \ldots, (x_n, y_n)\}$ be a sequence of data point-class label pairs, where x corresponds to the data, and y corresponds to the class labels.

Given a new test point x_{n+1}, the p-value for this test point with respect to the class y is defined as:

$$p_{n+1}^y = \frac{count\left\{i \in \{1, \ldots, n+1\} : \alpha_i^y \le \alpha_{n+1}^y\right\}}{n+1} \tag{1}$$

where α_{n+1}^y is the conformity measure[1] of x_{n+1}, assuming it is assigned the class label y. The *S-Criterion* of efficiency, introduced in [5], is defined as the average sum of the p-values, as follows:

$$\frac{1}{n}\sum_{i=1}^{n}\sum_{y} p_i^y \tag{2}$$

where n is the number of test data points and p_i^y are the p-values of the ith data point with respect to the class y.

Smaller values are preferable for the *S-criterion*, as given in [5]. This means that we would like all p-values to be low, which in turn ensures that the size of the prediction set, given by $\{y | p^y > \epsilon\}$, is small. In other words, for an incoming test point, we want as small a number of training data points to have a lesser conformity score than the test point as possible. To put it another way, we want most of the training data points to have a higher conformity score than the test point. This roughly translates to saying that we want a small value for each of the expressions $(\alpha_i - \alpha_j)$ for each test point x_i and training point x_j. By extension, we would like a small value for the sum of differences between the conformity scores of the incoming test points and the training data points, given by the following expression:

$$\sum_{i=1}^{n}\sum_{j=1}^{m}(\alpha_i - \alpha_j) \tag{3}$$

Here n is the number of test data points and m is the number of training data points.

For a k-NN classifier, the conformity score for a test point x_i is given as follows [1][2]:

$$\frac{\sum_{j=1}^{k} D_{ij}^{-y}}{\sum_{j=1}^{k} D_{ij}^{y}} \tag{4}$$

which is the ratio of the sum of the distances to the k nearest neighbours belonging to classes other than the hypothesis y (denoted by D_{ij}^{-y}), against the sum of the distances to the k nearest neighbours belonging to the same class as the hypothesis y (denoted by D_{ij}^{y}). Considering that we want to find the value of

---

[1] We use the term *conformity measure* in this work similar to the usage in [5]. Note that the conformity measure is simply the complement of the typical non-conformity measure terminology used in earlier work in this field.

the parameter k which minimises the *S-criterion* measure of efficiency, we write equation (3) in terms of k. Doing so allows us to formulate an objective function in terms of k. This leads us to the following objective function:

$$\underset{k}{\text{argmin}} \left(\sum_{i=1}^{n} \sum_{j=1}^{m} \left(\frac{\sum_{l=1}^{k} D_{il}^{-y}}{\sum_{l=1}^{k} D_{il}^{y}} - \frac{\sum_{l=1}^{k} D_{jl}^{-y}}{\sum_{l=1}^{k} D_{jl}^{y}} \right) \right) \tag{5}$$

In this work, we treat the aforementioned formulation as a score ranking problem, and arrive at the solution for the model parameter k by scoring the objective function value for various values of k and choosing the one which minimises the objective function value. The value of k is varied from 1 to 25 and that k is chosen which results in the least value of the objective function. We note here that there may be more efficient methods to solve this optimisation formulation, which we will attempt in future work. Our objective in this paper is to establish a proof-of-concept that such an approach can be useful in model selection. We now validate this approach through our experiments in Section 4.

4   Empirical Study

We tested the proposed model selection methodology for k-NN on four different datasets, which are described in Table 1[2]. The experiments were carried out

Table 1. Description of datasets

Dataset	Num of Classes	Size of Training Set	Number of Training Points	Number of Validation Points	Size of Test Set
USPS Dataset	10	7291	5103	2188	2007
Handwritten Digits Dataset (from UCI repository [10])	10	3823	2676	1147	1797
Stanford Waveform Dataset	3	300	210	90	500
Stanford Vowel Dataset	11	528	370	158	462

by randomly dividing the training set into training and validation subsets of sizes in a 70 : 30 ratio. To compute the objective function value as in Equation 5, the validation set was considered as the test set, and the conformity scores were computed for validation and training data points. These scores were then plugged into the objective function to finalise on a value for the parameter k. The value of k was varied from 1 to 25 and the objective function was evaluated using the same. The procedure was repeated 5 times to neutralise any impact of randomness bias, and the results shown in this paper have been averaged

---

[2] http://archive.ics.uci.edu/ml/
http://statweb.stanford.edu/~tibs/ElemStatLearn/data.html

over these 5 trials. We then tested the performance of the k-NN classifier, on independent test sets (different from the validation sets used to compute the objective function), with the same k values, and noted the accuracy obtained with each of these models. Our results are illustrated in Figures 1, 2, 3 and 4. For each dataset, the left sub-figure plots the values of the objective function against the values of the parameter k using the validation set. The value of k that provides the minimum objective function value is chosen as the best model parameter. The right sub-figure plots the accuracy obtained by the classifier on the test set, against all values of k. We observe that, in general, the value of the objective function (left sub-figures) is negatively correlated with accuracy (right sub-figures), which suggests the effectiveness of this methodology. The correlation coefficient ρ is calculated for each of the sub-figures, corroborating this point.

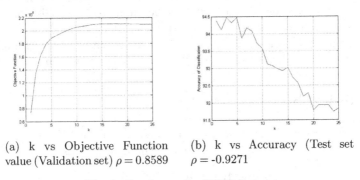

(a) k vs Objective Function   (b) k vs Accuracy (Test set
value (Validation set) $\rho = 0.8589$ $\rho = -0.9271$

Fig. 1. Results on the USPS Dataset

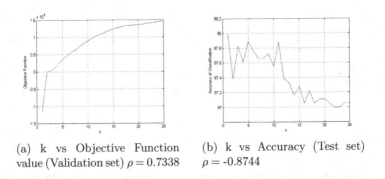

(a) k vs Objective Function   (b) k vs Accuracy (Test set)
value (Validation set) $\rho = 0.7338$ $\rho = -0.8744$

Fig. 2. Results on the Handwritten Digits Dataset

While we studied the performance of the classifier on the test set (in terms of accuracy) in the above experiments, we also performed a separate experiment to study if the final value of k obtained using our methodology results in efficient

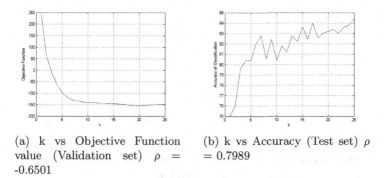

(a) k vs Objective Function value (Validation set) ρ = -0.6501

(b) k vs Accuracy (Test set) ρ = 0.7989

Fig. 3. Results on the Stanford Waveform Dataset

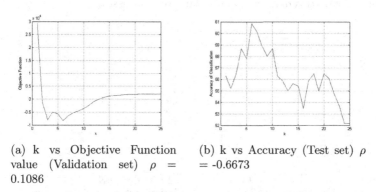

(a) k vs Objective Function value (Validation set) ρ = 0.1086

(b) k vs Accuracy (Test set) ρ = -0.6673

Fig. 4. Results on the Stanford Vowel Dataset

conformal predictions on the test set. Figures 5 and 6 show the size of the prediction sets, averaged over all the test points, plotted against the k values, for the Stanford Waveform and the USPS datasets, respectively.

While one approach to model selection would be to maximise accuracy on the validation set, this does not always result in the best performance of the classifier. As evidenced in Figure 7, maximising accuracy on the validation set results in $k = 1$ (left sub-figure), while the best performance on the test set is obtained when $k = 6$ (right sub-figure). However, in saying this, we concede that this approach, of maximising accuracy on the validation set, does not always falter in giving the optimum k which also maximises accuracy on the test set. Figure 8 shows that both approaches, one that maximises accuracy on the validation set and the other which is the proposed method for model selection (minimising an objective function which is essentially a proxy for the *S-criterion* of efficiency), result in the same value for the model parameter k.

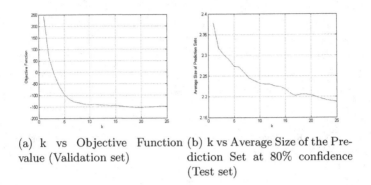

(a) k vs Objective Function value (Validation set)

(b) k vs Average Size of the Prediction Set at 80% confidence (Test set)

Fig. 5. Study of efficiency of k-NN conformal predictors on the test set of the Standard Waveform dataset (this dataset contains data from 3 classes)

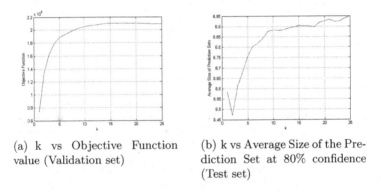

(a) k vs Objective Function value (Validation set)

(b) k vs Average Size of the Prediction Set at 80% confidence (Test set)

Fig. 6. Study of efficiency of k-NN conformal predictors on the test set of the USPS dataset (this dataset contains data from 10 classes)

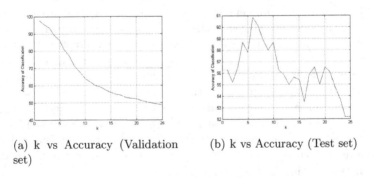

(a) k vs Accuracy (Validation set)

(b) k vs Accuracy (Test set)

Fig. 7. Using accuracy on validation set for model selection on the Stanford Vowel Dataset

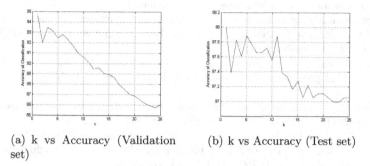

(a) k vs Accuracy (Validation set)   (b) k vs Accuracy (Test set)

Fig. 8. Using accuracy on validation set for model selection on the Handwritten Digits Dataset

5 Conclusions and Future Work

The Conformal Prediction framework has been gaining popularity as a robust methodology to associate measures of confidence with prediction outcomes in classification and regression settings. While the framework can be proved to be valid under any suitable definition of a conformity measure, its efficiency - the measure of narrowness of its prediction regions - can vary with different classification methods and different model parameters. In this paper, we propose a new methodology to use the efficiency of conformal predictors to perform model selection in classification methods. In particular, we use the *S-criterion* of efficiency to derive an objective function that can be minimised to obtain the model parameter k in the k-NN classifier. Our results with different standard datasets show promise in this approach.

In future work, we plan to incorporate other measures of efficiency (as described in [5]) to develop on the proposed idea. Besides, while we transformed the optimisation formulation into a score ranking problem, we believe that it is possible to solve this (or a related) optimisation problem more efficiently using known methods with performance bounds (such as, submodular optimisation). We intend to pursue these efforts in our ongoing and future work. We will also consider generalising this approach to other classifiers in the near future.

References

1. Vovk, V., Gammerman, A., Shafer, G.: Algorithmic Learning in a Random World. Springer-Verlag New York Inc., Secaucus (2005)
2. Balasubramanian, V., Ho, S.S., Vovk, V., eds.: Conformal Prediction for Reliable Machine Learning: Theory, Adaptations and Applications. Morgan Kaufmann, Amsterdam (2014)
3. Vovk, V.: On-line confidence machines are well-calibrated. In: Proceedings of the The 43rd Annual IEEE Symposium on Foundations of Computer Science, pp. 187–196 (2002)

4. Balasubramanian, V., Chakraborty, S., Panchanathan, S., Ye, J.: Kernel learning for efficiency maximization in the conformal predictions framework. In: 2010 Ninth International Conference on Machine Learning and Applications (ICMLA), pp. 235–242, December 2010

5. Vovk, V., Fedorova, V., Nouretdinov, I., Gammerman, A.: Criteria of efficiency for conformal prediction. Technical report, Royal Holloway University of London (April 2014)

6. Bishop, C.M.: Pattern Recognition and Machine Learning. 1st ed. corr. 2nd printing 2011, edition edn. Springer, New York (February 2010)

7. Pekala, M., Llorens, A., Wang, I.J.: Local distance metric learning for efficient conformal predictors. In: 2012 IEEE International Workshop on Machine Learning for Signal Processing (MLSP), pp. 1–6, September 2012

8. Yang, F., Chen, Z., Shao, G., Wang, H.: Distance Metric Learning-Based Conformal Predictor. In: Iliadis, L., Maglogiannis, I., Papadopoulos, H., Karatzas, K., Sioutas, S. (eds.) Artificial Intelligence Applications and Innovations, Part II. IFIP AICT, vol. 382, pp. 254–259. Springer, Heidelberg (2012)

9. Hardoon, D.R., Hussain, Z., Shawe-Taylor, J.: A nonconformity approach to model selection for SVMs. arXiv:0909.2332 [stat] (September 2009) arXiv: 0909.2332

10. Bache, K., Lichman, M.: UCI machine learning repository (2013). http://archive.ics.uci.edu/ml

Confidence Sets for Classification

Christophe Denis$^{(\boxtimes)}$ and Mohamed Hebiri$^{(\boxtimes)}$

Laboratoire d'Analyse et de Mathématiques Appliquées,
Université Paris Est – Marne-la-Vallée, UFR de Mathématiques, 5 Bd. Descartes,
Champs-sur-Marne, 77454 Marne-la-Vallée, Cedex 2, France
{Christophe.Denis,Mohamed.Hebiri}@u-pem.fr

Abstract. Conformal predictors, introduced by [13], serve to build prediction intervals by exploiting a notion of conformity of the new data point with previously observed data. In the classification problem, conformal predictor may respond to the problem of classification with reject option. In the present paper, we propose a novel method of construction of confidence sets, inspired both by conformal prediction and by classification with reject option. An important aspect of these confidence sets is that, when there are several observations to label, they control the proportion of the data we want to label. Moreover, we introduce a notion of risk adapted to classification with reject option. We show that for this risk, the confidence set risk converges to the risk of the confidence set based on the Bayes classifier.

Keywords: Classification · Classification with reject option · Conformal predictors · Confidence sets · Plug-in confidence sets

1 Introduction

Prediction is one of the main tasks people have to deal with in machine leaning. Indeed, based on a collection of n labelled observations (x_i, y_i), $i = 1, \ldots, n$, the statistician's interest is to build a rule which will be used for new and unlabeled observations. In this paper, we focus on prediction in the binary classification problem, that is, we aim at assigning a class beyond, says, 0 and 1, to each new covariate. However, it is not assumed that a covariate x fully determines the label y. Indeed, in difficult setting, such as when the conditional probability $\eta(x) = \mathbb{P}(Y = 1|X = x)$ $((X, Y)$ is the generic data-structure) is close to $1/2$, the covariate x might be hard to classify. Those cases rise the question of studying classification methods which allow to not classify observations when the doubt is too important; in such framework, we talk about *classification with reject option*. This problem is particularly relevant in some applications where a misclassification may lead to big issues: it is better to not assign a label than to assign one which is not confident. A great amount of authors have focus their effort in this problem in the machine learning community, see between many others [3,7,10] and references therein. On the other hand, in the statistical community,

A. Gammerman et al. (Eds.): SLDS 2015, LNAI 9047, pp. 301–312, 2015.
DOI: 10.1007/978-3-319-17091-6_25

an almost exhaustive list is [2,5,8,15]. These papers provide a deep understanding of some statistical aspects of the prediction in the classification problem with reject option in several contexts. However there is much to do yet. The present paper introduces a new way to tackle this problem: the classification rules rely on the transduction methodology as described in [11]. That is, we use the unlabeled data to improve the classification rule based on local arguments [6]. Here the labeled and the unlabeled data are part of the construction of the classifier (see for instance [14] for an example of such methods).

In the present paper, we introduce the *confidence set* which is a transductive rule that responds to the classification problem with reject option. An important feature of this work is to establish the connexion between such approach and the promising approach named *conformal prediction* presented in the references [12,13]. The methodology of conformal prediction relies on two key ideas: one is to provide a confidence prediction (namely, a confidence set containing the unobserved label with high probability) and the other is to take into account the similarity of an unlabeled covariate with the labeled covariates based on a so-called *non conformity measure, cf.* Chapter 2 in the book by [13]. While this method can be used in general frameworks, we observe that, applied to the classification problem, it appears to respond (in a transductive way) to the prediction with reject option task. On the other hand, even if the methodology of conformal prediction is clear, its statistical counterpart is not well understood. In the present paper, we aim at lighting some blurred points in the framework of conformal prediction. Draw ours inspiration from the works by Wegkamp and his various co-authors in the prediction with reject option problem [8,15], we propose in the same time a statistical founding to some kind of conformal predictors. However, our approach is different from the one introduced by Wegkamp and his co-authors in several aspects that will be detailed in Section 2.3.

The rest of the paper is organized as follows: in the Section 2, we introduce the confidence set based on the Bayes classifier and state some of its properties. We illustrate its performance in the Gaussian mixture model as well. The notion and the convergence of plug-in confidence sets are presented in Section 3. Section 4 is devoted to numerical experiments. The proof of the main result is postponed in Appendix.

2   General Framework

This section is devoted to the definition and the important properties of the confidence sets. We first introduce some useful notations and definitions in Section 2.1. The general definition of a confidence set is given in Section 2.2. We define the confidence sets that we consider in our work in Section 2.3 and apply it to Gaussian mixture models in Section 2.4.

2.1   Notations

In this section, we introduce the main notations and recall the background of the supervised classification.

Let (X, Y) be the generic data-structure taking values in $\mathcal{X} \times \{0, 1\}$ with distribution $\mathbb{P}$. Let $(X_\bullet, Y_\bullet)$ be a random variable independent from (X, Y) but with the saw law. We assume that we only observe $X_\bullet$ (and not the true label $Y_\bullet$). Hereafter, we recall some basics about supervised classification. The goal in classification is to predict the label $Y_\bullet$ for the observation of $X_\bullet$. A classifier (or classification rule) s is a function which maps $\mathcal{X}$ onto $\{0, 1\}$. Let $\mathcal{S}$ be the set of all classifiers. The misclassification risk R associated to $s \in \mathcal{S}$ is defined as

$$R(s) = \mathbb{P}(s(X) \neq Y).$$

The minimizer of R over $\mathcal{S}$ is the Bayes classifier, denoted by s^* and characterized by

$$s^*(\cdot) = \mathbf{1}\{\eta(\cdot) \geq 1/2\},$$

where $\eta(x) = \mathbb{P}(Y = 1 | X = x)$ for $x \in \mathcal{X}$. One of the most important quantities in our methodology is the function f defined by $f(\cdot) = \max\{\eta(\cdot), 1 - \eta(\cdot)\}$. It will play the role of some kind of score function. Throughout this paper, we assume that the random variable $\eta(X)$ is continuous: $\forall x \in (0, 1)$, $\mathbb{P}(\eta(X) = x) = 0$. This implies that the cumulative distribution function of $f(X)$ is continuous.

2.2   General Definition of a Confidence Set

Hereafter, we give the general definition of a confidence set and of the corresponding notion of risk. A confidence set Γ_s, associated to a classifier $s \in \mathcal{S}$, is defined as a function which maps $\mathcal{X}$ onto $\{\{0\}, \{1\}, \{0, 1\}\}$, such that for an instance X, the set $\Gamma_s(X)$ can be either $\{s(X)\}$ or $\{0, 1\}$. We decide to classify the observed data X, according to the label $s(X)$, if $\mathrm{card}\,(\Gamma_s(X)) = 1$. In the case where $\Gamma_s(X) = \{0, 1\}$, we decide to not classify that observed data X. Let $s \in \mathcal{S}$ and Γ_s be a confidence set associated to s. The former rule makes natural the following definition of the risk associated to Γ_s:

$$\mathcal{R}(\Gamma_s) = \mathbb{P}(Y \notin \Gamma_s(X) | \mathrm{card}\,(\Gamma_s(X)) = 1)$$
$$= \mathbb{P}(s(X) \neq Y | \mathrm{card}\,(\Gamma_s(X)) = 1). \tag{1}$$

The risk $\mathcal{R}(\Gamma_s)$ evaluates the misclassification error risk of s conditional on the set where X is classified. In this work, we investigate general but reasonable ways to construct confidence sets in the sense that we ask the confidence set to satisfy the following *Improvement Risk Property (IRP)*:

Property 1 (IRP). The considence set Γ_s associated to the classifier s is such that

$$\mathcal{R}(\Gamma_s) \leq R(s).$$

The former condition is a quite natural since it avoids to consider constructions of confidence sets that make the misclassification risk $R(s)$ worse. The following proposition provides a necessary and sufficient condition to get the IRP satisfied.

Proposition 1. *Let $s \in \mathcal{S}$ and Γ_s the associated confidence set. The confidence set Γ_s satisfies the IRP iff*

$$\mathbb{P}\left(\operatorname{card}\left(\Gamma_s(X)\right) = 1 | s(X) \neq Y\right) \leq \mathbb{P}\left(\operatorname{card}\left(\Gamma_s(X)\right) = 1 | s(X) = Y\right).$$

The proof of this result is straightforward and is then omitted. Before going in further considerations and, in the way the confidence sets are constructed, let us mention that the definition of the risk $\mathcal{R}$, given by (1), depends on the probability of classifying a covariate:

$$\mathcal{P}\left(\Gamma_s\right) := \mathbb{P}\left(\operatorname{card}\left(\Gamma_s(X)\right) = 1\right). \tag{2}$$

Then, it is important to evaluate the risk $\mathcal{R}$ while keeping under control the probability of classifying (2). This is partly the scope of the next paragraph.

2.3 ε-Confidence Set

In this section, we introduce a class of confidence set referred as *ε-confidence sets*. They rely on the Bayes classifier s^* and on the function f. The name ε-confidence sets reflects the fact that we exactly control the probability (2) of classifying a covariate by ε, where $\varepsilon \in (0,1)$ is a previously fixed.

Definition 1. *Let $\varepsilon \in (0,1)$, the ε-confidence set is defined as follows*

$$\Gamma_\varepsilon^\bullet(X_\bullet) = \begin{cases} \{s^*(X_\bullet)\} & \text{if } F_f(f(X_\bullet)) \geq 1 - \varepsilon \\ \{0,1\} & \text{otherwise,} \end{cases}$$

where F_f is the cumulative distribution function of $f(X)$ and $f(\cdot) = \max\{\eta(\cdot), 1 - \eta(\cdot)\}$.

The main feature of the ε-confidence set is that it assigns a label to a new data $X_\bullet$ if the corresponding score $f(X_\bullet)$ is large enough; more precisely, if it is larger than a proportion ε of $f(X)$ evaluated on former instances X for which the label is observed. In this sense, the ε-confidence set can be seen as a *conformal predictors*, cf. [13]. Indeed, its construction is based on the function f with can be seen as a conformity measure. This will be made clearer in Section 3 when we consider the empirical counterpart of this set. On the other hand, note that the ε-confidence sets is to be linked to the classifier with reject option introduced in [8]. Indeed, for $\epsilon \in (0,1)$, we have

$$F_f(X_\bullet) \geq 1 - \varepsilon \iff f(X_\bullet) \geq F_f^{-1}(1 - \varepsilon),$$

where F_f^{-1} denotes the generalized inverse of F_f. Let $\alpha = F_f^{-1}(1 - \varepsilon)$. Then $\alpha \in (1/2, 1)$ and the classifier with reject option introduced in [8] provides the following confidence set:

$$\Gamma_\alpha^W(X_\bullet) = \begin{cases} \{s^*(X_\bullet)\} & \text{if } f(X_\bullet) \geq \alpha \\ \{0,1\} & \text{otherwise.} \end{cases}$$

Hence, the covariate $X_\bullet$ is classified if $f(X_\bullet)$ is larger than the parameter α. Large values of α make us expect that a covariate $X_\bullet$ such that $f(X_\bullet) \geq \alpha$ is correctly classified. Nevertheless, the counterpart is that the probability of classifying the covariate is small. So, the choice of the parameter α is crucial. This is the main difference with the ε-confidence set. Indeed, the introduction of this approach is motivated by the fact that the definition of ε-confidence set ensures that we are able to control exactly the probability of assigning a label. This is reflected by the following equality

$$\mathcal{P}(\Gamma^\bullet_\varepsilon) = \mathbb{P}(F_f\left(f(X_\bullet)\right) \geq 1 - \varepsilon) = \varepsilon. \tag{3}$$

which holds since $F_f(f(X_\bullet))$ is uniformly distributed.

The rest of this section states two properties of the ε-confidence set. First, the ε-confidence set satisfies the IRP. Moreover, since $\varepsilon \leq \varepsilon' \Rightarrow F_f^{-1}(1 - \varepsilon) \geq F_f^{-1}(1 - \varepsilon')$, one shows that $\varepsilon \mapsto \mathcal{R}(\Gamma^\bullet_\varepsilon)$ is increasing. Finally we can set that the ε-confidence sets are optimal in the following sense:

Proposition 2. *Fix $\varepsilon \in (0,1)$. Let $s \in \mathcal{S}$ and Γ_s an associated confidence set such that $\mathcal{P}(\Gamma_s) = \varepsilon$. Then*

$$\mathcal{P}(\Gamma_s) = \mathcal{P}(\Gamma^\bullet_\varepsilon) = \varepsilon \text{ and}$$
$$\mathcal{R}(\Gamma_s) \geq \mathcal{R}(\Gamma^\bullet_\varepsilon).$$

2.4 ε-Confidence Set for Gaussian Mixture

In this section, we apply the ε-confidence set introduced in Definition 1 with the Bayes classifier to the particular case of Gaussian mixture model. We set $\mathcal{X} = \mathbb{R}^d$ with $d \in \mathbb{N} \setminus \{0\}$. Let us assume that the conditional distribution of X given Y is Gaussian and that, for simplicity, the marginal distribution of Y is Bernoulli with parameter $1/2$. To fix notation, we set

$$X|Y = 0 \sim \mathcal{N}(\mu_0, \Sigma)$$
$$X|Y = 1 \sim \mathcal{N}(\mu_1, \Sigma)$$

where μ_0 and μ_1 are vectors in $\mathbb{R}^d$ and Σ is the commun covariance matrix. We assume that Σ is invertible. The following theorem establishes the classification error of the ε-confidence set $\Gamma^\bullet_\varepsilon$ in this framework.

Theorem 1. *For all $\varepsilon \in (0,1)$, we have*

$$\mathcal{R}(\Gamma^\bullet_\varepsilon(X_\bullet)) = \frac{\mathbb{P}_Z\left(\phi\left(Z\right) + \phi\left(Z + \|\mu_1 - \mu_0\|_{\Sigma^{-1}}\right) \leq \varepsilon\right)}{\varepsilon}$$

where Z is normally distributed and ϕ is the normal cumulative distribution function.

The proof of this theorem brings into play heavy but simple computations. It is then omitted in this paper. Note that in the particular case where $\varepsilon = 1$.

It turns out that the ε-confidence set does not differ from the 'classical' Bayes classification rule, and then we get back

$$\mathcal{R}(\Gamma_1^\bullet(X_\bullet)) = R(s^*) = \mathbb{P}_Z\left(Z \geq \frac{\|\mu_1 - \mu_0\|_{\Sigma^{-1}}}{2}\right).$$

3   Plug-in ε-Confidence Set

In the previous section, the ε-confidence set relies on η which is unknown. We then need to build an ε-confidence set bayed on an estimator of η. To this end, we introduce a first dataset $\mathcal{D}_n^{(1)}$, which consists of n independent copies of (X, Y), with $n \in \mathbb{N} \setminus \{0\}$. The dataset $\mathcal{D}_n^{(1)}$ is used to estimate the function η (and then the functions f and s^* as well). Let us denote by $\hat{f}$ and $\hat{s}$ the estimators of f et s^* respectively. Thanks to these estimations, an empirical version of the ε-confidence set can be

$$\widetilde{\Gamma}_\varepsilon^\bullet(X_\bullet) = \begin{cases} \{\hat{s}(X_\bullet)\} & \text{if } F_{\hat{f}}(\hat{f}(X_\bullet)) \geq 1 - \varepsilon \\ \{0,1\} & \text{otherwise,} \end{cases}$$

where $F_{\hat{f}}$ is the cumulative distribution function of $\hat{f}(X)$ with $\hat{f}(\cdot) = \max\{\hat{\eta}(\cdot), 1 - \hat{\eta}(\cdot)\}$ and $\varepsilon \in (0,1)$. Hence, we observe that $\widetilde{\Gamma}_\varepsilon^\bullet(X_\bullet)$ invokes the cumulative distribution function $F_{\hat{f}}$ which is also unknown. We then need to estimate it. Let N be integer and let $\mathcal{D}_N^{(2)} = \{(X_i, Y_i), i = 1, \ldots, N\}$ be a second dataset that is used to estimate the cumulative function $F_{\hat{f}}$. We can now introduce the plug-in ε-confidence set:

Definition 2. *Let $\varepsilon \in (0,1)$ and $\hat{\eta}$ be any estimator of the η, the plug-in ε-confidence set is defined as follows:*

$$\widehat{\Gamma}_\varepsilon^\bullet(X_\bullet) = \begin{cases} \hat{s}(X_\bullet) & \text{if } \hat{F}_{\hat{f}}(\hat{f}(X_\bullet)) \geq 1 - \varepsilon \\ \{0,1\} & \text{otherwise,} \end{cases}$$

where $\hat{f}(\cdot) = \max\{\hat{\eta}(\cdot), 1 - \hat{\eta}(\cdot)\}$ and $\hat{F}_{\hat{f}}(\hat{f}(X_\bullet)) = \frac{1}{N}\sum_{i=1}^N \mathbf{1}_{\{\hat{f}(X_i) \leq \hat{f}(X_\bullet)\}}$.

Remark 1. Samples sizes] The dataset $\mathcal{D}_n^{(1)}$ and $\mathcal{D}_N^{(2)}$ can be constructed from an available dataset the statistician has in hand. The choice of n relies on the rate of convergence of the estimator $\hat{\eta}$ of η. Note that $\mathcal{D}_N^{(2)}$ is used for the estimation of a cumulative distribution function.

Remark 2. Connexion with conformal predictors] Definition 2 states that we assign a label to $X_\bullet$ if $\frac{1}{N}\sum_{i=1}^N \mathbf{1}_{\{\hat{f}(X_i) \leq \hat{f}(X_\bullet)\}} \geq 1 - \varepsilon$, in other words, if $X_\bullet$ is conform up to a certain amount. This approach is exactly in the same spirit as the construction of the conformal predictor for binary classification. Indeed, the construction of conformal predictors relies on a so-called *p-value* which can be seen as the empirical cumulative function of a given non-conformity measure. This is the counterpart of the empirical cumulative function of the score $\hat{f}(X_\bullet)$ in our setting (note that $\hat{f}(\cdot)$ is our conformity measure). In this point of view, conformal predictors and confidence sets differ only on the way the score (or equivalently the non-conformity measure) is computed. In our methodology, we use a first dataset to estimate the true score function f and a second one to estimate the cumulative distribution function of f. On the other hand, in the setting of conformal predictors , the non-conformity measure is estimated by Leave-One-Out cross validation. This makes the statistical analysis of conformal predictors more difficult, but they have the advantage of using only one dataset to construct the set of labels.

Furthermore, there is one main difference between confidence sets and conformal predictors. These last allow to assign the empty set as a label. which is not the case of the confidence set. In our setting, both of the outputs $\emptyset$ and $\{0, 1\}$ are referred as the rejecting of classifying the instance.

The rest of this section is devoted to establish the empirical performance of the *plug-in ε-confidence set*. The symbols $\mathbf{P}$ and $\mathbf{E}$ stand for generic probability and expectation. Before setting the main result, let us introduce the assumptions needed to establish it. We assume that

$$\hat{\eta}(X) \to \eta(X) \quad \text{a.s, when } n \to \infty,$$

which implies that $\hat{f}(X) \to f(X)$ a.s. We refer to the the paper [1], for instance, for examples of estimators that satisfy this condition. Moreover, we assume that $F_{\hat{f}}$ is a continuous function.

Let us now state our main result:

Theorem 2. *Under the above assumptions, we have*

$$\mathbf{R}\left(\widehat{\Gamma}_\varepsilon^\bullet(X_\bullet)\right) - \mathcal{R}\left(\Gamma_\varepsilon^\bullet(X_\bullet)\right) \to 0, \quad n, N \to +\infty,$$

where $\mathbf{R}\left(\widehat{\Gamma}_\varepsilon^\bullet(X_\bullet)\right) = \mathbf{P}\left(\hat{s}(X_\bullet) \neq Y_\bullet | \hat{F}_{\hat{f}}(\hat{f}(X_\bullet)) \geq 1 - \varepsilon\right).$

The proof of this result is postponed in the Appendix. Theorem 2 states that if the estimator of η is consistent, then asymptotically the plug-in ε-confidence set performs as well as the ε-confidence set.

4   Numerical Results

In this section we perform a simulation study which is dedicated to evaluating the performance of the plug-in ε-confidence sets. The data are simulated according to the following scheme:

1. the covariate $X \stackrel{\mathcal{L}}{=} (U_1, \ldots, U_{10})$, where U_i are i.i.d from a uniform distribution on $[0, 1]$;

2. conditional on X, the label Y is drawn according a Bernoulli distribution with parameter $\eta(X)$ defined by $\mathrm{logit}(\eta(X)) = X^1 - X^2 - X^3 + X^9$, where X^j is the jth component of X.

In order to illustrate our convergence result, we first estimate the risk $\mathcal{R}$ of the ε-confidence set. More precisely, for each $\varepsilon \in \{1, 0.5, 0.1\}$, we repeat $B = 100$ times the following steps:

1. simulate two data sets $\mathcal{D}_{N_1}^{(2)}$ and $\mathcal{D}_K^{\bullet}$ according to the simulation scheme with $N_1 = 1000$ and $K = 10000$;
2. based on $\mathcal{D}_{N_1}^{(2)}$, we compute the empirical cumulative distribution of f;
3. finally, we compute, over $\mathcal{D}_K^{\bullet}$, the empirical counterpart $\mathcal{R}_{N_1}$ of $\mathcal{R}$ of the ε-confidence set using the empirical cumulative distribution of f instead of F_f

From these results, we compute the mean and standard deviation of the empirical risk. The results are reported in Table 1. Next, for each $\varepsilon \in \{1, 0.5, 0.1\}$, we estimate the risk $\mathcal{R}$ for the plug-in ε-confidence set. We propose to use two popular classification procedures for the estimation of η: the random forest and logistic regression procedures for instance. We repeat independently B times the following steps:

1. simulate three dataset $\mathcal{D}_{n_1}^{(1)}, \mathcal{D}_{N_2}^{(2)}, \mathcal{D}_K^{\bullet}$ according to the simulation scheme. Note that the observations in dataset $\mathcal{D}_K^{\bullet}$ play the role of $(X_{\bullet}, Y_{\bullet})$;
2. based on $\mathcal{D}_{n_1}^{(1)}$, we compute an estimate, denoted by $\hat{f}$, of f with the random forest or the logistic regression procedure;
3. based on $\mathcal{D}_{N_2}^{(2)}$, we compute the empirical cumulative distribution of $\hat{f}(X)$;
4. finally, over $\mathcal{D}_K^{\bullet}$, we compute the empirical counterpart $\mathbf{R}_K$ of $\mathbf{R}$.

From these results, we compute the mean and standard deviation of the empirical risk for different values of n_1. We fix $n_2 = 100$ and $K = 10000$. The results are reported in Table 2.

Table 1. Estimation of $\mathcal{R}$ for ε-confidence set. The standard deviation is provided between parenthesis.

ε	$\mathcal{R}_{N_1}$
1	0.389 (0.005)
0.5	0.324 (0.006)
0.1	0.238 (0.013)

First of all, we recall that for $\varepsilon = 1$, the measure of risk of confidence sets match with the misclassification risk of the procedure we use to estimate η. Next, several observations can be made from the study: first, the performance of the Bayes classifier, illustrated in Table 1 when $\varepsilon = 1$ ($\mathcal{R}_{N_1} \approx 0.389$) reflects that

Table 2. Estimation of **R** for plug-in ε-confidence set. The standard deviation is provided between parenthesis.

ε	n_1	random forest	logistic regression
1	100	0.45 (0.02)	0.43 (0.02)
1	1000	0.42 (0.01)	0.40 (0.01)
0.5	100	0.42 (0.02)	0.39 (0.02)
0.5	1000	0.37 (0.01)	0.34 (0.01)
0.1	100	0.38 (0.04)	0.34 (0.05)
0.1	1000	0.32 (0.02)	0.25 (0.02)

the classification problem is quite difficult. Second, we can make two general comments: i) all the methods observe their risk diminishes with ε, regardless the value of n_1. This behavior is essentially expected since the methods classify the covariates for which they are more confident; ii) the performance of the methods are better when n_1 increases. This is also expected as the quality of estimation of the regression function η increases with the sample size. It is crucial to mention that our aim is not to build a classification rule that does not make errors. The motivation when introducing the plug-in ε-confidence set is only to improve and make more confident a classification rule. Indeed, since the construction of the confidence set depends on the estimator of η, poor estimators would lead to bad plug-in ε-confidence sets (even if the misclassification error is smaller). As an illustration we can see that the performance of the plug-in ε-confidence based on logistic regression are better than those of the plug-in ε-confidence based on random forest. Moreover, we remark that the logistic regression is completely adapted to this problem since its performance gets closer and closer to the performance of the Bayes estimator when n_1 increases (regardless the value of ε). Our final observation concerns some results we chose to not report: we note that, independently of the value of n_1, the proportion of classified observations is close to ε which is conform to our result (3).

5   Conclusion

Borrowing ideas from the conformal predictors community, we derive a new definition of a rule that responds to the classification with reject option. This rule named ε-confidence set is optimal for a new notion of risk we introduced in the present paper. We illustrate the behavior of this rule in the Gaussian mixture model. Moreover, we show that the empirical counterpart of this confidence set, called plug-in ε-confidence set is consistent for that risk: we establish that the plug-in ε-confidence set performs as well as the ε-confidence set. An ingoing work is to state finite sample bounds for this risk.

Appendix

Proof (Theorem 2). Let us introduce some notation for short: we note $U_\bullet$, $\hat{U}_\bullet$ and $\hat{\hat{U}}_\bullet$ the quantities $F_f(f(X_\bullet))$, $F_{\hat{f}}(\hat{f}(X_\bullet))$ and $\hat{F}_{\hat{f}}(\hat{f}(X_\bullet)) = \frac{1}{N}\sum_{i=1}^{N} \mathbf{1}_{\{\hat{f}(X_i) \leq \hat{f}(X_\bullet)\}}$. We have the folowing decomposition

$$\mathbf{1}_{\{\hat{s}(X_\bullet) \neq Y_\bullet \,,\, \hat{\hat{U}}_\bullet \geq 1-\varepsilon\}} - \mathbf{1}_{\{s^*(X_\bullet) \neq Y_\bullet \,,\, U_\bullet \geq 1-\varepsilon\}} =$$
$$\left\{ \mathbf{1}_{\{\hat{s}(X_\bullet) \neq Y_\bullet \,,\, \hat{\hat{U}}_\bullet \geq 1-\varepsilon\}} - \mathbf{1}_{\{\hat{s}(X_\bullet) \neq Y_\bullet \,,\, \hat{U}_\bullet \geq 1-\varepsilon\}} \right\}$$
$$+ \left\{ \mathbf{1}_{\{\hat{s}(X_\bullet) \neq Y_\bullet \,,\, \hat{U}_\bullet \geq 1-\varepsilon\}} - \mathbf{1}_{\{s^*(X_\bullet) \neq Y_\bullet \,,\, U_\bullet \geq 1-\varepsilon\}} \right\}$$
$$=: A_1 + A_2. \quad (4)$$

Since,

$$\left| \mathbf{P}\left(\hat{s}(X_\bullet) \neq Y_\bullet \,,\, \hat{\hat{U}}_\bullet \geq 1-\varepsilon \right) - \mathbf{P}\left(\{s^*(X_\bullet) \neq Y_\bullet \,,\, U_\bullet \geq 1-\varepsilon \} \right) \right| \leq |\mathbf{E}\,[A_1]| + |\mathbf{E}\,[A_2]|,$$

we have to prove that $|\mathbf{E}\,[A_1]| \to 0$ and $|\mathbf{E}\,[A_2]| \to 0$.

$$A_2 = \left(\mathbf{1}_{\{\hat{s}(X_\bullet) \neq Y_\bullet\}} - \mathbf{1}_{\{s^*(X_\bullet) \neq Y_\bullet\}} \right) \mathbf{1}_{\{U_\bullet \geq 1-\varepsilon\}} + \mathbf{1}_{\{\hat{s}(X_\bullet) \neq Y_\bullet\}} \left(\mathbf{1}_{\{\hat{U}_\bullet \geq 1-\varepsilon\}} - \mathbf{1}_{\{U_\bullet \geq 1-\varepsilon\}} \right),$$

so, we have

$$|\mathbf{E}\,[A_2]| \leq 2\mathbf{E}\,[|\hat{\eta}(X_\bullet) - \eta(X_\bullet)|] + \mathbf{E}\left[\left| \mathbf{1}_{\{\hat{U}_\bullet \geq 1-\varepsilon\}} - \mathbf{1}_{\{U_\bullet \geq 1-\varepsilon\}} \right| \right]. \quad (5)$$

Next, combining the fact that, for any $\delta > 0$,

$$\left| \mathbf{1}_{\{\hat{U}_\bullet \geq 1-\varepsilon\}} - \mathbf{1}_{\{U_\bullet \geq 1-\varepsilon\}} \right| \leq \mathbf{1}_{\{|U_\bullet - (1-\varepsilon)| \leq \delta\}} + \mathbf{1}_{\{|\hat{U}_\bullet - U_\bullet| > \delta\}},$$

and that

$$|\hat{U}_\bullet - U_\bullet| = \left| F_{\hat{f}}(\hat{f}(X_\bullet)) - F_f(\hat{f}(X_\bullet)) + F_f(\hat{f}(X_\bullet)) - F_f(f(X_\bullet)) \right|$$
$$\leq \left| F_{\hat{f}}(\hat{f}(X_\bullet)) - F_f(\hat{f}(X_\bullet)) \right| + \left| F_f(\hat{f}(X_\bullet)) - F_f(f(X_\bullet)) \right|$$
$$\leq \sup_{t \in [1/2,1]} \left| F_{\hat{f}}(t) - F_f(t) \right| + \left| F_f(\hat{f}(X_\bullet)) - F_f(f(X_\bullet)) \right|,$$

we deduce, using Markov Inequality and (5), that

$$|\mathbf{E}\,[A_2]| \leq 2\mathbf{E}\,[|\hat{\eta}(X_\bullet) - \eta(X_\bullet)|] + 2\delta_n + \sqrt{\beta_n}, \quad (6)$$

where $\beta_n = \mathbf{E}\left(\left| F_f(\hat{f}(X_\bullet)) - F_f(f(X_\bullet)) \right| \right)$ and δ_n is set depending on n as follows: $\delta_n = \alpha_n + \sqrt{\beta_n}$ with $\alpha_n = \sup_{t \in [1/2,1]} \left| F_{\hat{f}}(t) - F_f(t) \right|$.

By assumption, $\hat{\eta}(X_\bullet) \to \eta(X_\bullet)$ *a.s.* Moreover $|\hat{\eta}(X_\bullet) - \eta(X_\bullet)| \leq 1$, so $\mathbf{E}[|\hat{\eta}(X_\bullet) - \eta(X_\bullet)|] \to 0$. Since $\hat{f}(X_\bullet) \to f(X_\bullet)$ *a.s.* when $n \to \infty$ and F_f is continuous and bounded on a compact set, $\beta_n \to 0$. Moreover, Dini's Theorem ensures that $\alpha_n \to 0$. Therefore, we obtain with Inequality (6)

$$|\mathbf{E}[A_2]| \to 0.$$

Next, we prove that $|\mathbf{E}[A_1]| \to 0$. For any $\gamma > 0$,

$$|\mathbf{1}_{\{\hat{U}_\bullet \geq 1-\varepsilon\}} - \mathbf{1}_{\{\hat{U}_\bullet \geq 1-\varepsilon\}}| \leq \mathbf{1}_{\{|\hat{U}_\bullet - (1-\varepsilon)| \leq \gamma\}} + \mathbf{1}_{\{|\hat{U}_\bullet - \hat{U}_\bullet| \geq \gamma\}}. \quad (7)$$

We have, for all $x \in (1/2, 1)$, $F_{\hat{f}}(x) = \mathbb{E}_{\mathcal{D}_n^{(1)}}\left[\mathbb{P}\left(\hat{f}(X) \leq x | \mathcal{D}_n^{(1)}\right)\right]$. But, conditional on $\mathcal{D}_n^{(1)}$, $\hat{F}_{\hat{f}}(x)$ is the empirical cumulative distribution of $\mathbb{P}\left(\hat{f}(X) \leq x | \mathcal{D}_n^{(1)}\right)$ where $\hat{f}$ is view as a deterministic function. Therefore, the Dvoretzky–Kiefer–Wolfowitz Inequality (*cf.* [4,9]) yields

$$\mathbf{E}\left[\mathbf{1}_{\{|\hat{U}_\bullet - \hat{U}_\bullet| \geq \gamma\}}\right] \leq 2e^{-2N\gamma^2}, \quad \text{for } \gamma \geq \sqrt{\frac{\log(2)}{2N}}.$$

So, using (7) and choosing $\gamma = \gamma_N = \sqrt{\frac{\log(N)}{2N}}$, we obtain

$$\mathbf{E}[|A_1|] \to 0,$$

which yields the result. Now, it remains to prove that $\mathbf{P}\left(\hat{U}_\bullet \geq 1 - \varepsilon\right) \to \varepsilon$. By assumption, $\mathbf{P}\left(\hat{U}_\bullet \geq 1 - \varepsilon\right) = \varepsilon$. Since, we have proved that

$$\mathbf{E}\left[|\mathbf{1}_{\{\hat{U}_\bullet \geq 1-\varepsilon\}} - \mathbf{1}_{\{\hat{U}_\bullet \geq 1-\varepsilon\}}|\right] \to 0.$$

This ends the proof of the theorem.

References

1. Audibert, J.Y., Tsybakov, A.: Fast learning rates for plug-in classifiers. Ann. Statist. **35**(2), 608–633 (2007)
2. Bartlett, P., Wegkamp, M.: Classification with a reject option using a hinge loss. J. Mach. Learn. Res. **9**, 1823–1840 (2008)
3. Chow, C.K.: On optimum error and reject trade-off. IEEE Transactions on Information Theory **16**, 41–46 (1970)
4. Dvoretzky, A., Kiefer, J., Wolfowitz, J.: Asymptotic minimax character of the sample distribution function and of the classical multinomial estimator. Ann. Math. Statist. **27**, 642–669 (1956)
5. Freund, Y., Mansour, Y., Schapire, R.: Generalization bounds for averaged classifiers. Ann. Statist. **32**(4), 1698–1722 (2004)
6. Györfi, L., Kohler, M., Krzyżak, A., Walk, H.: A distribution-free theory of nonparametric regression. Springer Series in Statistics. Springer, New York (2002)

7. Grandvalet, Y., Rakotomamonjy, A., Keshet, J., Canu, S.: Support Vector Machines with a Reject Option. In: Advances in Neural Information Processing Systems (NIPS 2008), vol. 21, pp. 537–544. MIT Press (2009)
8. Herbei, R., Wegkamp, M.: Classification with reject option. Canad. J. Statist. **34**(4), 709–721 (2006)
9. Massart, P.: The tight constant in the Dvoretzky-Kiefer-Wolfowitz inequality. Ann. Probab. **18**(3), 1269–1283 (1990)
10. Naadeem, M., Zucker, J.D., Hanczar, B.: IN Accuracy-Rejection Curves (ARCs) for Comparing Classification Methods with a Reject Option. MLSB., 65–81 (2010)
11. Vapnik, V.: Statistical learning theory. Adaptive and Learning Systems for Signal Processing, Communications, and Control. John Wiley & Sons Inc., New York (1998)
12. Vovk, V., Gammerman, A., Saunders, C.: Machine-learning applications of algorithmic randomness. In: Proceedings of the 16th International Conference on Machine Learning, pp. 444–453 (1999)
13. Vovk, V., Gammerman, A., Shafer, G.: Algorithmic learning in a random world. Springer, New York (2005)
14. Wang, J., Shen, X., Pan, W.: On transductive support vector machines. In: Prediction and discovery, Contemp. Math., Amer. Math. Soc., Providence, RI, vol. 443, pp. 7–19 (2007)
15. Wegkamp, M., Yuan, M.: Support vector machines with a reject option. Bernoulli. **17**(4), 1368–1385 (2011)

Conformal Clustering and Its Application to Botnet Traffic

Giovanni Cherubin[1,2]([✉]), Ilia Nouretdinov[1], Alexander Gammerman[1],
Roberto Jordaney[2], Zhi Wang[2], Davide Papini[2], and Lorenzo Cavallaro[2]

[1] Computer Learning Research Centre and Computer Science Department, Royal
Holloway University of London, Egham Hill, Egham, Surrey TW20 OEX, UK
`Giovanni.Cherubin.2013@live.rhul.ac.uk`
[2] Systems Security Research Lab and Information Security Group, Royal Holloway
University of London, Egham Hill, Egham, Surrey TW20 OEX, UK

Abstract. The paper describes an application of a novel clustering
technique based on Conformal Predictors. Unlike traditional clustering
methods, this technique allows to control the number of objects that
are left outside of any cluster by setting up a required confidence level.
This paper considers a multi-class unsupervised learning problem, and
the developed technique is applied to bot-generated network traffic. An
extended set of features describing the bot traffic is presented and the
results are discussed.

Keywords: Information security · Botnet · Confident prediction ·
Conformal prediction · Clustering

1 Introduction

Within the past decade, security research begun to rely heavily on machine learning to develop new techniques to help in the identification and classification of
cyber threats. Specifically, in the area of network intrusion detection, botnets are
of particular interest as these often hide within legitimate applications traffic.
A botnet is a network of infected computers controlled by an attacker, the *botmaster*, via the Command and Control server (*C&C*). Botnets are a widespread
malicious activity among the Internet, and they are used to perform attacks
such as phishing, information theft, click-jacking, and Distributed Denial of Service (DDoS). Bots detection is a branch of network intrusion detection which
aims at identifying botnet infected computers (*bots*). Recent studies, such as [9],
rely on clustering and focus their analysis on high level characteristics of network traffic (*network traces*) to distinguish between different botnet threats.
We take an inspiration from this approach, and apply Conformal Clustering,
a technique based on Conformal Predictors (CP) [10], with an extended set of
features. We produce clusters from unlabelled training examples; then on a test
set we associate a new object with one of the clusters. Our aim is to achieve
a high intra-cluster similarity in terms of application layer protocols (**http**, **irc**
and **p2p**).

© Springer International Publishing Switzerland 2015
A. Gammerman et al. (Eds.): SLDS 2015, LNAI 9047, pp. 313–322, 2015.
DOI: 10.1007/978-3-319-17091-6_26

In previous work [4,5,8] the conformal technique was applied to the problem of anomaly detection. It also demonstrated how to create clusters: a prediction set produced by CP was interpreted as a set of possible objects which conform to the dataset and therefore are not anomalies; however the prediction set may consist of several parts that are interpreted as clusters, where the significance level is a "trim" to regulate the depth of the clusters' hierarchy. The work in [8] was focused on a binary (anomaly/not anomaly) unsupervised problem. This paper generalizes [8] for a multi-class unsupervised learning problem. This includes the problem of clusters creation, solved here by using a *neighbouring rule*, and the problem of evaluating clusters accuracy, solved by using Purity criterion. For evaluating efficiency we use Average P-Value criterion, earlier presented in [8].

In our approach we extract features from network traces generated by a bot. Then we apply preprocessing and dimensionality reduction with t-SNE; the use of t-SNE, previously used in the context of Conformal Clustering in [8], is here needed for computational efficiency, since the way we here apply Conformal Clustering has a time complexity increasing as $\Delta \times \ell^d$, where Δ is the complexity to calculate a P-Value and varies respect to the chosen non-conformity measure, ℓ is the number of points per side of the grid, and d is the number of dimensions. This complexity can be reduced further for some underlying algorithms. The dataset is separated into *training* and *test* sets, and clustering is applied to *training* set. After this the testing objects are associated with the clusters.

An additional contribution made by this paper is related to feature collection: an algorithm based on *Partial Autocorrelation Function* (PACF) to detect a periodic symbol in binary time series is proposed.

2   Data Overview

The developed system is run on *network traces* produced by different families of botnets. A network trace is a collection of network packets captured in a certain window of time. A network trace can be split into *network flows* (netflows), a collection of packets belonging to the same communication. A netflow contains high level information of the packet exchange, such as the communicating IP addresses and ports, a timestamp, the duration, and the number and size of exchanged packets (transmitted, received and total). As [9] suggested, a system using only netflows, thus not modelling the content of the packets, is reliable even when the traffic between *bot* and *C&C* is encrypted.

In the dataset creation phase we extract a feature vector from every network trace. A feature vector is composed of the following 18 features: *median* and *MAD* (Mean Absolute Deviation) of *netflows duration*, *median* and *MAD* of *exchanged bytes*, communication *frequency*, use *percentage* of *TCP* and *UDP* protocols, use *percentage* of *ports* respectively in three ranges[1], *median* and *MAD* of *transmitted* and *received bytes* considering the *bot* as source, *median* and *MAD* of *transmitted* and *received bytes* considering the connection initiator

---

[1] We base these ranges on the standard given by *IANA*: System Ports (0–1023), User Ports (1024–49151), and Dynamic and/or Private Ports (49152–65535).

as source. Duration of netflows, transmitted received and total exchanged bytes have been used in past research for bots detection [9]; these quantities were usually modelled by their mean value. We model them here by using median and MAD, since normal distribution is not assumed; furthermore, median is invariant in non-linear rescaling.

Since, as others observed [9], in most botnet families *bots* communicate periodically, we introduce the feature *frequency* which takes into account the period of communication, if any. We can detect the period of communication by looking at the netflows timestamps, and constructing a binary time series y_t as:

$$y_t = \begin{cases} 1, \text{if flow occurred at time } t \\ 0, \text{if no flow occurred at time } t \end{cases} \quad \text{for } t \text{ in } \{0,1,...\}, \quad (1)$$

where time t is measured in seconds.

For a period T we then define the feature frequency to be:

$$\text{frequency} = \begin{cases} 0, & \text{if } T = \infty (\text{no period}) \\ 1/T, & \text{otherwise} \end{cases} \quad \text{for } T > 0.$$

which is consistent whenever a period is found or not. Later in this section we introduce a novel approach for detecting periodicity within a binary time series defined as in Eq. 1.

The dataset we use contains traffic from 9 families of botnets and we will group them with respect to the application layer protocol they are based on. We hence define three classes of botnets: **http, irc** and **p2p** based. Our goal is to produce clusters containing objects from the same class. In this paper *objects* and *feature vectors* refer to the same concept; *example* refers to a labelled object.

2.1 Periodicity Detection Based on PACF

Equation (1) defines a binary time series y_t, such that $y_t = 1$ when some event has happened at time t, $y_t = 0$ otherwise. Our goal is to check whether the time series contains a periodic event, and if so we want to determine the period T of this event. The study [1] calls this task 'Symbol Periodicity' detection. Past studies in *bots* detection, such as [9], approached the problem by using Power Spectral Density (PSD) of the Fast Fourier Transform of the series.

We propose an algorithm based on Partial Autocorrelation Function (PACF) for achieving this goal, which is simple to implement, well performing under noisy conditions[2], and which may be extended to capture more than one periodic event.

Given a generic time series u_t, the PACF of lag k is the autocorrelation between u_t and u_{t-k}, removing the contribution of the lags in between, $t-1$ to $t-k+1$. The PACF coefficients ϕ_{kk} between u_t and u_{t-k}, are defined as [2]:

---

[2] By noise we mean events which can happen at any time t; let $W=\text{Integer}(L * \nu)$, where L is the length of y_t and $\nu \in [0,1]$ the percentage of noise (noise level), we simulate noise in our artificial time series by setting $y_t = 1$ for a number W of positions t uniformly sampled in $[1, L]$.

$$\phi_{11} = \rho_1$$
$$\phi_{22} = (\rho_2 - \rho_1^2)/(1 - \rho_1^2)$$
$$\phi_{kk} = \frac{\rho_k - \sum_{j=1}^{k-1} \phi_{k-1,j}\rho_{k-j}}{1 - \sum_{j=1}^{k-1} \phi_{k-1,j}\rho_j} \quad , k = 3, 4, 5, \ldots$$

where ρ_i is the autocorrelation for lag i, and $\phi_{kj} = \phi_{k-1,j} - \phi_{kk}\phi_{k-1,k-j}$ for $j = 1, 2, \ldots, k-1$.

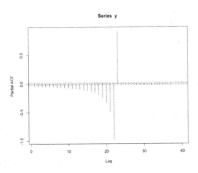

Fig. 1. PACF over a binary time series with one periodic event of periodicity $T = 23$ exhibits a peak at lag $k = 23$

From our experiments on artificial binary time series with one periodic event we noticed that PACF on them presents a high peak at the lag corresponding to the period T. For instance, Fig. 1 is the PACF over an artificial binary time series of 10^4 elements, having a periodic event with period $T = 23$. This fact holds true even under noisy conditions. We run our experiments on artificial binary time series of length 10^4, testing all the periods in $\{3, 4, \ldots, 100\}$, inserting different percentages of white noise and computing PACF over 150 lags. The period is estimated as the lag at which PACF is maximum, and checked if equal to the true period. The experiments show that for a time series of length $L = 10^4$ the accuracy remains 1 for the noise level $\nu = 0.05$ and becomes 0.83 for $\nu = 0.2$. If $L = 10^5$, then it is pure for up to $\nu = 0.1$, while for noise level $\nu = 0.2$ it is 0.96.

So far we assumed to know that a periodicity existed in y_t. In case, as for our dataset, we do not assume a priori a periodicity exists, we can use a threshold for performing detection. We noticed that relevant peaks in PACF are larger than 0.65. Hence we compute PACF, get the maximum of it, and consider its lag to be a valid period only if its value is larger than a threshold $\vartheta = 0.65$; otherwise, we consider the time series to be aperiodic.

3   Conformal Clustering Approach

We perform the following steps on a dataset X created as in Sect. 2:

1. Preprocessing of X;
2. Dimensionality reduction with t-SNE (produces Z);
3. Z is split into *training* (100) and *test* (34) set;
4. Conformal Clustering on *training* set;
5. Test objects are associated to the clusters following a neighbouring rule.

After this, evaluation criteria *Average P-Value* (APV) and *Purity* are computed.

3.1   Preprocessing and Dimensionality Reduction

We apply log-transformation to bytes-related features of the dataset because they take values in a large range. t-SNE requires the dataset to be consistently normalized before application. We apply normalization in $[0, 1]$ to all features u:

$$u_{01} = \frac{u - min(u)}{max(u) - min(u)},$$

Our application of Conformal Clustering requires to compute ℓ^d P-Values, where ℓ is the number of points per grid side and d is the number of features. We use t-SNE, as [8] did before, as a dimensionality reduction algorithm before clustering.

T-SNE [6] is originally developed as a visualization algorithm for high dimensional data. However, thanks to its ability of keeping far in the low dimensional projection dissimilar objects of the high dimensional data, and *vice versa* for similar objects, it reveals to be a good dimensionality reduction algorithm. We can trim a few parameters of it, such as *perplexity* and *distance metric*. Perplexity may be viewed as the number of effective neighbours each object has in high dimensional space; distance metric is a similarity measure between objects in high and low dimensional space. For our experiments we used *Euclidean Distance* as a distance metric, and trimmed the value of perplexity. By applying t-SNE to our preprocessed dataset we obtain $Z = \{z_1, z_2, ..., z_N\}$, a 2-D projection of it.

3.2   Conformal Clustering

CP allows to have a confidence measure on predictions. Given a bag of observations $D = \wr z_1, .., z_{n-1} \wr$, $z_i \in \mathbf{Z}$, a new object z and a significance level ε, CP allows to determine if z comes from D with an error on the long run of at most ε. The only property required by CP is that $\wr z_1, .., z_{n-1} \wr$ are exchangeable. Note that exchangeability property is weaker than *iid*, since:

$$iid \implies exchangeable.$$

We define a non-conformity measure $A : \mathbf{Z}^{(*)} \times \mathbf{Z} \longmapsto \mathbb{R}$, to be a function which accepts a bag of objects and an object z_i, and returns a scalar representing how much z_i is conform to the other objects. The result of CP is a P-Value p_n and a boolean answer indicating if the new object is conform to D. Follows a description of the algorithm.

Data: Bag of objects $D = \langle z_1, .., z_{n-1} \rangle$, non-conformity measure A,
significance level ε, a new object z
Result: P-Value p_n, *True* if z is conform to training objects

Set provisionally $z_n = z$ and $D = \langle z_1, .., z_n \rangle$
for $i \leftarrow 1$ **to** n **do**
$\quad | \quad \alpha_i \leftarrow A(D \setminus z_i, z_i)$
end
$\tau = U(0, 1)$
$p_n = \dfrac{\#\{i : \alpha_i > \alpha_n\} + \#\{i : \alpha_i = \alpha_n\}\tau}{n}$
if $p_n > \varepsilon$ **then**
$\quad | \quad$ Output *True*
else
$\quad | \quad$ Output *False*

Algorithm 1. Conformal Prediction using new examples alone

In the algorithm, τ is sampled in *Uni(0,1)* to obtain a *smoothed conformal predictor*, as suggested by [3]. Smoothed conformal predictor is *exactly valid*, which means that the probability of error equals ε on the long run. Confidence level is defined as $1 - \varepsilon$, which is the probability for a new example generated by the same distribution to be covered by the prediction set.

Conformal Clustering uses CP to create a set of predictions Γ^ε, which contains the new objects which are conform to old objects in D. These objects are then clustered by using a *neighbouring rule*. Follows a description of the algorithm. A d-dimensional grid of ℓ equally spaced points per side is created within the feature values range; d is the number of features. P-Values are computed using CP for each point of the grid considering them as new objects z respect to the bag of *training* observations Z. Conform points are predicted respect to a significance value ε. These points are then clustered by using a neighbouring rule: two points z_i, z_j are in the same cluster if they are neighbours on the grid. In this context, significance level ε can be used as a trim to regulate the depth of the clusters (see Fig. 2). In fact, ε is responsible for the percentage of instances left outside any clusters; the more of them there are, the less connected to each other are the remaining ones, which leads to a deeper level of hierarchical clustering.

Once created the clusters, *test* objects are associated to them by using the rule: a *test* object is from a cluster if its distance from one of the cluster point is smaller or equal to the grid unit. If a point is associated to more than one clusters, these clusters are merged.

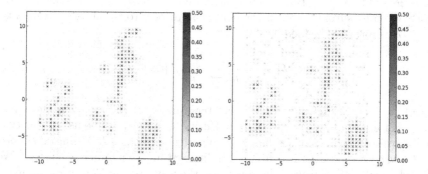

Fig. 2. Trimming significance level ε on P-Values grid. Non-conformity measure k-NN with $k = 1$ (*left*) and *KDE* with $h = 0.1$ (*right*) are used. Coloured points are the predicted ones with respect to a significance level.

3.3 Non-conformity Measures

A non-conformity measure is a function $A : \mathbf{Z}^{(*)} \times \mathbf{Z} \rightarrow \mathbb{R}$, where $\mathbf{Z}^{(*)}$ is the set of possible bags over $\mathbf{Z}$. CP is valid for every non-conformity measure, but some of them are more efficient; *efficiency* is later presented in this document as a performance criterion. In our experiments we used non-conformity measures *k-Nearest Neighbours* (k-NN) and *Kernel Density Estimation* (KDE).

A_i, k-NN non-conformity measure for object z_i, given δ_{ij} to be the j-th smallest distance between z_i and the objects in $\langle z_1, ..., z_n \rangle \setminus z_i$, is:

$$A_i = \sum_{j=1}^{k} \delta_{ij},$$

where k is the chosen number of neighbours.

A_i, KDE non-conformity measure for a kernel function $K : \mathbb{R}^d \rightarrow \mathbb{R}$, where d is the number of features, is:

$$A_i = -\left(\frac{1}{nh^d} \sum_{j=1}^{n} K\left(\frac{z_i - z_j}{h} \right) \right),$$

where h is the kernel bandwidth. We here use a Gaussian kernel:

$$K(u) = \frac{1}{2\pi} e^{-\frac{1}{2} u^2}.$$

4 Results

We measure the performances of our system by using two criteria: *Purity* and *Average P-Value* (APV). Purity is an accuracy criterion which measures the homogeneity of clusters. It is the weighted sum, for all the clusters, of the percentage of objects from the most frequent class respect to the cluster cardinality. Purity [7] is formally defined as:

$$Purity(\Omega, C) = \frac{1}{n} \sum_k \max_j \#\{\omega_k \cap c_j\},$$

where $\Omega = \{\omega_1, ..., \omega_K\}$ is the set of clusters, and $C = \{c_1, ..., c_J\}$ is the set of classes. For a parameter set we compare Purity for a fixed ε. The use of Purity is usually avoided for evaluating clustering algorithms such as *K-Means* or *Hierarchical Clustering*, because it is highly conditioned by the number of clusters. We although employ this criterion here because the way we trim Conformal Clustering parameters does not essentially influence the number of clusters for the same ε. APV is an efficiency criterion introduced by [8]; efficiency in CP measures the size of the prediction set Γ^ε. APV is defined to be the mean of P-Values of the P-Values grid. We want this parameter to be as small as possible.

Table 1. Conformal Clustering respectively with k-NN trimming k (*above*) and KDE gaussian kernel trimming bandwidth h (*below*)

k	1	2	3	4	5	6	7	8	9	10
APV	**0.129**	0.139	0.141	0.147	0.160	0.167	0.176	0.183	0.189	0.193
Purity ($\varepsilon = 0.2$)	**0.990**	0.970	0.970	0.960	0.960	0.960	0.960	0.940	0.920	0.920

h	0.001	0.005	0.01	0.05	0.1	0.2	0.3	0.4	0.5	1.0
APV	0.404	0.332	0.299	0.165	**0.130**	0.138	0.146	0.155	0.165	0.211
Purity ($\varepsilon = 0.2$)	**1.000**	0.980	**1.000**	0.990	0.990	0.990	0.970	0.970	0.950	0.920

In our first experiment we apply Conformal Clustering to a t-SNE projection with perplexity 50. Table 1 shows the results of using non-conformity measures k-NN and KDE trimming their parameters. The significance level was set to $\varepsilon = 0.2$. We notice that KDE manages to achieve perfect Purity, with the penalty of a larger APV. Non-conformity measure k-NN obtains its best Purity and APV for the value $k = 1$. K-NN also gets for this value the best APV overall. Further we will see from Fig. 3 that it is more robust on perplexity than KDE. KDE efficiency quickly fails for small bandwidth ($h < 0.05$), which may be due to high computational precision required by this method. Figure 2 shows k-NN and KDE predictions on P-Values grid respect to the significance level.

In the second experiment we inspect how t-SNE perplexity influences the results. We experiment with many values of perplexity, apply Conformal Clustering with k-NN ($k = 1$) and KDE (bandwidth $h = 0.1$) non-conformity measures, and measure APV and Purity. Figure 3 shows the results for k-NN and KDE non-conformity measures. The trends for Purity are both ascendant as perplexity increases, and after approximately 20 they get on average very close to perfect Purity. As for the efficiency, while for k-NN APV does not look strictly

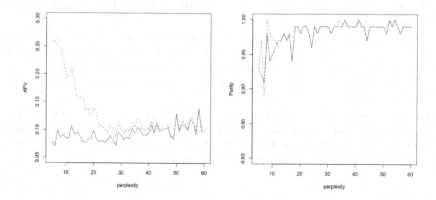

Fig. 3. Trimming t-SNE perplexity and evaluating Conformal Clustering for non-conformity measures KDE (gaussian kernel, bandwidth $h = 0.1$) in dashed brown line, and k-NN ($k = 1$) in blue line. We evaluate criteria APV (*left*) and Purity (*right*).

correlated to perplexity (despite a slow increasing trend as perplexity grows), for KDE APV decreases, which indicates that for KDE perplexity value can be set larger to get better performances. These results indicate k-NN to be a better candidate than KDE as a non-conformity measure for Conformal Clustering, but further experiments on different training sets should investigate this.

5   Conclusions and Future Work

We described here a novel clustering technique called Conformal Clustering, extending previous research for a multi-class unsupervised learning setting. We presented its application for clustering network traffic generated by *bots*. A neighbouring rule was introduced for creating clusters from a prediction set of objects. Purity and APV criteria were used for evaluating clustering performances. We also proposed a novel algorithm based on PACF for detecting a single periodicity in a binary time series.

For future research we plan to develop various criteria of accuracy and efficiency. Our aim is also to reduce the computational complexity of Conformal Clustering. If the problem does not require reduction of dimensionality then an application of t-SNE can be avoided. In high dimension a potential alternative to t-SNE is using an irregular (random) grid instead of the current one, but this would need some revision of the clustering definition. The methodology was shown on the example of two non-conformity measures, each having two parameters (including perplexity), and we compared their quality. Using more data, this can be extended further to find the best approach. We also plan to develop new non-conformity measures related to underlying algorithms like BotFinder [9]. The experiments for the proposed periodicity detection algorithm computed PACF for a number of lags close to the period to detect; future studies may investigate its performance when using a different number of lags. PACF-based periodicity detection can be also extended for detecting more than one period in an instance.

From a security perspective, our dataset contained only network traces from infected computers. One more direction is to consider extending this approach to model family-based clusters of botnets and on assessing its ability to detect bot-infected machines by monitoring real-world unknown network traffic.

Acknowledgments. This work is supported by EPSRC grants EP/K033344/1 ("Mining the Network Behaviour of Bots"), EP/K006266/1 and by the National Natural Science Foundation of China (No.61128003) grant. We are grateful to Vladimir Vovk, Zhiyuan Luo and Hugh Shanahan for useful discussions.

References

1. Elfeky, M.G., Aref, W.G., Elmagarmid, A.K.: Periodicity detection in time series databases. IEEE Transactions on Knowledge and Data Engineering **17**(7), 875–887 (2005)
2. Enders, W.: Applied econometric time series (1995)
3. Gammerman, A., Vovk, V.: Hedging predictions in machine learning. The Computer Journal **50**(2), 151–163 (2007)
4. Laxhammar, R., Falkman, G.: Sequential conformal anomaly detection in trajectories based on hausdorff distance. In: 2011 Proceedings of the 14th International Conference on Information Fusion (FUSION), pp. 1–8. IEEE (2011)
5. Lei, J., Rinaldo, A., Wasserman, L.: A conformal prediction approach to explore functional data. Annals of Mathematics and Artificial Intelligence, pp. 1–15 (2013)
6. Van der Maaten, L., Hinton, G.: Visualizing data using t-sne. Journal of Machine Learning Research **9**(2579–2605), 85 (2008)
7. Manning, C.D., Raghavan, P., Schütze, H.: Introduction to information retrieval, vol. 1. Cambridge University Press, Cambridge (2008)
8. Smith, J., Nouretdinov, I., Craddock, R., Offer, C., Gammerman, A.: Anomaly Detection of Trajectories with Kernel Density Estimation by Conformal Prediction. In: Iliadis, L., Maglogiannis, I., Papadopoulos, H., Sioutas, S., Makris, C. (eds.) Artificial Intelligence Applications and Innovations. IFIP AICT, vol. 437, pp. 271–280. Springer, Heidelberg (2014)
9. Tegeler, F., Fu, X., Vigna, G., Kruegel, C.: Botfinder: Finding bots in network traffic without deep packet inspection. In: Proceedings of the 8th International Conference on Emerging Networking Experiments and Technologies, pp. 349–360. ACM (2012)
10. Vovk, V., Gammerman, A., Shafer, G.: Algorithmic learning in a random world. Springer (2005)

Interpretation of Conformal Prediction Classification Models

Ernst Ahlberg[1], Ola Spjuth[2], Catrin Hasselgren[3], and Lars Carlsson[1] (✉)

[1] Drug Safety and Metabolism, AstraZeneca Innovative Medicines and Early Development, Mölndal, Sweden
{ernst.ahlberg,lars.a.carlsson}@astrazeneca.com

[2] Department of Pharmaceutical Biosciences and Science for Life Laboratory, Uppsala University, Uppsala, Sweden
ola.spjuth@farmbio.uu.se

[3] Internal Medicine, University of New Mexico, Albuquerque, NM, USA
chasselgren@unm.edu

Abstract. We present a method for interpretation of conformal prediction models. The discrete gradient of the largest p-value is calculated with respect to object space. A criterion is applied to identify the most important component of the gradient and the corresponding part of the object is visualized.

The method is exemplified with data from drug discovery relating chemical compounds to mutagenicity. Furthermore, a comparison is made to already established important subgraphs with respect to mutagenicity and this initial assessment shows very useful results with respect to interpretation of a conformal predictor.

1 Introduction

In drug discovery a huge amount of data is generated to understand the effect of compounds interacting with biological targets. This data is usually generated for compounds that are synthesized and progressed in the drug discovery process. However, to decide which compounds to synthesize and aid in the design of new compounds, modeling of data generated from experiments is required. In drug discovery this type of modeling is often referred to as Quantitative Structure-Activity Relationship (QSAR). QSAR models are applied to predict properties such as solubility or specific toxicity of chemical compounds using machine learning and are widely used within the pharmaceutical industry to prioritize compounds for experimental testing or to alert for potential toxicity during the drug-discovery process [9,11]. The requirements for building a QSAR model is a set of compounds and a property that has been determined experimentally. The compounds are represented by objects that relatively easily can be calculated from the chemical structure of the compound, like for example by viewing the compounds as graphs and counting subgraphs of particular types. The experimental property is used as the label to be learned. The models need to allow for ranking of the compounds but it is also important that a measure of

© Springer International Publishing Switzerland 2015
A. Gammerman et al. (Eds.): SLDS 2015, LNAI 9047, pp. 323–334, 2015.
DOI: 10.1007/978-3-319-17091-6_27

the associated risk can be obtained. For these reasons the conformal prediction framework [12,16] is well suited for this type of modeling and is gaining popularity. To influence the design of new compounds the model should also provide information about possible changes to a compound that is likely to affect the biological activity. In comparison to machine learning in general this amounts to determining important components of the objects. The determination of these components can be done with two different views, one where we consider what is of global importance, what is important considering all examples we have observed, and the other of local importance, what is important for a specific example that we have predicted. Conformal prediction [12,16] is a method that use existing data to determine valid prediction regions for new examples. Thus instead of giving a point estimate, a conformal prediction model gives a prediction region that contains the true value with probability equal to or higher than a predefined level of confidence. Such a prediction region can be obtained under the assumption that the observed data is exchangeable [16].

It is of great utility to have models that allow for interpretation of the prediction. Ideally a chemist should get information on what parts of a compound that could be removed or replaced to get closer to the property of interest of that particular compound. To be able to perform such actions is of general interest in machine learning. Given a prediction for a new example it would in most cases be valuable to understand if slight changes to the object can alter the prediction to something more favorable. This is what we, somewhat loosely, define as a model being interpretable. A method to interpret machine-learning models, where the objects are compounds, has been proposed by Carlsson *et. al.* [4]. The idea there was to view the model as function that maps the objects to the labels, that is in the drug-discovery setting, the compounds to the corresponding property. By computing the gradient of the function with respect to the components of the object, suggestions of possible changes to the objects are made that would change the label in a more favorable fashion. In the case of classification the function for which the gradient was computed is real valued, for example for SVM it was the decision function and for RandomForest the fraction of votes for one class.

Tremendous manual effort has been put into defining subgraphs of compounds that are highly correlated to the binary experimental properties mutagenic or non mutagenic. The procedure is based on manual inspection of the chemical compounds to define subgraphs. For each subgraph, all compounds in the data set are tested for the presence of the subgraph. This results in a contingency table with mutagenic or non mutagenic versus subgraph present or no subgraph present. A statistical test, usually based on standard scores, is then performed using the contingency table. The subgraphs are subsequently modified and re-tested in an iterative fashion until a sufficient number of subgraphs are identified that can be used to identify mutagenic compounds at a given level of significance. The manually derived subgraphs are commonly used as rules that provide both prediction and interpretation and an example of this procedure can be found in [10].

The remainder of this paper is organized as follows. In the next section we present how a component in an object of a particular prediction can be identified that would allow for a change in the credibility of a prediction. Next, we show results when the procedure is applied to fictitious data and to Ames mutagenicity data. In the last section we conclude the paper.

2 Method

Any machine-learning model is an approximation of a relationship between an object and its label, like a compound and its biological activity, and can be viewed as a mathematical function. The gradient of a function at a point in object space explains how this function behaves in the local neighborhood to that specific object and it can be calculated for any sufficiently smooth function. By computing the gradient of a label a local linear approximation, a truncated Taylor series expansion, is obtained and this enables the exploration of the function in that local neighborhood of the object space without an explicit differentiable analytical expression of the model.

In this work we focus on the component of an object that results in the largest change locally, by magnitude, of the function. We remark that one could also evaluate a set of the most important components of an object, defined by an arbitrary cutoff, either on the size of the components of the gradient or by taking a predefined number of the largest components of an object sorted in descending order by the size of the corresponding components of the gradient. This can be adjusted to the problem at hand. We will proceed in describing the proposed method assuming that we only need to consider one component of the gradient, without loss of generality.

Consider a set of examples $\{x_k, y_k\}$ where the object for the kth example is denoted x_k and the corresponding label is y_k, which can be either discrete or continuous. The number of components of an object x is M. These examples are used to train a model and we can regard this relationship as a function $y = f(x)$. In the case of conformal prediction, the interest is not primarily in the label itself but rather the change in the p-value, similarly to how a decision function value can be used when the underlying modeling algorithm is SVM, thus rather than looking at $f(x)$ we look at $p^c(x) = p(x, c)$, where c indicates the class label to be considered of all relevant labels, C. Since a conformal predictor produces a p-value for each possible label, we propose to calculate the gradient in object space for the most credible label, $\hat{c} : \max_c\{p^c(x)\}, c \in C$[1]. Assuming a sufficiently smooth function describing the p-values and the objects in metric spaces, then the jth component of a discrete gradient can be defined as a one-sided finite difference

$$p_j'^{\hat{c}}(x) = \frac{p^{\hat{c}}(x + h_j) - p^{\hat{c}}(x)}{h}, \tag{1}$$

where h_j denotes that the jth component of the otherwise all zeros vector is set to h. The step length, h, can also be allowed to vary for varying j based on knowledge

---

[1] This is equivalent to the definition of *Credibility* in [16]

about the distribution of objects, perhaps in what is observed from a training set. For a given object x to be predicted, we assume all possible class labels. This is identical to the procedure of a regular conformal predictor classification. When we have determined the most credible class, we proceed to compute the gradient of the corresponding p-value. We remark that the complexity of the proposed method in addition to the regular conformal predictor is M evaluations of $p^{\hat{c}}(x)$. We also note that the definition of a p-value, in most uses of conformal predictors, is piecewise constant and discontinuous as a function of the nonconformity score. However, wider finite-difference schemes can be used for smoothing of the discrete gradient, but they would be more computationally costly to evaluate. Another possibility is to use an interpolated p-value[2]. A pseudo code representation of the proposed method is described in Algorithm 1.

> **for** $c \in C$ **do**
> > $p^c(x) = p(x, c)$
>
> $\hat{c} : \max_c p(x, c)$
> $\hat{j} = 1$
> $\hat{p} = 0.0$
> **for** $j \in 1 \dots M$ **do**
> > $p_j'^{\hat{c}}(x) = \dfrac{p^{\hat{c}}(x + h_j) - p^{\hat{c}}(x)}{h}$
> > **if** $\hat{p} < p_j'^{\hat{c}}(x)$ **then**
> > > $\hat{j} = j$
> > > $\hat{p} = p_j'^{\hat{c}}(x)$
>
> **if** $\hat{p} > 0.0$ **then**
> > $\hat{j}$ is an important component of x
>
> **else**
> > no important component of x

Algorithm 1. This shows pseudo code for the proposed method. When a component of the gradient is positive the largest component, $\hat{j}$, is identified. If the most credible p-value is at a local maxima in object space, no component is identified.

3   Results

To evaluate the proposed method of interpreting conformal prediction models by computing the largest component of the gradient we will conduct two experiments. The first one will be on fictitious data and the second on a data set describing activities (labels) of compounds in the Ames mutagenicity test [3].

---

[2] A continuous p-value is defined in the paper *Modifications to p-values of Conformal Predictors*, also presented at COPA 2015

3.1   Experimental Results on Fictitious Data

Here we will use categorical data defined by the function

$$f(x_1, x_2) = \begin{cases} 0, \text{ if } & x_1 < 0, \\ 1, \text{ if } & x_1 \geq 0, \end{cases} \tag{2}$$

where the object $x_1, x_2 \in [-0.5, 0.5]$. The intention is to examine how our procedure behaves at and in a neighborhood to a transition between different values of a label. We randomly sampled 400 objects from a uniform distribution to create a training set with labels according to (2) and a corresponding test set of 1000 examples. A transductive Mondrian conformal algorithm was used to create a model, where calibration was done for each type of label. The algorithm was implemented using C-SVC in libsvm [5] with the cost coefficient (C in libsvm) set to 50.0 and the width of the kernel function, (g in libsvm) to 0.002. The nonconformity scores were defined by the Lagrangian multipliers and p-values were calculated by using the definition in [16, p. 27], a smoothed p-value. All predictions were carried out without updating the training set by learning from predicted examples. We chose $h = 0.01$, to avoid extremely large components of the gradient. The choice was based on assuming that the distribution of training objects could be represented by a uniformly spaced grid of the size 20×20 in object space and then assigning a slightly smaller value. Results showing p-values and components of the discrete gradient are shown in Figures 1 and 2. The most

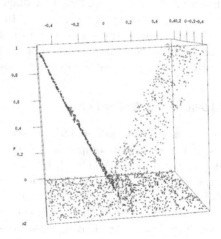

Fig. 1. The p-values for the label 1 are represented by red dots and those for the label 0 with blue dots. The vertical axis shows the value of the p-values and horizontal axes show values of x_1 and x_2.

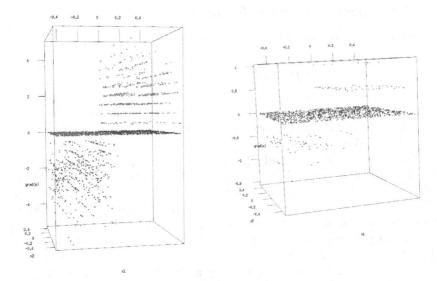

Fig. 2. The plots show partial derivatives of the p-values with respect to x_1 (left) and x_2 (right). The coloring corresponds to the coloring in Figure 1.

credible p-value corresponds to label 0 for $x < 0$ and otherwise it corresponds to label 1. We can see that a large proportion of the gradient components colored red in the left plot of Figure 2, for $x_1 > 0$ are larger by magnitude than the corresponding gradient components in the plot to the right. In Figure 1, the value of p-values colored red is increasing as x_1 is increasing for $x_1 > 0$. The results are consistent for p-values representing label 0 although the sign of the gradient components is opposite that of the gradient components based on label 1.

3.2   Experimental Results on Ames Data

For the Ames data there is a well established link between subgraphs of compounds and mutagenicity. The standard comparator here is a manual curation of compound subgraphs, encoded as SMARTS [1], by Kazius *et. al.* [10]. Using subgraphs to describe the underlying problem has another advantage in that it is easy to visually highlight the subgraphs on to the original compounds.

The object used when applying the proposed method to Ames mutagenicity data is the signature [7,8] descriptor. The signature descriptor describes a compound by a set of strings, representing subgraphs of the compound, and the associated counts. Each string is a canonical representation of a subgraph written as a directed acyclic graph. Signature descriptors are calculated for all atoms in a compound. The neighboring atoms are added layer by layer limited by a predefined distance threshold, called height. Each incrementation of the height adds all atoms reached by traversing an additional bond away from the originating atom. At height zero, the signature descriptors are simply an enumeration of atom types in a compound with their corresponding counts. The number of unique strings depends on the number of unique atom types and their neighboring atom types, see Figure 3 and Table 1. Table 1, originally presented in Eklund *et. al.* [6] and modified here represents the height zero and one signatures for the drug compound paracetamol. The lower part of the table shows the signature descriptors, as unique strings with corresponding counts. The signature descriptor represents very sparse objects with limited overlap between non-zero components of objects especially at high heights. The signature descriptors used in this work were generated by CDK [14].

In the evaluation of the proposed method inductive Mondrian conformal prediction has been applied using support vector machines with a radial basis function kernel as described in [6]. The Mondrian taxonomy was based on the individual labels (non mutagenic and mutagenic), thus ensuring class specific

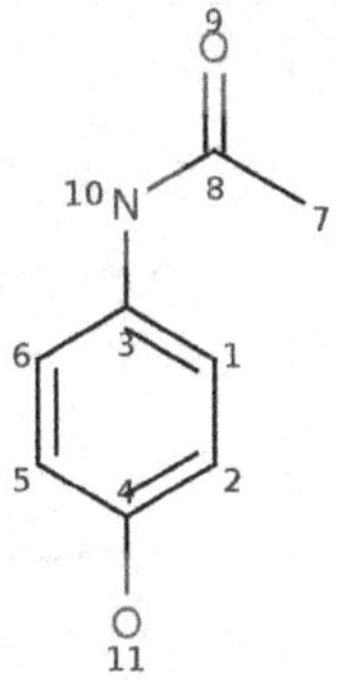

Fig. 3. Paracetamol is a drug compound for treatment of pain and fever. The atom numbers are displayed in this figure.

Table 1. The signatures of height zero and one for paracetamol. The atom number is denoted by w and the height by l.

w	$l = 0$	$l = 1$
1	[C]	[C]([C]=[C])
2	[C]	[C]([C]=[C])
3	[C]	[C]([C]=[C][N])
4	[C]	[C]([C]=[C][O])
5	[C]	[C]([C]=[C])
6	[C]	[C]([C]=[C])
7	[C]	[C]([C])
8	[C]	[C]([C][N]=[O])
9	[O]	[O](=[C])
10	[N]	[N]([C][C])
11	[O]	[O]([C])

Count	Signature
8	[C]
1	[N]
2	[O]
4	[C]([C]=[C])
1	[C]([C]=[C][N])
1	[C]([C]=[C][O])
1	[C]([C])
1	[C]([C][N]=[O])
1	[O](=[C])
1	[N]([C][C])
1	[O]([C])

Table 2. Examples of highlighted subgraphs by the proposed method in the second column from left, by a set of manually created SMARTS in the third column. The fourth column shows the predictions of the compounds when the subgraph identified as making the most change in the unfavorable direction is altered. The left column shows the experimental activity of the AMES mutagenicity test. The subgraphs were colored in red for predictions where the credibility is based on the p-value for the mutagenic label and in blue for the non-mutagenic label. If we were to chose one label from the conformal prediction without specifying a significance level it would be the most credible label. The SMARTS only predict the mutagenic label and this is also indicated by a red coloring of the important atoms. The figures predicted by the proposed method were visualized using Bioclipse [13] and the ones predicted by the manually created SMARTS using oechem [2].

Activity	Conformal Prediction	SMARTS Prediction	Modified Compound Conformal Prediction
Mutagenic			
Mutagenic			
Mutagenic			
Mutagenic			
Non mutagenic			
Non mutagenic			

Table 2. (*continued*)

Activity	Conformal Prediction	SMARTS Prediction	Modified Compound Conformal Prediction
Non mutagenic			
Non mutagenic			
Non mutagenic			
Non mutagenic			
Non mutagenic			
Mutagenic			

validity. Furthermore, libsvm [5] was used to implement the Mondrian conformal predictor where the nonconformity scores were defined as the decision function values of the C-SVC algorithm. The cost coefficient (C in libsvm) was set to 50.0, the width of the kernel function, (g in libsvm) to 0.002 and the signature descriptor heights were 0, 1, 2 and 3 leading to $M = 23226$. For any prediction made, only the non-zero components were considered when determining the most important component of an object. The reason for this limitation is that the objects are very sparse and that it is of higher interest, in a drug-discovery setting, to suggest changes to subgraphs present in the predicted compound. The gradient of the credible p-value was calculated using $h = 1$ due to the nature of the signature descriptor.

The interpretation of conformal predictors is demonstrated using the AMES mutagenicity data set described in Kazius *et al.* [10], as a training set. This set consisted of 4254 examples and was randomly divided in to a calibration and a proper training set. The calibration set contained 99 examples of each class and the remainder was used as a proper training set. Evaluation examples have been selected out of 880 compounds reported by Young *et al.* [17]. The compounds present in both data sets have been removed from the external validation set. We remark that this is an early investigation and that we here only show a few examples of how the interpretation of the conformal predictor can be applied to data from the drug-discovery domain. The compounds in Table 2 display highlighted subgraphs using the proposed method and the Kazius SMARTS along with Ames mutagenicity classification. All atoms belonging to the signature descriptor representing the most important component of the object were colored based on the label defining the credible p-value. If it was a mutagenic label then the atoms were colored red, otherwise they were colored blue. These examples show that the proposed method retrieves similar subgraphs as the Kazius SMARTS which is encouraging. Furthermore, the *Modified Compound Conformal Prediction* column shows examples where a change has been made to the highlighted part of the original compound. This shows that a change in the compound, affecting the predicted most important component, can change the prediction all together. This is of great importance when applying this type of predictors in the drug-discovery setting.

4   Discussion

By computing the gradient of the p-value as a function of the objects in a conformal prediction model it is possible to describe the behavior in a local neighborhood to a prediction. We can not always expect the model to be smooth or even have non-zero gradient components in object space as can be seen by our experiment using fictitious data. But, the experiment qualitatively showed that by understanding what the model looks like in a local neighborhood to an object is useful for understanding how changes to the object would change the p-value for the newly created object. When applied to mutagenicity data described by the signature descriptor, this method shows very nice correspondence to previously published Kazius SMARTS. Some of the changed compounds even completely changed in predicted activity upon a change of the most important subgraph of the initially predicted compound. For example, the compound in the first row of the Table 2 is predicted mutagenic and the substructure highlighted in red is indicated as the most important one. When changing the nitrogen (N) to a carbon and removing the highlighted oxygen (O) a new compound is formed. This new compound, showed in the modified compound column, is predicted to be non mutagenic which is known to be correct experimentally. For the remainder of the compounds we do not have this information but this highlights the value that the method can provide. The proposed method can be used with any type of conformal prediction based model, however the result may not have such a readily accessible visual representation. In the drug-discovery setting, a chemist using a QSAR model can often anticipate what some changes of compounds would lead to in terms of change in biological activity. Finally, additional information that the components of the gradient gives might improve the utility of the proposed method. When applied to problems with labels represented by real numbers, it should be possible to use the same approach at least when predicting with inductive conformal predictors as in [6]. In this case the midpoint of the predicted range can be used as the function to calculate the gradient of in object space. In future work, we plan a more exhaustive and rigorous evaluation on both fictitious data and data from the drug-discovery domain, similar to the work done in [15], as well as looking at regression problems. It is also of great interest if there could be a way of determining h based on a training set and verify this on data of general interest to the machine-learning community and not only the drug-discovery community.

Acknowledgments. The authors greatly appreciate the feedback given by the reviewers. The feedback helped clarifying several important aspects of the proposed method and the conducted experiments as well as identifying weaknesses.

References

1. Daylight Theory: SMARTS - A Language for Describing Molecular Patterns. http://www.daylight.com/dayhtml/doc/theory/theory.smarts.html (accessed January 13, 2015)
2. Openeye Scientific Software. http://www.eyesopen.com (accessed August 30, 2014)
3. Ames, B.N., Lee, F.D., Durston, W.E.: An improved bacterial test system for the detection and classification of mutagens and carcinogens. Proceedings of the National Academy of Sciences 70(3), 782–786 (1973). http://www.pnas.org/content/70/3/782.abstract
4. Carlsson, L., Helgee, E.A., Boyer, S.: Interpretation of nonlinear qsar models applied to ames mutagenicity data. Journal of Chemical Information and Modeling 49(11), 2551–2558 (2009). http://dx.doi.org/10.1021/ci9002206, pMID: 19824682
5. Chang, C.C., Lin, C.J.: LIBSVM: a library for support vector machines (2001), software available at http://www.csie.ntu.edu.tw/~cjlin/libsvm
6. Eklund, M., Norinder, U., Boyer, S., Carlsson, L.: The application of conformal prediction to the drug discovery process. Annals of Mathematics and Artificial Intelligence, pp. 1–16 (2013). http://dx.doi.org/10.1007/s10472-013-9378-2
7. Faulon, J.L., Churchwell, C.J.: Signature Molecular Descriptor. 2. Enumerating Molecules from Their Extended Valence Sequences. J. Chem. Inf. Comput. Sci. **43**, 721–734 (2003)
8. Faulon, J.L., Visco, D.P.J., Pophale, R.S.: Signature Molecular Descriptor. 1. Using Extended Valence Sequences in QSAR and QSPR Studies. J. Chem. Inf. Comput. Sci. **43**, 707–720 (2003)

9. Grover, M., Singh, B., Bakshi, M., Singh, S.: Quantitative structure-property relationships in pharmaceutical research. Pharm. Sci. & Tech. Today **3**(1), 28–35 (2000)

10. Kazius, J., McGuire, R., Bursi, R.: Derivation and Validation of Toxicophores for Mutagenicity Prediction. J. Med. Chem **48**, 312–320 (2005)

11. Lewis, R.A.: A General Method for Exploiting QSAR Models in Lead Optimization. J. Med. Chem. **48**(5), 1638–1648 (2005)

12. Shafer, G., Vovk, V.: A tutorial on conformal prediction. Journal of Machine Learning Research 9, 371–421 (2008). http://www.jmlr.org/papers/volume9/shafer08a/shafer08a.pdf

13. Spjuth, O., Eklund, M., Ahlberg Helgee, E., Boyer, S., Carlsson, L.: Integrated decision support for assessing chemical liabilities. J. Chem. Inf. Model. **51**(8), 1840–1847 (2011)

14. Steinbeck, C., Han, Y., Kuhn, S., Horlacher, O., Luttmann, E., Willighagen, E.: The chemistry development kit (cdk) an open-source java library for chemo- and bioinformatics. J. Chem. Inf. Comput. Sci. 43(2), 493–500 (2003). http://dx.doi.org/10.1021/ci025584y, pMID: 12653513

15. Stålring, J., Almeida, P.R., Carlsson, L., Helgee Ahlberg, E., Hasselgren, C., Boyer, S.: Localized heuristic inverse quantitative structure activity relationship with bulk descriptors using numerical gradients. Journal of Chemical Information and Modeling 53(8), 2001–2017 (2013). http://dx.doi.org/10.1021/ci400281y, pMID: 23845139

16. Vovk, V., Gammerman, A., Shafer, G.: Algorithmic Learning in a Random World. Springer-Verlag New York Inc., Secaucus (2005)

17. Young, S., Gombar, V., Emptage, M., Cariello, N., Lambert, C.: Mixture De-Convolution and Analysis of Ames Mutagenicity Data. Chemometrics and Intelligent Laboratory Systems **60**, 5–11 (2002)

New Frontiers in Data Analysis
for Nuclear Fusion

Confinement Regime Identification
Using Artificial Intelligence Methods

G.A. Rattá$^{(\boxtimes)}$ and Jesús Vega

Laboratorio Nacional de Fusión. CIEMAT, Madrid, Spain
giuseppe.ratta@ciemat.es

Abstract. The L-H transition is a remarkable self-organization phenomenon that occurs in Magnetically Confined Nuclear Fusion (MCNF) devices. For re-search reasons, it is relevant to create models able to determine the confinement regime the plasma is in by using, from the wide number of measured signals in each discharge, just a reduce number of them. Also desirable is that a general model, applicable not only to one device but to all of them, is reached. From a data-driven modelling point of view it implies the careful —and hopefully, automatic— selection of the phenomenon's related signals to input them into an equation able to determine the confinement mode. Using a supervised machine learning method, it would also require the tuning of some internal parameters. This is an optimization problem, tackled in this study with Genetic Algorithms (GAs). The results prove that reliable and universal laws that describe the L-H transition with more than a ~98,60% classification accuracy can be attained using only 3 input signals.

Keywords: L-H transition · Nuclear fusion · SVM · Genetic algorithms

1 Introduction

Harnessing controlled fusion reactions through MCNF is an ambitious goal the scientific community has pursuit during the best part of the last 70 years. Up to now, the most promising type of MCNF configuration is the one called 'tokamak' and it is the one chosen for the reference next step machine, ITER.

Beyond the technical difficulties still unsolved, the considerable advances in the field have cleared the path towards the future devices in which stable burning conditions with high gain factors are expected to be reached. If so, one of the main burdens affecting the mankind will be lightened or —let's be positive— even solved: safe, cheap, abundant and non-polluting energy could be released and collected for its use in industries and daily life.

MCNF has been under study from ~1950's with modest results until around 20 years ago, when one of the major breakthroughs in the field was attained in ASDEX [1]. It was observed that once an input heating power threshold was surpassed, pronounced gradients in the temperature and density profiles appeared and a considerable improvement of the energy confinement time of a factor ~2 was evidenced. The particle transport was significantly reduced in a fascinating self-organization phenomenon. This transport

© Springer International Publishing Switzerland 2015
A. Gammerman et al. (Eds.): SLDS 2015, LNAI 9047, pp. 337–346, 2015.
DOI: 10.1007/978-3-319-17091-6_28

barrier, formed almost spontaneously in the plasma edge, is a clear signature of an enhanced confinement. The regime, extensively replicated later in several devices, was called High confinement mode or simply H-mode [2]. Even now, the underlying physic of the L-H transition is not fully understood. Then, theoretical models [3, 4, 5, 6] and data-driven techniques [7, 8, 9, 10] aimed at shading some light upon the phenomenon's inner mechanisms are continuously created and discussed.

For research purposes, it is relevant to distinguish the plasma regime (L or H) of a running discharge by inspecting just few plasma measurements. This can lead to unweave the complex and non-linear relationships among different parameters for each state. From a data-driven perspective, the operational mode recognition can be seen as a binary classification problem, being the possible categories 'L mode' and 'H mode'. Yet, the optimal combination of input signals (if it is possible a reduced number of them to ease the interpretability of the results) is up to be properly chosen from a wide set of available plasma quantities. Also, in case the classification technique is based on a supervised system[1], some internal parameters tuning[2] are required to achieve reliable results.

In this study general models that satisfactorily fulfil all the above-mentioned requirements are developed. A wide international database collected from 19 different tokamaks containing several measurements of discharges at L and H mode is used to train and test the classification systems.

GAs are applied to automatically select a combination of a reduced number of inputs and appropriately adjusting the kernel parameters values to create the final models, whose testing accuracies overpass the 98,60%.

2   The International ITPA L-H Database

To get a model universally applicable to different tokamaks using supervised data-driven systems it is necessary to feed a machine learning engine with inputs from all these devices. For this specific study, an international L-H database has been addressed [11].

This particular database provides a broad diversity of measurements (156 plasma parameters from 19 different tokamaks) but it burdens the considerable problem of empty entries. Depending on the device the data came from, some of the parameters can be in blank.

Specifically, the database contents 9980 entries. Each entry is an n-dimensional row vector with $n=156=$number of parameters (i.e. 1x156 vector), labelled as belonging to L or H mode[3]. Still, only complete vectors are useful for the development of the models. Incomplete vectors must be deleted[4] and consequently the database suffers a

---

[1]   In this article it is SVM with an RBF kernel.

[2]   In this article they are the slack variable C and the parameter γ.

[3]   Other regimes (as Ohmic or ELMy H) are also specified in the database. For pragmatic reasons in this study only 'L' mode and 'H' mode classes have been considered.

[4]   Some imputation techniques can be applied to solve the problem of missing values but their application is out of the scope of this study.

reduction. In some cases, using exactly the same initial database, its final size has been drastically reduced by this 'cleaning' of empty entries, as in [9], where only 800 vectors were kept.

In this study a compromise was reached. Only 15 relevant parameters were kept, having in mind their relevance and availability.

The parameters are: 1) the effective atomic mass; 2) the plasma geometrical major radius; 3) the major radius of the magnetic axis; 4) the horizontal plasma minor radius; 5) the area of plasma cross section; 6) the plasma volume; 7) the minimum distance between the separatrix flux surface and either the vessel wall or limiters; 8) the toroidal magnetic field; 9) the plasma current; 10) the safety factor at 95%; 11) the line integrated density; 12) the neutral beam power in watts that is lost from the plasma; 13) the electron temperature at the magnetic axis; 14) the plasma energy in joules as determined from the diamagnetic loop; 15) the estimated Loss Power not corrected for charge exchange and unconfined orbit losses.

To improve the further inclusion in the SVM classifier, each one of the signal values has been normalized according the standard formula:

$$\text{Normalized signal value} = \frac{\text{Signal value} - \text{min}}{\text{max} - \text{min}}$$

where:
min= the minimum value of the signal (in all the database).
max= the maximum value of the signal (in all the database).

As consequence, the maximum and minimum values of the signals are bounded between 0 and 1.

The final database, with normalized vectors without any empty value, contains a total of 3580 entries (2176 H-mode and 1404 L-mode samples).

3   The Computational Problem

The main aim of this study is to obtain a good (hopefully the best) combination of plasma signals and RBF Kernel values to discriminate between L and H modes.

The possible combinations (without permutations) are ruled by:

$$\sum_{i=1}^{n} C_i^n$$

$$C_i^n = \frac{n!}{(n-i)!\,i!}$$

where:
n =number of possible values and i =possible groupings.

Assuming that 15 signals are going to be included (15 values) and 10 different values will be tested for C and for γ (a total of 20 values), then $n=i=35$.

The estimated time required to exhaustively explore all these combinations (assuming that each one, that includes the train and test of a SVM system, would take an gross estimated time of ~1 ms) is more than one year. It is obvious than an alternative technique is required for the computation of the models and that is the main reason of the application of GAs to accelerate the calculations.

4   The GAs Driven Models

4.1   Brief Introduction to GAs

GAs [12] emulates nature, where better adapted individuals have higher chances to survive and breed descendants. In this context, adaptation means to reach, among others, the objectives of survival and reproduction. The adapted ones are able to transfer to the next generation their genetic material and their offspring will inherit a combination of "well-adapted" parents' genes. Oppositely, individuals unable to survive and reproduce will not pass to the following generations their characteristics and therefore their configuration is destined to extinction.

Given a problem, GAs creates a population of solutions/individuals. Each individual is represented by a code (it can be imagined as a simplified version of DNA) that defines the characteristics of each solution/individual.

To measure which individuals are better solving a particular problem, a metric called Fitness Function (FF), that scores individuals performances, is applied. According the FF score, a higher possibility to mate and have descendants is assigned to individuals/solutions with better values. Descendants are created as a combination of parents characteristics/genes (i.e. interchanging the bits of the vectors).

Finally, and since descendants are a combination of promising genes (bits), it is expected that newer generations outperform the former ones.

The procedure can be summarized in few steps:

1- Creation of a population of individuals. Each individual represents a possible solution to a problem. They are codified as vectors (to provide them the future possibility of crossing their bits with other vectors/individuals to create offspring).

2- Evaluation of each individual of the population according the objectives of the problem. This requires defining a metric to test how good each individual is solving the problem (i.e. the FF).

3- Selection of parents (a higher probability to be chosen as parent is assigned to those individuals with higher FF values).

4- Creation of children as a combination of parents' genes/bits (using genetic operators as crossover, mutation, reproductor).

5- Unless an ending condition is satisfied, iterate from step 2, where the new population (created in step 4) is evaluated.

6- Selection of the best solution. Once the ending condition has been fulfilled, the best individual of all generations (highest FF value) is chosen as the final model.

The power of GA to reduce computational times in problems underlies in these basic principles. Instead of exploring all the possible combinations, the most promising ones are chosen and crossed to create new solutions prone to overmatch the former ones.

4.2   GAs Application to the Problem

Codification

An *ad hoc* GA was programmed to simultaneously select a reduced set of inputs (from the 15 available) and to tune the parameters C and γ for a SVM using a RBF kernel.

The codification of each individual of the GA was assigned as follows:

- A binary number to represent the inclusion ('1') or not ('0') of each one of the 15 signals.
- The possible assignations for the slack variable were: $C \rightarrow \{0,01; 0,5; 1; 5; 10; 50; 100; 10^3; 10^4; 10^6\}$.
- The possible values for γ were: $\rightarrow \{ 10^{-5} ; 10^{-4} ; 10^{-3} ; 0,005; 0,01; 0,1; 0,5; 1; 10\}$.

By this way, each individual is represented by a 1x17 vector where their 15 first values are '0' or '1', the 16th value is one of the above mentioned possible for C and the 17th value one of the above mentioned possible for γ. An example individual could be: $\{0; 1; 0; 0; 0; 0; 0; 0; 0; 0; 0; 0; 0; 0; 0; 5; 10\}$. This codification means that the individual will be a SVM system trained using only the signal number 2 (plasma geometrical major radius in the list given at Section 2) with the slack variable $C=5$ and a γ value of the RBF kernel of 10.

The total number of individuals per population was set as 2 times the length of each individual (17)=34, according with [13].

The initial population is created assigning random values to each individual. Then, it evolves automatically following the basic steps stated in Section 4.1.

Fitness Function

It was necessary to define a robust criterion to evaluate the performance (Fitness Function) of each one of the individuals. Then, a 2-fold cross validation algorithm was repeated 3 times for each individual. The mean of these 6 results is computed and assigned as FF value. This severe evaluation favours results with high generalization capabilities, since the individuals are repeatedly trained and tested with different sets of samples.

Other sub-objective was to create models as simple as possible due to two main reasons. The first is because simpler models normally have higher generalization capabilities. The second is because the interpretability of the models (which is relevant in physics) is clearer if the amount of involved variables is limited.

It was necessary, then, to somehow 'steer' the course of the evolutionary processes of the GAs towards solutions that include fewer signals. To do it, a 'reward' of an extra 1% of their FF value was assigned to those individuals that require fewer signals than the mean (number of signals) of the population in the evaluated iteration.

Parents Selection, Mutation Probability, Ending Condition

Parents were chosen using the *roulette* method. It consists of sorting all the individuals according their FF value and assigning a higher score (maximum equal to 1) to the ones with higher FF values and lower ones (minimum equal to 0) to the ones with lower FF values. A virtual roulette is spun and it randomly selects a number between 1 and 0 (e.g. 0,56). Those individuals with a score superior to the roulette's number are selected as parents.

To create children, parent's bits have to be mixed. A 2 points cross-over method has been chosen since this technique has proven to attain solutions in faster times than the conventional 1 point-crossover [14]. The method consists on randomly selecting 2 points in the parent's vectors (see Fig. 1) and to interchange the sections defined by these points to form 2 children.

The mutation probability (the chance of randomly changing a bit value) was standardly set as a 0.05%. After some testing runs it was seen that 50 iterations/generation was sufficient to achieve good results.

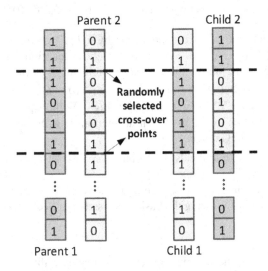

Fig. 1. Example of the 2-point cross-over method

5   Results

5.1   Temperature Related Results

One important quantity for the comprehension of the phenomenon is the electron temperature. The parameter, however, might not be the one that evidences more clearly the regime a discharge is in and therefore there are considerable chances that the GA does not select it for the final model. One of the advantages of the GA-driven optimization is that it allows conditioning the evolutionary process by modifying the codification of the individuals/solutions. Specifically in this case, the bit corresponding to the electron temperature (13th one) has been 'forced' to be always activated (i.e. equal to '1'). This means that the final solution has, mandatorily, to include the electron temperature in the model.

After 50 generations, the best individual/solution obtained by the algorithm included only three plasma signals (one of them, of course, the 'forced' electron temperature). The separating hyperplane, represented in Fig. 2, is a smooth dome-shaped solution that accurately isolates samples from L and H modes.

Notice that the axes in the figure are bounded between 0 and 1. This is due to the normalization performed over the signals.

A 98,63% of the samples are correctly classified by this model.

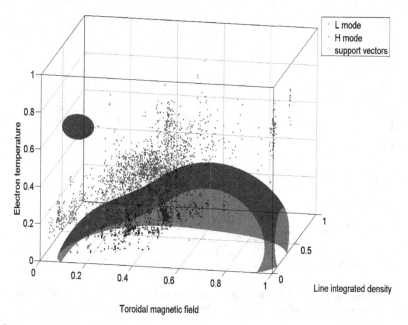

Fig. 2. A smooth dome-shaped hyperplane separates L mode and H mode samples. Values have been normalized between 0 and 1.

5.2   Power Related Results

Possibly the most studied models to understand the underlying physics that makes the L-H transitions occur are the ones that involve the input power or some derived measure of it. This is reasonable: the firsts observations of the phenomenon were directly related to the input power. Besides, it is a variable that can be externally controlled during the machine operation and it can be used to provoke the transition.

Therefore, it was interesting for this study to take advantage, one more time, of the 'forcing' mechanism that GAs permit to include one plasma power quantity into the final solution. In this case, the signal set to '1' was the Loss power (Ploss), defined as the total input power minus the time rate of change of the total plasma stored energy. This signal has been also used in other studies related to the L-H transition [15, 16].

In the results plotted in Fig. 3, attained by the same methodology explained in the previous Section 5.1. with a limit of 50 generation, it is clear that samples at higher Ploss are prone to have transited to the H-mode. This was the expected outcome. However, it is possible to notice a significant cluster of samples that, even at low Ploss, have transited to H-mode. This always occurs at ~0,5 plasma minor radiuses values. Also strikes the attention a grouping of isolated L-mode samples in the corner near the origin, correctly covered by a separate 'wing' of the hyperplane.

In this case, the solution accurately classified the 98,60% of the samples.

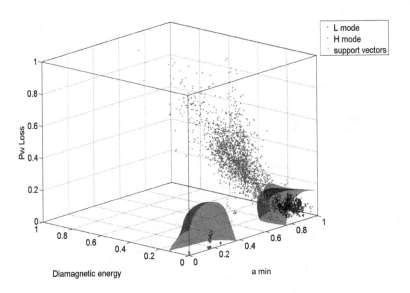

Fig. 3. Requiring again only 3 plasma signals, a consistent solution that accurately separates the operational regimes was reached. Values have been normalized between 0 and 1.

5.3   Computational Cost

The mean time required to train and test the SVM classifiers (each time for a cross-validation) was 9 ms per individual, nine times higher than the initially estimated one (see Section 3). An exhaustive analysis contemplating all possible combinations would have required around 9 years (instead of the initially estimated 1 year) using the same PC (Intel i7-3770, 3,40 GHz, 16 GB RAM memory).

Each one of the two results provided in this article took a total of ~8 minutes of computational time, attaining robust and high accuracy models and simultaneously allowing setting restrictions to force the inclusion of phenomenon-relevant variables.

Free licenced SVM-light software [17] with its MATLAB extensions [18, 19] was used for the calculations.

6   Discussion

In this article, a data-driven method has been applied to create models able to distinguish L and H mode samples from a wide number of tokamaks.

The approach faced a multi-objective optimization problem. The combination of the most adequate set of plasma measurement and the SVM parameters values was automatically selected to obtain accurate models. The technique also allowed the inclusion of some desirable constraints, as 'forcing' the presence of some physics-relevant plasma quantities into the models and to 'reward' those solutions that include fewer signals.

All the calculations have been performed using a public international database. It contains samples from 19 tokamaks placed around the world. This database provides the opportunity of creating universal models applicable to all these machines. Nevertheless, the variety of the data sources was counterproductive at the time of applying them into the main algorithm due to empty entries. The signals were not always measured in all devices and therefore a revision of the data had to be performed for its use as input vectors. This selection was conditioned by the number of samples it was necessary to retain. This number depended on the amount of plasma signals to include in the final database, having in mind that the larger the amount of variables, the higher the probability of having an unfilled entry (and therefore the higher the chances to discard that sample from the database). As final compromise it was decided to consider 15 signals. The consequence was the reduction of the original database from 9880 to 3580 entries. The decision is reasonable, especially taking into account other studies with the same database and considerably more radical sample eliminations [9].

Two models were developed, both of them attaining high accuracies (above 98,60% of correct classifications), each one of them requiring only three signals. The reduced number of parameters allowed drawing the separating hyperplanes into three-dimensional plots, which helps the understanding of the relationship among the involved measurements by simple visual inspections.

Another very important aggregate the GAs supplied was a drastic reduction of the computational times. An analogue procedure, using instead of GAs an exhaustive analysis, would have taken around 9 years with the same PC and software.

A noteworthy aspect of the achieved results is that the solutions, even if they are obviously non-linear, present a smooth shape, which suggests a high generalization power. This point was reinforced by the several (3, exactly) repetitions of a 2-fold cross-validation training/testing method to evaluate each one of the individuals in the main GA code. Finally, it is interesting to notice that regardless the 2 solutions are very different (not even one plasma signal is shared in the 2 models) they have converged into remarkably similar and high accuracy results.

References

1. https://www.ipp.mpg.de/16195/asdex
2. Wagner, F., et al.: Phys. Rev. Lett. **53**, 1453–1456 (1984)

3. Chankin, A.V.: Fusion. Plasma Phys. Control **39**, 1059 (1997)
4. Rogister, A.L.: Fusion. Plasma Phys. Control **36**, A219 (1994)
5. Scott, B., et al.: In: Proc. 16th Int. Conf. on Fusion Energy (Montreal, Canada, 1996), vol **2**, 649. IAEA, Vienna (1996)
6. Shaing, K.C., Crume, E.C.: Phys. Rev. Lett. **63**, 2369 (1989)
7. Vega, J., et al.: Nucl. Fusion **49**, 085023. doi:10.1088/0029-5515/49/8/085023
8. Rattá, G.A., et al.: Fusion Engineering and Design **83**(2–3), 467–470, April 2008
9. Murari, A., et al.: Nuclear Instruments and Methods in Physics Research Section A: Accelerators, Spectrometers, Detectors and Associated Equipment. **623**(2), 850–854 (November 11, 2010)
10. Yao, K., Huang, Y.: 39th EPS Conference & 16th Int. Congress on Plasma Physics (2012)
11. http://efdasql.ipp.mpg.de/threshold/Public/ThresholdDbInfo/ThresholdvarDB2_3.htm
12. Mitchell, M.: MIT Press. (1996) ISBN 780585030944
13. Alander, J.T.: Proceedings CompEuro, Computer Systems and Software Engineering, 6th Annual European Computer Conference, pp. 65–70 (1992)
14. De Jong, K.A., Spears, W.M.: Parallel Problem Solving from Nature. LNCS, vol. 496, pp. 38-47. Springer, Heidelberg (1991)
15. Liu, Z.X., et al: Nucl. Fusion 53, 073041 (2013)
16. Maingi, R., et al: Nucl. Fusion 45, 1066 (2005)
17. Joachims, T.: Advances in Kernel Methods - Support Vector Learning. MIT-Press (1999)
18. MATLAB and Statistics Toolbox. The MathWorks, Inc., Natick, Massachusetts, United States
19. Briggs, T.: MATLAB/MEX Interface to SVMlight. http://sourceforge.net/projects/mex-svm/

How to Handle Error Bars in Symbolic Regression for Data Mining in Scientific Applications

A. Murari[1], E. Peluso[2(✉)], M. Gelfusa[2], M. Lungaroni[2], and P. Gaudio[2]

[1] Consorzio RFX-Associazione EURATOM-ENEA per la Fusione,
Corso Stati Uniti, 4, 35127 Padova, Italy
[2] Associazione EURATOM-ENEA - University of Rome "Tor Vergata",
Via del Politecnico 1, 00133 Rome, Italy
emmanuele.peluso@uniroma2.it

Abstract. Symbolic regression via genetic programming has become a very useful tool for the exploration of large databases for scientific purposes. The technique allows testing hundreds of thousands of mathematical models to find the most adequate to describe the phenomenon under study, given the data available. In this paper, a major refinement is described, which allows handling the problem of the error bars. In particular, it is shown how the use of the geodesic distance on Gaussian manifolds as fitness function allows taking into account the uncertainties in the data, from the beginning of the data analysis process. To exemplify the importance of this development, the proposed methodological improvement has been applied to a set of synthetic data and the results have been compared with more traditional solutions.

Keywords: Genetic programming · Symbolic regression · Geodesic distance · Scaling laws

1 Introduction

One of the main objectives of data analysis in scientific applications consists of the task of extracting from the data mathematical expressions for the problem at hand, to be compared with theoretical models and computer simulations. In the last years, symbolic regression (SR) via genetic programming (GP) has proved to be a very useful approach to this task. The method allows exploring the available databases and identifying among the mathematical expressions produced, the Best Unconstrained Empirical Model Structure (BUEMS) to describe the phenomena of interest. The main advantage of the proposed approach consists of practically eliminating any assumption about the mathematical form of the models. The obtained equations are therefore data driven and not hypothesis driven. The basic elements of symbolic regression via genetic programming are covered in Section 2.

© Springer International Publishing Switzerland 2015
A. Gammerman et al. (Eds.): SLDS 2015, LNAI 9047, pp. 347–355, 2015.
DOI: 10.1007/978-3-319-17091-6_29

In the last years, SR via GP has been successfully applied in various fields and has obtained significant results even in the analysis of very complex systems such as high temperature plasmas for the study of thermonuclear fusion [1]. On the other hand, the methodology is still in evolution and would benefit from upgrades aimed at increasing both its versatility and the quality of its results.

In this paper, an approach to handle the error bars in the measurements is proposed, to increase the scientific relevance of the method. Indeed in many scientific studies, such as the extraction of scaling laws from large data sets, very often the measurements are taken as perfect or at least the consequence of their uncertainties is not properly evaluated. In this work, it is shown how the error bars of the measurements can be taken into account in a principled way from the beginning of the data analysis process using the concept of the Geodesic distance on Gaussian Manifolds (GD). The idea, behind the approach proposed, consists of considering the measurements not as points, but as Gaussian distributions. This is a valid assumption in many physics applications, because the measurements are typically affected by a wide range of noise sources, which from a statistical point of view can be considered random variables. Each measurement can therefore be modelled as a probability density function (pdf) of the Gaussian type, determined by its mean μ and its standard deviation σ. The distance between the measurements and the estimates of the various models can therefore be calculated using the GD using the Rao formula (see Section 4). This distance can be used as fitness function in the SR code to converge on the most suitable model taking into account the error bars of the measurements in a principled way, since the beginning of the data analysis process.

With regard to the structure of the paper, SR via GP is introduced in the next section. The mathematical formalism of the GD on Gaussian manifolds is presented in Section 3. The potential of the proposed technique to tackle the uncertainties in the data is illustrated with a series of numerical tests using synthetic data. Some examples of application are described in detail in Section 4. Summary and directions of future activities are the subject of the last section of the paper.

2   The Basic Version of Symbolic Regression via Genetic Programming

As mentioned in the previous section, this paper describes the refinement of advanced statistical techniques for the extraction of mathematical expressions from large databases to investigate the behaviour of scientific phenomena. The main advantage of the basic tools consists of practically eliminating any assumption about the form of the models. This section describes briefly the mathematical basis of the tools implemented to perform the analysis presented in the rest of the paper.

The objective of the method consists of testing various mathematical expressions to model a certain phenomenon, given a database. The main stages to perform such a task are reported in Figure 1. First of all, the various candidate formulas are expressed as trees, composed of functions and terminal nodes. The function nodes can be standard arithmetic operations and/or any mathematical functions, squashing terms as well as user-defined operators [2,3]. The terminal nodes can be independent variables or constants (integer or real). This representation of the formulas allows an easy implementation of symbolic regression with Genetic Programming. Genetic Programs (GPs) are computational methods able to solve complex and non-linear optimization problems [2,3]. They have been inspired by the genetic processes of living organisms. In nature, individuals of a population compete for basic resources. Those individuals that achieve better surviving capabilities have higher probabilities to generate descendants. As consequence, better adapted individuals' genes have a higher probability to be passed on to the next generations.

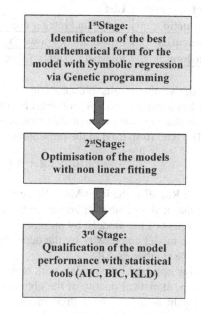

Fig. 1. The main steps of the proposed methodology to identify the best models without assumption on their mathematical form

GPs emulate this behaviour. They work with a population of individuals, e.g mathematical expressions in our case. Each individual represents a possible solution to a problem. A fitness function (FF) is used to measure how good an individual is with respect to the environment. A higher probability to have descendants is assigned to those individuals with better FF. Therefore, the better the adequacy (the value of the FF) of an individual to a problem, the higher is the probability that its genes are propagated.

In our application, the role of the genes is played by the basis functions used to build the trees representing the various formulas. The list of basis functions used to obtain the results described in the rest of the paper is reported in Table I. Evolution is achieved by using operators that perform genetic like operations such as reproduction, crossover and mutation. Reproduction involves selecting an individual from the current population and allowing it to survive by copying it into the new population. The crossover operation involves choosing nodes in two parent trees and swapping the respective branches thus creating two new offsprings. Mutations are random modifications of parts of the trees.

Table 1. Types of function nodes included in the symbolic regression used to derive the results presented in this paper, x_i and x_j are the generic independent variables

Function class	List
Arithmetic	c (real and integer constants),+,-,*,/
Exponential	exp(x_i),log(x_i),power(x_i, x_j), power(x_i,c)
Squashing	logistic(x_i),step(x_i),sign(x_i),gauss(x_i),tanh(x_i), erf(x_i),erfc(x_i)

To derive the results presented in this paper, the Akaike Information Criterion (AIC) has been adopted [4] for the FF. The AIC, is a well-known model selection criterion that is widely used in statistics, to identify the best models and avoid overfitting. The AIC form used in the present work is:

$$AIC = 2k + n \cdot \ln(RMSE/n) \qquad (1)$$

where RMSE is the Root Mean Square Error, k is the number of nodes used for the model and n the number of entries in the database (DB). The AIC allows rewarding the goodness of the models, by minimizing their residuals, and at the same time penalising the model complexity by the dependence on the number of nodes. The better a model, the smaller its AIC.

Having optimised the models with non-linear fitting, what remains is the qualification of the statistical quality of the obtained scaling laws. To this end, a series of statistical indicators have been implemented. They range from model selection criteria, such as the Bayesian Information Criterion (BIC), to statistical indicators, such as the Kullback-Leibler divergence (KLD) [5,6].

3   Geodesic Distance to Include the Effects of the Error Bars and Application to Scaling Laws

As seen in the previous sections, the goal of SR via GP is to extract the most appropriate formulas to describe the available data. To achieve this, typically the RMSE of the distances between the data and the model predictions is used in the FF. In this way, SR is implicitly adopting the Euclidean distance. The (dis)similarity between data points and predictions is measured with the Euclidean distance, which has a precise geometrical meaning and a very long historical pedigree. However, it implicitly requires considering all data as single infinitely precise values. This assumption can be appropriate in other applications but it is obviously not the case in science, since all the measurements typically present error bars. The idea is to develop a new distance between data, which would take into account the measurement uncertainties. The additional information provided by this distance should hopefully render the final results more robust. In particular, using the GD the final equations are more general and less vulnerable to the detrimental effects of outliers (see Section 4).

The idea, behind the approach proposed in this paper, consists of considering the measurements not as points, but as Gaussian distributions. This is a valid assumption in many scientific applications, because the measurements are affected by a wide range of noise sources, which from a statistical point of view can be considered random variables. Since the various noises are also typically additive, they can be expected to lead to measurements with a global Gaussian distribution around the most probable value, the actual value of the measured quantity. Each measurement can therefore be modelled as a probability density function (pdf) of the Gaussian type, determined by its mean μ and its standard deviation σ:

$$p(x|\mu, \sigma) = \frac{1}{\sqrt{2\pi}\sigma} exp\left[-\frac{(x-\mu)^2}{2\sigma^2}\right] \tag{2}$$

In this work, having in mind applications to experimental data, it is assumed that the measured values are the most likely ones, within the probability distribution representing the measurement errors. In the case of Gaussian distributions, the most likely value is the mean. Therefore, the individual measurements are assumed to be the means of the Gaussian distributions representing their uncertainties. This is the typical hypothesis adopted in the application of the GD.

Modelling measurements not as punctual values, but as Gaussian distributions, requires defining a distance between Gaussians. The most appropriate definition of distance between Gaussian distributions is the geodesic distance (GD), on the probabilistic manifold containing the data, which can be calculated using the Fischer-Rao metric [7]. For two univariate Gaussian distributions $p_1(x|\mu_1, \sigma_1)$ and $p_2(x|\mu_2, \sigma_2)$, parametrized by their mean μ_i and standard deviations $\sigma_i (i = 1,2)$, the geodesic distance GD is given by:

$$GD(p_1||p_2) = \sqrt{2}\ln\frac{1+\delta}{1-\delta} = 2\sqrt{2}\tanh^{-1}\delta, \text{ where } \delta = \left[\frac{(\mu_1-\mu_2)^2+2(\sigma_1-\sigma_2)^2}{(\mu_1-\mu_2)^2+2(\sigma_1+\sigma_2)^2}\right]^{\frac{1}{2}} \tag{3}$$

In the case of multiple independent Gaussian variables, it is easy to prove that the square GD between products of distributions is given by the sum of the squared GDs between corresponding individual distributions.

The last thing required consists of inserting the GD into the SR. To this end, a good solution has proved to be to insert the GD in the FF according to the following formula:

$$AIC = 2k + \sum_i GD_i \tag{4}$$

Where the symbols have the same meaning as in formula (1) and the index i runs over the entries of the database.

4   Example of Application: Scaling Laws

To exemplify the flexibility and power of the techniques described in the previous section, they are applied to the problem of deriving scaling laws from the data. Section 4.1 contains an introduction to the problem of data driven scaling laws. In Section 4.2 the capability of the upgraded methodology to identify also scaling laws is proven using synthetic data.

4.1   Scaling Laws

In various fields of science, such as Magnetic Confinement Nuclear Fusion, many systems to be studied are too complex to allow a treatment on the basis of first principle physical models. Therefore, to overcome the gap between theoretical under-standing and data, in order to profit from the deluge of experimental measurements of the last decades, data driven models have become quite popular. They are particularly useful to assessing how system properties scale with dimensions or other parameters. One major hypothesis is implicitly accepted in the vast majority of the most credited scaling laws reported in the literature [9,10]: the fact that the scaling laws are in form of power law monomials. Indeed the available databases have typically been studied using traditional log regression. This implies that the final scaling laws are assumed "a priori" to be power law monomials of the form: $B^\beta C^\chi \dots D^\delta G^{-\gamma} H^{-\lambda} \dots K^{-\mu}$; where the capital letters represent physical quantities [11]. This assumption on the form of these scaling equations is often not justified neither on theoretical nor on experimental grounds. Moreover, the use of log regression to analyse the data typically does not take into account the uncertainties in the measurements properly. The two develop-ments described in the previous sections overcome these limitations. SR via GP allows the freedom to identify scaling laws of very different mathematical forms and the GD can take properly into account the error bars in the measurements. The profit of combining these two approaches (SR via GP and a Gaussian manifold based me-tric) in the proposed tool are shown in the next Section using synthetic data.

4.2   Numerical Results

Synthetic databases have been generated to test the Euclidean metric and Geodesic metric as fitness function for SR via GP. Four formulas have been investigated , each one composed of two terms with three independent variables and one dependent vari-able, as showing the equations (5), (6), (7), (8). The range of variation of the three independent variables is also reported $x_1 \in [0.015, 3.9]$, $x_2 \in [0.044, 1.97]$, $x_3 \in [0.268, 2.178]$. Values are randomly generated, uniformly distributed within the vari-ation range of the independent variables, in relation to the size of the database. The study is performed by choosing the number of entries in the DB, then checking if the genetic algorithm, with the different metrics, gives in output the formulas used to generate the data.

$$f_1 = \cos(x_1 \cdot x_2) + \sin x_1^{0.5} \tag{5}$$

$$f_2 = \cos\left(\frac{x_1}{x_2}\right) + 2x_3 \cdot \{1/[1 + exp(-0.8 \cdot x_2)]\} \tag{6}$$

$$f_3 = x_2^{1.5} \cdot x_3 - 0.5 \cdot x_1^{0.5} \cdot \cos x_3 \tag{7}$$

$$f_4 = x_1 \cdot x_2 \cdot exp(-x_3) + 2x_3 \tag{8}$$

After the choice of the formula and the size of the inputs, it is possible to choose the type of noise to be applied to the analytical formulation: Uniform, Gaussian and Asymmetric. In the case of uniform noise, it is possible to set the percentage of noise compared to the average value of the chosen analytical formulation. Hence, a random uniform vector is generated, including values between +/- the percentage of the mean value of the used formula. This noise vector is then applied to the dependent variable to generate the noise-affected database. In the case of Gaussian noise, the standard deviation of the distribution of the noise can be selected. This way, a random noise of Gaussian distribution, which has zero mean and standard deviation equal to a percentage of the average value of the chosen analytical formulation, is generated. After that, this noise vector is applied to the dependent variable to generate the noise-affected database. The last type of noise is asymmetric. It consist of two random Gaussian distributions, in which the user can choose the standard deviations of the two distributions, always equal to a percentage of the average value of the analytical formulation. And more, the weight of the first distribution can be chosen, while the second is complementary to the first. The first Gaussian distribution always has zero mean, while the second has mean equal to two times the sum of the two standard deviations. Also, in this case the noise vector is then applied to the dependent variable to generate the noise-affected database.

Once the noise-affected databases are generated, as described before, Symbolic Regressions adopting the Euclidean metric and the Geodesic metric (introduced in section3) are used to study the behaviour of the algorithm. In all the cases in which the noise distributions are Gaussian noise or Uniform noise, the two metrics have provide exactly the same results. This is true for independently from the size of the databases. On the other hand, when the database contains outliers there is a significant improvement in the results of the Geodesic metric compared to the Euclidean metric. Table II shows the results of the SR conducted to database of 50 inputs (very few). This is challenging scenario to check which metric gives the best results in relation the presence of outliers (asymmetric database). In the columns the table shows the characteristic parameters of the asymmetric noise (described previously), the metric used and the standard deviations (for GD metric).The accuracy of algorithm in finding the right formula is shown in the last column. The results that can be found are classified as follows: Global, the algorithm finds perfectly the formulation expected; (1/2) the algorithm finds, at least, the first term of the formulation; (2/2) the algorithm finds, at least, the second term of the formulation; Negative, when the algorithm does not find any terms of the formulation.

Table 2. Summary table of tests carried out on the database of 50 inputs (where there are five points outliers) to the equations from (5) to (8), containing details of all the noise information and the metric listed in this section

Type Noise	Eq.	σ I Gauss [%mean value]	σ II Gauss [%mean value]	Weight I Gauss $\in[0,1]$	Metric	GD σ data [%]	GD σ model [%]	Goals
Asymmetric	(5)	15	30	0.9	EUC	---	---	(1/2)
Asymmetric	(5)	15	30	0.9	GD	20	0.1	Global
Asymmetric	(6)	10	50	0.9	EUC	---	---	Negative
Asymmetric	(6)	10	50	0.9	GD	20	0.1	(1/2)
Asymmetric	(7)	15	30	0.9	EUC	---	---	(1/2)
Asymmetric	(7)	15	30	0.9	GD	10	0.1	(1/2)
Asymmetric	(8)	10	50	0.9	EUC	---	---	Negative
Asymmetric	(8)	10	50	0.9	GD	10	0.1	Global

5   Discussion and Conclusions

In this paper, symbolic regression via genetic programming has been tested on different custom noise-affected databases to check the most challenging scenarios in relation to the fitness function (FF) of the algorithm. In the study, many variations of the parameters of the noise have been carried out on all four formulas presented. The obtained results demonstrate that the two metric, Euclidean and Gaussian, return the same performance, for all levels of Gaussian noise and dimensions of the database investigated. On the other hand, when the Geodesic distance is used, the method is significantly more robust to the presence of outliers because the GD tends to discriminate the data too far from the main trend.

So, to summarise, in the case of databases affected by Gaussian noise, SR via GP performs equally well irrespective of the fact the Euclidean or the Geodesic distance is used. In these cases, the using the GD simply provides an alternative way to double-check the quality of the results as it can be seen in Table III. In the case of small databases, affected by a significant percentage of outliers, the use of the GD improves the resilience and the reliability of the results compared to the RMSE. In these situations, as in the case of classification as reported in [12], the use of the GD provides a competitive advantage compared to the traditional RMSE based on the Euclidean distance.

Table 3. Summary table of tests carried out on the database of 50 or 500 inputs with Gaussian noise, using the formulations from (5) to (8), containing details of all the noise information and the metric listed in this section. Results show how both metric can be used as a double check of the quality of the results.

Inputs DB	Eq.	σ I Gauss [%mean value]	Metric	GD σ data [%]	GD σ model [%]	Goals
50	(5)	30	EUC	---	--	(1/2)
50	(5)	30	GD	30	0.1	(1/2)
50	(6)	30	EUC	---	---	(1/2)
50	(6)	30	GD	30	0.1	(1/2)
50	(7)	30	EUC	---	---	(1/2)
50	(7)	30	GD	30	0.1	(1/2)
50	(8)	30	EUC	---	---	(2/2)
50	(8)	30	GD	30	0.1	(2/2)
500	(5)	20	EUC	---	---	Global
500	(5)	20	GD	20	0.1	Global
500	(6)	20	EUC	---	---	(1/2)
500	(6)	20	GD	20	0.1	(1/2)
500	(7)	20	EUC	---	---	(1/2)
500	(7)	20	GD	20	0.1	(1/2)
500	(8)	20	EUC	---	---	Global
500	(8)	20	GD	20	0.1	Global

References

1. Wesson, J.: Tokamaks, 3rd edn. Clarendon Press Oxford, Oxford (2004)
2. Schmid, M., Lipson, H.: Science, vol. 324, April 2009
3. Koza, J.R.: Genetic Programming: On the Programming of Computers by Means of Natural Selection. MIT Press, Cambridge (1992)
4. Hirotugu, A.: A new look at the statistical model identification. IEEE Transactions on Automatic Control $19(6)$, 716–723 (1974)
5. Silverman, B.W.: Density Estimation for Statistics and Data Analysis. Chapmans & Hall (1986)
6. Burnham, K.P., Anderson, D.R.: Model Selection and Multi-Model Inference: A Practical Information-Theoretic Approach, 2nd edn. Springer (2002)
7. Amari, S., Nagaoka, H.: Methods of information geometry. Translations of mathematical monographs, vol. 191. American Mathematical Society (2000)
8. Connor, J.W., Taylor, J.-B.: Nuclear Fusion 17, 5 (1977)
9. Murari, A., et al.: Nucl. Fusion **53**, 043001 (2013), doi:10.1088/0029-5515/53/4/043001
10. Murari, A., et al.: Nucl. Fusion **52**, 063016 (2012), doi:10.1088/0029-5515/52/6/063016
11. Barenblatt, G.I.: Scaling. Cambridge University Press (2003)
12. Murari, A., et al.: Nucl. Fusion **53**, 033006, (9 p.) (2013)

Applying Forecasting to Fusion Databases

Gonzalo Farias[1]([✉]), Sebastián Dormido-Canto[2], Jesús Vega[3],
and Norman Díaz[1]

[1] Pontificia Universidad Catolica de Valparaiso, Valparaiso, Chile
gonzalo.farias@ucv.cl, christophare@gmail.com
[2] Departamento de Informática y Automática, UNED, Madrid, Spain
sebas@dia.uned.es
[3] Laboratorio Nacional de Fusión, CIEMAT, Madrid, Spain
jesus.vega@ciemat.es

Abstract. This manuscript describes the application of four forecasting
methods to predict future magnitudes of plasma signals during the discharge. One application of the forecasting could be to provide in advance
signal magnitudes in order to detect in real-time previously known patterns such as plasma instabilities. The forecasting was implemented for
four different prediction techniques from classical and machine learning
approaches. The results show that the performance of predictions can get
a high level of accuracy and precision. In fact, over 95 % of predictions
match the real magnitudes in most signals.

Keywords: Forecasting · Signals · SVR · ARIMA

1 Introduction

Every experiment in a nuclear fusion device produces thousands of signals with
enormous amounts of data. For instance, in JET (the biggest world fusion device)
every discharge of about tents of seconds, can generate 10GB of acquired data.
ITER (the international nuclear fusion project) could storage until 1 TByte per
shot. Bolometry, density, temperature, and soft X-rays are just some examples of
the thousands of data acquired during a discharge. Huge databases, with enormous amount of data, are a common situation in experimental fusion devices.

During last years, a great effort has been done in order to apply pattern
recognition and machine learning techniques to speed up the processing and
perform automatic analysis of the massive fusion databases. Some examples of
this work can be found in [1–3]. Despite of these advances, there is still a room
for improvements. In particular, this work proposes the use of several techniques
to perform forecasting in real-time of six different waveforms (temporal evolution
signals) of the experimental fusion device TJ-II.

Forecasting plasma behaviour requires appropriate models to capture the
dynamics of this physical phenomenon. Once the model is obtained, it can be
used to predict a signal n samples ahead into the future by using the current and

© Springer International Publishing Switzerland 2015
A. Gammerman et al. (Eds.): SLDS 2015, LNAI 9047, pp. 356–365, 2015.
DOI: 10.1007/978-3-319-17091-6_30

past values of acquired data. To this end, large fusion databases can be useful to build suitable data-driven models in order to perform predictions.

Such predictions could be used in order to anticipate off-normal plasma behaviour during a discharge. A suitable forecasting system could in theory predict plasma well-known patterns such as disruptions[3] with enough anticipation to mitigate or even avoid the disruptive event. Late detection of these plasma instabilities can affect the integrity of plasma-facing components, which could imply unexpected non-operation periods of the device[4].

The paper is structured as follows. Section 2 introduces the waveforms considered in this work. Section 3 describes how to perform forecasting by means classical and machine learning approaches. The criteria to assess the performance of the forecasting and the main results of the work are described in Section 4. Finally, Section 5 summaries the main results and discusses future works.

2   TJ-II Fusion Database

The CIEMAT, and specially the association EURATOM/CIEMAT for magnetic confinement fusion, have obtained through many different experiments a large number of signals in the nuclear fusion device TJ-II (see Fig. 1).

Fig. 1. TJ-II fusion device stellerator

TJ-II[5] is a medium sized stellarator fusion device (Heliac type, magnetic field $B_0 = 1.2T$, average major radius $R(0) = 1.5m$, average minor radius $\leq$ $0.22m$) located at CIEMAT (Madrid, Spain) that can explore a wide rotational transform range. TJ-II plasmas are produced using electron cyclotron resonance heating (ECRH) (two gyrotrons, 300 kW each, 53.2 GHz, second harmonic, X-mode polarization) and additional neutral beam injection (NBI, 300 kW).

Fusion devices generate massive databases and typically, thousands of signals with a high number of samples are collected per discharge. In the case of TJ-II, there are over one thousand digitization channels for experimental measurements. Each signal describes a particular measurement of a physical characteristic of the plasma. Most measurements that these sensors provide are univariate time-series data. Discharges last between 150-250ms, with a repetition frequency of about 7 minutes. Depending on the sampling rate, the number of samples could be in the range of 4000-16000 per discharge. In order to show the application of forecasting methods to the TJ-II database, 6 signals have been considered here. Table 1 shows the name and description of each signal. Fig. 2 depicts the plots of the signals for a typical shot.

Table 1. Selected signals of TJ-II

Signal	Description
S1	Spectroscopic signal (CV line)
S2	Bolometer signal
S3	Line averaged electron density
S4	Electron cyclotron emission
S5	H_α emission
S6	Soft X-ray emission

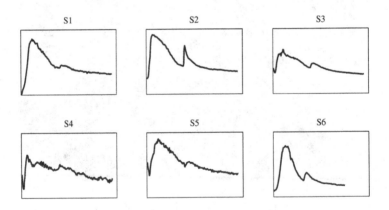

Fig. 2. Plots of signals for a typical discharge

3   Approaches to Forecasting

Before applying forecasting techniques, a pre-processing mechanism has been applied in order to reduce the number of samples of the signals. The sampling period of TJ-II raw signals is normally 0.01 ms. However, in order to make predictions from a practical point of view, a resampled version of the time serie is required. To this end, one sample of the resampled signal corresponds to the average of one hundred samples of the original version, reducing the sampling rate from 10^5 to 10^3 samples per second.

In this Section two kind of approaches will be briefly described: classical and machine learning techniques. In classical approach, the exponential smoothing (EXS)[6] and the autoregressive integrated moving average model (ARIMA)[6] are considered. On the second approach, the intelligent techniques and the training algorithm are introduced here. Experiments, testing and results are shown in next Section.

3.1   Forecasting with Classical Techniques

Prediction of future samples could be performed by considering old or past values of time serie. Classical approaches try to find mathematical relationships to make forecasting. Examples of that are the techniques such as moving average (MA), where the past observations are weighted equally, or exponential smoothing, where weights decrease exponentially over time. Equation 1 shows the mathematical relation of EXS models, where $0 < \alpha < 1$, and the variables $y(t)$ and $\hat{y}(t)$ represent the actual and predicted magnitudes. A big issue with the EXS models is to find a suitable value of α for all discharges of a signal.

$$\hat{y}(t) = \alpha y(t-1) + (1 - \alpha)\hat{y}(t-1) \tag{1}$$

On the other hand, ARIMA considers a temporal evolution signal as a stochastic process. ARIMA models are represented as ARIMA(p, d, q), where the parameters p, d, and q indicate the order of the components *autorregresive*(AR), *integrated*(I) and *moving average*(MA) respectively. ARIMA is usually applied to stationary signals in both mean and variance in order to get a model. In the case of non-stationary signals these are transformed before fitting the ARIMA model. In our case, since the data are non-stationary signals, we performed some pre-processing algorithms for normalization, logarithm transformation, and differentiation. Normalization is needed to set the range of the magnitudes from 0 to 1. To this end, the minimum and maximum magnitude for all discharges are computed. Thus, the minimum is subtracted from each sample of the signal. The result is divided by the subtraction between the maximum and the minimum. The steps for logarithm transformation and differentiation are required to get a signal with both variance and mean constants. Note that, these last steps could be applied as many times as required.

The whole process to get stationary time series data is shown in Fig. 3. After pre-processing, the order of the ARIMA model (p, d, and q) can be identified by using for instance, the autocorrelation function (AC) and the partial autocorrelation function (PACF). Once the model order is identified, all discharges of a given signal are concatenated in order to adjust the coefficients of each component of the ARIMA model.

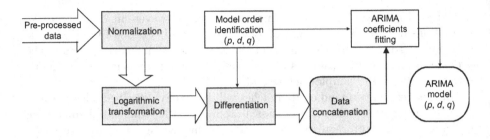

Fig. 3. Flowchart for ARIMA model fitting

3.2   Forecasting with Machine Learning Approaches

In the context of nuclear fusion databases, the main issue of classical approaches is to find an analytical mathematical expression that makes suitable predictions, which could be very hard and a very time consuming task. The process to identify the order of the ARIMA model is normally not straightforward, and the performance of the model depends strongly on the selection of the parameters and coefficients.

Rather than to find out a mathematical expression to forecast future samples, we could try to apply machine learning techniques[7] to train a data-driven model for a particular signal by considering all discharges of a campaign. To this end, we can use a scatter plot called here autoregressive map (AM), which relates past and future magnitudes of a signal (AMs are very similar to phase portrait or Forrester diagrams[8]). Fig. 4 shows an example of an autoregressive map.

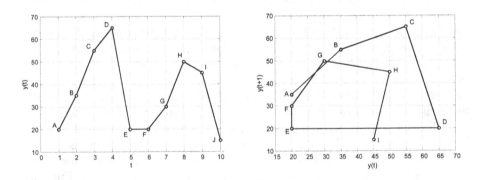

Fig. 4. A time serie and its autoregressive map for the relation $y(t) \rightarrow y(t+1)$

In this case, left plot is a time serie of 10 samples. We can build the relation $y(t) \rightarrow y(t+1)$ between current $y(t)$ and future sample $y(t+1)$ of the time serie, which is depicted on the right plot of Fig. 4. Note that the relation can take into account more past magnitudes such as $y(t-1)$ and $y(t-2)$ in order to avoid multi-valued functions of past and future samples.

Fig. 5 shows an example of an AM for the relation $[y(t), y(t-1)] \to y(t+1)$ of a particular shot of signal S2. Note that to predict future sample $y(t+1)$ we required the samples $y(t)$ and $y(t-1)$. Take into account also that a suitable predicting model for any signal should be trained considering not just one shot, but all discharges of a campaign.

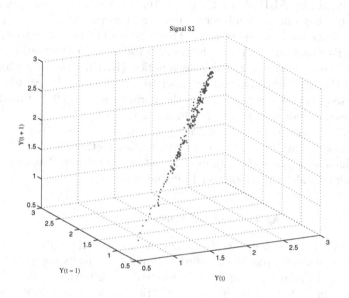

Fig. 5. An autoregressive map for the relation $[y(t), y(t-1)] \to y(t+1)$ of S2

Once we get the AM that relates past and future samples of a signal, we can use it to train a predicting model. Thus, when a new discharge is available, we can take the corresponding past values of the signal to feed the trained model and to perform forecasting. In this work, two regression techniques are considered from machine learning approach with the objective to predict future samples of a signal: artificial neural networks (ANN)[7] and support vector machines for regression (SVR)[9, 10].

4   Experimental Results

Four techniques are tested to perform forecasting with the TJ-II database: exponential smoothing (EXS), autoregressive integrated moving average models (ARIMA), artificial neural networks (ANN), and support vector machines for regression (SVR).

4.1   Experimental Setup of Forecasting Methods

Before building the models, we need to define the structure of each model. Thus, in the case of EXS it was necessary to set the weights of past samples. In the case of ARIMA, the order of p, q, and d was obtained by inspection of the PACF and ACF. After several experiments, it was concluded that a suitable structure should be ARIMA(5,1,1). Regarding to ANN, the structure includes for simplicity only one hidden layer with seven neurons. Input and output layer have five and one neuron respectively. The activation function of the output layer is the identity function, the rest of layers uses the sigmoid function. Finally, the kernel function of SVR was radial basis function (RBF). The parameters of the kernel and the regularization cost were set to $\gamma = 0.007$ and $C = 10$. The loss function used is the ϵ-insensitive with the parameter $\epsilon = 0.001$. Finally, in all cases five past values were considered to predict.

The training set includes 40 discharges, and the test set includes 27. The experiments were carried out under cross-validation methodology, which requires to select the discharges of the training and test sets randomly. The results shown in this work consider the average of 100 experiments.

4.2   Performance Assessment of Forecasting

To assess the performance of each forecasting method the criteria of accuracy and precision were selected. Both criteria are mathematically computed by using Equation 2 and Equation 3 respectively, where N denotes the number of samples of the time serie. Note that the accuracy tries to determine how close is the prediction $\widehat{y}(t)$ to the real value $y(t)$. Regarding to the precision, it intents to asses how repeatable and reproducible are the predictions (i.e., the standard deviation of predictions). The difference between both concepts can be observed in the example of Fig. 6.

$$MAPE = \frac{1}{N} \sum_{t=1}^{N} |y(t) - \widehat{y}(t)| \tag{2}$$

$$\sigma = \sqrt{\frac{1}{N} \sum_{t=1}^{N} ||y(t) - \widehat{y}(t)| - MAPE|^2} \tag{3}$$

4.3   Results

Table 2 and Table 3 show the accuracy and precision for the forecasting methods ANN, SVM, EXS and ARIMA (ARI for short). The assessment is done for 1, 3 and 5 samples ahead, i.e., $y(t+1)$, $y(t+3)$, and $y(t+5)$ respectively. Texts in bold are the best performance of each horizon of prediction.

Observing the assessment for accuracy and precision, we can conclude that both SVR and ARIMA are suitable techniques to perform forecasting with TJ-II

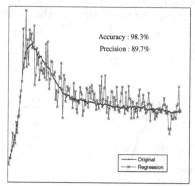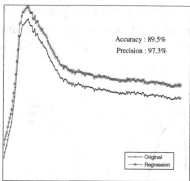

Fig. 6. Difference between accuracy and precision

Table 2. Forecasting accuracy in percentage

	ANN			SVR			EXS			ARI		
Signal	1	3	5	1	3	5	1	3	5	1	3	5
S1	96	95	93	**98**	96	94	94	92	88	**98**	**97**	**95**
S2	92	89	91	98	96	94	94	91	88	**99**	**98**	**97**
S3	97	96	94	98	96	94	94	92	88	**99**	**98**	**97**
S4	95	92	90	96	93	90	92	91	89	**99**	**98**	**97**
S5	95	93	92	96	94	92	94	92	88	**97**	**96**	**96**
S6	95	93	92	**98**	95	93	93	90	86	**98**	**96**	**94**

Table 3. Forecasting precision in percentage

	ANN			SVR			EXS			ARI		
Signal	1	3	5	1	3	5	1	3	5	1	3	5
S1	95	94	92	**98**	95	92	91	89	87	**98**	**97**	**96**
S2	95	93	92	98	94	92	91	90	90	**99**	**97**	**96**
S3	95	94	91	97	93	89	91	89	88	**99**	**98**	**97**
S4	93	90	87	96	91	88	90	89	89	**99**	**98**	**97**
S5	94	92	90	96	93	89	91	89	88	**97**	**96**	**94**
S6	94	92	90	**98**	93	90	91	88	86	**98**	**96**	**94**

signals. In both cases the accuracy and precision is over 90% for most signals. As it was expected, EXS is the worst option to make predictions. The results also shown that forecasting is much easier for 1 sample ahead than 3 or 5, no matter which method is selected. Note also that the best performance is obtained by the signal S3 and the worst performance is obtained by the signal S4, which is probably due to the noisy nature of this signal (see Fig. 2).

Fig. 7 shows the forecasting of signal S2 by using the prediction techniques SVR and ARIMA. Both plots depicts the complete predictions of the signal.The horizons of prediction are three and five samples ahead. Note that methods use five past magnitudes (lags) of the signal.

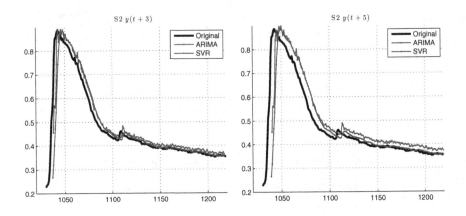

Fig. 7. SVR and ARIMA forecasting for 3 and 5 samples ahead of a signal S2

5   Summary and Future Works

This article describes the application and assessment of four different techniques to perform forecasting. Two techniques from classical approaches and two other methods from a machine learning approach. Six signals of the TJ-II databases have been selected. The results show that almost all predictions to five samples ahead reach a performance of accuracy and precision over 90% independently of the signal and the technique.

The signal S3 has the best performance (97% of accuracy and precision with ARIMA when predicting five samples ahead) and the S4 the worst (under 90% in four cases). Best predicting models were obtained in almost all cases with ARIMA, second best cases were found with SVR.

Regarding to the implementation of both ARIMA and SVR techniques, it is necessary to indicate that finding suitable ARIMA coefficients is a much more difficult task than training SVR model, this is because ARIMA needs first to identify correctly the orders p, d, and q of each component before fitting the model. In both cases, the computational costs are high, specially when involving massive databases.

Future works will focus on three big issues. Firstly, exhaustive searching could be applied in order to find better parameters (e.g. kernels, sigma, etc. in SVR or number of neurons and hidden layers in ANN) for building models. Secondly, testing other well-known techniques for prediction such as Bayes[11] theory and

Kalman filter, and finally to perform forecasting in order to detect in real time some well-known behaviours of plasma during a discharge.

Acknowledgments. This work was partially supported by Chilean Ministry of Education under the Project FONDECYT 11121590. This work was partially funded by the Spanish Ministry of Economy and Competitiveness under the Projects No ENE2012-38970-C04-01 and ENE2012-38970-C04-03.

References

1. Dormido-Canto, S., Farias, G., Vega, J., Dormido, R., Sanchez, J., Duro, N., Vargas, H., Murari, A., Contributors, J.-E.: Classifier based on support vector machine for jet plasma configurations. Review of Scientific Instruments **79**(10), 10F326–10F326 (2008)
2. Farias, G., Vega, J., Gonzalez, S., Pereira, A., Lee, X., Schissel, D., Gohil, P.: Automatic determination of l/h transition times in DIII-D through a collaborative distributed environment. Fusion Engineering and Design **87**(12), 2081–2083 (2012)
3. Vega, J., Dormido-Canto, S., López, J.M., Murari, A., Ramírez, J.M., Moreno, R., Felton, R.: Results of the JET real-time disruption predictor in the ITER-like wall campaigns. Fusion Engineering and Design **88**(6), 1228–1231 (2013)
4. Lehnen, M., Alonso, A., Arnoux, G., Baumgarten, N., Bozhenkov, S.A., Brezinsek, S., Brix, M., Eich, T., Gerasimov, S.N., Huber, A., Jachmich, S., Kruezi, U., Morgan, P.D., Plyusnin, V.V., Reux, C., Riccardo, V., Sergienko, G., Stamp, M.F., and JET EFDA contributors. Disruption mitigation by massive gas injection in JET. Nuclear Fusion 51, 123010 (12pp) (2011)
5. Alejaldre, C., Alonso, J., Almoguera, L., Ascasíbar, E., Baciero, A., Balbín, R., et al.: Plasma Phys. Controll. Fusion **41**(1), A539 (1999)
6. Peña, D., Tiao G., Tsay, R.: A course in time series analysis. John Wiley & Sons Inc., (2001)
7. Duda, R.O., Hart, P.E., Stork, D.G.: Pattern Classification. 2nd edn., John Wiley (2001)
8. Forrester, J.W.: Lessons from system dynamics modeling. Syst. Dyn. Rev. **3**, 136–149 (1987)
9. Vapnik, V.: The nature of statistical learning theory. Springer (1999)
10. Scholkopf, B., Smola, A.J.: Learning with kernels: Support vector machines, regularization, optimization, and beyond. MIT Press (2001)
11. Gelman, A., Carlin, J.B., Stern, H.S., Dunson, D.B., Vehtari, A., Rubin, D.B.: Bayesian data analysis. CRC Press (2013)

Computationally Efficient Five-Class Image Classifier Based on Venn Predictors

Jesús Vega[1(✉)], Sebastián Dormido-Canto[2], F. Martínez[2], I. Pastor[1], and M.C. Rodríguez[1]

[1] Laboratorio Nacional de Fusión, CIEMAT, Madrid, Spain
jesus.vega@ciemat.es
[2] Dpto. Informática y Automática, UNED, Madrid, Spain

Abstract. This article shows the computational efficiency of an image classifier based on a Venn predictor with the nearest centroid taxonomy. It has been applied to the automatic classification of the images acquired by the Thomson Scattering diagnostic of the TJ-II stellarator. The Haar wavelet transform is used to reduce the image dimensionality. The average time per image to classify 1144 examples (in an on-line learning setting) is 0.166 ms. The classification of the last image takes 187 ms.

Keywords: Venn predictors · Image classifier · Multi-class classifier · Thomson Scattering · Nuclear fusion

1 Introduction

The Thomson Scattering (TS) diagnostic is an essential measurement system in nuclear fusion research. It allows the simultaneous determination of two radial profiles: electron temperature and electron density. In the case of the TJ-II stellarator [1], a charge-coupled device (CCD) camera collects the light from a pulsed ruby laser that is scattered by the free electrons of the plasma. The images are two-dimensional spectra [2, 3] with the horizontal and vertical axes displaying respectively scattered wavelength and position along a plasma chord. In TJ-II, there are five different classes of images depending on the kind of measurement (fig. 1). Each class implies a different processing of the image data.

To automate the TS data processing after an image acquisition, a pattern classifier is required. A first automatic classifier [4] was based on a 5-class Support Vector Machine (SVM) predictor with the one-versus-the-rest approach (the terms predictor and classifier are used with the same meaning in this article). The TJ-II TS images have 385x576 pixels, i.e. 221760 possible attributes. To gain computational efficiency in the training process but without losing prediction efficiency, the number of attributes is reduced by means of a Haar wavelet transform [5, 6].

The classifier that is described in [4] produces non-qualified estimates, i.e. the accuracy and reliability of the predictions are not provided. After this, a specific classifier [7] based on conformal predictors [8] was developed to provide together with the image prediction, a couple of values (confidence and credibility) to show the

A. Gammerman et al. (Eds.): SLDS 2015, LNAI 9047, pp. 366–375, 2015.
DOI: 10.1007/978-3-319-17091-6_31

quality of the prediction. This specific classifier is based on the creation of a hash function [9] to generate several 'one-versus-the-rest' classifiers for every class and, finally, SVM is used as underlying algorithm. This predictor system is utilized in an on-line learning setting, i.e. examples are presented iteratively in a random order and, as images are classified, they are added to the training set with their real labels. After the classification of 600 images (whose dimensionality is reduced through the use of a Haar wavelet transform at level 4 of decomposition), the average computational time per image is 3750 ± 65 ms.

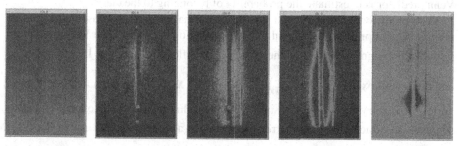

Fig. 1. Image patterns in the TJ-II Thomson Scattering. From left to right: CCD camera background (BKG), stray light without plasma or in a collapsed discharge (STRL), electron cyclotron heating (ECH) discharge, neutral beam injection (NBI) heating discharge and, finally, discharge after reaching the cut off density during ECH heating (COFF). The first two types of images are used for the diagnostic calibration and the rest are used for plasma analysis.

To significantly decrease the computation time per image, the previous conformal predictor was modified to use an SVM incremental training approach as underlying algorithm. In this case, [10], the average computational time per image after 1000 classifications is about 500 ms with a standard deviation around 20 ms. Again, the images are represented by their Haar wavelet transform at level 4.

The present article tackles the same 5-class prediction problem to automate the data analysis of the TJ-II TS diagnostic after the capture of an image. The objective is twofold. On the one hand, the computational time of the classifications will be drastically decreased. On the other hand, the predictions will be qualified with a probabilistic criterion. To accomplish both objectives, Venn predictors with the nearest centroid (NC) taxonomy will be used. Venn predictors with the NC taxonomy have shown not only a high computational efficiency but also a good predictive efficiency in several nuclear fusion applications [11, 12, 13].

Section 2 briefly describes the theory of Venn predictors. Section 3 presents the image pre-processing performed in this article. Section 4 shows the results with 15 different predictors and section 5 is devoted to briefly discussing the results.

2   Venn Predictors

In the general formulation of a classification problem with J classes, the training set is made up of pairs $(\mathbf{x}_i, y_i), i = 1,...,n$ where $\mathbf{x}_i$ is a feature vector with d attributes and $y_i \in \{Y_1, Y_2,..., Y_J\}$ is the label of its corresponding class. Given a new feature vector $\mathbf{x}_{n+1}$ to be classified into one (and only one) of the J classes, the objective of a Venn predictor is to estimate the probability of belonging to the class.

Venn predictors are a particular type of conformal predictors whose output can be interpreted as a probability interval that the prediction is correct. The Venn prediction framework assigns each one of the possible classifications $Y_j, j = 1,..., J$ to $\mathbf{x}_{n+1}$ and divides all examples $\{(\mathbf{x}_1, y_1),...,(\mathbf{x}_n, y_n),(\mathbf{x}_{n+1}, Y_j)\}$ into a number of categories. To carry out this division, Venn machines use a taxonomy function $A_n, n \in \mathbb{N}$, which classifies the relation between a sample and the set of the other samples:

$$\tau_i = A_{n+1}\left(\left\{(\mathbf{x}_1, y_1),...,(\mathbf{x}_{i-1}, y_{i-1}),(\mathbf{x}_{i+1}, y_{i+1}),...,(\mathbf{x}_{n+1}, y_{n+1})\right\},(\mathbf{x}_i, y_i)\right).$$

Values τ_i are called categories and are taken from a finite set $T = \{\tau_1, \tau_2,..., \tau_T\}$. Equivalently, a taxonomy function assigns to each sample $(\mathbf{x}_i, y_i)$ its category τ_i, or in other words, it groups all examples into a finite set of categories. This grouping should not depend on the order of examples within a sequence.

Categories are formed using only the training set. In each non-empty category τ, it is possible to compute empirical probabilities of an object to have a label y' within category τ as

$$P_\tau(y') = N_\tau(y') \Big/ N_\tau$$

where N_τ is the total number of examples from the training set that are assigned to category τ and $N_\tau(y')$ is the number of examples within category τ having label y'.

At this point, given a new example $\mathbf{x}_{n+1}$ with unknown label y_{n+1}, it has to be assigned to the most likely category of those already found using only the training set. Let this category be τ^*. The empirical probabilities $P_{\tau^*}(y')$ are considered as probabilities of the object $\mathbf{x}_{n+1}$ to have a label y'. The theory of conformal predictors [8] allows constructing several probability distributions of a label y' for a new object. First it is considered the hypothesis that the label y_{n+1} of a new object $\mathbf{x}_{n+1}$ is equal to y, $(y_{n+1} = y)$. Then, the pair $(\mathbf{x}_{n+1}, y)$ is added to the training set and the taxonomy function A is applied to the extended sequence of pairs. This groups all the elements of the sequence into categories. Let $\tau^*(\mathbf{x}_{n+1}, y)$ be the category containing the pair $(\mathbf{x}_{n+1}, y)$. Now, for this category, it is possible to calculate as previously the values N_{τ^*}, $N_{\tau^*}(y')$ and the empirical probability distribution

$$P_{\tau^*(\mathbf{x}_{n+1}, y)}(y') = {N_{\tau^*}(y')}\big/{N_{\tau^*}}.$$

This distribution depends implicitly on the object $\mathbf{x}_{n+1}$ and its hypothetical label y. Trying all possible hypothesis of the label y_{n+1} being equal to y, a set of distributions $P_y(y') = P_{\tau^*(\mathbf{x}_{n+1}, y)}(y')$ for all possible labels y are obtained. In general, these distributions will be different since when the value of y is changed, it is also changed (in general), firstly the grouping into categories, secondly the category $\tau^*(\mathbf{x}_{n+1}, y)$ containing the pair $(\mathbf{x}_{n+1}, y)$ and, finally, the numbers N_{τ^*} and $N_{\tau^*}(y')$. Therefore, the output of a Venn predictor is made up of as many distributions as the number of possible labels.

In other words, in a multi-class problem with J possible classes $\{Y_1, Y_2, ..., Y_J\}$, J different probability distributions are obtained. Each one is a row vector with J elements $\left(P_{y=Y_K}(Y_1), P_{y=Y_K}(Y_2), ..., P_{y=Y_K}(Y_J)\right)$ that are the probabilities of the several labels $Y_1, Y_2, ..., Y_J$ into the category τ^* with the assumption that $y = Y_K$. In this way, a square matrix of dimension J is obtained:

$$P_J = \begin{pmatrix} P_{y=Y_1}(Y_1) & P_{y=Y_1}(Y_2) & \vdots & P_{y=Y_1}(Y_J) \\ P_{y=Y_2}(Y_1) & P_{y=Y_2}(Y_2) & \vdots & P_{y=Y_2}(Y_J) \\ \hdashline P_{y=Y_J}(Y_1) & P_{y=Y_J}(Y_2) & \vdots & P_{y=Y_J}(Y_J) \end{pmatrix}$$

From this matrix, the Venn predictor outputs the prediction $\hat{y}_n = Y_{j_{best}}$, where

$$j_{best} = \arg \max_{j=1,\ldots,J} \overline{p(j)}$$

and $\overline{p(j)}, j = 1, \ldots, J$ is the mean of the probabilities obtained for label $Y_j, j = 1, \ldots J$ among all probability distributions (i.e. the mean of every column of matrix P_J). In words, the prediction is the label of the column with the maximum mean value. The probability interval for the prediction $\hat{y}_n = Y_{j_{best}}$ is $\left[L\left(Y_{j_{best}}\right), U\left(Y_{j_{best}}\right)\right]$, where $U\left(Y_{j_{best}}\right)$ and $L\left(Y_{j_{best}}\right)$ are respectively the maximum and minimum probability of the column j_{best}.

In this article, as mentioned in the introduction, the selected taxonomy has been the nearest centroid taxonomy [14]. Owing to the fact that there are five different types of images, the number of categories in the NC Venn taxonomy is also 5. This means that the NC taxonomy sets the category of a pair equal to the label of its nearest centroid. The mathematical formulation of the NC taxonomy is

$$\tau_i = A_n\left(\left\{(\mathbf{x}_1, y_1), \ldots, (\mathbf{x}_{i-1}, y_{i-1}), (\mathbf{x}_{i+1}, y_{i+1}), \ldots, (\mathbf{x}_n, y_n)\right\}, (\mathbf{x}_i, y_i)\right) = Y_j$$

where

$$j = \arg \min_{j=1,2,\ldots,5} \|\mathbf{x}_i - \mathbf{C}_j\|,$$

$\mathbf{C}_j$ are the centroids of the five classes and ‖.‖ is a distance metric. In this article, the Euclidean distance has been chosen.

For the reader convenience, it is important to mention other types of taxonomies that can be used with multi-class problems in the Venn prediction framework. Five different taxonomies are analyzed in [15], where the Venn predictors are based on neural networks. Lambrou et al. [16] shows an application of inductive conformal predictors to develop an inductive Venn predictor with a taxonomy derived from a multi-class Support Vector Machine classifier. Nouretdinov et al. [17] describes the logistic taxonomy, which is created from the method of logistic regression.

3   Image Pre-processing

As it was mentioned previously, the objective of this article is to develop a new automatic classification system for the TJ-II TS images to both reduce the classification computational time and obtain a prediction probability interval. To this end, Venn predictors with the NC taxonomy in an on-line learning setting are used. But it is well-known that any conformal predictor in an on-line learning setting can be very expensive from a computational point of view. In the present case, the images have

221760 possible attributes and, therefore, a first attempt to reduce the computational time is to decrease the signal dimensionality without losing essential information.

Analysis of bi-dimensional signals is getting great improvements by using Wavelet based methods. Due to the fact that the wavelet decomposition is multi-scale, images can be characterized by a set of approximation coefficients and three sets of detailed coefficients (horizontal, vertical and diagonal). The approximation coefficients represent coarse image information (they contain the most part of the image energy), whereas the details are close to zero (but the information they represent can be relevant in a particular context). Therefore, the initial TJ-II TS images (221760 attributes) have been decomposed with the Haar wavelet transform at different levels (from level 2 to level 6) and several combinations of approximation and vertical details coefficients have been taken into account (table 1). Due to the particular patterns of the TJ-II TS diagnostic, horizontal and diagonal detail coefficients are not useful for a proper discrimination of the classes.

Table 1. A total number of 15 Venn predictors with the NC taxonomy have been developed to analyse the effect of the decomposition level and the selection of coefficients on the prediction reliability and computational time. The last and last but one columns indicate de wavelet coefficients (approximation or vertical details) taken into account with each predictor. When both coefficients are set, the attributes are the sum of the approximation and vertical details coefficients.

#predictor	Haar decomposition level	Approximation coefficients	Vertical detail coefficients
1	2 (13968 attributes/image)	x	
2	3 (3528 attributes/image)	x	
3	4 (900 attributes/image)	x	
4	5 (234 attributes/image)	x	
5	6 (63 attributes/image)	x	
6	2 (13968 attributes/image)		x
7	3 (3528 attributes/image)		x
8	4 (900 attributes/image)		x
9	5 (234 attributes/image)		x
10	6 (63 attributes/image)		x
11	2 (13968 attributes/image)	x	x
12	3 (3528 attributes/image)	x	x
13	4 (900 attributes/image)	x	x
14	5 (234 attributes/image)	x	x
15	6 (63 attributes/image)	x	x

It should be noted the high dimensionality reduction carried out with the wavelet transform. According to table 1, the reduction with regard to the initial images goes from 93.70% (level 2) to 99.97% (level 6).

4   Results

A dataset of 1149 images has been used. The number of images corresponding to
the five classes BKG, STRL, ECH, NBI and COFF is respectively 107, 205, 461, 334
and 42.

As mentioned, the Venn predictors with the NC taxonomy are tested in an on-line
learning setting. The initial training set contains just one image of each type. The rest
of images (1144) are randomly chosen and classified one by one. After the prediction,
each image is added to the training set with each real class (the predicted class could
be different from the real one).

Fig. 2 shows the results of predictors 1-5, which correspond to use as attributes the
approximation coefficients of the wavelet transform at the selected decomposition
levels. The plots illustrate the cumulative success rate (CSR), the upper success probability curve (USPC) and the lower success probability curve (LSPC) after the classification of 1144 images.

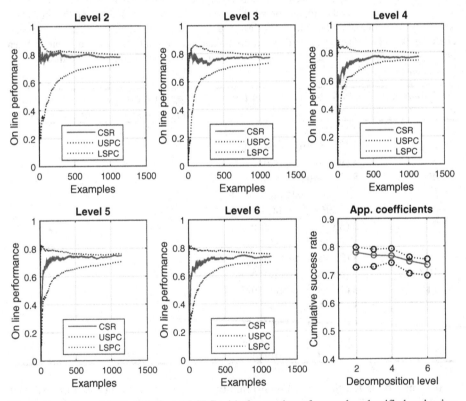

Fig. 2. Evolution of CSR, USPC and LSPC with the number of examples classified and using
as attributes the approximation coefficients of the Haar wavelet transform

The CSR is computed as

$$CSR_n = \frac{1}{n}\sum_{i=1}^{n} succ_i$$

where $succ_i = 1$ if the example is correctly classified at trial i and $succ_i = 0$ otherwise. In the same way, the LSPC and the USPC respectively follow

$$LSPC_n = \frac{1}{n}\sum_{i=1}^{n} l_i$$

$$USPC_n = \frac{1}{n}\sum_{i=1}^{n} u_i$$

where l_i and u_i define the probability interval of the prediction at trial i: $[l_i, u_i]$.

Table 2. Average computational time of Venn predictors and the NC taxonomy in the on-line learning setting

Wavelet transform decomposition level	Computation time (ms/example)
2	2.404
3	0.614
4	0.166
5	0.051
6	0.013

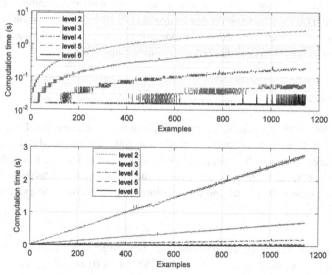

Fig. 3. Semilogarithmic and linear plots of the computational times with the Venn predictors and the NC taxonomy in the on-line learning setting

The plots at the different decomposition levels show that the probabilities provided by the Venn predictors are 'well calibrated'. This means that these probabilities have a frequentist justification because they contain the cumulative success rate in all cases. Also, it is important to note how the probability interval becomes narrower as more examples are included in the training set. In other words, the effect of the learning process produces more efficient predictions, i.e. narrower probability intervals.

The right-most bottom plot summarizes the result of example 1144 at the different decomposition levels. This last example result should be interpreted as a summary of the maximum knowledge acquired by each respective predictor (they have both the largest training set and the narrowest prediction interval). The predictors at levels 2, 3 and 4 can be considered equivalent since the probability prediction intervals are comparable. The preferred predictor is the one obtained at level 4 because it shows higher prediction efficiency, i.e. the tightest prediction interval.

Predictors 6-10 use only the vertical detail coefficients and provide very wide probability intervals at decomposition levels 2 and 3. In general, their predictions are worse than the ones obtained with predictors 1-5. The results with predictors 11-15, which use as attributes the sum of approximation and vertical detail coefficients, do not show better predictions, in spite of including a combination of predictors 1-10.

From the analysis of these predictors, it is possible to conclude that the best ones use the approximation coefficients as attributes and, in particular, the corresponding to a decomposition level of 4 (predictor #3 of table 1) allows obtaining the best predictive efficiency. It is important to emphasize that these predictors use just one example per class in the initial training set.

Finally, fig. 3 shows the computation time evolution as the number of training examples is increased. Of course, the highest times correspond to the case with higher number of attributes per image (Haar wavelet decomposition at level 2). It should be noted the linear behavior of the computational time with the number of examples. Table 2 presents the average times per image at different decomposition levels of the wavelet transform. The standard deviations are below tens of microseconds. These times are two orders of magnitude below the ones obtained in [10].

5   Discussion

Venn predictors with the nearest centroid taxonomy, on the one hand, allow for high success rates with narrow probability prediction intervals in the classification of the TJ-II TS images. On the other hand, the average computational time is orders of magnitude below previous results. In the case of the predictor #3 in table 1, the average computational time is 0.166 ms and the absolute time to classify the example #1144 is 187 ms.

Acknowledgments. This work was partially funded by the Spanish Ministry of Economy and Competitiveness under the Projects No ENE2012-38970-C04-01 and ENE2012-38970-C04-03.

References

1. Sánchez, J., et al.: Overview of TJ-II experiments. Nuclear Fusion 51, 094022 (10p.) (2011)
2. Barth, C.J., et al.: Review of Scientific Instruments 70, 763 (1999)
3. Herranz, J., et al.: Fusion Engineering and Design 65, 525 (2003)
4. Vega, J., Pastor, I., Cereceda, J. L., Pereira, A., Herranz, J., Pérez, D., Rodríguez, M.C., Farias, G., Dormido-Canto, S., Sánchez, J., Dormido, R., Duro, N., Dormido, S., Pajares, G., Santos, M., de la Cruz, J. M.: Application of intelligent classification techniques to the TJ-II Thomson Scattering diagnostic. In: 32th EPS Plasma Physics Conference, Junio 27-Julio 1, Tarragona (2005) (España). http://eps2005.ciemat.es
5. Daubechies, I.: Ten Lectures on Wavelets. SIAM. (1992)
6. Mallat, S.: A Wavelet Tour of Signal Processing, 2nd edn. Academia Press (2001)
7. Makili, L., Vega, J., Dormido-Canto, S., Pastor, I., Murari, A.: Computationally efficient SVM multi-class image recognition with confidence measures. Fusion Engineering and Design 86, 1213–1216 (2011)
8. Vovk, V., Gammerman, A., Shafer, G.: Algorithmic learning in a random world. Springer (2005).
9. Saunders, C., Gammerman, A., Vovk, V.: Computationally efficient transductive machines. In: Okamoto, T., Hartley, R., Kinshuk, Klus, J. (eds.) Proceedings of 11th International Conference on Algorithmic Learning Theory, pp. 325–333. IEEE Computer Society Press, Los Alamitos (2000)
10. Makili, L., Vega, J., Dormido-Canto, S.: Incremental Support vector machines for fast reliable image recognition. Fusion Engineering and Design 88, 1170–1173 (2013)
11. Vega, J., Murari, A., Dormido-Canto, S., Cruz, T.: Simulations of nuclear fusion diagnostics based on projections with Venn predictors and context drift detection. Annals of Mathematics and Artificial Intelligence (2014). http://dx.doi.org/10.1007/s10472-013-9393-3
12. Vega, J., Murari, A., Dormido-Canto, S., Moreno, R., Pereira, A., Acero, A., JET-EFDA Contributors.: Adaptive high learning rate probabilistic disruption predictors from scratch for the next generation of tokamaks. Nuclear Fusion 54, 123001 (17p.) (2014)
13. Acero, A., Vega, J., Dormido-Canto, S., Guinaldo, M., Murari, A., JET-EFDA Contributors.: Assessment of probabilistic Venn Machines as real-time disruption predictors from scratch: application to JET with a view on ITER. In: Conference Record of the 19th IEEE Real-Time Conference, May 26-30, Nara, Japan (2014). http://rt2014.rcnp.osaka-u.ac.jp/AbstractsRT2014.pdf
14. Dashevskiy, M., Luo, Z.: Reliable probabilistic classification and its application to internet traffic. In: Huang, D.-S., Wunsch II, D.C., Levine, D.S., Jo, K.-H. (eds.) ICIC 2008. LNCS, vol. 5226, pp. 380–388. Springer, Heidelberg (2008)
15. Papadopoulos, H.: Reliable Probabilistic Classification with Neural Networks. Neurocomputing 107, 59–68 (2013)
16. Lambrou, A., Papadopoulos, H., Nouretdinov, I., Gammerman, A.: Reliable probability estimates based on support vector machines for large multiclass datasets. In: Iliadis, L., Maglogiannis, I., Papadopoulos, H., Karatzas, K., Sioutas, S. (eds.) AIAI 2012 Workshops. IFIP AICT, vol. 382, pp. 182–191. Springer, Heidelberg (2012)
17. Nouretdinov, I., et al.: Multiprobabilistic venn predictors with logistic regression. In: Iliadis, L., Maglogiannis, I., Papadopoulos, H., Karatzas, K., Sioutas, S. (eds.) AIAI 2012 Workshops. IFIP AICT, vol. 382, pp. 224–233. Springer, Heidelberg (2012)

SOM and Feature Weights Based Method for Dimensionality Reduction in Large Gauss Linear Models

Fernando Pavón[1]([⊠]), Jesús Vega[2], and Sebastián Dormido Canto[3]

[1] GAMCO S.L., Alcalá 20, 28014 Madrid, Spain
fernando.pavon@gamco.es
http://www.gamco.es
[2] Laboratorio Nacional de Fusión, CIEMAT, Avenida Complutense 40,
28040 Madrid, Spain
jesus.vega@ciemat.es
http://www.ciemat.es
[3] Departamento Informática Y Automática, UNED, 28040 Madrid, Spain
sebas@dia.uned.es
http://www.dia.uned.es/

Abstract. Discovering the most important variables is a crucial step for accelerating model building without losing potential predictive power of the data. In many practical problems is necessary to discover the dependant variables and the ones that are redundant. In this paper an automatic method for discovering the most important signals or characteristics to build data-driven models is presented. This method was developed thinking in a very high dimensionality inputs spaces, where many variables are independent, but existing many others which are combinations of the independent ones. The base of the method are the SOM neural network and a method for feature weighting very similar to Linear Discriminant Analysis (LDA) with some modifications.

Keywords: Linear regression · Feature election · SOM · Artificial neural networks · Weighted euclidean distance

1 Introduction

A fundamental problem in signal processing and data analysis is to find out the linear combinations among the variables and to weight the importance of each signal or variable. It could be used, for instance, to reduce the amount of data to process, which is often a key factor in determining the performance of the information processing system.

Dimensionality reduction can be a very critical issue in the data analysis of the extremely large databases of fusion devices. For example, JET is the largest fusion device in the world and collects tens of thousands of signals per discharge (which means over 10 Gbytes of data per discharge). ITER, the next generation fusion device that is under construction, will acquire about five hundred

© Springer International Publishing Switzerland 2015
A. Gammerman et al. (Eds.): SLDS 2015, LNAI 9047, pp. 376–385, 2015.
DOI: 10.1007/978-3-319-17091-6_32

thousand signals per discharge and this will correspond to over 1 Tbyte of data per discharge. This massive amount of data are necessary to model the plasma behaviour that is ruled by highly complicated and extremely non-linear interactions. Therefore, the availability of intelligent methods for data reduction is a key aspect in nuclear fusion.

A linear regression is a way for modelling the relationship between a dependent variable and one or more independent variables. Given i independent variables X and the linear dependent variable Y, the linear regression problem can be defined like follows, using next matrices of data sets:

$$Variables = \begin{pmatrix} X_{1,1} & X_{1,2} & \cdots & X_{1,i} & Y_1 \\ X_{2,1} & X_{2,2} & \cdots & X_{2,i} & Y_2 \\ \vdots & \vdots & \ddots & \vdots & \vdots \\ X_{n,1} & X_{n,2} & \cdots & X_{n,i} & Y_n \end{pmatrix} \tag{1}$$

The linear model takes the form

$$Y_i = \theta_1 X_{i,1} + \theta_2 X_{i,2} + \ldots + \theta_n X_{n,1} + \varepsilon_i \qquad i = 1, \ldots, n \tag{2}$$

Where ε_i is the error or disturbance term.
Written in a matrix form:
$$\mathbf{Y} = \mathbf{X}\theta + \varepsilon \tag{3}$$

Where $\mathbf{X}$ is the sub-matrix of $X's$ in (1), and

$$\theta = \begin{pmatrix} \theta_1 \\ \theta_2 \\ \vdots \\ \theta_n \end{pmatrix} \qquad \varepsilon = \begin{pmatrix} \varepsilon_1 \\ \varepsilon_2 \\ \vdots \\ \varepsilon_n \end{pmatrix}$$

Nowadays with the advent of Big Data and sophisticated data mining techniques, the number of variables encountered is often tremendous making variable selection or dimension reduction techniques imperative to produce models with acceptable accuracy and generalization.

Artificial Neural Networks have been used for feature extraction, [1] and [2], and for feature selection [3]. In this paper a method based on well known Kohonen's Self Organized Maps (SOM) [4] and weighting features is presented. For weighting features a method similar to Linear Discriminant Analysis (LDA) [5] is used. A larger ratio value means it is a significant feature or signal and, on the contrary, a smaller value indicates it is an insignificant feature or a signal that we can discard, for example, in the creation of models for prediction or classification. The proposed method will be applied to an experiment using synthetic data where exist many independent and non-gaussian signals, and other ones with are the result of linear and nonlinear combination of the independent signals. The method has to find out not only the signals that show some type of correlation among them but also the signals with larger weights.

This paper is organized in the following: a briefing about the variable reduction and de Self Organized Maps are presented in the next two sections. The proposed feature weighting method is described in section 4, in section 5 some experimental results are presented. Finally future works and conclusions of this technique for weighting characteristics are showed in section 6.

2   Variable Reduction

Variable reduction is a crucial step for accelerating model building without losing potential predictive power of the data. The temptation to build a model using all available information (i.e., all variables) is hard to resist. But analytical limitations require us to think carefully about the variables we choose to model. Moreover the number of a parameters of a model (i.e., neuronal predictive model) depends of the number of inputs. A high number of parameters usually cause problems of over-fitting. In section 4 the method for automatic discover the importance of the variables is presented. In this section is described the classical approximation to discover the importance of variables and the relationship among them.

Before to describe different methods for discovering the relationship among variables is necessary to define two different concepts: variable independence and uncorrelated variables.

To define the concept of *independence*, consider two scalar-valued random variables y_1 and y_2. Basically, the variables y_1 and y_2 are said to be independent if information on the value of y_1 does not give any information on the value of y_2 and vice-versa. Independence can be defined by the probability densities. Let us denote by $\psi(y_1, y_2)$ the joint probability density function (pdf) of y_1 and y_2. Let us further denote by $\psi_1(y_1)$ the marginal pdf of y_1, i.e. the pdf of y_1 when it is considered alone:

$$\psi_1(y_1) = \int \psi(y_1, y_2) dy_2 \tag{4}$$

and similarly for y_2. Then we define that y_1 and y_2 are independent if and only if the joint pdf is factorizable in the following way:

$$\psi(y_1, y_2) = \psi_1(y_1)\psi_2(y_2) \tag{5}$$

This definition extends naturally for any number n of random variables, in which case the joint density must be a product of n terms.

The definition can be used to derive a most important property of independent random variables. Given two functions, h_1 and h_2, we always have

$$E\{h_1(y_1)h_2(y_2)\} = E\{h_1(y_1)\}E\{h_2(y_2)\} \tag{6}$$

After the definition of independence, is necessary to define the term of correlated or uncorrelated variables. A weaker form of independence is uncorrelatedness. Two random variables y_1 and y_2 are said to be uncorrelated, if their covariance is zero:

$$E\{y_1y_2\} - E\{y_1\}E\{y_2\} = 0 \tag{7}$$

If the variables are independent, they are uncorrelated, which follows directly from 6, taking $y_1(y_1) = y_1$ and $h_2(y_2) = y_2$. But uncorrelatedness does not imply independence. For example, assume that (y_1, y_2) are discrete valued and follow such a distribution that the pair are with probability 1/4 equal to any of the following values: (0,1),(0,21),(1,0),(21,0). Then y_1 and y_2 are uncorrelated, as can be simply calculated. On the other hand,

$$E\{y_1^2 y_2^2\} = 0 \neq \frac{1}{4} = E\{y_1^2\}E\{y_2^2\} \tag{8}$$

so the condition in 6 is violated and the variables cannot be independent.

The variables can have redundant information because they are not independent and then we can eliminate some of these variables.

There are different traditional methods to find out redundant variables:

- Graphical representation. Is simple: representation of each variable vs each other. If we have n variables, we need represent this one with the $n-1$ others variables. So we need $n(n-1)/2$ graphics. With the graphical representation we know if two variables are related if the points follow a defined function (in this case the variables are correlated), or they are dispersed (the variables are not correlated).
- Variable exploration using a tree (quasi brute-force). The method consists in to explore the possible combinations of the variable in the input vector of a model. The begining is generate models which have all the variables and models which have a one less variable. The model who has the minimum increase of error indicates the variable less useful. This variable is eliminated and the process begin again with a variable less.
  The figure 1 shows the process of election of variables. The variable combination is codified using ones and zeros. The position of the one or zero indicates the variable. One indicates that the variable is used and zero indicates the not used variable in the input vector. In each step of the process (horizontal row) the variable that will be discarded in next steps. That variable is indicated for the model which produce minor errors. The process finish when the errors grow up significantly.

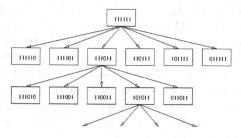

Fig. 1. Variable exploration using a tree

– Linear correlation coefficients. Using the correlation matrix we can check the close or not of each point is to a line. This matrix is calculated using the equation 9. The correlation coefficients are between 0 and 1. 1 indicates that the variables are perfectly correlated linearly.

$$corrcoef(i,j) = \left\| \frac{\sum_{k=1}^{n}(x(i)_k - \bar{x}(i))(x(j)_k - \bar{x}(j))}{\sqrt{\sum_{k=1}^{n}(x(i)_k - \bar{x}(i))^2 \sum_{k=1}^{n}(x(j)_k - \bar{x}(j))^2}} \right\| \qquad (9)$$

We are interested in very high dimensionality problems. With many variables or signals the graphical representation is not practical, variable exploration using a tree is complex and need very time and CPU resources. The correlation coefficients only discover linear correlated variables. In section 4 is explained our method for discovering the important variables in a very high dimension problems, through weighting features using like first step a Self Organized Maps. For that reason in the next section we give a brief explanation about SOM.

3 Self Organized Maps

In the feature weighted method presented, the SOM neural networks is used to "distribute" the input vectors in different classes. The feature method is a modification of a k-NN clasification problem presented in [6]. In every classification problem we need to classify input vectors into a pre-defined classes, in our case the classes will be the neurons of the SOM. In the next section we described the weighted features method in deep. Now we only need to know that the first step of the method is to create a SOM. And this method is not only limited to classification problems, it can be applied to interpolation problem too. The finality is to discover the most important features or signals independent of the problem that we will use these features.

Kohonens self-organizingmap (SOM) was originally devised by Kohonen in 1982, to model a biological phenomena called retinotopy, a process of self-organisation of the neural links between the visual cortex and the retina cells when excited by a succession of independent stimulus. One of the advantages of this algorithm in practical terms is its easy implementation, which is as follows.

There all a total of N neurons labelled with $1, ..., N$. Each neuron k has as associated position vector $I_k = (i_{k1}, i_{k1}, ..., i_{kM}) \in \mathbb{N}^M$, which describes the position of the neuron in an M-dimensional grid. This position vector does not change. The number of neurons B in any column of the neuron grid is the same.

The neuron weight vector for neuron i at iteration t is denoted by $\mathbf{X}_i(t) \in \mathbb{R}^D$, and where it only makes sense if $M \leqslant D$. Neuron weight j of neuron i is denoted X_{ij}. The neuron weights are initialised randomly or taking any of the input vectors like the first weighted vectors, and then the algorithm proceeds as follows. At iteration t an input vector $\xi(t) \in [0, 1]^D$ is presented to the network. The *winner* neuron ν is chosen such that

$$\|\xi(t) - \mathbf{X}_\nu(t)\| \leqslant \|\xi(t) - \mathbf{X}_i(t)\| \forall i \qquad (10)$$

In the ease where there is more than one possible choice of winner ($\|\xi(t) - \mathbf{X}_r(t)\| = \|\xi(t) - \mathbf{X}_s(t)\| < \|\xi(t) - \mathbf{X}_i(t)\| \forall i \neq r, s$) then a predefine rule is used to choose the winner, for example in the one-dimensional case the neuron with the smallest index could be chosen. The neuron weights are then updated as,

$$\mathbf{X}_i(t+1) = \mathbf{X}_i(t) + \alpha(t)h(d(\mathbf{I}_i, \mathbf{I}_\nu))\{\xi(t) - \mathbf{X}_i(t)\} \tag{11}$$

The function h is a "neighbourhood" function $h : \mathbb{R}^+ \to \mathbb{R}^+$. In practice it is a decreasing function about zero, such that for $|a| \leqslant |b| \in \mathbb{R}^+$ then $h(a) \geqslant h(b)$.

The function $\alpha(t)$ is a gain $\alpha(t) \in (0,1)$. $\alpha(t)$ could be constant or $\alpha(t) \to 0, t \to \infty$. The function d is a metric function which gives a measure of the distance between $\mathbf{I}_i$ and $\mathbf{I}_j$.

An important characteristic of de Kohonen's Self Organized Maps versus other competitive networks or self-organized is the SOM keep the neighbour relationships among the input data and represent the regions with an high dimensionality in the input signals over the equivalent topological structure of the network.

The main applications of the SOM are the 2D visualizations of N-Dimensional data and the clustering.

4   Feature Weighting Method Based on SOM

Our objective is to weight the different features, that is, each signal in the input space. We present a generalization of the approach in [6]. In this paper the authors improve a k-NN classifier by change the method for training a Self Organized Maps.

They proposed a revised version of SOM using weighted Euclidean metric in the learning phase.

First of all the weighted Euclidean metric have been calculated with the inputs vectors and the class what belongs that inputs vectors.

Using this new weighted Euclidean metric the SOM is generated. The next step is mapping, that is, draw all test samples to be projected to the SOM, and use the k-NN classifier in the two dimensional mapping samples.

A significant variation is proposed: the SOM is the first step for calculating the weights of the features. In our approach the SOM is the way for discovering the important features; and the focus is not only in classification problems, it could be applied to a prediction problems too.

The proposed procedure for discovering the most important signals and which are combinations of the others ones is:

1. Generate a SOM with all the signals configured as inputs vectors. An input vector is formed for the sampled signals in a time t. The winner neuron is calculated using the "non-modified" Eculidean distance (see 10).
2. Consider each neuron in the SOM like a class in a classification problem. Applied the feature weighted method using the trained SOM.

3. The signals with are linear or nonlinear combinations of others will be an high weight. The independent signals will be the lower one.

The $FeatureWeightingMethod$ is:

Let $\xi_i^j = [\xi_{i1}^j, \xi_{i2}^j, ..., \xi_{id}^j]$, $i = 1, ..., N_j$ and $j \in (1, ..., N_n)$, be the d-dimensional training sample of class or neuron j. Where N_n is the number of classes (is equal of the number of the SOM neurons). $N = \sum_{j=1}^{N_n} N_j$ is the total number of training samples. In order to measure the difference among features, the global mean of total training samples of feature v is calculated by

$$m_v = \frac{1}{N} \sum_{i=1}^{N_j} \sum_{j=1}^{N_n} \xi_{iv}^j, \qquad (v = 1, ..., d) \tag{12}$$

and local mean of class j of feature v is

$$u_v^j = \frac{1}{N_j} \sum_{i=1}^{N_j} \xi_{iv}^j, \qquad (v = 1, ..., d) \tag{13}$$

The way to estimate the weights of features is adapted from LDA, the between-class variance S_v^B of the feature v which is defined by the following formulation:

$$S_v^B = \frac{1}{N_c} \sum_{j=1}^{N_c} (m_v - u_v^j)^2, \qquad (v = 1, ..., d) \tag{14}$$

Similarly, the within class variance S_v^J of the feature v is computed by

$$S_v^J = \sum_{j=1}^{N_n} P_j S_{jv}, \qquad (v = 1, ..., d) \tag{15}$$

where $P_j = \frac{N_j}{N}$ is the prior probability of class j, and S_{jv} is the variance of class j of feature v. Finally, the weighting feature Ψ_v is acording to the ratioi of hte between-class variance S_v^B to the within-class variance S_v^J, that is

$$\Psi_v = \frac{S_v^B}{S_v^J}, \qquad (v = 1, ..., d) \tag{16}$$

According to this rule, if the value of variance of between classes is large, it implies that the distributions of classes are separate, and this feature is helpful for classification. On the hand, if the value of S_v^J is small, it indicates that inter class samples are closed. Therefore, a larger weight should give to this feature.

5 Experimental Results

We use a synthetic data set. 110 signals have been generated, and 10.000 values of each signal or variable.

The first 100 variables are uniformed distributed random values, and the next 10 are linear and nonlinear combinations of the first 100. There are 8 variables which are linear combination, and 2 which are nonlinear combination

We have generate the next matrices of signals and parameters:

$$Signals = \begin{pmatrix} X_{1,1} & X_{1,2} & \cdots & X_{1,100} & Y_{1,1} & Y_{1,2} & \cdots & Y_{1,10} \\ X_{2,1} & X_{2,2} & \cdots & X_{2,100} & Y_{2,1} & Y_{2,2} & \cdots & Y_{2,10} \\ \vdots & \vdots & \ddots & \vdots & \vdots & \vdots & \ddots & \vdots \\ X_{n,1} & X_{n,2} & \cdots & X_{n,100} & Y_{n,1} & Y_{n,2} & \cdots & Y_{n,10} \end{pmatrix}$$

$$\theta's = \begin{pmatrix} \theta_{1,1} & \theta_{1,2} & \cdots & \theta_{1,10} \\ \theta_{2,1} & \theta_{2,2} & \cdots & \theta_{2,10} \\ \vdots & \vdots & \ddots & \vdots \\ \theta_{100,1} & \theta_{100,2} & \cdots & \theta_{100,10} \end{pmatrix}$$

Where $n = 1...10000$ and

$$\theta_{1,j}...\theta_{90,j} \in [0,1] \ and \ \theta_{91,j}...\theta_{100,j} \in [50,100]; \ j = 1...10 \tag{17}$$

The linear combinations are:

$$Y_{1,1} = \sum_{i=1}^{100} \theta_{i,1} X_{1,i}$$
$$Y_{1,2} = \sum_{i=1}^{100} \theta_{i,1} X_{2,i}$$
$$...$$
$$Y_{2,1} = \sum_{i=1}^{100} \theta_{i,2} X_{1,i}$$
$$...$$

We can express the combinations before as:

$$Y_{t,k} = \sum_{i=1}^{100} \theta_{i,t} X_{k,i} \tag{18}$$

Where $t = 1...8$ and $k = 1...10$.

The nonlinear combinations are:

$$Y_{t,k} = \sum_{i=1}^{100} \theta_{i,t} \sin(X_{k,i}) \tag{19}$$

Where $t = 9, 10$ and $k = 1...10$

Using the synthetic data in the matrix *signals* we check the performance of the proposed method for reducing the number of variables, or finding out the most relevant variables. And discover the qualitative weight of the independent variables $X's$ in the linear and nonlinear combinations.

The execution time of proposed method is in seconds using a computer with a Xenon processor at 1.86 GHz and 6 GB of memory. For instance, using the

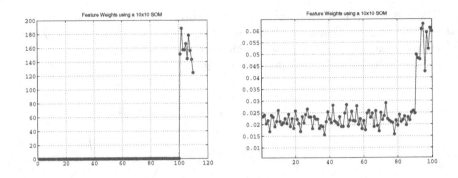

Fig. 2. Weights of the 110 features using a SOM of 100 neurons (10x10)

Fig. 3. Weights of the 100 first features using a SOM of 100 neurons (10x10)

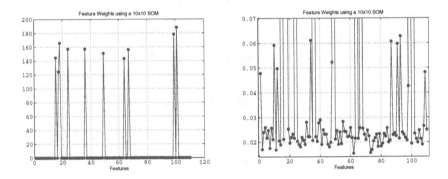

Fig. 4. Weights of the 110 first randomly permutation features

Fig. 5. Zoom: weights of the 110 first randomly permutation features

synthetic data set generated and a SOM with 100 neurons, the training time of the SOM is about 40 seconds and only 1,5 seconds for calculating the 110 weights.

The figure 2 shows the big difference among the last ten weights and the first one hundred weights, that is, the Ys and the rest. Ys are the linear and nonlinear combinations of the first 100 independent variables (18 and 19). Moreover the proposed method also can identifies the most relevant independent variables in the linear and nonlinear combinations 3. This figure is a zoom of the first 100 features, and the 91 to 100 features are the features with a greater θ (see 17) in the combinations that produces the signals Ys. The method for weighting features preponderate the variables which are the results of the combinations of the others. That are the signals which represent the most quantity of the information in the problem. And also the method discover which variables $X's$ are most important in the $Y's$ signals.

The capability of discover the important signal which is combination of the other ones no depend of the order of the variables in the input vectors. In the figure 4 is observed the 10 dependant variables which have been randomly permuted in their position in the input vector. And the figure 5 is a zoom of the former figure 4 in wich we can see the 10 variables with a greater θ in the linear and nonlinear combinations.

6 Conclusion and Aplicabilities

In this paper we have presented a method for discovering dependant variables which are the result of linear and nonlinear combination of the independent variables. This method also discovers the importance of the variables in the linear regression and in the nonlinear combinations. We can use the SOM networks for a first step for "splitting" the input vectors in the neurons and after this, to calculate the weight of each signal depending on their "within-class" and "between-class" variances.

This method can be applied to improve many areas, we will highlight two: in classification and visualization problems using a weighted euclidean distance for training a SOM; and applied this method to deep-learning techniques, in order to discover the most relevant characteristics for representation of a problem.

References

1. Oja, E.: Principal Components. Minor Components, and Linear Neural Networks Neural Networks **5**, 927–935 (1992)
2. Hyvärinen, A., Oja, E.: Independent component analysis: algorithms and applications. Neural Networks **13**, 411–430 (2000)
3. Castellano, G., Fanelli, A.M.: Feature selection: a neural approach. Neural Networks **5**, 3156–3160 (1999)
4. Kohonen, T.: Essentials of the self-organizing map. Neural Networks **37**, 52–65 (2013)
5. Theodoridis, S., Koutroumbas, K.: Pattern Recognition. 3rd edition. Academic Press (2006)
6. Wu, J.-L., Li, I.-J.: The Improved SOM-Based Dimensionality Reducton Method for KNN Classifier Using Weighted Euclidean Metric. International Journal of Computer, Consumer and Control (IJ3C) **3**(1) (2014)
7. Nathans, L.L., Oswald, F.L., Nimon, K.: Interpreting Multiple Linear Regression: A Guidebook of Variable Importance. Practical Assessment, Research & Evaluation **17**(9) (2012)
8. Haykin, S.: Neural Networks: A Comprehensive Foundation. Prentice Hall (1999)
9. Yuan, J.-L., Fine, T.L.: Neural-network design for small training sets of high dimension. IEEE Transactions on Neural Networks **9**(2), 266–280 (1998)

Geometric Data Analysis

Assigning Objects to Classes of a Euclidean Ascending Hierarchical Clustering

Brigitte Le Roux[1,2(✉)] and Frédérik Cassor[2]

[1] MAP5, Université Paris Descartes, 45 Rue des Saints Pères,
75270 Paris Cedex 06, France
Brigitte.LeRoux@mi.parisdescartes.fr
[2] CEVIPOF Sciences-Po, 98 Rue de l'Université, 75007 Paris, France

Abstract. In a Euclidean ascending hierarchical clustering (AHC, Ward's method), the usual method for allocating a supplementary object to a cluster is based on the geometric distance from the object-point to the barycenter of the cluster. The main drawback of this method is that it does not take into consideration that clusters differ as regards weights, shapes and dispersions. Neither does it take into account successive dichotomies of the hierarchy of classes. This is why we propose a new ranking rule adapted to geometric data analysis that takes the shape of clusters into account. From a set of supplementary objects, we propose a strategy for assigning these objects to clusters stemming from an AHC. The idea is to assign supplementary objects at the local level of a node to one of its two successors until a cluster of the partition under study is reached. We define a criterion based on the ratio of Mahalanobis distances from the object–point to barycenters of the two clusters that make up the node.

We first introduce the principle of the method, and we apply it to a barometric survey carried out by the CEVIPOF on various components of trust among French citizens. We compare the evolution of clusters of individuals between 2009 and 2012 then 2013.

Keywords: Geometric data analysis · Correspondence analysis and doubling coding · Ascending hierarchical clustering · Mahalanobis distance · Survey data

1 Assignment by Dichotomies to a System of Classes

Let I be a set of n objects, and C a set[1] of C classes $c \in C$ defining a partition of I. We suppose that we have a nested system, providing a hierarchy of classes and more precisely a dichotomic hierarchical clustering represented by a binary tree.

The end elements of the hierarchy are the classes $c \in C$, that we call "primary classes". The n objects of I are divided into the C primary classes, the absolute

---

[1] As a general convention, we denote the cardinalities of finite set as the sets themselves, except for set I.

© Springer International Publishing Switzerland 2015
A. Gammerman et al. (Eds.): SLDS 2015, LNAI 9047, pp. 389–396, 2015.
DOI: 10.1007/978-3-319-17091-6_33

frequencies of classes are denoted $(n_c)_{c \in C}$ (with $n = \sum n_c$). The classes of the hierarchy are denoted c_ℓ with ℓ going from 1 to C for the primary classes, and from $C + 1$ to $2C - 1$ for the classes associated with the nodes of the hierarchical tree. The top node $c_{\ell=2C-1}$ is the set I of all objects.

As an example, take the following hierarchy with four terminal elements: $C = \{c1, c2, c3, c4\}$.

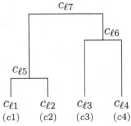

The assignment of a supplementary object i_s will be made downwards as follows:

- we first decide to which of the two immediate successors (here $c_{\ell 6}$ or $c_{\ell 5}$) of the top node ($c_{\ell 7}$) we assign the supplementary object i_s;
- once the assignment to a node ℓ is made (say here $c_{\ell 6}$), we decide to which of the two immediate successors ($c_{\ell 3}$ or $c_{\ell 4}$) of this node ($c_{\ell 5}$) we assign the supplementary object i_s;
- and so on until we reach a primary class.

In the sequel, we suppose that objects are represented by points in a Euclidean space. We apply a Euclidean clustering to the cloud of points, that is, an ascending hierarchical clustering using the variance criterion (Ward's method) [7].

2 Distance from Object to Class

We suppose that the space is referred to an orthonormal basis, for instance the basis associated with the principal axes of the cloud. We denote $\mathbf{c}_\ell$ the column–vector of the coordinates of the mean point of class c_ℓ and $\mathbf{V}_\ell$ its covariance matrix. If $\mathbf{y}$ denotes the column–vector of the coordinates of object i, the proximity index between object i and class c_ℓ [2], denoted $\kappa_\ell(i)$, is equal to the Mahalanobis distance [6] from object–point i to the center of class c_ℓ. One has:

$$\kappa_\ell^2(i) = (\mathbf{y} - \mathbf{c}_\ell)^\top \mathbf{V}_\ell^{-1} (\mathbf{y} - \mathbf{c}_\ell)$$

Comment

If, as an proximity index, we take the geometric distance from object–point i to the center of the class c_ℓ, that is $\left((\mathbf{y} - \mathbf{c}_\ell)^\top (\mathbf{y} - \mathbf{c}_\ell)\right)^{1/2}$, we do not take into account the fact that the classes differ in weight, shape and dispersion. Now it seems natural that a point that is equidistant from the center of a highly concentrated class and from the center of a very dispersed class will be assigned to the latter one. Hence, it is preferable to choose the κ-norm as a proximity index from a point to a class, since it takes into account the shape of the class.

3 Assignment Criterion

In order to decide if a supplementary object i_s is assigned to class c_ℓ or to class $c_{\ell'}$, we will compare the ratio $\rho_{(\ell,\ell')}(i_s) = \kappa_\ell^2(i_s)/\kappa_{\ell'}^2(i_s)$ to a threshold $\alpha_{(\ell,\ell')}$.

i_s is assigned to class c_ℓ if $\rho_{(\ell,\ell')}(i_s) < \alpha_{(\ell,\ell')}$ and to $c_{\ell'}$ if not[2].

Among the possible thresholds, we will choose the one, denoted $\widehat{\alpha}_{(\ell,\ell')}$, for which, if we assign the $n_{c_\ell} + n_{c_{\ell'}}$ basic objects $i \in c_\ell \cup c_{\ell'}$ according to the preceding rule, the number of errors (misclassified objects) is minimum ([1], [3]).

We denote:

- $N_\ell(\alpha)$ the number of basic objects i belonging to class c_ℓ that are misclassified at level α, that is, the number of $i \in c_\ell$ with $\rho_{(\ell,\ell')}(i) > \alpha_{(\ell,\ell')}$;
- $N_{\ell'}(\alpha)$ the number of objects belonging to class $c_{\ell'}$ that are misclassified at level α, that is, the number of $i \in c_{\ell'}$ with $\rho_{(\ell,\ell')}(i) < \alpha_{(\ell,\ell')}$;
- $N_{(\ell,\ell')}(\alpha) = N_\ell(\alpha) + N_{\ell'}(\alpha)$ the number of objects of the two classes c_ℓ and $c_{\ell'}$ misclassified at level α.

The threshold $\widehat{\alpha}_{(\ell,\ell')}$ is the value α corresponding to the *minimum* of $N_{(\ell,\ell')}(\alpha)$.

Calculation Algorithm. To calculate $\widehat{\alpha}_{(\ell,\ell')}$, the values $\rho_{(\ell,\ell')}(i)$ are ranked in ascending order, hence the sequence indexed by j (with $1 \leq j < n_{c_\ell} + n_{c_{\ell'}}$), with:

$$\rho_{(\ell,\ell')}(1) \leq \ldots \leq \rho_{(\ell,\ell')}(j) \leq \ldots \leq \rho_{(\ell,\ell')}(n_{c_\ell} + n_{c_{\ell'}})$$

- If $\alpha < \rho_{(\ell,\ell')}(1)$, then all basic objects are assigned to class $c_{\ell'}$, hence there are n_{c_ℓ} errors.
- If $\rho_{(\ell,\ell')}(j) < \alpha < \rho_{(\ell,\ell')}(j+1)$ $(j \geq 2)$, there is one less error if the basic object corresponding to j belongs to class c_ℓ and one additional error if it belongs to class $c_{\ell'}$, and so on.

We denote $j_{\min}$ the rank corresponding to the minimum of $N_{(\ell,\ell')}(\alpha)$, *i.e.* the rank of the object for which the ratio ρ is taken as threshold.

4 Application to the Survey Data of Trust Barometer (CEVIPOF)

4.1 Data Set

The data come from surveys initiated by CEVIPOF (Centre de Recherches Politiques de Sciences-Po Paris) that take account of several, and sometimes heterogeneous, components of trust. The aim of these surveys is to measure changes in trust between 2009 and 2012 then 2013 in France.

---

[2] If $\rho_{(\ell,\ell')}(i_s) = \alpha_{(\ell,\ell')}$, the more numerous class is chosen.

Six waves of on–line surveys has been conducted each year since 2009 by the research center CEVIPOF in partnership with the *Pierre Mendès France Institute* and the *Conseil Economique, Social et Environnemental*. The samples (about 1,500 persons) are designed to be representative of the French citizens registered to vote, by using the quota method (gender, age, CSP) and categorization by type of agglomeration and size of the home town. The data are collected by "OpinionWay" polling institute using a CAWI (Computer Assisted Web Interview) system (See www.cevipof.com/fr/le-barometre-de-la-confiance-politique-du-cevipof/).

4.2 Structure of the Space of Trust

In order to measure changes in trust [4], we take as a reference the 2009 survey (intermediate date between 2007 and 2012 presidential elections). In the analyses, the 1,375 individuals of Wave 1 (2009) are put as active elements, all individuals in the other two waves are put as supplementary [2].

In order to construct the space of trust and to make a typology of the French citizens registered to vote according to trust [4], we retained five components of trust measured by 24 questions:

1. *Political trust*: trust in political roles (7 questions: presidential institution, Prime Minister; your member of parliament (MP), mayor, general councillor; political parties, European Union);
2. *Institutional trust*: trust in large public or private institutions (5 questions: hospital, police, medias, Trade Unions, WTO);
3. *Economic trust*: trust in organizations of the economic world (4 questions: banks, public firms, private firms, trust/control firms);
4. *Interpersonal trust* (5 questions: trust in neighbors, people, foreigners, etc.);
5. *Individual trust* (3 questions: feeling of personal happiness, personal responsability, trust in one's own future):.

Almost all questions are in the same format: a four–level Likert scale (with levels: much trust, some trust, not much trust, no trust at all). In order to construct the space of trust, we use a procedure called doubling, that is, we attribute two scores per individual instead of a single score [6]. We respectively coded the four levels (3,0), (2,1), (1,2) and (0,3) for four–level scales and by (1,0), (0,1) for the two levels of the three dichotomous questions. Then the table is doubled with a "trust pole" and a "distrust pole" for each individual. We performed a correspondence analysis of the table with 2×24 columns and 1,375 rows. In the correspondence analysis display of this table, we obtain two points for each question and one point for each individual. The line joining two poles of one question goes through the origin (as shown in figure 1 for the question about "trust in police").

Furthermore, trust components have a different number of questions. Thus, each question is weighted by the inverse of the number of questions the component contains. Thus the components are roughly balanced in the analysis.

Their contributions to the cloud variance are respectively 22%, 19%, 21%, 23% and 15%.

The first axis is more important than the second. We will give the interpretation of the first two axes[3].

Table 1. Variances of axes λ (for $\lambda >$ to the mean $\bar{\lambda}$) and decreasing curve

axis	vaiance (λ)	cumulated rate
1	0.0721	23.80
2	0.0310	34.04
3	0.0229	41.59
4	0.0210	48.52
5	0.0162	53.88
6	0.0125	58.02

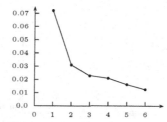

Interpretation of Axes. Axis 1 is an axis of trust/distrust: it opposes the trust poles of the questions (black markers) to the distrust poles (white markers). The political, then the economic components of trust account for 34% and 25% of the variance of axis 1.

For axis 2, the interpersonal component is predominant with a contribution of 63%, then the economic component contributes to 27%. It opposes, on the one hand (bottom in figure 1), interpersonal trust (neighbors, foreigners, people met for the first time, etc.) and distrust in banks, firms, and on the other hand, the opposite poles of these questions.

4.3 Clustering of Individuals

On the cloud of individuals, we perform a Euclidean clustering, precisely an AHC with variance criterion (Ward's method [7]).

We can distinguish four groups of individuals as regards trust. The superior hierarchical tree associated with the partition in four clusters is given in Figure 3 and the concentration ellipses represented in the plane 1-2 of the space of trust in Figure 4.

Interpretation of Classes. Class $c1$ ($n_{c1} = 402$) groups the "hyper-trusters"; class $c2$ ($n_{c2} = 396$) groups the "moderate trusters"; class $c3$ ($n_{c3} = 267$) groups the "moderate distrusters" and class $c4$ ($n_{c4} = 311$) groups the "hyper-distrusters".

---

[3] For more details and the interpretation of axis 3 see [3].

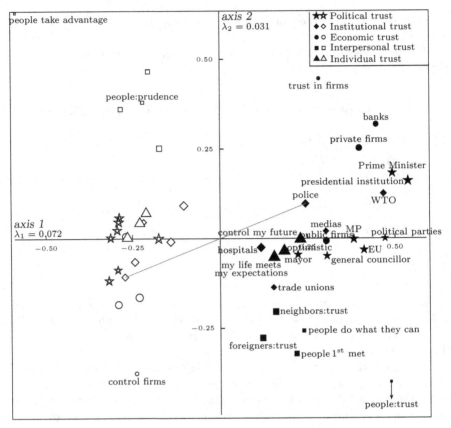

Fig. 1. Cloud of questions with their two poles: the trusted one with black markers and the distrusted one with white markers (the size markers are proportional to weights)

4.4   Assignment of Individuals of Waves 4 and 5

To complement this study, we use the procedure described above to assign the individuals of the other waves to the classes defined by the AHC of individuals of Wave 1 (2009). The percentages of individuals in each class for waves 1 (2009), 4 (2012) and 5 (2013) are given in table 2.

Table 2. Percentages of individuals in each class for the 3 waves

classes	Dec 2009	Dec 2012	Dec 2013
c1 hyper–trusters	29	29	28
c2 moderate trusters	29	20	17
c3 moderate distrusters	19	31	34
c4 hyper–distrusters	23	20	21

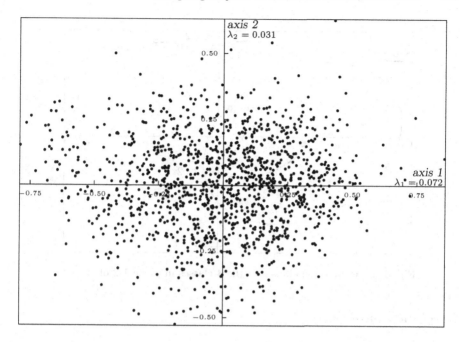

Fig. 2. Cloud of individual in plane 1-2 (the graphical scale is equal to three quarter of that of figure 1)

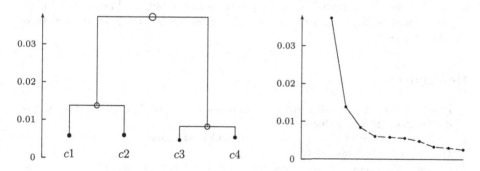

Fig. 3. Superior hierarchical tree and diagram of level indexes

Comment: The level of trust diminishes. The method used here enables us to specify the changes: from the above percentages, we can say there exists an important shift in moderate trust towards moderate distrust, and there is a little change in extreme classes.

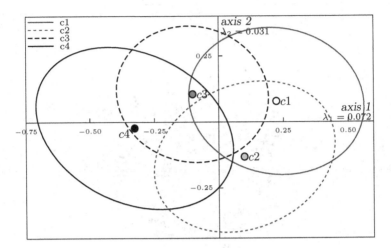

Fig. 4. Concentration ellipses of the 4 classes in plane 1-2 of the CA

5   Conclusion

As we have seen, this method is of particular interest for the study of data tables indexed by time, that is for longitudinal studies. It can also be used in the case of a cloud of individuals equipped with structuring factors, for instance for comparing, as Pierre Bourdieu says, "positions in the field and position taking".

A calculation algorithm program was written in R, and it is invoked from SPAD software[4].

References

1. Benzécri, J.-P.: Analyse discriminante et analyse factorielle. Les Cahiers de l'Analyse des Données **2**(4), 369–406 (1977)
2. Le Roux, B.: Geometric Data Analysis: from Correspondence Analysis to Structured Data Analysis. Kluwer, Dordrecht (2004)
3. Le Roux, B.: Analyse géométrique des données multidimensionnelles. Dunod, Paris (2014)
4. Le Roux, B., Perrineau, P.: Les différents types d'électeurs au regard de différents types de confiance. Les Cahiers du CEVIPOF **54**, 5–35 (2011). http://www.cevipof.com/fr/les-publications/les-cahiers-du-cevipof/
5. Mahalanobis, P.C.: On the generalized distance in statistics. Proceedings of the National Institute of Sciences (Calcutta) **2**, 49–55 (1936)
6. Murtagh, F.: Correspondence Analysis and Data coding with Java and R. Chapman and Hall, London (2005)
7. Ward, J.H.: Hierarchical grouping to optimize an objective function. Journal of the American Statistical Association **58**(301), 236–244 (1963)

---

[4] The analyses of the CEVIPOF barometer data were performed using SPAD (distributed by Coheris SPAD©).

The Structure of Argument: Semantic Mapping of US Supreme Court Cases

Fionn Murtagh[1]([✉]) and Mohsen Farid[2]

[1] Department of Computing, Goldsmiths University of London, London, UK
fmurtagh@acm.org
[2] Paul Quinn College, Dallas, TX, USA
m.farid@acm.org

Abstract. We semantically map out the flow of the narrative involved in a United States Supreme Court case. Our objective is both the static analysis of semantics but, more so, the trajectory of argument. This includes consideration of those who are involved, the Justices and the Attorneys. We study therefore the flow of argument. Geometrical (metric, latent semantic) and topological (ultrametric, hierarchical) analyses are used in our analytics.

Keywords: Data analytics · Multivariate data analysis · Correspondence analysis · Latent semantic analysis · Hierarchical clustering · Metric and ultrametric mapping

1 Introduction

In this work, we examine the argumentation used in US Supreme Court cases. We have at our disposal about 500 such cases. Future work will carry out comparative analyses of the trajectories of argument, and cross-argument, implying also cross-case, analysis. Our objectives will include both legal content and also a data-driven, contextually-based, and semantics-enabled analysis of this particular form of discourse. In this paper we examine one such case. The Annex to this paper provides details of the Supreme Court cases that we are using, and it provides some aspects also on the particular case at issue in this initial work. See this Annex for those involved, that included the plaintiff, the defendant, the *amicus curiae* (i.e., "friend of the court", an accepted role providing public policy perspective), and the Justices from the Supreme Court, including the Chief Justice. Furthermore, in the Annex, it is noted how this court case was one where the state of Kansas brought an action against the states of Nebraska and Colorado. This case was heard in late 2014.

In this work we use the Correspondence Analysis platform [9], together with chronological hierarchical clustering [1,8]. Background on many aspects can be found in [5,6]. The Correspondence Analysis methodology was introduced to mainstream legal and jurisprudence domains by Harcourt [4]. As a methodology, this offers a latent semantic analysis that is well integrated with

© Springer International Publishing Switzerland 2015
A. Gammerman et al. (Eds.): SLDS 2015, LNAI 9047, pp. 397–405, 2015.
DOI: 10.1007/978-3-319-17091-6_34

importance-based selection of observables and their attributes (for us in this paper, speech elements and the words used), with chronological aspects of the dynamics involved, with visualizations, to which we can add the statistically significant terms.

In [1], there is an in depth discursive analysis of the closing speech for the prosecution in a murder trial. The trajectory of the argument is studied using Correspondence Analysis and chronological hierarchical clustering. See e.g. [8] where this integrated toolset, for semantic analysis of the data and its dynamical, or chronological, aspect is applied to film script. In [1] the objective is to analyze the progression of the arguments. The broader objective is to understand what constitutes effectiveness, through the ability to map the flow of argument, and later to use such perspectives for teaching and training.

A starting point is the units of discourse that are used. Let us consider how thinking, and the expression of such thought in language, can be utilized. Chafe [2], in relating and establishing mappings between memory and story, or narrative, considered the following units.

1. *Memory* expressed by a *story* (memory takes the form of an "island"; it is "highly selective"; it is a "disjointed chunk"; but it is not a book, nor a chapter, nor a continuous record, nor a stream).
2. *Episode*, expressed by a *paragraph*.
3. *Thought*, expressed by a *sentence*.
4. A *focus*, expressed by a phrase (often these phrases are linguistic "clauses"). Foci are "in a sense, the basic units of memory in that they represent the amount of information to which a person can devote his central attention at any one time".

The "flow of thought and the flow of language" are treated at once, the latter proxying the former, and analyzed in their linear and hierarchical structure as described in other essays in the same volume as Chafe [2] and in [3].

In section 2, we describe the data, the discourse chronology, and characterizing terms. We apply McKee's ([7], p. 252) dictum that text is the "sensory surface" of the underlying semantics. In section 3, the semantic analysis is carried out. This includes semantic mapping and visualizing, and clustering of the personages involved, the Justices and Attorneys. In section 4, we segment the overall argument or discourse. We provide an initial visualization of the trajectory of this Supreme Court argument.

2   Data Preprocessing

The Annex describes the particular court case argument that we use, as a model case.

In this initial analysis, due to our objective of mapping the semantics of the discourse, we remove all punctuation, and we set all upper case to lower case. The widespread presence of "–", indicating a cut or a break in speaking, comes within the scope of our excluded punctuation.

In terms of the structure of the text, we have the following. A speaker is one of: the Chief Justice, the 7 other Justices, the 3 Attorneys (cf. Annex for their names). Each speaker name precedes a statement that consists of up to a number of successive sentences.

To begin with then, we have 567 sentences, arranged in 213 statements, with the text comprising 1396 words. By removing common grammatical words that are on a stopword list (from the SMART information retrieval system, in the R package, tm), the word set used decreases to 1063. Since we will take into consideration the speaker as well as what is said, and given the fact that there are 11 speakers, our analysis will be carried out on the statements. A further data preprocessing step is to remove words that are rare. We define rare words as words that appear in fewer than 10 statements, and also words that are used less than 10 times in the full argument. Such rare words are removed because we are less interested here in exceptionally occurring instances, but rather instead we are interested in underlying trends and patterns expressed by the speaking. Rare can also become important for Correspondence Analysis, due to their exceptionality (so they will have a small mass, but they will be at a great distance from the centre of gravity of the cloud of words, with the result that they will be of large inertia). Rare words may well determine some of the factors, in the output, latent semantic factor space. For these reasons, therefore, we remove such words. We are left with 59 words (from the previous 1063 words).

Because the Justice and Attorney names are of particular interest to us, we separate these from other words used, for the purposes of our analysis in the next section. We carry out our semantic analysis on the cloud of words that do not have these names. That analysis, i.e. determining the latent semantic, Euclidean metric, factor space, is simultaneously the analysis of the cloud of statements. Then we project the Justice and Attorney names into the factor space. In this way, we position them semantically in the factor space, as a function of the words they use in the statements expressed by them, and as a function of the statements they make.

3 Semantic Mapping Through Correspondence Analysis and Classificatory Analysis

Figure 1 displays the relative positioning of the plaintiff, Stephen R. McAllister, representing Kansas, and the defendant, David D. Cookson, from Nebraska. As is typical for such sparse input data, the inertia explained by the factors or axes, and therefore the corresponding eigenvalue, is small.

The Justices, plaintiff and defendant, and one term, "honor", were supplementary elements. That is to say, they were entered into the analysis following the construction of the factors. In the case of this term, "honor" (often used in the expression "Your Honor"), in an initial analysis, it influenced strongly the first two factors. Therefore, because of its exceptionality, it was put as a supplementary term.

With one exception, Justice Kagan, all other Justices are in the upper left quadrant of Figure 1. We left, for the present, the function words "you're" and "didn't" (through our preprocessing, written as "youre" and "didnt", respectively). While Figure 1 distinguishes, on the vertical axis, the issue of contention from the legal debate, we will flag some issues as deserving of further study, later. One such issue is why Justice Kagan is separately located from the other Court Justices. Due to limited statements, and hence limited interventions here, the Justices Alito, Ginsburg and Kennedy had insufficient data to be retained in these analyses.

Factors 1 and 2, and 20 most important terms

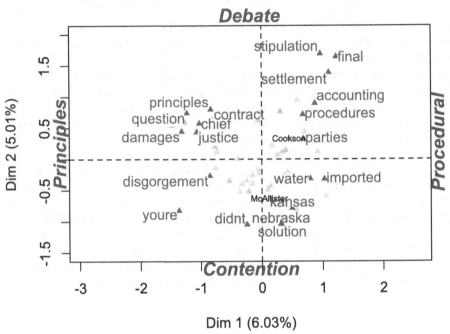

Fig. 1. The principal factor plane, where the first and second axes ("Dim 1", "Dim 2") explain 11.04% of the inertia. The 20 words that contribute most to the definition of the factors, are displayed. Words that are not displayed are located at the fainter pink triangle symbols. The names of just plaintiff McAllister and defendant Cookson are shown. In the upper left quandrant, the grey triangles are the locations of Justices: Roberts, Scalia and Sotomayor, and (closer to the origin) Breyer. Kagan and (amicus curiae) O'Connell are located in the lower left quadrant. The labelling of the axes is concluded from the words that are displayed.

Figure 2 shows that the plaintiff and defendants, McAllister and Cookson, together with the amicus curiae, O'Connell, are quite close semantically. This is an expression of the core discussion revolving around what they had to say. It is interesting to find how much Chief Justice Roberts differs, semantically, from other Justices.

Clustering, using argument content

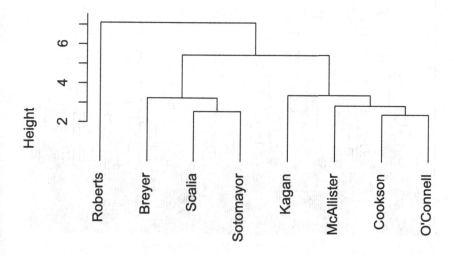

Attorneys: McAllister, Cookson; Amicus Curiae: O'Connell
Chief Justice Roberts, Justices Breyer, Kagan, Scalia, Sotomayor

Fig. 2. From their semantic coordinates in the full dimensionality factor space, the hierarchical clustering uses Ward's minimum variance agglomerative criterion. This is also a minimum inertia criterion for equiweighted points, endowed with the Euclidean metric that is defined in the latent semantic factor space.

4   Towards the Trajectory of Argument

We have already noted Chafe's description of the options for considering the segmentation of the flow of narrative and/or of thought. Here, we have multiple speakers. Using the semantic mapping provided by the Correspondence Analysis, in the full dimensionality space, we will apply a chronological clustering. That is to say, we use a clustering of the statements. (As noted in section 2, before our data preprocessing, we started out with 213 statements, that comprised the succession of 567 sentences. Each statement was a mini-speech by a Justice or by an Attorney.)

Such clustering uses the complete linkage agglomerative clustering criterion, in order to have a well-defined hierarchy. This has been used in [1, 8]. The hierarchy that is determined in this way is displayed in Figure 3. From the 213 statements that comprise the entire court argument, there are 195 that did not become empty of words, when the word corpus used was reduced as described in section 2.

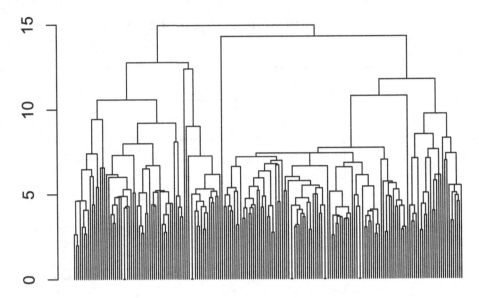

Fig. 3. From their semantic coordinates in the full dimensionality factor space, and taking the chronology into account, this contiguity constrained agglomerative hierarchical clustering uses the complete link cluster criterion (guaranteeing a well-formed hierarchy). 189 successive statements are clustered here. As described in the text, we implement an approach to select statistically significant cluster segments from this hierarchy.

We proceed as follows on the basis of Figure 3. Through permutation assessment of the statistical significance of cluster formation, or rejection of such a hypothesis associated with each and every agglomeration in the hierarchy building process, we arrive at a set of segments of the chronological sequence. See in particular [1] for application of the segmentation approach. Using a significance threshold of 15% and 5000 randomizations, we arrive at statistically permitted agglomerations that give rise to 26 successive segments. These are segments (in sequence, which implies chronological) of the 189 statements covering the entire discourse.

From these 26 segments, we carry our a semantic mapping analysis of the segments, crossed by the 59 terms that we have retained. These terms are the names of Justices and Attorneys and 51 other words. What we found as the more important words were displayed in Figure 1. In Figure 4, it can be seen that segments 1, 2, 3, 4 are somewhat outlying (not greatly so, of course, cf. the later segment 9). These segments are respectively statements 1–8, 9–13, 14–18, 19–29. Then the main part of the argument flow in this case, comprising segments 10 through to 21, are fairly centrally located in this planar map of the argument flow. These segments are defined from statements 60 to 149. We also note the semantic positioning of the Attorneys and Justices here.

26 successive argument segments

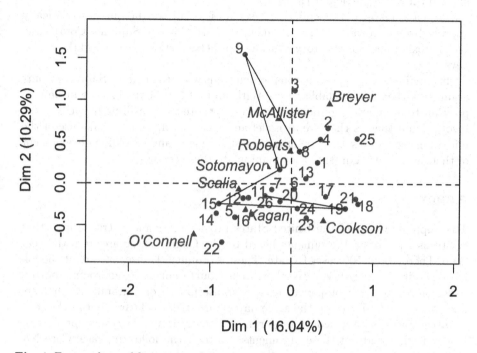

Fig. 4. Factor plane of factors 1 and 2, using 26 successive segments in the chronology of statements, crossed by 51 words used and the names of Justices and Attorneys. The longer segments, therefore being the most dominant, are traced out with connecting lines. These segments are: segments 4, 8, 9, 10, 15, 19 and 26. Visual proximity of any named individual and any segment of statements indicates an influence (by the individual on the semantic content of the segment of successive statements).

The segments are of differing lengths. Some are even of length 1, being just one single statement, by one Justice or Attorney, in the Court case transcript. We looked at all segments which had 10 or more statements, in order to have a set of sufficiently dominant or important segments. This was the case for the segments 4, 8, 9, 10, 15, 19 and 26, which had, respectively, the following number of statements: 11, 11, 10, 10, 18, 10, 26. Because we are taking these as dominant segments, there are connected with lines in Figure 4. This is our way, therefore, to display the general and overall trajectory of this Supreme Court case.

5   Conclusion

In this initial work, we have taken one Supreme Court case. We used the transcript of this session. It involved the plaintiff and defendant, the amicus curiae, the Chief Justice, and the four Supreme Court Justices (together with three other Justices who were not included in our analysis since they did not say much during this particular case).

We have mapped the underlying semantics and sought out a statistically approved segmentation of the argument flow. In this one Supreme Court case, we have examined classificatory relationships between the Justices and the Attorneys.

It remains now to generalize and extend this work to all other Supreme Court arguments that are available to us. With around 500 of these, we will be in a position to compare argument structures; to note relationships between those involved and themes that are at issue; and most of all, we can make use of the underlying semantics, that includes both static views and unfolding development of themes and of arguments that manipulate these themes.

Annex

The Supreme Court of the United States provides Argument Transcripts, that are transcripts of oral arguments heard by the Court. These are from the year 2000. There about 500 cases to date. These Argument Transcripts are at the following address, where it is noted that: "The Court's current Courtroom reporter, Alderson Reporting Company, provides transcripts of oral arguments that are posted on this Web site on the same day an argument is heard by the Court."

http://www.supremecourt.gov/oral_arguments/argument_transcript.aspx

In our initial study of these arguments, we took the following case, Case No. 126:

http://www.supremecourt.gov/oral_arguments/
argument_transcripts/126,%20orig_heim.pdf

This case is the following. "State of Kansas, Plaintiff v. State of Nebraska and State of Colorado", Washington, D.C., Tuesday, October 14, 2014.

This session, that we analyze in this article, started at 10:04 a.m. Appearances were: Stephen R. McAllister, on behalf of the plaintiff; Ann O'Connell, as amicus curiae; David D. Cookson, on behalf of the defendants; then there was a rebuttal argument by Stephen R. McAllister. Chief Justice Roberts concluded the session, with submission of the case, at 11:03 a.m.

This transcript is in double spacing, it has sequence numbers on all lines, pages 3–56 contain the court presentation and discussion. Pages 57–68 contain an index of all terms (including years and other numerical terms), with their page and line numbers.

Justices present are as follows, and representatives of the plaintiff and defendants.

1. Stephen R. McAllister, Esq., Solicitor General of Kansas, Topeka, Kansas; on behalf of the plaintiff.
2. Ann O'Connell, Esq., Assistant to the Solicitor General, Department of Justice, Washington, D.C.; on behalf of United States, as amicus curiae.
3. David D. Cookson, Esq., Chief Deputy Attorney General, Lincoln, Nebraska; on behalf of defendants.

4. Chief Justice Roberts
5. Justice Scalia
6. Justice Kagan
7. Justice Sotomayor
8. Justice Breyer
9. Not included in our analysis due to limited involvement: Justice Ginsburg, Justice Alito, Justice Kennedy

For background on this case, the following may be referred to.

No. 126, Original, In The Supreme Court of the United States, State of Kansas, Plaintiff, versus State of Nebraska and State of Colorado, Defendants.

"Final Report of the Special Master with Certificate of RRCA Groundwater Model", Vincent L. McKusick, Special Master, One Monument Square, Portland, Maine 04101, USA. September 17, 2003.

For this, see http://www.supremecourt.gov/specmastrpt/orig126_102003.pdf. It may be noted that the RRCA Groundwater Model is the Republican River Compact Administration Ground Water Model, for the Republican River Basin, developed for Colorado, Kansas and Nebraska.

References

1. Bécue-Bertaut, M., Kosvot, B., Morin, A., Naro, G.: Rhetorical strategy in forensic speeches. Multidimensional statistics-based methodology. Journal of Classification **31**, 85–106 (2014)
2. Chafe, W.L.: The flow of thought and the flow of language. In: Givón, T. (ed.) Syntax and Semantics: Discourse and Syntax, vol. 12, pp. 159–181. Academic Press, New York (1979)
3. Chafe, W.: Discourse, Consciousness, and Time: The Flow and Displacement of Conscious Experience in Speaking and Writing. University of Chicago Press (1994)
4. Harcourt, B.E.: Measured interpretation: introducing the method of Correspondence Analysis to legal studies, pp. 979–1017. University of Illinois Law Review (2002)
5. Le Roux, B., Rouanet, H.: Multiple Correspondence Analysis. Sage (2010)
6. Le Roux, B., Rouanet, H.: Geometric Data Analysis: From Correspondence Analysis to Structured Data Analysis. Kluwer (2010)
7. McKee, R.: Story - Substance, Structure, Style, and the Principles of Screenwriting, Methuen (1999)
8. Murtagh, F., Ganz, A., McKie, S.: The structure of narrative: the case of film scripts. Pattern Recognition **42**, 302–312 (2009)
9. Murtagh, F.: The Correspondence Analysis platform for uncovering deep structure in data and information. Computer Journal **53**, 304–315 (2010)

Supporting Data Analytics for Smart Cities: An Overview of Data Models and Topology

Patrick E. Bradley[(✉)]

Karlsruhe Institute of Technology, 76131 Karlsruhe, Germany
bradley@kit.edu

Abstract. An overview of data models suitable for smart cities is given. CityGML and *G*-maps implicitly model the underlying combinatorial structure, whereas topological databases make this structure explicit. This combinatorial structure is the basis for topological queries, and topological consistency of such data models allows for correct answers to topological queries. A precise definition of topological consistency in the two-dimensional case is given and an application to data models is discussed.

1 Introduction

Electronic government, planning systems, and citizen participation require data models suitable for performing such tasks. Geographic Information Systems (GIS) for smart cities are used for assessing transportation and mobility, urban risk management and GIS-assisted urban planning, including noise-mapping and solar energy issues [17].

In order to be useful for more than visualisation purposes, data models must be topologically consistent, meaning that the underlying combinatorial and geometric models must be compatible. The reason is that it is usually more efficient to use the combinatorial model for topological queries. The precise definition of topological consistency varies considerably in the literature. E.g. in [9], 3D-meshes via one-dimensional finite elements are considered. Their consistency rule is that line segments intersect only in boundary points. With this, they achieve self-correction of inconsistent meshes. In [3], topological-geometric consistency means that the interiors of 1-cells resp. 2-cells may not intersect. However, no statement about cells of different dimensions is made. The authors of [18] use only the geometric model for determining topological relations, and then make corrections of violations against topological integrity constraints. According to [1], a surface is consistent if and only if it is a valid 2D-manifold. In [8], the topological consistency of simplifications of line configurations is treated without defining topological consistency. The authors of [14] discuss arbitrary configurations of points, line segments and polygons in the plane, as well as their extrusions to 3D. Their consistency rules are that line segments may intersect only in their boundary points, and the interior of a polygon may not intersect any other object. Nothing is said about the intersection of a point with another

© Springer International Publishing Switzerland 2015
A. Gammerman et al. (Eds.): SLDS 2015, LNAI 9047, pp. 406–413, 2015.
DOI: 10.1007/978-3-319-17091-6_35

object, or how the boundaries of objects intersect. For [12], a surface in $\mathbb{R}^3$ is consistent if it is a so-called *2.8D map*. Gröger & Plümer extend this consistency rule by not allowing the interiors of points, lines, areas and solids to intersect [10,11]. An efficiently verifiable list of local consistency rules then requires a tesselation of $\mathbb{R}^3$. This excludes e.g. free or exterior walls, i.e. polygons which border at most one solid.

In the following section, we will discuss some data models for smart cities, namely CityGML, *G*-maps and topological databases. The next section gives some examples of queries involving topology in smart cities. This is followed by a section in which our point of view on topological consistency is made into a precise definition, and some consequences are discussed.

2 Data Models for Smart Cities

CityGML is an XML-based format for virtual 3D city models based on the Geographic Markup Language (GML). It is an international standard issued by the Open Geospatial Consortium (OGC) [13]. In essence, it models a configuration of points, line segments, polygons with holes, and solids together with a semantic structure by representing the thematic properties, taxonomies and aggregations. Solids and line segments are given by their boundary representations, and polygons with holes by their cycles of vertices under the tag `gml:LinearRing`. The combinatorial structure can be extracted from the xlink-topology together with the coordinate lists.

A *generalized map* (or short: *G*-map) is a topological model designed for representing subdivided objects in any dimension, and is an implicit boundary representation model. The definition of a *G*-map is given in [15] as

Definition 1. *An n-G-map is an $(n+2)$-tuple $G = (D, \alpha_0, \ldots, \alpha_n)$ such that*

- *D is a finite set of points called* darts
- *$\alpha_0, \ldots, \alpha_n$ are involutions on D, i.e. $\alpha_i \circ \alpha_i$ is the identity map on D*
- *$\alpha_i \circ \alpha_j$ is an involution if $i + 2 \leq j$ with $i, j \in \{0, \ldots, n\}$*

The combinatorial structure is given by *i*-cells which in turn are defined as *G*-maps whose underlying darts are an orbit of the group generated by the involutions other than α_i. *G*-maps can depicted in the following way:

- A dart is depicted as •——⊢
- An orbit under the group $\langle \alpha_0 \rangle$ generated by the involution α_0 is depicted as
  •——⊢ ⊢——•
- An orbit under the group $\langle \alpha_i \rangle$ generated by α_i with $i > 0$ is depicted by connecting darts with *i* strokes. E.g. for $i = 1$: ⊢——• •——⊢

An example of a *G*-map with two 2-cells, five 1-cells and four 0-cells is given in Figure 1 (left). The 2-cells are the orbits of $\langle \alpha_0, \alpha_1 \rangle$ which are the upper and lower triangles of Figure 1 (right); the 1-cells are the orbits of $\langle \alpha_0, \alpha_2 \rangle$ which are

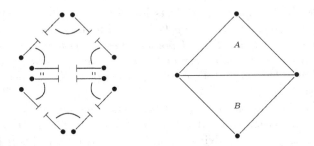

Fig. 1. Left: A G-map with two 2-cells, five 1-cells, and four 0-cells. Right: The cell complex associated with the G-map

the sides; and the 0-cells are the orbits of $\langle \alpha_1, \alpha_2 \rangle$ which are the vertices of the figure. Notice that involution α_2 leaves some darts fixed, i.e. has fixed points.

One problem with G-maps is their verbosity, especially in higher dimensions [6]. This means that it takes very many darts to describe a cell complex with relatively few cells. The reason is that a dart corresponds uniquely to a *cell tuple* which is a maximal sequence of cells $(c_n, \ldots, c_0)$ with c_i a face of c_{i+1}. The number of cell tuples is in general exponential in the number of cells for n large. The review article [7] contains some examples of urban models generated with G-maps.

A *topological database* [5,16] is mathematically given by a set of objects together with a binary relation on this set. As a relational database, it can be realised by two tables: one X for the objects, and one R for the relation. It is well known that a binary relation defines a topology on a set, and every finite topological space has a relation which defines the topology [2]. The table R can then be interpreted as the relation "bounded by" from which connectivity queries can be made.

It follows that in a topological database, the combinatorial structure is explicitly modelled. Additional orientation information yields an algebraic structure which turns R into a (partial) matrix, and under the condition $R^2 = 0$ this is a relational form of a chain complex with boundary operator R, important for some topological computations (e.g. Betti numbers). Figure 2 shows a cell complex with oriented cells and its relational boundary operator as a partial matrix. The orientation of the areas A, B is fixed here to be counter clockwise.

3   Topological Queries in Smart Cities

Once the combinatorial model underlying the data model has been established, topological queries can be made. A large class of topological queries are path queries: *Is there a path $A \to B$?* under some constraints. These constraints can be of geometric or of semantic nature. For example, the objects passed along a path must have a certain minimum size (geometric constraint) or the path must be inside a building (semantic constraint). Combinations of different types of constraints are also possible.

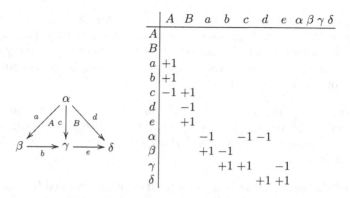

	A	B	a	b	c	d	e	α	β	γ	δ
A											
B											
a	+1										
b	+1										
c	−1	+1									
d		−1									
e		+1									
α			−1		−1	−1					
β			+1	−1							
γ				+1	+1		−1				
δ						+1	+1				

Fig. 2. Left: A cell complex with oriented cells. Right: Its relational boundary operator as a partial matrix

A particular type of path queries makes use of the *adjacency graph*. On a 2D-manifold, this is the *area adjacency graph*: the nodes are the polygons, and the edges are given by polygons adjacent along a common line segment. In 3D, it is the *volume adjacency graph*. Here, the nodes are the solids, and two solids are connected by an edge iff they share a common polygon at their boundaries. The advantage of the adjacency graph is that it does not use the complete dataset. However, it is quite common to have available only 2-dimensional data for city models. Then, in order to compute the volume adjacency graph of a complex building with many rooms, it is first necessary to fill all the shells surrounded by polygons with solids. This is a homology computation: the shells are the *second homology*. Homology computations are in essence algebraic computations, for which a chain complex derived from the data becomes useful. The number of shells is thus the *second Betti number*. The *first homology* is given by the loops, (window-like) openings, "inner courts", "tunnels" and "passages" of buildings. The *first Betti number* is their count. Consequently, the topological database enhanced with orientation information (i.e. the relational chain complex) has everything needed for homology queries.

4   Topological Consistency

As we have seen, topological queries exploit the combinatorial (or algebraic) model underlying the data model. This approach prefers the use of topological databases or relational chain complexes over data models which do not explicitly code the combinatorial structure. From CityGML or *G*-maps, a topological database can be extracted. In order for topological queries to yield correct answers, the geometric and combinatorial models must be compatible. This form of *topological consistency* means that both models must realise the same cell complex structure of the data. In other words, the data comprising of points, line segments and polygons must form a valid cell complex geometrically, and this is the combinatorial model underlying the data model. In Geographic Information

Systems, polygons may have holes. Such polygons are in general not cells, and we call these *quasi-cells*. A *quasi-cell complex* is obtained by sewing quasi-cells along their boundaries iteratively into the one-skeleton of the previously obtained quasi-cell complex. A one-dimensional quasi-cell complex is a cell complex. This generalises our notion of topological consistency:

Definition 2. *A finite set consisting of points, line segments, polygons with holes, together with the sides of each element is* topologically consistent *if its elements are closures of (quasi-)cells of a quasi-cellulation of the union of all elements in* $\mathbb{R}^3$.

A *quasi-cellulation* of a space is the quasi-cell complex obtained from a partition of the space into (quasi-)cells. The *combinatorial quasi-cell complex* associated with a configuration as in Definition 2 is the quasi-cell complex obtained by sewing each element along its boundary with each side as it occurs along the boundary. Such a configuration is topologically consistent if and only if the quasi-cellulation from Definition 2 coincides with the combinatorial quasi-cell complex associated with this configuration. Checking topological consistency amounts to computing pairwise intersections of elements. Such an intersection must then be a disjoint union of boundary elements plus possibly the interior of an element. Figure 3 shows an example of a consistent configuration. It consists

Fig. 3. A consistent configuration consisting of a square A, four line segments and four points

of a square, and the line segments and points at its boundary. These cells form a natural cellulation of the square, and coincide with the combinatorial cell complex associated with this configuration.

In [4], we prove the following intersection criterion:

Theorem 1. *A configuration as in Definition 2 is topologically consistent if and only if the intersection of any two distinct maximal elements A and B is the (possibly empty) disjoint union of boundary elements of A and B.*

An immediate consequence of Theorem 1 is that if an urban model is built up of polygons (with or without holes), topological consistency can be checked by computing the intersections of pairs of polygons. Line segments and points need not be intersected in this case. Figures 4–6 represent possible topological inconsistencies. Notice that in Fig. 5, the boundary vertices of polygon A are depicted as ○ and ⊙, whereas those of polygon B are ● and ⊙.

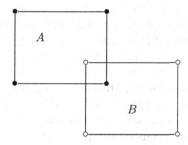

Fig. 4. A topologically inconsistent configuration where $A \cap B$ is not a union of objects

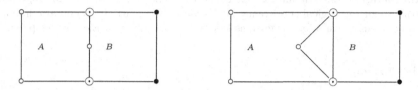

Fig. 5. Left: A topologically inconsistent configuration where $A \cap B$ is a non-disjoint union of objects. Right: The combinatorial cell complex associated with the configuration to the left contains a loop-hole.

Fig. 6. A topologically inconsistent configuration where $A \cap B$ is a point which is not a boundary element of both A and B

5   Conclusions

We have discussed data models for smart cities: CityGML, G-maps and topological databases. The first two indirectly model the combinatorial structure underlying the data, whereas topological databases explicitly model it, and can be enhanced with orientation information on the individual building blocks. This combinatorial model can then be exploited to retrieve answers to topological queries which are correct if the model is topologically consistent, i.e. the underlying combinatorial and geometric models are compatible. Topological consistency can be checked through computing intersections of maximal building blocks which are polygons with holes or line segments in 3D. It is well known that this can be done in polynomial time. Applications of topological consistency are also beyond purely topological queries: for example, our results can lead to more efficient GIS-assisted urban planning systems, transportation and noise management, or improved management and evaluation of Smart Cities and public Open

Linked Data repositories, exploiting the advantages of topological consistency in data. Examples of possible applications could include airport terminal buildings, or commercial application of flying robots, e.g. the logistics and delivery drones that are used in some warehouses. A validator for CityGML data is work in progress. Future research will include the extension of the notion of topological consistency to higher dimensions and to the case where objects may be contained in higher-dimensional objects, like e.g. points or line segments inside a polygon. This is relevant for applications in Geographic Information Systems: for example a town in a region should be consistently represented as a point inside a polygon in certain levels of detail.

Acknowledgments. The author would like to thank Fionn Murtagh for suggesting to write about topological consistency in the context of smart cities, and also him and the anonymous referees for suggestions leading to a better exposition of this paper.

References

1. Akleman, E., Chen, J.: Guaranteeing the 2-manifold property for meshes with doubly linked face list. Int. J. Shape Model. **5**, 159–177 (1999)
2. Alexandroff, P.: Diskrete Räume. Matematiećeskij Sbornik **44**(2), 501–519 (1937)
3. Boudriault, G.: Topology in the TIGER file. In: Proceedings of the International Symposium on Computer-Assisted Cartography, pp. 258–263 (1987)
4. Bradley, P.: Topological consistency of polygon complexes in CityGML. Work in progress
5. Bradley, P., Paul, N.: Using the relational model to capture topological information of spaces. The Computer Journal **53**, 69–89 (2010)
6. Bradley, P., Paul, N.: Comparing G-maps with other topological data structures. Geoinformatica **18**(3), 595–620 (2014)
7. Breunig, M., Zlatanova, S.: 3D geo-database research: Retrospective and future directions. Computers & Geosciences **37**, 791–803 (2011)
8. Corcoran, P., Mooney, P., Bertolotto, M.: Line simplification in the presence of non-planar topological relationships. In: Gensel, J., et al. (eds.) Bridging the Geographic Information Sciences. Lecture Notes in Geoinformation and Cartography, pp. 25–42. Springer (2012)
9. Gattass, M., Paulino, G., Gortaire, J.: Geometrical and topological consistency in interactive graphical preprocessors of three-dimensional framed structures. Computers & Structures **46**(1), 99–124 (1993)
10. Gröger, G., Plümer, L.: How to achieve consistency for 3D city models. Geoinformatica **15**, 137–165 (2011)
11. Gröger, G., Plümer, L.: Provably correct and complete transaction rules for updating 3D city models. Geoinformatica **16**, 131–164 (2012)
12. Gröger, G., Plümer, L.: Transaction rules for updating surfaces in 3D GIS. ISPRS Journal of Photogrammetry and Remote Sensing **69**, 134–145 (2012)
13. Kolbe, T.: Representing and exchanging 3D city models with cityGML. In: Lee, J., Zlatanova, S. (eds.) Proc. 3rd Int. Workshop on 3D Geo-Information. Lecture Notes in Geoinformation & Cartography (2009)
14. Ledoux, H., Meijers, M.: Topologically consistent 3D city models obtained by extrusion. IJGIS **25**(4), 557–574 (2011)

15. Lienhardt, P.: N-dimensional generalized combinatorial maps and cellular quasi-manifolds. International Journal on Computational Geometry and Applications **4**(3), 275–324 (1994)

16. Paul, N., Bradley, P.: Eine Erweiterung des Relationalen Modells zur Repräsentation räumlichen Wissens. Datenbank-Spektrum, Online First (August 2014)

17. Tao, W.: Interdisciplinary urban GIS for smart cities: advancements and opportunities. Geo-spatial Information Science **16**(1), 25–34 (2013)

18. Ubeda, T., Egenhofer, M.: Topological error correcting in GIS. In: Scholl, Michel O., Voisard, Agnès (eds.) SSD 1997. LNCS, vol. 1262, pp. 281–297. Springer, Heidelberg (1997)

Manifold Learning in Regression Tasks

Alexander Bernstein, Alexander Kuleshov, and Yury Yanovich[✉]

Kharkevich Institute for Information Transmission Problems RAS, Moscow, Russia
National Research University Higher School of Economics, Moscow, Russia
abernstein@hse.ru, {kuleshov,yury.yanovich}@iitp.ru

Abstract. The paper presents a new geometrically motivated method for non-linear regression based on Manifold learning technique. The regression problem is to construct a predictive function which estimates an unknown smooth mapping f from q-dimensional inputs to m-dimensional outputs based on a training data set consisting of given 'input-output' pairs. The unknown mapping f determines q-dimensional manifold M(f) consisting of all the 'input-output' vectors which is embedded in (q+m)-dimensional space and covered by a single chart; the training data set determines a sample from this manifold. Modern Manifold Learning methods allow constructing the certain estimator M* from the manifold-valued sample which accurately approximates the manifold. The proposed method called Manifold Learning Regression (MLR) finds the predictive function f_{MLR} to ensure an equality $M(f_{MLR}) = M*$. The MLR simultaneously estimates the m×q Jacobian matrix of the mapping f.

Keywords: Nonlinear regression · Dimensionality reduction · Manifold learning · Tangent bundle manifold learning · Manifold learning regression

1   Introduction

The general goal of Statistical Learning is finding a predictive function based on data [1-3]. We consider a regression task which is as follows. Let f be an unknown smooth mapping from a set $\mathbf{X} \subset R^q$ to m-dimensional Euclidean space R^m. Given a training data set $\{(x_i, u_i = f(x_i)), i = 1, 2, \ldots, n\}$ consisting of the input-output pairs, to construct the learned function f*(x) which maps the input to the output and can be used to predict output f(x) from future input x with small error.

There are various approaches and methods for a reconstruction of an unknown function from the training data, such as least squares technique (linear and nonlinear), artificial neural networks, kernel nonparametric regression and kriging, SVM-regression, Gaussian processes, Radial Basic Functions, Deep Learning Networks, Gradient Boosting Regression Trees, Random Forests, etc. [3-10]. Many methods (kernel nonparametric regression, kriging, Gaussian processes) use kernels that are typically stationary. However, as indicated in many studies [3, 8, 11], these methods have serious drawbacks for the functions with strongly varying gradients; thus, it is necessary to use non-stationary kernels with adaptive kernel width.

Statistical Learning, which is a part of Machine Learning, can be considered as a general problem to extract previously unknown information from a given data set; thus, it is

© Springer International Publishing Switzerland 2015
A. Gammerman et al. (Eds.): SLDS 2015, LNAI 9047, pp. 414–423, 2015.
DOI: 10.1007/978-3-319-17091-6_36

supposed that information is reflected in the structure of the data set which must be discovered from the data ('Machine learning is about the shape of data' [12]). Therefore, various geometric methods, which are used for finding of the geometrical and topological structure in data and based on topological data analysis, computational geometry and computational topology [13-14], have now become the central methodology for Machine Learning, including Statistical learning, tasks.

One of the emerging directions in the Geometric Data Analysis is the Manifold Learning (ML) which is based on an assumption that the observed data lie on or near a certain unknown low-dimensional data manifold (DM) $\mathbf{M}$ embedded in an ambient high-dimensional space [15-17]. A motivation for this assumption is that, typically, the real-world high-dimensional data lie on or near a certain unknown low-dimensional manifold embedded in a high-dimensional 'observation' space.

In general, the goal of the ML is to find the unknown DM $\mathbf{M}$ from the training manifold-valued data; thus, ML is a part of dimensionality reduction problems under the 'manifold assumption'.

In this paper, the ML is used to solve the regression task as follows. An unknown smooth function $f: \mathbf{X} \subset R^q \to R^m$ determines a smooth q-dimensional manifold

$$\mathbf{M}(f) = \{Z = F(x) = \begin{pmatrix} x \\ f(x) \end{pmatrix} \in R^{q+m}: x \in \mathbf{X} \subset R^q\} \tag{1}$$

which is embedded in an ambient space R^p, $p = q + m$, and covered (parameterized) by a single chart $F: x \in \mathbf{X} \subset R^q \to Z = F(x) \in \mathbf{M}(f) \subset R^p$. Its Jacobian

$$J_F(x) = \begin{pmatrix} I_q \\ J_f(x) \end{pmatrix} \tag{2}$$

is a (q+m)×q matrix which is split into q×q unit matrix I_q and m×q Jacobian matrix $J_f(x)$ of the mapping f(x). The q-dimensional linear space spanned by columns of the Jacobian $J_F(x)$ (2) is the tangent space to the DM $\mathbf{M}(f)$ at a point $F(x) \in \mathbf{M}(f)$.

Arbitrary learned function $f^*: \mathbf{X} \to R^m$ also determines a manifold $M(f^*)$ with use of the function $f^*(x)$ in the formula (1) instead of f(x). The proposed ML-approach to the regression task is as follows: to find the learned function f^* to ensure small Hausdorff distance $d_H(M(f^*), M(f))$ between the manifolds $M(f^*)$ and $M(f)$.

This approach is realized as follows. The manifold $\mathbf{M}(f)$ is considered as an unknown data manifold, and

$$\mathbf{Z}_n = \{Z_i = F(x_i) = \begin{pmatrix} x_i \\ u_i \end{pmatrix}, i = 1, 2, \dots, n\} \subset \mathbf{M}(f) \tag{3}$$

is a p-dimensional training data set sampled from the DM $\mathbf{M}(f)$.

The Grassmann&Stiefel Eigenmaps (GSE) algorithm [18-20] allows accurate reconstruction of the DM $\mathbf{M}(f)$ and its tangent spaces from the sample $\mathbf{Z}_n$ (3). The GSE-solution determines a q-dimensional reconstructed manifold (RM) $\mathbf{M}_{GSE}$ in R^p which also is parameterized by a single chart and ensures the manifold proximity property $d_H(\mathbf{M}_{GSE}, \mathbf{M}(f)) \approx 0$. For an infinitely increasing sample size n, the GSE has optimal convergence rate [21] coinciding with the asymptotically minimax lower bound for the Hausdorff distance between the DM and the arbitrary estimator for the DM [22]. The learned function f* is constructed as a solution of the equation $\mathbf{M}(f*) = \mathbf{M}_{GSE}$.

This ML-based approach to the regression can be called the Manifold Learning Regression (MLR). The constructed tangent spaces to the RM $\mathbf{M}_{GSE}$ allow accurate estimating of the Jacobian $J_f(x)$ also.

Note that an idea to solve the regression tasks using certain dimensionality reduction technique was earlier proposed in [23], but the idea could have been effectively realized only after creating of methods that allow sample-based reconstructing of the DM and its differential structure (the tangent spaces).

This paper is organized as follows. There is no generally accepted definition for the ML, and Section 2 contains a brief review of various formulations of the ML-problems including the Tangent bundle manifold learning (TBML) problem consisting in accurate reconstruction of both the unknown DM and its tangent spaces from the sample. The TBML-solution (the GSE algorithm) is briefly described in Section 3. Section 4 gives the proposed MLR-solution of the regression task. Results of numerical experiments are presented in Section 5.

2   Manifold Learning

2.1   Conventional Manifold Learning Setting

The conventional formulation of the ML called the Manifold embedding is as follows: Given a data set $\mathbf{Z}_n = \{Z_1, Z_2, \ldots, Z_n\}$ sampled from the DM $\mathbf{M}$, construct an embedding mapping h of the DM $\mathbf{M}$ to the Feature space (FS) $\mathbf{Y} = h(\mathbf{M}) \subset R^q$, $q < p$, which produces a low-dimensional parameterization (low-dimensional coordinates) of the DM and preserves specific properties of the DM. The manifold embedding is often limited to the construction of the mapping h only for the sample points and is to find an 'n-point' mapping $h_{(n)}$ of the sample $\mathbf{Z}_n$ to a q-dimensional dataset $\mathbf{Y}_n = h_{(n)}(\mathbf{Z}_n) = \{y_1, y_2, \ldots, y_n\}$ (feature sample) which faithfully represents the sample $\mathbf{Z}_n$. The corresponding problem can be called the Sample embedding; thus the embedding h is an extension of the embedding $h_{(n)}$ for the Out-of-Sample points $Z \in \mathbf{M} \setminus \mathbf{Z}_n$.

The terms 'faithfully represents' and 'preserves' are not formalized in general, and in different methods they can be different due to choosing an optimized cost function reflecting specific data properties to be preserved; as it is pointed out in [24], a general view on dimensionality reduction can be based on the 'concept of cost functions'.

2.2   Manifold Learning as Manifold Reconstruction Problem

We consider the ML problem in which the term 'preserves specific properties' has a specific meaning 'to preserve as much available information contained in the high-dimensional data as possible', which is determined by the possibility for reconstructing the initial vector $Z \in \mathbf{M}$ from the feature $y = h(Z)$ with small reconstruction error [24-25]. This formulation assumes the availability of a reconstruction mapping g from the FS $\mathbf{Y}$ to the ambient space R^p; the average reconstruction error $E_p|Z - g(h(Z))|$ is an adequate evaluation measure ('universal quality criterion') in this problem [24-25], here P is the probability measure on the DM $\mathbf{M}$ according to which the data are sampled. In some applications, in which the ML is the first step for reducing the initial 'high-dimensional' task to the learning procedures in the low-dimensional FS, one has to reconstruct a point $Z \in \mathbf{M}$ from its feature $y = h(Z)$ which does not belong to the feature sample $(y \in \mathbf{Y} \setminus \mathbf{Y}_n)$; such features arise as solutions of certain reduced problem in the FS (such as the examples that are contained in [19-20]).

A strict problem definition is as follows: Given an input data set $\mathbf{Z}_n$ randomly sampled from the DM $\mathbf{M}$, to construct a solution $\theta = (h, g)$ consisting of an embedding mapping $h: \mathbf{M} \to \mathbf{Y}_\theta = h(\mathbf{M}) \subset \mathbf{R}^q$ and a reconstruction mapping $g: \mathbf{Y}_\theta \to \mathbf{R}^p$ which ensure the approximate equality $r_\theta(Z) \approx Z$ for all $Z \in \mathbf{M}$; here the reconstructed value $r_\theta(Z) = g(h(Z))$ of a vector Z is a result of successively applying the embedding and reconstruction mappings to the vector Z. The reconstruction error $\delta_\theta(Z) = |Z - r_\theta(Z)|$ is a measure of the quality of the solution θ at the point $Z \in \mathbf{M}$.

The solution θ determines a q-dimensional manifold

$$\mathbf{M}_\theta = \{Z = g(y) \in \mathbf{R}^p: y \in \mathbf{Y}_\theta \subset \mathbf{R}^q\} \tag{4}$$

in $\mathbf{R}^p$ called the Reconstructed manifold (RM) which is parameterized by a single chart g defined on the FS $\mathbf{Y}_\theta$. Small reconstruction error means the manifold proximity property $\mathbf{M}_\theta \approx \mathbf{M}$ (determined by Hausdorff distance $d_H(\mathbf{M}_\theta, \mathbf{M})$) meaning that the RM $\mathbf{M}_\theta = r_\theta(\mathbf{M})$ accurately reconstructs the DM $\mathbf{M}$ from the sample. Therefore, the formulated problem can be called the Manifold reconstruction problem.

There are some (though a limited number of) methods for reconstructing the DM from the sample; such mappings are constructed in a natural way in the PCA (principal components analysis) and the nonlinear auto-encoder neural networks. Certain reconstruction procedures are proposed in [26] for the Locally Linear Embedding (LLE) [27]; Local Tangent Space Alignment (LTSA) technique [28] also provides certain reconstruction of original high-dimensional vectors from their features.

2.3   Manifold Learning as Tangent Bundle Manifold Learning

The reconstruction error $\delta_\theta(Z)$ can be directly computed at sample points $Z \in \mathbf{Z}_n$; for the Out-of-Sample point $Z \in \mathbf{M} \setminus \mathbf{Z}_n$, it describes the generalization ability of the solution θ at the specific point Z.

Local lower and upper bounds for the maximum reconstruction error in a small neighborhood $U_\epsilon(Z) = \{Z' \in \mathbf{M}: |Z' - Z| \le \epsilon\}$ of an arbitrary point $Z \in \mathbf{M}$ are obtained in [19]; these bounds are defined in terms of certain distance $d_2(L(Z), L_\theta(r_\theta(Z)))$ between the tangent spaces $L(Z)$ and $L_\theta(r_\theta(Z))$ to the DM $\mathbf{M}$ and the RM $\mathbf{M}_\theta$ at the points Z and $r_\theta(Z)$, respectively; here $L_\theta(r_\theta(Z))$ is the linear space $\mathrm{Span}(J_g(h(Z)))$ spanned by columns of the Jacobian matrix $J_g(y)$ of the mapping g at a point $y = h(Z)$.

Considering $L(Z)$ and $L_\theta(r_\theta(Z))$ as elements of the Grassmann manifold Grass(p, q) consisting of all q-dimensional linear subspaces in $\mathbf{R}^p$, the distance d_2 is the projection 2-norm metric [29] on the Grassmann manifold.

It follows from the bounds that the greater the distances between these tangent spaces, the lower the local generalization ability of the solution. Thus, it is natural to require that the solution θ ensures not only the manifold proximity but also the tangent proximity $L(Z) \approx L_\theta(r_\theta(Z))$ for all $Z \in M$ in selected metric on the Grassmann manifold. This requirement means a preserving of the differential structure of the DM and arises also in various applications.

The set $TB(M) = \{(Z, L(Z)): Z \in M\}$ composed of points Z of the manifold M equipped by tangent spaces $L(Z)$ at these points is known in manifold theory as the tangent bundle of the manifold M. Thus, the amplification of the ML consisting in accurate reconstruction of both the DM M and its tangent spaces from the sample can be referred to as the Tangent bundle manifold learning (TBML).

The below described GSE algorithm [18-20] solves the TBML and gives also new solutions for the Sample embedding, Manifold embedding and Manifold reconstruction problems.

3   Grassmann & Stiefel Eigenmaps

3.1   Structure of the GSE

The GSE consists of three successively performed steps: tangent manifold learning, manifold embedding, and tangent bundle reconstruction.

In the first step, a sample-based family $H = \{H(Z)\}$ consisting of $p{\times}q$ matrices $H(Z)$ smoothly depending on Z is constructed to meet the relations $L_H(Z) \approx L(Z)$ for all $Z \in M$; here $L_H(Z) = Span(H(Z))$ are q-dimensional linear spaces in R^p spanned by columns of the matrices $H(Z)$. The mappings h and g will be built in the next steps in such a way as that the linear space $L_H(Z)$ will be the tangent space $L_\theta(r_\theta(Z))$ to the further constructed RM M_θ at the point $r_\theta(Z)$, which yields the tangent proximity.

In the next step, given the family H already constructed, the embedding mapping h(Z) is constructed to meet the relations $Z' - Z \approx H(Z) \times (h(Z') - h(Z))$ for near points $Z, Z' \in M$; the FS $Y_\theta = h(M)$ is also determined in this step.

In the final step, given the family H and the mapping h already constructed, the mapping g(y), $y \in Y_\theta$, is constructed to meet the relations $J_g(h(Z)) \approx H(Z)$ and, then, $g(h(Z)) \approx Z$ (the tangent and manifold proximities, respectively).

3.2   GSE: Preliminaries

The tangent space $L(Z)$ at a point $Z \in M$ is estimated by the q-dimensional linear space $L_{PCA}(Z)$ spanned by the PCA principal vectors corresponding to the q largest eigenvalues which are a result of the PCA applied to sample points from an ε-ball $U_\varepsilon(Z)$, here ε is a small parameter of the GSE. If the DM M is 'well sampled' and ε is small enough (in future, $\varepsilon = \varepsilon_n = O(n^{-1/(q+2)})$) then $L_{PCA}(Z) \approx L(Z)$ [30].

Introduce the data-based kernel $K(Z, Z') = K_E(Z, Z') \times K_G(Z, Z')$ on the DM M, where $K_E(Z, Z') = I\{Z' \in U_\varepsilon(Z)\} \times \exp\{- t \times |(Z - Z')|^2\}$ is the 'heat' Euclidean kernel [31] and $K_G(Z, Z') = K_{BC}(L_{PCA}(Z), L_{PCA}(Z'))$ is the 'Grassmann' kernel, here t > 0 is a

GSE parameter and K_{BC} is the Binet-Cauchy kernel on the Grassmann manifold [29]. This aggregate kernel reflects not only 'geometrical' Euclidean nearness between the points Z and Z' but also 'tangent' nearness between the linear spaces $L_{PCA}(Z)$ and $L_{PCA}(Z')$, which yields nearness between the tangent spaces L(Z) and L(Z').

3.3   GSE: Tangent Manifold Learning Step

The matrices H(Z) will be constructed to meet the relations $L_H(Z) = L_{PCA}(Z)$, which yields the proximity $L_H(Z) \approx L(Z)$. To provide smooth dependence of $L_H(Z)$ on Z (to align the linear spaces $L_{PCA}(Z)$), the matrices H(Z) are chosen as a solution of two optimizing problems for the cost functions defined below: the tangent space alignment problem and the kernel interpolation problem.

In the tangent space alignment part, a matrix set $\mathbf{H}_n$ consisting of p×q matrices H_i which meet the constraints $\text{Span}(H_i) = L_{PCA}(Z_i)$, i = 1, 2, ... , n, is constructed to minimize the quadratic form $\sum_{i,j=1}^{n} K(Z_i, Z_j) \times \|Z_i - Z_j\|_F^2$ under the normalizing condition $\frac{1}{K} \sum_{i=1}^{n} K(Z_i) \times (H_i^T \times H_i) = I_q$ required to avoid a degenerate solution; here $K(Z) = \sum_{j=1}^{n} K(Z, Z_j)$, $K = \sum_{i=1}^{n} K(Z_i)$ and $\|\cdot\|_F$ is the Frobenius matrix norm. The exact solution of this minimizing problem is obtained in the explicit form as a solution of specified generalized eigenvector problems. The optimized cost function is an extension of the 'Laplacian' cost function in the Laplacian eigenmaps [31], and the proposed solution differs from the alignment problem solution in the LTSA [28].

In the kernel interpolation part, given the matrix set $\mathbf{H}_n$ already constructed, the matrix H(Z) for an arbitrary point $Z \in \mathbf{M}$ is chosen to minimize the quadratic form $\sum_{j=1}^{n} K(Z, Z_j) \times \|H(Z) - Z_j\|_F^2$ under the conditions $L_H(Z) = L_{PCA}(Z)$. A solution to this problem is given by $H(Z) = \pi(Z) \times \frac{1}{K(Z)} \sum_{j=1}^{n} K(Z, Z_j) \times H_j$, here $\pi(Z)$ is the projector onto the linear space $L_{PCA}(Z)$.

This Step gives a new nonparametric solution for a problem of estimating of the tangent spaces L(Z) in the form of a smooth function of the point $Z \in \mathbf{M}$ [32-33].

3.4   Manifold Embedding Step

This step consists of two parts which give the new solutions for the Sample embedding problem and the Manifold embedding problem, respectively.

First, given the matrices H(Z), a preliminary vector set $\mathbf{h}_n = \{h_1, h_2, ... , h_n\}$ is constructed as a standard least squares solution which minimizes the residual $\sum_{i,j=1}^{n} K(Z_i, Z_j) \times |Z_j - Z_i - H(Z_i) \times (h_j - h_i)|^2$ under the natural normalizing condition $h_1 + h_2 + ... + h_n = 0$. This set $\mathbf{h}_n$ is a new solution in the Sample embedding.

Then, given the set $\mathbf{h}_n$, the value h(Z) for an arbitrary point $Z \in \mathbf{M}$ is given by

$$h(Z) = h_{KNR}(Z) + V(Z) \times \frac{1}{K(Z)} \sum_{j=1}^{n} K(Z, Z_j) \times (Z - Z_j), \tag{5}$$

where $V(Z)$ is the explicit written $q \times p$ matrix and $h_{KNR}(Z) = \frac{1}{K(Z)} \sum_{j=1}^{n} K(Z, Z_j) \times h_j$ is the standard Kernel nonparametric regression estimator for $h(Z)$ based on the preliminary values $h_j \in \mathbf{h}_n$ of the vectors $h(Z_j)$ at the sample points Z_j, $j = 1, 2, \ldots, n$. The value (5) minimizes the residual $\sum_{j=1}^{n} K(Z, Z_j) \times |Z_j - Z - H(Z) \times (h_j - h)|^2$ over h and gives the new solution for the Manifold embedding problem.

3.5   Tangent Bundle Reconstruction Step

This step which gives a new solution for the Manifold Reconstruction problem and consists of several sequentially executed stages.

First, the data-based kernel $k(y, y')$ on the FS $\mathbf{Y}_\theta = h(\mathbf{M})$ is constructed to satisfy the approximate equalities $k(h(Z), h(Z')) \approx K(Z, Z')$ for near points $Z, Z' \in \mathbf{M}$. The linear space $L^*(y) \in Grass(p, q)$ depending on $y \in \mathbf{Y}_\theta$ which meets the condition $L^*(h(Z)) \approx L_{PCA}(Z)$ is also constructed in this stage.

Then, a $p \times q$ matrix $G(y)$ depending on $y \in \mathbf{Y}_\theta$ is constructed to meet the conditions $G(h(Z)) \approx H(Z)$. To do this, the $p \times q$ matrix $G(y)$ for an arbitrary point $y \in \mathbf{Y}_\theta$, is chosen to minimize over G the quadratic form $\sum_{j=1}^{n} k(y, y_j) \times \|G - H(X_j)\|_F^2$ under the constraint $Span(G(y)) = L^*(y)$. A solution to this problem is given by the formula

$$G(y) = \pi^*(y) \times \frac{1}{k(y)} \sum_{j=1}^{n} k(y, y_j) \times H(X_j), \qquad (6)$$

here, $\pi^*(y)$ is the projector onto the linear space $L^*(y)$ and $k(y) = \sum_{j=1}^{n} k(y, y_j)$.

Finally, the mapping g is built to meet the conditions $g(h(Z)) \approx Z$ and $J_g(y) = G(y)$ which provide the manifold and tangent proximities, respectively. To do this, the vector $g(y)$ for an arbitrary point $y \in \mathbf{Y}_\theta$ is chosen to minimize over g the quadratic form $\sum_{j=1}^{n} k(y, y_j) \times |Z_j - g - G(y) \times (y_j - y)|^2$. The solution to this problem is

$$g(y) = \frac{1}{k(y)} \sum_{j=1}^{n} k(y, y_j) \times Z_j + G(y) \times \left(y - \frac{1}{k(y)} \sum_{j=1}^{n} k(y, y_j) \times y_j \right), \qquad (7)$$

the first term is the standard kernel nonparametric regression estimator for $g(y)$ based on the values Z_j of the vector $g(y)$ at the sample feature points y_j, $j = 1, 2, \ldots, n$.

4   Solution of the Regression Task

Consider the TBML problem for the unknown manifold $\mathbf{M} = \mathbf{M}(f)$ (1) considered as the data manifold in which the data set $\mathbf{Z}_n \subset \mathbf{M}$ (3) is the sample from the manifold. Applying the GSE to this problem, we get the embedding mapping $h(Z)$ (5) from the DM $\mathbf{M}$ to the FS $\mathbf{Y} = h(\mathbf{M})$, the reconstruction mapping $g(y)$ (7) from the FS $\mathbf{Y}$ to the R^P and its Jacobian $G(y) = J_g(y)$ (6).

A splitting of the p-dimensional vector $Z = \begin{pmatrix} Z_x \\ Z_u \end{pmatrix}$ on the q-dimensional vector Z_x

and the m-dimensional vector Z_u implies the corresponding partitions $g(y) = \begin{pmatrix} g_x(y) \\ g_u(y) \end{pmatrix}$

and $G(y) = \begin{pmatrix} G_x(y) \\ G_u(y) \end{pmatrix}$ of the vector $g(y) \in R^p$ and p×q matrix G(y); the q×q and m×q

matrices $G_x(y)$ and $G_u(y)$ are the Jacobian matrices of the mappings $g_x(y)$ and $g_u(y)$.

From the representation $Z = \begin{pmatrix} x \\ f(x) \end{pmatrix}$ follows that the mapping h*(Z) = Z_x = x determines a parameterization of the DM. Thus, we have two parameterizations of the
DM: the GSE-parameterization y = h(Z) (5) and the parameterization x = h*(Z) which
are linked together by an unknown one to one 'reparameterization' mapping y = $\varphi(x)$.

After constructing the mapping $\varphi(x)$ from the sample, the learned function

$$f_{MLR}(x) = g_u(\varphi(x)) \tag{8}$$

is chosen as a MLR-solution of the regression task ensuring proximity $f_{MLR}(x) \approx f(x)$;
the matrix $J_{f,MLR}(x) = G_u(\varphi(x)) \times G_x^{-1}(\varphi(x))$ is an estimator of the Jacobian $J_f(x)$.

The simplest way to find $\varphi(x)$ is the choice the mapping y = $\varphi(x)$ as a solution of
the equation $g_x(y) = x$; the Jacobian matrix $J_\varphi(x)$ of this solution is $(G_x(\varphi(x)))^{-1}$. By
construction, the values $\varphi(x_j) = y_j$ and $J_\varphi(x_j) = G_x^{-1}(y_j)$ are known at the input points
$\{x_j, j = 1, 2, \ldots, n\}$; the value $\varphi(x)$ for an arbitrary point $x \in X$ is chosen to minimize
over y the quadratic form $\sum_{j=1}^n K_E(x, x_j) \times |y - y_j - G_x^{-1}(y_j) \times (x - x_j)|^2$, here
$K_E(x, x')$ is the 'heat' Euclidean kernel in R^q. The solution of this problem is

$$\varphi(x) = \frac{1}{K_E(X)} \sum_{j=1}^n K_E(x, x_j) \times \{y_j + G_x^{-1}(y_j) \times (x - x_j)\}, \quad K_E(X) = \sum_{j=1}^n K_E(x, x_j).$$

Denote $y_j^* = y_j + \Delta_j$, where Δ_j is a correction term, then $g(y_j^*) \approx g(y_j) + G(y_j) \times \Delta_j$.
This term is chosen to minimize the principal term $|g(y_j) + G(y_j) \times \Delta_j - Z_j|^2$ in the
squared error $|g(y_j^*) - Z_j|^2$, and $\Delta_j = G^-(y_j) \times (Z_j - g(y_j))$ is the standard least squares
solution of this minimization problem, here $G^-(y_j) = (G^T(y_j) \times G(y_j))^{-1} \times G^T(y_j)$.

The another version of the reparameterization' mapping

$$\varphi(x) = \frac{1}{K_E(X)} \sum_{j=1}^n K_E(x, x_j) \times \{y_j + G^-(y_j) \times (Z_j - g(y_j)) + G_x^{-1}(y_j) \times (x - x_j)\}$$

is determined by the choice of the points y_j^* as the values of the function $\varphi(x)$ at the
input points $x_j, j = 1, 2, \ldots, n$.

5   Results of Numerical Experiments

The function $f(x) = \sin(30 \times (x - 0.9)^4) \times \cos(2(x - 0.9)) + (x - 0.9)/2$, $x \in [0, 1]$, (Fig.
1(a)), which was used in [34] to demonstrate a drawback of the kernel nonparametric
regression (kriging) estimator with stationary kernel (sKNR) f_{sKNR}, was selected to
compare the estimator f_{sKNR} and the proposed MLR estimator f_{MLR} (8). The kernel
bandwidths were optimized for both methods.

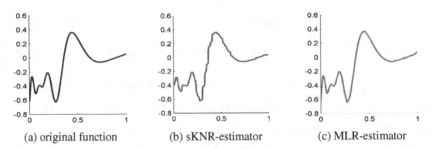

(a) original function   (b) sKNR-estimator   (c) MLR-estimator

Fig. 1. Reconstruction of the function (a) by the sKNR-estimator (b) and MLR-estimator (c)

The same training data set consisting of n = 100 randomly and uniformly distributed points on the interval [0, 1] was used for constructing the estimators f_{sKNR} and f_{MLR} (Fig. 1(b) and Fig. 1(c)). The mean squared errors MSE_{sKNR} = 0,0024 and MSE_{MLR} = 0,0014 were calculated for both estimators at the uniform grid consisting of 1001 points on the interval [0, 1]. Visual comparison of the graphs shows that the proposed MLR-method constructs an essentially smoother estimator for the original function.

Acknowledgments. The study was performed in the IITP RAS exclusively by the grant from the Russian Science Foundation (project № 14-50-00150).

References

1. Vapnik, V.: Statistical Learning Theory. John Wiley, New-York (1998)
2. James, G., Witten, D., Hastie, T., Tibshirani, R.: An Introduction to Statistical Learning with Applications in R. Springer Texts in Statistics, New-York
3. Hastie, T., Tibshirani, R., Friedman, J.: The Elements of Statistical Learning: Data Mining, Inference, and Prediction, 2nd edn. Springer (2009)
4. Bishop, C.M.: Pattern Recognition and Machine Learning. Springer, Heidelberg (2007)
5. Deng, L., Yu, D.: Deep Learning: Methods and Applications. NOW Publishers, Boston (2014)
6. Breiman, L.: Random Forests. Machine Learning **45**(1), 5–32 (2001)
7. Friedman, J.H.: Greedy Function Approximation: A Gradient Boosting Machine. Annals of Statistics **29**(5), 1189–1232 (2001)
8. Rasmussen, C.E., Williams, C.: Gaussian Processes for Machine Learning. MIT Press, Cambridge (2006)
9. Belyaev, M., Burnaev, E., Kapushev, Y.: Gaussian process regression for structured data sets. To appear in Proceedings of the SLDS 2015, London, England, UK (2015)
10. Burnaev E., Panov M.: Adaptive design of experiments based on gaussian processes. To appear in Proceedings of the SLDS 2015, London, England, UK (2015)
11. Loader, C.: Local Regression and Likelihood. Springer, New York (1999)
12. Vejdemo-Johansson, M.: Persistent homology and the structure of data. In: Topological Methods for Machine Learning, an ICML 2014 Workshop, Beijing, China, June 25 (2014). http://topology.cs.wisc.edu/MVJ1.pdf
13. Carlsson, G.: Topology and Data. Bull. Amer. Math. Soc. **46**, 255–308 (2009)

14. Edelsbrunner, H., Harer, J.: Computational Topology: An Introduction. Amer. Mathematical Society (2010)
15. Cayton, L.: Algorithms for manifold learning. Univ of California at San Diego (UCSD), Technical Report CS2008-0923, pp. 541-555. Citeseer (2005)
16. Huo, X., Ni, X., Smith, A.K.: Survey of manifold-based learning methods. In: Liao, T.W., Triantaphyllou, E. (eds.) Recent Advances in Data Mining of Enterprise Data, pp. 691–745. World Scientific, Singapore (2007)
17. Ma, Y., Fu, Y. (eds.): Manifold Learning Theory and Applications. CRC Press, London (2011)
18. Bernstein, A.V., Kuleshov, A.P.: Tangent bundle manifold learning via grassmann&stiefel eigenmaps. In: arXiv:1212.6031v1 [cs.LG], pp. 1-25, December 2012
19. Bernstein, A.V., Kuleshov, A.P.: Manifold Learning: generalizing ability and tangent proximity. International Journal of Software and Informatics 7(3), 359–390 (2013)
20. Kuleshov, A., Bernstein, A.: Manifold learning in data mining tasks. In: Perner, P. (ed.) MLDM 2014. LNCS, vol. 8556, pp. 119–133. Springer, Heidelberg (2014)
21. Kuleshov, A., Bernstein, A., Yanovich, Yu.: Asymptotically optimal method in Manifold estimation. In: Márkus, L., Prokaj, V. (eds.) Abstracts of the XXIX-th European Meeting of Statisticians, July 20-25, Budapest, p. 325 (2013)
22. Genovese, C.R., Perone-Pacifico, M., Verdinelli, I., Wasserman, L.: Minimax Manifold Estimation. Journal Machine Learning Research 13, 1263–1291 (2012)
23. Kuleshov, A.P., Bernstein, A.V.: Cognitive Technologies in Adaptive Models of Complex Plants. Information Control Problems in Manufacturing 13(1), 1441–1452 (2009)
24. Bunte, K., Biehl, M., Hammer B.: Dimensionality reduction mappings. In: Proceedings of the IEEE Symposium on Computational Intelligence and Data Mining (CIDM 2011), pp. 349-356. IEEE, Paris (2011)
25. Lee, J.A.: Verleysen, M.: Quality assessment of dimensionality reduction: Rank-based criteria. Neurocomputing 72(7–9), 1431–1443 (2009)
26. Saul, L.K., Roweis, S.T.: Think globally, fit locally: unsupervised learning of low dimensional manifolds. Journal of Machine Learning Research 4, 119–155 (2003)
27. Saul, L.K., Roweis, S.T.: Nonlinear dimensionality reduction by locally linear embedding. Science 290, 2323–2326 (2000)
28. Zhang, Z., Zha, H.: Principal Manifolds and Nonlinear Dimension Reduction via Local Tangent Space Alignment. SIAM Journal on Scientific Computing 26(1), 313–338 (2005)
29. Hamm, J., Lee, D.D.: Grassmann discriminant analysis: A unifying view on subspace-based learning. In: Proceedings of the 25th International Conference on Machine Learning (ICML 2008), pp. 376-83 (2008)
30. Tyagi, H., Vural, E., Frossard, P.: Tangent space estimation for smooth embeddings of riemannian manifold. In: arXiv:1208.1065v2 [stat.CO], pp. 1-35, May 17 (2013)
31. Belkin, M., Niyogi, P.: Laplacian eigenmaps for dimensionality reduction and data representation. Neural Computation 15, 1373–1396 (2003)
32. Bengio, Y., Monperrus, M.: Non-local manifold tangent learning. In: Advances in Neural Information Processing Systems, vol. 17, pp. 129-136. MIT Press, Cambridge (2005)
33. Dollár, P., Rabaud, V., Belongie, S.: Learning to traverse image manifolds. In: Advances in Neural Information Processing Systems, vol. 19, pp. 361-368. MIT Press, Cambridge (2007)
34. Xiong, Y., Chen, W., Apley, D., Ding, X.: A Nonstationary Covariance-Based Kriging Method for Metamodeling in Engineering Design. International Journal for Numerical Methods in Engineering 71(6), 733–756 (2007)

Random Projection Towards the Baire Metric for High Dimensional Clustering

Fionn Murtagh[1]([✉]) and Pedro Contreras[2]

[1] Goldsmiths University of London, London, UK
fmurtagh@acm.org
[2] Thinking Safe Ltd., Egham, UK
pedro.contreras@acm.org

Abstract. For high dimensional clustering and proximity finding, also referred to as high dimension and low sample size data, we use random projection with the following principle. With the greater probability of close-to-orthogonal projections, compared to orthogonal projections, we can use rank order sensitivity of projected values. Our Baire metric, divisive hierarchical clustering, is of linear computation time.

Keywords: Big data · Ultrametric topology · Hierarchical clustering · Binary rooted tree · Computational complexity

1 Introduction

In [18], we provide background on (1) taking high dimensional data into a consensus random projection, and then (2) endowing the projected values with the Baire metric, which is simultaneously an ultrametric. The resulting regular 10-way tree is a divisive hierarchical clustering. Any hierarchical clustering can be considered as an ultrametric topology on the objects that are clustered.

In [18], we describe the context for the use of the following data. 34,352 proposal details related to awards made by a research funding agency were indexed in Apache Solr, and MLT ("more like this") scores were generated by Solr for the top 100 matching proposals. A selection of 10,317 of these proposals constituted the set that was studied.

Using a regular 10-way tree, Figure 1 shows the hierarchy produced, with nodes colour-coded (a rainbow 10-colour lookup table was used), and with the root (a single colour, were it shown), comprising all clusters, to the bottom. The terminals of the 8-level tree are at the top.

The first Baire layer of clusters, displayed as the bottom level in Figure 1, was found to have 10 clusters (8 of which are very evident, visually.) The next Baire layer has 87 clusters (the maximum possible for this 10-way tree is 100), and the third Baire layer has 671 clusters (maximum possible: 1000).

In this article we look further at the use of random projection which empowers this linear hierarchical clustering in very high dimensional spaces.

© Springer International Publishing Switzerland 2015
A. Gammerman et al. (Eds.): SLDS 2015, LNAI 9047, pp. 424–431, 2015.
DOI: 10.1007/978-3-319-17091-6_37

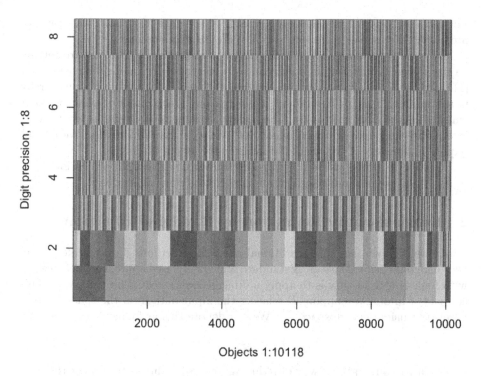

Fig. 1. The mean projection vector of 99 random projection vectors is used. Abscissa: the 10118 (non-empty) documents are sorted (by random projection value). Ordinate: each of 8 digits comprising random projection values. A rainbow colour coding is used for display.

1.1   Random Projection in Order to Cluster High Dimensional Data

In [3] we show with a range of applications how we can (1) construct a Baire hierarchy from our data, and (2) use this Baire hierarchy for data clustering. In astronomy using Sloan Digital Sky Survey data, the aim was nearest neighbour regression such that photometric redshift could be mapped into spectrometric redshift. In chemoinformatics using chemical compound data, we first addressed the problem of high dimensional data by mapping onto a one-dimensional axis. When this axis was a consensus of rankings, we found this approach, experimentally, to be stable and robust.

We continue our study of this algorithm pipeline here. Our focus is on the random projection approach, which we use. In this article, having first reviewed the theory of random projection, we note that the conventional random projection approach is not what we use. In brief, the conventional random projection approach is used to find a subspace of dimension greater than 1. In the conventional approach, the aim is that proximity relations be respected in that low dimensional fit to the given cloud of points. In our random projection approach, we seek a consensus 1-dimensional mapping of the data, that represents relative proximity. We use the mean projection vector as this consensus.

Since we then induce a hierarchy on our 1-dimensional data, we are relying on the known fact that a hierarchy can be perfectly scaled in one dimension. See [11] for the demonstration of this. Such a 1-dimensional scaling of a hierarchy is not unique. This 1-dimensional scaling of our given cloud of ponts is what will give us our Baire hierarchy. The mean of 1-dimensional random projections is what we use, and we then endow that with the Baire hierarchy. We do not require uniqueness of the mean 1-dimensional random projection.

Relative to what has been termed as conventional random projection (e.g., in [13]), our use of random projection is therefore non-conventional.

2   Dimensionality Reduction by Random Projection

It is a well known fact that traditional clustering methods do not scale well in very high dimensional spaces. A standard and widely used approach when dealing with high dimensionality is to apply a dimensionality reduction technique. This consists of finding a mapping F relating the input data from the space $\mathbb{R}^d$ to a lower-dimension feature space $\mathbb{R}^k$. We can denote this as follows:

$$F(x) : \mathbb{R}^d \rightarrow \mathbb{R}^k \tag{1}$$

A statistically optimal way of reducing dimensionality is to project the data onto a lower dimensional orthogonal subspace. Principal Component Analysis (PCA) is a very widely used way to to do this. It uses a linear transformation to form a simplified dataset retaining the characteristics of the original data. PCA does this by means of choosing the attributes that best preserve the variance of the data. This is a good solution when the data allows these calculations, but PCA as well as other dimensionality reduction techniques remain computationally expensive. Eigenreduction is of cubic computational complexity, where, due to the dual spaces, this is power 3 in the minimum of the size of the observation set or of the attribute set.

Conventional random projection [2,5–8,13,14,23] is the finding of a low dimensional embedding of a point set, such that the distortion of any pair of points is bounded by a function of the lower dimensionality.

The theoretical support for random projection can be found in the Johnson-Lindenstrauss Lemma [9], which is as follows. It states that a set of points in a high dimensional Euclidean space can be projected into a low dimensional Euclidean space such that the distance between any two points changes by a fraction of $1 + \varepsilon$, where $\varepsilon \in (0, 1)$.

Lemma 1. *For any $0 < \varepsilon < 1$ and any integer n, let k be a positive integer such that*

$$k \geq 4(\varepsilon^2/2 - \varepsilon^3/3)^{-1} \ln n. \tag{2}$$

Then for any set V of any points in $\mathbb{R}^d$, there is a map $f : \mathbb{R}^d \rightarrow \mathbb{R}^k$ such that for all $u, v \in V$,

$$(1 - \varepsilon) \parallel u - v \parallel^2 \ \leq \ \parallel f(u) - f(v) \parallel^2 \ \leq \ (1 + \varepsilon) \parallel u - v \parallel^2.$$

Furthermore, this map can be found in randomized polynomial time.

The original proof of this lemma was further simplified by Dasgupta and Gupta [4], also see Achlioptas [1] and Vempala [23].

We have mentioned that the optimal way to reduce dimensionality is to have orthogonal vectors in $\mathbb{R}$. However, to map the given vectors into an orthogonal basis is computationally expensive. Vectors having random directions might be sufficiently close to orthogonal. Additionally this helps solving the problem of data sparsity in high dimensional spaces, as discussed in [19].

Thus, in random projection the original d-dimensional data is projected to a k-dimensional subspace ($k \ll d$), using a random $k \times d$ matrix R. Mathematically this can be described as follows:

$$X_{k \times N}^{RP} = R_{k \times d} \, X_{d \times N} \tag{3}$$

where $X_{d \times N}$ is the original set with d-dimensionality and N observations.

Computationally speaking random projection is simple. Forming the random matrix R and projecting the $d \times N$ data matrix X into the k dimensions is of order $O(dkN)$. If X is sparse with c nonzero entries per column, the complexity is of order $O(ckN)$. (This is so, if we use an index of the nonzero entries in X.)

3   Random Projection

Random mapping of a high dimensional cloud of points into a lower dimensional subspace, with very little distortion of (dis)similarity, is described in [12]. Kaski in this work finds that a 100-dimensional random mapping of 6000-dimensional data is "almost as good". The background to this is as follows. Consider points $g, h \in \mathbb{R}^\nu$, i.e. ν-dimensional, that will be mapped, respectively, onto $x, y \in \mathbb{R}^m$, by means of a random linear transformation with the following characteristics. We will have $m \ll \nu$. Random matrix, R, is of dimensions $m \times \nu$. Each column, $r_j \in \mathbb{R}^m$ will be required to be of unit norm: $\|r_j\|_2 = 1 \ \forall j$. We have: $x = Rg$, and we have $x = \sum_{j=1}^{\nu} g_j r_j$ where g_j is the jth coordinate of $g \in \mathbb{R}^\nu$, in this mapping of $\mathbb{R}^\nu \to \mathbb{R}^m$. While by construction, the space $\mathbb{R}^\nu$ has an orthonormal coordinate system, there is no guarantee that all $x, y \in \mathbb{R}^m$ that are mapped in this way are in an orthonormal coordinate system. But (Kaski cites Hecht-Nielsen), the number of *almost orthogonal directions* in a coordinate system, that is determined at random in a high dimensional space, is very much greater than the number of orthogonal directions. Consider the case of $r_j \in \mathbb{R}^\nu$ being orthonormal for j. Then $X = RG$ for target vectors in matrix X, and source vectors in matrix G. Therefore $R'X = R'RG = G$ (where R' is R transpose), and hence $X'X = G'R'RG = G'G$. Since invariance of Euclidean distance holds in the source and in the target spaces, this is Parseval's relation. (For the Parseval invariance relation, see e.g. [20], p. 45.) Since the $r_j \in \mathbb{R}^\nu$

will not form an orthonormal system, we look instead, [12], at the effect of the linear transformation, given by R, on similarities (between source space vectors and between target space vectors).

For $g, h \in \mathbb{R}^\nu$ mapped onto $x, y \in \mathbb{R}^m$, consider the scalar product: $x'y = (Rg)'(Rh) = g'R'Rh$. Looking at the closeness to orthonormal column vectors in R makes us express: $R'R = I + \epsilon$ where $\epsilon_{ij} = r_i'r_j$, $i \neq j$, and $\epsilon_{ii} = 0$ because $r_i \in \mathbb{R}^\nu$ are of unit norm. The diagonal of $R'R$ is the identity: $\text{diag}(R'R) = \{r_i^2, 1 \leq i \leq \nu\} = I$. Now, take components of each r_j, call them $r_{jl}, 1 \leq l \leq m$. Our initial choice of random R used (in its vector components): $r_{jl} \sim$ iid $\mathcal{N}(0)$ (i.e. zero-mean Gaussian). Then normalization implies (vectors): $r_j \sim$ iid $\mathcal{N}(0,1)$. It follows that the orientation is uniformly distributed. We have $E[\epsilon_{ij}] = 0, \forall i, j$ where E is the expected value. Recalling that $\epsilon_{ij} = r_i'r_j$ and r_i, r_j are of unit norm, therefore ϵ_{ij} is the correlation between the two vectors.

If the dimensionality m is sufficiently large, then $\epsilon_{ij} \sim \mathcal{N}(0, \sigma_\epsilon^2)$, with $\sigma_\epsilon^2 \approx 1/m$. This comes from a result (stated in [12] to be due to Fisher), that $1/2 \ln(1 + \epsilon_{ij})/(1 - \epsilon_{ij}) \sim \mathcal{N}$ with variance $= 1/(m-3)$ if m is the number of samples in the estimate. If the foregoing is linearized around 0, then $\sigma_\epsilon^2 \approx 1/m$ for large m. Further discussion is provided by Kaski [12].

In summary, the random matrix values are Gaussian distributed, and the column vectors are normalized. This makes the column vectors to be Gaussian vectors with zero mean and unit standard deviation. Distortion of the variances/covariances, relative to orthogonality of these random projections, has approximate variance $2/m$, where m is the random projection subspace (or the number of random projections). With a sufficient number of random projections, i.e. a sufficiently high dimensionality of the target subspace, the distortion variance becomes small. In that case, we have close to orthogonal unit norm vectors being mapped into orthogonal unit norm vectors in a much reduced dimensionality subspace.

In [13], the use of column components r_j in R that are Gaussian is termed the case of conventional random projections. This includes r_j in R being iid with 0 mean and constant variance, or just iid Gaussian with 0 mean. The latter is pointed to as the only necessary condition for preserving pairwise distances. There is further discussion in [13] of 0 mean, unit variance, and fourth moment equal to 3. It is however acknowledged that "a uniform distribution is easier to generate than normals, but the analysis is more difficult". In taking further the work of [1], sparse random projections are used: the elements of R are chosen from $\{-1, 0, 1\}$ with different (symmetric in sign) probabilities. In further development of this, very sparse, sign random projection is studied by [13].

While we also use a large number of random projections, and thereby we also are mapping into a random projection subspace, nonetheless our methodology (in [3, 17], and used as the entry point in the work described in this article) is different. We will now describe how and why our methodology is different.

4   Implementation of Algorithm

In our implementation, (i) we take one random projection axis at a time. (ii) By means of maximum value of the projection vector (10317 projected values on a random axis), we rescale so that projection values are in the closed/open interval, $[0, 1)$. This we do to avoid having a single projection value equal to 1. (iii) We cumulatively add these rescaled projection vectors. (iv) We take the mean vector of the, individually rescaled, projection vectors. That mean vector then is what we use to endow it with the Baire metric. Now consider our processing pipeline, as just described, in the following terms.

1. Take a cloud of 10317 points in a 34352-dimensional space. (This sparse matrix has density 0.285%; the maximum value is 3.218811, and the minimum value is 0.)
2. Our linear transformation, R, maps these 10317 points into a 99-dimensional space. R consists of uniformly distributed random values (and the column vectors of R are not normalized).
3. The projections are rescaled to be between 0 and 1 on these new axes. I.e. projections are in the (closed/open) interval $[0, 1)$.
4. By the central limit theorem, and by the concentration (data piling) effect of high dimensions [10, 21], we have as dimension $m \to \infty$: pairwise distances become equidistant; orientation tends to be uniformly distributed. We find also: the norms of the target space axes are Gaussian distributed; and as typifies sparsified data, the norms of the 10317 points in the 99-dimensional target space are distributed as a negative exponential or a power law.
5. We find: (i) correlation between any pair of our random projections is greater than 0.98894, and most are greater than 0.99; (ii) correlation between the first principal component loadings and our mean random projection is 0.9999996; and the correlation between the first principal component loadings and each of our input random projections is greater than 0.99; (iii) correlations between the second and subsequent principal component loadings are close to 0.

In summary, we have the following. We do not impose unit norm on the column vectors of our random linear mapping, R. The norms of the initial coordinate system are distributed as negative exponential, and the linear mapping into the subspace gives norms of the subspace coordinate system that are Gaussian distributed. We find very high correlation (0.99 and above, with just a few instances of 0.9889 and above) between all of the following: pairs of projected (through linear mapping with uniformly distributed values) vectors; projections on the first, and only the first, principal component of the subspace; the mean set of projections among sets of projections on all subspace axes. For computational convenience, we use the latter, the mean subspace set of projections for endowing it with the Baire metric.

With reference to other important work in [12, 21, 22] which uses conventional random projection, the following may be noted. Our objective is less to determine or model cluster properties as they are in very high dimensions, than it is to extract useful analytics by "re-representing" the data. That is to say, we are having our data coded (or encoded) in a different way. (In [15], discussion is along the lines of alternatively encoded data being subject to the same general analysis method. This is as compared to the viewpoint of having a new analysis method developed for each variant of the data.)

Traditional approaches to clustering, [16], use pairwise distances, between adjacent clusters of points; or clusters are formed by assigning to cluster centres. A direct reading of a partition is the approach pursued here. Furthermore, we determine these partitions level by level (of digit precision). The hierarchy, or tree, results from our set of partitions. This is different from the traditional (bottom-up, usually agglomerative) process where the sequence of partitions of the data result from the hierarchy. See [3] for further discussion.

To summarize: in the traditional approach, the hierarchy is built, and then the partition of interest is determined from it. In our new approach, a set of partitions is built, and then the hierarchy is determined from them.

5   Conclusions

We determine a hierarchy from a set of – random projection based – partitions. As we have noted above, the traditional hierarchy forming process first determines the hierarchical data structure, and then derives the partitions from it. One justification for our work is interest in big data analytics, and therefore having a top-down, rather than bottom-up hierarchy formation process. Such hierarchy construction processes can be also termed, respectively, divisive and agglomerative.

In this article, we have described how our work has many innovative features.

References

1. Achlioptas, D.: Database-friendly random projections: Johnson-Lindenstrauss with binary coins. Journal of Computer and System Sciences **66**(4), 671–687 (2003)
2. Bingham, E., Mannila, H.: Random projection in dimensionality reduction: applications to image and text data. In: Proceedings of the Seventh International Conference on Knowledge Discovery and Data Mining, pp. 245–250. ACM, New York (2001)
3. Contreras, P., Murtagh, F.: Fast, linear time hierarchical clustering using the Baire metric. Journal of Classification **29**, 118–143 (2012)
4. Dasgupta, S., Gupta, A.: An elementary proof of a theorem of Johnson and Lindenstrauss. Random Structures and Algorithms **22**(1), 60–65 (2003)
5. Dasgupta, S.: Experiments with random projection. In: Proceedings of the 16th Conference on Uncertainty in Artificial Intelligence, pp. 143–151. Morgan Kaufmann, San Francisco (2000)
6. Deegalla, S., Boström, H.: Reducing high-dimensional data by principal component analysis vs. random projection for nearest neighbor classification. In: ICMLA 2006: Proceedings of the 5th International Conference on Machine Learning and Applications, pp. 245–250. IEEE Computer Society, Washington DC (2006)

7. Fern, X.Z., Brodly, C.: Random projection for high dimensional data clustering: a cluster ensemble approach. In: Proceedings of the Twentieth International Conference on Machine Learning. AAAI Press, Washington DC (2007)

8. Fradkin, D., Madigan, D.: Experiments with random projections for machine learning. In: KDD 2003: Proceedings of the Ninth ACM SIGKDD International Conference on Knowledge Discovery and Data Mining, pp. 517–522. ACM, New York (2003)

9. Johnson, W.B., Lindenstrauss, J.: Extensions of Lipschitz maps into a Hilbert space. In: Conference in Modern Analysis and Probabilities. Contemporary Mathematics, vol. 26, pp. 189–206. American Mathematical Society, Providence (1984)

10. Hall, P., Marron, J.S., Neeman, A.: Geometric representation of high dimension, low sample size data. Journal of the Royal Statistical Society Series B **67**, 427–444 (2005)

11. Critchley, F., Heiser, W.: Hierarchical trees can be perfectly scaled in one dimension. Journal of Classification **5**, 5–20 (1988)

12. Kaski, S.: Dimensionality reduction by random mapping: fast similarity computation for clustering. In: Proceedings of the 1998 IEEE International Joint Conference on Neural Networks, pp. 413–418 (1998)

13. Li, P., Hastie, T., Church, K.: Very sparse random projections. In: KDD 2006: Proceedings of the 12th ACM SIGKDD International Conference on Knowledge Discovery and Data Mining, vol. 1, pp. 287–296. ACM, New York (2006)

14. Lin, J., Gunopulos, D.: Dimensionality reduction by random projection and latent semantic indexing. In: 3rd SIAM International Conference on Data Mining. SIAM, San Francisco (2003)

15. Murtagh, F.: Correspondence Analysis and Data Coding with R and Java. Chapman and Hall (2005)

16. Murtagh, F., Contreras, P.: Algorithms for hierarchical clustering: an overview. Wiley Interdisciplinary Reviews: Data Mining and Knowledge Discovery **2**(1), 86–97 (2012)

17. Murtagh, F., Contreras, P.: Fast, linear time, m-adic hierarchical clustering for search and retrieval using the Baire metric, with linkages to generalized ultrametrics, hashing, Formal Concept Analysis, and precision of data measurement. p-Adic Numbers, Ultrametric Analysis and Applications **4**, 45–56 (2012)

18. Murtagh, F., Contreras, P.: Linear storage and potentially constant time hierarchical clustering using the Baire metric and random spanning paths. In: Proceedings, European Conference on Data Analysis. Springer (forthcoming, 2015)

19. Murtagh, F., Contreras, P.: Search and retrieval in massive data: sparse p-adic coding for linear time hierarchical clustering and linear space storage (in preparation, 2015)

20. Starck, J.L., Murtagh, F., Fadili, J.M.: Sparse Image and Signal Processing: Wavelets, Morphological Diversity. Cambridge University Press, Curvelets (2010)

21. Terada, Y.: Clustering for high-dimension, low-sample size data using distance vectors, 16 p. (2013). http://arxiv.org/abs/1312.3386

22. Urruty, T., Djeraba, C., Simovici, D.A.: Clustering by random projections. In: Perner, P. (ed.) ICDM 2007. LNCS (LNAI), vol. 4597, pp. 107–119. Springer, Heidelberg (2007)

23. Vempala, S.S.: The Random Projection Method, DIMACS: Series in Discrete Mathematics and Theoretical Computer Science, vol. 65. American Mathematical Society, Providence (2004)

Optimal Coding for Discrete Random Vector

Bernard Colin[1], Jules de Tibeiro[2]([✉]), and François Dubeau[1]

[1] Département de Mathématiques, Université de Sherbrooke,
Sherbrooke J1K 2R1, Canada
[2] Secteur Sciences, Université de Moncton à Shippagan,
Shippagan E8S 1P6, Canada
jules.de.tibeiro@umoncton.ca

Abstract. Based on the notion of mutual information between the components of a discrete random vector, we construct, for data reduction reasons, an optimal quantization of the support of its probability measure. More precisely, we propose a simultaneous discretization of the whole set of the components of the discrete random vector which takes into account, as much as possible, the stochastic dependence between them. Computationals aspects and example are presented.

Keywords: Divergence · Mutual information · Correspondence analysis · Optimal quantization

1 Introduction and Motivation

In statistics and data analysis, it is usual to take into account simultaneously, a given number of discrete random variables or discrete random vectors. This is particularly the case in surveys, censuses, data mining, etc. but also when some multidimensional discrete probabilistic models seem well suited to the phenomenon under study. In this context, one often wants to use data to adjust some statistical forecasting models or simply to account for the stochastic dependence between random variables or random vectors. For example, in the non-parametric framework, descriptive and exploratory models of data analysis as, among others, correspondence analysis, are dedicated to determining the stochastic dependence between random variables or random vectors, by means of their associations between their respective categories. Similarly, the parametric framework of usual discrete multidimensional distributions, leads to the estimation of the parameters of the joint distribution in order to estimate the stochastic dependence between random variables or vectors. However for various reasons (easy use, clearness of results and graphical displays, confidentiality of the data, etc.), one has in practice to create for each random variable or components of a random vector, new categories by grouping old ones. For instance, educational level such as "Primary", "Secondary", "College" and "University" is more often used than the exact number of years of studies.

For this purpose, one creates usually classes for each variable, regardless of the stochastic dependence that may exist between them. This approach however,

© Springer International Publishing Switzerland 2015
A. Gammerman et al. (Eds.): SLDS 2015, LNAI 9047, pp. 432–441, 2015.
DOI: 10.1007/978-3-319-17091-6_38

although very widespread, deprives the statistician of information that could be crucial in a predictive model since, in doing so, it degrades arbitrarily the information on the stochastic relationship between variables which could consequently, affect the quality of the forecast. To alleviate this problem, we propose to adapt to the discrete case, the approach introduced in the continuous case, by Colin, Dubeau, Khreibani and de Tibeiro [7], which is based on the existence of an optimal partition of the support of the probability measure of a random vector, corresponding to a minimal loss of mutual information between its components resulting from data reduction.

2 Theoretical Framework

2.1 Generalities

We briefly present hereafter the theoretical frame relative to determining a finite optimal partition of the support $S_{\mathbb{P}}$ of the probability measure of a discrete random vector. Let $(\Omega, \mathcal{F}, \mu)$ be any probability space, where Ω is a given set, where $\mathcal{F}$ is a σ-field of subsets of Ω and where the probability measure μ is supposed to be absolutely continuous with respect to a reference measure. Let $X = (X_1, X_2, ..., X_k)$ be a random vector defined on $(\Omega, \mathcal{F}, \mu)$ with values in a countable set $\mathcal{X}$, usually identical to $\mathbb{N}^k$, $\mathbb{N}^{*^k} = (\mathbb{N} \cup \{0\})^k$ or $\mathbb{Z}^k$. If $\mathbb{P}$ is the probability measure image of μ under the mapping X, one has:

$$\mathbb{P}(x_1, x_2, ..., x_k) = \mathbb{P}(X_1 = x_1, X_2 = x_2, ..., X_k = x_k)$$
$$= \mu \{\omega \in \Omega : X_1(\omega) = x_1, X_2(\omega) = x_2, ..., X_k(\omega) = x_k\}$$

where $x = (x_1, x_2, ..., x_k) \in \mathcal{X}$. Finally, $\mathbb{P}_{X_1}, \mathbb{P}_{X_2}, ..., \mathbb{P}_{X_k}$ denote respectively the marginal probability measures of the components $X_1, X_2, ..., X_k$ of the random vector X.

2.2 Mutual Information

As defined in the continuous case, the mutual information $\mathcal{I}_\varphi (X_1, X_2, ..., X_k)$ between the random variables $X_1, X_2, ..., X_k$ is nothing else than the φ-divergence $I_\varphi \left(\mathbb{P}, \otimes_{i=1}^{i=k}\mathbb{P}_{X_i}\right)$ between the probabiliy measures $\mathbb{P}$ and $\otimes_{i=1}^{i=k}\mathbb{P}_{X_i}$ given by:

$$\mathcal{I}_\varphi (X_1, X_2, ..., X_k) = I_\varphi \left(\mathbb{P}, \otimes_{i=1}^{i=k}\mathbb{P}_{X_i}\right),$$
$$= \sum_{x \in \mathcal{X}} \left[\varphi \left(\frac{\mathbb{P}(x)}{\otimes_{i=1}^{i=k}\mathbb{P}_{X_i}(x)}\right) \otimes_{i=1}^{i=k}\mathbb{P}_{X_i}(x)\right],$$
$$= \mathbb{E}^{\otimes_{i=1}^{i=k}\mathbb{P}_{X_i}} \left[\varphi \left(\frac{\mathbb{P}(X)}{\otimes_{i=1}^{i=k}\mathbb{P}_{X_i}(X)}\right)\right].$$

where φ is a convex function from $\mathbb{R}_+\backslash\{0\}$ to $\mathbb{R}$ (see Csiszár[10], Aczél and Daróczy[1], Rényi[20] for details). It is easy to check, using some elementary calculations, that all the properties of divergence and mutual information, as set out in the continuous framework, are also valid in a discrete setting (as positivity if $\varphi(1) \geq 0$, convexity with respect to the joint probability measure, independence of components, etc.) and, in particular, the one relating to the loss of information arising from a transformation of the random vector X. This property, known as *"data-processing theorem"*, states that it is not possible to strictly increase the mutual information between random variables or random vectors using a transformation on these last (see [1], [9], [10], [23]).

3   Optimal Partition

3.1   Mutual Information Explained by a Partition

Without loss of generality, and for sake of simplicity, it is assumed that, for $i = 1, 2, ..., k$, each component X_i of the random vector X, is a random variable with value in $\mathbb{N}^*$. Moreover, for every $i = 1, 2, ..., k$, we denote by $\eta_{il_i} \in \mathbb{N}^*$ any integer value of the random variable X_i, where $l_i \in \mathbb{N}^*$. Given k integers $n_1, n_2, ..., n_k$, we consider for every $i = 1, 2, ..., k$ a partition $\mathcal{P}_i$ of the support $S_{\mathbb{P}_{X_i}}$ of the random variable X_i, obtained by using a set $\{\gamma_{ij_i}\}$ of n_i intervals of the form:

$$\gamma_{ij_i} = [x_{i(j_i-1)}, x_{ij_i}[\text{ where } j_i = 1, 2, ..., n_i - 1 \text{ and } \gamma_{in_i} = [x_{i(n_i-1)}, \infty[$$

where the bounds of the intervals are real numbers such that: $0 = x_{i0} < x_{i1} < x_{i2} < ... < x_{i(n_i-1)} < \infty$.

Remark: the choice for real bounds for the half-open intervals γ_{ij_i} follows from the fact that it is not *a priori* excluded that one of the elements of the optimum partition be a single point x of $\mathbb{N}^{*^k}$.

The "product partition" $\mathcal{P}$ of the support $S_{\mathbb{P}}$ in $n = n_1 \times n_2 \times ... \times n_k$ cells, is then given by:

$$\mathcal{P} = \otimes_{i=1}^{i=k} \mathcal{P}_i = \{ \times_{i=1}^{i=k} \gamma_{ij_i} \}$$

where $j_i = 1, 2, ..., n_i$, for $i = 1, 2, ..., k$. If $\sigma(\mathcal{P})$ is the σ-algebra generated by $\mathcal{P}$ (the algebra generated by $\mathcal{P}$ in the present case), the restriction of $\mathbb{P}$ to $\sigma(\mathcal{P})$ is given by:

$$\mathbb{P}\left(\times_{i=1}^{i=k} \gamma_{ij_i}\right) \quad \text{for every } j_1, j_2, ..., j_k$$

and for which it follows easily that the marginal probability measures are given for $i = 1, 2, ..., k$, by: $\mathbb{P}_{X_i}(\gamma_{ij_i})$ where $j_i = 1, 2, ..., n_i$.

The mutual information, denoted by $\mathcal{I}_\varphi(\mathcal{P})$, explained by the partition $\mathcal{P}$ of the support $S_{\mathbb{P}}$ is then defined by:

$$\mathcal{I}_\varphi(\mathcal{P}) = \sum_{j_1, j_2, ..., j_k} \varphi\left(\frac{\mathbb{P}\left(\times_{i=1}^{i=k} \gamma_{ij_i}\right)}{\prod_{i=1}^{i=k} \mathbb{P}_{X_i}(\gamma_{ij_i})} \right) \prod_{i=1}^{i=k} \mathbb{P}_{X_i}(\gamma_{ij_i})$$

and the loss of the mutual information arising from data reduction due to the partition $\mathcal{P}$, is given by:

$$\mathcal{I}_\varphi(X_1, X_2, ..., X_k) - \mathcal{I}_\varphi(\mathcal{P})$$

which is positive due to the *"data-processing theorem"*.

3.2   Existence of an Optimal Partition

For any given sequence $n_1, n_2, ..., n_k$ of integers and for every $i = 1, 2, ..., k$, let $\mathcal{P}_{i,n_i}$ be the class of partitions of $S_{\mathbb{P}_{X_i}}$ in n_i disjoint intervals γ_{ij_i}, as introduced in the previous subsection, and let $\mathcal{P}_\mathbf{n}$ be the class of partitions of $S_\mathbb{P}$ of the form:

$$\mathcal{P}_\mathbf{n} = \otimes_{i=1}^{i=k} \mathcal{P}_{i,n_i}$$

where $\mathbf{n}$ is the multi-index $(n_1, n_2, ..., n_k)$ of size $|\mathbf{n}| = k$.

We define an optimal partition $\mathcal{P}$ as a member of $\mathcal{P}_\mathbf{n}$ for which the loss of mutual information $\mathcal{I}_\varphi(X_1, X_2, ..., X_k) - \mathcal{I}_\varphi(\mathcal{P})$ is minimum. Therefore, we have to solve the following optimization problem:

$$\min_{\mathcal{P} \in \mathcal{P}_\mathbf{n}} (\mathcal{I}_\varphi(X_1, X_2, ..., X_k) - \mathcal{I}_\varphi(\mathcal{P}))$$

or equivalently, the dual optimization problem:

$$\max_{\mathcal{P} \in \mathcal{P}_\mathbf{n}} \mathcal{I}_\varphi(\mathcal{P}) = \max_{\mathcal{P} \in \mathcal{P}_\mathbf{n}} \sum_{j_1, j_2, ..., j_k} \varphi \left(\frac{\mathbb{P}\left(\times_{i=1}^{i=k} \gamma_{ij_i}\right)}{\prod_{i=1}^{i=k} \mathbb{P}_{X_i}(\gamma_{ij_i})} \right) \prod_{i=1}^{i=k} \mathbb{P}_{X_i}(\gamma_{ij_i})$$

which is, in turn, equivalent to the problem of finding the real bounds x_{ij_i} of the intervals γ_{ij_i} for every $i = 1, 2, ..., k$ and for every $j_i = 1, 2, ..., n_i$. If the support $S_\mathbb{P}$ is finite, we have a finite number of members of $\mathcal{P}_\mathbf{n}$ so an optimal partition automatically exists, while if the support $S_\mathbb{P}$ is denumerably infinite, the set $\mathcal{P}_\mathbf{n}$ is denumerable. In that case, the countable set of the real numbers $\mathcal{I}_\varphi(\mathcal{P}_n)$ where $\mathcal{P}_n \in \mathcal{P}_\mathbf{n}$ for all $n \in \mathbb{N}^*$, may be ordered according to a non-decreasing sequence, bounded above by $\mathcal{I}_\varphi(X_1, X_2, ..., X_k)$. So in this case, the existence of an upper bound for the sequence $(\mathcal{P}_n)_{n \geq 0}$ ensures the existence of an optimal partition or possibly the existence of a "quasi optimal" partition, if the upper bound is not attained by a member of $\mathcal{P}_\mathbf{n}$.

As an example, let $X = (X_1, X_2)$ be a bivariate discrete random vector with a finite support $S_\mathbb{P} = [0, 1, 2, ..., p] \times [0, 1, 2, ..., q]$. If n_1 and n_2 are respectively the given numbers of elements of the partitions $\mathcal{P}_1$ and $\mathcal{P}_2$ of the sets $\{0, 1, 2, ..., p\}$ and $\{0, 1, 2, ..., q\}$, then $\mathcal{P} = \mathcal{P}_1 \otimes \mathcal{P}_2$ is a "joint" partition of the set $[0, 1, 2, ..., p] \times [0, 1, 2, ..., q] \subseteq \mathbb{N}^{*^2}$ with exactly $n_1 \times n_2$ non-empty cells. It is easy to check that the finite number of elements of the set $\mathcal{P}_\mathbf{n}$ where $\mathbf{n} = (n_1, n_2)$, is given by:

$$card(\mathcal{P}_\mathbf{n}) = \binom{p}{n_1 - 1} \binom{q}{n_2 - 1}$$

In order to find the optimal partition, it is sufficient to consider all possible values of $\mathcal{I}_\varphi(\mathcal{P}_n)$ where $\mathcal{P}_n \in \mathcal{P}_\mathbf{n}$, for all $n = 1, 2, ..., card(\mathcal{P}_\mathbf{n})$. If the support $S_\mathbb{P}$ is unbounded, it is possible for numerical reasons, to bring back the problem to one with a bounded support by the means of the transformation:

$$\mathcal{T} = \begin{cases} U = F(X_1) \\ V = G(X_2) \end{cases}$$

from $\mathbb{N}^* \times \mathbb{N}^*$ in $\overline{\mathrm{Im}(F)} \times \overline{\mathrm{Im}(G)} \subset [0,1] \times [0,1]$, where F and G are respectively the cumulative distribution functions of the random variables X_1 and X_2. One can check easily that for such transformation, one has:

$$\mathcal{I}_\varphi (X_1, X_2) = \mathcal{I}_\varphi (U, V)$$

In other words, T is a "mutual information invariant" transformation.

4   Computational Aspects

4.1   Example

In order to illustrate the process to determining the optimal quantization, let us consider the following contingency table $N = \{n_{ij}\}$, involving two random categorical variables X_1 and X_2:

Table 1. Contingency table involving two random categorical variables

$X_1 \backslash X_2$	1	2	3	4	5	6	7	8	9	10
1	80	36	87	47	99	42	23	28	11	58
2	60	20	89	61	60	21	19	10	11	4
3	168	74	185	127	137	112	96	53	21	62
4	470	191	502	304	400	449	427	164	45	79
5	236	99	306	187	264	188	93	56	36	87
6	145	52	190	91	133	65	70	30	20	54
7	166	64	207	194	193	33	94	23	28	129
8	160	60	160	110	110	51	29	20	21	80
9	180	60	211	111	194	97	79	30	27	49
10	125	55	187	115	53	82	43	17	15	41

from which we can easily deduce a joint probability measure $\mathbb{P} = \{p_{ij}\}$ by dividing each entry by $n = \sum_{i=1}^{10} \sum_{j=1}^{10} n_{ij}$. Let us suppose that we want to find an optimal partition of the support of this discrete probability measure in 3×3 elements. To this end, let $\{[1, \alpha_1[, [\alpha_1, \alpha_2[, [\alpha_2, 10]\}$ and $\{[1, \beta_1[, [\beta_1, \beta_2[, [\beta_2, 10]\}$ be respectively the elements of the partitions of the support of the probability measures $\mathbb{P}_{X_1}$ and $\mathbb{P}_{X_2}$, where $\alpha_1, \alpha_2, \beta_1$ and β_2 are of the form: $k + \frac{1}{2}$ with $k = 1, 2, ..., 9$. Let us suppose that function φ is the χ^2-metrics given by:

$$\varphi(t) = (1 - t)^2$$

where:

$$t = \frac{p_{ij}}{p_{i\bullet} p_{\bullet j}}$$

The mutual information is then given by:

$$\mathcal{I}_\varphi (X_1, X_2) = I_\varphi \left(\mathbb{P}, \otimes_{k=1}^{k=2} \mathbb{P}_{X_k}\right) = \sum_{i=1}^{10} \sum_{j=1}^{10} \left(1 - \frac{p_{ij}}{p_{i\bullet} p_{\bullet j}}\right)^2 p_{i\bullet} p_{\bullet j}$$

$$= \sum_{i=1}^{10} \sum_{j=1}^{10} \frac{p_{ij}^2}{p_{i\bullet} p_{\bullet j}} - 1 = .0650$$

For every choice of $\alpha = (\alpha_1, \alpha_2)$ and $\beta = (\beta_1, \beta_2)$ (there are exactly $36 \times 36 = 1296$ possible choices) resulting in a 9-cells $\{C_{lk}, l, k = 1, 2, 3\}$ partition $\mathcal{P}_{\alpha,\beta}$ of the support $S_\mathbb{P}$ of the probability measure $\mathbb{P}$, we have to calculate, using standard notations, the following probabilities:

$$\pi_{lk} = \sum_{(i,j) \in C_{lk}} p_{ij} \quad, \quad \pi_{l\bullet} = \sum_{k=1}^{3} \pi_{lk} \quad \text{and} \quad \pi_{\bullet k} = \sum_{l=1}^{3} \pi_{lk}$$

It follows that:

$$\mathcal{I}_\varphi(\mathcal{P}_{\alpha,\beta}) = \sum_{l=1}^{3} \sum_{k=1}^{3} \left(1 - \frac{\pi_{lk}}{\pi_{l\bullet} \pi_{\bullet k}}\right)^2 \pi_{l\bullet} \pi_{\bullet k}$$

and we have to solve the following optimization problem:

$$\max_{\alpha,\beta} \mathcal{I}_\varphi(\mathcal{P}_{\alpha,\beta})$$

For this elementary example, methods of exhaustion allow to find easily a solution (α^*, β^*) which satisfy the equality:

$$\mathcal{I}_\varphi(\mathcal{P}_{\alpha^*,\beta^*}) = \max_{\alpha,\beta} \left[\sum_{l=1}^{3} \sum_{k=1}^{3} \left(1 - \frac{\pi_{lk}}{\pi_{l\bullet} \pi_{\bullet k}}\right)^2 \pi_{l\bullet} \pi_{\bullet k}\right]$$

In the present case, using an enumeration algorithm[1], we have found:

$$\alpha^* = (3.5, 4.5) \quad \text{and} \quad \beta^* = (5.5, 8.5)$$

for which the partitions of the supports $\mathbb{P}_{X_1}$ and $\mathbb{P}_{X_2}$ are repectively given by:

$$(\{1, 2, 3\}, \{4\}, \{5, 6, 7, 8, 9, 10\}) \quad \text{and} \quad (\{1, 2, 3, 4, 5\}, \{6, 7, 8\}, \{9, 10\})$$

Furthermore, the ratio of the initial mutual information explained by $\mathcal{P}_{\alpha^*,\beta^*}$ is given by:

$$\frac{\mathcal{I}_\varphi(\mathcal{P}_{\alpha^*,\beta^*})}{\mathcal{I}_\varphi(X_1, X_2)} = \frac{.0326}{.0650} \approx .51$$

Similarly, for an optimal partition of $S_\mathbb{P}$ in 4×4 cells, we obtain respectively for $\alpha^* = (\alpha_1^*, \alpha_2^*, \alpha_3^*)$ and $\beta^* = (\beta_1^*, \beta_2^*, \beta_3^*)$:

$$\alpha^* = (3.5, 4.5, 9.5) \quad \text{and} \quad \beta^* = (4.5, 5.5, 8.5)$$

for which the corresponding partitions of the supports $\mathbb{P}_{X_1}$ and $\mathbb{P}_{X_2}$ are repectively given by:

$$(\{1, 2, 3\}, \{4\}, \{5, 6, 7, 8, 9\}, \{10\}) \quad \text{and} \quad (\{1, 2, 3, 4, \}, \{5\}, \{6, 7, 8\}, \{9, 10\})$$

Moreover:

$$\frac{\mathcal{I}_\varphi(\mathcal{P}_{\alpha^*,\beta^*})}{\mathcal{I}_\varphi(X_1, X_2)} = \frac{.0380}{.0650} \approx .59$$

For the resolution of the optimization problems arising from the examples presented thereafter, some more sophisticated numericals methods are needed. For example, we have to invoke in these cases some combinatorial algorithms (see B. Korte and J. Vygen [17]) or metaheuristics methods (see J. Dréo et al. [11] or T. Ibakari, K. Nonobe and M. Yagiura [15]).

---

[1] MathLab programs are available on request at the address: francois.dubeau@usherbrooke.ca

4.2   Some Usual Multivariate Distributions

Multinomial Distribution: One says that the random vector $X = (X_1, X_2, ...,$
$X_k)$ is distributed as a multinomial distribution, denoted by $\mathcal{M}n(n; p_1, p_2, ..., p_k)$,
with parameters $n, p_1, p_2, ..., p_k$, if its probability density function, is expressed
in the following form:

$$\mathbb{P}(X_1 = x_1, X_2 = x_2, ..., X_k = x_k) = \begin{pmatrix} n \\ x_1, x_2, ..., x_k \end{pmatrix}$$

$$\times \prod_{i=1}^{k} p_i^{x_i} \mathbb{I}_{\{S_{\mathbb{P}} \subseteq [0,1,2,...,n]^k\}}(x_1, x_2, ..., x_k)$$

where

$$\begin{pmatrix} n \\ x_1, x_2, ..., x_k \end{pmatrix} = \frac{n!}{x_1! x_2! ... x_k!}$$

where $0 \leq p_i \leq 1$ for all $i = 1, 2, ..., k$ with $\sum_{i=1}^{k} p_i = 1$ and where $S_{\mathbb{P}} \subseteq$
$[0, 1, 2, ..., n]^k = \{(x_1, x_2, ..., x_k) : \sum_{i=1}^{k} x_i = n\}$. In this case, each member of $\mathcal{P}_{\mathbf{n}}$
has exactly $\prod_{i=1}^{k} \binom{n}{n_i - 1}$ non-empty cells.

Multivariate Poisson Distribution:

Multivariate Poisson distribution of type I : Given two independent random variables X_1 and X_2 distributed as two *Poisson* distribution $\mathcal{P}(\lambda)$ and $\mathcal{P}(\mu)$ with
parameters λ and μ, one says that the bivariate random vector $X = (X_1, X_2)$ is
distributed as a bivariate *Poisson* distribution of type I $\mathcal{P}(\lambda, \mu; \gamma)$, with parameters λ, μ and γ, if its cumulative distribution function $H(x_1, x_2)$ is given by:

$$H(x_1, x_2) = F(x_1)G(x_2)\left[1 + \gamma\left(1 - F(x_1)\right)\left(1 - G(x_2)\right)\right]$$

where $-1 \leq \gamma \leq 1$, and where F and G are respectively the cumulative distribution functions of X_1 and X_2.

Multivariate Poisson distribution of type II : According to Johnson, Kotz and
Balakrishnan [16] , one says that the random vector $X = (X_1, X_2, ..., X_k)$ is
distributed as a multivariate *Poisson* distribution of type II $\mathcal{P}(\lambda_1, \lambda_2, ..., \lambda_k)$,
with parameters $\lambda_1, \lambda_2, ..., \lambda_k$, if its probability density function is given by:

$$\mathbb{P}\left(\cap_{i=1}^{k}\{X_i = x_i\}\right) = \left[\prod_{i=1}^{k} \frac{e^{-\lambda_i} \lambda_i^{x_i}}{x_i!}\right] \times$$

$$\exp\left\{ \begin{array}{l} \sum_i \sum_j \lambda_{ij} C(x_i) C(x_j) \\ + \sum_i \sum_j \sum_l \lambda_{ijl} C(x_i) C(x_j) C(x_l) \\ + ... + \lambda_{12...k} C(x_1) C(x_2) ... C(x_k) \end{array} \right\} \mathbb{I}_{\mathbb{N}^{*k}}(x_1, x_2, ..., x_k)$$

where $\lambda_i > 0$ for all $i = 1, 2, ..., k$, where $C(\bullet)$ is a *Gram-Charlier* polynomial of
type B (see [16]) and where

$$\lambda_{ijl...} = \mathbb{E}\left[X_i X_j X_l ...\right]$$

for all $i, j, l, ... \in 1, 2, ..., k$. See also Holgate [13],[14], Campbell [6], Aitken and
Gonin [3], Aitken [2], Consael [8], for more details.

Multivariate Hypergeometric Distribution: This distribution arises from random sampling (without replacement) in a population with k categories. The random vector $X = (X_1, X_2, ..., X_k)$ is said to have a multivariate hypergeometric distribution, denoted by $\mathcal{HM}(n; m; m_1, m_2, ..., m_k)$, with parameters $n, m, m_1, m_2, ..., m_k$, if its probability density function is given by:

$$P(X_1 = n_1, X_2 = n_2, ..., X_k = n_k) = \frac{\prod_{i=1}^{k} \binom{m_i}{n_i}}{\binom{m}{n}}$$

where one has: $\sum_{i=1}^{k} m_i = m; \sum_{i=1}^{k} n_i = n$ and $0 \leq n_i \leq \min(n, m_i) \ \forall i = 1, 2, ..., k$. Moreover, each marginal distribution is a univariate hypergeometric distribution $\mathcal{H}(n, m)$.

Negative Multinomial Distribution: The random vector $X = (X_1, X_2, ..., X_k)$ is distributed as a negative multinomial distribution, noted by $\mathcal{MN}(p_0, p_1, p_2, ..., p_k)$, with parameters $p_0, p_1, p_2, ..., p_k$, if its probability density function is given by:

$$P(X_1 = n_1, X_2 = n_2, ..., X_k = n_k) = \frac{\Gamma(n + \sum_{i=1}^{k} n_i)}{n_1! n_2! ... n_k! \Gamma(n)} p_0^n \prod_{i=1}^{k} p_i^{n_i} \mathbb{I}_{\mathbb{N}^{*k}}(n_1, n_2, ..., n_k)$$

where $0 < p_i < 1$ for $i = 1, 2, ..., k$ and where $\sum_{i=0}^{k} p_i = 1$. For more details and applications of this distribution one can see : Bates and Neyman [5], Sibuya, Yoshimura and Shimizu [21], Patil [18], Neyman [19], Sinoquet and Bonhomme [22], Guo [12], Arbous and Sichel [4].

5   Conclusions

Let $X = (X_1, X_2, ..., X_k)$ be a discrete random vector defined on a probability space $(\Omega, \mathcal{F}, \mu)$ with values in a countable set $\mathcal{X}$ (usually $\mathbb{N}^k$, $\mathbb{N}^{*k} = (\mathbb{N} \cup \{0\})^k$ or $\mathbb{Z}^k$), and with a joint probability measure $\mathbb{P}$ absolutely continuous with respect to a counting measure. For a given measure of mutual information $\mathcal{I}_{\varphi}(X_1, X_2, ..., X_k)$ between the components of X, we have shown, using a criterion based on minimization of the mutual information loss, that there exists for given integers $n_1, n_2, ..., n_k$, an optimal partition of the support $\mathcal{S}_{\mathbb{P}}$ of $\mathbb{P}$ in $\prod_{i=1}^{k} n_i$ elements, given by the Cartesian product of the elements of the partitions of the support of each components $X_1, X_2, ..., X_k$ in, respectively, $n_1, n_2, ..., n_k$ classes. This procedure allows to retain the stochastic dependence between the random variables $(X_1, X_2, ..., X_k)$ as much as possible and this may be significantly important for some data analysis or statistical inference as tests of independence. As illustrated by an example, this optimal partition performs, from this point of view, better than any others having the same number of classes. Although this way of carrying out a quantization of the support of a probability measure is less usual than those associated with marginal classes of equal *"width"* or of *"equal probabilities"*, one thinks that practitioners could seriously consider it, at least, in the case where the conservation of the stochastic dependence between the random variables seems to be important. Finally, from a practical point of view, we have paid attention to some semiparametric cases for which one can assume the probability measure $\mathbb{P}$ is a member of a given family depending on the unknown parameter θ.

References

1. Aczél, J., Daróczy, Z.: On Measures of Information and Their Charaterizations. Academic Press, New York (1975)
2. Aitken, A.C.: A further note on multivariate selection. Proceedings of the Edinburgh Mathematical Society **5**, 37–40 (1936)
3. Aitken, A.C., Gonin, H.T.: On fourfold sampling with and without replacement. Proceedings of the Royal Society of Edinburgh **55**, 114–125 (1935)
4. Arbous, A.G., Sichel, H.S.: New techniques for the analysis of absenteeism data. Biometrika **41**, 77–90 (1954)
5. Bates, G.E., Neyman, J.: Contributions to the theory of accident proneness. University of California, Publications in Statistics **1**, 215–253 (1952)
6. Campbell, J.T.: The Poisson correlation function. Proceedings of the Edinburgh Mathematical Society (Series 2) **4**, 18–26 (1938)
7. Colin, B., Dubeau, F., Khreibani, H., de Tibeiro, J.: Optimal Quantization of the Support of a Continuous Multivariate Distribution based on Mutual Information. Journal of Classification **30**, 453–473 (2013)
8. Consael, R.: Sur les processus composés de Poisson à deux variables aléatoires. Académie Royale de Belgique, Classe des Sciences, Mémoires **7**, 4–43 (1952)
9. Csiszár, I.: A class of measures of informativity of observations channels. Periodica Mathematica Hungarica **2**(1–4), 191–213 (1972)
10. Csiszár, I.: Information Measures: A Critical Survey. Transactions of the Seventh Prague Conference on Information Theory, Statistical Decision Functions and Random Proccesses **A**, 73–86 (1977)
11. Dréo, J., Pétrowski, A., Siarry, P., Taillard, E.: Metaheuristics for Hard Optimization. Springer (2006)
12. Guo, G.: Negative multinomial regression models for clustered event counts, Technical Report, Department of Sociology, University of North Carolina, Chapel Hill, NC (1995)
13. Holgate, P.: Estimation for the bivariate Poisson distribution. Biometrika **51**, 241–245 (1964)
14. Holgate, P.: Bivariate generalizations of Neyman's type A distribution. Biometrika **53**, 241–245 (1966)
15. Ibakari, T., Nonobe, K., Yagiura, M.: Metaheuristics: Progress as Real Problem Solvers. Springer (2005)
16. Johnson, N.L., Kotz, S., Balakrishnan, N.: Discrete Multivariate Distribution. John Wiley & Sons, Inc. (1997)
17. Korte, B., Vygen, J.: Combinatorial Optimization: Theory and Algorithms, 21 Algorithms and Combinatorics, Fourth Edition. Springer (2008)
18. Patil, G.P.: On sampling with replacement from populations with multiple characters. Sankhya, Series B **30**, 355–364 (1968)
19. Neyman, J.: Certain chance mechanisms involving discrete distributions (inaugural address). In: Proceedings of the International Symposium on Discrete Distributions, pp. 4–14, Montréal (1963)

20. Rényi, A.: On measures of entropy and information. In: Proceedings of the Fourth Berkeley Symposium of Mathematical Statistics and Probability, (I), pp. 547–561. University of California Press, Berkeley (1961)
21. Sibuya, M., Yoshimura, I., Shimizu, R.: Negative multinomial distribution. Annals of the Institute of Statistical Mathematics **16**, 409–426 (1964)
22. Sinoquet, H., Bonhomme, R.: A theoretical analysis of radiation interception in a two-species plant canopy. Mathematical Biosciences **105**, 23–45 (1991)
23. Zakai, J., Ziv, M.: On functionals satisfying a data-processing theorem. IEEE Transactions **IT–19**, 275–282 (1973)

Author Index